# THE
# TWO
# KOREAS

OTHER BOOKS BY DON OBERDORFER

*Tet!*

*The Turn: From the Cold War to a New Era*

*Princeton University: The First 250 Years*

# THE
# TWO
# KOREAS
## A CONTEMPORARY HISTORY

New Edition

# Don Oberdorfer

BASIC
BOOKS

A Member of the Perseus Books Group

A Member of the Perseus Books Group

Library of Congress Cataloging-in-Publication Data

Oberdorfer, Don.
    The two Koreas : a contemporary history / Don Oberdorfer.--New ed.
       p. cm.
    Includes bibliographical references and index.
    ISBN-10 0–465–05162–6 (pbk.)
    ISBN-13 978-0–465–05162–5 (pbk.)
    1. Korea (South)—History. 2. Korea (North)—History. 1. Title.
DS922.2.025 2001
951.904-dc21

                                                                                    2001043486

Published by Basic Books,
A Member of the Perseus Books Group
Revised Edition published December 2001

Jacket design by Suzanne Heiser
Text design by Karen Savary
Set in 11-point Calisto by GAC/Sheppard Poorman, Indianapolis

          DHAD   06  07  08  09    20  19  18  17  16  15  14  13  12  11  10  9

*For the people of the two Koreas*
*May they be one again, and soon.*

# CONTENTS

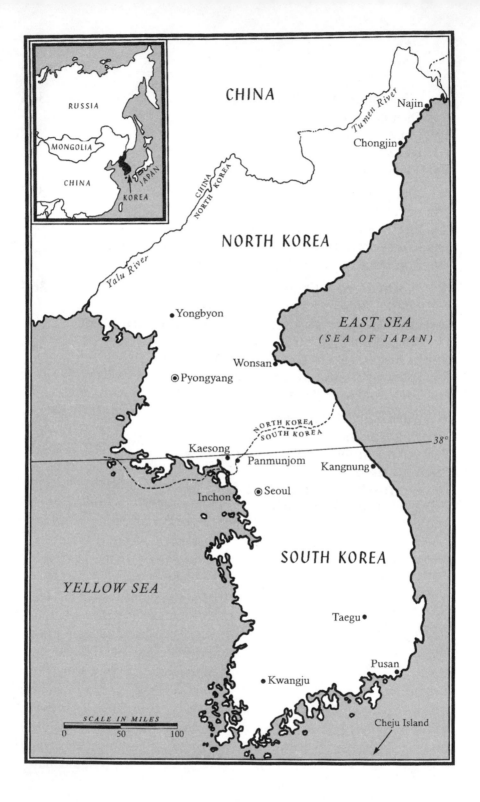

CHINA

RUSSIA

MONGOLIA

CHINA

JAPAN

KOREA

*Tumen River*

Najin

Chongjin

CHINA
NORTH KOREA

NORTH KOREA

*Yalu River*

• Yongbyon

EAST SEA
*(SEA OF JAPAN)*

Wonsan•

⊙Pyongyang

NORTH KOREA
SOUTH KOREA

Kaesong

Panmunjom

38°

Kangnung•

Inchon

⊙Seoul

YELLOW SEA

SOUTH KOREA

Taegu•

Pusan

• Kwangju

Cheju Island

*SCALE IN MILES*

0          50          100

# PREFACE TO THE NEW EDITION

*We are now traveling the length of free Korea by troop train, from the southern tip, the port of Pusan, to almost the farthest point therefrom, Inchon on the northwest coast . . . Our first impressions, at Pusan, were miserable and pathetic. The dirtiest children I have ever seen anywhere evaded MPs around the train to beg from GIs. One boy crawled around the train on his only leg; what had been his left one was off at the thigh. When our train pulled out, several boys threw rocks at the train . . . Out of Pusan, however, the picture is better. The Korean countryside is quite mountainous, with villages in the little stretches of valleys between the rugged, unadorned crags. The people in the villages till the soil and wash in the muddy water holes, and the children do God-knows-what. They line the sides of the railroad and shout, "hello, hello" at the troop train, hoping to be thrown cigarettes or candy or something of value.*

— FROM MY DIARY, *August 11, 1953*

This was my introduction to Korea as a U.S. Army lieutenant weeks after the armistice which ended the bloody three-year war on the peninsula, and the beginning of a lifelong interest in an embattled and amazing country. In my field artillery unit just south of the ceasefire line, we were dug in and ready to renew the battle against heavily armed North Korean units stationed across the hills only a mile or two away. We did not know how fragile or hardy the armistice would be or how long the truce would hold, but none of us would have believed that the state of no-war, no-peace would persist into the twenty-first century.

The massively fortified strip bisecting the Korean peninsula was one of the world's most dangerous potential flashpoints throughout the cold war. Although the barriers have come down nearly everywhere else, at this writing Korea remains—as President Bill Clinton said in his 1997 State of the Union address—"the Cold War's last divide." The misnamed "demilitarized zone," a verdant but heavily mined sanctuary for wild birds and animals, continues to be the focal point of the most powerful concentrations of opposing military forces of the post–cold war world despite both secret and open attempts at reconciliation. Close to 2 million troops, including 37,000 from the United States who would be instantly involved in new hostilities, are on duty in North or South Korea, with many on hair-trigger alert wielding powerful weapons of war. Today, despite dramatic and hopeful recent developments, American overseas commitments and military forces are at greater risk at the Korean DMZ than anywhere else on earth.

While the confrontation across the DMZ continues, almost everything else has changed dramatically. South of the dividing line, the Republic of Korea has developed since the 1970s into an economic powerhouse. By 1997 it was the world's eleventh largest economy and one of the foremost producers of ships, automobiles, electronics, steel, and a host of other goods, with a per capita income of more than $10,000 per year. By that time its fiesty democracy had thrown off all vestiges of military rule and imprisoned the two generals who had led the country in the 1980s. Late in 1997, it was suddenly beset by a massive financial crisis that began in Southeast Asia. In this atmosphere it elected longtime opposition leader Kim Dae Jung as its president for the next five years. He immediately set about to stabilize and reform the economy, and undertake new and positive engagement toward the North. Although economic reform is still incomplete, his determined and persistent policy toward the North paid off in an unprecedented summit meeting in June 2000 and the promise of extensive North-South interaction in economic, political, and even military fields.

North of the dividing line, the Democratic People's Republic of Korea, which developed its own unique brand of communist

Confucianism, remains militarily powerful but has lost the race in every other way. Early in the 1990s North Korea was abandoned by its former sponsor and ally, the Soviet Union, which established close relations with South Korea and then collapsed, and was devalued by its other major sponsor and ally, China, which became more interested in markets than in Marxism. Following the death of its founding leader in 1994, North Korea suffered a sharp economic decline, which was a central factor in a famine in outlying areas that led to massive loss of life.

Under the successor leadership of the enigmatic Kim Jong Il, the eldest son of the founder, Pyongyang was forced to turn to the outside world for humanitarian assistance in the mid-1990s. Late in the decade North Korea undertook new policies of engagement with South Korea, the United States, and a variety of other Asian and European countries. At this writing, it is yet uncertain whether Kim Jong Il's limited opening and cautious domestic reforms will continue and, if so, whether these actions will bring about a revival of the North Korean economy and secure the survival of the regime. In the preface to earlier editions of this book, I wrote that it seemed unlikely that the DPRK could survive in its existing form without such major changes. As risky as they may be, the North's new policies, I believe, have improved its odds.

I have sought to record here the ways in which the two halves of this ancient and homogeneous people, thoughtlessly divided at the end of World War II by the great powers, have grappled with each other for advantage and supremacy in the past three decades, and how they have dealt with the powerful forces all around them. The course of their struggle, like those that enveloped the Korean peninsula for many centuries past, has been deeply affected by actions of the surrounding powers—China, Japan, and Russia. Since World War II and especially since the Korean War, in which nearly 1,500,000 Americans served and 36,000 Americans were killed, the United States has played a major role. Korea is the only country in the world where the interests and security concerns of these four powers directly intersect. Although the major powers have had a large impact on Korea's fate, the hardy, gutsy, independent-minded Koreans on both sides of the DMZ have demanded and won for themselves important roles. Beginning with the North-South summit meeting of June 2000, they have begun to take their future into their own hands as never before.

Because of its turbulent history, its strategic location, and its enduring state of tension, Korea has often flitted across the world's newspaper headlines and television screens in the past thirty years, only to disappear from view when the immediate dangers seemed to pass. The episodic nature of the world's attention means that most people in most countries have little idea how the recurrent Korea crises developed or what their significance has been. Whether acts of war, terrorism or heroism, showdowns over nuclear weapons, the sudden deaths of Korean leaders, the starvation of the people of the North, or the turn toward peaceful engagement, the news from and about Korea has been marked by a remarkable absence of historical context, background, or basis for understanding.

Upon retiring from daily journalism in 1993, I set out to remedy this omission by producing a history of the North-South conflict and conciliation in contemporary Korea, with special attention to the roles of the outside powers. It seemed presumptuous for an American to undertake this task, but I realized I had advantages not available to most others. I was a witness to some of the events described here during my 1972–75 tenure as Northeast Asia correspondent for the *Washington Post* and lived through other major events in Washington or in nearly yearly trips to Korea as the newspaper's diplomatic correspondent in the seventeen years thereafter. I have met all of South Korea's presidents, except its founding president, Syngman Rhee, and most of the other senior political leaders of that country. Starting in the mid-1980s I met North Korea's foreign minister or his senior deputy almost every year during their annual trips to the United Nations General Assembly in New York. These and other contacts led to my visits to North Korea in 1991 and 1995. I have been fortunate to have had many associations with present and former officials of the governments in Washington, Beijing, Moscow, and Tokyo, who provided unusual access to international aspects of the story.

The original edition of this book was four years in the making, nearly equally divided between research and writing, during which I examined the past while keeping up with fast-paced current events. The sponsorship of Johns Hopkins University's Nitze School of Advanced International Studies, which appointed me journalist-in-residence upon my retirement from the *Washington Post* and grants from the Rockefeller Brothers Fund and the Korea Foundation made it possible for me to concentrate almost full time on this effort in 1993–97 and to travel extensively to interview hundreds of participants in the events described here. After the dramatic events of 1998–2000 I decided to add a new chapter to bring the story up to date.

Despite all efforts, I continue to be impressed with what I do not know, especially about North Korea. Despite the limited opening, the decision-making and moving forces behind the scenes in Pyongyang remain obscured in a secrecy that is unique in the world for its thoroughness and pervasiveness. Unlike the former Soviet Union and even China, North Korea has revealed virtually none of the documentation of discussions and decisions, even from its earliest era. Using sources available to me elsewhere, including archival materials from the Soviet Union and the [East] German Democratic Republic as well as former diplomats and experts from those countries, I have done my best to discover and understand what underlay thought and action in North Korea in earlier times.

This is my third book of what has been called "contemporary history," which seeks to transcend journalism but is written only a few years after the events it describes. Like my first book, *Tet!*, on the crucial battle of the Vietnam War, and *The Turn* (more recently republished as *From the Cold War to a New Era*), on the diplomacy of the United States and the Soviet Union between 1983 and 1991, this volume goes to press while the outcome of the drama on the Korean peninsula is still beyond our reach. As in my earlier works, I was inspired by a quotation from British historian Dame C. Veronica Wedgwood: "History is written backward but lived forward. Those who know the end of the story can never know what it was like at the time." What follows is intended to convey what it was like at the time, before the end of the story is known.

— WASHINGTON, March 2001

# A NOTE ON KOREAN NAMES

The remarkable thing about Korean names is that so many of them are almost the same. The three most common surnames, Kim, Lee, and Park, account for more than 40 percent of the entire population of South Korea, according to a recent census. The surname Kim is associated with the mythical founder of the Silla dynasty. Lee (or Yi, in Korean) is the name of the dynasty that ruled Korea from 1392 to the annexation of Korea by Japan in 1910. Park also has an ancient origin. Only about 250 different surnames are known to exist among South Korea's 44 million people.

As is the case with most other East Asian names, the surname is usually written first, as in Kim Il Sung or Kim Young Sam. I have followed this practice throughout the book, except for a few figures whose names are widely known in reverse order, such as South Korea's first president, Syngman Rhee.

A list and brief identification of the principal characters whose activities are described in this book can be found starting on page 447.

# 1

## WHERE THE WILD BIRDS SING

*A*loft on dazzling white wings, the great cranes wheel in the sky and float down for a landing in a richly forested, unspoiled two-and-a-half-mile strip of land that stretches like a ribbon for 150 miles across the waist of the Korean peninsula. Here several hundred rare white-naped cranes stop over each spring and autumn in migration between their breeding grounds in northeastern China and Russia and their winter home in Japan. Amid a profusion of wildflowers, the birds join even rarer endangered red-crowned Manchurian cranes, the most elegant and highly prized member of the crane family and a symbol of good luck, fidelity, and long life in the Orient for more than a thousand years. Ornithologists have recorded 150 species of cranes, buntings, shrikes, swans, geese, kittiwakes, goosanders, eagles, and other birds passing through or living in the verdant strip each year, joining other year-round residents such as pheasant, wild pigs, black bears, and small Korean deer.

Under the terms of the armistice that ended the Korean War in 1953, all civilian activity is banned in the zone except for one tightly controlled farming village on each side. Due to a densely planted underground garden of deadly land mines, which the birds and animals somehow use a sixth sense to avoid, military patrols stick closely to well-worn paths. For the most part, it is a unique and leafy sanctuary in the midst of a crowded, increasingly urbanized peninsula.

The serenity is deceptive. The demilitarized zone, or DMZ, between North and South Korea is bordered by high fences of barbed and razor wire on the north and south, and guarded on the two sides by more than a thousand guard posts, watch towers, and reinforced bunkers across the width of the peninsula. On hair-trigger alert behind the fortifications are two of the world's largest aggregations of military force—1.1 million North Koreans facing 660,000 South Koreans and 37,000 Americans, the latter backed by the full military power of the world's most powerful nation. All sides are heavily armed and ready at a moment's notice to fight another bloody and devastating war. Now that the Berlin wall has fallen and the Soviet Union has collapsed, this pristine nature preserve marks the most dangerous and heavily fortified border in the world. The common wisdom of American GIs on duty in the area is "there ain't no D in the DMZ."

Across these fortified lines have flowed the passion and invective of an ancient nation that was suddenly and cruelly divided in the twentieth century by the great powers. The DMZ has been violated by tunnels, defiled by infiltrators, and scarred by armed skirmishes. The melodic call of its birds has been marred by harsh propaganda from giant loudspeakers erected on both sides to harass or entice the troops on the opposite lines. At the Joint Security Area in the clearing at Panmunjom, the only place along the course of the buffer zone where the barbed wire and mines are absent, low-slung conference buildings have been placed squarely atop the line of demarcation, and the negotiating tables within them are so arranged that the dividing line extends precisely down the middle. Here the hostility is palpable and open. Northern and southern troops scowl, spit, and shout obscenities at each other outside the conference buildings, and there have been shoving matches, injuries, and even deaths.

Panmunjom has also seen hopeful moments: meetings of special emissaries and political leaders, both publicized and secret; the transit of official delegations from one side to the other; the passage of relief supplies to ameliorate the effects of floods and famines; the return of prisoners and detainees from both sides; and the arrival and departure of would-be peacemakers and political leaders from the United States and other countries. If the hostility and tension on the Korean peninsula are ever to be alleviated through negotiation, the clearing at Panmunjom is likely to play a major role.

## THE EMERGENCE OF TWO KOREAS

Korea is a peninsula of approximately 85,000 square miles, roughly the size of New York and Pennsylvania combined, which juts down from the northeastern part of the vast mainland of Asia. It is well defined, with seas on the east, west, and south and two large rivers, the Yalu and the Tumen, providing a natural boundary with the landmass on the north. Archaeological exploration has confirmed that it was inhabited at least 20,000 years ago, and some sites suggest that its human habitation began much earlier. By the fourth century B.C. the antecedents of the Korean state, a tribal kingdom called Choson, had emerged near the Chinese border in northern Korea. By A.D. 300 the Koreans had thrown off Chinese rule and developed three separate kingdoms in the north, southeast, and southwest of the peninsula. In A.D. 668 the Silla kingdom, with Chinese help, overwhelmed the other two and unified nearly all of Korea.

From that early time on, for nearly thirteen hundred years until the mid-twentieth century, Korea developed as a unified country under a single administration with a distinctive language and strong traditions. It invented its own ingenious writing system and the first known movable metal type a century before Gutenberg's invention in Europe.

Geography dealt Korea a particularly difficult role. Located in a strategic but dangerous neighborhood between the greater powers of China, Japan, and Russia, Korea has suffered nine hundred invasions, great and small, in its two thousand years of recorded history. It has experienced five major periods of foreign occupation—by China, the Mongols, Japan, and, after World War II, the United States and the Soviet Union.

Of the major powers, China had by far the greatest influence and was the most acceptable to Koreans. Like many others on the rim of the Middle Kingdom, the Korean kings embraced Chinese culture, paid tribute to the Chinese emperor, and received recognition and a degree of protection in return. When unified Japan began its major expansion in the sixteenth century, its leader Hideyoshi Toyotomi attacked Korea as the first phase of an invasion of the Chinese mainland. The Korean navy under Admiral Yi Sun Sin fought back with an early class of ironclad warships, known as turtle ships, which inflicted severe losses on the Japanese. Eventually the Japanese were driven out, but only after laying waste to the land, thus setting a lasting pattern of enmity.

In the wake of the Japanese invasion and a subsequent invasion by the Manchus, who were soon to take power in China, Korea established a rigid policy of excluding foreigners, except for the Chinese and a small Japanese enclave that had been established at the southern port of Pusan. The imperial rulers of the Hermit Kingdom, as it was often called, created a governmental and social system modeled on Chinese Confucianism, with strictly regulated relations between ruler and subject, father and son, and husband and wife.

Korea's isolation ended in the mid-nineteenth-century age of imperialism, when major powers, including the United States, European countries, and Japan, sent warships forcibly to open the country to trade. In 1882, as a defensive measure against its neighbors, Korea signed a "Treaty of Amity and Commerce" with the United States, its first with a Western power, in which the United States promised to provide "good offices" in the event of external threat. It was reported that the Korean king danced with joy when the first American minister to Korea arrived. Among the treaties that followed shortly was one with czarist Russia, which had recognized the importance of the strategic peninsula and would soon begin building the Trans-Siberian Railway. The Russian foreign minister, Count Vladimir Lamsdorff, would later write, "Korea's destiny as a component part of the Russian empire, on geographical and political grounds, had been foreordained for us to fulfill."

In 1902, Japan carved out a strong position for itself by entering into an alliance with Britain, the most important European power in the area. Japan recognized British interests in China in return for British recognition of Japanese special interests in Korea. Sensing the weakness along the rim of the Chinese mainland, Russia began moving forces into Korea and immediately came into conflict with Japan. In an attempt to head off a clash, Japan proposed that the two countries carve up Korea into spheres of influence, with the dividing line at the thirty-eighth parallel—the same line chosen by the United States for the division of Korea after World War II. Russia's refusal to accept this and other proposed compromises led eventually to the Russo-Japanese war of 1904. Japan's surprise victory, its first over a Western power, put the Japanese in a powerful position to dominate Korea.

In 1905, in what many Koreans consider their first betrayal by the United States, Secretary of War (later President) William Howard Taft approved Japan's domination of Korea in a secret agreement with the Japanese foreign minister, in return for assurances that Tokyo would not challenge U.S. colonial domination of the Philippines. Later the same year, Japan's paramount political, military, and economic interests in Korea were codified in the Treaty of Portsmouth (New Hampshire), in which President Theodore Roosevelt played peacemaker and dealmaker between Japan and Russia, and for which he was awarded the Nobel Peace Prize. With no opposition in sight, Japan occupied Korea in 1905 and annexed it outright as a Japanese possession in 1910. Japan then ruled as the harsh colonial master of the peninsula until its defeat in World War II.

What many Koreans consider the second American betrayal— the division of Korea—occurred in the final days of World War II. The United States, Britain, and China had declared in the Cairo Declaration in 1943 that "in due course, Korea shall become free and independent," and at the 1945 Yalta Conference President Franklin D. Roosevelt proposed a U.S.–Soviet–Chinese trusteeship over Korea. Beyond these few words, there was no agreement among the wartime allies and no practical planning in Washington about the postwar future of the peninsula. It was reported that in 1945 Secretary of State Edward Stettinius asked a subordinate in a State Department meeting to please tell him where Korea was.

Only in the last week of the war, when the Soviet Union finally declared war on Japan and sent its troops into Manchuria and northern Korea, did the United States give serious consideration to its postwar policy in the peninsula. Suddenly Washington realized that

Russian occupation of Korea would have important military implications for the future of Japan and East Asia.

At this point, according to Yale University historian Richard Whelan, "the U.S. government would probably have been happiest if Korea simply had not existed." About two thousand civil affairs officers had been trained for military government duty in Japan, and elaborate plans had been drawn up for that country, but no one had been trained and no plans had been made for Korea. Despite Korea's well-known antipathy to its Japanese overlords, Washington had rebuffed efforts by Korean exile groups for recognition during the war. Thus as World War II drew to a close, there had been no consultation with Koreans about the future of their country.

On the evening of August 10, 1945, with Tokyo suing for peace and Soviet troops on the move, an all-night meeting was convened in the Executive Office Building next to the White House to decide what to do about accepting the impending Japanese surrender in Korea and elsewhere in Asia. Around midnight two young officers were sent into an adjoining room to carve out a U.S. occupation zone in Korea, lest the Soviets occupy the entire peninsula and move quickly toward Japan. Lieutenant Colonels Dean Rusk, who was later to be secretary of state under Presidents Kennedy and Johnson, and Charles Bonesteel, later U.S. military commander in Korea, had little preparation for the task. Working in haste and under great pressure, and using a *National Geographic* map for reference, they proposed that U.S. troops occupy the area south of the thirty-eighth parallel, which was approximately halfway up the peninsula and north of the capital city of Seoul, and that Soviet troops occupy the area north of the parallel.

No Korea experts were involved in the decision. Rusk later confessed that neither he nor any of the others involved were aware that at the turn of the century the Russians and Japanese had discussed dividing Korea into spheres of influence at the thirty-eighth parallel, a historical fact that might have suggested to Moscow that Washington had finally recognized this old claim. "Had we known that, we almost surely would have chosen another line of demarcation," Rusk wrote many years later.

The thirty-eighth parallel line was hastily incorporated into General Order Number One for the occupation of Japanese-held territory.

Despite the fact that U.S. forces were far away and would not arrive on the scene for several weeks, the Soviets carefully stopped their southward advance at the parallel. Thus Korea came to be divided into two "temporary" zones of occupation that, as the cold war deepened, became the sites of two antagonistic Korean regimes based on diametrically opposed principles and sponsors.

U.S. forces were eventually sent from Japan for occupation duty, an assignment that was not popular with the troops. Colonel Harry Summers, who later became a prominent military strategist, recalls arriving for duty as a U.S. Army private and being lectured by the occupation commander, General John R. Hodge, that "there are three things American troops in Japan are afraid of: diarrhea, gonorrhea, and Ko-rea." Under Hodge's guidance, the U.S.-backed Republic of Korea was officially proclaimed on August 15, 1948. The Soviet-backed Democratic People's Republic of Korea (DPRK), in the North, was proclaimed on September 9, 1948. The South inherited a larger population and more of the agriculture and light industry, while the North obtained most of the heavy industry, electric power, and mineral resources. Each regime claimed sway over the entire peninsula; these claims persist today.

Summing up, Gregory Henderson, a former U.S. Foreign Service officer and noted Korea scholar, wrote in 1974, "No division of a nation in the present world is so astonishing in its origin as the division of Korea; none is so unrelated to conditions or sentiment within the nation itself at the time the division was effected; none is to this day so unexplained; in none does blunder and planning oversight appear to have played so large a role. Finally, there is no division for which the U.S. government bears so heavy a share of the responsibility as it bears for the division of Korea."

As these events and those of its more distant past illustrate, Korea has been a country of the wrong size in the wrong place: large and well located enough to be of substantial value to those around it and thus worth fighting and scheming over, yet too small to merit priority attention by more powerful nations on all but a few occasions. Korea's fate was often to be an afterthought, subordinated to more immediate or compelling requirements of larger powers, rather than a subject of full consideration in its own right.

Yet Koreans are neither meek nor passive, but a tough, combative, and independent-minded people with a tradition of strong centralized authority. They are characteristically about as subtle as *kimchi,* the fiery pepper-and-garlic concoction that is their national dish, and as timid as a *tae kwon do* (Korean karate) chop. Confronted with the reality of their bitter division, North and South Korea have grappled unceasingly for advantage and supremacy over each other—and with the greater powers outside. How they have done so in the past quarter-century, and with what risks and results, is recounted in these pages.

## WAR AND ITS AFTERMATH

To head its regime in the North, the Soviet Union chose a 33-year-old Korean guerrilla commander who had initially fought the Japanese in China but had spent the last years of World War II in Manchurian training camps commanded by the Soviet army. Kim Il Sung, as he called himself (his birth name was Kim Song Ju), had a burning ambition to reunite his country. In the South the United States gave the nod to 70-year-old Syngman Rhee, who had degrees from George Washington University, Harvard, and Princeton and had lived in exile throughout most of the Japanese occupation. Rhee had a messianic belief that he was destined to reunite Korea under an anticommunist banner.

Late in 1948 the Soviet army went home, turning North Korea over to the regime it had created. The following June, U.S. troops followed suit. Before the summer was over, civil war broke out in clashes of battalion size along the thirty-eighth parallel. Each side was building its forces with an eye to gaining military supremacy.

On June 25, 1950, North Korea, with Soviet and Chinese backing, invaded the South in an effort to reunify the country by force of arms. The invasion was contested and ultimately repulsed by the forces of the United States, South Korea, and fifteen other nations under the flag of the United Nations. The Chinese intervened massively on the other side to save North Koreans from defeat. Internationally, the bloody three-year Korean War was a historic turning point. It led the United States to shift decisively from post–World

War II disarmament to rearmament to stop Soviet expansionism, tripling U.S. military outlays and doubling its troop presence in Europe to bolster the newly formed North Atlantic Treaty Organization. The war cemented the alliance between the Soviet Union and China for most of a decade and made the United States and China bitter enemies for more than twenty years. The battle for Korea firmly established the cold war and brought the Korean peninsula to the center of global attention.

Until recently, the origins of the war have been a matter of intense dispute. As late as 1993, North Korea republished its version in a paperback volume titled *The US Imperialists Started the Korean War.* However, documents from the Soviet archives recently made available to historians show clearly that in March, August, and September 1949 and January 1950, Kim implored Stalin and his diplomats repeatedly to authorize an invasion of the South, at one point telling Soviet embassy officers, "Lately I do not sleep at night, thinking about how to resolve the question of the unification of the whole country. If the matter of the liberation of the people of the southern portion of Korea and the unification of the country is drawn out, then I can lose the trust of the people of Korea."

On at least two occasions in 1949, Stalin turned down Kim's requests, but the documents establish that in early 1950 he approved the war plan due to the "changed international situation." At this writing, scholars are still unsure what led to Stalin's reversal. Was it the victory of Mao's Communist Party in China, the development of the Soviet Union's atomic bomb, the withdrawal of U.S. forces from South Korea, or Secretary of State Dean Acheson's famous statement excluding South Korea from the U.S. defense perimeter—all of which took place in 1949 or early 1950—or a combination of these and other causes? We still do not know.

The Korean conflict was considered the prototype of a limited war in that none of the big powers used the nuclear weapons available to them, and the United States refrained from attacking Soviet or Chinese territory. On the peninsula, however, the war was savage in its destructiveness. Although the figures are uncertain, a widely accepted estimate is that 900,000 Chinese and 520,000 North Korean soldiers were killed or wounded, as were about 400,000 UN

Command troops, nearly two-thirds of them South Koreans. U.S. casualties were 36,000 dead.

In Korea the war devastated both halves of a country that had only just begun to recover from four decades of Japanese occupation and the sudden shock of division. Around 3 million people, roughly a tenth of the entire population of both sides at the time, were killed, wounded, or missing as a result of the war. Another 5 million became refugees. South Korea's property losses were put at $2 billion, the equivalent of its gross national product for 1949; North Korean losses were estimated at only slightly less.

When the fighting finally stopped in July 1953, the front line was an irregular tangent slanting across the thirty-eighth parallel very close to where it had all begun. In keeping with the armistice agreement, the forces on each side pulled back two thousand meters from the cease-fire lines to create the demilitarized zone. Although both sides were exhausted by three years of combat, there were fears— which have never died—that the battle might be resumed at any moment.

One of the most important consequences of the war was the hardening of ideological and political lines between North and South. The antipathy that had developed between the opposing regimes was deepened into a blood feud among family members, extending from political leaders to the bulk of the ordinary people who had suffered at the hands of the other side. The thirteen-hundred-year-old unity of the Korean people was shattered.

In the aftermath of the war, the Rhee regime in the South became increasingly dictatorial and corrupt until it was forced out of office in 1960 by a student-led revolt. After a year the moderate successor government was ousted by a military junta headed by Major General Park Chung Hee, a Japanese-trained officer who had flirted with communism immediately after the Japanese surrender. Park's background created concern in Washington and initial hope in Pyongyang. Early on, Kim Il Sung dispatched a trusted aide to the South to make secret contact with Park. But instead of exploring a deal, Park had the emissary arrested and executed.

In the North, Kim Il Sung systematically purged his political opponents, creating a highly centralized system that accorded him unlimited power and generated a formidable cult of personality. As the great communist divide between the Soviet Union and China emerged in the mid-1950s, Kim, though profoundly disturbed by it, learned to play off his communist sponsors against each other to his own advantage. In July 1961 he went to Moscow and persuaded Nikita Khrushchev, who was seeking to recruit him as an ally against China, to sign a treaty of "friendship, cooperation and mutual assistance," pledging to come to Pyongyang's aid in case of a new war on the divided peninsula. This done, Kim proceeded to Beijing, where he presented Chinese leaders with his Moscow treaty and asked them to match it, which they did by signing their own nearly identical accord.

While both North and South Korea gave lip service to eventual reunification, there was little but hostility between them in the 1950s and 1960s. In the most notable incident, in January 1968, a thirty-one-man North Korean commando team attempted to assassinate the South Korean president. The team penetrated to within a thousand yards of the Blue House, the South Korean equivalent of the White House, before being repulsed by police and security forces. The prospects for any sort of reconciliation on the divided peninsula appeared slim indeed.

## THE ORIGINS OF NEGOTIATION

On July 9, 1971, Henry Kissinger landed secretly in Beijing on a Pakistani airliner to begin the historic Sino-American rapprochement that openly split the communist world and changed global politics. At the time, North Korean leader Kim Il Sung, a familiar figure to Chinese elders and a frequent unannounced visitor, was also secretly in Beijing. But while Kissinger and the president he served, Richard Nixon, were thrilled by the prospect of a geopolitical shift of great importance, Kim found the maneuvering of the great powers distinctly unsettling.

So far as can be determined, Korea did not figure in Nixon's desire to end the two decades of hostility with China, which had begun with Chinese intervention in the Korean War. However, among the factors uppermost in Nixon's triangular diplomacy with

Moscow and Beijing was its potentially alarming effect on North Vietnam, another Asian client of the two giants of international communism. By simultaneously improving ties with both of Hanoi's sponsors, Nixon hoped to demonstrate that North Vietnam was expendable and vulnerable in a larger game being played by major powers. Though probably unintended, the same sets of pressures were felt by North Korea and, to Washington's eventual dismay, by South Korea as well. As a result both Korean regimes felt more insecure than ever before. Both, for the first time, decided to try to take the settlement of their conflict into their own hands.

From Kim Il Sung's vantage point China's sudden shift toward amicable relations with the United States represented a betrayal of the common struggle against U.S. imperialism, leaving him in an exposed position against the American military power, still entrenched on the other side of the DMZ. The astute Chinese were sensitive to his problem. In his initial talk with Kissinger, Premier Chou Enlai went out of his way to urge that all U.S. troops be withdrawn from South Korea, although Chou may have done this more for Kim's reassurance than for any expectation of results. Immediately after Kissinger's departure, the leaders in Beijing dispatched two high-ranking officials to Pyongyang to give Kim a full report on the discussions with the Americans.

Later in the year, the Chinese approved new economic aid and signed the first agreement on military aid to North Korea in fifteen years. The results began to appear the following April, when newly arrived Chinese tanks clanked through Pyongyang's Kim Il Sung Square in the parade for the North Korean leader's birthday. At the same time, China began supplying North Korea with its models of Russia's MiG-19 supersonic fighter planes.

After holding his silence about the Sino-American developments for three weeks, Kim finally spoke out on August 6, 1971, at a mass rally in Pyongyang honoring his closest foreign friend, Cambodian head of state Prince Norodom Sihanouk. In a surprise move, Kim announced that "we are ready to establish contact at any time with all political parties, including the [ruling] Democratic Republican Party, and all social organizations and individual personages in South Korea." This was an abrupt reversal of the long-standing position, reiterated by North Korea's foreign minister only four months earlier, that the ouster of the ruling party was an essential condition for negotiations with the South.

In Seoul, President Park Chung Hee was also shaken by the news of Nixon's opening to China. Like the rest of America's allies, Park had had no advance notice from Washington, and he too found it shocking because it raised new doubts about the constancy and reliability of his great power sponsor. To Park, the rapprochement implied U.S. acceptance of a hostile, powerful, and revolutionary country in South Korea's immediate neighborhood, tied by a military alliance to North Korea. Since the announcement of the "Nixon Doctrine" in mid-1969—that Asians should provide the manpower for their own wars—the United States had appeared to be moving steadily toward disengagement. Early in 1971, over Park's vehement objections, Washington had withdrawn 20,000 of the 62,000 American troops stationed in South Korea, at the same time that it was pulling back American forces from South Vietnam. Despite the reassuring words of U.S. political leaders and diplomats, Park took these developments as "a message to the Korean people that we won't rescue you if North Korea invades again," according to his longtime aide, Kim Seong Jin. Now on top of everything else, the White House was suddenly, and without notice to him, consorting with Beijing.

Meeting privately with reporters at the Blue House on the day Kissinger's secret trip to China was announced, the South Korean president was gloomy. "The United States has long been trying to reach a rapprochement with Red China, but China has not changed," Park complained, suggesting that Washington had made all the concessions. In a subsequent off-the-record dinner with Blue House correspondents, Park declared that 90 percent of the Nixon visit to China was a domestic maneuver intended to aid the president's reelection. In view of Nixon's "low-posture diplomacy" toward Beijing, Park told reporters, the pressing question for South Korea was, "How long can we trust the United States?"

Weeks later, Park addressed his concerns directly to Nixon in a letter that was delivered to Secretary of State William Rogers by Foreign Minister Kim Yong Shik. The South Korean president was particularly worried that deals might be made about the Koreas during Nixon's forthcoming trip to Beijing, and he wanted to discuss it with Nixon at a meeting. But in Washington Park's concern was such a low-priority question that it took three months for the State Department and Nixon's National Security Council staff to frame and present a presidential reply. When it finally came, it was a ritual declaration from Nixon that during his Beijing trip he would not seek accommodation with China at the expense of South Korea's national interest. Park was told that a summit meeting was out of the question. Recalling his feelings about the maneuvering surrounding the U.S. rapprochement with China years later, Park wrote that "this series of developments contained an unprecedented peril to our people's survival. . . . [The situation] almost reminded one of the last days of the Korean Empire a century earlier, when European Powers were similarly agitating in rivalry over Korea."

Even before Kissinger's secret trip to Beijing, North Korea had been putting forth discreet feelers for direct talks with the South, and Park's government had been quietly discussing how to respond. After Kim Il Sung's August 6 announcement the South moved quickly by proposing a meeting in the context of Red Cross societies. The North immediately accepted.

On August 20, 1971, eighteen years after the armistice ended the Korean War, representatives of the two Red Cross societies met in Panmunjom for the first exploratory discussions between the two halves of the divided peninsula. To no one's surprise, the talks did not go smoothly.

On November 20, after three months and nine rounds of fruitless sparring, South Korean "Red Cross delegate" Chong Hong Jin, who actually was deputy director of the international affairs bureau of the South Korean Central Intelligence Agency (KCIA), handed a note proposing private and separate meetings at Panmunjom to his counterpart, North Korean "Red Cross delegate" Kim Duk Hyun, actually a senior official of the Workers Party Organization and Guidance Department, the DPRK control mechanism. Like these two, many of the participants in the Red Cross exchanges actually were intelligence or party officials. In the decades to come, because these agencies were powerful, discreet, and tightly controlled by their respective leaders, they would become frequently used channels for the many secret communications between North and South.

The South's bid for higher-level talks was promptly accepted. North Korean leaders were ready and very willing. A plenary meeting of the Central Committee of the Workers Party, gathering in secret as the contacts were beginning, approved a large-scale peace offensive toward the South in response to "the changing domestic and foreign political situation."

On March 28, 1972, following eleven rounds of secret contacts with his counterpart, South Korea's Chong slipped out the northern door of the North Korean pavilion of Panmunjom instead of returning to the southern side. He was taken by car to the nearby North Korean city of Kaesong and then by helicopter to Pyongyang—the first of many South Korean officials to go to that capital for talks. There it was arranged for the secret contacts to go to a higher level: the chief of South Korea's intelligence agency would come to Pyongyang for talks, and a senior North Korean would reciprocate by making a trip to the South. In late April, a direct telephone line linking the offices of the KCIA and the Workers Party was secretly installed between Seoul and Pyongyang.

The man in charge in the South was Lee Hu Rak, a former noncommissioned officer in the Japanese army and former chief of staff to President Park before being named to head the KCIA. While it took its name and some of the functions from its U.S. model, in many respects the KCIA was more like the prewar Japanese *kempeitai* or the Soviet KGB in its unbridled power in the domestic as well as the foreign arena. The former U.S. diplomat and Korea scholar Gregory Henderson called the KCIA "a state within a state, a vast shadowy world of . . . bureaucrats, intellectuals, agents and thugs." By the early 1970s, the director of the KCIA was more powerful and more feared at home than the prime minister or any other governmental figure except the president himself.

After receiving written instructions from the president about visiting the "special zone," Lee traveled secretly through Panmunjom to Pyongyang in early May. Looking back on it, Lee recalled that "I felt the kind of anxiety that is quite indescribable" because "we simply had no ghost of a precedent to guide me as to how to open up some sort of mutually acceptable communication." He was also mindful that, as the chief of intelligence for the Republic of Korea (ROK), he was the person the northern communists would like most to get their hands on, after Park himself.

His hosts took him to see the sights of Pyongyang and to a revolutionary opera extolling Kim's anti-Japanese exploits. Then on his second night in Pyongyang, Lee was awakened and driven through a rainstorm to a well-guarded building in the hills around the North Korean capital. He was not told where he was being taken. At fifteen minutes after midnight, at the end of the harrowing ride, the thoroughly shaken KCIA director, who thought he might never live to see the dawn, found himself face to face with Kim Il Sung.

## KIM IL SUNG

The Great Leader, as he was known to his subjects, is among the most fascinating figures of the twentieth century, dominating his country during his lifetime as few individuals are ever able to do. From the late 1950s his power was virtually unlimited within the borders of North Korea, and his decisions often had repercussions involving life and death in South Korea and beyond. As a national leader, Kim surpassed all others of his time in longevity. When he died in July 1994 at age 82, he had outlived Joseph Stalin by four decades and Mao Tse-tung by almost two decades, and he had remained in power throughout the terms of office of six South Korean presidents, nine U.S. presidents, and twenty-one Japanese prime ministers.

The future founder and leader of North Korea was born in Pyongyang on April 15, 1912, the day the *Titanic* sank. His parents were both Christians. His mother was the devout, churchgoing daughter of a Presbyterian elder, and his father had attended a missionary school.

Kim had only eight years of formal education, the last two in Chinese schools in Manchuria, where his father moved to operate an herb pharmacy. When he was 17 years old, he was expelled from school for revolutionary activities and never returned to the classroom. After being jailed briefly, in the early 1930s he joined guerrilla bands fighting the Japanese who, after turning Korea into a Japanese colony in 1910, had invaded and occupied Manchuria. The Korean guerrillas were organized by and attached to an army led by the Chinese Communist Party.

Although Kim's activities fell short of the brilliant, war-winning exploits later concocted by North Korean propagandists, he was successful enough that the Japanese put a price on his head. By 1941, Kim's unit and other parts of the Chinese guerrilla army were forced to retreat across the Manchurian border to Soviet army training camps, where they spent the next four years. During these years Kim married a Korean partisan and fathered two sons, the elder of whom was Kim Jong Il, his eventual political heir and successor.

It is still unclear how Kim was selected to lead North Korea. Having spent years in a Soviet training camp, Kim was well known to the Soviet officers who occupied the area north of the thirty-eighth parallel in 1945, and he had a reputation for being reliable and courageous. He appeared in Pyongyang immediately after the war in the uniform of a Soviet army captain, according to a Soviet general who served in the occupation force. Some accounts suggest that Joseph Stalin himself made the final choice of Kim from several candidates. Stalin is reported to have said, "Korea is a young country, and it needs a young leader."

As a leader, Kim was cordial to and comfortable with ordinary people. He emerged from a family of hard-working ordinary people and described himself in his memoirs as "an ordinary man." Vadim Medvedev, a Gorbachev aide who was Kim's escort for several days in Moscow in 1986, wrote later that he was "greatly surprised" to find in him "an absolutely normal person, with whom you could talk not only about politics but also weather, exchange opinions on events happening around and impresssions on what we saw."

Yet at the same time Kim came to live in luxury and exclusiveness beyond the dreams of kings. He inhabited at least five sumptuous palaces in North Korea and innumerable guest houses built for his comfort and amusement, all completely cut off from anyone except servants, bodyguards, and carefully screened guests. Uninvited people were barred from even setting foot on the wide and well-tended road leading to his Pyongyang residence. Like Stalin and

Mao, whose cults of personality he emulated but far outdistanced, his automobile used special lanes, and other traffic was banished when he moved through the streets of his capital. When he went to the Soviet Union by train in 1984, all rail traffic was stopped along his route at the demand of the North Koreans, so that his luxurious special train could travel unimpeded by any competing or oncoming trains. (This caused massive tie-ups in the Soviet rail system.) When his train stopped to take on supplies or to give Kim a breath of air along the way, the station platforms were cleared of their normal throngs, left vacant except for specially authorized people, some of whom had been recruited to applaud and cheer him.

In deference to his health, a special institute was established in Pyongyang to concentrate on the aging process of this one man, with doctors and medical specialists monitoring his every move, and special fruits and vegetables produced solely for his consumption. When Kim traveled to Berlin on his 1984 European trip, according to a former East German diplomat who helped arrange the visit, Kim's aides arranged for a special bed to be flown ahead for his sleeping comfort (as was often the case with Ronald Reagan as U.S. president). In addition, they brought a special toilet with built-in monitoring equipment that instantly analyzed whatever the Great Leader eliminated for any sign of health problems. The former German diplomat said that medical specialists from different friendly countries were assigned primary responsiblity for consultation on different parts of the leader's body, with East German doctors being given responsibility for Kim's head and neck, including the large but benign tumor on the back of his neck that had been visible since the early 1970s.

From his education in Chinese schools and his four years in a Soviet military camp, Kim was fluent in Chinese and conversant in Russian. His complex relationship with the two giants of communism—his neighbors, sponsors, and for most of his life, his allies—was central to nearly all that he did or said. To a large extent, he owed his career as well as his country's well-being to China and Russia, yet he was always wary of their dominant power. In a tradition practiced by Koreans throughout their history, Kim went to extraordinary lengths to gain and maintain as much independence as possible.

Oleg Rakhmanin, a former Soviet official who had extensive meetings with Kim over a twenty-five-year period, said that when Kim was being actively wooed to take Moscow's side against Beijing, he was "careful and prudent, weighing his every word. He was afraid the Chinese would learn what he said to us. . . . [Kim was] a calculating character—a chess player who calculates his every move." Another former Soviet official, who had been posted in the Soviet Embassy in Pyongyang, described Kim as "a flexible and pragmatic politician, an Oriental Talleyrand. He would agree with our leaders and give a lot of promises, but afterward he would pursue the same line, his own line."

Due perhaps to his limited formal education, Kim was not a book reader and could not be fairly described as an intellectual. In deference to the intellect, he added a pen to the traditional communist hammer-and-sickle as North Korea's official emblem, but in personal conversations he rarely referred to world history or to any work of serious literature. "He knows a lot of Confucianism and a smattering of Marx, Lenin, Hegel, and such," said a former communist diplomat who dealt with Kim extensively.

Most of his government's philosophical utterances dealt with "the *juche* idea," which has been hailed in North Korea as Kim's original, brilliant, and revolutionary contribution to national and international thought. But Kim acknowledged on occasion that *juche* was not original with him. While the fact was rarely mentioned in the North, the term and concept go back at least to Korean scholars in the early years of the twentieth century. Kim explained that "I have just laid special emphasis on it."

Kim's version of *juche,* which emanates from North Korea's militant nationalism, is usually described in shorthand as "self-reliance," but there is much more to it. According to Han S. Park of the University of Georgia, a leading American expert on *juche* as a philosophical system and state religion, "*Juche* views Korea as a chosen land, as people are told consistently that world civilization originated from the Korean peninsula." A much-publicized tenet of *juche* is the people-centered view that "man is the master over all things" and creates his own destiny, but according to Park, this humanistic-sounding precept is firmly embedded in and qualified by a collective consciousness guided by a Great Leader—in this case, Kim Il Sung and his successor, Kim Jong Il.

In an explicit analogy to the human body, in *juche* the Great Leader is the brain that makes decisions and commands action, the Workers Party is the nerve system that mediates and maintains equilibrium between the brain and the body, and the people are the bone and muscle that implement the decisions and channel feedback to the Leader. However bizarre this belief system seems to outsiders, North Koreans are systematically instructed in it and walled off from contrary views. The great unanswered question is how many North Koreans are true believers and how many have their private doubts.

Beyond its sanctification of Kim's decisions, *juche* was a declaration of political independence from his two communist sponsors. Although it was originally called "a creative application of Marxism-Leninism," eventually all reference to Marxist connections was abandoned. The *juche* philosophy has deep traditionalist roots and great appeal to the Korean antipathy for external domination. In practice, it became synonymous with North Korea's famous autarky.

For a visitor from afar, the most extraordinary thing about the Kim Il Sung era was the unrestrained adoration, bordering on idolatry, built up around the Great Leader, which seemed to reflect a craving for adulation that could never be sated. Kim's photograph, later joined by a separate picture of his son, Kim Jong Il, was on the wall in every home as well as every shop and office. Starting in the 1960s, every North Korean adult wore a badge bearing Kim's likeness on his or her suit, tunic, or dress. Within his country Kim was nearly always referred to as *suryong* or Great Leader, a term referring to the greatest of the great that Kim reserved for Lenin, Stalin, and Mao before he began applying it to himself in the 1960s.

In the late 1980s, according to one count, there were at least 34,000 monuments to Kim in North Korea, not including benches where he once sat, which were protected with glass coverings, and other memorabilia of his many visits throughout the country. The main square in the capital, the leading university, the highest party school, and many other places and institutions were named for him. During Kim's travels as well as his everyday meetings, an aide followed behind him writing down his every observation, many of which were published in several languages and considered holy writ by North Koreans. In the 1960s, near the beginning of the buildup, a Soviet party official who had experienced the deification and later downfall of Stalin had the temerity to ask Kim directly, "How is it possible there is this cult of personality in your country?" Kim's answer was, "You don't know our country. Our country is used to paying respect to elders—like China and Japan, we live by Confucian culture." It is unlikely that anyone was bold enough to ask this question of him in more recent years.

Kim created an impermeable and absolutist state that many have compared to a religious cult. No dissent from or criticism of Kim Il Sung, his tenets, or his decisions was permitted. Citizens were arrested, and some even sent off to one of the country's extensive gulags, for inadvertently defacing or sitting on a newspaper photograph of the Great Leader or his son and chosen successor. Reports of inhuman treatment, torture, and public execution for failure to conform with Kimism were rife. According to defectors and U.S. State Department Human Rights reports, twelve prison camps were established in remote areas containing as many as 150,000 people, many of whom were held in ghastly, inhuman conditions with little chance of ever being released.

Kim's biographer, Dae-Sook Suh of the University of Hawaii, wrote that Kim became "a ruler who wields more power than the notorious monarchs of the old Korean kingdom," building a state that practices "a peculiar brand of oriental despotism" rather than communism. "There was no such thing as a conversation with Kim Il Sung," said a prominent South Korean who was Kim's guest on numerous occasions. "If he spoke to a North Korean, that person stood up, in effect at attention, to receive instructions or orders." With his personal guests who were important to him or his state, Kim was a stickler for detail. While in Pyongyang, "he would call me every day," said this South Korean, always asking, "How are you feeling? Is everything all right?"

In a revealing speech in the 1970s, Kim told government officials that "whatever I am doing, I cannot rest easy unless I have the whole situation at my fingertips." As the restless and energetic leader of a small country, Kim telephoned the chief of the general staff every night for a report on the military situation, and the foreign minister for a report on diplomatic developments. Based on the reports, he said he issued immediate instructions.

During most of his years in power, Kim traveled incessantly within the country on personal inspection tours giving "on-the-spot guidance." As late as 1980, Kim told Representative Stephen Solarz, the first U.S. political figure to visit Pyongyang, that each year he spent ten to fifteen days on such tours in each of the ten provinces and three special cities. Kim boasted to Solarz that as a result of his conversations with farmers in their fields, he had personally counter-manded government instructions about the planting time for rice—and claimed that the amended policy produced a bumper crop.

Because his many directives took on the aura of holy writ, they proved difficult to change if they became outdated or were mistaken from the start. Even Politburo members and government ministers were forced to undergo "self-criticism," and some were ousted from their jobs, for making proposals that inadvertently breached policy lines previously laid down by the Great Leader. "Once said by Kim, it is said forever," according to a diplomat who spent four years in Pyongyang. "Nobody is allowed to change anything; the smallest sign of deviation means the system has developed a dangerous crack."

In the spring of 1972, Kim had just celebrated his sixtieth birth-day with great fanfare, a traditional milestone for Korean elders, after which they are greatly venerated. Kim's *hwangop* birthday was the occasion for the opening of the ninety-two-room Museum of the Revolution, devoted to glorifying him, and the unveiling of his sixty-six-foot-high bronze likeness, painted in gold, on a scenic spot over-looking Pyongyang, where a shrine had been erected for worship of the Japanese emperors during the Japanese occupation. It was the largest statue ever built by Koreans for any leader in their long his-tory. Still in his physical prime, Kim was a burly man with a rolling walk and heavy-rimmed glasses. *New York Times* correspondent Har-rison Salisbury, the first American correspondent granted an inter-view with the Great Leader, called him "a big, impressive man with a mobile face and a quick chuckle" and nearly constant gestures to emphasize his words. At this point in his long career, Kim turned his attention and his considerable charisma to creating his first political opening to South Korea.

## CONVERSATIONS WITH THE SOUTH

The historic initial secret meeting between Kim Il Sung and the second most powerful figure in the South began with an exchange of pleasantries and assurances of trust. In the early morning hours of May 4, 1972, Lee Hu Rak, director of the ROK intelligence agency, broke the ice by praising the achievements of construction he had been shown on his first day in Pyongyang. Kim Il Sung responded by praising the South Korean president for sending Lee as "an expression of his trust," and he commended Lee as "a very bold person" and "a hero" for making the journey to the opposite camp.

The meeting, whose record was kept by Lee's aide and not disclosed until seventeen years later, was remarkable for the shared antipathy to the major powers and the heavy emphasis by both sides on reaching accords and eventual reunification.

> LEE: President Park Chung Hee and I believe unification should be achieved by ourselves without interference of the four powers [the United States, China, Japan, the Soviet Union]. . . . We are never front men of the United States or Japan. We believe we should resolve our issues by ourselves. . . .
>
> KIM: Our position is to oppose reliance on external forces on the issue of unification. This is where I agree with Park Chung Hee. . . .
>
> LEE: I'd like to tell you that President Park is a person who detests foreign interference most.
>
> KIM: That being so, we are already making progress to solve the issue. Let us exclude foreign forces. Let's not fight. Let's unite as a nation. Let's not take issue with communism or capitalism. . . .
>
> LEE: A nation with 40–50 million people is a powerful country. [The population of the South in 1972 was 32 million; that of the North 14 million.] One hundred years ago we

yielded to big powers because we were weak. In the future the big powers will yield to us. I'd like to make it clear to you, the big powers only provide lip service to our hope for unification. But in their hearts, they don't want our unification.

KIM: Big powers and imperialism prefer to divide a nation into several nations.

In a further attempt to clear the air, Kim apologized for the actions of the North Korean commando team that had attempted to assassinate Park in 1968. Kim suggested, improbably, that he did not know of the famous Blue House raid in advance, blaming it on "leftist chauvinists within our structure" and saying that when he had learned of it, he fired his chiefs of espionage and security. (In fact, there was a purge of military and paramilitary officials afterward.) "Tell President Park I feel very sorry," said Kim.

After the secret return visit to Seoul by the DPRK deputy premier Park Sung Chul, who conferred with President Park, North and South Korea surprised the outside world by publicly issuing a joint statement on July 4, 1972, a date that seemed to have been chosen to illustrate their independence from the nation that celebrates its own independence then.* The statement declared that the two sides had reached full agreement on three principles:

First, unification shall be achieved through independent efforts without being subject to external imposition or interference.
    Second, unification shall be achieved through peaceful means, and not through use of force against one another.
    Third, a great national unity, as a homogeneous people, shall be sought first, transcending differences in ideas, ideologies, and systems.

*The ROK government notified the U.S. Embassy in Seoul several days in advance of the announcement and gave American diplomats an advance look at the text. Although supposedly a state secret, news of the statement circulated freely in Seoul. The 21-year-old son of Francis Underhill, the deputy U.S. ambassador, shocked his father the night before the announcement by telling him he had heard about the secret diplomacy and the impending joint statement from Koreans at a tea shop along the main street in Seoul.

As part of the joint statement, the two sides agreed "not to defame and slander one another" and to take positive measures to prevent inadvertent military incidents. In order to avoid officially granting recognition to each other, however, the statement was not signed by the two governments but simply by KCIA director Lee Hu Rak and Director of Organization and Guidance Kim Young Joo, Kim Il Sung's brother, "upholding the desires of their respective superiors."

In a press conference Pyongyang's emissary to the South, Deputy Premier Park, announced the North's interpretation of these accords. He declared, "Now that there exists no threat of aggression in South Korea from the North, nor . . . any need of protection and [since] our nation is settling its internal problems according to its own faith, the U.S. imperialists must no longer meddle in the domestic affairs of our country; they must withdraw at once, taking with them all their forces of aggression."

Kim Il Sung saw the North-South dialogue as a way to wean the South Korean regime away from the United States and Japan and to bring about the withdrawal of U.S. troops. Shortly after the July 4, 1972, joint statement, Kim's ambassador in Berlin, Lee Chang Su, in a confidential presentation to the East German Politburo, said that "the [communist] party and government of North Korea will concentrate on forcing South Korean leaders into agreement, to free them from U.S. and Japanese influence and to allow no U.S. intervention." He revealed that a North Korean peace offensive had been authorized in meetings of the Workers Party in November 1971 and July 1972, and he said the effort had "undermined the attempts of the U.S. imperialism to retain its troops in Korea, as well as the attempts of the Japanese imperialists to invade Korea again. . . . The Park Chung Hee clique will capitulate to this peace offensive. The tactical measures we adopted proved successful with the holding of talks with the enemy."

President Park, according to his longtime aide, Kim Seong Jin, saw the dialogue as a helpful tactic in a harsh environment in which North Korean military power was a serious threat. "As long as you can touch an opponent with at least one hand," said Park, "you can tell whether he will attack." Park had no belief or interest in unification in his lifetime, his aide said, and little interest in making compromises to bring fruits from the North-South contacts. Unlike his successors, Park also expressed no interest in meeting Kim Il Sung. "He told me directly, I have no intention at all [to meet Kim Il Sung]," said his aide. "Why should I meet that fellow?"

Most of the world, however, greeted the surprising news of the conciliatory joint statement with soaring optimism about the chances for a rapprochement between the two bitter enemies. Among those most fascinated were the veteran correspondents who had covered the Korean War and were still following events on the divided peninsula. Keyes Beech, Tokyo correspondent of the *Chicago Daily News,* was among the most eminent of these. At the outset of the war in 1950, Beech had telephoned NBC correspondent John Rich in the Japanese capital to tell him that hostilities had broken out at the thirty-eighth parallel. "We'd better get over to Korea, there's a war on," said Beech. Twenty-two years later, after hearing the dramatic news of the North-South joint statement, Beech again telephoned Rich and reminded him of their 1950 discussion. This time it had a different twist. "We'd better get over to Korea," said Beech, "there's a peace on." Both men were in Seoul within days.

# 2

## THE END OF THE BEGINNING

The fifty-four members of the North Korean Red Cross delegation, each wearing a Kim Il Sung badge and some dressed in the high-necked cadre suits typical of the Chinese communists, walked across the dividing line at Panmunjom a few minutes before ten A.M. on September 13, 1972. As they stepped into the South for the first time since the bloody war that had left millions dead, the northerners were greeted with embraces, handshakes, and laughter from their southern counterparts and bouquets of flowers from pigtailed schoolgirls. For one emotional moment the two delegations seemed to transcend the bitter ideological and political conflict that had plagued the peninsula for decades. Suddenly they showed themselves to be brothers, sisters, and cousins—all Koreans.

The first visit of North Koreans to the South, openly and in peace, since the Korean War, came two months after the July 4 joint statement, which had surprised Koreans on both sides and the rest of the world. Although their leaders were more skeptical, for the ordinary people of the two Koreas this was among the most hopeful moments in the second half of the twentieth century. There was widespread popular anticipation that the beginning of the North-South dialogue could mean the dawning of an era of peace and the reuniting of divided families and the nation.

On the roadsides leading to the center of Seoul, hundreds of thousands, perhaps a million people turned out to stare and wave at the visitors from across the lines. Streets and roadways along the route had been washed and swept, new shrubs had been planted and anticommunist signs taken down or painted over. Very few of the 43,000 American troops who were then in Korea were in evidence; only ten, many fewer than usual, were on duty at Panmunjom, and the rest had been instructed to stay out of sight.

The first exchange of North-South Red Cross delegations had had taken place two weeks earlier in the North. There everything had been meticulously prepared: People along the route to Pyongyang had lined up to greet the visitors dressed in their Sunday best; shops in the capital had been specially stocked for the occasion, and public buildings illuminated. It was all too perfect for Chung Hee Kyung, the principal of Ehwa Girls High School in Seoul, and the only woman among the southern delegates. The North Koreans she saw and met seemed to her dolls who had been programmed to say and do as they were told. When she returned to a large, loud, and unruly welcome in the South, to her own surprise she began weeping uncontrollably with relief and joy to be among familiar human beings with human reactions. "It was my most genuine experience of patriotism," Chung recalled.

The North Koreans who came to Seoul, following an afternoon of leisure, were taken to an elaborate reception at historic Kyongbok Palace, the seat of the Choson dynasty, the country's long-lasting and final royal kingdom. With an eye to history, the ROK government staged the reception in the Pavilion of Joyous Meeting, first built in 1412 as a greeting place for diplomatic delegations and royal visitors to the Korean court.

Inside the historic two-story pavilion, which is anchored in a pond near the former quarters of the Korean queens, were banks of colorful flowers, a sumptuous buffet, and several dozen gorgeous young women, many wearing filmy dresses, miniskirts, or other alluring modern garb. I walked up to one of the beautiful hostesses and asked who she was and why she was there. "I'm a Red Cross volunteer," she replied firmly, refusing to answer further questions. After receiving the same answer from another hostess of stunning beauty, I turned to a South Korean journalist familiar with the preparations. From him I learned that the KCIA, which had devised the program of the North Koreans, had asked for and received the services of some of the country's most beautiful young women from the national airline, modeling firms, and television companies and provided each one with a substantial sum of money to buy whatever dress she thought showed off her features best. In return, she was to show up as a hostess for the North Korean visitors, without revealing how this had come about.

The communist visitors professed to be unimpressed by the glamor of the hostesses or the symbolism of the reception in the historical surroundings. An austere man wearing a Mao jacket and a Lenin cap to complement his Kim Il Sung button, Yun Ki Bok, who was the chief political adviser of the North Korean delegation, observed sourly that the palace buildings were "outright testimony that the ruling class in the past exploited the people." The following night, the visitors were guests at a risqué display of bikini-clad, high-kicking South Korean dancers at Walker Hill, which had been built as a rest-and-recreation center for American troops. Some of the North Koreans, whose society was officially prudish, covered their faces or averted their eyes. They complained that the show was "the result of American imperialism" and lodged an official protest about the sexy display.

The visitors were lodged in the Tower Hotel, located on a mountain overlooking the capital city. Businesses in the city's tall buildings were asked to leave their lights on all night to present a more impressive view and, not incidentally, to prove that Seoul had electricity to spare. At the time of the division of the country, North Korea had inherited the main municipal power plant, which had been located well north of the city. Until the South built a new power plant, the North had caused privation and consternation by shutting off the electricity whenever it chose.

In yet another effort to impress, the government took the visitors for a drive on the recently opened expressway that ran from Seoul down the length of the peninsula to the southern city of Pusan. To create more traffic, Seoulites were asked to drive their cars on the highway even if they had no place to go, and a transport firm was asked to drive its big trailers along the nearby parts of the road. A northern visitor, perhaps getting wind of this exercise in mobilization (the kind of thing that was commonplace in Pyongyang), congratulated one of the heads of the southern delegation for his success in "bringing all the vehicles in the country to Seoul" to buttress its claims to prosperity. "That was difficult, but not nearly as hard as bringing all the tall buildings here for you to look at" was the reply.

The opening ceremony in a hotel ballroom dramatized the political character of the meeting. Believing that the highly ideological northerners would overreach and offend the broad mass of the generally conservative South Korean public, which was passionately in favor of unification but also fearful of communism and imbued with the memory of the 1950–53 war, the Seoul government had decided to televise the speeches live. The North Korean political adviser, Yun Ki Bok, attacked the United States, referred to "the nation's glorious capital, Pyongyang," and praised "the Great Leader," whereupon hundreds of telephone calls of protest, some stimulated by Seoul's ubiquitous intelligence agency, flooded the switchboards of the television station and local police. Responding in part to signals from the top, the country's mood shifted abruptly, from hope to anger. When the North Koreans left the hotel after the opening ceremony, for the first time they encountered silence rather than applause. A North Korean delegate waved to a crowd outside, but this time nobody waved back.

As a spectacle and a roller-coaster ride of deeply felt emotions, the first open diplomatic foray by northerners to the South was impressive. As a negotiating forum, however, it was a flop. It quickly became apparent that the North had little interest in the limited accommodations for divided families that were proposed by the South, demanding instead such moves as repeal of the South's Anti-Communist Law and extensive exchange of political cadres down to the lowest governmental levels.

Rather than have the talks fall apart in Seoul, however, President Park ordered his delegation to sign a meaningless joint agreement extolling the spirit of "brotherly love" and "Red Cross humanitarianism" and postponing serious negotiation to a future meeting in the North Korean capital. Park decided it would not be in keeping with Korean courtesy to clash sharply with the visitors and have the talks collapse at such an early point while he was the official host.

## PARK CHUNG HEE

The dominant figure in South Korea was in many respects almost the opposite of his North Korean counterpart. Whereas Kim Il Sung had been an anti-Japanese guerrilla fighter, Park Chung Hee had attended the Japanese military academy, had become an officer in the Japanese army, and, as required at the time, had even temporarily taken a Japanese name, Masao Takagi. And while Kim was a big man, who tended to dominate with his presence and his outgoing, confident personality, Park Chung Hee was small and wiry, seemingly self-contained and often aloof. During my one personal interview with Park, in June 1975, this powerful and greatly feared political leader seemed reticent and shy, almost smaller than life, as he sat in a big chair in his Blue House office. As we talked, he toyed with a tiny chihuahua dog in his lap and rarely looked me in the eye.

Responding to different sets of external relationships and espousing different ideologies, Park and Kim had one thing in common: Each had come to dominate his respective section of the Korean landmass. In his eighteen-year reign, from the military coup he led in 1961 to his assassination in 1979, Park left his mark on South Korea to a greater extent than any other person in modern times; his tenure and his impact were equaled only by Kim's extraordinary run of nearly half a century in the North. Both men were strong rulers who owed much to the Confucian tradition of deference to authority that long predated twentieth-century Korea.

Park was born in a village near Taegu on September 30, 1917, the son of a small farmer who had been a minor county official. At age 20, he graduated from a teachers' college and taught primary school for three years before volunteering for the Japanese army. Soon his record was so outstanding that he was sent to the Japanese military academy in Manchuria and was commissioned a lieutenant. His orderly mind and neat handwriting from his teaching days proved to be lifelong attributes, as did the sense of organization and use of power that he learned in military training. When his private safe was opened after his death, aides discovered files of handwritten personal notes on individuals, meticulously arranged in Park's own indexing system.

After the Japanese surrender and the division of the country in 1945, Park joined the newly established South Korean military academy and graduated as an officer the following year. In a much-disputed episode of his life, Park was arrested as leader of a communist cell at the Korean Military Academy following the 1948 Yosu rebellion, in which army troops under communist leadership refused to follow orders and proclaimed a short-lived "people's republic." Park was sentenced to death by a military court, but his sentence was commuted by President Syngman Rhee at the urging of several Korean officers and on the recommendation of Rhee's American military adviser, James Hausman, who knew him "as a damned good soldier." Park then switched sides, turning over a list of communists in the armed forces and becoming an intelligence official at army headquarters whose job it was to hunt them down.

This bizarre history caused worry in Washington when then–Major General Park suddenly emerged as leader of the 1961 military coup. At Park's request, Hausman flew to Washington and told high officials that despite his early history, Park was no communist and "there is nothing to worry about." The U.S. Embassy, in a cable to the State Department, rejected the possibility that Park could be a secret communist, "mainly because his defection from communists and turnover apparatus would make him victim no. 1 if communists ever took power." Park's political opponents sought to use his early leftist activities against him, but when he was strong enough he prohibited further public mention of it. In the early 1970s, an American correspondent, Elizabeth Pond of *The Christian Science Monitor,* was barred from the country for writing an article discussing Park's past.

Given his prewar Japanese education, his Confucian heritage, and his military background, there was nothing in Park's previous life to suggest fealty to democracy American-style, which he considered an inconvenient and unproductive practice. After he led the 1961 coup, it took heavy pressure from the Kennedy administration to persuade him to return the country to nominal civilian rule and to run for election as president. He successfully did so in 1963 and 1967, then insisted on a change in the constitution permitting him a third term. He narrowly won that third election in 1971 against opposition leader Kim Dae Jung after pledging never to ask the people to vote for him again. In 1972 he redeemed that pledge literally, though certainly not in spirit, by abolishing direct presidential elections and creating a method of indirect election, under which he could be (and was) reelected by an easily controlled national convention for the rest of his life.

An assessment by the U.S. military command in Korea in 1975 noted, "From the time he led the 1961 coup, it has been evident that President Park had little admiration for or interest in the craft of politics. His approach to his stewardship as ROK head of state has remained that of a general who desires that his orders be carried out without being subjected to the process of political debate."

South Korea under Park was dependent militarily and to a large degree economically on the United States. This dependence grated on Park, who worked steadfastly to increase his independence from Washington, much as Kim Il Sung struggled to gain independence from his Soviet and Chinese sponsors. Park's relationship with his principal foreign backer was fundamentally lacking in trust. The extent of American confidence in Park in the 1960s is suggested by the later disclosure of former Ambassador William J. Porter that U.S. intelligence had installed listening devices in Park's Blue House office, though he said they had been removed by the time of his arrival in 1967. Following disclosure of the bugging, Park had the Blue House swept by his own surveillance experts and installed special multilayered glass windows with static between the panes to foil electronic eavesdropping from outside, activated by a switch near his desk. "Whenever he'd call me to his office, he'd turn on the switch and lower his voice," one of Park's ministers recalled.

Today, however, Park is remembered less for his conflicts with Washington and successive waves of political repression than as the father of his country's remarkable economic progress. More than two-thirds of South Koreans polled by a Seoul daily in March 1995 said Park was the country's greatest president, more than five times the number that gave that honor to any other chief executive. The overwhelming reasons cited were the economic progress and development under his regime, and its relative stability.

South Korea's economic rise under Park started from a low point. Looking back after a decade in power, Park wrote that when he took over the country as leader of the 1961 coup, "I honestly felt as if I had been given a pilfered household or a bankrupt firm to manage. Around me I could find little hope. . . . I had to destroy, once and for all, the vicious circle of poverty and economic stagnation. Only by reforming the economic structure could we lay a foundation for decent living standards." For Park, rapid economic growth was essential not only as the source of prosperity but also for two other goals, which he held even higher: enhancing national security, in an era when U.S. willingness to protect the country against the North was waning, and winning political legitimacy for his regime, which had taken power by force of arms against a legitimately elected government.

Only a month after seizing power, Park established the Economic Planning Council, which later became the Economic Planning Board, to provide central governmental direction for the economy. The first five-year development plan, produced shortly thereafter, declared that "the economic system will be a form of 'guided capitalism,' in which the principle of free enterprise and respect for freedom and initiative of free enterprise will be observed, but in which the government will either directly participate in or indirectly render guidance to the basic industries and other important fields."

As that passage suggests, Park's model for economic development was the highly successful postwar Japanese system. In 1965, in a very unpopular personal decision that nonetheless gave a powerful boost to the Korean economy, Park normalized relations with Japan. Despite fierce domestic opposition based on antipathy to the former colonial masters, the Seoul-Tokyo normalization, which was strongly encouraged by Washington, brought an immediate Japanese assistance package of $800 million and led to many more millions in Japanese investments and valuable economic tie-ups with Japanese firms. In another far-reaching decision of the mid-1960s, Park sent two divisions of Korean troops to fight alongside American forces in South Vietnam, for which he received Washington's gratitude and

Korean firms received a major share of war production and construction contracts. In 1966 revenues from the war made up 40 percent of South Korea's foreign exchange earnings, making Vietnam the country's first overseas profit center.

Park took personal charge of the economy, bringing highly professional economists, many of them American-educated, into the planning agencies. He established an economics situation room next to his office in the Blue House to monitor the implementation of the plans, and he frequently met with economic officials and businessmen who were developing projects with government support. Much like the "on-the-spot guidance" practiced by Kim Il Sung in the North, Park incessantly visited government offices in the economic area and construction sites in the field to check up on what was happening.

Park refused to be guided by economists when he was determined to move ahead with one of his visionary projects. When American and World Bank economists said that South Korea could not successfully build, operate, or support an integrated steel mill and refused to approve financing, Park remained determined to build it. Declaring that "steel is national power," he obtained Japanese loans and personally pushed through construction of a massive mill at Pohang, on the southeast coast, which became the world's largest steel-production site and a foundation of Korea's heavy industry. Park was the driving force behind the ambitious Seoul-to-Pusan expressway, which experts had also said was impractical. An engineer on the project recalled that "after a while, I found myself thinking of him, of all things, as a sort of conductor of an orchestra—with his helicopter as his baton. Up and down he would go, this time with a team of geologists to figure out what was wrong with some mountainside that had crumbled on our tunnel-makers, the next time with a couple of United Nations hydrologists to figure out how our own surveyors had got some water table wrong. If he didn't know the answer on Tuesday, Mr. Park was back with it on Thursday or Saturday."

"President Park monitored the progress of every single project, both public and private, and closely governed the industrialists by the stick-and-carrot method," according to Kim Chung Yum, who was a senior economic aide to Park and eventually his chief of staff. Park

chose the firms that would be awarded contracts on large govern-
ment-backed projects and provided or withheld credit through government banks, depending on their performance. The growth sectors
of the national economy came to be dominated by a few highly organized, diversified industrial-business conglomerates known as
chaebols, loosely modeled on the Japanese prewar zaibatsu or its postwar zaikai. While this facilitated Korea's dramatic economic rise in
the 1970s and beyond, the intimate relations between government
and business also set the mold for the corruption charges that later
were to plague the retirement years of Park's successors.

Although he wielded enormous economic power, Park never
became a rich man and was not personally corrupt. He usually had a
simple bowl of Korean noodles for lunch and ate rice mixed with
barley, to save on rice. He had bricks placed in his Blue House toilet
to conserve water. Setting a modest style, he wore open-collar shirts
without neckties in the summer months and encouraged civil servants
to do the same.

Park's personal hold over the economy was embodied by his
ambitious Heavy and Chemical Industries Promotion Plan, a massive
program to build up six strategic industries—iron and steel, shipbuilding, chemicals, electronics, nonferrous metals, and machinery. Initiated in late 1971 and formally announced in January 1973, the plan
was designed by Park to enhance his political legitimacy and to respond to what he saw as a perilous security combination: the North
Korean military buildup, which became intensive as Pyongyang asserted greater independence from the Soviet Union and China in the
mid-1960s; and his decreasing confidence in American security assurances, as the United States disengaged from the Vietnam War and
sought to reduce its commitments elsewhere in East Asia.

The Heavy and Chemical plan, which Park conceived and
rammed through despite the misgivings of the Economic Planning
Board and other economists, was the foundation of Korea's later
success in automobiles, shipbuilding, and electronics, but it was also
very costly and eventually was scaled back considerably. Cho Soon, a
prominent economist and scholar who later became mayor of Seoul,
wrote in a retrospective analysis that the scale of Park's projects "ex-
ceeded by far what the country could accommodate" and substituted

government decision-making for private initiative in the economy. Accordingly, Cho wrote, "The results were waste and distortions in resource use, inflationary pressure, the emergence of immense conglomerates, and widening inequality in the distribution of income and wealth."

Nevertheless, the overall results of the development program that Park put in place between 1961 and 1979 were spectacular. In broad terms, according to the World Bank, South Korea's inflation-adjusted GNP tripled in each decade after Park's first year in office, thereby condensing a century of growth into three decades. At the same time, the country dramatically reduced the incidence of poverty, from more than 40 percent of all households living below the poverty line in 1965 to fewer than 10 percent in 1980. Per capita income shot up from less than $100 annually when Park took power to more than $1,000 at the time of his death and more than $10,000 today. In view of these achievements, it is small wonder that he is viewed by most South Koreans in retrospect as a leader of unparalleled greatness.

## WASHINGTON BLINKS AT PARK'S COUP

At six P.M. on October 16, 1972, Park's prime minister, Kim Jong Pil, notified U.S. ambassador Philip Habib of a sweeping change in the country's political direction, requesting that it be kept secret until made public twenty-five hours later. The surprise announcement by Park, a copy of which was handed to Habib, declared martial law, junked the existing constitution, disbanded the National Assembly, and prepared a plan for indirect election of the president. At the same time, to silence opposition, Park arrested most of the senior political leaders of the country.

Park called his new system *yushin*, which his spokesmen translated as "revitalizing reforms," and justified his actions on the grounds that the nation must be strong and united to deal with the North and maintain its independence in a changing international environment. The proposed announcement laid heavy stress on perils beyond Korea's shores, as "the interests of the third or smaller countries might be sacrificed for the relaxation of tension between big powers."

Despite the emphasis on external threats, Habib had no illusions about the real purpose of Park's dramatic moves. He cabled Washington within a few hours to say that "the measures proposed are designed to insure that President Park will stay in office for at least twelve years with even less opposition and dissent and with increased excutive powers" and that "if these proposals are carried out Korea will indeed have, for all practical purposes, a completely authoritarian government." While the ambassador conceded that Park might believe that he must strengthen his domestic position to deal with the North, Habib informed Washington that "there is little doubt that these measures are unnecessary given any objective view of the situation."

The pressing question was what the United States should do in view of its extensive interests and its historic leverage in South Korean politics. In the aftermath of World War II and the division of the peninsula, Washington had played the central role in anointing Syngman Rhee as the country's first president, and in 1960, in the face of a student-led popular uprising, it had also played a major role in forcing him to leave power. In 1961, the U.S. Embassy and the U.S. Command had spoken out publicly but ineffectually against General Park's military coup against the constitutionally elected post-Rhee government, but it had then successfully applied steady and persistent pressure to force Park to reestablish civilian government. Now the United States was confronted with what amounted to a coup in place, a power grab by Park to eliminate all legal opposition and retain power for as long as he wished.

Habib, a tough-talking, politically astute Foreign Service veteran from Brooklyn with extensive previous experience in Korea, was furious that his embassy had obtained no early warning of Park's surprise from its own sources. As he was well aware, the timing for the move had been chosen with care. Only three weeks earlier, Washington had done nothing when Philippine president Ferdinand Marcos, in a very similar maneuver that had been closely watched by Park, declared martial law and jettisoned his country's existing political institutions. Both Marcos and Park had sprung their power grabs during the campaign period of a U.S. presidential election, when American presidents are more reluctant than usual to make controversial decisions in foreign affairs. The Nixon–Kissinger White House, which prided itself on realpolitik in diplomacy, was fixated on the politically difficult situation in Vietnam, according to then–Assistant Secretary of State Marshall Green, at the time the State Department's senior Asia expert. "They didn't have time to be bothered" by Korea developments, he recalled.

With the plans drawn up and already in motion, Habib reported to Washington that "only the most drastic, positive and immediate actions by the U.S. might turn Park from the course on which he has embarked." In a pivotal judgment that established the limits of American engagement, Habib declared that "it is not incumbent upon the U.S. to take on the responsibility of getting Park to reverse his course within the next few hours. Nevertheless, we believe that in the long run, Park is creating major problems for himself and for his relationship with us and with others." Habib recommended that "we should be extremely circumspect in our public comments while making it clear that we are not in any way associated with the government's internal actions."

Washington accepted the advice of its ambassador and decided not to oppose Park's actions. The State Department cabled Habib, "We agree that [Park's] contemplated measures are unnecessary, and have grave reservations about the course he has embarked upon." Habib was instructed to tell Park that taking such a far-reaching decision without a serious exchange of views with the United States, was "incomprehensible in light of the past sacrifices and present support which we have given to the Republic of Korea and specifically to the present government." Nevertheless, no action was recommended to change Park's mind. If he were asked whether the United States would recommend against imposing martial law, Habib was instructed to answer that "this is an internal matter. . . . It is up to him to decide."

Washington's main concern seemed to be the proposed public statement accompanying the announcement, citing the American rapprochement with China and the resulting international fluidity as among the new perils to the Republic of Korea that justified drastic action. Habib was instructed to protest these statements, and in Washington Secretary of State William Rogers took them up personally with Korean ambassador Kim Dong Jo—all before the bombshell declaration was made public in Seoul. The references to U.S. policy in the prepared announcement were dropped, although to Washington's displeasure some references to maneuvering by "big powers" were retained. The Korean foreign minister solemnly told Habib that the phrase "big powers" was not intended to include the United States.

After Park's announcement had been made and tanks and troops had been put into the streets to implement martial law, after political figures had been arrested or silenced and the sometimes-fiesty Korean press had been placed under heavy censorship, Habib took a more careful look at the implications of what was being done. In an October 23 cable to Washington, the ambassador reported:

> It is clear that Park has turned away from the political
> philosophy which we have been advocating and supporting in
> Korea for 27 years. The characteristics of the discarded system
> which he regarded as weaknesses—the limitations on executive
> powers, the dissent and inherent uncertainties which arise in
> direct presidential elections—we regard as strengths. Because
> of our historic relationship with Korea, our security
> commitments, and the presence of a sustantial number of
> American troops, we are confronted with the problem of our
> reaction to these developments.

Habib reported that attempting to dissuade Park from the course of action he had chosen would be "impractical," but that seeking to soften the repressive aspects of new policies would be seen as giving tacit U.S. endorsement to the *yushin* plan as a whole. What remained, Habib concluded, was "a policy of disassociation," in which the United States would say it had not been consulted or involved in Park's actions and would stay clear of involvement in the reorganization of the Korean political system. In his cable, the ambassador faced squarely the consequences of the hands-off policy he recommended:

> In following such a course we would be accepting the fact that
> the U.S. cannot and should no longer try to determine the
> course of internal political development in Korea. We have
> already begun a process of progressively lower levels of U.S.

engagement with Korea. The process of disengagement should be accelerated. The policy we propose would be consistent with the disengagement trend, and Park's actions will contribute to the process.

Three days later Washington responded: "We agree with the Embassy's preference for a posture of disassociation. . . . In further-ance of this policy, we intend to refrain from arguing with the ROK in public, and seek to advance our counsel privately only where nec-essary and appropriate." When Prime Minister Kim Jong Pil visited the U.S. capital three months later, President Nixon told him pri-vately that "unlike other presidents, it is not my intention to interfere in the internal affairs of your country." With these decisions, most of which were never announced, the United States acquiesced in a di-minished role in South Korea's political future.

North Korea did not seem to mind Park's shift to a more author-itarian system that was more like its own arrangements, possibly be-lieving that this would make it easier to negotiate accords with him. On October 21, in the immediate aftermath of martial law, the two Koreas jointly announced that KCIA chief Lee Hu Rak would travel to Pyongyang on November 2 for another meeting with Kim Il Sung and that North Korea would send a top-level negotiator to Seoul shortly thereafter. The joint announcement was taken as a sign that the North-South dialogue remained on track.

### THE IMPACT OF *YUSHIN*

Within the South Korean body politic, the imposition of Park's *yushin* system provoked intense opposition from many quarters. Acting through the KCIA, the Army Security Command, and his increas-ingly powerful personal bodyguards, Park sought to silence all those who interfered or disagreed with his policies by temporary detention, arrest or imprisonment. In a brutal procedure known as the Korean barbecue, some opponents were strung up by their wrists and ankles and spread-eagled over a flame in KCIA torture chambers; others were subjected to water torture by repeated dunking or the forcing of water down their throats.

Chang Chun Ha, a distinguished Korean nationalist, told me how he had been seized on his way downtown and taken to a KCIA jail for a week of nearly continuous interrogation, in an unsuccessful effort to persuade him to endorse Park's martial-law "reforms." Meanwhile his distraught family, as his captors repeatedly pointed out to him, did not know what had happened to him or if he would ever return. Three years later Chang, an independent-minded man who had fought for Korean independence while Park was in the Japanese army, was killed under mysterious circumstances that the government attributed to a mountain-climbing mishap but that his family and friends believed was political assassination. A doctor who examined Chang's body was beaten and intimidated by the secret police, but he broke his silence many years later to declare that Chang's wounds were inconsistent with a fall from a cliff and to suggest that he had been murdered.

Security organs worked hard to stifle the Korean press. For more than a year following the *yushin* decree, KCIA operatives came daily to major Korean newspapers and broadcast stations to tell them what news they could or could not report, at times specifying the size of the headlines and the prominence of the display to be given to particular items. Due to this system, Park's picture and activities dominated the news. If Korean editors or reporters resisted, they were called in for grilling and often beaten.

Not all dissent was silenced. The most articulate, authoritative, and unbridled voice of opposition was Kim Dae Jung, Park's opponent in the hotly contested 1971 presidential race and a favorite son of the rebellious southwestern provinces of Cholla, where long ago an independent Korean kingdom had existed. Before the voting Kim accurately predicted that if Park won, he would become a "generalissimo" and arrange to be in office forever. Kim escaped being silenced with other political leaders in October 1972, because he happened to be in Japan when martial law was imposed. He immediately condemned the action as dictatorial, unconstitutional, and unjustified. Rather than return home to be arrested, Kim kept up his caustic criticism from abroad.

On August 8, 1973, Kim was lured to a luncheon meeting with two visiting Korean parliamentarians in a suite at a Tokyo hotel. As he said good-bye in the corridor, he was shoved into a nearby room by three men in dark suits, then punched, kicked, and anesthetized. He was taken by car down an expressway to a port and placed aboard a motorboat and then a large ship, where he was tightly trussed and weights placed on his hands and legs.

Kim's abduction was sensational news in Japan, where externally directed political violence was rare and, coming from Korea, a particularly painful affront to Japanese sovereignty. In Seoul, Ambassador Habib decided that strong and immediate action was necessary to save Kim's life and avert a serious crisis within South Korea and between South Korea and Japan. Calling in senior embassy officials, Habib instructed them to find out within twenty-four hours who had kidnapped Kim. U.S. intelligence officers quickly identified the KCIA as the culprit, whereupon the ambassador, in his characteristically blunt and salty language, laid down the law to the high command of Park's government, declaring that there would be grave consequences for relations with the United States if Kim did not turn up alive.

Habib's quick action probably saved Kim's life. After a few hours at sea, the weights were suddenly taken off Kim's body, and his bonds were loosened. Five days after his abduction, he was released, battered and dazed, a few blocks from his residence in Seoul. After thirty-six hours during which Kim was permitted to speak publicly of his ordeal, he was placed under house arrest. Park's government made no effort to identify or penalize his abductors.

Three weeks after Kim's kidnapping, North Korea suspended both the North-South political-level talks and the Red Cross talks, invoking the kidnapping of the popular opposition politician as the reason for its action. However, Pyongyang had been losing interest in the dialogue even in the months before the kidnapping. It was increasingly clear that the inter-Korean talks were not leading to the withdrawal of U.S. military forces. Moreover, the exposure of North Korean delegates to the more prosperous South was making Pyongyang's leaders uncomfortable.

Park's regime, which had used the North-South talks to justify its brutal political coup, now sought to salvage the talks. Late in the year the South proposed a series of meetings of the vice chairmen of the political-level North-South Coordinating Committee. The first meeting coincided with a major event in the South—the ouster of the powerful KCIA director, Lee Hu Rak, who had negotiated with Kim Il Sung but had also engineered the kidnapping of Kim Dae Jung.

After a prominent Seoul National University law professor was tortured to death in October 1973, CIA station chief Donald Gregg protested the killing and told the Blue House he found it personally difficult to work further with Lee. A week later, Lee was fired by President Park and replaced with a former justice minister, who initiated reforms in KCIA operations. With Lee out of the picture as chief contact with the North, the prospects seemed better to revive the discussions with Pyongyang. From December 1973 to March 1975, ten North-South vice-chairmen meetings were held under the aegis of the North-South Coordinating Committee, at Panmunjom, but they accomplished little.

Why did the initial attempt at North-South dialogue flower and then wither? How sincere were Park Chung Hee and Kim Il Sung? What did their initial contacts suggest for the future?

From a historical perspective, it seems clear that both Korean leaders had been jarred out of their previous patterns of inflexibility by fast-moving international developments. Whether through hope or fear, each had decided he had more to gain than to lose by dealing directly with the opposing state, something that had never been done before. As it turned out, both benefited in important ways from the experiment in coexistence, even though the practical results were nil.

The dialogue proved extremely useful to Park. It was helpful to his regime internationally, especially in the United States, whose previous ambassador, William J. Porter, had been promoting the case for dialogue for several years. Domestically, the opening to the North was broadly popular with the South Korean public, raising hopes for family reunions, a lowering of tension, and eventual unification, all of which were held out as potential benefits by Park's government. Most importantly, Park used the requirement for national strength and unity in dealing with the North to justify his *yushin* regime, which gave him the upper hand against the civilian politicians whom he despised and guaranteed him an unlimited tenure in the presidency.

Kim Il Sung also found the dialogue with the South to be beneficial, especially in breaking out of his diplomatic isolation. At the end of 1970, before the move toward talks began, North Korea had diplomatic relations with only thirty-five countries, nearly all of them socialist regimes, while South Korea had diplomatic relations with eighty-one countries. Immediately following the start of North-South dialogue, Pyongyang gained recognition from five Western European nations and many more neutral countries. Within four years, North Korea was recognized by ninety-three countries, on a par with South Korea's relations with ninety-six. The North also gained entry for the first time to the UN's World Health Organization and, as a result, sent its first permanent UN observer missions to New York and Geneva.

Also for the first time, as part of its peace offensive, North Korea communicated directly with the United States, initially by inviting journalists from *The New York Times* and *The Washington Post* to Pyongyang for extensive interviews and then by addressing a diplomatic message directly to Washington. In April 1973, North Korea's legislature, the Supreme People's Assembly, sent a telegram to the U.S. Congress referring to the developments on the divided peninsula and asking the American lawmakers for help in removing U.S. troops from South Korea, as they had just been removed from South Vietnam. Congress did not reply, but this letter set the stage for a succession of direct and indirect communications to Washington in the years to come.

Near the end of 1972, both Park and Kim reaped some personal rewards from their headline-making interaction. In November, using the dialogue with the North as his justification, Park won approval, through a nationwide referendum, of the new constitution granting him virtually unchecked and unlimited power. The charter was approved after an extensive sales campaign that took place under martial law, with newspapers censored and the opposition unable to be heard. In December, Park was elected unanimously, with no debate permitted, to a new six-year term as president by the hand-picked National Conference of Unification.

Not to be outdone, Kim put through a new constitution in the North, also without objection or dissent. Under the new charter, the nation was to be guided by the *juche* idea "as a creative application of Marxism-Leninism." Kim, who had held the title of prime minister as well as general secretary of the ruling Workers Party, promoted himself to president. Although this did not increase his already all-encompassing power, the new title put him on a semantic par with the leader of the South.

Neither Kim Il Sung nor Park Chung Hee harbored the belief that his indirect dialogue would lead to unification of the divided peninsula, although this hopeful prospect was, at least briefly, widespread among the respective publics of both men. Neither leader was willing to seriously compromise the policies and interest groups on which their respective regimes were based to pursue the long-term goal of national unity. To a great degree, the military-backed governments of both the North and the South had been shaped by the rivalry between them. While both Kim and Park were in favor of unification, each was fiercely opposed to a merger on the other leader's terms. Without a strong push from the outside powers, who had conflicting interests and who were paying little attention to the Korean peninsula, the two rival states were incapable of sustaining their dialogue.

Nonetheless, the exchanges of the early 1970s were a turning point in the cold war on the Korean peninsula, holding out the possibility, for the first time, of mutual cooperation and eventual peaceful reunification. An aspiration of immense appeal on both sides had flickered into life in tangible and tantalizing fashion. It would never be entirely extinguished, despite the many trials to come.

# 3

## THE TROUBLE DEEPENS

President Park Chung Hee was droning on, reading his prepared speech in Korean without flourishes or gestures, rarely pausing to look up from his papers at the audience of distinguished citizens and foreign diplomats. I was nodding off from boredom. The scene was the National Theater in Seoul, on a national holiday, August 15, 1974—the twenty-ninth anniversary of the country's liberation from Japan. Suddenly a loud *pop* from the back of the hall broke the monotony, and I turned to see a figure in a dark suit running down the center aisle of the theater, firing a weapon as he ran. More shots rang out, and presidential security guards raced onto the stage from the wings, guns drawn, some blazing. Amid the pandemonium in the hall, Korea's first lady slumped to the floor from her seat on the stage and was carried out by attendants, her bright orange *hanbok*, the traditional flowing Korean gown, stained with blood. She would die within hours from a bullet wound to her head.

As the final shots were heard, the assassin was lost from view in a pile-up of security men, then hustled from the hall. A high school girl, who was part of the chorus singing for this state occasion, was also carried out. She later died of her wounds, apparently from a presidential bodyguard's wild shot.

Startled by the eruption of violence, I had lost sight of Park during the melee. But now, as it subsided, he reappeared from behind the bulky—and bulletproof—lectern, where he had taken refuge when the shooting began. As he rose, he waved his hand to the stunned crowd, which broke into loud applause. Park told an aide later that he never saw the assassin's face.

Order was restored in surprisingly few minutes. Then to my astonishment, Park resumed the reading of his prepared speech. At the end, he sat patiently while the high school chorus—minus the unfortunate 16-year-old victim—calmly sang a musical selection as planned. On his way out Park noticed his wife's shoes and handbag under the chair where she had been sitting, and he picked them up as he left. Explaining Park's impassive behavior at a moment of supreme stress, his longtime aide Kim Seong Jin described the president as "a man of responsibility, who has got to finish what he set out."

The gunshots in the National Theater marked the start of a period of intensified tension on the Korean peninsula, during which earlier moves toward North-South rapprochement were replaced with undisguised hostility. The impetus for the deepening struggle came in part from the failure of the decade-long U.S. military effort in Indochina. While Saigon was falling, Kim Il Sung made a bid to renew his open warfare against the South, but China refused to go along, and the Soviet Union avoided even inviting Kim to visit Moscow to make his case. By the mid-1970s, both the giants of international communism had much too great a stake in their own relations with the United States to risk another international war on the Korean peninsula. At the same time, U.S. diplomats intervened with secret persuasion and powerful threats to stop Park Chung Hee from proceeding with a South Korean nuclear weapons program that could bring new dangers of escalation that nobody, including the great powers, would be able to control. Washington's veto of Seoul's nuclear ambitions proved that the United States could still wield impressive clout on security issues when convinced that its most vital interests were at stake.

◆　　◆　　◆

For months before the Independence Day shooting, tension in Seoul had been building toward a crisis as Park and his domestic opponents engaged in an escalating political struggle. As the shock of martial law had worn off, protests had grown—especially after the kidnapping of opposition leader Kim Dae Jung from Tokyo, which galvanized anti-Park forces. Pyongyang's subsequent suspension of the North-South dialogue robbed the government of its strategic justification for the internal crackdown.

Two of the most important groups in the growing democratic opposition were students and the Christian community, both of which were traditional foes of tyranny in Korea, and both of which had grown rapidly in the late twentieth century.

The unusual stature of students in Korean society and especially in political activism is the product of a tradition stretching back over many centuries. Undergirded by the Confucian emphasis on scholarship, students had spearheaded nationalistic movements against Japanese colonial rule. They saw themselves, and were often seen by others, as guardians of state virtue and purity, and they were expected to demonstrate their opposition to compromise with those ideals.

The practice of student political activism had been powerfully reinforced in the early 1960s. Massive student protests in 1960 against Syngman Rhee's increasingly authoritarian government were halted by police gunfire that killed 130 students and wounded another thousand in Seoul alone. The government's brutality robbed it of legitimacy in the eyes of the public and led to its replacement. The military coup led by General Park that took over the government by force in 1961 was never accepted as legitimate by many activist students, who passionately opposed the existence of military-dominated regimes.

After liberation from Japan, the thirst for education had led to rapid growth in the South Korean student population, from fewer than 8,000 college and university students in 1945 to 223,000 by 1973. While only a small percentage of Korean students were politically active, this vanguard was intensely engaged, prone to rigid, often radical political and social theories, and ready to do battle with government authority by employing their bodies as well as their voices.

Christianity, too, was strongly associated with Korea's resistance to Japan's colonial rule. As advocates and symbols of Western-oriented modernization, Christians have had high prestige in Korean society. From an estimated 300,000 in North and South Korea in

1945, the number of Christians had grown rapidly by 1974 to an estimated 4.3 million in South Korea (3.5 million Protestants and 800,000 Roman Catholics). Except for the largely Catholic Philippines, South Korea is the most Christianized country in Asia.

As the dissident movement broadened and deepened, the government periodically cracked down with detentions and arrests. Virtually no news of this confrontation between Park and the most politically active portions of his populace appeared in the tightly controlled Korean press. However, due to the international press and the many outside connections of regime opponents, the struggle was well publicized outside Korea. The governments of the United States, Japan, and a number of European countries were uncomfortable and made their views known in official démarches and unofficial statements urging Seoul to take a path of caution and moderation.

In Washington, congressional criticism of Park's human rights policies and the activities of the KCIA in intimidating Korean Americans led to Capitol Hill hearings and congressionally mandated cuts in U.S. military aid to South Korea. Seoul's response to these political pressures was to try, in time-honored Korean fashion, to purchase favor in ways that presaged scandals in the 1990s over Asian efforts to influence U.S. politics.

One major effort was led by Park Tong Sun, a young Korean graduate of Georgetown University who had set himself up as a Seoul government–backed dealmaker and agent of influence in Washington. The payoffs to members of Congress he arranged would later blow up into an influence-peddling scandal that, following the Watergate scandal that brought down President Nixon, was given the name Koreagate.

Direct government efforts to curry favor with American officials were equally lacking in subtlety. When Nixon aide John Niedecker came to Seoul in May 1974 as the official U.S. representative to a Korean presidential prayer breakfast, he was handed a sealed envelope just prior to his departure by President Park's powerful chief of presidential security, Park Jong Kyu. To Niedecker's surprise and discomfort, the envelope contained $10,000 in hundred-dollar bills. He quickly turned the money over to the U.S. Embassy, which returned it to the security chief in short order with a stern rebuke for attempting to bribe an American official. Later Niedecker was offered political money from Seoul of up to $5,000 for each U.S. House of Representatives candidate selected by the Nixon administration and up to $30,000 for each U.S. Senate candidate. Niedecker rejected the offer and reported the approach to his superiors.

Early in 1974, Park used his martial-law powers to issue emergency decrees making criticism of the constitution a crime and outlawing a student federation on the grounds it was subversive. Violators faced trial by closed military courts. A U.S. military assessment, which was kept confidential at the time, quoted intelligence sources as saying that "there was little or no validity to the charge of communist activity by the students" but that the accusation appeared to be designed "to tarnish opposition to the government with a communist image and to justify the repressive measures."

By the time of the August 15 Independence Day celebration, nearly two hundred people had been sentenced to death or long prison terms under the emergency decrees. Among those found guilty were a prominent Roman Catholic bishop, a popular dissident poet, and the only living former president of South Korea, Yun Po Sun. The struggle within the South, added to the permanent conflict with the North, made the city as tense as a war zone. When Park moved from room to room in his presidential mansion, the corridors were cleared of all but essential people because of what a senior U.S. Embassy official called his "morbid fear of assassination" by North Koreans. When Park's bulletproof limousine rolled down the street, traffic was stopped, and all windows along the route were ordered shut on pain of arrest.

All this was in the background when the gunshots rang out in the National Theater. In view of the intensity of the internal struggle, there had been a growing sense that Seoul's crisis was reaching an explosive point. A sudden act of violence was not so surprising. But from what direction had the gunshots come? Political dissidents? A rival military group? And what would happen next, now that Park had survived the attack?

## THE STRUGGLE WITH JAPAN

The man who tried to change Korean history with a .38 caliber pistol was a 22-year-old Korean resident of Osaka, Japan, who confessed to being instructed and assisted by an official of a North Korea–oriented residents association in Japan. The identity of the would-be assassin and the fact that his attack had been launched from Japan led to a serious crisis between the two U.S. allies in Northeast Asia, which were closely intertwined economically but had never come to terms politically with their unhappy history.

Mun Se Kwang had flown from Japan to South Korea on August 6, bringing a handgun—which had been stolen from a Japanese police station—concealed in a radio. He checked in to Korea's best hotel and on the morning of the Independence Day ceremony hired a limousine and driver from the hotel, paying him extra to perform obsequious bows at the entrance to the National Theater. Mun then strode inside past dozens of security officers as if he were an important guest.

The assassin had planned to shoot Park in the lobby of the theater, but failed to get an unobstructed view. As the ceremony began, he was swept inside and was only able to find a seat close to the back of the large hall. Near the middle of Park's address, he rose from his seat, intending to stride quickly down the center aisle, pause, and take careful aim with his gun, as he had been trained to do. But as Mun sought to move into position, his finger accidentally squeezed the trigger of his pistol, and the gun went off, grazing his left thigh. At that point, the unplanned shot having alerted security guards, the gunman made a run for it down the aisle, firing rapidly—but not accurately—as he ran.

Taken to KCIA headquarters and treated for his superficial wound, the gunman initially insisted he was "a revolutionary warrior" who should be treated as a prisoner of war. For a full day, he refused to say anything more than his name, Mun Se Kwang, and his address in Osaka. On the second day, one of the Korean prosecutors said to Mun, "You are a jackal, aren't you?" With this reference to the Frederick Forsythe novel, *The Day of the Jackal,* about a plot to assassinate French president Charles De Gaulle, Mun for the first time looked startled and showed emotion. He answered, "Yes." Assured that he would be treated not as a common criminal but as a man who was "looking for something big," Mun began to confess.

Korea and Japan, which are separated only by a narrow body of water, have a complex and tangled history, with more periods of conflict than friendly relations. Continental Asian culture originally made its way to Japan via the Korean peninsula. The two countries share an overlapping cultural heritage, yet in many ways the tension between them is more impressive. For all their recorded history, Japan has been more populous and militarily stronger. In modern times, imperial Japan's occupation of Korea from 1905 until its downfall in 1945 left bitter resentment on the part of Koreans. The Japanese, for their part, mixed feelings of superiority with trepidation about the Koreans in their midst and abroad.

During the Japanese occupation and especially during World War II, more than 2 million Koreans were forcibly brought to Japan, mainly as laborers. While most of them were repatriated after Japan's defeat, about 600,000 remained, mostly in the lowest-paying and least-skilled jobs. By 1974, they comprised the main exception to Japan's famed homogeneity, making up nearly nine-tenths of the entire "alien" population living amid 108 million Japanese. Although Mun Se Kwang, like many others, was born in Japan, raised in Japan, and could not even speak Korean, his birth certificate and alien registration papers described him as a South Korean whose permanent home was in a province near Pusan. Under law and practice in Japan, he and others like him had little hope of ever becoming Japanese citizens and were relegated to secondary jobs and status.

One year earlier, Japan had been furious at the violation of its sovereignty in the Tokyo kidnapping of South Korean opposition leader Kim Dae Jung. Now, after Mun Se Kwang's deadly run down the aisle of the National Theater on the day commemorating Korean liberation from Japan, it was Seoul's turn to be furious. Mun, although an ethnic Korean, was a resident of Japan, had used a Japanese police pistol, and had entered Korea on a Japanese passport obtained under false pretenses. Citing these facts, the South Korean president demanded an apology from Japan, punishment of all those in Japan who were connected with the case, and disbandment of the pro–North Korean residents' association, the Cho Chongryon, popularly known as Chosen Soren. Japan balked at such strong measures, and to make matters worse, the Japanese Foreign Ministry issued a statement refusing to accept any Japanese responsibility for the assassination attempt.

Park and others were outraged. The speaker of the ROK National Assembly, Chung Il Kwon, said Japan's reaction "shows how much they despise and look down on Koreans. . . . If [Chinese leader] Mao's wife had been killed by a Chinese raised in Japan, the Japanese prime minister would crawl on his hands and knees from Tsingtao to Beijing to apologize for Japan's responsibility, but they sneer at us because we're Korean." Because of Japanese mishandling and latent anti-Japanese sentiments, South Korea seemed more furious about the involvement of Japan than about that of the North Koreans who hatched the assassination plot.

Park personally summoned the Japanese ambassador, Torao Ushiroku, and threatened dire consequences if Japan did not cooperate. To emphasize his anger, Park refused to speak to the ambassador in Japanese—though, having been a lieutenant in the Japanese army, he knew the language perfectly—insisting that his foreign minister interpret his words instead. As added pressure, Park instigated and orchestrated daily anti-Japanese demonstrations in the capital, during one of which protesters chopped off their fingers in ritual sacrifice against Japan and marched on to storm the Japanese Embassy and smear its walls with blood. Most importantly, Park made serious preparations to break off diplomatic relations with Japan and nationalize all Japanese assets in Korea if satisfaction was not forthcoming.

At that moment the United States was transfixed with its own domestic crisis. Just six days before the assassination attempt in Seoul, Richard Nixon resigned the presidency as a result of the Watergate scandal, and Gerald Ford became president. Although Asia experts in Washington were aghast at the dangerous breach between the two U.S. allies, the orders to American diplomats were to stay out of the dispute.

Disregarding the instructions, Deputy Chief of Mission Richard Ericson, in charge of the embassy in Seoul after the departure of Philip Habib to be assistant secretary of state, placed his career on the line and worked out a face-saving accommodation. In secret meetings with Japanese Embassy officials and South Korean prime minister Kim Jong Pil, Ericson arranged a carefully phrased Japanese letter of regret, pledges of a limited crackdown on "criminal acts" of pro–

North Korean elements in Japan, and a peacemaking visit to Seoul by a respected Japanese elder statesman.

The showdown with the mistrusted Japanese and the venting of national emotion over the killing of Park's wife temporarily unified the South Korean body politic behind Park. He took advantage of the changed political climate to repeal the most draconian of the emergency decrees, for the moment easing the confrontation with his domestic opponents.

The most profound impact of the shooting, however, was to remove the influence of the first lady, who had been highly popular among even those who feared or disliked her husband. Yook Young Soo (Korean women keep their maiden names after marriage) had been Park's second wife, or third if one counts a common-law liaison in the late 1940s. She had come from a prominent family and was graceful, physically attractive, and articulate—all the things he was not. She had been a check and balance for her husband, a sounding board and humanizing influence. Following her death, Park became even more isolated, withdrawn, and remote.

Ten weeks after his wife's death, Park wrote in the diary that he kept,

> Already into the last week of October! The dying fall holds only loneliness. In the garden the chrysanthemums bloom, beautiful, peaceful, as they did a year ago, but the autumn leaves, falling one by one, only make me sad.

Mun Se Kwang was convicted of attacking the president and killing his wife and on December 20, 1974, was hanged in Seoul prison.

On August 15, 1975, the first anniversary of her death, Park wrote in his diary:

> A year ago on this day around 9:45 A.M. you came downstairs dressed in an orange Korean dress and we left together for the ceremonies. You were leaving the Blue House for the last time in your life.
> This day a year ago was the longest of my life, the most painful and sad. My mind went blank with grief and despair.

I felt as though I had lost everything in the world. All things became a burden, and I lost my courage and will.

A year has passed since then. And during that year I have cried alone in secret too many times to count.

## THE UNDERGROUND WAR

Three months after the assassination attempt on Park, a South Korean army squad on a routine patrol discovered steam rising from high grass in the southern part of the demilitarized zone, about two-thirds of a mile south of the military demarcation line that marks the border. Hoping to find a hot spring, a soldier poked his bayonet into the ground, which gave way to a widening hole, revealing the top of a reinforced tunnel about eighteen inches below the surface. As the soldiers began to probe further, they were interrupted by automatic weapons fire from a nearby North Korean guard post. They returned fire before breaking off the engagement. The incident of November 15, 1974, was the first clash of arms between the two opposing armies in twenty months.

Further exploration revealed a sophisticated underground construction about four feet high and three feet wide, with walls of reinforced concrete, complete with electric lines and lighting, areas for sleeping and weapons storage, and a narrow-gauge railway with carts for excavating soil. The U.S. Command calculated that about two thousand troops could be sqeezed into the tunnel from its source, about two miles away in North Korea, to its planned exit south of the DMZ, and that additional troops could be put through the tunnel at a rate of 500 to 700 men per hour. Suddenly American and South Korean forces faced a threat of surprise attack from beneath behind their forward defense lines.

North Koreans are masters of tunneling, a practice they developed to a fine art when protecting themselves against American air power during the Korean War. Late in 1970 and early in 1971, five attempts by North Korean forces to tunnel under the south fence of the DMZ had been detected, usually from areas not under direct American or South Korean observation. These were small tunnels, which military experts concluded had been dug by reconnaissance personnel in an effort to observe southern positions.

In November 1973, a year before the discovery of the steam rising from high grass, the search for tunnels was redoubled when a sentry in the southern part of the DMZ heard a faint tapping beneath his feet in the early morning, as if someone were knocking softly at a door. Although listening devices and seismic instruments were put in place, efforts to pinpoint the source of the noise were unsuccessful.

An important break came in September 1974, when a North Korean Workers Party functionary from the city of Kaesong, just north of the DMZ, defected, bringing with him valuable knowledge and diagrams of some tunnel locations beneath the southern lines. The defector, Kim Pu Song, said that extensive tunnel digging had been ordered from the highest echelons of the party in late 1972, not long after the North-South joint statement in which the two sides agreed to work for peaceful unification and "not to undertake armed provocations against one another, whether on a large or small scale."

According to the defector, the tunnel digging was highly organized, with North Korean army teams of about twelve members each working in shifts around the clock, augmented by supervisors, engineers, technicians, and guards. The defector said that the wartime purpose of the tunnels would be to infiltrate light infantry and special forces personnel into the South to participate in a lightning attack; in peacetime the tunnels were intended to facilitate the infiltration of North Korean agents.

Based on Kim's information as well as its own estimates, the South Korean Command projected the existence of fifteen tunnels under the DMZ. Later the U.S. Command increased the number of actual or suspected tunnel locations to twenty-two.

Even after the defector's information, it took the accident of the steam rising in tall grass to locate the precise location of the first intercepted tunnel in November 1974. In February 1975 the second tunnel was found by extensive exploratory drilling at a suspect site and confirmed by lowering a specially developed camera into a tiny borehole. At the time of its discovery, the tunnel had progressed three-fourths of a mile into the South Korean side of the DMZ. Aerial photography eventually identified its starting point at the base of a mountain nearly three-fourths of a mile into North Korean territory.

Tunnel number two, as it was called, was an extraordinary engineering feat, even bigger and longer than the first one, constructed through solid granite more than fifty yards below ground using modern drilling machinery that had been imported from abroad. Several months after it was found, I made my way down the steep-sloped intercept passage to inspect this impressive construction, accompanied by an American explosive ordnance team and South Korean troops. The floor and ceiling were uneven, but my six-foot frame was able to stand erect at most points along the two hundred yards where I was permitted to go. I could stretch both arms toward the sides of the chamber without touching them. The U.S. Command estimated that the dark, dank chamber could accommodate about 8,000 troops and put through another 10,000 men per hour with light artillery and other supporting weapons. Its intended discharge point would have been well behind South Korean forward defense lines.

Outside the tunnel, I saw South Korean soldiers digging new lines of trenches and bunkers at the approaches to the DMZ to protect themselves against North Korean troops who might pour out of underground structures. The most suprising thing was that, despite the discovery of two tunnels, formal U.S. and ROK protests, and much publicity, the sounds of digging continued to be detected under the surface of the DMZ. All indications were that Kim Il Sung had authorized the digging, and nobody else could give an order to stop.

The U.S. Command and the ROK military responded to the underground challenge by making increasingly sophisticated efforts to locate tunnels far below the surface. In addition to the borehole cameras, the largely secret detection efforts utilized standard and experimental seismic listening devices, complete with soundproof booths for analyzing tapes. Eventually a total of 245 such devices were placed along the DMZ to record underground activity at suspect sites; the tapes were picked up at least once a week for examination. One technique involved sending electromagnetic pulses between two holes deep into the ground, in an effort to detect cavities between the two sites. In view of the length of the DMZ—it stretches across 151 miles—and the complex geology of the Korean peninsula, an American physicist who examined the effort called it "worse than looking for a needle in a haystack; more like looking for a vacuum in space." The Pentagon tried everything—even hiring psychics to find more tunnels. Without their help, but through the use of highly sophisticated drilling and listening equipment, two more fully developed tunnels were found, in 1978 and 1990.

How much danger the tunnels posed to South Korea, once the first ones were detected, is questionable. U.S. and ROK forces quickly adjusted their defense lines to take account of possible incursions from underground. There is no doubt, though, that the intercepted tunnels served Seoul and Washington as tangible evidence of North Korea's aggressive intentions. According to Nathanial Thayer, the CIA national intelligence officer for East Asia in the mid-1970s, "Anytime anyone wanted more money for CIA, I would go up to see [House Speaker] Tip O'Neill. The argument was, if [North Koreans] are not aggressive, why are they building these tunnels?" The money was always forthcoming.

## CHALLENGE FROM THE NORTH

As the underground war suggests, the struggle for military supremacy did not stop or even slow because of the North-South contacts of 1971–72; on the contrary, the fluidity and uncertainty that gave rise to the dialogue also gave rise to an intensified arms race on the divided peninsula. Instead of a turn toward peace, the two Koreas were competing to build and import more and deadlier weapons of war.

A highly respected study by Robert Scalapino and Chong Sik Lee published in the early 1970s described North Korea as "perhaps the most highly militarized society in the world today," and it became even more so as the decade wore on. A retrospective U.S. military analysis of North Korea's development identified 1972–77 as a time of "remarkable North Korean Army growth" surpassing any other period since the Korean War. In parallel fashion, it was also a period of remarkable growth in South Korean military power.

Divided against each other at the DMZ and backed by rival world powers, both Korean states had become heavily militarized following the mutual devastation of the 1950–53 war. In May 1961 Major General Park Chung Hee seized power in Seoul at the head of a military group. Four months later Kim Il Sung finally cemented his undisputed authority over rival factions at the Fourth Workers Party Congress, buttressed by his military comrades-in-arms from his years as a guerrilla fighter. The militarized ruling group in the North promulgated the slogan "Arms on the one hand and hammer and sickle on the other." Kim also formulated a policy known as the Four Great Military Lines, which has become permanent doctrine in North Korea: to arm the entire populace, to fortify the entire country, to train each soldier to become cadre, and to modernize military weapons and equipment.

Tracking North Korean military activity is immensely difficult for any outsider, since virtually all aspects have been and remain closely guarded secrets in Pyongyang. North Korea has never published realistic information on its military forces, procurement, or operations. Fiercely independent and worried about the intentions of its communist allies, North Korea shared remarkably little information even with Moscow and Beijing after the 1950s. A retired Chinese officer who served twelve years as a Chinese military attaché in Pyongyang told me that North Korean officials would not disclose even to their close allies the size or organizational structure of their army. On infrequent visits to North Korea units in the field, he said, "we were just like sightseers" and were given no detailed information.

For all these reasons former CIA director Robert Gates described North Korea as "a black hole" and "without parallel the toughest intelligence target in the world." Donald Gregg, a career intelligence officer who served as CIA station chief in South Korea in the early 1970s and as U.S. ambassador to Seoul in 1989–93, said, "North Korea is the longest-running intelligence failure in the world."

Aside from the rare defector with operational details, such as the liaison agent who disclosed information about the tunnels under the demilitarized zone, the best source of information about the North Korean military has been aerial photographs and electronic intercepts provided by U.S. reconnaissance satellites. However, in these expensive operations, Korea only intermittently had a high priority. As U.S. forces withdrew from Vietnam in 1972 and détente seemed to be breaking out between Seoul and Pyongyang, the Joint Chiefs of Staff reduced American military intelligence resources devoted to the Korean peninsula by more than 50 percent. Given all this, estimates of North Korea's military buildup—and especially of the motivations behind it—must be treated with caution.

What is clear from a variety of sources is that in the 1970s Pyongyang was very active militarily. In May 1972, Kim Il Sung himself told Harrison Salisbury and John Lee of *The New York Times* that due to the hostile attitude of the United States, "we frankly tell you, we are always making preparations for war. We do not conceal this matter." In the early 1970s, Beijing renewed its military assistance to North Korea even as China moved toward rapprochement with the United States. Military supplies from the Soviet Union were still at a high level, although beginning a slow decline as Pyongyang found it harder to pay and as U.S.–Soviet détente flourished. In addition to the supplies from its allies, the North by the end of the decade was producing large quantities of its own field artillery pieces, rocket launchers, armored personnel carriers, main battle tanks, and surface-to-air missiles.

By 1974, according to the U.S. Command's intelligence estimate at that time, the North Korean army had grown to 408,000 troops, the fourth largest among the world's communist armies, and was described as "an efficient, well trained, highly disciplined force which is undergoing continual modernization." Of its twenty-three infantry divisions, fourteen were lined up from east to west close to the DMZ. Moreover, North Korea was developing a formidable air force of Chinese and Soviet bombers and fighters and a small but highly versatile navy.

In mid-1973, concerned by the buildup in the North, the U.S. Army assigned to Korea one of its ablest and most flamboyant combat leaders, Lieutenant General James F. Hollingsworth, who had extensive battle experience in World War II and Vietnam. Given command of the ROK/U.S. I Corps forces charged with defense of Seoul, Hollingsworth was visited at his new command post one night by a worried President Park, who asked, "Are you going to do the same thing here you did in Vietnam?" Hollingsworth's response: "I'm here to fight and die to save your country. That's what I'm going to do."

The existing war plan was an essentially defensive document calling for American and South Korean forces, in case of attack, to pull back in phases to the Han River, which bisects the capital city. But in 1974 Hollingsworth, telling his ROK subordinate commanders,

"I'm going to turn you into an offensive army," began moving the bulk of his artillery as far forward as possible, near the southern edge of the DMZ, where it was in position to strike well into North Korean territory. Two brigades of the U.S. Second Division were targeted to seize Kaesong, the most important city in the southern part of North Korea, in case of attack from the North. Hollingsworth's forward defense concept envisioned a massive use of U.S. and ROK firepower, including around-the-clock B-52 strikes, to stop a North Korean advance north of Seoul and deliver a powerful offensive punch to win the war within nine days.

Donald Gregg, CIA station chief in Seoul at the time, recalls Hollingsworth standing on the southern shore of the Imjin River, just a mile south of the DMZ, and declaring with bravado, "We'll kill every son of a bitch north of the forward edge of the battle area, and we won't retreat one inch." Privately, said Gregg, Hollingsworth wasn't sure he had enough firepower to do the job, but his offense-minded battle plan helped to calm the jittery South Koreans, as it was intended to do. Park, an enthusiastic supporter, supplied millions of dollars in construction funds for new roads, ammunition bunkers, and other facilities near the DMZ.

North Korea did not have to learn about Hollingsworth's new strategy from spies or other clandestine sources. In a press conference widely reported in Seoul, the colorful general announced his "violent, short war concept" before the plan had the approval of the Joint Chiefs of Staff or other military elements in Washington. There were unpublicized objections from the staff of the White House National Security Council on grounds that the nine-day war plan involved "almost immediate U.S. air interdiction, and possible use of nuclear weapons" for which there was no prior authorization. Hollingsworth got away with it because of the strong backing of the South Koreans and Secretary of Defense James Schlesinger.

North Korea responded in kind to the augmentation and repositioning of U.S. and ROK forces and Hollingsworth's aggressive plans to use them in case of war. Just as the growth spurt in North Korean forces stimulated the United States and South Korea to increased efforts, so the changes in firepower and strategy south of the DMZ helped stimulate large increases in North Korean forces and their repositioning closer to the dividing line with the South. With the failure of the initial efforts at productive North-South dialogue, the arms race could not be restrained by the two regimes themselves; nor did the outside powers have sufficient will or consensus to call a halt. The buildups, therefore, continued strongly.

The crucial military question in the mid-1970s was whether North Korea's allies in Beijing and Moscow would give military backing to a new attempt to unite the peninsula by force. The U.S. Command's 1974 intelligence estimate pointed out that while Pyongyang was "capable of initiating offensive action," it was unlikely to do so in the short run without Chinese and Soviet assistance. In the view of the U.S. Command, "these countries would not likely support adventurism on the part of NK's leader, Kim Il Sung. They probably would, however, assist NK against any invasion mounted by the ROK."

These assumptions were tested in the spring of 1975 as the massive U.S. effort in Indochina was collapsing in the face of communist guns. On April 18, the day after the Chinese-backed Khmer Rouge took over the Cambodian capital, Phnom Penh, and as the final battle for Saigon was getting under way, Kim Il Sung was received in Beijing with elaborate ceremony at the start of an eight-day state visit. In a famous speech at a welcoming banquet, the North Korean leader celebrated the communist victories in Indochina and forecast the collapse of the U.S.-backed regime in Seoul and the worldwide victory of Marxism-Leninism.

"If revolution takes place in South Korea we, as one and the same nation, will not just look at it with folded arms but will strongly support the South Korean people," Kim declared. Then, in a takeoff on Karl Marx's famous dictum that in revolution, the working class has nothing to lose but its chains, Kim added, "If the enemy ignites war recklessly, we shall resolutely answer it with war and completely destroy the aggressors. In this war we will only lose the Military Demarcation Line and will gain the country's unification."

According to a Chinese source with intimate knowledge of Korean affairs, Kim told Chinese leaders it would be "no problem" to liberate South Korea, but Premier Chou Enlai and his colleagues opposed any such idea. Without addressing Kim's ideas specifically, according to this source, Chinese leaders stressed the need for stability on the Korean peninsula, and "Kim was clever enough to understand" without having to lose face. About the same time, according to a former Soviet diplomat who was working on Korean issues at the time, Moscow made it explicitly clear to Kim that "we only support peaceful means for solution of the [South Korean] problem." Significantly, Kim did not stop in Moscow during an extensive trip to Eastern Europe and North Africa immediately following his Beijing visit. In a sign of discord between Kim and his senior communist sponsor, the North Korean leader even flew many hundreds of miles out of his way to avoid passing through Soviet airspace.

### ECHOES OF SAIGON

Even more than flirtation with China or other American actions he found difficult to accept, Park was shocked and alarmed by the U.S. failure in Vietnam. The prospects and plight of South Vietnam, the U.S.-backed anticommunist half of another divided country, bore an uncomfortable resemblance to the situation in South Korea. At the American behest, Park's government sent two divisions of Korean troops to fight in Vietnam, and they had remained until 1973, when the slow withdrawal of American forces was nearly complete. Although Korea was well paid for its efforts through procurement and construction contracts, to the point that revenues from the Vietnam War made up as much as 40 percent of its foreign exchange earnings, Park considered his troop commitment to be a self-sacrificing contribution to the anticommunist cause and a payback to Washington for saving the South in the Korean War. In Park's view, the American pullout from Vietnam and especially the betrayal of South Vietnam in the Paris negotiations with communist North Vietnam raised agonizing doubts about the reliability of the United States in his own case.

As South Vietnam was collapsing that April, Ambassador Richard Sneider in Seoul appealed to Washington for an urgent review of American policies in view of "declining ROK confidence in [the] U.S. commitment," accompanied by a "risk of North Korean provocation to test both U.S. intentions and ROK capabilities." Sneider, a cerebral State Department officer who had studied communist political operations during the Korean War, wrote in a secret cable that "Korea is not repeat not yet in a crisis era" but that this could come. To head it off, he recommended a long list of potential confidence-building measures, ranging from more weapons and economic support for the Seoul government, to contingency planning for special U.S. air and naval deployments to Korea in case of a serious threat of a North Korean attack.

The broader and longer-term problem, Sneider wrote, was the need for a fundamental shift in the U.S. relationship with a Korea that, "while still dependent on us, is no longer [a] client state." Sneider recommended immediate initiation of a major review of Korea policy in Washington.

Two months later, in June 1975, Sneider fired off a more extensive rendition of his views to a U.S. capital that was still preoccupied with the aftermath of the failure in Vietnam. Sneider wrote in a remarkable twelve-page secret cable:

> Our present policy toward Korea is ill-defined and based on an outdated view of Korea as a client state. It does not provide a long-term conceptual approach to Korea, geared to its prospective middle power status. It leaves the ROKG [ROK government] uncertain what to expect from us and forces us to react to ROKG on an ad hoc basis. We have not for example made clear to the Koreans what the prospects are for a continued, long-term U.S. military presence. Nor have we clarified what the ROKG can expect from us in the way of military technology, although we discourage President Park's efforts to develop his own sophisticated weapons. These uncertainties lead President Park into preparations for what he sees as our eventual withdrawal, preparations which include internal repression and plans for the development of nuclear weapons. They also induce optimism on the part of North Korea about our withdrawal and doubts in Japan about our credibility and about the future of Korea.

Sneider saw two main alternatives to the existing policy: disengagement or the establishment of a new basis for durable partnership.

Habib, his predecessor as ambassador, was back in Washington on the receiving end of his cables as assistant secretary of state for East Asian and Pacific affairs. Habib had observed at the time of Park's martial-law takeover in October 1972 that the process of U.S. disengagement from Korea had "already begun" and "should be accelerated." However, in the wake of the debacle in Vietnam, Sneider made the case that "disengagement, whether gradual or otherwise, is now far too risky as long as the North Korean posture remains militant; it would escalate the possibility of conflict and risks a breakdown of Japanese confidence in our treaty commitment." Perhaps as a gesture to the views of Habib, Sneider wrote, "Under different circumstances, a gradual disengagement could be worth serious consideration."

Sneider called his preferred and recommended alternative "durable partnership" with long-term guarantees for Korea, along the lines of the NATO and Japanese partnerships. He wrote, "The longer we stave off the inevitable decision as to whether our relationship, including our military presence, is temporary or durable, the more President Park and Kim Il Sung will pursue their premises that it is in fact temporary, adding further to the instability on the Korean peninsula."

As he saw it, an improved relationship would involve such things as greater Washington–Seoul consultation, a transition from economic aid to private investment (which was already happening), and a higher priority for Korea on the U.S. negotiating agenda with China and the Soviet Union. However, the most important element he recommended was "a significant U.S. force presence with indefinite tenure . . . publicly projected with major reductions linked to changes in the security situation in Northeast Asia and arrangements between North and South reducing tensions on the Korean peninsula."

In the aftermath of Vietnam, Washington was wary of open-ended commitments. President Gerald Ford, who had taken office in August 1974 after Nixon's forced resignation, had told Park during a brief visit to Seoul in November 1974 that "we have no intention of withdrawing U.S. personnel from Korea." However, this statement was interpreted by the Ford National Security Council staff as applying only to total withdrawals, not to partial withdrawals. Responding to the concern of Sneider and others about South Korean fears of a U.S. pullout during a visit to Seoul in August 1975, Secretary of Defense James Schlesinger privately reassured Park that "he foresees no basic changes over the next five years" in the level of U.S. forces. But when this comment got back to the White House via a memorandum of the conversation, a National Security Council staff aide objected that Schlesinger had gone beyond administration policy.

In any case, it was obvious that Ford would face serious Democratic opposition the following year, which could bring about a change in the situation. Schlesinger told Park that "he expects President Ford to be reelected, but if not the Democrats are not likely to eliminate U.S. support for South Korea." Schlesinger may not have known or cared that Democrat Jimmy Carter, then considered a longshot contender for his party's presidential nomination, had already begun advocating the complete withdrawal of American ground troops from Korea.

With the election looming ahead, no new American relationship along the lines of Sneider's recommendation was instituted. Despite U.S. attempts at reassurance, Park continued to feel a deep sense of vulnerability. In mid-1975 he put three laws through the National Assembly that were intended to put the nation on a wartime footing: a tightened public security law, coming on top of the issuance of Emergency Decree Nine, which in effect banned all political criticism of the government; a civil defense law creating a paramilitary corps of all males between ages 17 and 50; and a new defense tax levied on a wide range of items.

The government doubled defense expenditures in the 1976 budget and continued to increase them sharply each of the next three years of Park's rule. In 1979 they doubled again, bringing them to four times the expenditure level of 1975. Although the South was devoting a far smaller percentage of its economic output to the military than the North, in absolute terms ROK military spending began outpacing that of the North in the mid-1970s, according to estimates of the International Institute of Strategic Studies. Although military spending on both sides was rising, the South's by the end of the decade was more than double that of the North.

Following the fall of Saigon, Park gave high priority to his Heavy and Chemical Industries Promotion Plan, which had been initiated earlier to provide the sinews of enhanced military power. Between 1975 and 1980, more than 75 percent of all manufacturing investment in South Korea was committed to this industrial base. With these resources, Park created a mechanized army division and five special forces brigades for mobile warfare, doubled the size of his navy, purchasing U.S. ships and missiles, and modernized his air force with faster, deadlier U.S. jets and missiles.

North Korea could not keep up with the South's rapidly rising military expenditures nor its increasing lead in military technology. On the other hand, North Korea continued to increase the numbers of its troops under arms and to move more of its forces closer to the DMZ and therefore closer to Seoul, the fast-growing South Korean capital, whose center was only thirty miles south of the dividing line. Increasingly, parts of Seoul were coming within range of North Korean heavy artillery and rockets. The upshot of all this was to heighten the military tension on the divided peninsula.

### THE SOUTH KOREAN NUCLEAR WEAPONS PROGRAM

Park's ultimate effort to secure the country's future was to launch a secret and serious effort to develop a South Korean nuclear bomb. According to Oh Won Chol, a senior adviser to Park on nuclear and military production programs, Park created an Agency for Defense Development, which included a clandestine Weapons Exploitation Committee, answerable only to the Blue House, after faster and better armed North Korean speedboats overwhelmed a South Korean patrol boat in June 1970 and forced it to the North. Only weeks later Park was shocked by the decision of the Nixon administration to withdraw the U.S. Seventh Division from Korea, despite his vehement protests. Park believed that the South Korean army was simply incapable of defending the country by itself with its outmoded arms and equipment, according to Oh. His nuclear adviser said that Park had not decided actually to produce a South Korean bomb, but that he was determined to acquire the technology and capability to do so on a few months' notice, as he and many others believed the Japanese could do. "Park wished to have the [nuclear] card to deal with other governments," Oh told me in 1996. In this field, the capability to produce nuclear weapons is almost as potent as possession of the bomb itself.

A major element in Park's effort was to acquire a reprocessing plant to manufacture plutonium, the raw material of atomic weapons, from irradiated uranium fuel, which could be produced in civilian power plants. Although most of South Korea's ambitious civil nuclear power program was based on American equipment and technology, Park steered clear of Washington in seeking reprocessing equipment and technology, and in 1972 he began working with France in this high-priority effort. By 1974 the Korean–French collaboration produced the technical design of a plant to manufacture about twenty kilograms of fissionable plutonium per year, enough for two nuclear weapons with the explosive power of the atomic bomb that the United States dropped on Hiroshima.

Work on an independent South Korean nuclear program and the rest of Park's defense development was centered in Taeduk, a science center south of Seoul. In 1973 South Korea began a quiet drive to recruit ethnic Korean nuclear, chemical, and engineering specialists from the United States and Canada. It also began shopping abroad for exotic materials and equipment useful for nuclear weapons.

India's nuclear test in 1974, the first by a developing nonaligned country, jolted the world awake to the dangers of the spread of nuclear weapons. Suddenly nuclear proliferation became a high-priority concern in Washington. U.S. intelligence officials began giving renewed scrutiny to import data on sensitive materials, and "when they got to Korea, everything snapped into place," an American analyst recalled years later. Based on these telltale hints, according to Paul Cleveland, who was political counselor of the U.S. Embassy in Seoul, "people were sent to work, and in a relatively short period of time developed absolute confirmation from clandestine sources" that South Korea was secretly embarked on a program to build the bomb.

In November 1974 the Embassy sent to Washington a highly classified intelligence assessment that South Korea "is proceeding with initial phases of a nuclear weapons development program." This kicked off an interagency intelligence study in Washington that concluded that the ROK could develop a limited nuclear weapon and delivery capability within ten years, but that its efforts to build a bomb would become known well before that time, with significant political impact on neighboring countries. A secret cable to the Embassy in Seoul from Secretary of State Henry Kissinger, with the concurrence of the Ford White House, emphasized the gravity of the issue:

> In the case of Korea our general [proliferation] concerns are intensified by its strategic location and by the impact which any Korean effort to establish nuclear capability would have on its neighbors, particularly North Korea and Japan. ROK possession of nuclear weapons would have major destabilizing effect in an area which not only Japan but USSR [Soviet Union], PRC [Peoples Republic of China] and ourselves are directly involved. It could lead to Soviet or Chinese assurances of nuclear weapons support to North Korea in event of conflict. . . . This impact will be complicated by fact that ROK nuclear weapon effort has been in part reflection of lessened ROKG [ROK government] confidence in U.S. security commitment, and consequent desire on Park's part to reduce his military dependence on U.S.

American policy as set forth in the secret instructions was "to discourage ROK effort in this area and to inhibit to the fullest possible extent any ROK development of a nuclear explosive capability or delivery system."

The administration decided on a multifaceted approach, using both direct U.S. pressure and the development of common policies with other nuclear supplier nations to inhibit South Korean access to nuclear weapons technology. The tough issue was how to accomplish this without a serious rift in the U.S.–ROK alliance, especially at a time when Korean confidence in the United States was plummeting due to the developments in Saigon.

Initially the emphasis was on indirect action to persuade France to revoke its offers of nuclear cooperation. U.S. ambassador Sneider cautioned the French ambassador in Seoul, Pierre Landy, that "the United States has no doubts that the Koreans have in mind putting to ulterior military ends what they can make use of such as plutonium." The French refused to give up their potential sales to Seoul, saying they would cancel their plans only if the Koreans asked them to do so.

South Korean officials denied they were embarked on a nuclear weapons program. Many of those who denied it probably didn't know the carefully hidden truth. "We have the capability," Park told columnist Robert Novak in early June 1975, but he denied that his government was using it. He added, in a plea for continuing U.S. support, "If the U.S. nuclear umbrella were to be removed, we have to start developing our nuclear capability to save ourselves." He said much the same thing in an interview with me several weeks later.

U.S. officials decided at the outset not to reveal to South Korea their certain knowledge of its clandestine nuclear weapons program, but instead centered their attack on its openly acknowledged plans to import a reprocessing plant. In July 1975, Ambassador Sneider was authorized to begin taking the American objections to reprocessing directly to South Korean officials. A National Security Council memorandum recognized that the campaign to persuade Seoul to forgo the planned reprocessing plant would approach the limit of what the South Korean government would accept from the United States. In order not to confront Park and to allow him to save face, Sneider took the case against the reprocessing plant methodically up the chain of command, first to the minister of science and technology, then to the foreign minister, and eventually to the secretary general of the Blue House. The U.S. ambassador never made direct allegations that Seoul was embarked on a weapons program, recalled Cleveland, who accompanied him on the visits, but emphasized "how important it was that Korea not buy this because of the appearances of things and the kinds of suggestions this would make back in the United States and the difficulties that it would cause."

Sneider's efforts in Seoul were closely coordinated with those of Washington officials. On his morale-boosting visit to South Korea in August 1975, Secretary of Defense James Schlesinger personally told Park that a South Korean nuclear weapons program was the one thing that could endanger U.S.–ROK relations. In what he later called "an elliptical conversation," Schlesinger did not refer to the U.S. intelligence findings, and Park did not admit to a secret weapons program. The U.S. defense secretary got the feeling, though, that "he knew that I knew."

In Washington that fall and winter, Philip Habib, the assistant secretary of state for East Asian and Pacific affairs who had preceded

Sneider as U.S. ambassador, held a series of increasingly intense conversations with South Korean ambassador Hahm Pyong Choon. By this time the French contract had been signed, but Habib demanded the Koreans cancel it. Park refused through his ambassador, declaring that this could not be done "as a matter of honor."

Washington concocted a number of incentives that it offered in return for cancellation of the French plant, including guaranteed access to reprocessing under U.S. auspices when it was needed by the ROK civilian nuclear industry, and access to additional American technology under a formal science and technology agreement. On the disincentive side, the U.S. administration, with congressional help, threatened to block Export-Import Bank financing of the next steps in Seoul's ambitious civil nuclear power program if the proliferation concerns were not resolved.

Finally both Sneider and Habib were authorized to employ the heaviest threat ever wielded by the United States against South Korea: that the entire U.S. security relationship would be put in doubt if Seoul went through with the plan.

At the height of the campaign in December 1975, Sneider pointedly informed a senior ROK official that the "real consideration" for Koreans was "whether Korea [is] prepared [to] jeopardize availability of best technology and largest financing capacity which only U.S. could offer, as well as vital partnership with U.S., not only in nuclear and scientific areas but in broad political and security areas." In deciding what to do, said Sneider, the ROK government "had to weigh the advantages of this kind of support and cooperation which USG could provide against the French option." According to an ROK participant, Donald Rumsfeld, who succeeded Schlesinger as secretary of defense, bluntly told his ROK counterpart in May 1976 that the United States "will review the entire spectrum of its relations with the ROK," including security and economic arrangements, if Seoul insisted on developing nuclear weapons.

Faced with such powerful and adamant U.S. opposition—all done in secret—Park reluctantly canceled the contract. The episode demonstrated that when the United States was determined—and when it believed its security interests on the peninsula were at stake—

it retained the clout in the mid-1970s to overwhelm even the most determined intentions of the Seoul government.

In the aftermath Sneider worried that this was not the end of the affair. What concerned him most about Korea's future, he told National Security Adviser Brent Scowcroft in a White House meeting, was "Park's emotionally charged drive to seek self-sufficency and self-reliance through a program of nuclear weapons and missile development." He recommended that after a decent interval, the United States begin confronting Park anew on the issue, lest the program be revived, resulting in the temptation for North Korea "to go the same route." Sneider observed that "Park was guilty of sloppy thinking in believing he could somehow obtain greater security by these policies; yet, given U.S. attitudes, one had to admit that South Koreans had some reason for their concern over their future security."

Although Park was forced to give up the French reprocessing plant and later to forgo purchasing a new Canadian heavy water reactor, the program refused to die. Rather than disband his clandestine nuclear team, Park gave it a new organizational parent, the Korean Nuclear Fuels Development Corporation, and a new objective, the manufacture of nuclear fuel rods for the country's reactors. In 1978 South Korea once again began discussions with France about reprocessing facilities. Again Washington blocked the deal, this time with the personal intervention of President Carter with French prime minister Valery Giscard d'Estaing.

Nonetheless, Son U Ryun, one of Park's former press secretaries, later wrote that during a walk on a beach in January 1979, the president confided in him that "we can complete development of a nuclear bomb by the first half of 1981." When this happens, Park went on, "Kim Il Sung won't be able to dare to invade the south." In an account that has been challenged by some of those who knew Park well, the former aide quoted Park as saying he planned to show the bomb to the world in the Armed Forces Day parade in 1981 and then announce his resignation as president. Son's account is widely disputed by former officials who were close to Park. However, it is consistent with the testimony of Kang Chang Sung, chief of the powerful Defense Security Command under Park. Kang said Park told him personally in September 1978 that 95 percent of the nuclear weapons development had been completed by the Agency for Defense Development, and that atomic bombs would be produced by South Korea in the first half of 1981.

## MURDER IN THE DEMILITARIZED ZONE

On the morning of August 18, 1976, five South Korean workmen, accompanied by a ten-man American and South Korean security detail, gathered around a prominent poplar tree near the western edge of the Joint Security Area at Panmunjom. The JSA, roughly circular and about eight hundred yards in diameter, is the only part of the demilitarized zone without fortifications, barbed wire fences, and land mines marking the division between the North and South. On that day tension was unusually high due to recent frequent threats, obscenities, and shoving matches. A year earlier an American officer had been kicked in the throat by a North Korean guard outside the building where the Military Armistice Commission met.

The purpose of the work detail on that steamy August day was to trim the boughs of a forty-foot-high tree that, in its summer foliage, obstructed the view between two guard posts manned by U.S. and ROK forces within the Joint Security Area. As the work got under way, two North Korean officers and nine enlisted men appeared on the scene and asked what was going on. After first seeming to approve, the Korean People's Army (KPA) commander, Lieutenant Pak Chul, a hostile and combative eight-year veteran of the JSA, demanded that the trimming stop, warning that "if you cut more branches, there will be a big problem." The senior American officer, Captain Arthur Bonifas, a West Point graduate who was within three days of ending his one-year tour in Korea, ignored the protest and ordered the work to continue. Lieutenant Pak then sent for reinforcements, who arrived by truck carrying metal pipes and ax handles, raising the KPA total on the scene to about thirty men. They surrounded the tree trimmers. The North Korean officer again demanded that the work stop, saying to the South Korean officer who served as the interpreter, "The branches that are cut will be of no use, just as you will be after you die." Captain Bonifas confided to the interpreter that he believed the North Koreans were only bluffing. He ordered the work to proceed.

Bonifas turned away from the North Korean officers, and Pak removed his watch, wrapped it in a handkerchief, and put it in his pocket. The other KPA officer rolled up his sleeves. Pak then shouted, "*Chookyo!*" (Kill!), and smashed Bonifas from behind with a karate chop, knocking him to the ground. This signaled a general KPA attack, first with fists and feet and then with clubs and iron pipes, which had been stored in the truck, and axes seized from the work party. Bonifas was beaten to death by five or six North Koreans wielding clubs and with the blunt edge of an ax. Lieutenant Mark Barrett, the other American officer present, tried to come to the aid of an enlisted man and was also knocked down and beaten to death. The South Korean interpreter was injured, along with four of the U.S. and ROK enlisted men. A U.S. Quick Reaction Force, which had been stationed nearby as a precaution, arrived after the fight had ended and the North Koreans had regrouped on their side of the lines. A camera with a telephoto lens, prepositioned following normal practice at a U.S. observation post, provided crucial evidence of the killings.

The deaths of the two American officers were the first fatalities in the Joint Security Area since it had been established at the end of the Korean War. Within days the killings would result in the gravest threat of all-out war from the 1953 armistice to the nuclear crisis of the 1990s. As in the nuclear crisis, Kim Il Sung showed his pragmatic side at the crucial moment, narrowly averting a widening clash. But the fact that the United States and North Korea were the principal actors left the leadership of South Korea on the sidelines and therefore far from satisfied with the outcome.

When news of the fatal skirmish reached the U.S. capital, President Ford was at the Republican National Convention in Kansas City, where he was competing for his party's presidential nomination against Ronald Reagan, who accused him of being too conciliatory to communists. In his absence, Secretary of State Henry Kissinger chaired the meeting of Washington Special Actions Group (WASAG), the top-level crisis committee of the Ford administration, in the White House Situation Room, the secure basement-level conference room replete with maps, briefing materials, and sophisticated communications.

A CIA briefer, making the initial presentation, noted there was no indication of North Korean troop movements or other preparations for a general attack. But he also expressed the view that the killings were not spontaneous. The agency submitted a written report, saying, "We are virtually certain that this incident was a deliberate provocation. We believe it was intended to support North Korea's diplomatic offensive against the US and South Korea . . . and also to arouse US public opinion about the American troop presence in Korea during the presidential election campaign."

The chief of naval operations, Admiral James L. Holloway, representing the uniformed Joint Chiefs of Staff, said that given "a military stand-off" on the peninsula, a North Korean attack could be successful only if it was a surprise, and since the killings had put everyone on alert, "we therefore do not believe that the North had a major attack in mind."

As in many such emergencies, the policy makers had only a dim idea about how the clash had arisen. Neither the CIA nor other agencies at the table seemed to know that this was not the first encounter over the poplar tree, until a cable on the history of the clash was handed to Kissinger while the meeting was already under way. It revealed that twelve days earlier, a South Korean work party and accompanying guards had approached the big poplar tree with saws and axes intending to cut it down, but had withdrawn after a North Korean guard ordered them to leave it alone. This incident had not been reported to military headquarters in Seoul. "They told us not to do it," commented William Hyland, the deputy national security adviser, when the cable was handed around the White House meeting.

The U.S. policy makers did not discuss the broader background of sharply rising tension on the peninsula, which in retrospect was a crucial factor in the clash. Within a little more than a year, Defense Secretary Schlesinger had threatened North Korea with nuclear attack in response to ROK concern following the fall of Saigon; nuclear-capable F-111 swing-wing fighter-bombers, the most advanced in the American arsenal, had landed in South Korea for military exercises amid great publicity; and the United States and South Korea had staged Team Spirit 76, the first of a long-running series of large-scale joint manuevers east of Seoul. The parachute drops, amphibious landings, and other maneuvers provoked a near-hysterical reaction from the North, which saw Team Spirit as a dress rehearsal for an invasion from the South.

On August 5, the day before the initial tree-cutting incident, North Korea had issued a lengthy government statement charging that the United States and South Korea were stepping up plans to invade the North. Pyongyang claimed they "have now finished war preparations and are going over to the adventurous machination to directly ignite the fuse of war." The declaration was highly unusual, being only the third official government statement on a Korea peninsular issue since the armistice. Puzzled, several American intelligence analysts attempted to have a warning sent to U.S. forces in Korea. However, this was not done. Instead, on August 6, the day following the alarmist statement from North Korea, the first abortive attempt was made to trim the poplar tree in the Joint Security Area.

For the policy makers in the White House meeting following the killings, the central topic was the means of retaliating against North Korea. Kissinger, who had spoken with Ford by telephone, was in a brutal mood. "The important thing is that they beat two Americans to death and must pay the price," the secretary of state announced. One participant in the meeting came out of it quoting Kissinger as saying, "North Korean blood must be spilled."

According to the minutes of the meeting, the discussion was remarkably free from many of the restraints that complicated U.S. policy making in other circumstances during the cold war. There was no expression of concern about the potential for touching off a wider war; nor was there any discussion of the likely reaction of China or the Soviet Union to an American action, although Kissinger met with the senior Chinese diplomat in Washington immediately after the meeting and issued a blunt warning through him to North Korea. Policymakers recognized a requirement to consult Japan under treaty arrangements about redeploying U.S. forces based on its territory, and Kissinger asked who would inform the South Korean president, but there was no discussion of the probable views of these Asian allies or the repercussions for them. As for Pyongyang's reaction, Kissinger observed that "it will be useful for us to generate enough activity so that the North Koreans begin to wonder what those crazy American bastards are doing or are capable of doing in this election year."

Even before the meeting was convened, General Richard Stilwell, the UN and U.S. commander in Korea, had recommended one potential response: to return to the JSA and cut down "the damned tree," as it was referred to during nearly all the governmental deliberations. This quickly won approval of the policy makers at the White House, but Kissinger wanted to do much more. After some discussion the group set in motion—and Ford subsequently ordered—(1) the raising of the American (and South Korean) alert status to greater readiness for war; (2) deployment of a squadron of F-4 fighters from Okinawa and F-111 fighter-bombers from Idaho to Korea; (3) preparations for "exercise" flights of B-52 heavy bombers from Guam to make practice bombing runs close to North Korea; and (4) preparations for redeploying the aircraft carrier USS *Midway* from Japan to the Korean straits.

While deciding on this massive show of American force in the area—and the felling of the tree—the WASAG meeting left undecided the punitive military action that Kissinger favored, and that he told the meeting Ford wished to explore. During the meeting Admiral Holloway suggested U.S. forces could lay mines or seize a North Korean ship. Another participant, according to Hyland, suggested that a nuclear weapon be exploded at sea near the North Korean coast as a warning. In discussion with Kissinger following the meeting, Hyland suggested an air strike in the eastern end of the DMZ, "where it would be unexpected and where it would not necessarily touch off something we couldn't handle." Kissinger seemed interested.

At Kissinger's request, the uniformed military explored two other options for punitive American actions to be taken at the time of the tree cutting. One was to destroy the nearby Bridge of No Return, across which prisoners of war had moved at end of the Korean War, by artillery fire, demolition charges, or precision guided missiles. The other option was an artillery attack against the DMZ barracks of the North Korean border guards. Both were strongly opposed by the Joint Chiefs of Staff on the grounds that they would put UN and ROK forces at the DMZ at great risk.

The JCS, however, told Kissinger it was exploring other punitive options to use "precision guided air munitions, surface-to-surface missiles, and unconventional warfare (SEAL) teams to destroy North Korean installations of military or infrastructure significance" after the tree felling was complete. "Henry thought we were being wimpish" by simply cutting down the tree, recalled National Security Adviser Scowcroft, who was with Ford in Kansas City but in constant touch with Kissinger. At a crucial point in the deliberations—after a second WASAG meeting to discuss U.S. responses—Deputy Secretary of Defense William Clements and Admiral Holloway called at the White House to see Hyland, who recalled them "wringing their hands that we may be headed into another Korean War" by taking strong action. In a sentiment characteristic of many near the top of government, they told Hyland, "These [North] Koreans are wild people."

In the end, Ford decided against any military reprisals because of their potential for escalation into a general war on the Korean peninsula. He explained later, "In the case of Korea to gamble with an overkill might broaden very quickly into a full military conflict, but responding with an appropriate amount of force would be effective in demonstrating U.S. resolve."

While the United States was pondering its course, the rival Korean states were reacting in very different ways. In response to the upgrading of American and South Korean alert status, North Korean radio broke into regular programming to announce that the entire army and reserve force was being placed into "full combat readiness." A strict blackout was imposed in Pyongyang, and the populace was crowded into underground shelters as air raid sirens wailed. Front-line troops were prepared for battle. From the DMZ to the capital, senior North Korean officials were evacuated into previously prepared and fortified tunnels.

Foreign Minister Ho Dam, speaking at a summit meeting of the nonaligned movement in Sri Lanka, depicted the ax killings as "intentional provocative acts against our side in the joint guard area of Panmunjom" intended to "directly set fire on the fuse of war." While keeping up a bellicose stand publicly, North Korea quickly agreed to a meeting of the Military Armistice Commission to discuss the clash. This suggested to Stilwell, he told the Pentagon privately, that the killings might well have been "a spontaneous, low-level overreaction" by North Korean guards.

In Seoul, President Park was privately furious at the killings, writing in his diary that "I cannot tolerate this barbaric act by crazy Kim Il Sung's gangs. . . . You stupid, cruel, violent gangs—you should know there is a limit to our patience. Mad dogs deserve clubs." In an initial meeting to discuss the military response, however, Park impressed General Stilwell as "calm, deliberate and positive throughout." Park advocated (1) "the strongest possible protest" to Pyongyang, including demands for an apology, reparations, and guarantees against repetition, all of which he admitted were not likely to be forthcoming; and (2) "appropriate counteraction" by military force to teach North Korea a lesson, but without the use of firearms. Stilwell believed Park did not wish to break the long-standing ban on using firearms in the Joint Security Area.

To improve the balance of forces there without introducing heavy arms barred by agreement from the DMZ, Park offered—and Stilwell accepted—the services of battle-ready ROK special forces troops with multiple black-belt honors in *tae kwon do* as reinforcements in case of trouble. (As it turned out, U.S. commanders learned later, the "unarmed" ROK troops were carrying grenades and had M16 rifles, antitank weapons, grenade launchers, and light machine guns hidden in their truck as they stood by waiting for action.) In a second meeting to go over Stilwell's plans, Park expressed a firm belief that the military response should be limited to removal of the poplar tree, and that "escalation should only evolve if the North escalates." Otherwise, he added, "the matter drops."

At seven A.M. August 21, three days after the killings, a convoy of twenty-three American and South Korean vehicles rolled into the JSA without warning to the North Koreans to begin what was named Operation Paul Bunyan. Aboard was a sixteen-member U.S. engineering team with chain saws and axes, who immediately began working on the massive trunk of the poplar and also removing two unauthorized barriers that had been erected in the JSA by North Korea. They were accompanied by a thirty-man security platoon armed with pistols and ax handles, and sixty-four ROK special forces *tae kwon do* experts.

This little band of troops, with its narrowly limited mission, was backed up by a mighty array of forces appropriate to the initiation of World War III. Hovering overhead with a noisy whirl of rotors was a U.S. infantry company in twenty utility helicopters, accompanied by seven Cobra attack helicopters. Behind them on the horizon were the B-52 bombers, escorted by the U.S. F-4 fighters and ROK F-5 fighters. Waiting on the runway at Osan Air Base, armed and fueled, were the F-111 fighter-bombers. The *Midway* aircraft-carrier task force was stationed offshore. On the ground at the approaches to the DMZ were heavily armed U.S. and ROK infantry, armor, and artillery backup forces.

Stilwell's battle plan, approved by Washington, called for mortar and artillery fire to cover the withdrawal of the tree-cutting force in case KPA guards resisted the operation with small arms. Under a last-minute White House order, American artillery were to open fire on the North Korean guard barracks in the DMZ in case of armed resistance. In the event of a KPA ground attack, the backup forces were to assist the withdrawal of all UN elements from the JSA while hundreds of rounds of heavy artillery rained down on nearby North Korean targets. That would have been the opening round of a wider war.

Five minutes into the operation, North Korean officials of the Military Armistice Commission were notified that a UN work party would enter the JSA "in order to peacefully finish the work left unfinished" on August 18. If not molested, the notification said, the UN force would take no further action. Within a few minutes five North Korean trucks and about 150 troops armed with automatic weapons gathered on the far end of the Bridge of No Return, looking across at the poplar. The troops watched in silence as the big tree was felled in forty-two minutes, three minutes fewer than Stilwell had estimated.

"We know it was very scary to the North Koreans, because we were listening," said an American official in Washington with access to North Korean front-line communications. A U.S. intelligence analyst monitoring the radio net said that "it blew their fucking minds."

The North Korean leadership quickly recognized that the killings at the DMZ were a dangerous mistake and moved to reduce the danger. Kim Il Sung claimed later that the Americans had started the fighting to help Ford win the U.S. presidential election but that the incident "no sooner happened than we realized that our soldiers had been taken in by the enemy's political scheme. So, we decided not to aggravate the incident any further."

Within an hour after the operation, the senior North Korean representative to the armistice commission, Major General Han Ju Kyong, requested a private meeting with the chief American representative, Rear Admiral Mark Frudden, to convey a message from Kim Il Sung. The personal message was Kim's first to the UN Command in the twenty-three-year history of the armistice. The usual fierce rhetoric was absent as Kim declared it "regretful" that an incident had occurred in the JSA and proposed that "both sides should make efforts" to avoid future clashes. The State Department initially rejected the Kim message as unacceptable because it did not forthrightly admit guilt, but then reversed itself after Habib and other Korean experts said that it was as close to an apology from Kim that could be obtained.

On August 25, in another surprise, North Korea proposed that to prevent future incidents, the Joint Security Area should be divided at the military demarcation line, which runs through it, and that henceforth KPA guards should stay north of the line and UN guards should stay south. The UN Command had made similar proposals several times in the past, but North Korea had not agreed. This time the concept was approved and details worked out with a minimum of controversy.

In the aftermath, some South Korean officials and the Seoul press harshly criticized the United States for not taking stronger action. As his fears subsided in the face of the U.S. buildup and North Korea's soft reaction, Park's belligerence toward North Korea seemed to grow. Questioned about Park's attitude at a White House meeting in mid-September, Sneider said that Park has "a parochial, Israeli complex stemming in part from the protection we have accorded to Korea for so long—Park tends to ignore or discount the costs we have to calculate in deciding how to react to North Korean provocations." The ambassador added, "Park may also have been influenced by his generals who were egging him on."

The brutal actions of the North Korean guards added immeasurably to the American perception of North Koreans as almost inhuman. Jimmy Lee, who served as the permanent U.S. Army civil servant on the Military Armistice Commission for almost thirty years, kept in his desk the gruesome photographs of the bloodied and battered bodies of Major Bonifas and Lieutenant Barrett. Bonifas was so badly beaten with the blunt end of an ax that his face was no longer recognizable. "Beneath the surface civility, this is what you are dealing with," Lee cautioned incoming U.S. officers at the DMZ.

Had different decisions been made in Washington on punitive actions or Kim Il Sung's statement of regret, the brutal killings in the DMZ might have led to a wider conflict on the peninsula with unknown results. A different set of decisions by Kim or a subordinate commander—especially an attempt to contest Operation Paul Bunyan with force of arms—would almost certainly have led to a sharp escalation. Had this happened, the course of history could have been changed in the United States as well as in Korea. In Scowcroft's view, which is hard to dispute, if North Korean belligerence had generated a war in August 1976, three months before the presidential election, "Ford would have won the election."

As it was, the assertions of U.S. power and authority—secretly against South Korea's nuclear weapons program, and very openly against North Korea's barbaric actions in the Joint Security Area—demonstrated that despite its failure in Indochina, the United States continued to be a potent force on the Korean peninsula. Washington did not, however, heed Ambassador Sneider's call to establish a more durable partnership with the ROK. Instead, U.S. policy in the period to come intensified the discord between Washington and Seoul.

# 4

## THE CARTER CHILL

*A*merica's reaction against military commitments abroad in the wake of the Vietnam disaster found its voice in its first post-Vietnam president, Jimmy Carter. As early as January 1975, in the first days of his candidacy for president, Carter advocated the withdrawal of U.S. troops from South Korea, which after the pullout from Vietnam were the only remaining U.S. military deployment on the mainland of Asia and a tripwire that guaranteed immediate U.S. involvement in case of a North Korean attack. After the little-known former governor of Georgia surprisingly won the nomination of his party and then the presidential election, he ordered that his idea be put into practice despite the absence of serious consideration within the government, despite the opposition of South Korea, which was alarmed, and Japan, which was gravely concerned. He also made little effort to negotiate with China and the Soviet Union, the other major powers involved, or with North Korea, to facilitate the American withdrawal.

For two and a half years, as opposition mounted both inside and outside his administration, Carter stubbornly fought to sustain his plan with the same dogged persistence he deployed in successfully pursuing the Camp David agreements on the Middle East and the Panama Canal Treaty. In the end, he was forced to give it up, even though in theory he had the power to order the troops home from Korea with the stroke of his pen as commander-in-chief of U.S. armed forces.

Carter's ill-fated withdrawal effort is a case study in the hidden limitations on presidential power in the American system. It is also a study in unintended consequences, which in this case included the fatal weakening of a South Korean president and the inoculation of the U.S. body politic for years to come against further attempts to withdraw forces from Korea.

Nobody, including Carter himself, seems to know precisely how and when he developed his unyielding determination that American forces should be withdrawn from Korea. "The origin of my position is not clear to me," the former president wrote me while I was preparing this book. Zbigniew Brzezinski, Carter's White House national security adviser and his closest collaborator on the troop withdrawal plan, called its origin "a mystery not yet unraveled." Cyrus Vance and Harold Brown, who grappled with the proposal and its author as secretary of state and secretary of defense, respectively, were equally uninformed about the roots of Carter's resolve, as were many others I interviewed from the Carter campaign staff and administration. Apparently nobody had the temerity to ask Carter at the time how and why he had concluded that U.S. troops were no longer needed.

Even before his policy began to run into trouble, Carter was reluctant to discuss its substance or consider alternatives; he knew what he wanted to do, and his mind was made up. During the transition period between his election and his inauguration as president, he turned down an offer of a CIA briefing on Korea, and he rarely attended any of the National Security Council discussions of Korea in the course of his administration. In *Keeping Faith,* Carter's lengthy memoir of his presidency, he devoted much space to foreign affairs but never mentioned the withdrawal issue.

## CARTER'S WITHDRAWAL: ORIGINS AND IMPLEMENTATION

As it happened, I was among the earliest to learn firsthand of Carter's determination. In late May 1975, he visited Tokyo for a meeting of the United States–Europe–Japan Trilateral Commission, while I was serving as *Washington Post* correspondent for Northeast Asia, based in the Japanese capital. Over drinks with me and *New York Times* correspondent Richard Halloran and in a speech the following day, Carter said he favored withdrawing all U.S. troops, both ground and air force, from Korea over a period of perhaps five years. To accomplish this, he advocated a major buildup of South Korea's own air force. When Halloran observed that the ROK air force had deliberately been kept weak so that it would not be used to attack North Korea and start another war, Carter began to have second thoughts. Within days he limited his withdrawal proposal to ground troops only, proposing to leave the U.S. Air Force in place or even build it up.

My story on Carter's statements in Tokyo was reduced by *Post* editors from eight paragraphs to two sentences. This was typical of the short shrift that would be given his views on Korea during the campaign, during which it never became a high-profile issue.

In itself, the idea of reducing or even completely withdrawing U.S. ground troops from Korea was hardly novel. In 1971, President Nixon had withdrawn the Seventh Infantry Division, which constituted roughly 20,000 of the 60,000 U.S. troops then on duty in Korea, despite passionate opposition from the Seoul government. Later Nixon's secretary of defense from 1969 to 1972, Melvin R. Laird, signed off on a plan within the Pentagon to reduce the remaining U.S. ground combat unit, the Second Infantry Division, to a single brigade, but its implementation was blocked by Alexander Haig and Henry Kissinger, who feared its political effects in Asia after the American opening to China. By coincidence, the very day I met Carter in Tokyo, May 27, 1975, the Ford White House launched a secret study of American policy toward Korea, specifically including the question of reducing the American military presence. No decisions were reached.

In 1977 Carter's White House press secretary, Jody Powell, in seeking to explain the roots of the policy, told me that Carter had been familiar with the discussions in Washington surrounding Laird's withdrawal plan. Powell added that Carter's views arose from "his basic inclination to question the stationing of American troops overseas." Carter, in his 1994 letter to me about his views, said, "Contrary to the opinion of many U.S. leaders, then and now, it was not a goal of mine just to deploy as many of our forces around the globe as host countries would accommodate.''

While Carter was making his run for the presidency, the post-Vietnam aversion to military involvement abroad was at a high point. In the month that Saigon fell, April 1975, only 14 percent of Americans responding to a Louis Harris public opinion poll favored U.S. involvement if North Korea attacked the South, while 65 percent said they would oppose it. This made a strong impression on Carter, who still recalled the results in his letter to me two decades later.

Two weeks before Inauguration Day, when the first informal meeting of the Carter administration's National Security Council team took place, policy toward Korea was one of fifteen items Carter selected for priority review and decision making. Presidential Review Memorandum/NSC 13 (PRM-13)—issued January 26, 1977, six days after Carter's inauguration, and sent to the heads of key national security departments and agencies—ordered "a broad review of our policies toward the Korean peninsula," including "reductions in U.S. conventional force levels." Despite the neutral-sounding words, officials of the new administration were shocked to discover that the basic decision had already been cast in concrete. The new secretary of state, Cyrus Vance, returned from the White House with instructions that the review should not consider *whether* to withdraw American ground troops from Korea, but only *how* to withdraw them.

The "review" was hardly under way before Carter sent Vice President Walter Mondale to Tokyo, at the end of January, to inform the Japanese of his determination to withdraw American ground troops over a period of years. Publicly the Japanese were understanding, but privately they were deeply worried about the potential for a general American pullback to affect their own security. Deputy Assistant Secretary of Defense Morton Abramowitz, a career holdover from previous administrations who accompanied Mondale on the trip, argued it was a serious mistake to move so quickly and especially not to fly on to Seoul to inform South Korean leaders in person of the decision, which was bound to be deeply upsetting. Summing up his strong belief, Abramowitz, who later loyally defended in public the policy he opposed in private, told Mondale, "We *can't* withdraw." The new vice president retorted breezily, "Hey, Mort, there's been an election."

On February 15, Carter sent a letter to South Korean president Park Chung Hee affirming the U.S. commitment to ROK security but broaching the issue of troop withdrawals and urging him to take steps to improve his human rights posture. The letter was presented to Park by Ambassador Richard Sneider and General John Vessey, the U.S. military commander in Seoul. Vessey, who had met Carter in the White House a few days before, said no decision had been made about withdrawal of American troops. Moreover, Vessey said Carter asked him to convey to Park that he "would make no changes in the troop deployments until after careful consultations with President Park." Park, citing many press stories about withdrawal plans, asked that quiet consultations begin very soon.

In early March, when ROK foreign minister Park Tong Chin came to Washington to begin the consultations, however, he found a U.S. president whose mind was made up. In a handwritten memo to Brzezinski and Vance on March 5, shortly before meeting the Korean minister, Carter said bluntly that Park must understand:

a) American forces will be withdrawn. Air cover will be continued.
b) US–Korean relations as determined by Congress and American people are at an all time low ebb.
c) Present military aid support and my reticence on human rights issue will be temporary unless Park voluntarily adopts some open change re political prisoners.

In the talking points for the meeting sent to Carter by Brzezinski, it was suggested that Carter justify his decision by saying, "In view of the expansion in South Korea's economy and military strength as well as the apparent desire of all the great powers to avoid war on the peninsula, our ground forces will be withdrawn." Minister Park, however, recalled that Carter's main justification was that "troop withdrawal is my campaign pledge." The meeting made it crystal clear that Carter was determined to go ahead with the withdrawal. Carter also said that the withdrawal would be gradual and that Washington would support the strengthening of South Korean defense capabilities to compensate for the American troop cutbacks.

Before he became president, Carter said he would seek guarantees of South Korea's security from China and the Soviet Union, before making a decision to withdraw troops. In fact, he did not. As late as mid-June 1977, well after the withdrawal plan had been established and announced, the administration still had not provided even an authoritative briefing for the Chinese and Soviets on what the United States had in mind.

In July 1977, Vance wrote in a memorandum to Carter that a diplomatic initiative involving the two Koreas with possible Chinese participation was "the missing dimension in our troop withdrawal policy." Carter responded favorably, and the State Department was authorized to begin consultations initially with Seoul and then with Beijing on a possible four-power conference to seek a political settlement on the peninsula. Vance took up the proposal with Foreign Minister Huang Hua on a trip to Beijing in late August but met with no enthusiasm from the Chinese side. There the idea seems to have been dropped for nearly two years, possibly because of South Korea's strongly negative reaction to Carter's troop withdrawal plans.

Carter had declared during the presidential campaign that "we've got 700 atomic weapons in Korea. I see no reason for a single one." (According to government documents, there were actually 683 warheads in South Korea at the time, remarkably close to Carter's statement.) His plan had been to order their removal as the first order of business. Defense Secretary Harold Brown, a physicist and nuclear expert, spearheaded a successful drive to persuade Carter to consider the removal of nuclear weapons along with, rather than ahead of, withdrawal of U.S. troops, lest sudden action in this sensitive area destabilize the situation on the Korean peninsula.

Carter's iron-willed resolve to move ahead posed an ethical and professional dilemma for many officials of his government, who believed in loyalty to presidential decisions yet who increasingly believed Carter's policy courted unnecessary and possibly unacceptable political and military risks. Unlike the classic Washington struggle of contending forces within the executive branch engaged in "a battle for the president's mind," this came to be "a battle against the president's mind." There were increasingly explicit private conversations among the conspirators, who might have been fired if their conniving had come to light. According to Richard Holbrooke, who was assistant secretary of state for East Asian and Pacific affairs and in the middle of the battle, it was "a full-scale rebellion against the president."

Somehow news correspondents covering the administration, including me, never grasped the full extent of the guerrilla war within the administration.

Facing fundamental questions of loyalty and responsibility, Brown's guideline was to "obey direct orders, but otherwise try to turn the president around." The most difficult thing for Brown was defending a policy in public that he opposed in private. Vance, who resigned on principle in 1980 in opposition to the hostage rescue mission in Iran, was able to maneuver within the limits of his conscience on the Korea withdrawal, keeping his misgivings to himself while vowing that he had to "find a way to change the president's mind." Brzezinski, who knew better than anyone else that Carter's view on the Korean issue was "strongly held, almost emotional," stuck with the president in high-level meetings until the bitter end, although he did nothing to stop the maneuvering of others to thwart Carter's idea.

On the military side, the politically appointed Joint Chiefs of Staff accepted the withdrawal policy on condition that American support elements remain and that South Korea receive adequate compensation for the reduction in American strength. The officers in the field, however, did not disguise their opposition. Major General John Singlaub, the chief of staff of the U.S. Command in Korea, told *Washington Post* correspondent John Saar that "if U.S. ground troops are withdrawn on the schedule suggested, it will lead to war." Stung by what he considered military insubordination, Carter summoned Singlaub to the White House, reprimanded him, and summarily removed him from Korea, reassigning him to a domestic post. The Singlaub episode created a political storm, deepening the controversy over the withdrawal plan.

The initial tactic of the internal opposition to the pullout was to seek to delay, modify, and water down the plans so that initial withdrawals would be minor, with lots of room for reflection and reversal. Carter, however, insisted on pushing ahead. In early May he signed a top-secret order containing a clear timetable: one brigade of the Second Division—at least 6,000 troops—was to be withdrawn by the end of 1978; a second brigade and its support elements—at least 9,000 troops—was to be withdrawn by the end of June 1980. American nuclear weapons in Korea were to be reduced and eventually re-moved along with the troops. Undersecretary of State Philip Habib, formerly U.S. ambassador to Korea, and General George Brown, chairman of the Joint Chiefs of Staff, were sent to brief the South Korean and Japanese governments.

In Seoul, President Park had not taken the withdrawal idea seriously at first, telling Korean reporters in an off-the-record luncheon that "I don't think it's going to happen soon." When Carter announced his decision publicly, Park summoned his national security advisers to the Blue House. Doing his best to control his emotions, the ROK president surprised his aides by saying he would not openly oppose the proposed withdrawal but would ask for compensation to maintain the North-South military balance. Park's attitude arose from his searing personal experience in 1970, when he had passionately opposed withdrawal of the Seventh Division, only to have all his objections overridden by Vice President Spiro Agnew, who had been sent to deliver the news. Agnew had emphasized that a U.S. president could assign his forces wherever and whenever he wished. In the face of this White House trump card, Park decided it would be unavailing and demeaning to mount a frontal attack on Carter's program.

Spurred on by doubts or outright opposition in the executive branch and the military, American domestic opponents of the withdrawal became more numerous and more vocal. To compensate for the withdrawal of American forces, Carter promised that $1.9 billion in military aid would be provided "in advance of or parallel to the withdrawals." This required congressional approval, but in July 1977, when Defense Secretary Brown briefed lawmakers at the White House, not a single senator or representative spoke up in support of the withdrawal, and many expressed their opposition. "It is clear that we face an uphill battle on this issue with Congress," Brzezinski reported in a memorandum to Carter.

Congressional support for South Korea had become a contentious topic independent of the troop withdrawal issue. Abuses of human rights and, especially, the arrest and conviction of eighteen prominent Christian leaders for issuing a manifesto complaining of the lack of freedom, provoked strong reactions from American churches and the public. In April 1976, shortly after the arrest of the

Christian leaders and while Carter was still campaigning, 119 senators and representatives signed a letter to President Ford condemning "continuing suppression" in Korea and warning that ongoing U.S. military support could make the United States "an accomplice to repression." Six months later, after conviction of the Christians, 154 members of Congress wrote President Park to protest "disrespect for human rights," which they said was undermining American–South Korean relations. Carter, who sought to make human rights and morality central tenets of his foreign policy, found the Park regime's abuses particularly offensive.

Another intense controversy had erupted on October 24, 1976, when *The Washington Post* reported that a Korean agent, Park Tong Sun, had distributed $500,000 to $1 million a year to bribe as many as ninety members of Congress and other officials, and that U.S. eavesdropping devices had recorded the planning for the bribery scheme. The *Post* story, by Maxine Cheshire and Scott Armstrong, was based on leaks from a secret grand jury investigation initiated by the Justice Department. Coming on the heels of the Watergate scandal, which had driven President Nixon from office, the bribery saga quickly became known as Koreagate. Carter took a posture of full cooperation with congressional probes, writing in a confidential memo to his staff that "we should move without reticence to provide all possible informations re: violations of U.S. law."

By the end of 1977, Carter's first year in office, four full-scale congressional investigations of Korean activities were under way, and the FBI and Internal Revenue Service had launched additional investigations. Eventually only one member of Congress, Representative Richard Hanna, was convicted of being bribed. But with charges of bribery and an avalanche of investigations filling the news, nobody wanted to vote for compensatory aid for the South Korean military. "By the spring of 1978," according to Robert Rich, the State Department country director for Korea, "Congress probably could not have passed a bill stating that Korea was a peninsula in Northeast Asia."

The showdown on the withdrawal issue came on April 11, when Brzezinski met with the secretaries of state and defense and senior Asia experts of the administration. Brzezinski informed Carter in advance that based on his soundings, "everybody, even Vance, is

against you" on proceeding with the troop withdrawal. Carter
pleaded with his subordinate, "Zbig, you've got to protect me. This is
my last foreign policy proposal from the campaign I haven't walked
away from."

By this time, most of the policy advisers privately had grave
doubts about the U.S. troop withdrawal or even opposed it for strategic reasons, but none was so bold as to say so in the White House
Situation Room. They believed, as Brown acknowledged later, that
officials "had either to support [Carter's] decision or resign." Instead
the officials made a case for delaying the withdrawal because of the
unwillingness of Congress to approve funds to compensate South
Korea as promised. "The issue is not the withdrawal but the Park
Tong Sun affair," Assistant Secretary of State Richard Holbrooke
told the meeting. "Because of 'Koreagate,' congressmen fear political
retribution at the polls if they vote for any sort of aid to Korea this
year." Moreover, Holbrooke said, to proceed with withdrawal without the aid package would be seen "as part of a retreat from East
Asia" and could torpedo the administration's plans to normalize
American relations with China. Michael Armacost, then a National
Security Council staff member and much later U.S. ambassador to
Tokyo, said "it will have extraordinarily adverse consequences in
Japan" to withdraw troops without providing compensating aid as
promised. The Defense Department's Morton Abramowitz said that
proceeding without the compensation package would likely bring
about the resignation of General Vessey, the U.S. military commander in Korea. He added that such a move "will lose the Joint
Chiefs of Staff," which had reluctantly accepted the withdrawal
policy.

With Brown, Vance, and most of the others counseling delay or
cancellation of the next withdrawal element, only Brzezinski addressed the real but unspoken issue. "This [withdrawal policy] may
have been the wrong decision, but now it has been made. We cannot
afford to go back on it," the NSC adviser said. In the end Brzezinski
devised and sold Carter on a plan to water down rather than delay the
first pullout of combat troops, limiting the immediate withdrawal to
only one battalion of troops, about 800 men, plus about 2,600 noncombat personnel, instead of the planned 6,000 combat troops, with

the rest theoretically to come out later. As many in the meeting hoped and assumed, the administration's rollback signaled a weakness that made further withdrawals much less likely.

Carter reluctantly accepted the face-saving maneuver, which was announced on April 21. In private he bitterly upbraided Brown for seeking to stymie his program. He expected more loyalty, he told his defense secretary heatedly. Brown was surprised at Carter's outburst but stood his ground, saying he felt obligated to give his best advice and judgment in private, especially since he had been the administration's point man in defending the withdrawal in congressional testimony. Earlier in his long governmental career, Brown had found himself intimidated by the powerful opinions of presidents John Kennedy and Lyndon Johnson. Now he was determined to tell Carter what he really thought despite the potential damage to their relationship. "Carter felt he was up against the establishment" on the touchy withdrawal issue, said Brown, "whereas we felt we were trying to save him from doing things that would cause big trouble with allies."

## THE VIEW FROM PYONGYANG

In Pyongyang, Kim Il Sung was keenly aware of Carter's proposal to withdraw American troops from South Korea. Such a move had long been one of Kim's central goals, in the belief that this would lead inevitably to reuniting the peninsula under his leadership, whether by peaceful or violent means. In public and in private, Kim had made Washington his enemy number one, blaming the United States for dividing the peninsula in 1945, intervening in 1950 to prevent reunification on Kim's terms, turning South Korea into its colony, elevating and sustaining Park Chung Hee as a military dictator, and a variety of other offenses, real or imagined. In the North Korean *Dictionary of Political Terminologies,* published in 1970, "U.S. imperialism" was defined as the work of the "most barbarously piratical invader and head of all other imperialistic countries." On the eve of Carter's inauguration, however, the fierce rhetoric was dropped, and the "American imperialist aggressor army" became simply "American forces" in Pyongyang's statements. The DMZ killings were blamed on the outgoing Ford administration by name, giving the incoming president a clean slate in Pyongyang.

Behind the scenes, Kim made energetic efforts to engage Carter directly. Beginning with an open letter to the U.S. Congress in 1973, Pyongyang had been appealing to Washington to open direct negotiations on replacing the existing armistice agreement with a peace treaty to pave the way for withdrawal of American troops and weapons from South Korea. In November 1976, immediately after Carter's election, Kim stepped up the campaign, sending a personal letter through the president of Pakistan to the U.S. president-elect at Plains, Georgia, asking for direct contacts. This was followed in February 1977 by a message to Secretary of State Vance from North Korean foreign minister Ho Dam, through the U.S. Embassy in Pakistan, expressing Pyongyang's desire to avoid confrontation with the United States, to pursue reunification peacefully, and to open direct U.S.– DPRK peace talks, which at least initially would exclude South Korea. The American reply expressed interest in discussions with the North, including discussions of "more permanent Armistice arrangements," but only if Seoul was permitted to participate fully.* At the time, this was a nonstarter in Pyongyang. In gestures to Pyongyang, Carter lifted the ban on travel to North Korea by U.S. citizens in March and for the first time invited North Korea's UN representative to an official U.S. reception.

In July 1977, in this era of high expectations, a U.S. Army helicopter was shot down by North Korean forces after it strayed over their side of the DMZ, killing three crewmen and leaving the fourth a captive. In a remarkably mild reaction, Carter described the flight as a mistake and played down the conflict. In response, North Korea returned the bodies and the captured American within three days, an unprecedentedly short time for such a move.

---

*Over the succeeding months, Kim Il Sung sent messages to Carter through President Bongo of Gabon in May 1977, Yugoslav president Tito in October 1977, and President Ceauşescu of Romania in April 1978. In each case, Kim declined to deal with the ROK government while it was under Park's leadership; in each case, Carter replied that he would negotiate with the North only with South Korean participation.

Yet as Carter was forced to modify and stretch out his program of American withdrawal, Kim became increasingly critical. "Carter has not kept his election pledges," Kim told visitors, charging that the withdrawal pledges were "aimed at deceiving the world." In a talk with a Japanese editor, Kim bitterly called the U.S. president "a con man" because of his position on Korean issues.

On December 8, 1977, Kim received a three-day visit from Erich Honecker, the general secretary of the East German Socialist Unity (Communist) Party, who came to be one of Kim's closest and most useful overseas friends. Both were lifelong revolutionaries who had advanced to high places with Soviet backing. Like Korea, Germany had been divided as a result of World War II. East Germany, like North Korea, was struggling to survive against a more populous and more prosperous capitalistic regime across a heavily militarized dividing line. Encouraged by the Soviet Union and recognizing the similarities, the German Democratic Republic (GDR, the formal name of East Germany) had been an important source of economic aid during all of North Korea's existence.

Kim prepared meticulously to receive Honecker, whom he had never met. To flatter Honecker and contribute to a positive atmosphere, he staged a mass rally of close to half a million people honoring Honecker, including North Korean musicians performing revolutionary German songs from Honecker's glory days as a youth leader. "It was the biggest reception of his lifetime. This old man was in tears," said an East German diplomat who was present.

The transcript of the confidential discussions with Honecker on December 10, preserved in the GDR archives, provides a rare snapshot of Kim's private views in the late 1970s. While acknowledging that his country faced problems, many of which he attributed to "American imperialism," Kim was supremely confident of his position and the ascendency of his self-reliant *juche* ideology. Wearing horn-rimmed glasses and an elegantly tailored cadre suit of the sort worn by Chinese leaders, Kim at 65 was still in the prime of his life. Only a few flecks of gray could be seen in his full head of hair.

Kim, according to the transcript, declared that his number one priority was unification of the country, and he outlined three strategic directions that he had set forth in the early 1960s and adhered to for the rest of his life: "first, to successfully carry out the organization of socialism in the northern part of the country; second, to support the revolutionary struggle in South Korea; third, to develop solidarity and unity with the international revolutionary forces." He discussed the status of each in turn.

Kim first described the extraordinary mobilization of the population that distinguished North Korea from nearly every other country, and that he justified as necessary to create a powerful revolutionary base for the Korean peninsula and beyond. He told Honecker without overstatement that "everyone, apart from infants, is included in the organizational life" of the nation. Of North Korea's 17 million people, at that time 2.2 million were in the Workers Party, and all the others, except for infants, belonged to various organizations of children, youths, women, farmers, or workers.

Education was compulsory through the eleventh grade. However, ideological instruction took up more than half the day in North Korean elementary schools in the 1970s, and Kim had decreed that this emphasis should be even greater in the upper grades. A U.S. Central Intelligence Agency analysis of the economic competition on the peninsula, issued a month after the Kim-Honecker meeting, cited the priority on teaching ideology over useful skills in the education system as a key reason why North Korea had fallen behind in labor productivity and a well-educated South Korea had surged ahead.

In his talk with Honecker, Kim described in general terms the social engineering that was so much a part of North Korea. To "revolutionize and reform women, according to the example of the working class," according to Kim, they were being "freed from heavy domestic work" and placed in jobs outside the home. About 80 percent of farmworkers were women, he said, and over 90 percent of workers in light industry. Without giving numbers, he explained that this was necessary because "many young people in our country are in the army." To compensate for the absence of mothers and to start inculcating its ideology early, North Korea had built nurseries and kindergartens for 3.5 million children so they could be "taken care of and educated by society."

Kim made no mention of this to Honecker, but the fact was that despite North Korea's strenuous efforts, by 1977 the balance of economic power on the peninsula was shifting decisively in favor of the South. In the first years after the Korean War, the centrally directed economy of North Korea had grown more rapidly than the more loosely controlled economy of South Korea. But in the early 1960s, the two economies took decisive turns: the North opted for an inner-directed economy, centered on building its heavy industry at home and shying away from commitments abroad; the South, guided by American-trained Korean economists and the promise of a share in the American and Japanese markets, turned toward an externally directed economy centered on exports and initially on light industry. These fateful turns eventually determined the outcome of the economic race on the peninsula, and they deeply affected the political and diplomatic spheres as well.

By the mid-1970s, by most outside estimates, the North's *juche* economy was falling behind. North Korea's gross national product, adjusted for inflation, doubled between 1965 and 1976, a highly creditable performance for a developing economy. But at the same time, South Korea's real GNP more than tripled. In the mid-1970s, as poverty was reduced below the thirty-eighth parallel, South Korea passed the North in per capita GNP for the first time since the division of the country.

Part of North Korea's economic problem was its very heavy spending for military purposes. From the mid-1960s to the mid-1970s, the North devoted an estimated 15 to 20 percent of its economy to its military. The South spent an average of 5 percent on its military, though due to Park's massive armament program the proportion briefly jumped to near 10 percent in the mid-1970s.

In the early 1970s, in an attempt to override the South's growing advantage, Pyongyang abruptly shifted its autarkic policies to a "great leap outward," purchasing entire factories from Western Europe and Japan, in a burst of economic activity that matched its sudden outwardly directed drive for negotiations with the South. One Japanese–Danish venture, for example, was to provide North Korea with the largest cement factory in the world. But in the worldwide economic dislocation following the 1973 Middle East war and oil embargo, North Korea found itself unable to meet the fast-rising payments on its external debts. As a result, North Korea's access to international credit was severely restricted, while South Korea's growing international trade made it a major player on the global scene.

In his conversation with Honecker, Kim conceded none of this but reiterated his belief in the superiority of the North, based in large part on his second strategic direction, the revolutionary struggle in the South. Referring to the fight that he and his guerrilla band had waged against the Japanese, while Park Chung Hee and others were serving in the Japanese army, Kim expressed confidence in his superiority because "the leading circles of South Korea are traitors, whereas we here are patriots." Contrary to existing evidence and belief in the South, Kim claimed that North Korean communists had been behind the student revolution that overthrew the regime of Syngman Rhee in 1960, and that the United States had organized the military junta headed by General Park Chung Hee that took power in 1961. In all these years, said Kim, the South Korean students had supported North Korea and "have not demonstrated against us even a single time," although they had demonstrated repeatedly against "the puppet regime."

Kim expressed certainty that after the withdrawal of U.S. troops, when the South Korean people chose their own way, "then they would choose the way of socialism." In the meantime, he said the crucial objective for the North was to isolate Park and his government rather than return to the 1972–73 era of North-South dialogue. The Americans were trying to get the dialogue restarted, he said, but "if we get together with Park Chung Hee and hold negotiations, there is the danger of weakening the South Korean political forces who are opposing Park Chung Hee."

On the first day of his visit, Honecker had committed East Germany to have "no relations" with South Korea, but Kim continued to stress the need to isolate the South, perhaps in hopes that his visitor would pass along his views to Moscow. Honecker's pledge would prove to be costly to East Germany; over the years that followed, each time the GDR was tempted to trade with the South, a sharp protest from Pyongyang reminded Honecker of his commitment, and the proposed deal was squelched.

Honecker at the time was considered a slavish follower of Soviet leadership, and thus Kim made special efforts to persuade him that he was not leaning to the Chinese side of the Sino-Soviet struggle for leadership in the communist world, which had broken out in the 1960s and had yet to be ended. The North Korean leader emphasized his troubles with Beijing during the Cultural Revolution, revealing that the Chinese had set up giant loudspeakers at the Sino-Korean border and delivered deafening attacks on "Korean revisionists" from five A.M. to midnight every day. On a later occasion, Kim told Honecker that at the height of the Sino-Soviet conflict in 1969, Chinese troops had threatened to march into Korean territory near the Soviet border, and he had ordered DPRK forces not to shoot. The Chinese withdrew, Kim reported. Since those days, relations with China had been repaired, but "we do not follow China blindly," Kim emphasized to Honecker. On the other hand, he added, "we also do not participate in the Soviet Union's polemics against China." Opting out of the Sino–Soviet conflict "does not mean that we are opportunists, but that the situation does not allow us anything else."

Finally, the Kim–Honecker talks dealt with North Korea's great power adversaries. While he was concerned about the danger of a revival of Japanese militarism, Kim conceded that "the Japanese nation is not as it was before" due to the lessons learned from World War II and the U.S. atomic bomb attacks. Looking to the future, he declared that a triumph of communism on the Korean peninsula would be "beneficial for stimulating the revolution in Japan."

As for the United States, Kim was scornful about Carter, after nearly a year of trying to make contact with the new American president. The decision to stretch out the U.S. troop withdrawal from South Korea was "a deceitful maneuver against the people" and an attempt to manipulate public opinion, he told Honecker. While pretending to prepare to withdraw, the American military was actually "carrying out war drills and importing weapons [to South Korea] every day."

Kim confided that his military reconnaissance teams constantly observed U.S. maneuvers in South Korea but kept their spying a secret. American officers were uncomfortably aware of this aspect of the internecine war on the divided peninsula. In 1975 a North Korean reconnaissance team was discovered while photographing and sketching the U.S. air base at Kwangju and a nearby ROK missile site, and in 1976 a North Korean team wearing ROK-style uniforms covered sixty to seventy miles on foot south of the DMZ before being caught. By the time of the Kim-Honecker meeting, the U.S. Command in Seoul had acknowledged in a confidential report that "the North can infiltrate or exfiltrate its agents or special warfare units by land, sea or air to virtually any location within the ROK." On the other hand, American and South Korean operations inside North Korea were extremely limited. U.S. knowledge of North Korean military affairs, however, was beginning to receive much higher priority.

## END OF THE CARTER WITHDRAWAL

An important assumption underlying Carter's withdrawal plan was that during and after the departure of American ground troops, the military balance on the peninsula would continue to be favorable to the South. In the late 1970s, however, this assumption was thrown into doubt by a new set of U.S. intelligence estimates that depicted the North's military forces as much more numerous and much better armed than previously believed. The new estimates proved to be a fatal blow to Carter's already embattled withdrawal plan.

The beginning of the end started with a 29-year-old intelligence analyst named John Armstrong, who in May 1975 was bent over a light table at Fort Meade, Maryland, scrutinizing aerial photographs of North Korean tanks. Armstrong, a West Point graduate who had served in Vietnam before becoming a civilian analyst for the army, had been laboriously counting the tanks when he reached a surprising conclusion: there were many more than expected on the basis of earlier reports. Within a few weeks, Armstrong identified an entirely new tank division (about 270 tanks and 100 armored personnel carriers) in a valley about fifty miles north of the DMZ.

For many years the principal source of intelligence on North Korea had been aerial photography from the cameras of American spy planes and reconnaissance satellites, augmented by electronic eavesdropping. Since the central U.S. military concern was a potential surprise attack, the photographs were carefully examined by combat units for evidence of southward movement or other signs of impending assault, then filed away. Until Armstrong came along, however, there had been little effort to compare the overall strength of North Korean units in the latest pictures with those of previous months or years.

Armstrong's first intensive study, completed in December 1975, reported North Korean tank forces to be about 80 percent larger than had been previously estimated. Armed with this alarming finding, he persuaded the army to assign six more full-time analysts to his project. Over the next two years, his team documented the development of North Korean special forces units, which were training on mock-ups of South Korean highways and terrain, and a major increase in the number and forward deployment of North Korean artillery.

When Armstrong finally took his findings to the U.S. command in Seoul in December 1977, he found a receptive audience in General Vessey, the U.S. commander, and others who were fighting the Carter withdrawal program. The following month, Vessey requested a complete intelligence reassessment of North Korea's strength, complaining to the Pentagon of the adverse effects "on overall U.S. military policy and decision-making" of overly conservative estimates of the enemy. In response, the army initiated a much more extensive study in Washington, with a reinforced team of thirty-five analysts summoned from all over the world. They went to work reexamining all the intelligence reports on North Korean forces since the armistice, and scrutinizing every frame of overhead photography and all the signal intelligence obtained since 1969. The results, officially reported in classified briefings beginning in mid-1978, were startling.

Due to a strong and steady buildup since 1971–72, North Korea was credited in the new estimate with about seven hundred maneuver battalions, nearly twice the number carried on the books a decade earlier and nearly double the size of the South Korean force structure. Moreover, the North was estimated to have many more tanks and artillery pieces than previously known, giving it a more than two-to-one advantage over the South in terms of the numbers of those weapons. The study, which eventually identified every North Korean unit down to the infantry company and artillery battery level, found the bulk of the forces positioned closer to the DMZ than had been expected. The overall size of the North Korean ground forces, previously estimated at 485,000, was now put at 680,000, an increase of about 40 percent. For the first time, the North was estimated to have more men under arms than the South, whose population was twice as large. In North Korea, according to the new data, one out of every twenty-six persons was on active duty in the army, the highest proportion of any major nation.

Senior officials were quick to recognize that the new findings had tremendous implications for the withdrawal program. Nathanial Thayer, who was national intelligence officer at the CIA, recalled that "everyone was thinking the same thing—this is a good way for Carter to get off this issue. Nobody I knew was for pulling out the troops; we all saw it as trouble." In early January 1979, results of the new estimate leaked to *The Army Times* and became front-page news in other papers, including my report in *The Washington Post.*

The new findings sharply intensified congressional pressure to halt the withdrawal program. Carter, however, was skeptical of the validity of the intelligence reassessment, and decades later he remains so. Recalling the immediate leaks and political impact of the report, Carter wrote me while I was preparing this book, "I have always suspected that the facts were doctored by DIA [Defense Intelligence Agency] and others, but it was beyond the capability even of a president to prove this."

By late January 1979, Carter himself was just about the only person in the administration who favored continuing with the troop withdrawal, and even he was aware that support for his views on Korea—and nearly everything else—was eroding drastically. He was being battered from every side following the forced departure of the shah from Iran and the triumph of the Iranian revolution earlier in the month, which led to a redoubling of world oil prices, intensified inflation, and other economic dislocations worldwide.

On January 22 he was persuaded to authorize a new review of Korea policy, chaired by the State Department, "in the light of recent developments affecting the Korean peninsula," including the "new judgments on North Korean order of battle." This artful piece of bureaucratic prose never explicitly mentioned the U.S. withdrawal as a matter for review, but everyone except Carter knew that that was its central topic. Unlike most other such studies, which aimed at bringing the bureaucracy into line behind new presidential policies,

Presidential Review Memorandum/NSC-45 was aimed by the bureaucracy at persuading the president to abandon an old policy he continued to cherish.

In order to avoid disclosing their real intent or backing Carter into a corner, his senior lieutenants conducted the "review" in extraordinary secrecy worthy of the most sensitive covert operation. The usual interagency channels of communication for the exchange of classified information were bypassed in favor of hand-carried memoranda between the offices of the top national security officials of government. For once, news of a major policy-making enterprise did not leak.

In the spring, aides recommended an idea that had been under discussion for many months: Carter should make a visit to Korea, following his trip to Tokyo for the June summit meeting of the Group of Seven industrialized nations. The advisers saw the trip as an integral part of a scenario to lead inexorably to further adjustment of the withdrawal plans: first absorb the new intelligence, then discuss it with leaders in Tokyo and Seoul, then report back to the U.S. congressional leadership on changes required by the altered circumstances. Carter reluctantly agreed to the visit, realizing it would probably be the occasion for reconsideration of his plan. He made it clear, however, that he did not wish to discuss the withdrawal issue with President Park, whom he had never met but whose record and regime were distasteful to him.

As the trip preparations were under way, Carter arrived at the Oval Office one morning with a novel—and startling—idea of how to ease the North-South confrontation on the Korean peninsula. Following the precedent of the Camp David accords the previous September between the leaders of Egypt and Israel, Carter proposed to invite Park and North Korean president Kim Il Sung to meet him in the demilitarized zone during his forthcoming trip, to establish a path toward peace. The Asia experts among the aides were horrified because they believed Park and Kim would not agree to meet, and that the proposal would be seen as a "flaky" stunt. The plan also met massive resistance from the U.S. ambassador in Seoul, William Gleysteen. A career Foreign Service expert on Asia who had grown up in China, the son of missionary parents, Gleysteen "just fell out of my chair" when informed of it. The experts persuaded Brzezinski and, through him, Carter to abandon the scheme. The idea was quietly dropped, without the South Korean leadership or anyone else getting wind of it.

As this incident suggests, Carter had been turning over in his mind the possibility that U.S. diplomacy could encourage a North-South settlement that would make the long-term presence of the American troops unnecessary. The four-power talks involving China as well as the United States and the two Koreas that Vance had suggested early in the adminstration had gone nowhere. However, the establishment of full U.S. diplomatic relations with China on January 1, 1979—a major accomplishment of the Carter administration—revived the possibility that Beijing might help to defuse the conflict on the divided peninsula. At the end of January, when Chinese leader Deng Xiaoping visited Washington, Carter asked him to help arrange North-South talks. Deng responded that the North was ready to talk to Americans, the Park government, and others in the South on the terms that it had previously proposed (which were unacceptable in Seoul and Washington). Deng said China would not pressure North Korea, lest it lose its influence there, but he assured Carter there was absolutely no danger of a North Korean attack.

Rebuffed in his June 1979 plan for a grand three-way summit meeting in the DMZ, Carter settled for proposing three-way talks of lesser diplomats. The South Koreans, however, had strongly resisted such an idea for many months, fearing a sellout by the United States in the pattern of Vietnam diplomacy. Ambassador Gleysteen, directed by Washington to obtain agreement in Seoul, found that the entire South Korean government was adamantly opposed to three-way talks except for Park himself, who was persuaded to consider it in the context of ending the U.S. withdrawal program. In the end, Park ordered his government to accept the proposal, possibly believing that he would win points with Carter and that Pyongyang would reject it anyway. The proposal, which was announced during Carter's trip to Seoul, appeared to be stillborn when North Korea lodged the expected objections. But as Korean diplomacy developed later on, the idea of three-way talks came back to life in a variety of circumstances.

On the evening of June 29, Carter arrived in Seoul aboard Air Force One from the G-7 summit meeting in Tokyo and immediately helicoptered to Camp Casey, the headquarters of the Second Infantry Division, to spend the night. After jogging with and addressing the troops, he traveled back to Seoul for a rousing official welcome by an estimated 500,000 people and bands playing such Carter favorites as "Onward, Christian Soldiers," lining the motorcade route to the Blue House.

Inside the presidential palace, Carter and six aides settled down across a long table for the talks with Park and his delegation. The South Korean president had been asked in advance by American officials to say little or nothing about the withdrawal issue so as not to upset the delicate minuet they had devised for Carter, but Park had his own ideas. The former schoolteacher had written out in his neat hand a lengthy presentation of the strategic and peninsular reasons why withdrawing American troops would be a cataclysmic mistake in view of the North's growing strength, and he boldly delivered it to the increasingly furious American president.

Nicholas Platt, the National Security Council expert on Asia, could see Carter silently working his jaw muscles, as he tended to do under great tension, and on the other side of the table he observed Park snapping his fingers to make his points, as he did unconsciously under extraordinary stress. Vance could feel the temperature in the room drop with Carter's cold fury. As Park continued his forty-five-minute oration, the president passed a note to Vance and Defense Secretary Brown: "If he goes on like this much longer I'm going to pull every troop out of the country." Instead of responding at once, Carter adjourned with Park to the next room for a private talk where he brought up human rights issues and demanded to know why the ROK, with a far bigger economy, did not match the North militarily. It was, as Assistant Secretary of State Holbrooke later observed, "as terrible a bilateral meeting between treaty allies as you can have."

When the meeting was over, Carter, Vance, Brown, and Brzezinski climbed into the presidential limousine for the short ride to the U.S. ambassador's residence. Gleysteen, summoned by Carter to join them, sat on a jump seat facing the president. Berating Park, Carter threatened to continue the withdrawal despite all opposition and accused his aides of conspiring against him. Gleysteen, who barely knew the president and had never had a serious discussion with him before, took the brunt of Carter's anger, responding in strong terms about the vast diffi-culties of continuing the pullout and the benefits that might be gained by calling it off. After what seemed to Gleysteen an eternity, with the angry president wagging his finger in his face, Vance and Brown joined the argument on his side. Brzezinski remained silent. For more than ten minutes, the top policy makers of the Carter administration contin-ued their heated debate in the closed car, sitting under the front portico at the ambassador's residence, with a long motorcade of puzzled offi-cials stalled and stretched out behind them. In the second car, which could see but not hear the animated argument, Holbrooke turned to Platt and said, "I guess the meeting on Korea that we've been trying to arrange all this time is finally taking place."

When he cooled off, Carter agreed to return to the previously suggested scenario for reconsidering the withdrawal program, on two conditions: first, that Park order a further substantial increase in ROK military expenditures along the lines the two presidents had discussed in their contentious private meeting; and second, that Park make a significant move in the human rights field, such as release of a large number of jailed dissidents. That afternoon, Vance wrote later, "our Korean policy hung in the balance" while the U.S. team sought and won agreement to Carter's demands from Park's government. Ironi-cally in view of later events, the aide designated by Park to negotiate with the Americans on the prisoner release, which ultimately involved eighty-seven dissidents, was KCIA director Kim Jae Kyu.

By the time Carter left Seoul, his demands had been agreed to, a Korean band had serenaded the first family with "Sweet Georgia Brown," and the withdrawal minuet was back on track. In the limou-sine en route to the airport, Carter tried in a most unusual way to reach out to Park. The devout U.S. president asked his counterpart about his religious beliefs. When Park replied that he had none, Car-ter said, "I would like you to know about Christ." He proposed to send Chang Hwan (Billy) Kim, an American-educated Baptist evan-gelist who fashioned himself as the Korean Billy Graham "to explain our faith." The Korean president agreed to receive him and did so shortly thereafter.

On July 20, three weeks later, Brzezinski announced at the White House that further withdrawal of U.S. combat elements was being suspended until 1981, which would have been the start of Carter's second presidential term, to "await credible indications that a satisfactory military balance has been restored and a reduction in tension is under way." Carter had no second term. In 1981, having been defeated for reelection, he was on his way home.

In the two and a half years of the withdrawal program, only one combat battalion of 674 ground troops was actually withdrawn, while twelve more air force F-4 fighters and their crews, totaling 900 troops, had been sent to augment those already in Korea. Including various noncombat units and some that had previously been scheduled for reduction, Carter reduced the total U.S. military strength in Korea by only about 3,000 troops, leaving nearly 37,000 in place. While Carter did not achieve his fervent aim of eliminating all U.S. nuclear weapons from Korean soil, he did reduce their number from nearly 700 to around 250 and consolidated them all at a single site, Kunsan air base, rather than having them spread around several locations.

In his haste and lack of finesse, an inexperienced president had transformed a general impulse to reduce U.S. military forces in South Korea into a highly controversial policy with which he was personally, and negatively, identified. Many of the American diplomatic and military officials dealing with the issue were not opposed to substantial reductions if pursued in well-planned fashion, but they were horrified by the peremptory and damaging way the issue was pursued by the Carter White House. By refusing to heed or even hear the objections until he finally was backed into a corner, Carter undermined his own position.

Even a determined president proved unable to decouple the United States from the high-stakes military standoff on the Korean peninsula. The major impact of Carter's unsuccessful effort was to intensify the concern among his Asian allies that had been generated by the American withdrawal from Vietnam. In Seoul, Carter's conflict with Park inadvertently diminished the standing of the South Korean president. The consequences were soon to come.

# 5

## ASSASSINATION AND AFTERMATH

On the evening of October 26, 1979, President Park Chung Hee dined with KCIA director Kim Jae Kyu, with whom he was increasingly at odds, in a KCIA safe house, or clandestine operations building, on the grounds of the Blue House. The president was accompanied by the powerful chief of presidential security, Cha Chi Chol, and the chief of the Blue House secretariat, Kim Kye Won. Like the president, all three of the other men were former military officers. Sitting on the floor on either side of Park at a traditional Korean low dining table and pouring liberally from a bottle of Chivas Regal were two young women, a model and a well-known singer.

As the dinner proceeded, Park criticized KCIA director Kim for failing to keep abreast of the massive domestic disorders that had erupted over political and economic issues. Security Chief Cha, who was advocating a harsher crackdown on students and strikers, also berated the KCIA director for contributing to the unrest by espousing policies that were too conciliatory. After a few minutes of abuse, the intelligence chief left the dining room and went to his office on the second floor of the building, where he picked up his .38 Smith & Wesson pistol and hid it in his pocket. He instructed his own guards to shoot the presidential bodyguards, who were waiting outside the dining room, if shots were fired inside.

After checking to make sure his aides were ready, Kim pulled out his pistol and demanded of Park, "How can you have such a miserable worm as your adviser?" Then he opened fire at point-blank range, first at Cha, then at Park, severely wounding them both. When his gun jammed, he borrowed another .38 pistol from a KCIA guard and finished the two men off. KCIA aides took the shooting as their signal to attack and kill five presidential bodyguards. Within minutes, the turbulent and historic eighteen-year reign of Park Chung Hee ended in a blaze of gunfire.

The assassination of Park opened a new era of transition and uncertainty, during which the United States sought unsuccessfully to nudge South Korean leaders toward a more democratic and participatory system to replace the authoritarianism of the past. U.S. influence had some small successes, but as American officials had learned in previous crises, their power to affect Korean politics was limited when the stakes were high for the domestic actors involved. At the end of the 1970s, the United States was still at the center of South Korea's external world, but the balance of power between the two countries had shifted dramatically.

South Korea was no longer an economic-aid client of the United States but had emerged as a rising middle power with a large and complex economy. The United States was still expected to deter the North by providing troops that would guarantee automatic U.S. involvement in case of war, but nearly all the Americans had been pulled back to reserve positions, leaving South Korean troops to defend most of the DMZ front line. Reflecting these changes, Ambassador Gleysteen reported to Washington in one of his first dispatches after the killing, "We should keep in mind that the Korea of 1979 is not the Korea of the early '60s when we were able to bully the early Park regime into constitutional reforms." Instead, the U.S. Embassy and the government in Washington limited themselves to subtler pressures, such as public statements and denial of symbolic meetings, in an attempt to affect the Korean future.

One of the first things Korean authorities did on the night of October 26 was to notify Ambassador Gleysteen that the Park regime had ended. General Lew Byong Hyon, the senior Korean officer in the recently established Combined Forces Command involving

American and South Korean officers, came to Gleysteen's residence around midnight and reported that "there's been an accident" involving Park. Lew didn't know how much to say and, at that point, did not know all the facts himself. Gleysteen went to the embassy to use his secure line to telephone National Security Adviser Brzezinski in Washington (where it was early afternoon) and to alert the State Department.

About two hours later, when it was clear that Park was dead and that Prime Minister Choi Kyu Ha would take over, at least temporarily, as mandated by Park's 1972 constitution, Jimmy Carter's National Security Council convened at the White House. The president had left for a previously planned weekend at Camp David.

As always in moments of crisis on the peninsula, Washington's first and foremost concern was for the security of South Korea and the U.S. troops stationed there to defend it. As was the case after the DMZ ax murders, American forces and South Korean forces under U.S. operational control were placed on a higher degree of alert, and an aircraft-carrier task force was ordered to Korean waters as a show of force intended to impress and deter the North. Two Airborne Warning and Surveillance (AWACS) radar planes were placed on station to monitor North Korean military movements. The State Department quickly announced that the United States would "react strongly in accordance with its treaty obligations to the Republic of Korea to any external attempt to exploit the situation in the Republic of Korea." Washington privately passed the same message, intended for North Korea, to China and the Soviet Union. Unannounced, the United States also stepped up spy plane surveillance of North Korea and closely monitored electronic intercepts. For the moment, Pyongyang remained quiet.

◆    ◆    ◆

In the months preceding the assassination, Park's regime had been under great strain. After a long period of rapid growth, South Korea had been afflicted by the worldwide inflation and recession, that arose from the redoubling of oil prices after the Iranian revolution early in 1979. An unprecedented wave of bankruptcies and strikes had swept the country. The large-scale release of dissidents under the unannounced agreement with Carter during his visit in early July had emboldened Park's critics, especially opposition New Democratic Party leader Kim Young Sam, who began denouncing the government in scathing terms.

On August 11, the government outraged Kim Young Sam and exacerbated its problems when steel-helmeted riot policemen invaded NDP headquarters and dragged out 190 female employees of the bankrupt Y. H. Industrial Company, who had staged a sit-in to enlist public sympathy. A month later, as part of a continuing political struggle, Kim publicly appealed to the United States in a *New York Times* interview to end its support of Park's "minority dictatorial regime." In response, on Park's instructions, Kim was expelled from the Korean National Assembly, precipitating the mass resignation of opposition party deputies and plunging the country into a political crisis.

In mid-October antigovernment demonstrations in Kim's home area of Pusan spread from campuses to the rest of the city, prompting the imposition of martial law in Pusan for the first time since Park's muscular imposition of his unchallenged rule in 1972. The Pusan protests, the U.S. Embassy reported to Washington, "probably resulted from a combination of political and economic frustrations including considerable weariness with the Park government and widespread objection to the government's recent heavy-handedness." Massive protests also erupted in the nearby industrial city of Masan.

As a show of American disapproval of Kim Young Sam's ouster from the National Assembly, Ambassador Gleysteen was briefly but publicly recalled to Washington. But on October 18, Gleysteen was back in Korea to accompany Secretary of Defense Brown, who was in Seoul for the annual high-level military consultations, to an intimate meeting with Park. There they presented a personal letter from Carter expressing concern about the political developments. Brown warned Park that Washington's security ties with Seoul could be affected if he did not return to a more liberal path. In this period, Gleysteen reported to Washington, "I was struck by the pervasiveness within the establishment of worry about where the government's hardline policies were leading Korea. People in almost all sectors and all levels told us of their anxiety and were becoming increasingly bold in identifying President Park as the man making the wrong decisions, listening to advisors who were telling him what they thought he wanted to hear." Gleysteen sensed that Park was losing his way, seeming to be uncertain about the wisdom of his own decisions.

In the last years of his life, especially after the assassin's bullets in 1974 that narrowly missed him and killed his wife, Park was the subject of extraordinary security measures imposed to protect him from outside threats. A half mile from the presidential mansion, windows in hotels had been taped or shaded to obstruct outsiders from getting a view of the Blue House. When Park appeared in public, guests were required to be in their places an hour before he appeared. Becasue of these draconian measures, Park was increasingly cut off from normal human contacts. But as it turned out, not even these measures could provide absolute security for a chief executive who had outlived his welcome.

By the time of his death, Park's regime was held together by fear and force—and undergirded by the remarkable economic growth he had fostered. But with his popularity waning and the economy temporarily faltering, Park was in trouble even in his own entourage. Seemingly immune to all external pressures to step aside, Park was removed by a privileged insider across the dinner table in his own presidential compound. When American officials, headed by Vance, flew into Seoul for Park's funeral, which was attended by huge crowds, they initially found surprisingly little sincere grief in the general public or among the officials who had served the late president. "His time had come," a senior ROK official told Assistant Secretary of State Holbrooke privately. "There wasn't a wet eye in Seoul," Holbrooke observed.

The motives of Kim Jae Kyu, Park's assassin, have never been fully established. Kim, a classmate of Park's in the second postwar ROK officers training course, had been considered a close friend of the president. His selection in 1976 to head the KCIA, the most sensitive instrument of Park's personal control, testifies to their intimate relationship. Like a number of other senior officers and officials, however, Kim felt increasingly alienated from Park's policies. At his trial, he told the court he had decided to kill Park years earlier in order to end the dictatorial *yushin* system, and he claimed that his objective was "a revolution for the restoration of democracy." On the basis of conversations with Kim, his lawyer, Kang Sin Ok, told me that Kim had decided a few weeks earlier to kill Park at his first opportunity.

On the other hand, there were signs that Kim's plot was hastily improvised. The first pistol he used had not been fired for a long time, and it misfired when he was killing Cha and Park. More telling, Kim had not devised a serious plan or set in motion an organization for taking over the government, although he had made arrangements before the dinner to meet Army Chief of Staff Chung Seung Hwa, a close friend, who was dining nearby in another Blue House facility. There had been rumors beforehand that Kim would soon be ousted from his job by the dissatisfied president, giving rise to the theory that he had acted in part from fear of dismissal or worse. Along with many other officials, Kim had clashed bitterly with chief bodyguard Cha in the past, adding a personal factor to their policy dispute.

Given Washington's well-known unhappiness with Park's policies, there was immediate speculation among conspiracy-minded Koreans and some Americans that the United States had had a hand in the assassination, especially when the news of Park's death was reported by American news agencies from Washington, following the afternoon White House meeting, before it was officially announced in Seoul, where it was still in the middle of the night. Nearly a month after the assassination, Gleysteen reported in a cable to Washington that suspicion of U.S. complicity persisted in Korea, but that "I have checked with Dick Sneider [his predecessor] and can state flatly that neither of us ever signalled to Kim Jae Kyu or any other Korean that we thought the Park government's days were numbered or that we would condone Park's removal from office." In the immediate aftermath of the assassination, James V. Young, assistant military attaché at the U.S. Embassy, reviewed the previous intelligence reporting and cable messages in embassy files and found nothing that indicated any physical danger to Park.

A more difficult question is whether the American clashes with Park over the withdrawal of American troops, the Koreagate scandal, and human rights abuses had weakened the Korean president in a way that contributed to his demise. Kim Kyung Won, who was special assistant to Park for international affairs, pointed out that the

KCIA had full access to the barrage of negative information about Park in the U.S. administration, Congress, the press, and elsewhere. "It is not implausible to me that [KCIA Director Kim] may have convinced himself that if he got rid of this Park Chung Hee, then his action would be welcome," the former aide said. Gleysteen, while convinced that the KCIA director's violent act resulted from madness of some kind, also believes that American behavior inadvertently fed it. Kim Jae Kyu, who had been the interlocuter with Americans on human rights issues during the Carter visit and at other times, "misread us," said Gleysteen. "He thought we saw him as kind of a guy in a white hat. In a way we did, but we saw him as the KCIA director, a white hat on a black head. And I think that contributed to his crazy decision."

Immediately after the killings, Kim Jae Kyu met Army Chief of Staff Chung and tried to persuade him to join him at KCIA headquarters and declare martial law, although the assassin did not disclose that he had killed the president. Instead Chung convened a meeting at Korean military headquarters, in which Kim participated—again without disclosing his role in the president's death. The truth came out when the other surviving principal from the fatal dinner, the chief of the Blue House secretariat, Kim Kye Won, finally turned up several hours later. At that point, the KCIA-chief-turned-assassin was arrested. He was later found guilty of murder and executed, along with his aides who had killed the president's bodyguards.

An emergency cabinet meeting named Prime Minister Choi Kyu Ha, a soft-spoken former diplomat, acting president as specified in Park's *yushin* law constitution. With American concurrence, martial law was declared over most of the country, and Army Chief of Staff Chung was named martial-law commander.

In Pyongyang, two days after Park's assassination, Kim Il Sung addressed a military meeting, drawing a stark contrast between South Korea, "one half of our territory . . . under the occupation of the U.S. imperialists and reactionaries, landlords and capitalists," and the DPRK, where "our people are enjoying a happy life to the full, without any worries about food, clothing, medical treatment and education." Kim announced, "There is no better 'paradise' and no better 'land of perfect bliss' than our country. Our country is truly a socialist paradise." While approving the elimination of "traitor" Park Chung Hee, the North Korean leader cautiously told the military assembly, "We must wait and see what change this will bring about in the revolutionary situation in South Korea." Other than this, North Korea said and did very little except to heighten the readiness posture of its armed forces, probably in response to similar actions south of the DMZ. The U.S. Command in Seoul and the Carter administration leadership in Washington, however, remained concerned about the possibility of North Korean efforts to take advantage of turbulence or turmoil in the South.

With the demise of Park and the nominal passage of power to a civilian authority, South Korea entered a delicate transitional period. Acting President Choi, taking U.S. advice, repealed Park's emergency decree forbidding criticism of the constitution and released the most prominent opposition leaders and dissidents from house arrest or prison. An outpouring of ideas and emotions came from an uncertain yet excited populace. Apparently becoming ambitious in his own right, Choi spurned U.S. advice that he announce he would serve as interim president for only a year—which American officials hoped would buttress his standing and encourage a peaceful transition.

Although both Washington and a Korean consensus favored changes in the constitution, the government and military leaders insisted that Park's discredited *yushin* charter remain in effect through the selection of Park's successor rather than open the process to the popular political contenders. Using its easily controlled procedures, Acting President Choi was elected to the presidency on December 6. Choi, who had no independent political backing, was not a forceful leader. It seemed likely that the military leadership was the real power. The question was, who would be the military leaders?

## THE COMING OF CHUN DOO HWAN

The answer came suddenly on the night of December 12, when a group of generals headed by Chun Doo Hwan shifted troops into key positions and used force to depose the existing military authorities. Moving without warning, they arrested the martial-law commander and army chief of staff, General Chung Seung Hwa, and commanders loyal to him and occupied army headquarters, the Defense Ministry, media outlets, and key bridges and road junctions. The takeover was so swift and decisive that firefights were rare and there were few casualties.

The justification for the mutinous action was suspicion that General Chung had had a hand in Park's assassination, which Chun Doo Hwan, as defense security commander, was charged with investigating. Another reason, more cogent to U.S. military officers, was that the established army leaders were making plans to rid themselves of the ambitious and troublesome Chun Doo Hwan by reassigning him to a distant command. Ignoring lawful procedures, Chun and his coconspirators took their dramatic actions before obtaining the approval of President Choi.

Ambassador Gleysteen and the senior U.S. commander in Korea, General John Wickham, spent a tense and surreal night in the fortified command bunker at Yongsan, the headquarters of the joint U.S.–ROK Combined Forces Command, headed by Wickham, which had been created a year earlier to provide continued American military leadership even if U.S. ground troops were being withdrawn. In theory, the underground bunker was the most important control center for military forces in South Korea. Like the sprawling central Seoul base where it is located, the bunker had been built by the Japanese army during its long occupation of Korea and was inherited by the U.S. Army after World War II. Nearly thirty-five years later, the Americans still commanded the base and the bunker, but on this night their influence did not go much further. The U.S. ambassador and senior commander were important onlookers as power was wrested from one Korean group by another almost before their eyes, with massive implications for the future of the country.

Gleysteen and Wickham, sitting at the worn wooden table in the VIP section of the bunker, received fragmentary reports of ROK troops moving in and around Seoul and of a shoot-out at the residence of General Chung. American and South Korean officers were unable to contact some major units, which did not answer telephones or radios, but Washington came through loud and clear on a secure telephone line from half a world away, demanding to know what was happening and offering advice. From time to time, the occupants of the bunker could hear shooting nearby. Out of growing concern for the security of the ambassador and the U.S. commander, a detail of American troops was summoned for guard duty around the underground facility.

Powerless to command a halt to the action, Gleysteen and Wickham drafted a statement in the name of the U.S. government warning "any forces within the ROK" that disruption of progress toward a broadly based government would have a "seriously adverse impact" on U.S.–ROK relations. The statement was conveyed to the Blue House and both factions of the Korean military and was broadcast by Voice of America and other official American media, but it had no effect. Most Koreans were not aware of it because all Korean news outlets had been seized by the insurgents. Ignoring calls from the U.S. commander, the CIA station chief, and others, the coup leaders refused direct contact with the Americans until they had established effective control.

In mid-evening, South Korean defense minister Ro Jae Hyun and the chairman of the Joint Chiefs of Staff, General Kim Chong Hwan, both looking pale and nervous, arrived at the bunker. Using U.S. communications, they sought to establish the loyalty of subordinate commanders, with mixed results. Wickham urged them not to order an attack on the insurgents at least until daybreak, fearing a nighttime battle with bloody and even more divisive results. Later Ro left for Defense Ministry headquarters nearby, where he was seized by plotters and compelled to assist in obtaining ex post facto authorization from President Choi for the arrest of the martial-law commander.

The nighttime takeover was in part a generational battle within the military. The deposed army chief of staff and many other occupants of top military posts were members of the eighth class of the Korean Military Academy; Chun Doo Hwan and his coconspirators were largely members of the younger eleventh class. To the shock and dismay of Wickham, who was charged with operational control of U.S. and ROK forces defending South Korea, part of a front-line division headed by Chun's classmate and close friend General Roh Tae Woo had left its positions near the DMZ without authorization, to take part in the intramilitary showdown in Seoul.

"We have been through a coup in all but name," Gleysteen reported to Washington when the morning dawned. "The flabby facade of civilian constitutional government remains but almost all signs point to a carefully planned takeover of the military power positions by a group of 'Young Turk' officers" headed by Major General Chun, the ambassador cabled Washington. As to his first "groggy conclusions," Gleysteen wrote,

> the December 12 incident is bad news from our point of view. The military of Korea who have remained remarkably united for 18 years under the firm, authoritarian hand of Park Chung Hee have now engaged in actions of insubordination which have not only generated animosities that may take years to work their way out but have also set a precedent for others to follow. In doing so, they totally ignored the Combined Forces Command's responsibilities, either ignoring the impact on the U.S. or coolly calculating that it would not make a difference. By their actions they have also run a serious risk vis-à-vis North Korea without giving it much thought.

The events of 12/12, as the night of the generals came to be called in Korean lore, cut short the reemergence of democratic and civilian rule, to which South Korea aspired after nearly two decades of domination by Park and his uniformed friends. Over the coming months, as the military once again took power, many Koreans felt that, once more, the government had been hijacked by a new and unknown ruling group using force of arms rather than the mandate of heaven or the consent of the governed. The showdown between opposing forces illuminated the real political landscape of South Korea as in a flash of lightning: U.S. control of the ROK military was purely nominal in a domestic struggle for power, civilian control over the military under President Choi was nonexistent, and a little-known figure named Chun was now the man to see in South Korea.

◆   ◆   ◆

Chun Doo Hwan was born on January 18, 1931, in a village near Taegu, a major city in southeastern Korea, the home region of Park Chung Hee and many other political leaders of modern Korea.

Chun's father, a Confucian scholar, was forced to flee with his family to Manchuria in 1939 because of a violent feud with a Japanese policeman. After returning to Korea, Chun's family was poor but proud. Chun graduated from Taegu Technical High School in 1951, in the midst of the Korean War, and joined the Korean Military Academy. He graduated in 1955 in the Academy's eleventh class—the first class to receive a full four-year military education and the first to have its curriculum based on an American rather than a Japanese model. Members of the eleventh KMA class, who maintained a special bond, formed the inner circle of the insurgent group that ousted their seniors in the 12/12 military showdown.

As a junior officer in 1959–60, Chun spent a year in American military schools at Fort Bragg, North Carolina, and Fort Benning, Georgia, which left him with a tenuous command of English and a sense of easy familiarity with the United States. Unlike Park Chung Hee, who was Japanese educated and never entirely comfortable with Americans, Chun felt he knew Americans and could deal with them without complexes. As a foreign military student, he bought a used car, obtained a U.S. driver's license, and often traveled on weekends. He was fond of telling aides—and he once recounted to me—his surprise, while driving through a small town well past midnight, to see the driver in a car ahead of him stop for a traffic light, even though no police or anybody else could be seen for miles. This impressed Chun with the law-abiding spirit of the American people, a trait he proclaimed was "essential for freedom and democracy."

After Park's military coup in 1961, Chun served for a year as a secretary for civil affairs to Park at the Supreme Council for National Reconstruction, the official name of the ruling junta. Turning down Park's suggestion that he embark on a political career, Chun opted to return to army duty. Nonetheless, his military duties were often entwined with politics. In 1964 he, Roh Tae Woo, and a handful of other Korean Military Academy graduates formed a secret club within the military that they named Hana-hoe, or "One Group," devoted to solidarity and patriotism and, as it turned out, self-advancement. Park gave the members of the club, which was headed by Chun, fast promotions and special perks. Hana-hoe members made up the core of the group that took power by force after Park's death.

As a battalion commander of the politically sensitive Capital Security Command in 1968, Chun led the chase against North Korean commandos who had attempted unsuccessfully to attack Park's Blue House. After a tour as regimental commander of ROK forces fighting in Vietnam, he became assistant director for operations of the presidential security force at the Blue House, where he had frequent personal contact with Park. In February 1979, eight months before Park's assassination, he became commanding general of the Defense Security Command, which Park also used for political control and as a check on his politically active bodyguard force and the KCIA. It was in this post that Chun became chief investigator of the assassination, paving the way for his clash with Army Chief of Staff Chung Seung Hwa.

On December 14, two days after his midnight takeover of the military, Chun engineered sweeping changes in the ROK army, moving the old guard aside and placing his classmates and close friends in sensitive posts. Roh became commanding general of the Capital Security Command; others of the Taegu Seven Stars, as the innermost group of insurgent generals were called, became commanders of the Special Warfare Command, the ROK Third Army, and other key units.

The same day, Chun held his first meeting with Gleysteen, coming at the ambassador's invitation to the U.S. Embassy. In response to Gleysteen's plea for a return to constitutional order, Chun insisted that he supported President Choi, that the events of December 12 were an accidental outgrowth of his investigation of Park's assassination, and that he harbored no personal ambition. The purge of the army, which had resulted in Chun's unchallenged control of the most important levers of power, was a glaring contradiction of this claim. While recognizing his intelligence and drive, Gleysteen came to distrust Chun and eventually consider him "almost the definition of unreliability . . . unscrupulous . . . ruthless . . . a liar." Gleysteen's successor as U.S. ambassador, Richard L. Walker, considered Chun "one of the shrewdest, most calculating, politically smart people I've known."

The events of December brought American officials face to face with the limited extent of their leverage on South Korean political developments. As in the 1961 military coup that brought Park to power, the military showdown of December 1979 was an accomplished fact before the United States was able to react. The U.S. Embassy had sought briefly but unsuccessfully to reverse the 1961 coup by announcing its continuing support of the elected government, but its effort was an embarrassing failure, a cautionary reminder to officials who came later. When a Korean academic urged Gleysteen through an American friend to "nullify what General Chun did and kick him out . . . teach Koreans a lesson that the United States does not support just anyone," the ambassador rejected the idea out of hand. "Cannot act as a colonial governor," Gleysteen responded.

American officials in both Seoul and Washington, realizing it would be fruitless, made no effort at any time to undo what Gleysteen privately called Chun's "power grab." Gleysteen explicitly told Chun's military colleagues that "we are not trying to reverse the events of December 12." Instead, the United States pressed Chun to refrain from interfering with the Korean political process or taking political power in his own right, both of which he soon did in contravention of their advice.

No one could deny that the United States had important stakes in the future of South Korea, but by 1979 it was unclear how far Washington could go in shaping that future. American diplomats relied mainly on attempts at persuasion, telling Chun and his colleagues that their takeover threatened national security and economic growth, in which the United States had major interests. In arguments that were often repeated, Gleysteen told Chun in their initial meeting that "the [December 12] actions had set a dangerous precedent within the ROK military, run great risks in light of the North Korean threat, and raised further questions internally about the ability of the Choi government to sustain progress toward orderly political liberalization, and externally about the prospects for stability." Gleysteen went on to stress that "the ROK had to maintain a civilian government and could not afford to lose the support of the U.S. military and businessmen who were deeply disturbed by what had happened."

Chun received these arguments politely but was not swayed by them. He and his fellow generals believed they knew more about the

North Korean threat than did the Americans, and they did not consider it an imminent danger. Indeed, in view of the recently proposed U.S. pullout, it was arguable how much danger the United States actually perceived from the North. As for the economic issues, the economy was still in trouble, exacerbated by uncertainty about the political future in Seoul; however, it was questionable whether U.S. business leaders seeking profits had clear-cut views on who should lead the country. The generals also sensed, correctly, that Washington, which was obsessed by the plight of American diplomats held hostage in Tehran since November 4, felt under great pressure not to push so hard in Seoul that they created "another Iran."

In an effort to press Chun and deny him full legitimacy, Gleysteen and Wickham, with Washington's approval, avoided meeting with him on a regular basis and sought to do as much business as possible through the official channels of the Choi government. The U.S. Embassy and the State Department pressed Choi to take bolder steps to assert his authority, but without much success. He was increasingly a figurehead. Nonetheless, Carter sent a personal letter to Choi in early January saying he was "deeply distressed" by the events of December 12 and that any similar actions "would have serious consequences for our close cooperation." In an unusual gesture, the embassy distributed the letter widely throughout the ROK government and military establishment.

In a message to Washington at the end of January, Gleysteen summed up the dilemma he felt in accepting "an unprecedentally activist role" in Korean domestic affairs. "If we don't do enough, dangerous events could occur; if we try to do too much, we may provoke strong, chauvinist reactions." This is particularly difficult, he observed, because "most Koreans sense a reduction in the real power of the U.S. and are increasingly concerned over what they perceive as our unwillingness to face up to the Soviet challenge, and they are also somewhat skeptical of our ability to handle Beijing." Apparently referring to the Iran hostage crisis, Gleysteen added that Koreans "suspect that we may be too preoccupied elsewhere to respond resolutely to difficulties on the peninsula."

Nevertheless, he concluded, "All significant political elements seek the image of U.S. support and many seek rather crude U.S.

intervention to shore up their weaknesses; ultimately we will therefore be criticized for undue interference in domestic affairs by those
who see our support for them as less helpful than desired. Few of
them realize that our influence is limited in large part by the fact that
we could not pull our powerful security and economic levers without
risk of destroying the ROK's stability.''

## THE KWANGJU UPRISING

In early 1980, with the economy sagging and the country still under
partial martial law, the South Korean government modestly began to
relax the repression. Opposition politicians began to speak up, and
student demonstrations, which are traditional in the spring, began on
an increasingly large scale to demand that martial law be lifted and an
early date be established for a presidential election. Well-known political figures began maneuvering publicly with an election in mind.
Chun, operating with the immense power of martial law, was at the
same time extending his personal network throughout the armed
forces from his post as chief of the Defense Security Command. In
mid-April he had Choi name him acting KCIA director, an act that
provided him immense new authority and that convinced the U.S.
Embassy that he was bent on taking over the presidency. In a gesture
of disapproval of Chun's move, Washington "indefinitely postponed" the annual Security Consultative Meeting between the top
defense officials of the two countries and informed ROK officers of its
reasons for doing so.

As the number of student demonstrators demanding elections
grew to the tens of thousands and spilled off the campuses into the
streets, both the civilian and military sides of the South Korean government raised with American officials the possibility of using military forces to back up the hard-pressed police. On May 8, Gleysteen
reported that he would try to defuse "this uncomfortable situation"
the following day in separate meetings with Chun and with Choi
Kwang Soo, the civilian chief of staff at the Blue House. After describing Korean attitudes on several sides, Gleysteen told Washington, "In none of our discussions will we in any way suggest that the
USG [U.S. government] opposes ROKG [ROK government] contin-

gency plans to maintain law and order, if absolutely necessary by reinforcing the police with the army. If I were to suggest any complaint on this score, I believe we would lose all our friends within the civilian and military leadership." The State Department responded, "We agree that we should not oppose ROK contingency plans to maintain law and order, but you should remind Chun and Choi of the danger of escalation if law enforcement responsibilities are not carried out with care and restraint."

In conversation with Gleysteen, Chun blamed the unrest on "a small number" of student radicals, professors, and ambitious politicians. He described the situation as not critical and said military force would be used only as a last resort. Wickham, meeting with the ROK defense minister and chairman of the Joint Chiefs of Staff the same day, emphasized the dangers of escalation if troops were used against civilians. The exchanges left Gleysteen with the impression that the student demonstrations might be handled with moderation, although they were reaching massive proportions and becoming larger by the day.

On May 13, however, Chun suddenly played the North Korean card, telling Wickham that Pyongyang was the "hidden hand" behind the students and that the decisive moment for a North Korean attack on the South might have arrived. Wickham reported to Washington that Chun's stress on danger from the North appeared to be a pretext for a move into the Blue House. American scrutiny of its intelligence turned up no sign of preparations for attack, and the State Department, concerned about rumors in Seoul, made a public statement to that effect. Years later a Korean military intelligence officer said he had been ordered by officials close to Chun to fabricate the supposed threat.

On the night of May 17 and the early morning hours of May 18, military authorities began widespread arrests of student leaders and senior political figures, including the three most likely candidates for president, the "three Kims"—opposition leaders Kim Dae Jung and Kim Young Sam and former prime minister Kim Jong Pil. All political activity was banned under a declaration of full martial law, as opposed to the partial martial law that had previously been in effect. The National Assembly was closed at bayonet point, and heavy censorship was reimposed on the Korean press. The army seized control, occupied many campuses, and closed all universities.

Gleysteen reported to Washington that the actions meant that "the military [have] all but formally taken over the country." In a "flash" cable, reserved for communications of the highest urgency, he declared that "the military leaders have shown disregard for constituted authority in the ROK—and for us. We have been presented with a *fait accompli* suggesting that the military leaders either do not know or care about the consequences of treating us in this manner." The ambassador, presenting sharp protests to President Choi and to the army chief of staff, said the United States found the actions "shocking and astounding." The CIA station chief in Seoul, Bob Brewster, made a similar protest to Chun. The State Department issued an unusually strong statement about an American ally, saying the United States was "deeply disturbed" and concerned that the use of military force will "exacerbate problems" in Korea.

One of the most serious issues was the fate of late President Park's old rival and nemesis, Kim Dae Jung. Because of his spectacular kidnapping from Tokyo by KCIA agents in 1973 and his subsequent persecution by the Park government, the opposition figure and former presidential candidate was better known abroad than any other living South Korean. At home he inspired passionate loyalty, especially among the regional constituents in his native Cholla provinces, but also fierce antipathy among conservatives, especially in the military. His release from house arrest and reemergence to prominence after Park's assassination was considered particularly threatening by those who had been close to Park.

As the country moved toward elections, it seemed distinctly possible, perhaps likely, that Kim could win a free and fair presidential balloting in the light of his popularity, the widespread respect for what he had suffered at the hands of Park, and the strong popular reaction against military rule. As early as mid-March, Gleysteen had observed the inherent contradiction in the emergence of Chun and the reemergence of Kim, and he reported to Washington that this ultimately would have to be resolved, "yet no one knows exactly how and when this will occur."

A large number of soldiers had invaded Kim's house as martial law was declared, and they searched it thoroughly as they took the political leader away. Soldiers also arrested at least nine of his secretaries, bodyguards, and close political associates. Just a few hours earlier, as rumors circulated that Kim would be arrested on charges of inciting student demonstrations, Gleysteen had warned the Blue House chief of staff, Choi Kwang Soo, that arrests of any politicians amid the growing tension was "ill advised" and that the arrest of Kim Dae Jung could be "incendiary."

The ambassador's prediction proved to be accurate. While troops quickly imposed a sullen order on Seoul, the declaration of martial law and especially the arrest of Kim touched off passionate protests in Kwangju, the capital of Kim's home region of southwestern Korea. After relatively routine early clashes between students and combat police early that Sunday, aggressive black-beret special forces troops arrived to quell the demonstrations. Tim Warnberg, a Peace Corps volunteer, recounted what he saw next:

> The soldiers charged and began swinging their clubs. We ran along with the panicked crowd and I ended up in a small store along with about 15 other people, including one other PCV [Peace Corps Volunteer]. A soldier came into the store and proceeded to club everyone over the head with his truncheon until he came to the other volunteer and me. He stopped, startled, hesitated a moment, and then ran out. We went out into the side street and found that the troops had retreated to the main street, leaving behind wounded people everywhere. Most of the injured had suffered serious blows to the head, arms or legs. . . . One young boy, bleeding from a gash on his forehead, told us he had been playing billiards when the paratroopers burst in and beat each person sharply on the head and then withdrew. The others had similar stories—though some were actively demonstrating, many were simply attending to their business when the troops indiscriminately began to beat them.

Martha Huntley, a missionary who had lived in Kwangju for nearly fifteen years, reported that

> one man we knew, a businessman about thirty, was pulled off the bus he was riding (along with other youngish-looking

people), and was kicked about the head so bad he lost an eye. Another young mother about the same age, thirty or early thirties, was taking her two children to Sunday school, was beaten and left unconscious on the sidewalk—she had to have stitches in her scalp and was incoherent for four months—her husband joined the students Sunday afternoon when they fought with the soldiers. No one knew what was happening or why.

Early on May 21, after three days of indiscriminate attacks by special forces and increasingly large, passionate, and violent opposition from Kwangju residents, townspeople commandeered military vehicles and raided weapons dumps to seize pistols, rifles, and thousands of rounds of ammunition. After a pitched battle with the special forces, a group of students set up a machine gun on the roof of a local hospital. When it became clear that the brutal tactics of the troops were not succeeding, they were withdrawn to the outskirts, where they proceeded to seal off the city.

The following day, more than 30,000 Kwangju people gathered in front of the provincial administration building, now taken over by protesters, to cheer demands that the troops stay out of town and that the government release all those in detention and pay compensation for the dead and wounded. Based on information supplied by the government, Gleysteen, in a cable to Washington, called the Kwangju events "a massive insurrection" that is "out of control and poses an alarming situation for the ROK military." He said much the same in a briefing for American news correspondents.

As the standoff continued, the lull in the crisis provided the opportunity for a negotiated settlement, which Washington strongly favored. On May 22 the State Department and the U.S. Embassy issued a statement calling for maximum restraint on both sides and a peaceful settlement, and also warning North Korea against attempting to exploit the situation. As a precaution, the U.S. military had moved AWACS surveillance planes to the area again and prepared to shift an aircraft-carrier task force. The South Korean news media, now under heavy censorship, did not report the statement. Seoul's military authorities agreed to air-drop leaflets containing the statement into Kwangju, but in fact they never did so. On the contrary, the government-controlled radio station heard in Kwangju reported that the United States had approved the dispatch of the hated special forces troops into Kwangju. Gleysteen protested and demanded a retraction. It was never given.

At the White House on May 22, a National Security Council meeting involving the top U.S. government officials except for Carter and Vice President Mondale considered the Korea crisis. According to the highly classified report on the meeting, "There was general agreement that the first priority is the restoration of order in Kwangju by the Korean authorities with the minimum use of force necessary without laying the seeds for wide disorders later. Once order is restored, it was agreed that we must press the Korean Government, and the military in particular, to allow a greater degree of political freedom to evolve." Regarding the immediate next steps, "We have counselled moderation, but have not ruled out the use of force, should the Koreans need to employ it to restore order," the meeting agreed. National Security Adviser Brzezinski summed up the American approach: "in the short term support, in the longer term pressure for political evolution."

The final military assault on Kwangju, using the ROK Twentieth Division and some special forces troops wearing regular army uniforms to disguise their identity, began at three A.M. on May 27. Compared with the early brutal and bloody encounters, the military action was relatively swift and effective. By the time the city was retaken, 170 people had been killed, by official government estimate, most of them in the first few days. The official death toll was raised to 240 in 1995 as a result of a reinvestigation, but Kwangju people claim that the real number of casualties was far higher than either official number. The outcome fueled a long-lasting and intense opposition to Chun, Roh, and the other generals and fervent anti-Americanism among citizens of the Cholla provinces and many Korean students.

Charges of American acquiescence or even approval of the Kwangju events reverberated in Korea. On May 16, before martial law was declared, the Korean military made the required notification to remove two elements of the ROK Twentieth Infantry Division from operational control of the Combined Forces Command, which directed the U.S.–ROK defense against North Korea. Before the Twentieth Division was sent to Kwangju to retake the city in the second week of conflict there, Wickham was asked to approve its redeployment to Kwangju, even though such an approval was not required once the division was out from U.S. operational control. After checking with Washington, Wickham and Gleysteen agreed it would be preferable to deploy the Twentieth Division rather than the hated special forces units, which had never been under U.S. command. These facts were used by Chun's propaganda organs to suggest U.S. sponsorship of the crackdown in Kwangju.

The "Kwangju massacre," as it was called, remained a central issue in Korean life for many years thereafter. It was the focus of much bitterness against Chun. The United States, which was also held responsible by many Koreans, for a long time spoke only sparingly and ineffectively about its role, evidently out of consideration for Chun. In 1985, after the U.S. Information Agency library was occupied by students protesting Kwangju, the Embassy recommended that it be permitted to make an extensive statement of the facts about American involvement, but this was rejected in Washington. It was not until June 1989, nine years after the fact and with Kwangju still a traumatic issue, that the United States responded to questions from a special committee of the ROK National Assembly by making public an extensive account of its involvement in the Kwangju events.

Charges of American complicity were given new currency in 1996 in reports by Tim Shorrock, a *Journal of Commerce* correspondent who obtained more than two thousand declassified U.S. documents on the events of 1979–80 under the Freedom of Information Act. Shorrock cited Gleysteen's statements of May 9 that the United States would not oppose contingency plans involving the use of the army to reinforce Korean police, as well as a U.S. military intelligence report transmitted to Washington on May 8 listing the whereabouts of seven special forces brigades and battalions. It included the information that "the 7th bdg [brigade] was probably targeted against Chonju and Kwangju universities." Gleysteen and Wickham told me they did not recall seeing this report, which in any case gave no hint of the wanton brutality that would be wielded by the special forces against the citizenry of Kwangju. At this writing, the 1980 events in Kwangju still remain a controversial and painful subject in South Korean–American relations.

In the immediate wake of the violent denouement, the United States adopted a "cool and aloof" public stand toward Chun and the other generals in order to signal disapproval and in hopes of affecting their future behavior. Washington indefinitely postponed a planned U.S. economic mission to Seoul and asked the Asian Development Bank to delay action on two pending loans to South Korea. In Seoul, Gleysteen met Chun twice in June, the month after the Kwangju uprising, and again in early July to advocate political liberalization and, on the last occasion, to emphasize the U.S. view that Chun had "abused" the U.S.–ROK security relationship. Nonetheless, U.S. intelligence reported, "Chun feels that he can more or less do as he pleases, irrespective of U.S. warnings." Donald Gregg, now an NSC official, commented that "We do have limited leverage, and Chun knows this." He thought Gleysteen's strong words might strengthen the U.S. hand. But Deputy National Security Advisor David Aaron argued that these arc "all empty words . . . the only way to get leverage on this guy is to start a dialogue with the North." That course was rejected.

It was in this chilly diplomatic climate, on a week-long visit in mid-July 1980, that I first met Chun and Roh Tae Woo. My meetings with them were arranged by Sohn Jang Nae, the KCIA minister in the ROK Embassy in Washington, a retired major general who had been Chun's and Roh's English teacher at the Korean Military Academy. To my surprise, I found two very different personalities: one decisive, strong, and ambitious; the other conciliatory, flexible, and much less openly ambitious.

Roh, whom I met at his Seoul Security Command headquarters, was so eager to explain himself that a conversation of several hours in length was continued at his request over lunch at his home the following day. I had never met a senior ROK general on active duty before—they had usually stayed away from American correspondents—and was impressed by Roh's openness, intelligence, and supple mind. I was also surprised, in view of what I had heard and read about Chun, that Roh said emphatically that he did not believe any military man was ready to become Korea's political leader. "We are not expert in economics or politics," he insisted, and should leave those issues to people who are. The crucial thing for the next leadership is a strong national consensus, Roh told me. "Our intention is very sound: defending the nation and not becoming involved in politics."

The conversation with Chun was very different. He saw me at the headquarters of the recently formed standing committee of the

Special Committee for National Security Measures, of which he was chairman and chief executive. Situated in a small building across from the historic Kyongbok Palace, the place where North Korean delegates had been welcomed to Seoul in 1972, the standing committee was a shadow government with far more clout than the official one in the nearby Blue House, as it demonstrated nearly every day with arrests, edicts, and press attention. Rather than wearing a uniform like Roh, Chun was dressed in a blue suit with a light blue shirt and sat in a wicker chair simpler than the others in the room, occasionally smoking a cigarette. He impressed me as a physically powerful man operating for the moment under great restraint. As a symbol of his unlimited ambition, there was a large globe in the office, which was unusual even for civilian officials of the South Korean government.

Chun began by saying, with a grin, that he felt like a schoolboy undergoing examination in being interviewed by me. If so, he had done his lessons well. He proceeded to answer my questions with an impressive directness and self-assurance that contrasted with my memory of interviewing Park Chung Hee and other Koreans of an earlier generation. Chun was coy only about his ambition for the presidency, and then only to preserve the formalities. Asked point-blank if he would seek the office, he said he was unable to foresee the future or answer with confidence but quickly added, "I've never run away from problems since the sudden death of the president." He had not planned or scheduled what had happened to him since October, he said, but attributed it largely to "divine providence," which had given him few choices about his course of action. He spoke of the importance of a strong presidency, given the external and internal challenges before the country. As a former political reporter, I had little doubt that he was preparing to move to the Blue House.

On August 7, Chun had himself promoted to four-star general in preparation for retiring from the army. The next day he received a political boost from an unexpected source: the U.S. military commander. General Wickham told Sam Jameson of *The Los Angeles Times* and Terry Anderson of the Associated Press in an interview that Chun might soon become president and that "lemming-like, the people are kind of lining up behind him in all walks of life." Speaking with astonishing frankness on background as a "highly placed U.S.

military official," but one whose identity became quickly known, Wickham said the United States would support Chun's move into the Blue House if he came to power legitimately, demonstrated a broad base of support over time, and did not jeopardize the security situation on the peninsula. Declaring that "national security and internal stability surely come before political liberalization," the U.S. general declared, "I'm not sure democracy the way we understand it is ready for Korea, or the Koreans ready for it." The State Department disavowed Wickham's remarks, but the disavowal had little effect.

Shortly thereafter Choi resigned the presidency, publicly claiming he was doing so to set a precedent for the peaceful transfer of power. Privately he told a military-led committee that he was resigning to take responsibility for the Kwangju events, which he called "a grave mistake" by the armed forces. On August 27, after receiving the endorsement of the ranking commanders of the armed forces, Chun Doo Hwan was elected president without opposition by the rubber-stamp National Conference for Unification. Carter sent him a private message that pointedly did not include congratulations but that urged early elections under a new constitution and "greater personal freedom" to enhance stability. Holding the new regime at arm's length, Washington banned cabinet-level visits to Seoul and postponed the annual U.S.–Korea security conference. Chun's main bid for popularity was his "purification" drive, in which close to ten thousand people were dismissed from government or arrested on corruption charges. The embassy learned to its dismay, however, that the new president and his aides were handing out cash to their followers on an even bigger scale than their predecessors had. "We had to deal with these guys. We had no choice," explained Gleysteen, who recommended the "cool and aloof" policy. "At the same time, we couldn't go along and get in bed with them."

## THE FIGHT TO SAVE KIM DAE JUNG

Chun's trump card with the United States was the nemesis of the ROK military, Kim Dae Jung. Formally accused of plotting the insurrection in Kwangju that was touched off by his arrest on May 18, Kim was put on trial by court-martial, found guilty, and sentenced to death on September 17. The U.S. Embassy had protested every step of the way, beginning with a strong démarche the day after Kim's arrest. Under heavy pressure from the embassy, the Martial Law Command permitted an American diplomat to attend the trial. When it was over, the State Department publicly described the charges against Kim as "far-fetched."

Several senior military figures insisted, in talks with me in 1980, that Kim, whom most of them had never met despite his national prominence, was or had been a communist working for North Korea. I had had numerous interviews with Kim over the years and never believed the accusations. While he was a man of immense ambition, he was also the political figure with more innovative ideas about his country's present and future than anyone else on the scene. Later in the decade, U.S. ambassador James Lilley, who had been a career CIA official, made a detailed study of Kim's record, including confidential reports and police files, and concluded that there was no evidence for the allegations of communist affiliation.

In a midsummer meeting presided over by Deputy Secretary of State Warren Christopher, the Carter administration decided to make a high-priority effort to free Kim and later to save his life. This decision, taken on humanitarian grounds, played into the hands of Chun, whose pride and political position were suffering from the undisguised U.S. disapproval of his regime. As the year wore on, the Chun government linked Kim's fate to normalization of the chilly relations between Washington and Seoul. In the final months of the Carter administration, the fate of Kim Dae Jung dominated American–South Korean relations, despite the wide variety of other issues at stake. It was also a major issue between South Korea and Japan, largely due to the residue of Japanese anger over Kim's abduction from Tokyo in 1973.

In mid-December, in an exception to its ban on cabinet-level visits to Seoul, the outgoing Carter administration sent Defense Secretary Brown to see Chun with an appeal for clemency toward Kim Dae Jung. According to Donald Gregg, who accompanied the defense secretary, Chun told him, "I am under terrific pressure from the military to execute him." Chun insisted that despite the intense feelings abroad, "I can't possibly succumb to foreign pressure."

After the American election on November 4, 1980, the defeated Carter team rapidly lost its clout with Chun, who eagerly awaited the new, more conservative Reagan administration. Reagan had made it clear from the start that he wanted no part of withdrawing U.S. troops, an initiative that was thoroughly associated with Carter and, by now, thoroughly discredited. However, his views on the Kim Dae Jung case were unknown. Carter administration officials were alarmed to learn of a pre-election remark to a Korean official in Washington by Alexander Haig, soon to become Reagan's first secretary of state, that the Seoul government should consider itself free to make any decision it chose about Kim Dae Jung and suggesting that the new administration would keep its hands off the case. The Carter team feared that the remark and the attitude it conveyed would be an open invitation to execute Kim.

Reagan's incoming national security adviser, Richard Allen, was more sympathetic and more concerned about the international repercussions of Kim's fate. At the end of November, Allen met General Lew Byong Hyon, chairman of the ROK Joint Chiefs of Staff, who had been sent from Seoul to discuss the case. The meeting was arranged by General John Vessey, the former U.S. commander in South Korea, who had returned to Washington as vice chief of staff of the U.S. Army. Without being explicit, Lew spoke of the serious insurrection that had been put down and said that "as long as the source of the trouble remains, we strongly feel that we should deal with it appropriately." Allen concluded Lew was telling him that Kim Dae Jung would be executed. Not knowing what to do or say, Allen made no comment but stalled for time.

There followed a series of confidential meetings between Allen and Korean officials on December 9, December 18, and January 2, orchestrated and led by Sohn Jang Nae, the KCIA minister in the ROK Embassy who had arranged my meeting with Chun the previous July. The key South Korean participant in the most important meeting was Lieutenant General Chung Ho Yong, commander of ROK special forces who had been so abusive in Kwangju and who was a member of Chun's inner circle. According to Korean notes of the meeting, Chung bluntly said that Kim Dae Jung was "the most dangerous person" to Korean national security and "must be executed in accordance with law." Allen responded that the execution of Kim would jeopardize the otherwise excellent chance for a major improvement in American–South Korean relations. In an interview in 1994, the former lieutenant general told me he personally opposed executing Kim and did not believe that Chun would carry it out but used the possibility as "a card" to obtain what he badly wanted—an early official visit to Reagan in the White House.

By the end of the third meeting, Allen, with encouragement from the outgoing administration, had arranged a deal to save the condemned dissident in return for a Chun visit to the White House and normalization of Chun's relationship with Washington. On January 21, 1981, the very day after Reagan's inauguration, the White House announced Chun's impending visit. Three days later, Chun announced the lifting of martial law and commutation of Kim's death sentence to life imprisonment.*

On February 2, less than two weeks after taking the oath of office, Reagan welcomed a broadly smiling Chun and his party at the diplomatic entrance of the White House with ruffles and flourishes and a trumpet fanfare. The controversial Korean was received at the White House before the leaders of such important American allies as Britain, France, or the other NATO countries, Japan, or even Canada or Mexico. In a cable from Seoul in preparation for the visit, Gleysteen reported that "to a considerable extent Chun will see the visit as made possible by his decision in the Kim Dae Jung case, but he will not wish to have it characterized as a crude tradeoff."

Tossing aside the restrained remarks drafted for him by the State Department, Reagan delivered a wholehearted embrace of the leader whom the Carter administration had held at arm's length. In his toast at a glittering East Room luncheon for more than fifty guests, Reagan reminisced about General Douglas MacArthur's handing back the battered city of Seoul to President Syngman Rhee after liberating the capital from North Korean occupation in 1950. With his accustomed oratorical skill, Reagan declared, "We share your commitment to

---

*In December 1982, Kim was released from confinement and permitted to fly to exile in the United States.

freedom. If there's one message that I have for the Korean people today, it is this: Our special bond of freedom and friendship is as strong today as it was in that meeting thirty years ago."

The Americans were under no misconception about what the reversal of the chilly Carter era relationship would do for Chun. A memorandum from Haig to Reagan in advance of the meeting pointed out that the first visit by a Korean president to the United States in twelve years would "symbolize the normalization of US–ROK relations after a period of prolonged strain" and "consolidate [Chun's] position within South Korea and legitimatize his new government in the eyes of the world." Haig pointed out in the secret assessment that while Chun "has preserved democratic forms, like his predecessor, his style is Confucian and authoritarian," backed by the army. Reagan was informed that "Chun expects us to be concerned with Korean internal developments and is prepared to consider our advice when it is offered privately and in the context of basic cooperation. His ability and willingness to accommodate foreign concerns over the Kim Dae Jung issue is a measure of how much he has matured."

In a complete reversal of what the incoming administration viewed as Carter's wimpish attitude toward Korea, Reagan publicly assured Chun that the new adminstration had no plans to withdraw American troops—in fact, Reagan eventually increased the forces to 43,000 Americans, the largest number on duty in Korea since 1972 and 3,000 more than when Carter had begun his withdrawal program. The two presidents announced they would immediately resume the previously postponed military and economic consultations. Although not publicly announced, Reagan formally informed Chun in their White House conversation that the United States was prepared to sell Korea F-16 warplanes, the most modern in the U.S. inventory, an arrangement that had been agreed to in principle during the Carter administration, but which Carter personally prevented from coming to fruition. On hearing the news from Reagan, Chun immediately accepted.

Reagan's warm White House reception was a major turning point for Chun, convincing most South Koreans that his takeover was a fait accompli. By his actions, Reagan built a store of obligation and goodwill with Chun that he drew upon later in connection with other issues. He also left a store of bitter antagonism and a sense of betrayal among Koreans who had previously admired the United States but who now held it responsible for Chun's December 12 military coup, the bloody suppression of opposition in Kwangju, and the high-profile endorsement of Chun's rule.

How much Reagan understood—or cared—about the political situation in Seoul is doubtful. At the November 20 meeting of the outgoing and incoming American presidents, their only meeting during the postelection transition period, Carter thanked Reagan for sending a message to Chun urging that Kim Dae Jung's life be spared. Up to that point in the extensive briefing, the newly elected U.S. president had had nothing to say. Carter discussed such issues as control of nuclear weapons in times of crisis and a long list of foreign policy issues, from the Soviet Union and the Middle East to China. However, when Carter touched on Korea and the Kim case, Reagan suddenly exclaimed, "Mr. President, I'd like to have the power that Korean presidents have to draft dissenters." The outgoing chief executive, who had championed human rights in quarrels with South Korean presidents, was startled by his successor's comment.

# 6

## TERROR AND TALK

Families and friends of the passengers of Korean Air Lines flight 007 waited with growing apprehension at Seoul's Kimpo airport on the morning of September 1, 1983. The flight, which originated in New York and refueled in Alaska, had mysteriously disappeared from the skies overnight en route to Seoul. Within a few hours, American intelligence agencies pieced together radio intercepts that told the grisly story of the discovery, tracking, pursuit, and destruction of the civilian airliner by Soviet air defense forces as it strayed over Soviet territory north of Japan. Playing back the tapes of transmissions recorded during the night, officials at an American–Japanese listening post heard the chilling report of a Russian fighter pilot to his headquarters: "The target is destroyed."

The first public revelation of the fate of KAL 007 came not from Seoul but from Washington, where Secretary of State George Shultz grimly announced that a Soviet fighter plane had shot down the airliner. Shultz called this "an appalling act" for which there was no excuse. President Reagan in subsequent statements called the action a "massacre," an "atrocity," and a "crime against humanity." The Soviet Union initially denied destroying the plane but later admitted it and justified the action on grounds that the airliner had violated its

139

"sacred" borders on an espionage mission concocted by the United States and its South Korean ally.*

The shooting down of KAL 007, whose passengers were predominantly Koreans and Americans, soon became a white-hot issue in international politics. It drove U.S.–Soviet relations to new depths of tension at a moment when relations were already extremely tense due to the imminent deployment of American missiles in Europe. For a time, it also slowed progress toward healing the breach between the Soviet Union and South Korea, which bitterly denounced the destruction of its airliner. Prior to the shootdown, the Soviet government, over the passionate objections of the North Koreans, had for the first time quietly decided to permit Soviet trading companies to deal with South Korean firms through third parties. In a bolder move, a delegation of Soviet parliamentarians had been preparing to travel to Seoul to participate in the International Parliamentary Union convention when KAL 007 was shot down. Due to the international furor, the trip was canceled. For the time being, the warming of Soviet–South Korean ties was put on a back burner.

A second severe shock to South Korea came little more than a month later, on October 9, 1983, during the state visit of President Chun Doo Hwan to Rangoon, Burma. At the ceremonial beginning of the visit, the best and the brightest of the South Korean government stood side-by-side in the Martyr's Mausoleum at the National Cemetery, awaiting the Chun's arrival for a wreath-laying in honor of Burma's founder. Some of the Korean officials were chatting, and a

---

*Due to the "spy plane" charges and the failure to locate the airplane's black box, or inflight data recorder, the circumstances of the tragedy would be controversial for nearly a decade. It was only in January 1993, a year after the Soviet Union had collapsed, that the long-hidden black box and recordings of air defense conversations were unveiled by the Russian government that had succeeded to power in the Kremlin. These records conclusively established that the airliner had strayed 360 miles off its scheduled course due to a series of innocent navigational errors and that a trigger-happy Soviet air defense commander had ordered the plane shot down by air-to-air missiles on the mistaken assumption it was on an espionage mission. The tapes also disclosed that the KAL cockpit crew members were unaware that they had strayed off course, oblivious to the danger they were in, and never knew what hit them when they and their passengers tumbled uncontrollably for twelve minutes to a watery grave.

few were standing with their hands by their sides, looking off in the distance. The Korean ambassador had arrived ahead of the president in his official car, with its ROK flag flapping in the breeze, and an anxious Burmese trumpeter was practicing his part in the ceremony to follow.

At that moment, North Korean army major Zin Mo, mistaking the ambassador's arrival and the bugler's call as the start of the wreath-laying ceremony, detonated a powerful bomb that he and two North Korean army captains had planted two days previously in the roof of the mausoleum. In the thunderous explosion, four members of the South Korean cabinet, two senior presidential advisers, and the ambassador to Burma were blown to bits by shrapnel and deadly steel pellets. Among those killed were Foreign Minister Lee Bum Suk, who as chief of the South Korean Red Cross delegation had welcomed and hosted the North Koreans in Seoul in September 1972; Presidential Secretary General Hahm Pyong Choon, former ROK ambassador to Washington and a leading foreign-policy intellectual; and Presidential Secretary Kim Jae Ik, an architect of South Korea's economic development. Due to his delayed arrival, Chun himself escaped injury.

Before the explosion, reclusive Burma and reclusive North Korea, each pursuing a distinctive brand of Asian socialism, had been the best of friends. High-level visits had been exchanged, and Burma had supported North Korean positions at the United Nations. This collegiality was put aside in Burma's fury and embarrassment over the deaths of seventeen visiting South Koreans and four Burmese at the nation's most revered ceremonial site. Burmese police quickly apprehended the North Korean military officers responsible for the deed. One of the North Koreans, Captain Kang Min Chul, made a full confession, which exposed the elaborate planning in Pyongyang that had gone into the attack.

Despite its earlier friendship and its neutralist stand, Burma broke diplomatic relations with North Korea and expelled all its diplomats. Japan, which had no diplomatic relations with North Korea, imposed restrictive sanctions on travel and official contacts. Pyongyang denied all complicity, as it has done in other instances of terrorism, but its denials were unconvincing in view of physical evidence linking it to the bombing, the confession of Captain Kang, and Burma's famous neutralism.

A year before the Rangoon bombing, in 1982, North Korea's clandestine foreign operations had been placed under the control of Kim Jong Il, the eldest son of Kim Il Sung, who had emerged as his father's anointed successor two years earlier, according to American terrorism expert Joseph Bermudez. In the fall of 1982, plans had been made to kill Chun in Gabon while the South Korean president was on a state visit to Africa. According to Koh Yong Hwan, a North Korean diplomat who took part in the plot but later defected to the South, the operation had been called off at the last minute on the personal instructions of the younger Kim. Koh, a sophisticated man who later became the Great Leader's French-language interpreter, said he believed the cancellation was ordered because the assassination of the South Korean president in an African country could have devastated North Korea's important African support in the UN General Assembly.

South Korea did not know of the Gabon plot at the time, but concerns about Chun's safety in his overseas travels probably saved his life in Rangoon in 1983. Asked to provide surveillance of Chun's plane by airborne radar (AWACS) aircraft during his trip, U.S. experts suggested that the route be moved farther away from the Vietnamese and Chinese coastlines, causing a change in the ROK president's planned schedule. Instead of arriving at four P.M. and going by motorcade directly to the ceremony at the Martyr's Mausoleum, where the North Korean agents doubtless would have been waiting, Chun arrived after 6 P.M., putting off the ceremonial visit to the following morning. Chun was still on his way from the ROK ambassador's residence, about a mile away from the mausoleum, when the powerful bomb went off.

The sudden deaths of South Korea's leading high officials caused a new outpouring of anger and grief in Seoul, and much of the same in official Washington, where the Rangoon victims were all well known. As a show of resolve and warning to North Korea, the aircraft carrier USS *Carl Vinson* and its battle group were kept in Korean waters beyond their scheduled departure date, and heightened security measures were taken along the DMZ. No unusual

North Korean troop movements were observed, but a few weeks later South Korean officials charged that Pyongyang had planned to launch commando raids after Chun's expected assassination. Kang Myung Do, a well-connected North Korean who defected in 1994, told me that a mass insurrection on the order of the 1980 Kwangju uprising had been anticipated if Chun had been killed. He said discharges from the North Korean army had been slowed or stopped in the months preceding the Rangoon bombing, apparently in preparation for what might occur.

A shaken Chun flew home with what was left of the elite governmental team he had taken to Rangoon. He traveled directly from the airport to a meeting of the surviving members of his cabinet and security team at the Blue House. At the meeting, Minister of Defense Yun Song Min proposed that the South Korean air force bomb the North in retaliation, but Chun rejected the proposal. U.S. intelligence learned that a senior South Korean commander at the DMZ was also advocating a punitive response. Chun said later he met with commanders who were eager to attack the North and declared that only he would decide whether to take military action—and that anyone who jumped the gun would be guilty of disloyalty. In a visit to Chun, Ambassador Richard Walker prepared to make a strong argument against retaliation, even though he said the United States had no doubt that North Korea was behind the attack. Chun responded, "I want to assure your president that I'm in full control of this government and military officers, who report to me. I have no intention of doing anything foolish or anything without full consultation with your government."

In fact, no retaliatory action was taken. When President Reagan visited Seoul the following month, he made a point of telling Chun in a private meeting that "we and the whole world admired your restraint in the face of the provocations in Rangoon and over Sakhalin Island [referring to the downing of KAL 007]." Reagan had come from Japan, where he had discussed the Rangoon bombing with Prime Minister Yasuhiro Nakasone, and told Chun he was pleased to learn that the Japanese were "doing whatever they can to punish the North Koreans." Secretary Shultz informed the ROK government that Washington would lead a worldwide campaign to censure and isolate North Korea in the aftermath of the bombing.

## THE NEGOTIATING TRACK

Oddly enough, as the Rangoon bombing plot developed, North Korea was simultaneously pursuing its most important diplomatic initiative toward the South in more than a decade. On October 8, 1983, the day before the bombing, Chinese diplomats passed a message to Washington from North Korea saying for the first time that it would take part in three-way talks with the United States and South Korea to bring peace to the peninsula, accepting Seoul as a full participant. For Pyongyang, this was a major departure from long-standing policies, and it established the basis for much of its diplomacy for the rest of the decade.

It was hardly surprising that Kim Il Sung decided to use the Beijing channel for his initiative toward the United States and South Korea. Since the initial breakthrough between the United States and China in 1971, Beijing had consistently played the role of diplomatic messenger between Washington and Pyongyang. Henry Kissinger had discussed Korea with Chinese premier Chou Enlai or other officials on at least eleven occasions during the Nixon and Ford administrations. In the mid-1970s, Kissinger sought secretly but unsuccessfully to use the Chinese contacts to persuade North Korea to accept the continued presence of American troops in the South "for at least the short term," in return for a commitment "to reduce and ultimately withdraw U.S. forces as the security situation on the peninsula is stabilized."

In the fall of 1983, Kim paved the way for his diplomatic bid with a speech in which he dropped his previously standard condition that the Chun regime be replaced before talks begin. In a conversation with U.S. secretary of defense Caspar Weinberger later that month, Chinese leader Deng Xioaping proposed that the United States and China work together to reduce tension and promote peaceful reunification on the Korean peninsula. Deng said that North Korea had "neither the intention nor the capability" to attack the South but that if the South attacked the North, "China will not be able to stay out."

American policy makers may have been mindful of this warning when they insisted that Chun not permit military retaliation for the Rangoon bombing.

In the aftermath of Rangoon, Deng was furious at Pyongyang for staging the bombing immediately after he had passed along Pyongyang's conciliatory diplomatic initiative to the Americans. For weeks afterward, Deng refused to see any North Koreans. The controlled Chinese media did not accept its ally's denials of complicity in the bombing, giving precisely equal treatment to the North Korean denials and the damning official reports from Rangoon.

The overlapping of Pyongyang's peace initiative and Pyongyang's act of bloody terrorism is a puzzle that has never been conclusively solved. Some American and South Korean experts believe the peace offensive was a diversionary tactic aimed at avoiding responsibility for the bombing, had its agents not been caught. Others believe it was undertaken by elements in North Korea that were unaware of the Rangoon plot. Still others suggest that the juxtaposition of such disparate events reflected internal discord in Pyongyang about the course of the struggle with the South and relations with the United States.

The available evidence does not support the diversionary tactic theory, because the North continued to pursue its diplomatic initiative with even greater intensity in the months and indeed years after Rangoon. The second theory seems unlikely: From what is known about the highly centralized decision-making apparatus in Pyongyang, it is hardly credible that Kim Il Sung and Kim Jong Il were unaware of either the talks initiative or the plan to assassinate Chun. The most likely explanation is that the diplomacy toward the South and a standing order to assassinate Chun were on separate tracks in Pyongyang, with initiatives in both areas going forward without much consideration of the impact of the one on the other. On several later occasions as well, North Korean diplomatic initiatives were closely trailed by public statements warning against concessions. This suggests that departures from the hard line were controversial in leadership circles in Pyongyang.

The idea of three-way peace talks involving the United States as well as the two Koreas had been discussed in Washington in the spring of 1978 by two maverick communists close to Kim Il Sung, Yugoslavia's president, Marshal Josip Broz Tito, and Romanian President Nicolae Ceauşescu, in separate conversations with President Carter. The idea had received a big boost in connection with Carter's 1979 trip to Seoul, when President Park Chung Hee agreed to back the proposal despite the misgivings of nearly everyone else in his government. The South Koreans feared a repetition of the Paris talks on Vietnam, where the South Vietnamese had been overshadowed by Hanoi and Washington and relegated to a devastating secondary role.

At the beginning of the Reagan administration in 1981, Secretary of State Alexander Haig had rejected the idea of three-way talks and instructed the State Department to oppose them. However, a number of American diplomats did not agree, and the American Embassy in Beijing continued to promote the plan in discussions with the Chinese. Moreover, a U.S. démarche to North Korea through Beijing in September 1983 mentioned trilateral talks among a list of items that could improve relations with the United States.

North Korea's three-way-talks proposal in October 1983 was given much less credence than it otherwise would have had because of the Rangoon bombing the next day. Nonetheless, the following month, Reagan, addressing the South Korean National Assembly on a trip to the Far East, personally endorsed three-way talks, declaring that "we would, as we've often stressed, be willing to participate in discussions with North Korea in any forum in which the Republic of Korea is equally represented." According to then–Assistant Secretary of State Paul Wolfowitz, the words were "boilerplate" and did not reflect actual administration thinking.

North Korea, however, took Reagan's words at face value, as was made clear in a speech by Politburo member and former foreign minister Ho Dam, who cited Reagan's remarks and proclaimed that Pyongyang's position had been taken "in full consideration of the long-maintained demand of the United States." North Korea continued to advance its proposal in December 1983, and in January 1984 it put it forth publicly in very high-level and high-profile fashion: During an official visit to Washington, Chinese Premier Zhao Ziyang brought it in writing to Reagan and Shultz at the White House. Hours after Zhao's presentation, North Korea broadcast the full text.

Once Pyongyang endorsed three-way talks, however, Washington rejected the very idea it had previously espoused. Reagan counterproposed, in discussions with Zhao, that peace talks on the peninsula should begin with North-South bilateral negotiations, and if that did not suffice, four-way talks that also involved China should begin. South Korea took the same position and also declared that Pyongyang must apologize for the Rangoon bombing before talks could begin. China seemed to be interested in participation in four-way talks, but the independent-minded North strongly opposed China's entry. The Soviet Union, not surprisingly, was cool to Chinese participation.

It is questionable how much sincerity was behind this maze of proposals and counterproposals in any of the capitals. Both the Reagan administration in Washington and Chun Doo Hwan's government in Seoul were leery of becoming involved in formal talks with Pyongyang. A window on Kim Il Sung's private thinking is provided by his conversation with Eric Honecker in May 1984. Kim confided that a major aim of his tripartite-talks proposal had been to make it more difficult for Reagan to increase U.S. troop strength in South Korea. Besides, he told Honecker, "with these talks [proposals] we want to expose the United States excuses" for staying in Korea. "To show the world that the United States does not want reunification, it is necessary to keep making new peace proposals. This is also necessary to encourage the South Korean population in their struggle."

## FLOODS AND FACE-TO-FACE TALKS

The leaderships and publics of both North and South Korea saw the struggle for influence and supremacy on the peninsula as a zero-sum game, in which any gain for the South was a loss for the North and vice versa. Moreover, for both regimes, considerations of "face" or prestige were often more important than issues of substance. Thus North-South discussions in the public arena tended to bear fruit only when both countries could credibly claim victory, which was uncommon. A parallel secret dialogue between Pyongyang and Seoul, only hints of which were made public when they occurred, was less constrained but often even more difficult, because the issues involved were more important.

In early September 1984, discussions between North and South were given sudden and unexpected momentum by an act of nature—torrential rains and landslides in the region near Seoul that killed 190 people and left 200,000 homeless. North Korea, in a gesture implying superiority, grandly offered to send relief supplies to its better-heeled cousins in the South. To everyone's surprise, Chun's government did not spurn the offer but prepared to receive rice, cement, textiles, and medical supplies. "Along a worn concrete road gone to weeds, hundreds of North Korean trucks entered South Korean territory today carrying the first supplies to pass between the two countries since the Korean war ended 31 years ago," wrote *The New York Times'* Clyde Haberman, who was on the scene at the DMZ. Some of the rice turned out to be wormy and the cement nearly unusable, but the South did not highlight the deficiencies or complain, even as Pyongyang hailed the flood relief in *Nodong Sinmun* headlines as a "Great Event, the First in the History of Nearly 40 Years of Division."

As the relief goods were delivered, the chairman of the North Korean Red Cross Society urged that success in this venture be used to launch "multisided collaboration and exchange." Capitalizing on the moment, the South proposed, and the North accepted, the opening of North-South economic talks and the resumption of the Red Cross talks.

With this surprising beginning, the North and South in a period of a little more than a year held thirteen public discussions, including five economic meetings, three Red Cross meetings, three working-level Red Cross contacts, and two preliminary contacts for a North-South parliamentary exchange proposed by Pyongyang. In September 1985, thirty-five South Koreans were permitted to cross the DMZ to visit family members in Pyongyang, and thirty North Koreans crossed in the other direction to meet family members in Seoul. After years of formal meetings, most of them sterile recitations of fixed positions, the emotional reunions of even a few divided families seemed at last to be a tangible payoff for the intra-Korean talks and a promise of better times to come.

Unknown to all but a few on each side, the progress was facilitated by secret talks at a high level, which had also resumed late in 1984 and reached a peak in the fall of 1985 as the family reunions were taking place. One of the lessons of the quarter-century of North-

South dialogue is that it rarely made progress unless the top leaders were involved. In the early 1970s and mid-1980s, most of the involvement of the heads of state was in secret; exchanges involving top leaders would emerge in the public arena only in the early 1990s.

The mid-1980s secret diplomacy began on the day after Christmas 1984, when a tall, urbane Korean who had lived in the United States for many years sat down to a four-hour meeting and luncheon with Kim Il Sung in Pyongyang. Channing Liem, who at 74 was two years older than the Great Leader, had been South Korean delegate to the United Nations under the short-lived reform government that was toppled by the 1961 military coup. After the coup he became a political science professor at the State University of New York at New Paltz and a vocal critic of the Park regime. Liem had previously visited Pyongyang in 1977 as a private citizen. This time, however, he came as an emissary of South Korean president Chun Doo Hwan, recruited for the task by Sohn Jang Nae, the activist intelligence chief in the ROK Embassy in Washington who had played a key role in negotiating Chun's triumphal visit to Reagan (and who had arranged my earlier meeting with Chun).

In his discussion with Liem, Kim Il Sung agreed to explore a North-South summit. The following week, Kim used his annual New Year's message to the Korean people to make an unusual endorsement of North-South dialogue, saying that success in the ongoing rounds of lower-level public talks could lead gradually to higher-level talks and "culminate in high-level political negotiations between North and South."

The meeting with Liem was unpublicized and known only to senior echelons in North and South. But the very next day, in one of those incidents that suggest pulling and hauling in influential circles in Pyongyang, *Nodong Sinmun,* the Workers Party newspaper, carried an oblique and, at the time, puzzling attack on accommodation with the South. "Sacrifice" and "struggle" are the keys to the victory of the revolution, said the paper, arguing that those who retreat from this road "in fear of being sacrificed" will inevitably "surrender" or become "turncoats."

In Seoul, the secret meeting with Kim whetted the appetite of those few who were aware of it. This was especially true of Chang Se Dong, another former general and chief presidential bodyguard who became director of the ROK intelligence apparatus in February 1985. With the confidential contacts with the North beginning to show promise, he took them under his direct control.

To aid him in this delicate work, Chang in March 1985 brought in a rising young star from the Blue House staff, the 42-year-old presidential secretary for political affairs, Park Chul Un. Park soon became the South's most energetic practitioner of secret diplomacy, not only in North Korea but in Hungary, the Soviet Union, and other countries as well, eventually earning acclaim in the Seoul newspapers as "the Korean Henry Kissinger." Park was bright, having graduated from Seoul National University Law School at the top of his class, and also well connected, being a cousin of the wife of General Roh Tae Woo, Chun's classmate, comrade, and eventual successor. Bold and ambitious—traits in short supply among South Korea's cautious senior bureaucrats—Park quickly made contact with senior figures in the North.

Within a short time, Park was authorized by Chun and later by Roh to be the South Korean secret channel to the North. His counterpart in Pyongyang was Han Se Hae, a 50-year-old graduate of Kim Il Sung University who had taken part in the Red Cross talks in 1972 under an assumed name and subsequently was vice minister of foreign affairs and DPRK ambassador at the United Nations. A fluent English speaker who was considered one of the North's most urbane and accomplished diplomats, Han became attached to the staff of the Central Committee of the Workers Party to pursue his contacts with the South.

Park and Han established a direct telephone connection between their desks in Seoul and Pyongyang, on which they had frequent conversations. The two met face-to-face a total of forty-two times between May 1985 and November 1991 in a wide variety of places, including Pyongyang, Seoul, Panmunjom, Paektu Mountain in North Korea, Cheju Island in South Korea, Singapore, and elsewhere. Some of the meetings lasted as long as five days, but except for a few sightings, most of this diplomacy remained secret.

Chun had repeatedly proposed a summit meeting with Kim Il Sung and recently had said he was willing to meet Kim anywhere in the North, South, or a third country, except for Panmunjom. To advance the summit diplomacy, a five-member North Korean delegation headed by former foreign minister Ho Dam and special envoy Han Se Hae secretly visited the South on September 4–6, 1985, and met Chun Doo Hwan at the private mansion of a Korean industrialist on the outskirts of Seoul. Chun had heard that Kim had seven presidential mansions in the North and wanted to show that luxurious accommodations outside the Blue House were available to him as well. The North Korean emissaries brought a letter from Kim Il Sung to Chun sending "warm regards" and saying "I sincerely hope to see you in Pyongyang." The letter from Kim to the man who had narrowly missed assassination by a North Korean bomb two years earlier ended, "Be well." In the secret talks, the former North Korean foreign minister insisted that the Rangoon killings "had nothing to do with us" and warned that if Pyongyang were required to apologize, it would mean the end of the talks.

The South Korean president spoke at length in the secret discussions about the military situation on the peninsula, including its nuclear dimensions. After taking power in 1980, Chun had decisively—some say, harshly—shut down the clandestine South Korean nuclear program, dispersing its scientists and engineers, in response to intense American concern about the project. However, he told Ho it would not be technically difficult for either the North or the South to produce nuclear weapons, should it decide to do so. The restraining factor, he declared, was the strong desire of both the Soviet Union and the United States to prevent nuclear wars involving small countries, which inevitably would spread to the great powers. Chun urged that Kim Il Sung, then 73 years old, turn away from conflict so that North-South issues could be resolved while he was still alive.

In a return visit the following month, Chang Se Dong, chief of the Agency for National Security Planning (NSP), the renamed South Korean intelligence agency; senior emissary Park Chul Un; and three others secretly visited the North Korean president. The southerners brought a letter from Chun calling for an early summit meeting "as a shortcut to peace where both of us meet face to face and open hearts to exchange conversation, build up trust and prevent a war." Kim appeared appreciative and friendly, but on the final day of talks, his aides presented their draft of a North-South nonaggression pact, which the southerners considered full of unacceptable rhetoric. The North also demanded, as it had the previous month, that the coming U.S.–ROK military exercise, Team Spirit '86, be called off. The South rejected both proposals.

After the October meeting, the prospects of an early summit meeting between Kim Il Sung and Chun Doo Hwan rapidly diminished. According to Sohn Jang Nae, who had returned to Seoul as a deputy director of South Korean intelligence, the summit negotiations failed because Chun lacked the strong will to proceed in the face of North Korean demands and bureaucratic rivalries in the South. "The talks bogged down in arguments over details," Sohn said in an interview for this book. An American intelligence official, who was given full access to the transcripts of the talks by Chun's government around the time that they took place, said that the two sides "got tied up in all sorts of linguistic tangles" such as what words to use to describe the level and nature of the proposed summit meeting. It seemed from the transcripts, the U.S. official said, that "the North was not very interested in making progress, and the South was also bringing up things that would irritate the North."

The final blow was the approach of the Team Spirit exercise, which under Chun had been built up to a powerful array of about 200,000 U.S. and ROK troops in increasingly realistic—and threatening—military maneuvers south of the DMZ, involving ground, sea, and air forces. Chun's intention in working with the Americans to enlarge Team Spirit, according to a former aide, was to scare the North Koreans. If so, he succeeded, because Pyongyang in most years put its own forces on full alert during the maneuvers, which lasted up to two months, and acted as if it feared a real attack. "Every time the opponent carries out such a maneuver we must take counteractions," Kim Il Sung told Erich Honecker. Citing the need to mobilize large numbers of reservists to supplement regular troops on guard against attack, Kim estimated that these annual mobilization exercises cost the country "one and a half months of working shifts . . . a great loss." Beyond the practical considerations, the North Korean leader considered the U.S.–ROK exercises an effort to intimidate him, and he reacted bitterly.

On January 20, Pyongyang issued a joint statement in the name of all its public negotiating teams—economic, Red Cross, and parliamentary exchange—denouncing this "nuclear war maneuver intended against North Korea" and indefinitely postponing all further discussions. With that, talk of an early summit meeting faded from view.

## KIM IL SUNG AND THE SOVIET CONNECTION

The railroad platform at Chongjin, a North Korean seaport city near the Soviet border, was decked out in festive colors as Kim Il Sung boarded a luxurious special train on May 16, 1984, for an eight-day ride to Moscow, with ceremonial stops in Siberia and European Russia. For his first official trip to the Soviet Union since 1961, the Great Leader traveled in imperial fashion, leading a huge entourage of 250 members including bodyguards, interpreters, pretty young female aides and even a masseuse, as well as his prime minister, foreign minister, defense minister, and other officials. One railroad car was set aside for Kim's meetings, another for his dinners, still another as his bedroom. At North Korea's request, all other rail traffic near the train was halted to allow his unimpeded passage in the Soviet Union, as had been done decades before when Joseph Stalin traveled. Internal security troops were posted at frequent intervals along the route of thousands of miles in the Soviet Union, after which Kim went on by rail to Poland, East Germany, Czechoslovakia, Hungary, Yugoslavia, Bulgaria, and Romania.

The Soviet Union played a powerful role in North Korea. To a great extent it had created the regime during its occupation of the northern half of the peninsula after the division of the country in 1945. The Soviet Union had selected and installed Kim as North Korea's leader, a selection that may have been made by Stalin himself. Soviet approval and support had been essential to Kim's ill-fated attempt to conquer South Korea in 1950. Materials recently made public from Soviet archives depict a central role for Stalin, suggesting that he personally insisted on continuing the war for well over a year after Kim was ready to seek a negotiated way out. Then, two weeks after Stalin's death, the Soviet leadership reversed his position and issued secret orders to communist negotiators to end the fighting.

Following the Korean War armistice in 1953, Kim remained heavily dependent on the Soviet Union economically and militarily, and he visited Moscow often before the full onslaught, in the early

1960s, of the great schism between the Soviet Union and China. The split between the two giants of international communism, which were also his most important patrons, created enormous problems for Kim, who struggled to keep on good terms with both of them even while being denounced for his internal policies and independent stance. Kim reacted bitterly to Nikita Khrushchev's reformist policies and his denunciations of his idol Stalin and the Stalinist "cult of personality" that Kim emulated. He was even more offended when the Chinese attacked him as a counterrevolutionary revisionist, aristocrat, and capitalist during the radical phase of the Cultural Revolution. At the same time, the Sino–Soviet dispute gave Kim space to maneuver between the two great powers of communism, each of which was forced to tolerate his independence for fear of pushing him decisively to the opposite camp.

Vadim Tkachenko, a leading Korea expert on the staff of the Central Committee of the Soviet Communist Party from 1962 to 1991, said Moscow was concerned about Pyongyang's often surprising and uncontrollable policies: "North Korea was an independent country which took the kind of actions that were difficult to explain. They would down a plane, capture a ship, join the nonaligned countries, and we would only learn of it from the newspapers." According to Tkachenko, "We didn't know [KCIA director] Lee Hu Rak was in Pyongyang in 1972; the Americans told us. We didn't know about the negotiations when the [U.S. spy ship] *Pueblo* was seized [in 1968]; the Americans told us. You'd make a mistake to think that Kim Il Sung was Moscow's man."

However much the Russians privately distrusted Kim and his regime, they saw North Korea as a strategic ally in Asia. A Central Committee official put it well at a closed conference in Moscow in 1984: "North Korea, for all the peculiarities of Kim Il Sung, is the most important bastion in the Far East in our struggle against American and Japanese imperialism and Chinese revisionism." For this reason, the Soviet Union continued to fuel North Korea's economy and military machine throughout the cold war, although the nature and extent of the support varied over time.

In early 1984, China's relations with the United States were improving rapidly, with President Reagan planning a trip to Beijing in late April, and Kim was once again worried about the direction of Chinese policy. At this juncture he decided to move toward closer ties with the Kremlin by asking for and receiving an invitation to pay an official visit to meet Konstantin Chernenko, who had become general secretary of the Soviet Communist Party on the death in February of his predecessor, Yuri Andropov.

When the Chinese learned of Kim's planned trip, they hurried to pay court to him. In their Beijing talks with Reagan, Chinese leaders stressed their backing for Kim's three-way-talks proposal, and Communist Party general secretary Hu Yaobang urged Reagan to withdraw U.S. troops from Korea, saying, "they could return in a day" if hostilities should start again. On May 4, three days after Reagan flew home, Hu traveled to Pyongyang for an eight-day official visit. Two million people turned out to greet him in what North Korea called "the greatest welcome in Korean history." For Kim, Hu's visit was an important part of his delicate balancing act between his two communist sponsors and an impressive prelude to his Moscow trip.

In the Kremlin talks with Chernenko and other officials, Kim's central purpose was to reconnoiter the likely course of Soviet politics, according to Oleg Rakhmanin, longtime Asia expert of the Communist Party Central Committee, who took part in the talks. "Kim understood the position of Chernenko perfectly" as a transitional leader, Rakhmanin recalled. Among those on hand for the talks and related social occasions was Politburo member Mikhail Gorbachev, who received his first personal exposure to this "socialist monarchy" in Asia, as he later referred to North Korea. Kim told his Soviet interlocutors, according to a confidential report on the talks furnished to Eastern European communist officials, that he expected this to be his last foreign journey—that henceforth his son and heir Kim Jong Il, who this time remained behind to run the country, or Prime Minister Kang Song San would visit foreign countries in his behalf.

Sitting with Soviet leaders in the Kremlin, Kim volunteered to discuss his relations with China and declared them to be good. Yes, it was true that China was flirting with the Americans and Japanese, but Kim declared that this was because "China is a poor country with a population of one billion people and its leadership is seeking help with modernization from the United States and Japan." At another point in his tour, Kim said that despite his confrontation with the United States and Japan, his greatest fear was "of socialism not being maintained in China." With Deng Xiaoping moving rapidly into market economics and hosting Reagan, "we must all insure that they follow a socialist way and none other," Kim told an Eastern European communist leader.

In the Kremlin, Kim told Chernenko that North Korea had no intention of attacking the South and spoke of his recent proposal for three-way talks with the United States and South Korea. While Washington was insisting on bringing in the Chinese to make a four-party negotiation, Kim said that "China is against such an arrangement." Kremlin officials responded that "the Americans are urging the Chinese toward a solution that suits them and their allies, but which creates the danger of the Korean problem being solved behind the backs of the Koreans themselves." Not surprisingly in view of the acute Korean sensitivity to outside interference, "we got the impression that the approach of China to solving the Korea problem was also causing some anxiety in Pyongyang," wrote a Soviet official who made notes on the Kremlin talks.

Kim assured Chernenko that in the future North Korea would give closer study to "the experience of the construction of socialism in the Soviet Union." Then, having refurbished high-level Communist Party and government ties between the two countries, Kim asked for more Soviet economic and military assistance. He was remarkably successful.

The Soviet Union had been North Korea's main source of external economic support since the creation of the DPRK, regardless of the ups and downs of political relations. By 1983, however, Soviet trade had fallen to less than 40 percent of Pyongyang's exports to all countries and about 25 percent of its imports. After Kim's 1984 visit, the flow of goods to and especially from the Soviet Union increased rapidly. Due initially to an extensive aid package approved as a result of Kim's visit, imports from the USSR jumped from $471 million in 1984 to $1,186 million in 1986 and $1,909 million in 1988, when they accounted for roughly two-thirds of North Korea's imports from all countries. Moscow not only financed a growing trade deficit with Pyongyang but also provided Soviet coal and oil at cut-rate prices, well below those of the world market.

On the military side, Chernenko was equally forthcoming. Since the early 1970s, Moscow had refused to provide sophisticated war-

planes to North Korea despite supplying them to such nations as
Egypt, Libya, and Syria, because of a Soviet fear that Kim might use
the planes rashly. However, on the basis of the newly improved
USSR–DPRK relationship and because the Reagan administration
was supplying the South with high-performance F-16s, Chernenko
promised to supply North Korea with sixty MiG-25 fighters—probably no match for the F-16s but a quantum jump beyond the DPRK's
previous weapons. The planes began showing up in North Korean
skies the following spring. The Kremlin's military aid package also
included SAM-3 surface-to-air missiles, and Soviet surface-to-surface
SCUD missiles with a fifty-mile range.

In return, Soviet military aircraft were permitted to begin regular
overflights of North Korean airspace before the end of 1984. By the
end of the following year, they had flown twenty-one missions over
North Korea. Soviet warships also began making port calls in North
Korea. Even before this flowering of Moscow–Pyongyang military
cooperation, the U.S. Command in South Korea was sufficiently concerned that it notified American forces whenever Soviet satellites
were expected overhead, in order to implement "avoidance tech-
niques" to mask American activities from overhead spying.

Besides obtaining military and economic assistance, another
top-priority aim of Kim Il Sung's 1984 trip was to persuade the Soviet
Union to forswear relations or even contacts with the South. Having
failed to unify the country through military means in the Korean
War, Kim was passionately opposed to the development of "two
Koreas," which implied a long-lasting division of the country. He
was particularly allergic to any dealings with or recognition of South
Korea by the Soviet Union or China—but his own dealings with the
South sapped the force of his argument. If he could deal with Seoul,
his allies reasoned, why couldn't they? Moreover, the South's rapid
economic growth and growing international stature made contacts
with Seoul increasingly attractive to members of the communist bloc.
South Korea fought hard to undertake and improve these relationships, step by step. And in zero-sum fashion, North Korea fought
hard against them, each step of the way.

For a long time, the Soviet Union rejected all relations with
South Korea. But in 1973, following the North-South joint statement

and President Park's drive for normal relations with communist countries, the Soviet Union began to permit South Korean citizens to participate in international conferences and sports events in the USSR. Pyongyang immediately protested, but Moscow responded that if it barred South Koreans from legitimate international activities, its own participants could be barred, and "there is even a danger that the Soviet Union would be expelled from important organizations."

Around the same time, North Koreans protested sharply after spotting a Soviet correspondent dining in a fashionable Paris café with two South Korean diplomats. The Soviet Foreign Ministry denied any wrongdoing but cabled its overseas posts that "unauthorized, reckless encounters with South Koreans harm our national interests and undermine trust in the integrity of Soviet foreign policy by the DPRK leadership." On another occasion, eagle-eyed North Korean diplomats detected a few South Korean stamps in an international postal exhibition in Moscow, prompting a high-level complaint and hurried removal of the offensive stamps from the display cases.

With South Korea's growing stature and strength in the 1980s, however, a more realistic assessment was beginning to permeate academic and governmental ranks in Moscow. Following Kim Il Sung's 1984 trip, the Korean-born deputy director of the Institute of Oriental Studies, Georgi Kim, said at a closed meeting of the Communist Party Central Committee that the Soviet Union should stop looking at Seoul through Pyongyang's biased eyes. He declared, "It is obvious that South Korea is a successful and respected country which is genuinely interested in being our friend. To respond positively to Seoul's overtures correlates with the U.S.S.R. national interest." This viewpoint was becoming increasingly influential in Moscow.

The slowly emerging Soviet relationship with South Korea was one of the principal issues on Kim Il Sung's mind in October 1986, when he flew to Moscow to meet Mikhail Gorbachev, who had taken power the previous year after the death of Chernenko.* Kim also

---

*In explaining Kim's decision to make an imperial-style rail trip across the Soviet Union in 1984, North Koreans had told Soviet officials that Kim's doctors recommended that he not fly, due to back trouble. In 1986 they said the doctors no longer objected to his flying.

sought to persuade the new Soviet leader to press the United States to remove its nuclear weapons and troops from South Korea, suggesting that the Seoul regime would be in trouble if its U.S. props were removed. Kim told Gorbachev with considerable exaggeration, "There is a big movement in favor of socialism in the South, and work is underway to create a national front. One third of South Korean parliamentarians support the North. Unlike the recent past when Americans were perceived as liberators and supporters, now many, not to mention the students, speak against the American presence." According to Vadim Medvedev, a senior aide to Gorbachev who participated in the talks, Kim was openly concerned that the interests of North Korea might be ignored in the heightened Soviet-American dialogue, just as he believed was happening in the Sino-American dialogue.

Several months before Kim Il Sung arrived, the Soviet Politburo had decided to shift to a more conciliatory economic and political posture toward South Korea that, a May 1986 Politburo document acknowledged, "was becoming a factor [in the] global, military-strategic balance." Trade with South Korean firms through third countries was encouraged and began to increase rapidly. Exchanges were permitted with South Korea in art, sports, and culture. Nevertheless, in his meeting with Kim in the Kremlin, Gorbachev unexpectedly excoriated China for doing business with South Koreans and declared flatly that "the Soviet Union won't engage with them." Vadim Tkachenko, the Korea expert on the Central Committee, was thunderstruck by Gorbachev's declaration, which contradicted the policy decisions that had been recently made with Gorbachev's participation. When Tkachenko asked higher-ups the next day what policy to follow, he was told to ignore Gorbachev's surprising declaration and "work as before."

When Kim and Gorbachev met, the Soviet leader had been in power nineteen months but, as Gorbachev told me in a 1994 interview, "we ourselves by that time had not yet moved very far in developing and shaping the new Soviet line" in foreign and domestic affairs. Earlier in the month, Gorbachev had met Reagan in a high-stakes bargaining match over nuclear weapons at the Icelandic capital of Reykjavik and had returned to Moscow without an agreement.

The Soviet leader was coming under fire for the first time from conservatives and some of the military for giving away too much to the West; this criticism may have accounted for his surprising declaration of solidarity in the meeting with Kim. In private, "Gorbachev had an ironical attitude to the claims of the Great Leader and considered him as a burden he had from the past," recalled Anatoly Chernyayev, Gorbachev's national security assistant. As Gorbachev would write in his memoirs, despite his misgivings about Kim's unusual ideology and a personality cult unique in the world, "North Korea was seen as a privileged ally, close to us through the socialist family group and the treaties of mutual friendship and protection. For this reason, we fulfilled virtually all of Pyongyang's wishes for weapons deliveries and economic help."

During the talks with Gorbachev, Kim was able to reconfirm the pledges of economic and military aid that had been offered by Chernenko two years earlier. Specifically, he obtained promises of thirty MiG-29 fighters, supersonic warplanes more advanced than those he had received from Chernenko, plus SU-25 fighters, SAM-5 missiles, and an advanced radar system for early warning and control of ground forces. As the pledges became realities, Soviet military aid to North Korea reached its post–Korean War peak levels, even while Gorbachev was reducing tensions on other fronts and dissolving conflicts with the West.

As a result of Kim Il Sung's diplomacy and the intensification of the cold war in the early years of the Reagan presidency, cooperation between Moscow and Pyongyang flourished in many fields in the mid-1980s. In 1987, the year following Kim's meeting with Gorbachev, the Soviet Union sent forty-five delegations to North Korea, while North Korea sent sixty-two delegations to Moscow. Nonetheless, there is considerable evidence that Kim Il Sung did not trust the new Soviet leader, especially as his liberalizing reforms, glasnost and perestroika, began to take hold and his relations with the capitalist world improved. Word was circulating among Pyongyang's diplomatic elite that Kim considered Gorbachev even more of a revisionist than the dreaded Nikita Khrushchev had been. Pyongyang increasingly feared a turn for the worse in relations with Moscow.

# 7

## THE BATTLE FOR DEMOCRACY
## IN SEOUL

For nearly all its existence since the liberation from Japan and the division of the country in 1945, South Korea had been dominated by strong rulers exercising virtually unchecked powers. As in the Kim regime in the North, this was in part a legacy of the leadership style of the Japanese colonial rulers, validated and justified by the national security requirements of the life-or-death struggle on the divided peninsula. During General Park Chung Hee's lengthy reign and the successor rule of General Chun Doo Hwan, the South experienced dramatic economic gains, but its political arrangements seemed frozen in time. This discrepancy gave rise to growing public discontent, expressed passionately by potent antigovernment political and social forces that even the strongest rulers had never been able to stifle. As the end of Chun's regime approached, the sense of imminent danger from North Korea diminished and South Koreans demanded an end to military rule enforced by the heavy-handed activities of secret police agencies and other repressive organs.

"The June Resistance," as the political crisis of mid-1987 is sometimes known, was the turning point for South Korea in its shift from authoritarianism toward democratic practice, from strong-arm politics to civil society and the rule of law. Although many trials and controversies still lay ahead, by the end of 1987 South Korea had taken a new road from which there was no turning back. At a crucial moment, the United States played an important supporting role.

## CHUN'S SUCCESSION STRUGGLE

The opportunity for peaceful transition emerged in the first instance from Chun's pledge, soon after taking office, to serve only a single presidential term, after which he would retire. Chun made his pledge, according to a close associate, because he drew a profound lesson from watching the regime of his mentor, President Park, decline, decay, and collapse in a hail of gunfire when its leader stayed on too long. In June 1980, while dominating the political scene as the top-ranking general before assuming the presidency, Chun told Richard Walker, a conservative professor with extensive Asian experience who later would become U.S. ambassador to Korea, "If I were to become president, I would like the history books to say that I was the first one in Korea to turn over power in a legitimate and constitutional manner."

The fears and wishes of his family also had a major impact on Chun. In 1981, Lee Soon Ja (Mrs. Chun) told me that their children had asked Chun not to become president, because they were happy with their lives and did not wish to change them so drastically. Furthermore, she said, when her husband was inaugurated on September 1, 1980, they asked him to finish his presidency properly and hand over the office to his successor. On Chun's first day in office, in a small meeting with her husband and his top aides, the First Lady repeated this advice, according to a participant. She added that George Washington was eternally revered in the United States because he refused to be installed permanently in office but insisted on leaving the presidency. "Please help my husband act like that," she implored the officials present. Two days later, while presenting letters of appointment to the members of his initial cabinet, Chun publicly declared, "More than anything else, I am fully determined to establish a tradition of peaceful transfer of power." Subsequently he announced at a press conference that he would serve a single term—which was set by his new constitution at seven years—and then return to private life.

Chun's declarations were greeted with great skepticism in political circles. Having seized power through military means and cemented his power in the Kwangju bloodbath—and having subsequently been elected president by a rubber-stamp college of electors— Chun lacked legitimacy and stature in the eyes of his people. Initially it seemed unlikely that this stern, aloof, and unpopular general would be the person to inaugurate a democratic tradition. Chun, however, took his one-term pledge seriously. He made plans to center his postpresidential life in a one-story marble office building constructed for this purpose in a parklike setting, replete with fruit trees, behind high steel gates south of Seoul. "Chun's fortress," as it was dubbed by Seoulites, was the headquarters of the Ilhae Foundation, a think tank named for Chun's honorific pseudonym and financed with $90 million in forced contributions from South Korea's big businessmen. Showing a keen interest in his postpresidential life, Chun quizzed FBI director William Webster, on a visit to Seoul, about the U.S. system for protecting former presidents.

Reagan and other senior American officials repeatedly and publicly praised Chun's "far-sighted" commitment to turn over power through constitutional processes, statements intended to lay down markers so that the pledge could not be ignored. "Chun Doo Hwan had made a commitment, and we wanted him to realize that the United States expected him to keep it," according to Secretary of State Shultz, who suspected that Chun would abandon the commitment if he could devise a way to do so. Yet Chun insisted he was sincere, volunteering to Reagan, in a private meeting at the Blue House in November 1983, that because of the precedents of Presidents Rhee and Park, who unilaterally extended their terms of office and were finally ousted by force, "the people believe that a change of presidents is possible only through violence. This is a very dangerous way of thinking. . . . My term is scheduled to end in 1988 and it will."

Nevertheless, Chun found it more difficult than he expected to keep his promise. "In a country like ours, it requires a lot more courage to give up power than to grab it," he confided at a dinner for Blue House reporters. He was well aware of the immense personal risks of dismounting from the tiger he had been riding since December 1979, including political and legal retribution from those who had suffered under his rule.

An important factor in the Korean political transition was the worldwide trend in the mid-1980s, in which the United States played a supporting role, toward democratization of authoritarian, military-backed regimes. The most dramatic case in Asia was the Philippines. Ferdinand Marcos's 1972 power grab, in which Washington had acquiesced, had encouraged Park Chung Hee to impose his authoritarian *yushin* system in Korea weeks later. But in 1986 Washington approved the "people power" revolution in Manila that ousted Marcos, and it prodded the falling dictator to leave the country for exile in Hawaii aboard a U.S. Air Force plane. These spectacular events emboldened the Korean opposition and focused an international spotlight on South Korea as the next potential flashpoint.

The opposition was also emboldened by the approach of the 1988 Summer Olympic Games to be held in Seoul, an event that promised greatly to enhance their country's international recognition and prestige and thus was of towering importance to all Koreans. The president of the International Olympic Committee, Juan Antonio Samaranch, had made it known that the games might be moved elsewhere in case of massive disorders in Seoul. This added substantially to the government's reluctance to use lethal and overwhelming force to put down protest demonstrations.

By the start of 1986, Korean public life was focused on post-Chun political arrangements. In April the president returned from a European trip convinced that a parliamentary system of government would best suit South Korea and, many people suspected, that it might permit him to retain power as prime minister or power broker after the end of his presidency. The opposition saw such a change as a threat. It demanded a return to the earlier practice of direct election of the president rather than election by an easily controlled college of electors, which had been established in President Park's martial-law "reforms." With the press still muzzled and the National Assembly a toothless body, the political contest was waged in the streets, with the opposition seeking to demonstrate insurmountable national support.

In keeping with tradition, politically active elements of the one million college and university students from Korea's 104 higher education institutions constituted the bulk of the participants in public demonstrations, joined in some cases by industrial workers. I watched the activist students in action on a May 1986 visit to the port city of Inchon, where General MacArthur had landed U.S. troops in one of the most successful engagements of the Korean War. The occasion was an opposition party rally to protest Chun's policies, but nearly an hour before the rally was to begin, the students precipitated a battle with police. First I heard the pop of tear gas canisters, and then, rounding the corner of a central plaza, I saw students charging the police lines, hurling Molotov cocktails, bricks, and rocks. Soon they were pushed back by a phalanx of law officers—many about the same age as the students. The rout became complete when police brought up a big tanklike vehicle spewing great clouds of tear gas, to which generous amounts of noxious pepper had been added to make it more unbearable. I watched in fascination—until my burning eyes and throat forced me to retreat inside Citizens' Hall, where opposition party leaders were placing wet compresses over their painful eyes and expressing dismay.

The following day, with the help of friends, I was able to meet three of the student leaders who were on the run from arrest warrants issued by police. The students, one of whom was an elderly 28 years old, said they had deliberately disrupted the opposition rally out of anger at the opposition's alleged willingness to compromise with Chun and his "fascist" regime. These young insurgents were also virulently anti-Chun and anti-American, insisting that the United States was responsible for Chun's rule and that Washington was manipulating Korea for its own cold war purposes. The killings at Kwangju in 1980 were cited as the moment when "imperialism [the United States] and fascism [Chun] got together" in Korea. I found the students wildly unrealistic but learned that their ideas were not atypical of campus thinking. In a survey at the elite Seoul National University, 59 percent of the student respondents characterized the United States as "neocolonialist" or "imperialist," and 80 percent were dissatisfied with U.S.–ROK relations (compared with only 9 percent dissatisfaction expressed by adults in a separate newspaper poll.)

With Chun relying on Washington for political as well as military backing, U.S. policy makers were in a delicate position. While it was clear that a large proportion of Koreans strongly favored a transition to a more democratic and open regime, American officials were leery of undermining Chun and thereby destabilizing the country with unpredictable results. With North Korea still a military threat and more than 40,000 American troops at risk, stability in Seoul was a central U.S. objective, at times an overriding one. Adding to the reluctance to intervene was the recognition of the great sensitivity of Koreans about the American role in their political affairs.

In February 1987 the State Department put its toe in the water with a New York speech by Assistant Secretary of State Gaston Sigur. In a calculated attempt to affect the political transition in Seoul, Sigur announced U.S. backing for creation of "a new political framework" through constitutional and legislative reform. He specifically advocated the "civilianizing" of the country's military-dominated politics. Sigur, considered a conservative in the Washington political spectrum, was also a committed advocate of democratic reforms in Asia. Surprisingly, he made this important policy speech without prior clearance from his superiors. Shultz initially termed the speech "outrageous" when he learned of its clear-cut prescriptions, but he later backed it strongly, telling Chun in Seoul that spring that "every sentence, every word, every comma is the policy of our government."

In mid-April, despite Sigur's call for "accommodation, compromise and consensus," Chun suddenly banned all further consideration of constitutional revision until after the 1988 Olympics. If permitted to stand, this ban meant that the next president, who was to be chosen before the end of the year, would be elected by a five-thousand-member electoral college that Chun could easily control. In practical effect, it meant that Chun could dictate the selection of his successor. Washington had only brief advance notice of Chun's decision but did not object forcefully. The opposition, however, began to protest immediately and vociferously.

On June 2, Chun summoned the Central Executive Committee of the ruling Democratic Justice Party to dinner at the Blue House and announced that he had chosen his longtime associate and friend, Roh Tae Woo, as the party's presidential candidate. Roh had retired from the army as a four-star general when Chun became president, and then held a succession of civilian jobs, including minister of sports, minister of home affairs, president of the Seoul Olympics Organizing Committee, and ruling party chairman. Nevertheless, he was seen by much of the public as "the bald man with a wig," meaning Chun in disguise—just another general who would continue dictatorial rule with support of the army.

Within hours of Roh's formal nomination on June 10 by the ruling party convention, massive and often violent protests erupted across the country, spreading to more than thirty cities. Pitched battles, the largest since the 1960 student revolution that had toppled President Syngman Rhee, broke out between demonstrators and police, more than seven hundred of whom were injured in the first two days. Tens of thousands of protesters were arrested. Citizens suffered in clouds of tear gas as the demonstrations paralyzed the central districts of Seoul and other cities, where such violence had rarely been experienced before. In an ominous development that threatened long-term stability, usually conservative middle-class Koreans displayed widespread sympathy and support for the protests as never before.

Coming on the heels of the Philippine revolution and before the Seoul Olympics, the Korean political crisis attracted extensive international attention. In the last two weeks of June, it was the single largest story in the American press, even surpassing the ongoing hearings on the Iran-Contra political scandal. An outpouring of resolutions, bills, hearings, speeches, and press conferences about the Korean crisis came to the fore in Congress. The Reagan administration, already under siege due to the Iran-Contra scandal, was under heavy domestic pressure to take a stand.

From the beginning of June, a principal concern in Washington was that military force might be used to suppress the demonstrations. Another concern was the possibility that a coup might impose a new era of military rule on the country, although this was considered less likely in view of Chun's control of his former army colleagues and Roh's standing with them. Even before the eruption of the extensive protests on June 10, administration officials were considering how they might exert American influence to head off a potential disaster.

As in earlier internal South Korean crises, Washington believed that its central role was to protect the external security of the South.

This time it did so in a message sent via Beijing warning North Korea not to take advantage of the trouble in the South. Pyongyang limited itself to rhetoric, and was cautious even in its comments about the dramatic developments in the South.

One idea discussed at high levels in Washington was to send a presidential emissary—perhaps Vice President George Bush or former ambassador Philip Habib—to take the administration's views directly to Chun, much as Reagan's friend, Senator Paul Laxalt, had gone to see Marcos at a crucial point in the Manila developments. The ROK ambassador in Washington, Kim Kyung Won, strongly advised against this plan on the grounds that it would put Chun on the defensive publicly and complicate the situation.

Officials then developed the idea of issuing a personal letter from Reagan to Chun calling for restraint and compromise—but how to do this without seeming to interfere in Korea's domestic affairs was a problem. Ambassador Kim recalled that in April, during an official visit to Washington, the ROK defense minister had carried a letter from Chun to Reagan. It was decided that Reagan's intervention in the increasingly turbulent Korean scene would take the form of a belated reply to the forgotten letter.

Composed in the White House and State Department and sent to California for the president's signature, the missive was couched in sympathetic, gentle, and inoffensive language, which Reagan preferred when dealing with allies. Saying that he was writing "as a friend," Reagan seemed to endorse ideas that Chun had already expressed. Yet its unmistakable meaning was a call for political rather than military solutions:

> I believe that political stability based on sound democratic
> institutions is critical to insuring the long-term security of your
> country, and you have often expressed the same sentiments.
> . . . Therefore, I applaud your commitment to a peaceful
> transfer of Presidential power next year as a crucial—and, as
> you say, unprecedented and historic—step in strengthening
> that institution of democratic government. . . .
> The release of political prisoners, and further steps along the
> lines you have recently taken toward effectively dealing with

police officials who abuse their authority, would send to the world a dramatic signal of your intent to break free of what you correctly term "the old politics." A free press and balanced coverage by television and radio are essential to realizing your commitment to fair elections. Dialogue, compromise, and negotiation are effective ways to solve problems and maintain national unity. Let me assure you that we will support all significant steps in these directions.

Finally, Reagan held out a personal sweetener—the promise of a visit to the United States by Chun after leaving office peacefully in 1988.*

The U.S. Embassy in Seoul received word on Wednesday night, June 17, that a letter from Reagan calling for restraint would soon be on its way, and asked for an appointment with Chun for Ambassador James Lilley to present it in person. The Korean government stalled—or in the word of the American political counselor, Harry Dunlop, "stonewalled"—on making an appointment as dozens of Korean cities became war zones. In the capital, thousands of protesters virtually took over many central streets. They overran a unit of eighty policemen, beat some of them badly, and burned their shields, masks, and tear-gas rifles in bonfires. In Pusan, the hometown of opposition leader Kim Young Sam, hundreds of police officers were injured as 15,000 protesters battled with rocks and firebombs against tear-gas assaults. Protesters in Taegu, the hometown of Chun and Roh, set several police posts on fire, overturned a fire truck, and turned its water cannon on riot police.

The usually decisive Chun was worried and frustrated. He had been telling aides for days that putting down the protests under the guns and bullets of martial law would damage the nation domestically and internationally and would constitute "a sad chapter in history," but at the same time he said that if the police lost control, he would be forced to take that step. By Friday morning, Chun seemed to have made up his mind to use the army. Meeting at ten A.M. with

---

*In fact, Chun did come in April 1988, two months after leaving office, and was welcomed as an elder statesman.

his defense minister, uniformed service chiefs, and the director of the intelligence agency, he ordered deployment, by four A.M. the next day, of battle-ready troops on a variety of campuses and cities. The U.S. Command was to be notified, as required, about those forces that would be withdrawn from the front lines. Student demonstrators were to be arrested. Under the emergency decree he was preparing, Chun told the meeting, he could dissolve political parties and open military courts to deal with dissenters. Another meeting with the military leaders was scheduled for five P.M.

The Blue House, meanwhile, finally acceded to the insistent American demands that Lilley deliver Reagan's letter. At two P.M. Lilley, an Asia expert who had been born in China and spent a career in the CIA before becoming an ambassador, presented Chun with the letter. Aware that the situation was extremely serious, Lilley had met beforehand with the U.S. military commander in Korea, General William J. Livesey, and obtained his verbal agreement that the use of military force was undesirable in the political crisis. Armed with this assurance, Lilley went beyond the gentle language of the Reagan letter to warn that intervention by the military would stretch the alliance in dangerous fashion and court a repeat of the damaging events of the 1980 Kwangju uprising. "This is the American position. The [U.S. military] command is with me. I speak for all of the United States," Lilley declared. Chun, who by that stage of his presidency often monopolized meetings with visitors, this time listened intently. He did not say what he would do, but he left Lilley with the belief that the presentation had made a serious impression. About an hour after Lilley left the Blue House, aides to Chun were told that the mobilization order had been suspended. Chun had put his sword back into the scabbard and turned to a political solution.

How much of a role the United States played in staying Chun's hand is difficult to determine. At the time and in retrospect, American officials gave principal credit to Koreans, while acknowledging that Washington played a supporting role. This view is given considerable credence by former general Chung Ho Yong, one of the inner circle of the Chun-Roh group of military leaders. Chung had resigned as minister of home affairs the month before the June crisis and would become defense minister after it was over. According to Chung, he was visited by younger generals and colonels who were alarmed by the extensive preparations that had been made to use force against the demonstrations. These military leaders—like the rest of society—thought the demonstrators had a just cause and that a crackdown would be a disaster. Chung took their concerns to Roh, telling him that the use of the military would have grave consequences for society and Roh's own political future. According to Chung, Roh saw the president within hours and strongly recommended against using military force. Roh recalled in an interview for this book that at that "very difficult moment," he had taken his opposition directly to the president. Of crucial importance, he said, was that "the military themselves felt the army should not be mobilized," which was a significant sign of the growing maturity of the ROK armed forces. Another Korean official close to the situation said Reagan's letter added to the impact of advice from a senior aide to Chun that if he put tanks and troops into the streets, the military commanders might develop a mind of their own about the uses of their power, much as Chun had challenged his own seniors and gained control of Seoul in December 1979.

After June 19 emphasis shifted from the streets to a negotiating track. On June 21 the National Assembly members of the ruling party held an unusual day-long caucus, at which the issue of compliance with the opposition demand for direct presidential elections was seriously raised and extensively discussed for the first time. On June 22, Chun announced a plan to meet opposition leader Kim Young Sam to seek a political solution to the crisis. Surprisingly, the two men had never met. After negotiations about the terms, the meeting took place on June 24 but ended without agreement.

On June 25, Assistant Secretary of State Gaston Sigur, who had peeled off from a Shultz trip in Australia shortly after the presentation of the Reagan letter, met Chun to observe the political situation firsthand and to reiterate that military force should not be used. Sigur found a distraught and nervous Chun, quite unlike the confident and decisive leader he had known before. While Chun did not confide his views about settlement of the crisis, he made it dramatically clear he would not seek to stay in office. "Don't you think I know what my people think about me? They don't want me in here anymore. And I don't want to stay under those circumstances," Chun confided to his American caller. "Tell the president, don't worry about that. I'm getting out. I'm not going to stay." At a private dinner arranged by the foreign minister, a cabinet member who had been counted among the most militant Chun loyalists told Sigur, "There's a fever going on and that fever is democracy. And we cannot turn it back."

On June 29, Roh stunned Koreans by accepting the central opposition demand and agreeing to the direct election of the next president—a daring move in view of the unpopularity of the ruling party. Roh's eight-point program also advocated a complete amnesty for Kim Dae Jung, freedom of expression for the tightly controlled press, and autonomy for the nation's closely monitored colleges and universities. According to a key adviser, Roh came close to advocating an official apology for the Kwangju massacre but backed away at the last minute due to concern about the military reaction. Roh made his startling announcement in the form of recommendations to Chun, whose views were not immediately known but who endorsed Roh's program two days later.

In the national jubilation that followed, Roh was acclaimed a hero by many Koreans, especially since there was widespread speculation that he had taken the bold steps with only grudging assent from Chun. The president said nothing to refute this belief and steadfastly refused to discuss his role in Roh's decisions. In early 1992, more than four years later, Chun's former press secretary published detailed notes of presidential conversations from June 1987, indicating that Chun had originated the decision to accept direct elections and arranged for Roh to take the credit in order to enhance his candidacy. Late in 1996, Lee Soon Ja (Mrs. Chun) said much the same in a document presented to a Seoul court. Whatever the true origin of Roh's dramatic reversal, it ended the crisis of June 1987 and put South Korea decisively on the path to political reform.

## THE ELECTION OF 1987

The South Korean election of December 1987, coming on the heels of the political breakthrough of June, was the first popular balloting for president since President Park Chung Hee's narrow victory in 1971.

Roh Tae Woo was praised for his summertime role in agreeing to a direct presidential election, but it was widely assumed that he could not win in December because of his military background. Military rule was just too unpopular, as was the would-be kingmaker, Chun. The president, on the other hand, was confident. Even before Roh's dramatic June 29 declaration, Chun told aides he had no worry that the ruling party would lose a popular vote "because the government has made numerous accomplishments and the economy is doing well." He also began to believe that clashes between the two most important opposition figures would sap their strength.

Indeed, a central problem for the opposition, as had often been the case before, was the presence of two powerful leaders who were rivals more than colleagues, each with a different geographical and political base. Both Kim Young Sam and Kim Dae Jung were civilian leaders who had long been persecuted while carrying the banners of political opposition and democracy. Together they represented a formidable force, but the big question was whether they could work together.

I was in Seoul that August and took the opportunity to meet separately with Roh and the two Kims, all of whom I had known for years.

The meeting with Roh took place amid the trappings of his political power in the spacious corner office he occupied in the National Assembly building as leader of the ruling party. Since our lengthy first meeting in 1980, I had seen him several times in his different civilian capacities in Washington and Seoul, and it seemed to me this time he was more articulate as well as a bit grayer. Wearing a conservative business suit, he nevertheless hooked his thumbs into his belt as we talked, as if he missed his uniform. When I reminded him of his statement at our first meeting that soldiers should not become involved in politics, he responded that he had not changed his mind. He went on to say, in the whispery voice he used to discuss sensitive topics, "I found myself in this situation. It may be the will of heaven—this is my destiny. That's my best answer."

The contrast with the hard-edged, decisive Chun could not have been greater. I noticed that in an hour's conversation, Roh never mentioned Chun except when I brought up his name, although the office contained a framed photograph of the two men in their shirt-sleeves, in addition to the obligatory official presidential portrait. When I asked about Chun, Roh said that their relationship had changed somewhat since the announcement of direct popular ballot-ing but that "our friendship to each other, loyalty to each other, has not changed." Although it was not generally known at the time, Chun was privately agonized about whether he could really trust Roh as his successor, according to Kim Yoon Hwan, who has known both men since high school days and who held senior Blue House posi-tions under both men.

Roh Tae Woo was born on December 4, 1932, in a farming village near Taegu. His father, who worked in the village office, was killed in an automobile accident when he was seven, and he was brought up by his mother. After brief military service at the start of the Korean War, he joined the Korean Military Academy in its first four-year class, the famous eleventh class, which included Chun and many others who later came to power as political and military leaders.

Chun and Roh became close friends. Chun, who attended a technical high school in Taegu, is two years older. He was almost always in the leadership role, with Roh a supportive follower. Before becoming president, Roh had been the successor to Chun in at least five official posts, including senior aide to the ROK army chief of staff, assistant director of operations for President Park's Blue House security force, and commanding general of the Defense Security Command. Chun was the leader of the December 1979 military coup that vaulted a new generation to power; Roh played an essential supporting role in bringing troops from his Ninth Infantry Division from the front lines to Seoul to support the facedown with the ex-isting authorities.

A person who has known both men well since their military academy days described Chun as "a very simple man who sees pic-tures in black and white" and Roh as "a man of environment and situation." Another Korean, who had watched both men as political leaders at close range, said that "the secret of Chun's leadership was his assertiveness," while Roh was "calculating and cautious" as well as surprisingly artistic, being interested in music, poetry, and novels.

My second candidate interview, with opposition leader Kim Young Sam, took place over breakfast at the Japanese restaurant of

South Korean CIA chief Lee Hu Rak secretly meets North Korean leader Kim Il Sung in May 1972 to begin the high-level dialogue between the two Korean states. (*Joong-ang Photo*)

Justifying his action on the need for national unity to confront the North in talks, South Korean president Park Chung Hee declares martial law in October 1972 to crush all domestic opposition. (*Photo by Kim In Kon / Joong-ang Photo*)

North Korean troops beat two American officers to death with clubs and ax handles in a 1976 melee in the DMZ to stop the trimming of a poplar tree (right). In reaction, the United States deploys massive ground, air, and naval forces to back up an operation to chop down the tree. (*Department of Defense*)

Presidents Park Chung Hee and Jimmy Carter review troops during Carter's 1979 visit to Seoul. While cordial in public, the two presidents quarreled bitterly in private over the U.S. troop withdrawal policy. (*Jimmy Carter Library*)

22

3-5-77

Zbig & Cy:

I'll see the S.Korean Foreign Minister next week. Park must understand:

a) American forces will be withdrawn. Air cover will be continued.

b) U.S.-Korean relations as determined by Congress and American people are at an all time low ebb.

c) Present military aid support and my reticence on human rights issue will be temporary unless Park voluntarily adopts some open change re political prisoners.

J.C.

Electrostatic Copy Made
for Preservation Purposes

DECLASSIFIED
E.O.12958, Sec.3.6
PER _____ NLC letter NLC-96-40
BY _____ NARS DATE 12/6/96

Copy Carter Library

Carter's secret memorandum to Zbigniew Brzezinski and Cyrus Vance six weeks after becoming president illustrates his iron determination on Korean issues. (*Jimmy Carter Library*)

The assassin of president Park, KCIA director Kim Jae Kyu (right) reenacts the fatal dinnertime shooting for prosecutors. (*Joong-ang Photo*)

Citizens of Kwangju parade through the streets in a popular uprising in May 1980 after brutal ROK special forces units temporarily withdraw. Many Koreans hold the United States partly to blame. (*Photo by Lee Chang Sung / Joong-ang Photo*)

President Ronald Reagan, Vice President George Bush, and their wives welcome President Chun Doo Hwan and his wife to the White House in 1981, despite previous U.S. opposition to Chun's assumption of power by a "a coup in all but name." (*Ronald Reagan Library*)

South Korea's cabinet and senior aides line up for a ceremony in Rangoon during Chun's state visit in 1983. Moments later, most of them were killed by a powerful North Korean bomb planted in the ceiling above them. (*Joong-ang Photo*)

President Kim Il Sung (center) meets Soviet leader Konstantin Chernenko (on Kim's right) and other leaders in his 1984 visit to Moscow. Politburo member Mikhail Gorbachev, later to be the Soviet leader, is third from right.

Kim is on outwardly cordial terms with Gorbachev in his 1986 visit to Moscow. Privately, however, they distrusted each other.

Two clandestine envoys from the North, Ho Dam (left) and Han Se Hae are greeted by President Chun in a mansion near Seoul in 1985. Such secret North-South meetings were numerous. (*Joong-ang Photo*)

In the mid-1980s thaw, two brothers of a divided family say goodbye after an emotional reunion in Seoul. (*Photo by Kim Joo Man / Joong-ang Photo*)

Bold protesters battle riot police in 1987 demonstrations demanding direct presidential elections in the South. Faced with widespread protests, the government gave in. (*Photo by Kim Hyung Soo / Joong-ang Photo*)

North Korean agent Kim Hyon Hui, trained from age 18 for espionage, planted a bomb that blew up a South Korean airliner with 115 aboard. She later was pardoned in Seoul and received many marriage proposals. (*Photo by Choi Jae Young / Joong-ang Photo*)

The 1988 Olympic games in Seoul generate South Korean diplomatic break-throughs in the communist world. Here Soviet athletes march in the opening ceremony. (*Photo by Chae Heung Mo / Joong-ang Photo*)

An exhilarated President Roh Tae Woo meets a reserved President Mikhail Gorbachev in San Francisco in 1990, ending the historical enmity in South Korea-Soviet relations. (*Joong-ang Photo*)

Chinese Foreign Minister Qian Qichen and party (foreground) are welcomed in 1991 to Pyongyang by DPRK Foreign Minister Kim Young Nam. Only eight commercial flights a week entered the country of 21 million people. *(Photo by author)*

Fourth graders in a sword drill in Pyongyang display childhood vigor and regimentation in 1991. In the background, the Pyongyang skyline and the Arch of Triumph, larger than the one in Paris, a tribute to Kim Il Sung. *(Photo by author)*

The United States feared that North Korea's indigenous 5-megawatt nuclear reactor, photographed surreptitiously by a Western visitor, would be the first element of a massive nuclear weapons program.

President Clinton, alarmed by the North Korean nuclear program and the confrontation of armies, visits the DMZ in 1993 and calls it "the scariest place on earth." (*AFP Photo*)

Former president
Carter meets President
Kim Il Sung in June
1994 to head off a mili-
tary crisis over nuclear
issues on the peninsula.
(*The Carter Center*)

As Carter appears on live CNN television from Pyongyang at the height of White
House policymaking on Korea, Vice President Gore and other top U.S. officials are
reduced to being amused but powerless onlookers. (*The White House*)

A limousine bearing a giant picture of Kim Il Sung leads his funeral procession in July 1994 through the broad avenues of the monumental capital he built. (*Wailing People: Summer of 1994, Pyongyang*, Gendai Shokan, *1994*)

Kim Jong Il, who inherited power after his father's death, waves to his people but remains mysteriously silent on public occasions.

Formerly close friends who grew apart in public life, ex-presidents Roh and Chun join hands at sentencing in court on corruption and treason charges in August 1996. (*Photo by Kim Chul Ho / Joong-ang Photo*)

A North Korean submarine, discovered by a cab driver at the South Korean coast, drives North-South relations to a new low in autumn 1996. (*Photo by Kim Chul Ho / Joong-ang Photo*)

Presidents Clinton and Kim Young Sam (second from right), accompanied by interpreters, walk through a field of flowers on Cheju island in April 1996 before announcing their proposal for four-party talks on permanent peace in the peninsula. (*Joong-ang Photo*)

The leaders of the two Koreas, Kim Dae Jung of the South and Kim Jong Il of the North, raise their hands together at the Pyongyang summit in June 2000, a high point of promise for an unprecedented era of cooperation on the divided peninsula. (*Korean Overseas Information Service*)

Four sorrowful children in a hospital at Pyongsong, who are years smaller than normal for their ages, illustrate the tragic long-term consequences of famine in parts of North Korea since the mid-1990s. (*Norbert Vollertsen*)

the modern and expensive Lotte Hotel. A man at ease with himself, he quickly discarded his suit jacket and rolled up his sleeves as we ate fish, rice, miso soup, and pickles. Kim had met the rival opposition leader, Kim Dae Jung, ten times in the previous six weeks and said he planned to continue meeting at least weekly until they reached a joint decision about which of them would run for president. "The public expectation is for the nomination of one [opposition] candidate as soon as possible," he said. In the meetings, "we promised each other we would have a united front to achieve democracy."

The personal rivalry between the two Kims went back to 1970, when they had contended for the presidential nomination of the major opposition party against incumbent President Park. Kim Dae Jung had been the victor in the nominating convention due to deft maneuvering that won the support of a third faction. Though the two Kims and their respective factions worked together at times, they were never comfortable with each another.

Kim Young Sam was born on December 20, 1928, on Koje Island near Pusan, at the southeastern tip of the Korean peninsula. His father, a successful island businessman, sent him to the elite high school in Pusan and to Seoul National University, the nation's most prestigious university. Kim was elected to the National Assembly on the government ticket at age 25, the youngest national legislator on record. He soon rebelled against the Syngman Rhee government's dictatorial tactics and was an original member of the opposition Democratic Party, embarking on a lifelong advocacy of democracy.

In 1960 the Koje Island home of Kim's parents was invaded while they slept by two men demanding money. As Kim's mother grappled with one of the men, she was fatally wounded by a gunshot to the abdomen. A year later one of the robbers was caught and confessed to being a North Korean agent seeking money to buy a boat. The family tragedy, which was well known in Korea, colored Kim's attitude toward the North and shielded him from the red-baiting that was common against opposition politicians. His elite schooling and establishment roots also made him unusually acceptable to the middle and upper ranks of Korean society. Of the three leading presidential contenders in 1987, he was the closest to a normal politician.

As an opposition leader, Kim had long been outspoken and undaunted by oppression. During the Park era, he was jailed for opposing military rule and in 1969 was the victim of an acid attack while opposing Park's drive to amend the Constitution to allow him a third term. A decade later he was expelled from the National Assembly for publicly calling Park a dictator and asking the United States to intervene. After Chun took power, Kim was placed under house arrest for two years for demanding democratic reforms and went on a twenty-three-day hunger strike. In our conversations while he was in opposition, I found Kim Young Sam a steadfast advocate of reform and democracy but vague on other issues.

The setting for my meeting with Kim Dae Jung was very different—his house in central Seoul, a walled compound I had visited many times while he was under various forms of house arrest. This time his front parlor was crowded with a claque of supporters, many of them from his home region of southwest Korea. That area, the current North and South Cholla Provinces, has had a distinctive history, going back at least thirteen hundred years to the time when it was the site of a separate Korean dynasty. Eventually overwhelmed by more powerful neighbors, Cholla was disadvantaged under President Park, who like both Chun and Roh was a native of a rival political center around Taegu. In the mid-1980s Cholla had notably fewer government ministers, generals, and heads of large conglomerates and a lower average income than most other regions. Kim Dae Jung was the hero and standard-bearer of Cholla and other downtrodden people in Korea, but at the same time he was distrusted and even feared by many people from other regions.

Kim Dae Jung was born on January 6, 1924, on a small island off the southwest Korean coast. Unlike his long-standing rival, however, he was not born to wealth or privilege and was an outsider to the mainstream of Korean elite society. To my surprise, I learned in 1987 that despite his fame and his important role in so many historic political developments, many leading Koreans had never met him in person.

After his victory over Kim Young Sam for the opposition party nomination in the 1971 presidential election, he vaulted to the top rank of political leadership by winning 46 percent of the vote against President Park in an election that was heavily rigged for the incumbent. Park hated and feared him. Park's KCIA kidnapped Kim in Tokyo and brought him home to Korea bound and gagged. Park then placed him under house arrest, while his captors went free, and later imprisoned him for sedition. After Park's assassination, Chun continued the vendetta. He had Kim arrested and sentenced to death on trumped-up charges and eventually, in a deal with the Reagan administration, sent him off into exile abroad. After he voluntarily returned home in 1985, Kim was placed under house arrest again.

Shortly before I saw him in 1987, Kim had finally been cleared of all outstanding charges and had his full political rights restored. Until then, he told me, there had been only two months since his kidnapping from Japan fourteen years earlier when he had been free of house arrest, prison, exile, or some other serious official restriction. The years in isolation and adversity had deepened his self-knowledge and political awareness. He had worked out his answers to major questions facing the country and could articulate them clearly.

In the weeks before our meeting, the army chief of staff, General Park Hee Do, had publicly expressed military opposition to Kim Dae Jung's potential candidacy. There was very serious doubt that military leaders would permit Kim to take office if he should be elected, and many supposed they would kill him. As we sat in the family dining room of his house, eating a Western breakfast of eggs and bacon from atop a red-checkered table cloth covered by plastic, Kim declared his refusal to give in to such threats. In contrast to 1979–80, when Chun and Roh seized power, he was sure the Korean people would fight this time rather than submit to continued military rule. "Democratization means neutralization of the military," he said.

I did not visit the fourth serious candidate, Kim Jong Pil, who had created his own minor political party and was thought to have little chance of being elected. (Eventually he won only 8 percent of the vote.) This Kim had been an architect of Park's 1961 military coup, the founder of the KCIA, and, when I knew him best in the early 1970s, Park's prime minister. Later he was temporarily banished from politics by Chun, and the great wealth he had accumulated was confiscated. Now he was seeking restoration of his honor. For most Koreans in 1987, he was a voice from their past.

Several weeks after I saw the two leading opposition figures, Kim Young Sam and Kim Dae Jung pledged publicly that they would not oppose each other, in order not to betray the people's wishes for political change. Nevertheless, a few days after that, Kim

Dae Jung appeared at a huge public rally in Kwangju in his home region of Cholla and began touring the country like a candidate. Later Kim Young Sam did the same, starting with his hometown of Pusan. Each claimed the right to be the opposition's choice on the basis of a long history of standing up for democracy, and each became convinced he would win the election. Heedless of their pledges, both of them ran for president.

Roh Tae Woo, meanwhile, enjoyed the advantages of leading the incumbent party, including massive funding and extensive coverage on television, which was heavily controlled by the government, and in newspapers, which were partly controlled. At the same time, he sought to separate himself from Chun in the public mind. Although the U.S. Embassy was under orders to remain strictly neutral, Roh managed to meet President Reagan at the White House in a mid-September trip to Washington to burnish his image as an internationally respected figure. This seemed to many Koreans to be a virtual endorsement by the United States. Neither of the opposition competitors sought to test that by arranging his own trip to the American capital.

On December 16, election day, Roh won the presidency with 36 percent of the popular vote, as Kim Young Sam (28 percent) and Kim Dae Jung (27 percent) split the opposition majority in half. Manwoo Lee, a Korean-American professor who made an intensive study of the election, wrote that "each candidate was like a Chinese warlord occupying his own solid territory" based on his region of origin. Lee also expressed doubt that either Kim Young Sam or Kim Dae Jung could have won even if running alone, due to the deep regional antagonism that had characterized the electioneering.

Roh's victory in a hotly contested direct election gave him the political legitimacy that Chun had lacked. It made it possible for him to permit a greater degree of free speech and free press than his predecessors had and to reduce government control of business. Roh's victory also permitted him to ease South Korea's hard anticommunist stance and to bid successfully for amicable ties and eventual diplomatic relations with Eastern European communist countries, the Soviet Union, and China, thereby undercutting North Korea's alliances and drastically changing the strategic situation in Northeast Asia.

# 8

## THE GREAT OLYMPIC
## COMING-OUT PARTY

For most of the world, the 1988 Olympic games at Seoul were a great sporting festival. Global television brought the opening ceremonies on September 17 to the eyes of more than a billion people, the largest television audience in history for any event until that time. But for Koreans, the games were much more. As the government and people in the South saw it, the Twenty-fourth Olympiad was their international coming-out party, an opportunity to show the world that South Korea was no longer a poverty-stricken Asian war victim but a strong, modern, increasingly prosperous country with a vibrant society. The South hoped the 1988 Olympics would enhance its economic growth and global stature as the 1964 Tokyo Olympics had famously done for Japan. Moreover, the universality of the games provided a golden opportunity for South Korea to play host to the Soviet Union, China, and the communist-led countries of Central and Eastern Europe, which were North Korea's allies and which, at the North's insistence, had shunned the South. For much the same reasons, North Korea loathed and feared the coming of the Seoul Olympics, seeing the games as an essentially political enterprise that would permit the South to improve its image in the world arena and move toward relations with Pyongyang's communist allies. North Korea waged a strenuous battle, month by month, to halt or downgrade the games. But its effort failed. The Olympics marked major strides in South Korea's drive to win recognition and accommodation from the communist world.

## THE COMING OF THE OLYMPICS

From the very first, South Korea recognized the political possibilities. President Park Chung Hee, who had approved the plan to bid for the 1988 Olympics shortly before his death in 1979, specified that one of the major objectives would be "to demonstrate Korea's economic growth and national power," and another would be "to create favorable conditions for establishing diplomatic relations with both communist and non-aligned nations." The potential diplomatic payoff added a unique and powerful incentive to South Korea's drive.

It was generally accepted that an Asian city would have first claim as host in 1988, following Mexico City (1968), Munich (1972), Montreal (1976), Moscow (1980), and Los Angeles (1984). For this reason, Seoul's most important competitor was Japan's entry, the city of Nagoya. Seoul had several advantages. Japan, a developed country, had already hosted one Olympics. Because of the intense rivalry between the two Koreas, which had often been played out in UN General Assembly votes, South Korea had embassies and consulates in nearly all third-world countries, which made up the bulk of the Olympics participants, while Japan had substantially fewer. Furthermore, many developing countries were sympathetic to one of their own.

In the end, Seoul simply worked harder. Four months before the voting, Chung Ju Yung, chairman of the giant Hyundai group, was named chairman of the committee to bring the Olympics to Seoul. As the vote approached, he and other Korean industrialists traveled widely, wining and dining Olympic committee delegates of other countries. South Korean prime minister Lho Shin Yong led an intense lobbying campaign with foreign diplomats in the corridors of the annual UN General Assembly session in New York.

In September 1981, when the Olympic delegates arrived at Baden Baden, West Germany, for the voting, they found impressive scale models of the Olympic Village that Seoul pledged to construct for the games. They were also greeted by dazzling smiles from dozens of Korea's most beautiful young women, including five former Miss Koreas and ten beautiful Korean Air Lines hostesses. According to a member of the victorious Korean delegation, Chung spent several million dollars in obtaining goodwill the same way he won construction contracts for Hyundai in the Middle East, with offers of airplane tickets, women, and money to any wavering delegates. Korea won over Japan by a resounding two-to-one margin.

North Korea was slow to react to the South's Olympic victory. It was more than two months after Seoul was awarded the games that *Nodong Sinmun* informed its readers, "Recently South Korean military fascists have been mobilizing high-ranking officials and related staff of the puppet government as well as pro-government trumpeters to raise a ridiculous hullabaloo every day about the Olympics, which are said to be going to be held in Seoul in 1988. Now the puppets of South Korea are approaching socialist nations and nonaligned countries in the hope of establishing diplomatic and official relations in order to have their 'state' recognized as a legitimate one."

As the time for the games approached, Pyongyang became less flippant and more apprehensive, portraying the issue to its communist allies in momentous terms. In June 1985, Hwang Jang Yop, then secretary for international affairs of the Workers Party, wrote the East German Socialist Unity (Communist) Party that the Seoul games were not merely an athletic issue but "an important political question touching on the basic interests of world revolution, of whether the attraction of socialism or capitalism will be strengthened on the Korean peninsula."

Following a suggestion from Cuba's Fidel Castro, North Korea proposed that the Seoul Olympics be recast as the "Chosun games" or the "Pyongyang-Seoul games," with North Korea as cohost, sharing equally in the sports events as well as the television revenues. North Korea insisted to its allies that "if the U.S.A. and the South Korean puppets do not accept our justified suggestions, then the socialist countries—as in the case of the Olympic games in Los Angeles—should collectively carry out a mighty strike and stand up against holding the games in South Korea."

While South Korea and the International Olympics Committee were willing to offer a few events to Pyongyang, full cohosting of the games awarded to Seoul—1,030 sports contests in all—was never a serious possibility. Neither was a boycott of the games by the Soviet Union and its Eastern European allies, which had boycotted the 1984 Los Angeles games and whose athletes and sports authorities were determined to participate this time.

Soviet foreign minister Eduard Shevardnadze made it clear on a visit to Pyongyang in January 1986 that Soviet bloc athletes were not prepared to sit out another Olympics, no matter what Pyongyang's problems might be. In a confidential report on his visit, Shevardnadze wrote, "We have the impression that internally [North Koreans] have already come to terms with the unavoidable participation of the USSR and the other brother countries in the games." He added that North Korea had asked him emphatically to delay announcing Soviet participation for as long as possible, and to support the cohosting proposal. Moscow agreed to keep its planned participation in Seoul a secret and gave lip service to the cohosting idea. Nonetheless, Soviet Olympics officials took an active part in preparations for the games, attending the convention of national Olympic committees in Seoul in April 1986, although they requested that their presence be given as little publicity as possible.

Meanwhile, negotiations were under way between the two Koreas, under the auspices of the International Olympic Committee (IOC), on possible North Korean participation. South Korea initially agreed that preliminary contests for four events could be held in Pyongyang, while North Korea initially proposed a fifty-fifty split of all events and then demanded one-third of the events. Gradually Seoul improved its proposal, offering all table tennis and fencing events to Pyongyang. The IOC, under pressure from North Korea's allies, suggested transferring a few more events. South Korea accepted the compromises, but North Korea rejected them as insufficient.

In May 1987, in a cable to Berlin authorities after talks with "leading comrades" in Pyongyang, East German ambassador Hans Maretzki reported that in the view of North Korea, the issue was "a strategic political fight against the Seoul regime and its imperialistic supporters," with sports considerations given second priority or no priority at all. Maretzki reported that with its inflexible and impractical positions on Olympics issues, "North Korea is once again putting itself in self-imposed isolation. Through its stubborn behavior, North Korea is granting advantages to South Korea, which will enjoy an improved image."

According to Park Seh Jik, president of the Seoul Olympics Organizing Committee, he and IOC president Juan Antonio Samaranch agreed to try to keep North Korea under control by dragging out the bargaining for as long as possible, even though they saw little hope for final agreement. In the end, they believed, North Korea would never agree to grant full access to tens of thousands of athletes, officials, and accompanying journalists from the West. But while the negotiations continued, it was difficult for North Korea to exert its maximum pressure against the participation of its communist allies in the games.

The talks came to a head in August 1987, when Pyongyang refused to accept a final IOC compromise proposal. On September 24, South Korea rejected a North Korean proposal for another direct North-South meeting on the issue. With this, in the view of the ROK Olympics chief, "North Korea was completely cornered. . . . Patience, mutual cooperation and careful planning by the IOC and South Korea for three years had finally succeeded in isolating North Korea. By the demonstration that the IOC and South Korea were doing their best to appease North Korea, the USSR and Eastern European countries were granted the option to participate freely in the Seoul Olympics."

## THE BOMBING OF KAL FLIGHT 858

North Korea did not take its defeat lying down. Two weeks later, on October 7, 1987, two highly trained espionage agents, a veteran operative and a young woman who had posed abroad as his daughter, were summoned to their headquarters in Pyongyang and assigned to destroy a South Korean airliner. They were told that the order came directly from Kim Jong Il, son of the North Korean president, and that its aim was to dissuade the nations of the world from participating in the Seoul Olympics. On November 29, a powerful bomb planted by the two operatives destroyed Korean Air Lines flight 858, flying across Southeast Asia on its way from Abu Dhabi to Seoul. All 115 persons onboard, mostly young South Korean men on their way home from engineering projects in the Middle East, were killed.

Kim Seung Il, a 70-year-old veteran North Korean espionage agent posing as a Japanese tourist, and Kim Hyon Hui, a 25-year-old agent on her first espionage operation, had boarded the flight in Baghdad and disembarked at the next stop, Abu Dhabi. They left behind, tucked away in an overhead luggage rack, a time bomb concealed in the hollowed-out innards of a portable radio. The original plan called for the two agents to immediately board a flight from Abu Dhabi back to Rome and then Vienna, where they would meet North Korean diplomats who would arrange their trip home. However, unexpected airport procedures in Abu Dhabi forced them to fly to Bahrain instead. There they languished for two days waiting for seats on a Rome-bound flight while the world absorbed the news of the mysterious airline explosion and intelligence agencies gradually zeroed in on the father-and-daughter "Japanese tourists" who had briefly traveled on the ill-fated plane.

Japanese police were quickly able to determine that the young woman's passport was a forgery. She and her companion were arrested at Bahrain airport while preparing to board their Rome-bound plane. As they were seized, both of them bit into poison ampules hidden in the filter tips of cigarettes they carried. The veteran agent died instantly, but Kim Hyun Hui survived, due to the quick reaction of a Bahraini policewoman who snatched the cigarette from her mouth before she had ingested enough of the poison. After Bahrain was convinced she was a North Korean, she was flown under heavy guard to Seoul, where for eight days she steadfastly held to a prepared cover story before finally confessing to her true identity and details of her act. Miss Kim was tried and sentenced to death for the bombing but eventually was given a presidential pardon on grounds that she was merely a brainwashed tool of the real culprits, the leaders of North Korea.

Years later I sat in a downtown Seoul office with Miss Kim, who told me the story of her life as a diplomat's daughter, a trained terrorist, and, lately, a devout Christian who had substituted Jesus for

Kim Il Sung as her savior. Although I had interviewed many defectors in the course of decades of reporting, this interview was uniquely unnerving. I found Miss Kim to be very beautiful, elegant, demure, and calm, tastefully dressed. I did not know then that she had been trained in North Korea to run ten miles in a single stretch, to bench-press 150 pounds, to shoot a silenced pistol with great accuracy, and to deliver karate chops that would swiftly kill. It was chilling to connect this attractive and intelligent young woman to the murder of 115 innocent people traveling home to their families.

As she had flown amid the passengers who would soon be killed by the powerful bomb in the luggage rack above her head, she did not dwell on the lives she would destroy but on her challenging mission. She had been told and believed, she said, that her act "was for national unification, which was a great purpose and aspiration of the nation" and therefore justified the human sacrifices. "People in democratic countries find it hard to believe, but I thought about it as a military order, to be accepted without question," she said.

From her youngest days, Miss Kim had been a star. As the daughter of a diplomat, she was selected as a small child to be a leading actress in the country's first Technicolor film, playing a little girl whose family flees to the Socialist Paradise from the poverty and misery of South Korea. At age 10, she was chosen to present a bouquet of flowers to the senior South Korean delegate to North-South talks in Pyongyang. At age 18, while attending Pyongyang Foreign Language College, she was selected for espionage work, given an assumed name, and sent to a military camp for rigorous ideological and physical training. Later she was intensively trained in passing herself off as Japanese or Chinese, and in clandestine communications and other espionage arts. North Korea carefully molded her for seven years before assigning her and her veteran partner in October 1987 to bomb the South Korean airliner.

When she was captured and brought to Seoul, her initial resolve was to maintain at all costs her false front. Miss Kim told me, "I had heard so many things about the torture and cruelty of the South Korean CIA that I was full of uneasiness and fear. I made up my mind I would have to face the worst part of this to keep my secret." In reality, however, she found that her captors treated her sympathetically and that South Korean television and walking tours of Seoul contradicted North Korean depictions of a corrupt, poverty-stricken American colony. "I began to doubt that the order [to bomb the airliner] was for unification of the country. I discovered I had just committed the crime of killing compatriots. . . . I thought I would die whether or not I confessed. I thought again and again. Finally I decided I had to tell the truth." After eight days of insisting she was a Chinese native who had lived in Japan, she suddenly spoke to her interrogators for the first time in her native Korean, "Forgive me. I am sorry. I will tell you everything."

In the wake of Miss Kim's confession, Washington assigned a senior Korean-speaking diplomat to make sure her story was true and had not been coerced. Once satisfied, the United States placed North Korea on its list of countries practicing state terrorism, triggering new economic and political sanctions, and it instituted an interagency drive to assist the South in sophisticated security arrangements for the upcoming Olympics. President Reagan and Secretary of State Shultz personally took up the threat of North Korean efforts to disrupt the games with Soviet foreign minister Shevardnadze in March 1988. "Do not worry," Shevardnadze told Reagan and Shultz. "We [the Soviet Union] will be in Seoul to compete. There will not be any terrorism." From that time on, he proved to be right.

### THE RISE OF *NORDPOLITIK*

The Twenty-fourth Olympiad, September 17–October 2, 1988, provided the pivot for South Korea's foreign policy at the end of the 1980s. Roh's "northern politics" shifted South Korea's declared policy toward Pyongyang and eventually launched new rounds of public and secret negotiations with North Korea's leaders. More immediate, dramatic, and lasting were the fruits of Roh's drive to establish relations with the allies of North Korea, as a new pragmatism and efforts at reform swept over communist regimes in the Soviet Union, China, and Eastern Europe. In time, these changes would alter the strategic alignments around the Korean peninsula in historic fashion.

*Washington Post* Tokyo correspondent Fred Hiatt and I interviewed Roh on July 1, 1988, midway between his inauguration in

February and the opening of the Olympic games in September. In this first meeting with Roh as president, I found him more relaxed and confident than I had seen him before, even though the government party had surprisingly lost its parliamentary majority in April elections and he was undergoing a rough political shakedown. Speaking to us in the ceremonial reception room of the Blue House, Roh described a fundamental change in policy toward North Korea. In the past, Roh noted, Seoul and Pyongyang had tried hard to isolate each other, each doing all in its power to retard and interfere with the adversary's relations with outside powers. "We have changed this," he said. "We will ask our allies, our friends, to induce North Korea to come out into international society as a regular member of the international community." Six days later, on July 7, Roh formally announced a new national policy toward the North and an intensified effort to establish relations with North Korea's communist allies.

Roh's effort to establish relations with North Korea's allies followed a previously established path. Contacts with the Soviet Union and China had long been a goal of Seoul governments, in the belief that such relationships would enhance the South's security and potentially undercut the North. In June 1983, Foreign Minister Lee Bum Suk declared the effort to normalize relations with the Soviet Union and China to be a formal objective of South Korean diplomacy. Lee, who was killed in the Rangoon bombing four months later, called the policy *Nordpolitik,* after the West German *Ostpolitik* policy with East Germany. In early 1985 specialists from several ROK ministries systematically studying the issue concluded that for the *Nordpolitik* policy to succeed, it was necessary to synchronize it with a more positive effort to negotiate with North Korea, lest it merely alarm Pyongyang as well as its allies. The task of implementing a more assertive negotiating strategy toward both North Korea and its allies was placed in the hands of Park Chul Un, the ambitious relative-by-marriage of Roh Tae Woo, who was made a special assistant to the chief of the ROK intelligence agency.

During his campaign for the presidency in 1987, Roh pledged to pursue a northern policy vigorously, declaring in a speech at Inchon that "we will cross the Yellow Sea" to China in order to resume a historic relationship with Korea's giant neighbor and promising new prosperity to the country's west coast areas. While on the surface China was cool to Roh's entreaties, Deng Xiaoping's market-oriented reforms in China augured well for eventual success, as did Mikhail Gorbachev's reformist "new thinking" in foreign policy that was sweeping the Soviet Union and Eastern Europe.

To implement his policies, Roh recruited as his special assistant for foreign affairs Kim Chong Whi, a 52-year-old U.S.-educated defense intellectual who had strong ideas about both the conception and the execution of South Korea's external affairs. With Roh's consistent backing, Kim steadily increased the authority of his office to hold sway over diplomacy, defense issues, and eventually North-South relations as well. During his five years at Roh's side he outlasted five prime ministers, four defense ministers, three foreign ministers, four ministers in charge of national unification, and five directors of the NSP intelligence agency. Kim energized previously reactive South Korean policy, taking the initiative on a variety of issues regarding North Korea and its communist allies, taking advantage of Seoul's swiftly growing economic strength and the approaching end of the cold war.

The first high-profile public initiative was Roh's *Nordpolitik* speech on July 7, 1988, less than a week after his remarks to Hiatt and me. Addressing himself to "my sixty million compatriots," a figure that included the people of both North and South, Roh unveiled a six-point program, including promotion of trade, exchanges of visits at all levels, and humanitarian contacts between the two Koreas. He also announced that Seoul would no longer oppose non-military trade with North Korea on the part of its allies, and that Seoul would cooperate with the North in its efforts to improve its relations with the United States and Japan. In parallel, he announced, "we will continue to seek improved relations with the Soviet Union, China and other socialist countries." Although he made no mention of the Olympics in his announcement, Roh's aides said at the time and later that the northern policy was explicitly designed, in part, to smooth the way politically for communist nations to participate in the Seoul games.

To nobody's surprise, North Korea reacted coolly to the new policy directions and rejected the proposals announced in Seoul. Kim

Il Sung, in private conversations with the East German defense minister later in July, declared that Roh's declaration "was intended to permanently split the country." Kim blamed the interruption of Red Cross talks and other North-South contacts on the annual Team Spirit military maneuvers of South Korean and American forces. "Peaceful negotiations cannot be reconciled with the fact that they are aiming cannons at us and sharpening their swords," he said, seemingly oblivious to the continuous military buildups on both sides. In an effort to regain the initiative, Pyongyang was in the process of proposing that members of the new opposition-dominated South Korean National Assembly meet with North Korean parliamentarians to discuss a "nonaggression declaration." Kim conceded to his German visitor that this, like so many proposals from one side to the other, was a nonstarter. The North Korean leader maintained that even if Seoul were willing, Washington would veto a nonaggression deal because it would destroy the justification for continued stationing of U.S. troops in the South.

The first benefits of South Korea's intensified effort to establish relations with North Korea's allies came in Hungary, whose pragmatic "goulash communism" made it the least ideological of the Eastern European countries, even though it was a member of the Warsaw Pact and Comecon, the East bloc economic organization. A pathfinder for this breakthrough was a businessman, Chairman Kim Woo Choong of the giant Daewoo group, an energetic and successful salesman who became increasingly close to Roh during his presidency. Always looking for new fields to conquer, Kim had pioneered the establishment of business deals and official ties with Sudan, Nigeria, Libya, Algeria, and Somalia, all of which had previously had relations with Pyongyang but not with Seoul. In the early 1980s he began knocking on the door of China but concluded that an early breakthrough was too difficult due to the close relations of Kim Il Sung with Chinese leaders. The Daewoo chief thereupon turned his attention to Eastern Europe and the Soviet Union.

In December 1984 the Daewoo chairman flew to Budapest aboard his private jet for conversations that broke the ice between the two countries. With Hungarian government and party acquiescence, a series of business exchanges took place, culminating in an agreement between the two chambers of commerce and the opening of trade promotion offices in each other's capitals in late 1987 and early 1988.

As Roh's *Nordpolitik* drive gathered force, Seoul pressed for full diplomatic relations with Hungary. Its timing was fortunate. In May 1988 a new and more Western-oriented team of officials took office, moving Hungary's orientation sharply toward the West. The following month, word came to Seoul from the chairman of the newly organized Hungarian Credit Bank, Sandor Demjan, who was struggling to bring market forces to an antiquated command economy, that Hungary would be willing to establish diplomatic relations before, during, or after the Olympics on the condition that Korea provide $1 billion in economic aid. The Hungarians were also very interested in increased trade with Korean firms.

Demjan's proposition touched off a series of secret negotiations between the two governments, in which financial aid was a key element. From July 5 to 14, a Korean team headed by Park Chul Un, Seoul's special negotiator with communist countries, visited Budapest, staying in a guarded villa on the outskirts of the capital. Intense bargaining sessions took place, centered on discussions between Park and Ferenc Bartha, the newly appointed president of the Hungarian national bank. The Koreans offered $400 million in loans, while Hungary reduced its asking price to $800 million. In further negotiations, Hungary agreed to establish an official mission in Seoul short of full relations in return for $400 million in loans, and to go all the way to diplomatic relations in return for an additional $400 million.

A second round of secret talks in Seoul, August 8–12, produced a tentative agreement to establish consular-level missions before the Olympics and full diplomatic relations within six months. Having the announcement of a breakthrough with at least one communist country before the Olympics was important to Seoul, which believed this would improve the political atmosphere for the games and lead to a series of steps by other nations afterward.

A third round of secret diplomacy in Budapest, August 22–27, sometimes eight or nine hours a day lasting until long past midnight, was required to make the deal. In the end, Hungary settled for $625 million in loans, mostly on a commercial basis, to take the first dramatic step. The exchange of ambassadorial-level missions was announced by the two nations on September 13, just four days before the opening ceremonies for the Seoul Olympics. Full diplomatic relations were established less than five months later, on February 1, 1989.

The reaction from North Korea was vehement and bitter, especially because Pyongyang recognized that Hungary's act would have important significance for other East bloc countries. Natalia Bazhanova, a Russian researcher who has studied the record of secret policy making in Moscow regarding Korea, reported that as North Korea suspected at the time, Hungary did consult the Soviet Union before establishing relations with Seoul and obtained approval. After the September announcement, an authoritative "commentator" article in *Nodong Sinmun* accused Hungary of committing "a treacherous grave act against the principles of Marxism-Leninism and the revolutionary cause of the working class." The lengthy denunciation asked, "Is Hungary so strapped that it has no choice but to beg for a few dollars even from the South Korean puppets, breaching faith with a friend to survive?"

Pyongyang was particularly embarrassed because Kim Pyong Il, Kim Il Sung's eldest son by his second wife and the younger half-brother of Kim Jong Il, had arrived in Budapest as North Korean ambassador only two weeks before the announcement of ties with the South. Afterward, he was quickly reassigned. North Korea downgraded its relations after the establishment of full Seoul-Budapest diplomatic relations but did not break them off. Moreover, barter trade between the two countries continued to flourish. "North Korea is very pragmatic" when its economic interests are concerned, commented a Soviet bloc diplomat who observed the Hungarian developments from Pyongyang.

Not surprisingly, as athletes of 160 nations marched into Olympic Stadium in Seoul for the opening ceremonies of the games on September 17, Hungary's Olympic team was deliriously cheered by the predominantly Korean audience. Cheers were also notably enthusiastic for the ground breaking appearance by athletes of the Soviet Union, which in the past had been South Korea's greatest extrapeninsular nemesis. Korean spectators cheered wildly for the Soviet basketball team as it vanquished the American team, to the shock and dismay of many American viewers.

In the new era of Soviet public diplomacy under Gorbachev, Moscow's athletes had been preceded in Seoul by an impressive procession of cultural and political emissaries, including the Bolshoi Ballet, the Moscow Philharmonic Orchestra, and the Moscow State Radio and TV Choir, the latter group including two Soviet-Korean vocalists.

Korean Air Lines, the national flag carrier whose Boeing 747 airliner had been shot down by a Soviet fighter plane five years earlier, was given special permission to fly over Soviet territory in connection with the Olympics. The Seoul government, in return, played host in Inchon harbor to the 12,800-ton *Mikhail Sholokov,* a floating hotel for nearly two hundred Soviet athletes and officials. In a deal that was made initially with Kim Woo Choong, the Daewoo conglomerate chairman, the Russians took home with them the computers they were given in Seoul to record the games and the cars and buses that were used to transport the Soviet delegation.

Of the 160 nations participating in the games, twenty-four had no diplomatic relations with South Korea. Nevertheless, global television via satellite leaped across nearly all political boundaries. The nations of the world broadcast an average of ten to twelve hours of the Olympics per day to a huge audience, ranging from the modern cities of Europe, Asia, and North America to tiny villages in remote parts of the third world. Ironically, the one political boundary that proved to be impervious was on the Korean peninsula. The games were ignored in North Korea, where most television and radio sets could receive only highly propagandistic channels and stations operated by the government. The Olympics were not broadcast in North Korea, and its athletes did not participate.

## WASHINGTON LAUNCHES A MODEST INITIATIVE

On July 5, 1988, Vice Minister of Foreign Affairs Shin Dong Won traveled from the Foreign Ministry, just across a broad boulevard in downtown Seoul, to the American Embassy on the opposite side. Calling on Ambassador James Lilley, Shin brought a copy of the special six-point declaration on North Korea that President Roh planned to make public two days later, which had been developed within the Blue House independently of the United States. Since South Korea lacked direct communication with the Soviet and Chinese governments, however, Washington loomed large as a transmission belt and potential influence on Moscow and Beijing. Shin asked for U.S. support and requested that the United States pass advance copies to the two big communist powers.

Lilley pointed out to his visitor that the planned ROK declaration "implies changes in U.S. policy toward North Korea," which previously had required that Pyongyang take specific steps to improve relations with the South before any improvement in American–North Korean relations could be made. The South Koreans fully understood that their shift would have consequences for U.S. policy, but they were cautious about what this would mean in practice. When I had asked Roh in the July 1 interview if South Korea would now stop objecting to North Korean applications for visas to visit the United States, he replied, "The change of government policy cannot be too drastic. There is a risk involved in changing everything too quickly." Nonetheless, he added, the basic policy would be to ask the United States and others "to help us draw [North Koreans] out to the international community."

U.S. diplomats passed advance copies of Roh's announcement to the Soviets and Chinese as requested, and they publicly praised the South Korean initiative as "positive and constructive." (In private, the State Department was more effusive, calling the move in an internal document "a major—indeed historic—reversal of traditional ROKG [ROK government] policy.") At the same time, however, Washington announced that no immediate U.S. action toward North Korea was required, though it would keep the issue under review. The United States passed word to Pyongyang that it would consider taking some positive steps if North Korea did not attempt to disrupt the Olympic games and if the North-South dialogue were to be resumed.

The principal leverage for Washington and the main issue under review was the touchy question of direct talks between the United States and North Korea. Kim Il Sung's regime had been appealing for such discussions with its archenemy since 1974, in hopes of persuading the Americans to withdraw from the divided peninsula.

Washington consistently refused even to talk without South Korean participation.

For many years the standing orders to American diplomats permitted them to speak to North Korean officials only about "nonsubstantive" matters when meeting them in social situations, and even then to terminate discussions as quickly as common courtesy allowed. Twice before, in September 1983 and March 1987, the State Department had issued new orders permitting substantive discussions with North Koreans in neutral settings. Nothing much came of this except for a few "getting to know you" chats at foreign embassies because both times the more flexible rules were soon canceled, due to North Korean acts of terrorism: the Rangoon bombing in October 1983 and the bombing of Korean Air Lines flight 858 in November 1987. Following Roh's declaration, Assistant Secretary of State Gaston Sigur and his senior deputy, William Clark, who had served earlier as political counselor in Seoul, became convinced it was time to move again with Pyongyang—this time more seriously.

In internal discussions regarding North Korea, "we came to the conclusion that if you're really going to achieve some sort of a semblance of peace on the Korea peninsula, the only way to do that is to take some steps to try to open the place," recalled Sigur. The Soviets and Chinese, he pointed out, had forever been pushing Washington to deal with Pyongyang. A central barrier had been Seoul's objections, and now those seemed to have lessened. That being so, the main issue at hand was one of tactics. Here Clark suggested a "modest initiative" that would be unilateral rather than conditional on North Korea's response.

In October 1988, following the successful completion of the Seoul Olympics, the State Department drew up and won White House approval for its plan, consisting of four points:

• A new policy of encouraging unofficial, nongovernmental visits by North Koreans to the United States. Since the beginning of 1988, only eight visas had been requested by North Koreans, and four of those—to attend a speed skating event in St. Louis—had been denied.

• Easing of stringent financial regulations that impeded travel to North Korea by American citizens.

• Permission for limited commercial export of American humanitarian goods, such as food, clothing, and medicine, to North Korea.

• Renewed permission for substantive discussions with North Koreans in neutral settings, with the expectation that this time serious communication might take place.

While no North Korean steps would be required to trigger these limited U.S. moves, Pyongyang would be asked for a "positive, constructive response." In private and public statements Washington listed five items that could be considered encouraging symbols of a more constructive policy. These were progress in the North-South dialogue, return of the remains of Americans missing in action from the Korean War, the elimination of anti-American propaganda, the implementation of confidence-building measures along the DMZ, and credible assurances that North Korea had abandoned terrorism as an instrument of state policy.

The American steps were discussed with Roh at the White House on October 20, when he met Reagan and Shultz during a four-day U.S. visit to address the UN General Assembly. Roh, who had been publicly appealing for a summit with Kim Il Sung and whose UN address was unusually conciliatory, approved the American initiative but asked that it not be made public until a few days after he returned to Seoul, which was done. In the meantime, U.S. diplomats briefed foreign governments on the initiative, with special attention to Soviet bloc countries in Europe, which were not usually briefed on American policies in Asia. In an October 25 cable to its embassies, the State Department emphasized that "these proposed measures are being taken both to stay in step with (but not in advance of) the ROKG in this matter, but also because we have substantial interests of our own in seeking to reduce tensions on the Korean peninsula and in promoting dialogue between the North and the South."

On October 28, three days before the public announcement, the State Department sent out instructions for special presentations of the new policies to the Soviet and Chinese governments, with the Chinese explicitly asked to pass along the briefing to Pyongyang. "The door is open for the DPRK to pursue an improvement of relations with the United States, if the DPRK abandons belligerence, confrontation and terrorism in favor of dialogue," Moscow and Beijing were told. The American briefers added that Washington hoped for a "constructive response."

It did not take long for North Korea to test the "modest initiative" by asking for a bilateral meeting with U.S. diplomats in Beijing. While Washington did not consider this a truly "neutral setting," it approved the meeting between a North Korean diplomat and the political counselor of the U.S. Embassy in Beijing, Raymond Burkhardt, to take place at the Chinese Foreign Ministry's International Club. There in a small second-floor room, which Americans assumed was bugged by the Chinese, the U.S.–North Korean talks began on December 5, 1988. Burkhardt, who had never dealt with North Koreans before, was surprised that their representatives turned out to be serious and businesslike diplomats who wasted no time with bluster or the usual obligatory praise of Kim Il Sung and *juche*. The discussions were centered squarely on the main issues of the day as seen in the two capitals.

Thus in late 1988 for the first time, North Korea achieved the mutually authorized, direct channel for diplomatic business with the United States that it had long been seeking. This, however, was fundamentally the result of Seoul's policy reversal rather than a reflection of new thinking in Washington. U.S. diplomats made it clear from the beginning that the Beijing talks were for communications but not for negotiations. The United States continued to insist that any dealmaking regarding the divided peninsula would have to involve Seoul.

As it turned out, the meeting between American and North Korean diplomats in the International Club in Beijing was the first in a series of thirty-four such sessions, in which messages were passed but little progress was made, between December 1988 and September 1993.

# 9

## MOSCOW SWITCHES SIDES

*A* month after the successful conclusion of the Seoul Olympics, the Soviet Union's ruling Politburo took up for the first time the question of its relations with South Korea. This unheralded Politburo meeting of November 10, 1988, whose decisions as usual were taken in secret, marked the start of a historic Soviet drive toward friendly accommodation with a long-standing antagonist on the Korean peninsula. As was often the case in major power deliberations regarding Korea, the Politburo decisions that day were based almost entirely on considerations of Russian national interest, with their impact in the peninsula given secondary consideration. Nonetheless, the reversal that was set in motion reverberated powerfully on both sides of the thirty-eighth parallel. Prodded and induced by the ROK, the Soviet Union was transformed over the next two years from godfather, superpower guarantor, and economic benefactor of North Korea to partner and, in some respects, client of South Korea. This was of monumental importance.

◆　　◆　　◆

By the time of the Politburo meeting, the cold war ice was breaking up between the Soviet Union and the United States, and Mikhail Gorbachev was at the height of his powers. The previous month

197

Gorbachev had ousted from the Politburo Yegor Ligachev, the most influential critic of the shift away from the traditional Soviet foreign policy support for "class struggle" and ideological allies, and he had placed foreign affairs under the supervision of Alexander Yakovlev, a leading exponent of a foreign policy based on "new thinking" and accord with the West. Gorbachev had been to Washington to sign a nuclear-weapons reduction treaty with the United States, and Ronald Reagan had been to Moscow to celebrate their new relationship and walk in Red Square with Gorbachev. Just two days earlier, on November 8, Vice President George Bush had been elected U.S. president to succeed Reagan, prompting Gorbachev to plan a December visit to New York to meet the president-elect and proclaim from the rostrum of the United Nations a new Soviet foreign policy based on "universal human values." In describing his new foreign policy, Gorbachev declared at the UN, "Today, the preservation of any kind of 'closed' society is hardly possible"—words that must have chilled Pyongyang. To confirm the seriousness of his policy, he took the occasion to announce a massive unilateral reduction of Soviet military forces and conventional armaments, and a large-scale military pullout from Eastern Europe, Mongolia, and the Asian part of the Soviet Union.

In the case of Korea, the fundamental reason for the Soviet policy shift was economic. Among the documents considered in the Politburo meeting of November 10 was a glowing memorandum from Vladimir Kamentsev, deputy prime minister in charge of foreign economic ties, who shared the view earlier endorsed by the ministers of foreign trade, finance, and oil and gas industries that the dynamic economy of South Korea was "the most promising partner in the Far East." Trade with Seoul, which was still being conducted in cumbersome fashion through unofficial contacts and third countries, was climbing steadily, and eager South Korean businessmen were knocking on Moscow's doors with attractive offers of more lucrative trade and potentially even subsidies and outright aid, on condition that state-to-state relations be established. The conclusion of Kamentsev's memorandum, according to the notes of a participant in the meeting, was that "unless we undertake to normalize our relations with South Korea, we may be late."

Gorbachev announced that he agreed with Kamentsev's recommendation to move toward South Korea. There was no dissent, and the decision was made. At the same time, the Soviet leader expressed the need for caution in implementing the shift, saying that the Korean issue "should be approached in the context of our broad international interests, as well as our domestic interests." In this respect, he said it was too early to establish political relations with the South before discussing the matter with other members of the Soviet bloc. In the meantime, he decided, cultural, sports, and other ties should be opened wider. "This will come as a signal to Kim Il Sung and to the United States," Gorbachev commented.

Having decided to move in a decisive although evolutionary way, Gorbachev sought to rationalize the action by suggesting it could add to a strong wave of nationalism in South Korea and thereby provide impetus for the withdrawal of U.S. military forces there. This proved to be wildly unrealistic.

Ruling out "shock methods" with respect to Moscow's old dependency and ally in the Korean peninsula, Gorbachev suggested that Foreign Minister Eduard Shevardnadze stop in Pyongyang during the course of a forthcoming trip to Japan to explain to the North Koreans the evolution of Soviet relations with South Korea. When Prime Minister Nikolai Ryzhkov remarked that Kim Il Sung might refuse to see Shevardnadze to receive such a message, Gorbachev acknowledged this could happen—but in any case "we will make this gesture, and give North Korea a notice."

Nobody had any illusion that the explanation would be easily accepted. The Politburo had before it classified reports, which had arrived in code, from the Soviet Embassy in Pyongyang reporting that Gorbachev's perestroika reform was already coming under sharp criticism from Kim Il Sung's regime, which increasingly considered Gorbachev a "revisionist" departing from the true faith of Marxism-Leninism. Gorbachev reacted calmly to these reports, noting that he had already experienced similar opposition in several other fraternal countries. Whatever the repercussions in North Korea, the Soviet leader was determined to change Moscow's long-standing Korea policies. He summed up the discussion by announcing, "We will firmly proceed on the way to rapprochement and establishing relations with South Korea. We are now taking this necessary decision."

## THE ROOTS OF CHANGE

The ground had been prepared for Moscow's shift in policy several months earlier, by Soviet participation in the Seoul Olympics, which had dramatically altered official, journalistic, and popular attitudes toward South Korea.

Until the Gorbachev era, very little information about South Korea had appeared in the Soviet press, and nearly all of that negative. However, in the Olympic year of 1988, there were 195 stories in leading Soviet newspapers and magazines, most of them firsthand accounts by Soviet correspondents. In addition to sports news, the correspondents had covered Korean economic achievements, culture, and lifestyle, with authentic impressions of Korean reality.

Remarks by Soviet reporters illustrate the overnight change in attitudes toward South Korea. Vitaly Ignatenko, who served as leader of the Soviet press at the Seoul games and later became Gorbachev's press secretary and director general of Tass, the Soviet news agency, said his first visit to Seoul had been "a shock" to him. "Everything I had read before turned out to be outdated; I arrived into the 21st century." Correspondent Vitaly Umashev of the influential weekly *Ogonyok* said, "My vision of South Korea as a Third World country disappeared." He reported that "in South Korea, Xeroxes are sold everywhere . . . but in our country they are still considered a tool of dissidents." The Communist Party newspaper *Pravda,* which had previously depicted South Korea mainly as a bastion of American militarism, summed up its impression after the close of the games: "The sports facilities in Seoul are the best in the world, and the values of the Korean traditional smile and etiquette have been greatly underestimated."

Even more powerful was the impact of television. Almost 200 million Soviet viewers watched the ceremonial opening of the games, with attention also directed outside the stadium to scenes of Seoul. Soviet television carried fourteen to sixteen hours daily from the ROK during the games. In an informal survey of 167 Muscovites, more than 70 percent had watched some of the Olympic telecasts. Many Russians had been stunned and delighted to see Korean spectators rooting for Soviet teams in the games, even against American competitors, and they were elated when the Soviet teams walked off with the highest national total of Olympic gold medals. An aide to Gorbachev told the Soviet leader, "There is definitely no other place on earth where people so heartily welcome Soviets."

Even before the games were held, South Korea took advantage of the change in the atmosphere with a persistent series of probes to Moscow. In the summer of 1988, Park Chul Un, the Blue House point man for northern politics, managed to travel to Moscow and deliver a letter to Foreign Ministry officials addressed to Gorbachev. The letter, signed by President Roh, praised the very perestroika policies that were being damned in Pyongyang and called for establishing Soviet–South Korean diplomatic relations as a step toward peace and stability in Asia. Park also handed over a Korean translation of Gorbachev's recently published book on his reformist policies. A few weeks later Gorbachev sent a return letter, which was delivered to Roh in Seoul via Georgi Kim, an ethnic Korean academician at the Soviet Institute of Oriental Studies.

As the Blue House emissary prepared to leave Moscow on September 9, he was informed that the Soviet Union intended to improve its unofficial ties. He was tipped off to look for important news in a speech to be delivered by Gorbachev in Krasnoyarsk in Siberia on September 16, the day before the opening of the Seoul Olympics. In the speech Gorbachev addressed himself for the first time in public to the potential thaw, declaring that "within the context of a general improvement in the situation on the Korean peninsula, opportunities can open up for forging economic ties with South Korea." He also proposed a multinational initiative to limit and reduce military forces and activities "in the areas where the coasts of the USSR, PRC, Japan, DPRK and South Korea merge close." In October, in a deliberate signal of approval, Roh in a speech to the UN General Assembly called for "a consultative conference for peace" involving the five powers mentioned by Gorbachev plus the United States. The Soviet ambassador to the United Nations and other officials noted the resemblance between the two proposals.

Quite apart from politics, the South's large and growing economic dominance on the peninsula made the country difficult to ignore. Although in the first decade after the Korean War the economies of the two Koreas had been roughly on a par, by 1988 the GNP of South Korea was at least seven times larger than that of the North and the gap was growing rapidly.

Up to 1984, the Soviet Union had provided more than $2 billion in foreign aid and credits to North Korea, much of it in the form of whole factories financed by soft loans that were never repaid. Following the trips to Moscow by Kim Il Sung in 1984 and 1986, the Soviet Union had provided an increasing quantity of oil and gas, weapons, and a variety of other goods on easy credit and concessional terms to its Northeast Asian ally. In 1984, however, Pyongyang stopped paying even interest on its smaller debt to Western creditors, and three years later it was officially declared in default, making it ineligible for further commercial loans. By 1988, Moscow was shipping $1.9 billion in goods to North Korea while receiving less than $.9 billion in return. This heavily subsidized Moscow–Pyongyang trade made up nearly three-fifths of North Korea's total trade turnover.

The vibrant economy of South Korea, on the other hand, was booming, with economic growth rates over 10 percent annually and a large global trade surplus, as its automobiles, ships, television sets, and computer chips made their mark on the international economy. No longer the object of foreign aid from the United States and Japan, Seoul in mid-1987 had become an aid-dispensing nation by establishing an Economic Development Cooperation Fund to assist developing countries. In their contacts with Moscow, leaders of South Korea's highly successful international conglomerates, known as *chaebols,* were expressing intense interest in investment and trade in Siberia, a high priority in Soviet economic plans for which massive foreign investment was needed. Moscow initially had hoped for major Japanese funds, but the unresolved dispute over the Soviet-held Northern Islands interfered with this prospect. The ROK was the logical substitute.

Even before the Politburo decision to move toward ties with the South, North Korea demanded an explanation from its Soviet ally for its growing trade relations with Seoul. In a memorandum in late

September, the international department of the Soviet Communist Party's Central Committee responded in astonishingly frank terms:

> The USSR, to solve its economic problems, is interested in new partners. South Korea possesses technology and products that can be of use, especially in the Far Eastern regions of our state. As is well known, South Korea maintains commercial links with almost all countries in the world, including such socialist states as the People's Republic of China. The opening up of direct economic contacts between the Soviet Union and South Korea will also benefit peace and stability in the Asia-Pacific region. We don't want to rush developing these ties. We'll move gradually, measuring progress in the economic field with the political trend in the region.

The international department added, "At the same time the USSR remains loyal to obligations to the DPRK. We don't intend to start political relations with South Korea."

In December 1988, a month after the unannounced Politburo decision to move toward normalized relations with the South, Seoul passed word that it would favorably consider Moscow's request for a $300 million commercial loan and also study a possible $40 million project to build a trade center in the Soviet Far East.

As Gorbachev had directed in the Politburo meeting, Foreign Minister Shevardnadze traveled to Pyongyang that month to inform the North Korean leadership directly of Moscow's decision to grow closer to South Korea. The North Korean capital struck members of the Soviet traveling party as depressingly cold and gray with unsmiling people and little clouds of dust in the streets. Kim Il Sung, however, did his best to stay on the good side of his important visitors. The great leader Kim Il Sung did not take issue with Moscow in his talk with Shevardnadze, which the Soviet foreign minister described in an internal report as "especially cordial."

It was left to Foreign Minister Kim Yong Nam, the official who often performed the job of putting forth Pyongyang's most intractable positions, to fiercely attack Moscow's shift on trade and economic relations with Seoul. According to Shevardnadze's internal report, his North Korean counterpart "rather sharply accused the socialist countries of not evaluating the situation in South Korea correctly, of deepening the division of the country and hindering inter-Korean dialogue and [charged that] some socialist countries are betraying socialism for the sake of money." Shevardnadze reported that "these fabricated accusations were firmly rejected by us." The Soviet foreign minister assured the North Koreans that Moscow's relations with Seoul would continue to be unofficial, and he included this commitment in the formal communiqué issued at the end of the talks.

Shevardnadze did not repeat in public or in his internal report his most emphatic statement in Pyongyang. At the height of the argument with his North Korean counterpart, he declared heatedly that "I am a communist, and I give you my word as a party member: the USSR leadership does not have any intention and will not establish diplomatic relations with South Korea." This would be thrown back in his face later by North Korea—and sooner than anyone guessed.

### GORBACHEV MEETS ROH

In 1989, a year of dramatic change in the external relations of the Soviet Union, ideology gave way to pragmatism and internationally accepted standards. The last Soviet troops left Afghanistan in February, ending an occupation that had severely damaged Moscow's standing abroad. In May, Mikhail Gorbachev traveled to Beijing to terminate once and for all the decades-long dispute between the two giants of communism. The live television coverage that had been authorized for the auspicious occasion turned out to be a disaster for Chinese leaders when American network cameras recorded the demonstrations of student protesters during Gorbachev's visit and their bloody suppression on June 4, shortly after he left.

In August, with Gorbachev's approval, the Polish Communist Party gave up power to a coalition headed by the noncommunist trade-union movement Solidarity. This spelled the end of the Brezhnev doctrine, under which Soviet military power enforced the loyalty of its peripheral satellite states. A series of spectacular events in Eastern Europe followed, in which the communist governments of Hungary, Czechoslovakia, Bulgaria, and Romania were ousted or their leaders forced to reverse their political direction. In November, the crossing points in the Berlin wall were flung open, bringing the symbolic end of the iron curtain that had divided Europe since World War II and leading in time to the absorption of communist East Germany by the West. At a windblown, sea-tossed summit meeting with President George Bush in Malta in December 1989, Gorbachev gratefully accepted American economic aid and declared that the United States and the Soviet Union were no longer enemies.

While his foreign policy was winning praise abroad, Gorbachev was coming under growing criticism at home. The Soviet Union was in the first stages of a painful economic transition, with consumer-goods shortages causing longer and longer lines and the budgetary deficit soaring to 12 percent of GNP, roughly six times the equivalent figure for the United States. Public confidence in the Soviet leadership was sharply declining, at a time when loosening controls on expression made it possible for the first time for the public to declare its views.

In these circumstances, Gorbachev saw a profitable relationship with Seoul as a promising new source of economic help for the embattled Soviet leadership. Moreover, by forging a visibly close relationship with South Korea, Moscow was poking a finger in the eye of the standoffish Japanese, who were refusing to provide economic assistance because of the Northern Islands issue. Gorbachev had diminished concern about North Korea, which was seen as a holdover from the Stalinist era and the epitome of the cold war states that were rapidly passing from the scene in Europe.

Looking back on the Korean developments, Gorbachev wrote in his memoirs, "Our interest in South Korea, one of the East Asian dragons which had succeeded in creating an economic miracle, grew in relation to the worsening of the economic situation in the USSR." In an interview for this book, the former Soviet leader also pointed out other factors, noting that he took up relations with Seoul "after a serious change in U.S.–Soviet relations and after the concept of New Thinking began to materialize, after the important process of change got under way in Eastern Europe, and after we abandoned the so-called Brezhnev doctrine."

In Seoul, President Roh was closely watching the signs of a developing Soviet shift, particularly Gorbachev's two policy speeches on Asian affairs in July 1986 in Vladivostok and September 1988 in Krasnoyarsk. As Roh interpreted their cautious phrases, Gorbachev was saying that the Soviet Union wanted cooperation with South Korea, especially economic cooperation. "I took this as an indication that the time was right, the opportunity had come to make ourselves available for the realization of this goal [of establishing relations]," Roh told me in 1993. "I would say I started smelling their real intention."

At the end of 1988, Moscow lifted restrictions on entry to the Soviet Union by South Koreans, giving them for the first time the same treatment as citizens of other capitalist and developing countries. Shortly thereafter, the two nations opened postal, telegraph, telephone, and telex links. In January 1989, Korea's most senior business figure, Chung Ju Yung of Hyundai, Korea's largest conglomerate, visited Moscow and reached a joint agreement on business cooperation with the Soviet Chamber of Commerce. Two weeks later the deputy chairman of the Soviet chamber, Vladimir Golanov, traveled to Seoul and agreed on the exchange of unofficial trade offices in the two capitals. When the South Korean office in Moscow opened, it was immediately mobbed by hundreds of Soviet entrepreneurs and government officers proposing deals.

Many Korean industrialists flocked to Moscow, where they were feted by Soviet officials and presented with requests to undertake a wide variety of enterprises, ranging from the construction of factories to produce consumer goods to help in the conversion of Soviet military industries to civilian uses. Trade between the two nations increased rapidly.

In early 1989 North Korea, in response, put on a spirited campaign to persuade Gorbachev to visit Pyongyang, hoping that this could reverse or at least halt the drift toward Seoul. It was widely known that Gorbachev planned to visit China in the spring, which would provide a convenient occasion for a stopover in Pyongyang. High-ranking North Korean leaders and their ambassador in Moscow used every possible tactic to get Gorbachev to add Pyongyang to his itinerary, including begging, demanding, and threatening. "It was very hard for us to invent new reasons all the time why he couldn't come," said a Gorbachev aide who prepared his trip to Beijing. Gorbachev's national security assistant, Anatoly Chernyayev, said Gorbachev feared his reformist reputation would suffer in Pyongyang because "he realized that once he went [to Pyongyang] and they staged a performance of hugging and kissing, everyone would accept it as a double standard."

Gorbachev's refusal to visit during his trip to Beijing in May 1989 was difficult for Pyongyang to swallow. This was especially so because the resolution of the Sino–Soviet dispute—which the Gorbachev journey symbolized—created a new situation in which neither major communist power would be fearful about pushing Kim Il Sung's regime into the arms of the other. Kim was worried about losing leverage with them both.

In Beijing, Gorbachev spoke of his fast-developing friendship with South Korea in a frank manner that would have been impossible during the Sino–Soviet split. The briefing materials prepared for him in Moscow by the Communist Party Central Committee noted that "Beijing energetically promotes unofficial ties with Seoul. The PRC's volume of trade with South Korea is $3 billion, ours is less than $200 million. This connection with Seoul does not harm China's relations with Pyongyang and at the same time helps the peace process on the Korean peninsula." Reflecting this view, Gorbachev told Chinese premier Li Peng, "We think that the USSR is behind China in developing ties with South Korea. Very far behind." The Chinese premier responded, "If you mean trade volume, you are right."

On the political side, Moscow was reaching out to Seoul through the activities of its party-dominated think tanks. With each passing month, more exchanges were proposed or consummated, especially with unofficial and opposition leaders in South Korea. In February 1989 the Institute of the U.S.A. and Canada, headed by the influential Georgi Arbatov, hosted Kim Dae Jung, the most internationally prominent opposition leader. The Institute of World Economic and International Relations (IMEMO), headed by the redoubtable Yevgeni Primakov, invited Kim Young Sam, his political rival.

Kim Young Sam's visit in June 1989 coincided with a trip to Moscow by North Korean Politburo member Ho Dam. Soviet authorities arranged a meeting of the two. Acting on the basis of an understanding reached with the Blue House before his trip, Kim Young Sam declined his North Korean interlocutor's invitation to visit Pyongyang, insisting that a North-South summit meeting come first. Had Kim accepted the invitation and traveled to Pyongyang, the contacts and understandings with the North that resulted might have changed Korean history. As it turned out, Kim's careful handling of his initial Moscow visit and the invitation from Pyongyang won acclaim from the government in Seoul and paved the way for Kim's political alliance with Roh Tae Woo in January 1990—an alliance that eventually resulted in Kim becoming Roh's successor as president. Nine months later, after becoming chairman of the ruling party, Kim returned to the Soviet capital and even managed a brief unofficial chat with Gorbachev.

Throughout this period, a struggle over Korea policy was taking place in Moscow. On one side were most Foreign Ministry officials, the Soviet military, and the Korea experts in the Central Committee, who favored caution because of the long-standing ties to North Korea; on the other side were members of the Soviet political and economic leadership, who considered the North Korean tie an anachronism and were eager to move ahead quickly with the South to obtain economic assistance. The central issues were those of pace and procedure rather than direction. "We understood the inevitability of future recognition of South Korea, but we were calling for going to this aim step by step," said a senior Foreign Ministry official. However, he said some departments in the Central Committee and some personal aides to Gorbachev insisted on taking dramatic steps at once, due to their urgent desire for financial aid. Vadim Tkachenko, the veteran Korea expert on the Central Committee staff, who favored a measured approach, said the top decision-makers "from the beginning converted the issue into trade [where] the most important thing was money. . . . [They were] doing everything on the spot, without thinking."

The moment of truth arrived in May 1990, when Gorbachev met privately in his office with the veteran former Soviet ambassador to the United States, Anatoly Dobrynin, who had returned to Moscow to become a senior foreign policy adviser to the Soviet leader. Dobrynin had been invited to visit Seoul for a conference of the

InterAction Council, an unofficial group of former heads of state and senior diplomats organized by former West German chancellor Helmut Schmidt. In view of the sensitivity of a trip to Seoul by a high-ranking Soviet official, Dobrynin was required to obtain Gorbachev's permission.

The day they met, Gorbachev had just received a report from his finance minister on the dire state of the Soviet Union's coffers. Foreign goods were urgently needed in an effort to keep living standards from sinking while reforms were under way, but financial markets were refusing to supply further credit because of Moscow's inability to pay its debts. Searching for money wherever he could, Gorbachev was in the process of authorizing a series of secret financial appeals to the West German government as part of the intense negotiations on the future of Germany.

Dobrynin recalled that Gorbachev's words to him were "we need some money." With that practical preamble, Gorbachev proposed that Dobrynin, in accepting the invitation to Seoul, use the occasion to explore the possibility of a major loan from the South Korean government. At this stage, Gorbachev was not ready to go to Seoul himself, but he told Dobrynin that he would be willing to meet Roh somewhere else, perhaps in the United States, where he was scheduled to have a summit meeting with Bush in late May or early June.

Dobrynin arrived in Seoul on May 22 and the following day was taken to a secluded Korean-style building on the grounds of the Blue House. There he met secretly with Roh and his security adviser, Kim Chong Whi, the architect of the *Nordpolitik* maneuvers. Dobrynin brought the news that Gorbachev was willing to meet the South Korean leader, a powerful symbolic step that was tantamount to official recognition and was certain to lead to full diplomatic relations in the near future. "You are the third to know," Dobrynin told the Korean president, "and you are the fourth," he said to Roh's aide. Emphasizing the need for secrecy, the Soviet emissary obtained a commitment that the Korean Foreign Ministry would not be informed until the last minute, because the Soviet Foreign Ministry had also been kept in the dark. It was agreed that the meeting would take place two weeks later in San Francisco, which Gorbachev planned to visit after the completion of his Washington summit with Bush. Dobrynin did not inform Foreign Minister Shevardnadze of the meeting until shortly before it was publicly announced, and the Soviet Foreign Ministry took no part in the session—an extraordinary omission in an important diplomatic event.

According to Dobrynin, he discussed with Roh in Seoul a loan of some billions of dollars without being specific on figures. In a 1993 interview for this book, Roh quoted Dobrynin as telling him that Soviet leaders "were in a desperate situation for their economic development." Having seen what Korea had done economically, Roh recalled, "they expected that South Korea could somehow play a role in the success of *perestroika*. As a model, they were attracted by the Korean economic development. That was their top priority at the time, and they naturally expected that South Korea could contribute to this." Roh told Dobrynin that Korea would make a major contribution to the Soviet Union, but only if and when full diplomatic relations were established.

From the Korean point of view, a full breakthrough with the Soviet Union was a development of immense importance. It would deprive North Korea of the undivided support of its original sponsor, its most important source of economic and military assistance and an important security guarantor against American power under the 1961 Soviet–DPRK treaty. Moreover, the spectacle of the general secretary of the Communist Party of the Soviet Union—the world's senior communist figure—meeting with the president of South Korea meant the legitimization of the Seoul government virtually everywhere and the final collapse of North Korea's long-standing effort to wall off the southern regime from communist nations. There was little doubt that in time China would follow the Soviet example in its own self-interest.

Although the meeting of Gorbachev and Roh took place on American soil, the United States played only a minimal role in bringing it about. Secretary of State James Baker had discussed Korea with Shevardnadze in separate meetings in February, March, April, and May, but these talks centered on the North Korean nuclear problem and, in any case, Shevardnadze was not involved in setting up the breakthrough with South Korea. The subject of a possible South Korean connection with the Soviet Union had been discussed in the spring by Roh's foreign policy aide, Kim Chong Whi, with Assistant Secretary of State Richard Solomon and U.S. ambassador to Korea Donald Gregg. Solomon agreed to help but offered the opinion that a breakthrough was unlikely during 1990.

Once the Gorbachev-Roh meeting was arranged, the United States did all it could to facilitate it. At the urging of the Blue House, which considered a signal of continued U.S. alliance to be vital, President Bush agreed to receive Roh at the White House following the California event. The visible show of American support for the breakthrough, Gregg reported to Washington, "may finally drive a stake through the heart" of a widespread South Korean belief that the United States was opposed to direct contacts between Seoul and Moscow.

The site for the meeting in San Francisco turned out to be more of a problem than anyone had anticipated. For security, convenience, and possibly symbolic reasons, the Soviet side proposed the Soviet Consulate General in the northern California city, but the Koreans adamantly resisted this because of historical overtones they considered shameful. In 1896, King Kojong had taken refuge in the Russian legation in Seoul for a year to escape assassination by the Japanese, with the result that Russia won special rights and benefits in a weakened Korea. This humiliation had never been forgotten in Korea, where historians coined a special word, *akwanpachon*, for "kings taking refuge in the Russian legation." After much discussion, the Soviets agreed to hold the meeting in Gorbachev's suite at the Fairmont Hotel.

Although the meeting itself was an unremarkable exchange of generalities, the event marked "a radical change" in Soviet policy from exclusive alliance with North Korea, as Gorbachev acknowledged later in an internal Kremlin report. There was no explicit decision to move to full diplomatic relations, though this was clearly implied and rapidly accomplished after Gorbachev and Roh shook hands. According to Kim Jong In, who was then Roh's senior economic aide, Roh stated near the end of the meeting that the Korean government was prepared to offer "several billion dollars" in economic support. Soviet notes taken at the meeting said Roh "announced a readiness to grant considerable credit" for the purchase of South Korean consumer goods and also pledged cooperation in creation of joint enterprises and in the opening of Soviet Asia. Others who were interviewed for this book insisted that money was not discussed, though everyone knew the issue was an important one.

When Gorbachev asked if Roh had a message for Kim Il Sung, Roh replied that he would welcome Soviet efforts to bring about a North-South rapprochement. Specifically, he asked Gorbachev to do three things: first, to tell Pyongyang that Seoul was ready to meet officially for the discussion of any outstanding question; second, to use Soviet influence to place the North on the path of external opening and internal reform; and third, to convey ROK willingness to discuss and take steps to reduce military confrontation on the peninsula. When Soviet diplomats tried to pass on Roh's message, Pyongyang refused to accept it, calling it "an unbelievable concentration of lies and slander."

At the end of the brief meeting, Roh eagerly asked for a photograph to record the two men together, knowing its political impact on both sides of the thirty-eighth parallel. Gorbachev was reluctant but was finally persuaded by Dobrynin, who argued that "it won't get published in Russia." The official Korean photographer recorded a broadly beaming Roh with his left arm in friendly fashion on the elbow of Gorbachev, who managed only a wisp of a smile.

Roh's press conference immediately afterward was broadcast live to South Korea. With the fall of the Berlin wall and the prospect of German unification, Roh noted, Korea remained in June 1990 the only nation still divided by cold war politics. "As a result of today's meeting, the cold war ice on the Korean peninsula has now begun to crack. We expect that this will be the first major step toward a peaceful and unified Korea," he declared. Roh repeated that Seoul did not wish to isolate the North Korean regime but that the ultimate objective of his *Nordpolitik* policy was to induce North Korea to open up. He told the assembled reporters, "The road between Seoul and Pyongyang is now totally blocked. Accordingly, we have to choose an alternative route to the North Korean capital by way of Moscow and Beijing. This may not be the most direct route but we certainly hope it will be an effective one."

## THE SHEVARDNADZE MISSION

In September 1990, three months after the Gorbachev-Roh meeting and less than two years after swearing "on my word as a party member" that the Soviet Union would not grant diplomatic recognition to South Korea, Soviet foreign minister Shevardnadze returned to Pyongyang to break the news that Moscow had decided to do just that. Shevardnadze's special Aeroflot plane arrived in a gusty wind so strong, there was doubt whether it could land, and his awkward mission met turbulence throughout. When he flew out of Pyongyang two days later, an angry Shevardnadze was smarting from accusations and threats, including a threat of accelerated nuclear weapons development, hurled at him by his North Korean counterpart, Kim Yong Nam. The Soviet foreign minister told his party, as his plane took off, that the experience had been "the most difficult, most unpleasant talk of my life."

◆　◆　◆

Eduard Shevardnadze, the white-maned politician who had succeeded the long-serving Andrei Gromyko as foreign minister in 1985, was a remarkable figure. A native of the southern republic of Georgia (and after the collapse of the Soviet Union, the embattled president of the struggling independent state of Georgia), Shevardnadze had had no diplomatic experience before being chosen by Gorbachev, an old friend, to be his foreign minister in 1985, the first year of the Gorbachev era. Perhaps because of his minority-group status as a Georgian in the Russian-dominated Soviet Union, Shevardnadze proved to be sensitive to the concerns of smaller nations and troubled peoples. While he was among the strongest advocates of democratic policies in domestic affairs and of the New Thinking in relations with the West, Shevardnadze was notably cautious about a rapid policy change on Korea. Alexander Bessmertnykh, who was a senior deputy to Shevardnadze and later his successor as foreign minister, said "he reasoned we have an ally, not an attractive one but a powerful one. He didn't want to give this up by forcing the pace." Another senior Foreign Ministry official, who worked closely with him on Asian matters, called Shevardnadze a very wise man. "He said it is very easy to worsen our relations with North Korea, but it would be extremely difficult to restore them."

How strongly Shevardnadze argued these points within the Kremlin inner circle during the consideration of Korea policy is uncertain. Gorbachev's aide Anatoly Chernyayev, who sat in on Politburo meetings, recalled that "Shevardnadze more than once reminded the Politburo that certain things might evoke irritation on the part of North Korea." According to his account, however, Shevardnadze did not throw the full weight of his influence against the rapid improvement of relations with the South in 1990 but instead told Gorbachev, "You do whatever you want but without me."

Following Gorbachev's meeting with Roh in San Francisco, the decision had been made in Moscow to establish full diplomatic relations with South Korea as of January 1, 1991. In discussing how to tell Pyongyang, it was suggested that Shevardnadze send his Asia chief, Deputy Foreign Minister Igor Rogachev, as a special envoy to do the distasteful job. However, Shevardnadze, a man of courage and honor, felt obligated to go himself, knowing that convincing North Korea to accept the change would be formidable.

On his plane en route to Pyongyang, Shevardnadze worked hard on his brief and his tactics. He decided to tell North Korean foreign minister Kim Yong Nam in a one-on-one meeting at the start of his talks, then to try to persuade Kim Il Sung, later in the visit, to accept the Soviet reversal calmly.

In the one-on-one meeting he had requested, Shevardnadze gave the bad news to Foreign Minister Kim. He argued that North Korea would benefit from Moscow's diplomatic relations with Seoul because Soviet officials would be able to talk directly with the South on North-South issues, the problem of U.S. troops and nuclear weapons, and other topics of importance to Pyongyang. Kim responded with passion against recognition of the South, saying it would reinforce the division of the country and severely aggravate relations between Moscow and Pyongyang. He asked that it be reconsidered.

After more than an hour of private discussion, the two ministers brought the other members of the two delegations into the large, high-ceilinged conference room. With the obligatory portrait of Kim Il Sung peering down at them, the two delegations were placed on opposite sides of a highly polished conference table, marked by North Korean and Soviet flags. Shevardnadze repeated the decision he had brought from Moscow and elaborated the reasons for it. He said the Soviet Union could not ignore such an important country as South Korea, which had become a major economic and political factor in the region and the world. He insisted that recognition of the South would not change the nature of Soviet relations with the North nor Moscow's views on Korean unification. Specifically, he declared, all Soviet obligations toward North Korea, including the 1961 treaty of alliance, would remain in force.

There were three microphones on each side of the long conference table, and the Soviet officials noticed that the Korean foreign minister spoke into his microphone as if he were addressing an unseen audience of greater importance than the delegation in front of him. At first he said he was not ready to reply to Shevardnadze's presentation but would do so later. Then, after being handed a note by an aide who entered the room from outside, he pulled out a prepared document and launched into a lengthy and bitter response, which featured the following points:

- Establishment of ties between the Soviet Union and South Korea would give international legitimacy to the permanent division of Korea. Formal recognition by Moscow would be fundamentally different from and more serious than that by other nations because the Soviet Union, along with the United States, had been responsible for the division of the country in 1945, and because the Soviet Union had been the first to recognize the DPRK as the sole legitimate state in Korea.

- Recognition by Moscow would embolden South Korea to try harder to destroy socialism in the North and swallow it up, along the lines of the East German scenario. It would lead to deepening confrontation in the peninsula.

- If Moscow recognized another part of Korea as legitimate, Pyongyang would be free to recognize other parts of the Soviet Union, which would create trouble for Moscow. (According to one participant, Kim named several places where Pyongyang might establish diplomatic relations, including Khazhakstan and other Central Asian republics of the USSR and the Baltics, which were straining to obtain independence.)

• Soviet recognition of the South would destroy the basis of the 1961 security treaty. Then the North would feel free to take its own actions in the Asia-Pacific region and not be obligated to consult the USSR in considering its policy.

• With the alliance a dead letter, North Korea would consider itself no longer bound by pledges not to create any weapons it desired. (On this point, some Soviet participants recall Kim specifically threatened to create nuclear weapons, but in any case the meaning of his words was clear.)

At the end of the meeting, Shevardnadze asked for time to consider what Kim had said, and he promised to reply the following morning. When he did so, he reiterated that the Soviet Union intended its relationship with North Korea to remain unchanged despite impending recognition of South Korea. As to the threat to take up relations with Soviet republics, Shevardnadze was unconcerned, saying that such contacts could be in the mutual interest of everyone.

Shevardnadze bore down hardest on the threat to create nuclear weapons. As a friend, he said, he would advise against this. Production of nuclear weapons would severely harm the DPRK's relations with the West and the international community, and the Soviet Union would have to react as well. He added, in an echo of Kim Il Sung's official line for years, that there was no possibility of using nuclear weapons on the Korean peninsula, because they would devastate not only the South but the North as well, and also damage China.

In reply, Kim Yong Nam repeated his statements from the previous day, even more harshly than before. In response to a direct question, he said it would be "very difficult" for the Soviet foreign minister to see President Kim Il Sung, who—he said—was out of Pyongyang.

Shevardnadze took this news in good grace at the meeting, but privately he was angry and upset, inasmuch as trying to explain the Soviet policy to the Great Leader had been his principal purpose in coming to Pyongyang. Back at his guest house—a notably smaller and less well-appointed one than that he had occupied two years earlier—Shevardnadze decided to leave at once, abruptly gathering his staff and departing several hours earlier than scheduled.

The Soviet foreign minister was still smarting from his treatment in Pyongyang when he went to New York for the UN General Assembly meetings later in September. While there, he planned to make a joint announcement with South Korea to establish Soviet–ROK diplomatic relations as of January 1. At a diplomatic reception several days before their planned announcement, South Korean foreign minister Choi Ho Joong, under instructions from Seoul, buttonholed Shevardnadze and pleaded with him to move up the date, arguing that "this is a good and right thing, so why not do it immediately?" To Choi's surprise, at their meeting on September 30, Shevardnadze readily agreed. With a flourish, the Soviet foreign minister took out his pen and struck through "January 1, 1991" on the prepared announcement, substituting "September 30, 1990" as the date for inaugurating the new relationship. As Shevardnadze crossed off one date and entered the other, he said under his breath in Russian, loud enough for his party to hear, "That will take care of our friends," meaning the North Koreans.

Pyongyang responded with a bitter denunciation in *Nodong Sinmun,* under the headline, "Diplomatic Relations Sold and Bought With Dollars." Citing past promises from Gorbachev and Shevardnadze not to recognize South Korea, the article declared that "the Soviet Union today is not the Soviet Union of past days when it adhered to socialist internationalism but it has degenerated into a state of a certain other character. . . . The Soviet Union sold off the dignity and honor of a socialist power and the interests and faith of an ally for $2.3 billion" [the amount of a reported South Korean economic cooperation fund for Moscow.] The article was written under the byline of "commentator," a designation given only to the most authoritative statements from North Korea's ruling hierarchy.

North Korea's relations with its original sponsor were headed into a deep freeze, with immense practical as well as political consequences. The Soviet Union was by far Pyongyang's most important trading partner, providing North Korea with most of its imports of weapons and weapons technology and large amounts of machinery

and equipment. Moscow was also an important supplier of petroleum, though not as large as China. Soviet exports to North Korea
were supplied on a highly concessional basis that most other nations
would not have accepted. Even so, North Korea had failed to pay for
much of what it bought, leaving huge overdue bills to the Soviet
Union. Now that trading relationship and more was in doubt.

## "HOW LONG WILL THE RED FLAG FLY?"

The Soviet Union's rapid movement to diplomatic relations with
Seoul was only the latest in a succession of international developments that were making Kim Il Sung's globe spin out of control.
Within little more than a year, the South had established full diplomatic ties and important economic ties with Hungary, Poland, Yugoslavia, Czechoslovakia, Bulgaria, and Romania, all of them Kim's
former allies, all of which had previously shunned the Seoul regime.
The maverick Romanian communist leader Nicolae Ceauşescu, who
had been Kim's special friend, had been overthrown and executed.
Kim's other special European friend, East German leader Erich Honecker, had been deposed and the Berlin wall opened. The former
East German communist regime, North Korea's close European ally,
was in the process of being taken over by the capitalistic West. As a
result of the fall of communism in Europe, there was intense speculation that Kim Il Sung and his regime would be the next to go.

In advance of the sensational Gorbachev-Roh meeting in San
Francisco, it had been highly uncertain how North Korea would
react. Three days before the meeting, the State Department's Korea
desk had speculated in a confidential briefing paper that "the shock of
Gorbachev's meeting with Roh—especially when he has avoided visiting North Korea—could spark a major leadership crisis in Pyongyang, which could heighten military tensions on the peninsula. It will
be hard for the North to let an insult of this magnitude pass. In their
rage and frustration, Kim Il Sung and Kim Jong Il might lash out at
the USSR, the ROK, or us." The chief of the State Department's
Bureau of Intelligence and Research, in a separate confidential memorandum to his superiors, said that in the aftermath of the San Francisco meeting, a "firestorm" was likely in Pyongyang. In talking

points submitted by the State Department to the White House in preparation for President Bush's conversation with Roh following the meeting, a central question on the minds of American officials was, "Could Pyongyang strike out irrationally?"

In fact, rather than turn inward or "lash out," as feared after the Soviet setback, Pyongyang sharply intensified a flurry of diplomatic activism with China, Japan, and South Korea that it had started several months earlier. Overtures were also being made to the United States, but Washington wasn't listening. In sum, North Korea sought at least briefly to match the diplomatic accomplishments of its rival below the thirty-eighth parallel. However, it was less prepared and less well equipped to make serious gains.

Only a week after Shevardnadze's abrupt departure from Pyongyang, Kim Il Sung traveled by train to Shenyang, in northeast China, for unannounced meetings with Jiang Zemin, general secretary of the Chinese Communist Party, on September 11 and Deng Xiaoping, the senior Chinese leader, on September 12. Among old friends, Kim did not disguise the fact that he had been severely shaken by the loss of his friends and allies in Europe and even more by the Soviet Union's decisions. According to a former Chinese diplomat who had access to the details, Kim Il Sung's central question for Deng was, "How long will the red flag fly?" In other words, how long will communism last, in view of the European and Soviet developments? Deng responded optimistically that the outlook was still bright. Although the Soviet Union was faltering, Deng insisted that Asian countries were defending the faith and that Marxism-Leninism was still strong in China, Vietnam, and Cuba as well as in North Korea.

Kim also raised the question of North Korean economic reforms. Deng, who had been urging Kim for years to follow his reformist example, encouraged him anew. The North Korean leader also made a subtle plea that China not follow the Soviet lead in recognizing the South, or at least slow down its moves in this direction. Beijing's trade with Seoul had been rapidly growing, sea and air routes had been opening up, and informal contacts among business and government leaders had been initiated. Despite Kim's plea, China agreed with South Korea a month after the Shenyang meeting to exchange trade offices equipped with quasi-diplomatic consular functions, an important step but not a widely noted or dramatic one. Chinese officials were willing to go slow but not to stop their advance toward Seoul.

Kim Il Sung's interaction with the other great Asian power, Japan, was more dramatic. On September 24, as a result of contacts that had begun in the spring and accelerated after the Gorbachev–Roh meeting in June, a chartered Japan Air Line jet landed in Pyongyang bearing forty-four Japanese Diet members with accompanying Foreign Ministry officials, aides, and journalists—by far the most important Japanese official mission ever to visit the North. Over the next four days, the Great Leader deployed all his personal charm and diplomatic skill to negotiate an unexpected breakthrough with the country he had fought in World War II and had long treated as an unregenerate antagonist.

Japan had normalized its relations with South Korea in 1965, expressing deep regret for the "unfortunate period" of Japanese occupation from 1910 to 1945 and providing $800 million in grants and credits as compensation. In the years that followed, Japanese trade, investment, and technology had been powerful forces behind the South's rapid economic development. Allied with both countries, the United States strongly supported the South Korean rapprochement with Japan and worked to reduce subsequent threats to the relationship.

North Korea's relations with Japan had been much more tenuous. Kim Il Sung had made modest overtures in the early 1970s, at the time of the U.S.–China opening and the initiation of the North-South talks, but such a Pyongyang-Tokyo rapprochement was vehemently opposed by Seoul and given no encouragement from Washington. Unofficial contacts between the Japanese government and North Korea were carried on mainly through parliamentarians of the Japan Socialist Party. The abnormal relationship between the two countries was dramatically illustrated by the legend printed on Japanese passports, "This passport is valid for all countries and areas except North Korea (Democratic People's Republic of Korea.)"

Late in 1988, behind the scenes, Pyongyang began reconsidering its Japan policy and making cautious overtures to Tokyo. The first clear sign of Japanese receptiveness was a January 1989 Foreign Ministry statement declaring that "Japan does not maintain a hostile policy toward North Korea" and that it would be appropriate "to move positively toward improved relations" if Pyongyang so desired. The statement also expressed hope for the release of two Japanese fishermen who had been held on espionage charges by North Korea since 1983 for permitting a stowaway to leave aboard their ship.

The Diet delegation that flew into Pyongyang was unique in containing leaders of Japan's ruling Liberal Democratic Party (LDP) as well as those of the Socialists, and especially because it was headed by the most powerful figure in Japanese politics, Shin Kanemaru. The gruff 75-year-old LDP kingmaker held no formal government post but was widely considered the power behind several prime ministers, including the incumbent Toshiki Kaifu, who had provided a "party to party" letter for Kanemaru to take to Pyongyang.* Kanemaru, who had no foreign policy experience, overrode objections from the Foreign Ministry in accepting the North Korean invitation at the time he did.

On the second day of the visit, the entire Japanese delegation was put aboard a special train in Pyongyang and taken to a resort in the Myohyang Mountains, one of North Korea's great scenic spots and the site of Kim Il Sung's favorite villa. After a morning of high-level meetings and a luncheon hosted by Kim, the delegation returned to Pyongyang—minus Kanemaru and a few aides, who had remained behind at Kim's insistence. That evening and the following morning, Kim and Kanemaru had two lengthy and intimate meetings, joined only by Kim's Japanese-language interpreter, in which Kim won Kanemaru's confidence and trust. There were no Japanese witnesses and no notes taken, but a Japanese official who spoke to Kanemaru soon after the meetings said Kim was furious at the Soviet Union and spoke of the necessity for "yellow skins" to stick together against "white skins." The official said it was clear to him that Kim was worried about the Russians most of all, even more than the

---

*Two years later, when Kanemaru fell from power and was jailed for tax evasion after $51 million in gold bars, cash, and other assets were found in his home, the scandal helped drive the LDP from power for the first time in thirty-eight years.

Americans. Kanemaru came out of his conferences with Kim with tears in his eyes and praise for the sincerity of the Great Leader.

During these and parallel meetings among the officials who had returned to Pyongyang, North Korea made a surprise proposal for immediate normalization of relations with Japan. Reversing Pyongyang's previous position, this proposal implied forthright Japanese acceptance of two Koreas, which North Korea had always opposed. The payoff for North Korea would be a large sum of Japanese reparations, in keeping with the precedent of the 1965 Japan–South Korea accord. In hopes of getting quick cash, Pyongyang proposed that some of the reparations money, which it reckoned in the billions of dollars, be paid even before diplomatic relations were established.

After a marathon negotiating session from which the accompanying Foreign Ministry representatives were excluded, the Japanese delegation, composed of the ruling LDP and the Socialist parties, issued a three-party declaration with the North Korean Workers Party. Among other things, the joint statement declared that Japan should "fully and formally apologize and compensate the DPRK" for the thirty-six years of Japanese occupation of Korea and also for the forty-five years of abnormal relations after World War II. This created a furor in Tokyo and Seoul because it was issued without coordination with South Korea, because its went well beyond the 1965 Tokyo–Seoul accord, and because of fear that some of Japan's funds could be used to support North Korea's military and nuclear weapons program.

As a result of the uproar, Kanemaru flew to Seoul to express regrets to President Roh, and apologized to U.S. Ambassador to Japan Michael Armacost for not consulting the United States. The negotiations with North Korea for the normalization of relations were turned over to the Foreign Ministry, which stiffened the Japanese position on the nuclear question and other issues. Not surprisingly, under Foreign Ministry leadership the talks got nowhere. The only tangible and lasting result of Kim Il Sung's initiative with Kanemaru was release of the two Japanese fishermen shortly after Kanemaru went home.

Another impor     North Korean initiative in this period was to restart high-level public talks—and high-level secret talks as well—with South Korea. On May 31, just days before the Gorbachev-Roh meeting, the Supreme People's Assembly called for the North-South dialogue to resume immediately across the board after months of inactivity. The North had frozen the talks early in the year after the United States and South Korea announced their annual Team Spirit military exercise.

Three weeks later, the North sent a telephone message to the South denouncing its "flunkyist and divisive antinational acts" with the Soviet Union but, more importantly, proposing to restart preparations for high-level North-South talks. Preliminary meetings continued over the summer, resulting in an agreement that a delegation headed by the North Korean prime minister would visit Seoul September 4–7 and that the South Korean prime minister would lead a high-level delegation to Pyongyang October 16–19. These meetings were at a higher level than previous North-South exchanges.

In early October, between the first and second round of the prime ministerial talks, a three-man delegation headed by NSP (formerly KCIA) director Suh Dong Kwon met secretly in a Pyongyang villa with Kim Il Sung and Kim Jong Il. A month later the North sent Yun Ki Bok, a Workers Party secretary who had been the political commissar for the 1972 Red Cross talks, and two other officials to meet Roh secretly in Seoul.

Suh told me in an interview for this book that these meetings came close to agreement on a North-South summit conference, to be held in North Korea early in 1991, but failed due to disagreement on a proposed joint declaration dealing with unification. Another senior ROK official familiar with the meetings, however, scoffed at this idea, saying that the two sides were never close to bridging fundamental disagreements.

The Pyongyang meeting with Suh was the first and only time that Kim Jong Il met with senior representatives of the South during his father's lifetime. While his father did most of the talking, the younger Kim occasionally interjected an opinion in a seemingly insecure way that did not impress the Seoul officials. When asked at the meeting, Kim Jong Il readily agreed to a separate meeting with Suh, but later the visitors were told he was unable to keep this promise because he was "too busy." Kim Il Sung pointedly told the South Koreans, "As long as I'm alive, I will rule the country."

Leaving no stone unturned, Kim Il Sung also made efforts to achieve a breakthrough in ties with the United States, which he had always regarded as the real power in the opposition camp. On May 24, 1990, the day after Dobrynin's secret meeting with Roh in Seoul, Kim delivered an important policy speech to a formal meeting of the North Korean legislature, the Supreme People's Assembly. Departing from his unyielding stand against the acceptance of U.S. military forces in the peninsula, Kim declared, "If the United States cannot withdraw all her troops from South Korea at once, she will be able to do so by stages." In case Washington was not paying attention, Pyongyang used the tenth meeting of American and North Korean political counselors in Beijing on May 30 to pass along the text of Kim's policy speech. In the meantime, on May 28, North Korea made its first positive response to U.S. requests for the return of Korean War remains, handing over five sets of remains it said were American. On May 31, the day that the Gorbachev–Roh meeting was publicly announced, North Korea made public a new disarmament proposal that was notably free of anti-U.S. or anti–South Korean rhetoric and that appeared to be more realistic than earlier proposals.

At this point the United States, which had become increasingly alarmed at the progress of North Korea's nuclear program, was in no mood for conciliatory responses. State Department talking points drafted for Bush's June 6 meeting with Roh, following the San Francisco meeting with Gorbachev, did not reflect any of Pyongyang's moves except for a brief mention of the return of the U.S. remains. Nevertheless, White House press secretary Marlin Fitzwater, in an effort to mitigate a deepening North Korean sense of isolation, made an unusual unsolicited announcement following the Bush–Roh meeting: "The United States reaffirms that it is not a threat to North Korean security, and we seek to improve relations with that country." He added that "the pace and scope of any improvement will depend importantly on North Korea's actions," mentioning specifically North Korea's willingness to permit international nuclear inspections. Beyond the press secretary's remarks, however, Washington made no effort to engage the unpopular—and stricken—North Koreans.

In retrospect, Washington's failure to explore improvement in relations with Pyongyang in the last half of 1990, when North Korea was still reeling from the blow inflicted by the Soviet Union, was an opportunity missed. The chances seem strong that Kim Il Sung would have responded eagerly to a U.S. initiative at a time when his traditional alliance with Moscow was in shambles and his alliance with Beijing was under growing stress. But while the United States continued to pressure North Korea on the nuclear issue in public and private, it offered no incentives to Pyongyang to take the actions it sought, even "modest initiatives" of the kind that had been taken near the end of the Reagan administration. This was due in part to the Bush administration's preoccupation with the Persian Gulf following the Iraqi invasion of Kuwait on August 2, 1990, but it was also due to the inability of Washington policymakers to agree on any actions regarding North Korea. The gridlock would continue until Bush's nuclear initiatives in September 1991, which were prompted by developments in the Soviet Union rather than Korea-related considerations.

## SOVIET–SOUTH KOREAN ECONOMIC NEGOTIATIONS

The months following the Gorbachev-Roh meeting in San Francisco were busy ones for Soviet–South Korean negotiations, most of which centered on the Soviet requests for aid. Two weeks after meeting Roh in June, Gorbachev wrote to him inviting a Korean economic delegation to Moscow to work on the issue. Headed by Roh's senior economic and foreign policy advisers at the Blue House, the delegation went to the Soviet capital in early August. It discussed forty potential projects in the Soviet Union but insisted that no economic aid programs could be made final until after the establishment of official diplomatic relations. Shevardnadze's impromptu action at the United Nations on September 30, recognizing South Korea, took care of that problem and cleared the way for further economic negotiations.

After correspondence in October between the two heads of state, in which Roh expressed his desire to meet Gorbachev in Moscow, Gorbachev aide Vadim Medvedev, a member of the newly empowered Presidential Council, traveled to Seoul in November with an invitation to Roh to make a state visit before the end of the year. Medvedev also brought a request from Gorbachev for $4 billion in credits, some to finance purchases of Korean goods and some in untied loans. The visitor suggested that this be announced by Roh during his forthcoming meetings in Moscow.

In the Kremlin on December 13–16, Roh met Gorbachev and with him issued a Declaration of General Principles of Relations. In deference to North Korea, the Declaration was careful to state that "the development of links and contacts between the ROK and the USSR must not in any way affect their relations with third countries or undermine obligations they assume under multilateral or bilateral treaties and agreements." In a private meeting, Roh asked Gorbachev to "exert an appropriate influence" on North Korea to develop a more cooperative relationship. The Soviet leader said he was doing what he could—which wasn't much, in view of Pyongyang's angry reaction to his new friendship with Seoul.

As an honored guest in the formerly forbidden capital, Roh also met Russian president Boris Yeltsin, spoke at Moscow State University, and laid a wreath with full Soviet military honors at the tomb of Moscow's Unknown Soldiers. Roh brought with him to Moscow twenty Korean business leaders as a sign of interest in the Soviet economy, but he declined to discuss aid projects or figures in detail. According to a former Soviet official, Roh told Gorbachev, "Don't worry about the aid; just take my word for it."

The two sides agreed that an aid program would be negotiated in Seoul in mid-January by Deputy Prime Minister Yuri Maslyukov, who had handled the Soviet side of the preliminary discussions. Before this could happen, however, Gorbachev on December 31 suddenly decided to send Deputy Foreign Minister Igor Rogachev to Seoul as a special envoy, seeking a major infusion of cash to help see the Soviet Union through the winter. This was dismaying to Gorbachev's professional Korea-watchers and much of his economic team, who feared that cash aid from Seoul would be wasted on short-term spending rather than applied to productive long-term projects. But Gorbachev was desperate. That fall he had even made a private and personal appeal for immediate financial help to Secretary of State James Baker, who then solicited a $4 billion line of credit for Moscow from traditionally anticommunist Saudi Arabia.

On January 6, Rogachev flew into Seoul with a team of economic and diplomatic officials aboard a special Aeroflot plane, carrying a letter from Gorbachev asking for $5 billion in aid, including $2 billion in an immediate untied bank loan—in effect, ready cash. The Koreans were shocked by the size and nature of the request. Roh had said publicly on his trip to Moscow that cash grants were "out of the question" because such a big country as the Soviet Union "would not accept grants from a small country like ours even if we offered them."

To Rogachev's unexpected request, the Koreans initially offered $350 million in ready cash. Rogachev declared the offer "unacceptable" in view of his long journey and the many statements of support that had been made by Koreans during earlier discussions. After intense bargaining and a threat to break off the talks and return home premptorily, Rogachev was able to raise the offer to $500 million. Suddenly the tables had been turned on the Moscow-Seoul relationship; the supposed superpower was the supplicant and the Korean side was deciding what it could provide. On the third day of negotiations, the Koreans agreed to supply $1 billion in cash and to negotiate later with Maslyukov on the rest of the aid program.

Maslyukov's mission three weeks later resulted in an agreement to supply $1.5 billion more in loans to finance Soviet imports of Korean consumer goods and industrial raw materials, and $500 million for the financing of plants and other capital goods. Together with the $1 billion bank loan obtained by Rogachev, the total was $3 billion, all of which was to be repaid at prevailing interest rates after a three-year grace period.

The deal was controversial in Seoul, especially because Korea had to borrow the money to lend to the Soviet Union. Korean officials justified the arrangement by arguing that the relationship with Moscow was a valuable asset to national security. According to a senior Korean official, Kim Chong Whi told Maslyukov during the negotiations that it would be politically impossible to aid the Soviet Union while Moscow continued to supply arms to North Korea. Maslyukov responded that he had personally rejected a recent North Korean request to Moscow for a new tank factory and would take similar action on future requests. Soviet exports of military equipment to North Korea dropped sharply in 1991, but it is unclear whether this was due to changed political decisions or simply to the economic straits of both Moscow and Pyongyang.

The last official meeting of Gorbachev and Roh, when the Soviet leader stopped at Korea's Cheju Island after a state visit to Japan in April 1991, included a financial transaction of a different sort. Gorbachev returned to Moscow with an unannounced gift from Roh of $100,000 in U.S. currency. An aide to Roh told me later that the money was at least nominally intended for "victims of Chernobyl," the Soviet civil nuclear disaster that had taken place five years earlier. Gorbachev's chief of staff, Valery Boldin, said the Soviet leader eventually had papers drawn up contributing the money to a children's hospital.

Slightly less than half ($1.47 billion) of the ROK aid for the Soviet Union was actually paid out before the collapse of the USSR in December 1991. As the successor state, Russia assumed the debts but lacked the money to make more than token repayments. Eventually Russia began providing tanks, helicopters, missiles, and spare parts to Seoul in partial repayment of the loans. By then Russia had again become an arms exporter to the world, but this time to nations that could pay with hard cash rather than to those with which it shared ideological solidarity. In supplying South Korea with arms, Moscow reversed its historic role as an armorer and ally of the state it had created north of the thirty-eighth parallel.

The Soviet reversal and later the Soviet collapse would have a powerful impact on North Korea. Strategically, it left Pyongyang more vulnerable and more isolated than before. Economically, the loss of North Korea's most generous and most important trading partner began a steady decline that would increasingly sap the strength of the Kim regime.

# 10

## CHINA SHIFTS ITS GROUND

In mid-June 1991 a Chinese civil airliner bringing Foreign Minister Qian Qichen and his official party from Beijing floated down slowly over a flat green landscape toward a landing on the outskirts of Pyongyang. Making its gradual approach to the capital's airport, the plane passed over a seemingly deserted country, with ribbons of roadways nearly empty of traffic and hardly any people visible in the neatly divided plots of farmland or around big apartment houses and other buildings. Seated in the tourist section of the plane, behind the foreign minister's first-class compartment, I peered down for the first time at the territory of North Korea and wrote in my journal that it looked to be a strange land "left deserted by some invisible plague."

Then as the plane roared down the runway, hundreds of people came into view: a colorful crowd lined up in well-ordered rows on the tarmac, enthusiastically waving pink plastic boughs. As we taxied up and the motors were turned off, we could hear martial music from a khaki-clad military band. From the roof of the terminal building, a giant portrait of Kim Il Sung looked down on the scene.

Waiting near the foot of the steps to welcome the high-ranking Chinese guest and his party was North Korean deputy premier and foreign minister Kim Yong Nam, the man who was also instrumental in my own invitation to visit. It was pure coincidence that I arrived on the same plane and was in Pyongyang at the same time as the Chinese foreign minister. Although secretive North Koreans had told me nothing of the discussions between the two neighbors, I realized later that I had witnessed the launching of an episode of diplomatic theater that had led to a major readjustment of the relations between Beijing and Pyongyang.

From its short-lived conquest of ancient Choson before the time of Christ until the twentieth century, China had been the foreign nation with the greatest importance in the Korean world. For more than a thousand years, until Korea's invention of its *hangul* alphabet in the fifteenth century, Chinese characters formed the basis of the Korean written language, and they remained important in classical writing into the modern era. Korea adopted not only Buddhism from China but also Confucianism, which remains at the heart of many Korean relationships, public and private. Throughout most of its history, Korea paid tribute to its giant neighbor at the court of the Middle Kingdom. Koreans called China *daeguk,* "big state" or "elder state."

China's intimate alliance with North Korea dates back to the Chinese communist sponsorship of Kim Il Sung's rebel bands against the Japanese in World War II. In the Korean War, China saved North Korea from defeat by sending its "volunteer" troops across the Yalu River, at the cost of 900,000 of its own soldiers killed or wounded.

Even more than the Soviet Union, China maintained a warm official friendship with the North Korean state through most of its existence, marred only by the revolutionary tumult of the Cultural Revolution. For decades both sides professed that China and North Korea were as closely linked as "lips and teeth." In 1970, shortly before Beijing's opening to Washington and Tokyo, Premier Chou Enlai declared that "China and Korea are neighbors linked by mountains and rivers. . . . This friendship cemented in blood was forged and has grown in the course of the protracted struggle against our common enemies, U.S. and Japanese imperialism. . . . Common interests and common problems of security have bound and united our two peoples together." Even after the 1971–72 shift in Beijing's foreign policy, Chinese leaders were careful to maintain close ties with North Korea, which was seen as an important ideological client and ally on China's border. On the North Korean side, Kim Il Sung in 1982 called the DPRK–China friendship "an invincible force that no one can ever break. . . . It will last as long as the mountains and rivers to the two countries exist."

Until recent years, the government in Beijing had kept aloof from anticommunist South Korea, which was the only Asian nation to continue to recognize the Nationalist regime on Taiwan as the legitimate government of China into the 1990s. Although Sino–South Korean trade had grown steadily after China opened up to market economics, the Chinese leadership was much more cautious than that of the Soviet Union in moving toward normalization of political relations with the South.

Nonetheless, by mid-1991 Beijing was following Moscow's lead in moving toward a much closer relationship with Seoul. The previous year, according to Beijing's figures, Chinese trade with South Korea had been seven times larger than its trade with the North and was increasing rapidly, bringing with it a greater need for multifaceted relations. Moreover, the termination of the Sino–Soviet dispute and Moscow's sharply diminished ties with North Korea made Chinese leaders less concerned with the possibility that adjusting their policy toward South Korea could push Kim Il Sung into the arms of the Soviet Union. In addition, China could see a potential domestic political gain in establishing diplomatic relations with South Korea, because it would force Seoul to terminate its long-standing official relationship with Taiwan, thus giving a sharp blow to the island state.

The seriousness of its new situation with China had been brought home dramatically to North Korea during the four-day visit of Chinese premier Li Peng in May, the month before Foreign Minister Qian's trip to Pyongyang. According to a variety of reports, Li broke the unwelcome news that China did not oppose admission of both North and South Korea to the United Nations and would not veto South Korea's application, despite the opposition of Pyongyang to dual admission. China's refusal to veto would assure Seoul's entry because the only other obstacle—a possible veto by the Soviet Union—had been eliminated in April when Gorbachev, during his visit to South Korea's Cheju Island, had promised that Moscow would support Seoul's application for UN membership.

On May 27, North Korea announced it had "no choice" but to apply for UN membership—even though dual membership would be an obstacle to unification—because otherwise the South would join the United Nations alone. This forced reversal at the hands of Moscow and Beijing was a symbol of North Korea's diminished clout with its former communist sponsors. It also may have been the underlying reason for Foreign Minister Qian's visit three weeks later, which was long on ceremony and short on substance. It appeared to be China's way of mending relations after forcing the North Koreans to swallow the bitter pill of dual North-South admission to the UN.

## A VISIT TO NORTH KOREA

Although it was a coincidence that I arrived with the Chinese minister, it was hardly surprising that someone of diplomatic importance shared my commercial airline flight. The Chinese civil aviation jet was the only plane to arrive from the outside world that day in the entire country of more than 20 million people. Only eight scheduled airplane flights and seven trains entered North Korea in a week in 1991, making it one of the most reclusive and mysterious nations on earth.

My traveling companion, *Washington Post* Tokyo correspondent T. R. Reid, and I were greeted in the airport terminal by our official hosts from the Society for Cultural Relations with Foreign Countries and transported to our hotel in two chauffeured red Mercedes sedans from the government motor pool. So few other vehicles were visible in either direction on the twelve-mile road into town that I could easily count them: twenty-three cars, six buses, three minivans, three trucks, and two jeeps—at midday Monday, or about three vehicles per mile, on the main highway into North Korea's capital city. Hundreds of people could be seen walking along the roadside or waiting patiently for the few overcrowded buses. Several days later, when Reid and I traveled by train to the southernmost city of Kaesong and the nearby DMZ, we learned that a special allocation of gasoline, approved at high levels, had been required to take us by car less than five miles from town to an observation post looking across at South Korea. The energy shortage seemed to have idled much of North

Korea's industry as well. I saw a number of overhead construction cranes during my week of travels, but not one that was in operation.

For North Korea, 1991 was a terrible year economically. Beginning in January, the Soviet Union demanded hard currency for its exports to Pyongyang rather than continue the traditional concessional arrangements of the past. As a result, North Korean imports from its most important trading partner declined precipitously. The drop was particularly sharp in energy imports, which fell by 75 percent from the 1990 level. This cutback made North Korea dependent on China for more than two-thirds of its imported energy. However, China was unwilling or unable to make up for the Soviet losses and in May notified Pyongyang that it would soon discontinue its concessional sales. The dire result was that in 1991–92 North Korea was forced to abruptly reduce its total petroleum consumption by between one-fourth and one-third, resulting in the deserted roadways and idle construction projects that I observed.

One might expect from all this to find a regime in a deep funk, fearful of the future and uncertain about which way to go. The greatest surprise to me was that Pyongyang's officialdom was, outwardly at least, undaunted by the revolutionary reversals in their alliances. In the North Korean worldview, the faltering of communism in the Soviet Union and its collapse in Eastern Europe proved the correctness of Kim Il Sung's independent policy of *juche* and his consistent refusal to formally join the Soviet bloc. Deputy Premier and Foreign Minister Kim Yong Nam spoke optimistically to me of "our people advancing along the road of the socialism they have chosen—socialism of their own style." This phrase, reminiscent of China's "socialism with Chinese characteristics," which justified Beijing's swing toward market economics, had first appeared the previous December in a Workers Party organ. In this case, "our own style" justified the absence of change rather than a deviation from the previous well-worn path.

To the evidence before my eyes in 1991, North Korea was unique, a land unlike any other I had seen in my extensive travels as a correspondent. The capital, Pyongyang, had been so leveled by American bombing in the Korean War that the head of the U.S. bomber command had halted further air strikes, saying that "there is nothing standing worthy of the name." Kim Il Sung had rebuilt it

from the ashes to a meticulously planned urban center of broad boule-
vards, monumental structures, and square-cut apartment buildings
that resembled a stage set more than a working capital. Indeed, it was
a synthetic city in many respects: according to foreign diplomats, the
population was periodically screened, and the sick, elderly, or disabled, along with anyone deemed politically unreliable, were evicted
from the capital.

Pyongyang was dominated by homage to Kim Il Sung. Among
its most imposing features was the Tower of the *Juche* Idea, an obelisk
almost as high as the Washington Monument, which was erected for
the Great Leader's seventieth birthday to celebrate his self-reliance
dogma; an Arch of Triumph larger than the one in Paris, celebrating
Kim's return from victory over Japan in 1945; and Kim Il Sung Stadium, seating 100,000 people for mass demonstrations of loyalty to
the ruler and the regime. Less celebrated but equally prominent was a
mammoth 105-story hotel, built to be the tallest in Asia but that
contained architectural defects so serious that it had never been occupied and probably never will be. Pyongyang struck me as a city designed by Russian-trained architects with some nods to Mao at the
height of the allegiance to the Little Red Book. It appeared well
suited for gigantic displays but not very convenient for people, who
had few cars and buses and, unlike Beijing, no bicycles to help them
traverse the capital's massive spaces.

On a guided tour of the city, we encountered several hundred
fourth-grade boys, led by an adult instructor, doing mass exercises
with wooden swords or, lacking these, pieces of flat wood cut to the
length of swords. The boys slashed, jumped, and shouted with enthusiasm and on cue. This was only one of many manifestations of the
collective activities that were being emphasized. People on the streets
avoided glancing at us when we approached, and the children in a
model school did not even look up from work when their headmaster,
two strange Westerners, and guides invaded their classroom—evidently because they had been instructed to take no notice. I found this
chilling and dehumanizing.

On the other hand, there were signs that behind the public
facade, North Koreans had not lost their individuality and humanity.
During a performance at the Pyongyang Circus, a spectacular display

of acrobatic talent, children squealed with laughter and uninhibited delight at an act featuring trained dogs. Another evening at the apartment of the sister of one of our guides, we experienced the warmth of Korean family life as a 7-year-old in pigtails played a small piano and her reluctant 5-year-old sister was coaxed into doing a little dance. The apartment, while modest by Western standards, was doubtless better than most, and a special allocation of food had apparently been granted to provide the guests with an abundant home-cooked dinner. Although hardly typical, it was the closest to everyday life that we were permitted to come.

Outside the capital and away from the country's few superhighways, the landscape reminded me of what I had seen in the South in the 1950s and 1960s. The overnight train to Kaesong, the city just north of the demilitarized zone, took six hours to go about 120 miles, with antiquated equipment over a rough roadbed. Along the way, I saw a steam locomotive still in use, no doubt burning coal from North Korean mines. I awoke early in the morning to look out at hills and rice paddies shrouded with the familiar heavy morning mist and small houses with chimney pipes on the side arising from traditional under-the-floor heating. Here and there the landscape was broken by dreary gray buildings that had been thrown up to house members of collective farms.

All this was in startling contrast to the traffic-choked, neon-lit modernity of Seoul and the dramatically improved living conditions of the South Korean countryside I had seen in recent years. While poverty had not been abolished, the wealth and health of most South Korean citizens had undergone revolutionary change for the better since I first observed them in the immediate aftermath of the Korean War, and immense change from the early 1970s when I spent so much time in South Korea as a correspondent. In the 1970s the South had the look and feel of a rawboned, gutsy frontier country with garlic on its breath, where its cities gave rise to a hundred pungent odors and even the newsprint had a peculiar musky smell. By 1991, South Korea had arrived, with high-rise buildings crowding out most of the slanting roofs of traditional houses in Seoul and other cities, and good roads and modern conveniences in the countryside. Nearly 10 million people, close to one in four of South Korea's 43 million citizens, were licensed drivers of the country's 4.2 million motor vehicles. More than 3 million foreign tourists visited the South, and close to 2 million ROK citizens traveled abroad during the year. In Seoul, nearly all white-collar workers now brushed their teeth after each meal, causing the pervasive garlic smell to nearly disappear from the capital's elevators and subway cars. From rock music to high fashion, South Korea was connected to the world.

The nexus between North and South was the Joint Security Area at Panmunjom, the principal destination on our trip from Pyongyang. Approaching from the North through the DPRK's hilltop pavilion, the JSA appeared benign and ordinary. Compared with the heavily manned southern side, we saw remarkably few troops. Dozens of schoolboys wearing the red kerchiefs of a youth organization were posing for a group picture with their teachers on the steps overlooking the small, temporary one-story buildings straddling the dividing line where Military Armistice Commission meetings took place.

As our small party of myself, fellow correspondent Tom Reid, and North Korean escorts approached the military demarcation line between North and South, an American sailor and two American MPs stood just across the line assiduously taking our pictures, most likely for U.S. and ROK intelligence. I felt little of the atmosphere of menace that I recall from visits to Checkpoint Charlie in Berlin before the wall came down, or even from my earlier visits to Panmunjom from the southern side. Perhaps it was because I was inside the enemy tent, having just been briefed by a North Korean major who was accompanying us, and for once I was not concerned about an imminent breach of the peace from the North, or from the South either.

Earlier in Pyongyang, Foreign Minister Kim Yong Nam had emphasized the high priority his government placed on negotiations to reduce tension at the DMZ and on the peninsula generally, because "we still have heavy danger of war." Kim painstakingly recounted North Korea's efforts to begin direct talks with the United States or three-way talks that would also include South Korea. "We have the intention and willingness to improve relations with the United States, but we cannot accept all the unjust demands of the U.S. side," he said. Recognizing that the issues are deeply rooted in history, he said, "the two countries must first of all officially make public their will to improve bilateral relations and start negotiations." Knowing the apprehension about North Korea in Washington and the deep reluctance to engage its diplomats, I had great doubt this would happen anytime soon.

Minister Kim Yong Nam, born on February 24, 1928, had risen step by step, by diligence and loyalty, through the ranks of the Workers Party to become party secretary for international affairs and, two months after the Rangoon bombing of October 1983, vice premier and foreign minister. The disaster in Rangoon had touched off an extensive reorganization of the bureaucracy dealing with North-South and international affairs. As the new foreign minister, Kim had set about restructuring DPRK diplomacy along more professional lines, in the process becoming the sponsor of many of the country's career diplomats.

A Chinese official who has known Kim for many years said that he has extremely good literary skills and that he drafted many speeches for Kim Il Sung. This may have been the source of his unusually close relationship to the Great Leader, who elevated him to full membership in the Politburo in 1980, while he was still party secretary for international affairs—a job that does not usually carry such weight or power. Kim's younger brother, Kim Du Nam, was also close to Kim Il Sung, being a four-star general and military secretary to the Great Leader.

I had met Kim Yong Nam during his first trip to the United Nations as foreign minister in 1984—at the time, a rare visit to New York by a high-ranking North Korean. My persistent requests for an interview finally won out over the extreme caution and skepticism of Pyongyang's UN observer mission. A lengthy first meeting in a cavernous Manhattan hotel suite was notable for Kim's prepared declaration, which he read from a cloth-covered notebook he took from his pocket, that North Korea was interested in talks with the United States on the "confidence building measures" mentioned by President Reagan in his UN address several weeks earlier. This was a reversal of the previous North Korean dismissal of confidence-building proposals and was clearly intended to be an important signal to Washington.

The Reagan administration, which at this point was contemptuous of North Korea and busily preparing for the U.S. presidential election in November, did not respond. But when *The Washington Post* placed my account of the interview on page one, the North Korean diplomatic hesitation about me vanished, at least temporarily. After that, I saw Kim or his senior deputy, Kang Sok Ju, nearly every time they came for their annual UN visits, even though their interview pronouncements never made the front page again.

In my 1991 meeting in Pyongyang, as in other meetings with him over the years, I found Kim Yong Nam a puzzling figure. In greetings before business began, he was cordial and relaxed, but once at work, he relentlessly followed his script in a way that reminded me of former Soviet foreign minister Andrei Gromyko. An American diplomat described his performance as resembling a robot's. Koh Yong Hwan, a former North Korean diplomat and high-level interpreter who defected to the South, called him a "model" for North Korean officialdom: "If Kim Il Sung was pointing to a wall and said there is a door, Kim Yong Nam would believe that and try to go through it." Yet by all accounts he is highly intelligent and, due to his high position and prestige within the system, an important behind-the-scenes figure in Pyongyang.

The foreign minister's polar opposite in demeanor was the colorful and flamboyant Kim Yong Sun, another important figure in Pyongyang's diplomacy, whom I met for the first time on my 1991 trip. Born in 1934, his career path was notable for its craggy leaps and reverses. Originally a politically minded provincial official in the southeastern part of the country, he served in political posts in other areas before joining the International Department of the Workers Party. In the mid-1980s, he was ousted and reportedly sent to work at hard labor in a coal mine as punishment for decadent behavior in organizing Western-style dancing at party headquarters. According to North Korean lore, he was rescued from oblivion by his friendship with Kim Kyong Hui, Kim Il Sung's youngest daughter by his first wife and the younger sister of Kim Jong Il. In contrast to the austere foreign minister, Kim Yong Sun is reputed to be a hard-drinking, partying buddy of Kim Jong Il, a ladies' man and devotee of high living.

Unlike all others whom I interviewed in Pyongyang in 1991, Kim Yong Sun did not wear a Western coat and tie but a zippered olive-drab short jacket similar to the U.S. Army's "Ike jacket." Sitting across a conference table at Workers Party headquarters, he apologized for his casual dress, saying that he had come straight from a meeting with workers and peasants in the countryside, who had encouraged him to return quickly to the capital when he told them he had an appointment with *Washington Post* reporters. It was a somewhat flattering touch, until I learned from a delegation of American Quakers months later that he had told them the same story, wearing the same jacket, at the start of their meeting.

Kim Yong Sun had more self-confidence and flair than anyone else I met in North Korea. His authoritative yet freewheeling style appeared to be grounded in intimacy with the Dear Leader, as Kim Jong Il was then known. It was notable that of a half-dozen senior officials I saw, only Kim Yong Sun volunteered to discuss the role of the Dear Leader, whom he described as "giving guidance in all fields: politics, economics, national defense, and diplomacy." The party secretary said he received frequent personal instructions, including telephone calls, from Kim Jong Il.

While Kim Yong Sun's fundamental positions did not deviate from the policy line of the party he served, he managed to present them in more accessible and impressive ways. At the end of our long conversation, which contained a plea for dialogue and cooperation with the United States, the party secretary said to me, "I understand you know Baker," referring to the U.S. secretary of state. "Please tell him I want to meet him." Although he and other officials were highly critical of American policy, the fact of my presence and the messages they gave me suggested eagerness for a direct relationship with the United States. North Korea, it seemed, was seeking in its "own style" to compensate for its losses in the communist world.

## CHINA CHANGES COURSE

The Chinese foreign minister left Pyongyang several days before the end of my own week-long trip, but the change in the relationship of the two Koreas to its giant neighbor continued to be a subject of immense importance on both sides of the thirty-eighth parallel. And in the early 1990s, those relationships, like others involving the outside powers, were in flux. For China, the challenge was to adjust its relations from one-sided support of the North Korean ally to productive ties with both South and North. It was of great importance to Beijing to do so without suffering a precipitous loss of influence with Pyongyang, as had been the case with the Soviet Union. This required diplomatic adroitness and careful handling, of which China is a master.

As late as January 1979, senior leader Deng Xiaoping told President Carter that North Korea "trusts China" and that "we cannot have contact with the South, or it will weaken that trust." Ironically, Deng's own reformist policies of pragmatism and emphasis on market economic forces made it imperative for China to amend its one-sided policy of ignoring the South.

China and South Korea, situated across the Yellow Sea from one another and with complementary and increasingly vibrant economies, proved to be natural trading partners. Beginning with indirect commerce through Hong Kong and other places, Sino–ROK trade leaped from $19 million in 1979, to $188 million in 1980, to $462 million in 1984, to $1.3 billion in 1986, to $3.1 billion in 1988. Chinese trade with North Korea was left far behind, stagnating at about $.5 billion in the late 1980s, much of it heavily subsidized by China. Although other aspects played their roles, this natural economic affinity with South Korea was of fundamental importance in overcoming Beijing's inhibitions about dealings with Seoul. Party elders and aged former generals could reminisce about their exploits with North Korea in bygone times, but South Korea loomed much larger for officials dealing with the economy.

In March 1988, with the ROK trade boom well under way, the Central Committee of the Chinese Communist Party set up an "economic team in relation to South Korea" with the mission of promoting economic relations. This unannounced decision proved to be the mechanism for implementing important changes. Although strategic and ideological factors had previously been the central considerations of China's Korea policy, the economic working party, headed by a deputy prime minister, made most of the day-to-day decisions regarding South Korea until the establishment of diplomatic relations.

Like so much else that happens on the Korean peninsula, the first crack in the political firewall between Beijing and Seoul had emerged from a violent incident—the hijacking in May 1983 of a Chinese airliner by six Chinese, who shot and wounded two crew members and forced the pilot to fly to South Korea. China sent a thirty-three-member official delegation to Seoul, where the two nations smoothly negotiated a deal for the return of the plane, its passengers, and its crew.

North Korea was quick to protest to China about this first official contact between Beijing and the Seoul government. Chinese officials responded that this was a special case and renewed the pledge that they would not depart from "China's firm stance" against ties with the South.

In March 1985, in another violent incident, two mutinous seamen opened fire with AK-47s aboard a Chinese navy torpedo boat in the Yellow Sea, killing the captain and five other crewmen. As the vessel ran out of fuel and drifted helplessly at sea, a South Korean fishing boat towed it to a nearby South Korean port. China sent three warships steaming into Korean territorial waters in search of the missing torpedo boat, and ROK air, naval, and coast guard forces were mobilized. In an atmosphere of impending crisis, Seoul CIA station chief James Delaney and Ambassador Richard Walker urgently communicated with Beijing to urge caution, Delaney through the American intelligence communications network and Walker through the U.S. Embassy in Beijing. The Chinese warships backed off, and the United States helped arrange the Sino–ROK negotiations that returned the ship and its crew to China in exchange for Beijing's apology for "inadvertently" entering Korean waters.

The amicable settlement of these unexpected emergencies coincided with the erosion of Chinese relations with North Korea as Kim Il Sung's trips to Moscow in 1984 and 1986 led to warming Soviet security ties and large new shipments of Soviet weapons. Chinese military officials were also unhappy with Soviet air force overflights of North Korean territory and Soviet navy visits to North Korean ports, all on the rim of China.

According to the account of a former Chinese official, a very senior North Korean military official, probably Defense Minister O

Jin U, sought to match the Soviet weaponry with Chinese weaponry in the mid-1980s, making extensive requests for ships, planes, and other major weapons during an unpublicized trip to Beijing. After a study by the Defense Ministry of the requirements and costs, Deng rejected the entire request and directed his aides to supply nothing. The North Korean minister left for home furious about the denial of military aid.

While unofficial contacts with South Korea continued to develop—most prominently, the participation of several hundred Chinese athletes in the 1986 Asian games in Seoul—the greatest shifts developed after the advent of President Roh Tae Woo. During his campaign for the presidency in 1987, Roh had pledged at the west coast port city of Inchon to "cross the Yellow Sea" to China during his term in office. China thus became the highest-priority target of his *nordpolitik* policy. This had an important domestic political component because the west coast areas of South Korea facing China were much less developed economically than the more prosperous east coast areas facing Japan. Perhaps because of his promises regarding China, Roh carried Inchon, normally a stronghold of the political opposition, in the presidential vote.

Roh began working on China relations immediately after taking office. Only eight days after his inauguration, he invited to the Blue House an old friend, a Chinese-born medical doctor who had lived three decades in Korea, and authorized him to go to China as an unofficial emissary to pave the way for diplomatic relations. This was the first of a large number of unofficial approaches by Korean businessmen and others authorized by Roh to make the case for full-scale ties. A number of influential Chinese, including Deng's daughter and his handicapped son, visited Seoul as guests of Korean industrialists. "We were sure they would send back their impressions to Deng and higher-ups without any filter," said a senior aide to Roh.

While the Soviet Union and Eastern European countries were moving toward political ties with South Korea in the wake of the Seoul Olympics, China remained cautious, insisting on the clear-cut separation of politics from economics. Roh, however, continued to signal his interest to Beijing in every way possible. When the Chinese government's June 1989 suppression of prodemocracy demonstrators in Tiananmen Square created widespread revulsion and endangered China's hosting of the 1990 Asian games, Roh lobbied Asian sports leaders, whom he knew well from the Seoul games, not to penalize China. He also urged Bush and British prime minister Margaret Thatcher, among other world leaders, to restrain their reactions to the Tiananmen crackdown, and he made sure that Beijing leaders knew of his efforts.

In the spring of 1990, China finally activated a channel for unofficial contacts aimed at eventual diplomatic relations with Seoul. The initial discussions, resembling the meetings of go-betweens exploring a marriage to unite two Asian families, involved Lee Sun Sok, president of the Sunkyung corporation in Seoul, whose board chairman's son had married Roh Tae Woo's daughter, and a Chinese Army colonel who was the son-in-law of Li Xiannian, a prominent member of the Chinese leadership. A subsequent series of meetings between the Korean businessman and high-ranking Chinese trade officials led to the establishment of semiofficial trade offices with consular functions in the two capitals at the end of 1990. The South Korean "trade representative" in the Chinese capital was not a businessman or economic official but in fact a veteran and senior diplomat, Ambassador Roh Jae Won (no relation to the president), who assumed a key role in the quasi-diplomatic negotiations with China.

The year 1991 was crucial in the revision of China's policy. Beginning with Deng Xiaoping's travels in southern China, the Beijing regime regained the confidence and momentum it had briefly lost in the bloody tumult of Tiananmen Square two years earlier. Once more it attuned its diplomacy to the external sources of capital, markets, and technology for rapid economic growth, which meant the capitalistic nations of North America, and Western Europe—and South Korea, just across the Yellow Sea. Unproductive ideological commitments, such as that to North Korea, slipped down on the priority list.

In May 1991, during Premier Li Peng's official visit to Pyongyang, China changed its basic trade policy with Pyongyang from concessional and barter exchanges to trade based on convertible currency at international prices. The new policy was implemented over a two-year period. It was on the same trip to Pyongyang that the Chinese premier officially informed Kim Il Sung of the decision not to veto South Korea's entry into the United Nations.

Later that year, Seoul's new status as a full member of the world body provided a venue and a rationale for upgrading Sino–South Korean ties. Immediately after its UN entry (and that of North Korea) in September 1991, Chinese foreign minister Qian Qichen met for the first time with South Korean foreign minister Lee Sang Ok in a UN conference room in New York. Although Qian was noncommittal about early normalization of bilateral relations, the meeting itself was unprecedented, and a landmark.

On November 21, Foreign Minister Qian became the first Chinese official to meet Roh Tae Woo, when he traveled in Seoul on the occasion of the third general meeting of the Asia Pacific Economic Coordination organization (APEC), a new and broadly inclusive institution that provides a forum for high-level discussions in Asia. As host for the meeting, South Korea had rendered great service to China by adroitly working out arrangements for Taiwan and Hong Kong to participate in this and future meetings alongside the representatives of Beijing, and doing so in a manner that was politically acceptable to all sides. This won China's gratitude and created a desire to respond.

Roh, who had prepared extensively for the session, observed that the Korean relationship with China "had a 5,000 year history, going back to ancient days, of good neighbors closer to each other than any other country" and that the period of severed relations since World War II was without precedent and cause for shame. He reminded Qian that in the sixteenth century Korea refused to permit the Japan warlord, Hideyoshi Toyotomi, to use Korean territory to stage an attack on the Chinese Ming dynasty—after which the Japanese invaded Korea and laid waste to the peninsula.

Roh assured his visitor that "we fully understand China's loyal relationship with North Korea that was forged through the Korean war." Nonetheless, he went on, "I believe that China, [South] Korea and North Korea can build a relationship without betraying that loyalty. As I have stated several times, we are not thinking, not even in dreams, of a German style unification by absorption, which North Korea is worried about. What we want to do with North Koreans, who are of the same nation, is to abandon hostility and restore confidence and to establish a cooperative relationship. It is not our position to dominate them based on our economic power."

Qian responded by addressing the long historical relationship of Korea and China and, invoking a common enemy, spoke of their "similar experiences of historic sufferings, which were caused by Japan." As for the unnatural absence of relations with South Korea, Qian blamed this on the outcome of World War II. He added that as North-South relations, Japanese–North Korean relations, and American–North Korean relations improved, normalization between China and South Korea would be easy. "I would like to tell you that China encourages North Korea to have a dialogue with South Korea. We believe the United States and Japan can be helpful in improving the position of North Korea."

Roh was ecstatic about the results of the meeting. He reminded his aides that during their interaction over many centuries past, the Korean kings always sent their emissaries to pay court to China, "but this time I received a kowtow" from the Chinese foreign minister.

In January 1992, in the wake of the Roh-Qian meeting and of a formal Sino–South Korean trade agreement signed in December, the Chinese Foreign Ministry held a series of strategic planning meetings that ended with a recommendation for full normalization with Seoul. A Chinese source said that, as a result, the Foreign Ministry listed normalization as one of its priority diplomatic objectives for 1992.

The timing of China's move was still uncertain until Qian confidentially informed the South Korean foreign minister, Lee Sang Ok, on the morning of April 13, 1992, that China was ready to open negotiations leading to full-scale relations. The revelation was made in a conference between the two ministers at the State Guest House in Beijing, where Lee was staying as a participant in a meeting of a UN agency, the Economic and Social Commission for Asia and the Pacific. The Chinese foreign minister, delivering the news in a matter-of-fact and soft-spoken way, emphasized that secrecy was essential.

Qian's declaration caused great excitement in Seoul among the handful of officials who were told of it. The ensuing secret negotiations, including a month-long pause while the Chinese prepared North Korea to absorb this new blow, took only four months. Together with the Korea policy reversal and subsequent collapse of the Soviet Union, the establishment of diplomatic relations between China and South Korea on August 24, 1992, and the state visit of Roh Tae Woo to Beijing two months later created a dramatically changed geopolitical situation around the divided peninsula.

What brought about the Chinese resolve to move quickly, according to sources on both sides, had less to do with the Korean peninsula than with China's sensitivity to developments on Taiwan, where a campaign for greater international recognition had been intensifying. The worldwide flowering of Taiwan's informal and paradiplomatic contacts and visits was disturbing to the leaders in Beijing, and its few breakthroughs were maddening. In January 1992 the Baltic nation of Latvia, newly freed to seek its own destiny by the collapse of the Soviet Union, established official relations with Taiwan, despite intense protests from China. Shortly before the April decision to begin negotiations with South Korea, Beijing learned that the west African nation of Niger had decided to establish full diplomatic relations with Taiwan. The way to retaliate, Chinese leaders reasoned, was to move quickly to establish diplomatic relations with Seoul, thus forcing South Korea to drop its diplomatic ties with Taiwan and depriving Taiwan of its last remaining official toehold in Asia.

Breaking off its diplomatic relations with Taiwan as demanded by China, was no easy task for South Korea. When Taiwanese authorities got wind of the secret PRC–ROK negotiations, they sent a high-ranking envoy, the secretary general of the presidential office, to remind Seoul that the Nationalist governments of China, the lineal ancestors of the current Taiwan regime, had supported the Korean nationalists in exile during the Japanese occupation, had given strong support to the independence of South Korea in UN politics in 1948, and had been close comrades-in-arms in anticommunist struggles after Chiang Kai-shek had been forced into exile.

If Seoul snubbed Taiwan in the face of this long relationship, its representatives implied, Taiwan would retaliate by opening official relations and expanding its trade with North Korea. But if on the other hand, Seoul managed to continue its diplomatic relations with Taiwan, South Korean firms would receive top priority in construction contracts and special trade benefits for five years. No such deal was in the cards, however. Taiwan had little bargaining power, since for strategic as well as economic reasons, fully normalized relations with China were far more important to South Korea than its ties with Taiwan.

For China, the delicate question was how to manage the establishment of diplomatic relations with the South in a way that did not alienate the North, as the Soviet Union had done with Gorbachev's abrupt maneuvers. This Beijing accomplished with great political and diplomatic finesse. While moving cautiously toward ties with Seoul in October 1991, Chinese leaders hosted Kim Il Sung with elaborate ceremony in what they announced was his thirty-ninth visit since the founding of the DPRK, a ten-day tour in which he was accompanied for several days by Communist Party general secretary Jiang Zemin. In April 1992, as Seoul was being secretly informed of China's willingness to initiate negotiations, Yang Shangkun, the president of the People's Republic, traveled to Pyongyang and personally intimated to Kim Il Sung that the change was coming. In the midst of negotiations with Seoul, China sent its president's brother, Yang Baibing, another powerful figure who was secretary-general of the Communist Party's Central Military Commission, on an eight-day "goodwill visit" to North Korea.

After July 29, when the substance of the Sino–South Korean arrangements were fully agreed and secretly initialed by both sides, the Chinese insisted on delaying the announcement for nearly a month until August 24, evidently for the sole purpose of further preparing the way in Pyongyang. During this time Foreign Minister Qian took the news to Pyongyang in an unannounced trip that met with much greater understanding than had Shevardnadze's tumultuous mission of the same sort two years earlier. Qian maintained that the normalization of relations with Seoul had been undertaken at the order of senior leader Deng Xiaoping, which left the North Koreans little room for argument.

Chinese officials later confided to a Japanese diplomat that flattery and saving face had been keys to obtaining North Korea's acceptance of the change. According to this account, Beijing told the North Koreans that "we need your help, because China has to respond to

Taiwan's gaining recognition abroad." The Chinese called on North Korea as old friends to magnanimously assist by permitting Beijing to recognize South Korea, thereby penalizing Taiwan for its actions.

When the Beijing-Seoul rapprochement was announced, North Korea accepted the blow with official silence. A month later, at the United Nations, I asked North Korean foreign minister Kim Yong Nam about the switch; he replied that China's new relationship with Seoul was "nothing special . . . nothing [that] matters to us."

In fact, the newest change in the great power alignments around the peninsula mattered greatly to Pyongyang, which was seeking to establish relations with the United States and Japan and hoped that China would withhold its official ties with South Korea until a package deal could be arranged. Pyongyang had elaborate warning that the Chinese shift was coming, but the timing of it must have been galling, because it arose from Beijing's desire to slap back at Taiwan rather than from any consideration of its impact on the Korean peninsula. North Korea's realization of its true standing in the priorities of its giant neighbor, along with sharply rising international pressures to curb its nuclear program, contributed to its growing troubles.

# *11*

## JOINING THE NUCLEAR ISSUE

I n the early 1990s, North Korea's program to develop nuclear weapons concentrated the minds of many of the world's political and military leaders and held their attention to an unprecedented degree. This frightening development was a potential threat not only to South Korea, the American troops on guard there, and the immediate Asian neighborhood; it was a threat as well to international stability and world order. A North Korean bomb could touch off a dangerous nuclear arms competition involving South Korea, Japan, and perhaps other industrialized nations and spread nuclear weapons materials to pariah nations in the Middle East through North Korean sales. More than that, an atomic weapon in the hands of an isolated and unpredictable regime with a record of terrorism would be a nightmare. It was, as South Korea's presidential national security adviser, Kim Chong Whi, told me while he was in office, not an issue of normal politics but "a question of civilization."

The more the outside world feared it, the more its nuclear program was a valuable asset to North Korea, which had few other resources of external worth after the decline of its alliances with the Soviet Union and China. There is no evidence that Pyongyang saw the nuclear program as a bargaining chip at its inception, but the record is clear that by the 1990s it had learned the program's value in relations with the world outside.

North Korea's nuclear debut, in the eyes of outsiders, dated back to April 1982, when an American surveillance satellite whirring unseen in the skies photographed what appeared to be a nuclear reactor vessel under construction in the bend of a river at Yongbyon, sixty miles north of the capital. When the photographs were examined in Washington a few days later, they drew the intense interest of American intelligence analysts, who marked the spot for special attention. In March 1984, as construction proceeded, a satellite pass showed the outline of a cylindrical nuclear smokestack rising from the site. Another set of photographs taken in June 1984 clearly showed the reactor, its cooling tower, and some limited power lines and electrical grid connections for local transmission of the energy to be produced.

Intelligence experts in Washington concluded from the photographs that the reactor utilized two minerals found in abundance in North Korea: natural uranium, to create an atomic reaction, and graphite, to moderate and control it. The layout was startlingly similar to old-model French and British reactors of the late 1950s, built to produce material for atomic weapons.

Taken alone, the North Korean reactor, while highly suspicious, was not conclusive evidence of a weapons program because it could also be the initial element of a civil nuclear power program. However, suspicions were heightened in March 1986, when satellite photographs of the Yongbyon area detected cylindrical craters in the sand of the nearby river bank. Analysts believed they were the residue of experimental high-explosive detonations in a certain pattern familiar to nuclear weapons experts: the precisely simultaneous explosions that are basic to implosion, one of the standard means of detonating an atomic bomb. After this discovery, restudy of earlier photographs produced evidence of similar craters in the same area since 1983.

With a reactor set to burn uranium and the technique of finely honed explosions appearing to be under development, the principal missing element in a serious atomic weapons program was a reprocessing plant. Using a complex chemical process, such a plant can separate plutonium, the raw material for a nuclear weapon, from other by-products of spent uranium fuel. Starting in March 1986, satellite photographs detected the outlines of a huge oblong building, nearly the length of two football fields, under construction at Yongbyon. In February 1987 the U.S. cameras looked down into the unroofed plant to see a long series of thick-walled cells in the typical configuration for separation of plutonium. A short time later, when the plant was roofed, U.S. intelligence could only guess at what was going on inside.

The first indigenous reactor at Yongbyon was a relatively modest plant rated by the North Koreans as producing 5 megawatts of electric power. But in June 1988 a much larger reactor, eventually described by the North Koreans as intended to produce 50 megawatts of power, was photographed under construction at Yongbyon. Such a plant, in combination with the huge reprocessing facility under construction, convinced most Washington officials with access to the closely held photography that North Korea was launched headlong on a drive to create its own nuclear weapons, and a highly ambitious drive at that. In what had been the middle of nowhere—a place famous in Korean poetry for its budding azaleas and little more—a stark and imposing industrial works of more than one hundred buildings was rising, surrounded by high fences and antiaircraft weapons and heavily guarded. As these facilities progressed toward completion and North Korea moved closer to being able to produce weapons of immense destructive power, the busy construction site at Yongbyon became increasingly an international problem that could not be ignored.

## THE ORIGINS OF THE NUCLEAR PROGRAM

Korea's involvement with nuclear weapons goes back to the dawn of the nuclear age. During World War II, Japan was vigorously pursuing a nuclear weapons program, though it lagged behind the all-out campaigns of the United States, Germany, and the Soviet Union. As U.S. bombing of the home islands increased, Japan moved its secret weapons program to the northern part of its Korean colony to get away from the attacks and take advantage of the area's undamaged electricity-generating capacity and abundance of useful minerals. After the division of Korea in 1945, the Soviet Union mined monazite and other materials in the North for use in its own atomic weapons program.

During the 1950–53 Korean War, General Douglas MacArthur requested authority to use atomic weapons and submitted a list of targets, for which he would need twenty-six A-bombs. His successor, General Matthew Ridgway, renewed MacArthur's request, but such weapons were never used. In early 1953 the newly inaugurated U.S. president, Dwight Eisenhower, began dropping hints that the United States would use the atom bomb if the deadlock persisted in the negotiations to conclude an armistice ending the war. Eisenhower, Secretary of State John Foster Dulles, and Vice President Richard Nixon all claimed later that the nuclear threats had played a major role in bringing about the truce, although recent revelations from Soviet archives cast doubt on that analysis.

Following the end of the war, the Soviet Union and North Korea signed two agreements on cooperation in nuclear research, and a small number of North Korean scientists began to arrive at the Soviet Union's Dubna Nuclear Research Center near Moscow. The Soviet Union also provided a small experimental nuclear reactor, which was sited at Yongbyon. At Soviet insistence, the reactor was placed under inspection by the International Atomic Energy Agency to ensure that material was not diverted to weapons, even though at that time North Korea was not a party to the Nuclear Non-Proliferation Treaty (NPT). The Soviet Union maintained that its assistance to North Korea did not include weapons development but was limited to civilian activities.

In its own quest for nuclear weapons, North Korea had turned to China shortly after its giant neighbor detonated its first atomic blast in 1964. Kim Il Sung sent a delegation to Beijing asking for assistance to mount a parallel program and, in a letter to Mao Zedong, declared that as brother countries who shared fighting and dying on the battlefield, China and North Korea should also share the atomic secret. Two former Chinese officials and a Japanese expert familiar with Chinese affairs told me that Mao turned down the North Korean request. "Chinese leaders thought this was a very expensive project," said an official who was in the Korea section of the Chinese Foreign Ministry at the time. "North Korea is a very small country. [Chinese leaders thought] it wasn't needed." Kim Il Sung is reported to have made another request for Chinese aid in 1974, when the South Korean nuclear weapons program was under way, a fact that may have influenced his thinking. Like the earlier appeal, this one was also unsuccessful.

When and why North Korea secretly launched its own program as a major enterprise is still the subject of speculation, in the absence of hard information. American experts believe site preparation for the first North Korean indigenous reactor, the one photographed by U.S. intelligence cameras in the spring of 1982, began around 1979. In the late 1970s, according to an official of the Russian Foreign Intelligence Service, Kim Il Sung authorized the North Korean Academy of Sciences, the army, and the Ministry of Public Security to begin implementation of a nuclear weapons program, including rapid expansion of existing facilities at Yongbyon.

After a high-level delegation from the international department of the East German Communist Party visited Pyongyang in May 1981, it reported in a memorandum to its Politburo, "The DPRK is strongly interested in the importation of nuclear power stations. Here it is estimated that they do not by any means exclude the military use of the nuclear technology." A former East German official said the cautiously worded report, which was written after extensive informal talks with North Korean officials, seriously understated Pyongyang's ardor. "They said very frankly, 'We need the atom bomb,'" according to this source.

North Korea's nuclear weapons program from the first was very self-reliant. Its "godfather" was Dr. Lee Sung Ki, a Korean born in the south who had earned his Ph.D. in engineering from Kyoto Imperial University in prewar Japan and served as dean of Seoul National University's college of engineering before crossing to the northern side during the Korean War. Lee, who became Kim Il Sung's intimate friend and closest scientific adviser, had won worldwide fame by developing vinalon, a synthetic fiber made from coal. Other members of the core group of nuclear weapons designers are believed to have been two South Koreans who were the products of prewar Japanese educations in physics and chemistry, respectively, before crossing to the north, and two North Koreans who were trained in nuclear physics at Moscow University.

The indigenous nature of the program facilitated the extreme secretiveness in which it proceeded. Not even officials of the North Koreans' close allies, the Soviet Union and China—both nuclear weapons powers—were permitted to visit the key facilities at Yongbyon once the nuclear program was under way.

In the 1980s, in addition to its clandestine program, North Korea sought to obtain civil nuclear power stations from the Soviet Union to alleviate its growing power shortages. Kim Il Sung took up the subject with Soviet leader Konstantin Chernenko in his May 1984 visit to Moscow and won agreement to additional talks on the subject. The United States, which was watching the developments in Yongbyon with growing apprehension, urged Moscow to persuade North Korea to sign the Nuclear Non-Proliferation Treaty, hoping this would lead to international inspection and control of Pyongyang's nuclear facilities.

In December 1985, Moscow agreed to supply four light-water nuclear power reactors—the type the Soviets operated at Chernobyl in Ukraine—but only if North Korea would join the NPT. North Korea joined the treaty on December 12, and two weeks later the Soviet and North Korean prime ministers agreed in principle on the power reactor deal.

It is unclear what significance North Korean leaders placed on signing the NPT at the time, or what they expected its obligations would be, but it is unlikely that they understood the pressures that would eventually be brought to bear as a result of their adherence. Under the pact, North Korea agreed not to receive or manufacture nuclear weapons and to accept international inspection of all its nuclear facilities to verify that weapons were not being produced. This commitment later provided the legal justification for intervention by the United States, the United Nations, and the international community generally to curb North Korea's nuclear program.

Under provisions of the treaty, North Korea was allowed eighteen months to negotiate and sign a safeguards (inspection) agreement with the International Atomic Energy Agency, which conducts the inspections. In mid-1987, near the end of the eighteen-month period, the IAEA learned that it had mistakenly sent Pyongyang the wrong kind of agreement document—one designed for individual sites rather than general inspections—as a model for negotiations. Because of the error, the IAEA bureaucracy gave Pyongyang another eighteen months, but that deadline passed in December 1988 with no accord and no movement from Pyongyang. By then, North Korea's prospects for acquiring the Soviet-built power reactors—the reason why it had joined the NPT in the first place—had sharply diminished with its declining relations with Moscow and the dwindling fortunes of the Soviet economy. Yet unless North Korea was willing to make a big international stir by withdrawing from the pact, it was stuck with the treaty commitments it had made. There was little indication then, however, that the IAEA's inspections, if North Korea were forced to endure them, would be very onerous.

## NUCLEAR DIPLOMACY: THE AMERICAN WEAPONS

When the Bush administration took office in Washington in January 1989, information and concern about the North Korean nuclear program was limited to a small group of American officials with access to the satellite photographs. Although most intelligence officials had no doubt about the seriousness of the danger, a nuclear analyst at the Department of Energy suggested that the North Koreans might be building a chemical fiber factory. There was also the puzzling question of why Yongbyon was not better hidden: on a clear day the outline of the nuclear complex could be seen with the naked eye from airliners taking off and landing at Pyongyang airport. Such questions were excuses for inaction by a U.S. governmental apparatus that was anything but eager to grapple with this complex and explosive topic. "The real problem was the policymakers' reluctance to face the issue, an avoidance of reality that probably flowed from the realization of the scope and difficulty of the problem," according to a former official who dealt with it in both the Reagan and Bush administrations.

The first impulse of the Bush administration was to inform others with potential influence about what Washington's space satellites had seen rising at Yongbyon. If the North Koreans were to be stopped or even slowed, it was clear that the United States would have to gain the cooperation of the other major powers with interests in the Korean peninsula. For this reason, the chief of the State

Department's Korea desk, Harry Dunlop, briefed Soviet and Chinese officials in February 1989 about the North Korean nuclear program during visits to their capitals. Later Secretary of State James Baker took up the issue repeatedly with senior officials of the two communist giants. According to Baker, "Our diplomatic strategy was designed to build international pressure against North Korea to force them to live up to their agreement to sign a safeguards agreement permitting inspections."

In May a five-member U.S. team of experts traveled to Seoul and Tokyo to provide the first extensive briefing for those governments. By then, word of the American findings was trickling out, and the State Department feared that failure to provide information could be a blow to South Korean confidence in the United States. Washington was also eager to put its own spin on the news it was imparting.

Before the briefing, an Arms Control and Disarmament Agency official wrote to her superiors, "I think the South Koreans need to be convinced that their interests would not be served by embarking on a weapons program of their own, or allowing our conclusions to become public." The second of those concerns turned out to be well taken. The highly classified briefing in Seoul, with its gripping conclusion that North Korea might be able to produce atomic bombs by the mid-1990s, leaked almost immediately to the South Korean press, and from there to U.S. and international news media.

After an article that I wrote about the briefing appeared in *The Washington Post,* the North Korea Mission to the United Nations issued a press release denying any nuclear weapons activity and calling my report "an utterly groundless lie." Despite the denial, the intelligence briefing and the notoriety it attained launched the public and political tumult over the North Korean nuclear program.

The issue was to dominate U.S. policy regarding the divided peninsula for five years to come, at times to the exclusion of almost anything else.

◆ ◆ ◆

The North Korean response to growing pressure to permit IAEA inspections was to insist it would never agree while being threatened by American nuclear weapons, especially those based in South Korea. The argument had undeniable logic and appeal. As officials in Washington studied the issue, they also realized it would be difficult to organize an international coalition to oppose North Korean nuclear weapons activity as long as American nuclear weapons were in place on the divided peninsula. A Bush administration interagency committee on the North Korean nuclear issue kept coming back to whether the American nuclear deployments should be removed but was unable to reach a decision.

American nuclear weapons had been stationed on the territory of South Korea for more than three decades, since President Eisenhower authorized the deployment of nuclear warheads on Honest John missiles and 280-millimeter long-range artillery in December 1957. As South Vietnam was faltering in the early 1970s, creating fears about South Korea's future, American deployments became notably more prominent. By 1972, according to U.S. documents obtained by nuclear researcher William Arkin, 763 nuclear warheads were deployed in South Korea, the peak number ever recorded.

In 1974 congressional committees began raising questions in public about the security and usefulness of the atomic weapons. As a correspondent who often visited Korea, I learned and reported at that time that American nuclear weapons were stationed uncomfortably close to the DMZ and that nuclear warheads had been flown by helicopter almost routinely to the edge of the DMZ in training exercises.

Public threats to use nuclear weapons were part of the U.S. response to nervousness in Seoul following the fall of Saigon. Secretary of Defense James Schlesinger, publicly acknowledging the presence of American atomic weapons in Korea, declared in June 1975 that "if circumstances were to require the use of tactical nuclear weapons . . . I think that that would be carefully considered." He added, "I do not think it would be wise to test [American] reactions." A year later, well-publicized temporary deployments of nuclear-capable U.S. warplanes to Korea in February 1976 and the first of the annual U.S.–ROK Team Spirit military maneuvers that June involved large-scale movements of troops and practice for use of nuclear weapons. In August 1976 nuclear-capable air and naval assets were massively deployed to Korea after the killing of the two American officers in the DMZ tree-cutting episode.

Thereafter, the trend reversed as the Carter administration reduced the number of American nuclear weapons deployed in Korea to about 250 warheads. Part of the reduction was due to Carter's withdrawal policies and part to the replacement of some obsolete nuclear weapons by highly accurate conventional weapons. By the onset of the Bush administration in 1989, the Korean deployments had been reduced to about 100 warheads. The cutbacks had been made without public notice, in keeping with the long-standing U.S. policy to "neither confirm nor deny" deployments of nuclear weapons abroad.

American military commanders saw little practical requirement in Korea for the remaining weapons, which were artillery warheads and gravity bombs stored at Kunsan air base on the west coast, south of Seoul. In October 1990, U.S. ambassador Donald Gregg, after consulting General Robert RisCassi, the U.S. military commander in Korea, and also the general's two immediate predecessors, recommended to Washington that the weapons be removed to facilitate the negotiations with the North and to avoid their emergence as a serious political issue in the South. The following spring, Admiral William J. Crowe, former chairman of the Joint Chiefs of Staff and an Asia expert, publicly recommended that the nuclear weapons be withdrawn as part of a deal with North Korea. Crowe spelled out in public what others were saying in private, that due to the mobility of U.S. forces, "the actual presence of any nuclear weapons in South Korea is not necessary to maintain a nuclear umbrella over the R.O.K."

These recommendations, however, ran into deep reservations in Washington. President Bush's national security adviser, retired Lieutenant General Brent Scowcroft, was strongly opposed to removing the American weapons as a concession to the North on grounds that Pyongyang had done nothing to earn this reward. Equally serious was concern that removal of the weapons would be seen by the South, and especially by its military, as weakening both the U.S. deterrent against the North and the U.S. commitment to defense of the South.

In the spring of 1991, the topic of the nuclear weapons was broached, gingerly at first, in a series of intimate meetings in Seoul involving Gregg, RisCassi, and several senior officials of the Blue House and ROK Defense and Foreign ministries. Under previous U.S. practice, only the South Korean president—with no aides present—had been briefed on the nature and location of American nuclear weapons in the country. Until the highly confidential "inner circle meetings" began in Seoul, a Korean civilian participant recalled, "it was taboo even to talk about the American tactical nuclear weapons; for us, they were shocking to consider."

The discussions deepened in a two-day meeting of American and South Korean military and civilian officials at U.S. Pacific Command headquarters at Honolulu, Hawaii, in early August. While other issues were mentioned, Washington's real purpose was to be sure that the Koreans would be comfortable with removal of the remaining American nuclear weapons. At the high point of the sessions, the representative of the U.S. Joint Chiefs of Staff announced the Pentagon's conclusion that the nuclear deployments in South Korea were not necessary for the country's defense. While no strong objections to removal of the weapons were raised by the Koreans, some suggested that they be used as a bargaining chip for concessions from Pyongyang. The meeting concluded without formal agreement.

What finally broke through the inertia in Washington was a dramatic and unexpected development in a different part of the world: the failed coup in mid-August 1991 of hard-liners against Soviet president Mikhail Gorbachev. Although the plotters were arrested, the coup marked the transfer of real power from Gorbachev to his rival, Russian president Boris Yeltsin, and the beginning of the rapid move toward dissolution of the Soviet Union. On September 27, in an initiative calculated to bring forth reciprocal steps from Moscow, Bush announced the removal of all ground-based and sea-based tactical nuclear weapons from U.S. forces worldwide. The withdrawal of the nuclear artillery from South Korea would leave in place there only some sixty nuclear warheads for air-delivered gravity bombs.

After consulting his advisers, Bush secretly decided to remove these last American nuclear deployments on the peninsula. He also decided in principle to permit North Koreans to inspect the U.S. base at Kunsan where the nuclear weapons had been stored, to meet another of North Korea's demands. "We were able to hook a ride on a Soviet-related decision," said Richard Solomon, who as assistant secretary for East Asian and Pacific affairs had tried unsuccessfully for many months to deal with the issue of the American nuclear weapons in Korea.

Before making his formal decisions, Bush privately informed South Korean president Roh Tae Woo in a meeting at the United Nations that the United States would continue to provide the nuclear umbrella—that is, nuclear protection against threats to South Korea's security—whether or not American nuclear weapons were in place on the peninsula.

In December, when the last of the nuclear bombs had been removed, Roh was permitted to announce officially that "as I speak, there do not exist any nuclear weapons whatsoever, anywhere in the Republic of Korea." The withdrawal of the American nuclear weapons had a powerful effect in North Korea, contributing in important fashion to an era of compromise and conciliation.

## THE DECEMBER ACCORDS

The winter of 1991 inaugurated a period of unusual progress in North-South relations and in North Korea's relations with the United States. It was one of those rare periods when the policies of the two Koreas were in alignment for conciliation and agreement, with all of the major outside powers either neutral or supportive.

Economically and politically, 1991 had been a very bad year for Kim Il Sung. His estrangement from the Soviet Union the previous year had cost him a crucial alliance and left him with a painful energy shortage and worsening economic problems. North Korean leaders were briefly cheered in August 1991 by the coup attempt against Mikhail Gorbachev, and they quickly made it known they hoped it would succeed. However, when the coup failed and Russian president Yeltsin became the de facto leader of the failing Soviet Union, Kim could expect no help or even sympathy from Moscow.

In the spring of 1991, Kim's other major ally, China, had forced him to reverse his long-standing opposition to dual entry with South Korea to the United Nations. Now Beijing was moving toward normalization of relations with Seoul. When Kim visited China in October, he was advised to open up economically as China had done and to undertake a rapid settlement with South Korea in the interest of regional peace and stability. Chinese leaders also urged him to give credence to Bush's announcement that American tactical nuclear weapons were being withdrawn and to resolve the concern over the North Korean nuclear program as soon as possible. After returning from Beijing, Kim convened a Politburo meeting, from which emerged new efforts at reconciliation with the South and the world outside.

Simultaneously, South Korea had been shifting toward a more conciliatory posture regarding the North in preparation for the final year of Roh Tae Woo's presidency, during which he hoped to have a summit meeting with Kim Il Sung. High-level talks led by the two prime ministers visiting each other's capitals, which had begun in the fall of 1990, resumed in the fall of 1991. In a private conversation with the visiting North Korean prime minister, Roh sent word to Kim of his desire for a summit meeting as a step toward an improved relationship between the North and South. Kim responded, through the next visit to Pyongyang of the South Korean prime minister, that he was willing to meet if there was something important to be achieved, but not under other circumstances.

Starting with the October 22–25, 1991, prime ministerial meeting in Pyongyang, rapid progress was made between North and South. Before the southerners went home, the two Koreas had agreed in principle to work out and adopt at their next meeting a single document setting the terms for broad-ranging accord. When the northern team came to Seoul on December 10, it was prepared to compromise and, as southern delegates saw it, ready to sign an agreement. "This time we brought the seal with us," said a visitor from Pyongyang, referring to the official stamp used to authenticate documents in Asia. This was an astonishing change from the months and years of sterile negotiations in which the two Koreas had refused to budge from fixed positions.

The result of three days of intense bargaining was by far the most important document adopted by the two sides since the North-South joint statement of July 4, 1972. In the "Agreement on Reconciliation, Nonaggression and Exchanges and Cooperation between the South and the North," adopted and initialed on December 13, 1991, the two Koreas came closer than ever before to accepting each other's regime as a legitimate government with a right to exist. The document portrayed the two Koreas as "recognizing that their relations, not being a relationship between states, constitute a special interim relationship stemming from the process toward unification." The guidelines of the "special interim relationship," if implemented, would have meant a nearly complete cessation of the conflict on the peninsula and a reversal of decades of policy on both sides:

• Mutual recognition of each other's systems, and an end to interference, villification, and subversion of each other.

• Mutual efforts "to transform the present state of armistice into a solid state of peace," with continued observance of the armistice until this was accomplished.

• Nonuse of force against each other, and implementation of confidence-building measures and large-scale arms reductions.

• Economic, cultural, and scientific exchanges, free correspondence between divided families, and the reopening of roads and railroads that had been severed at the North-South dividing line.

Three separate subcommittees on political and military activities and on exchanges were authorized in the agreement, to work out the many details, none of which were specified in the accord.

North Korea refused to deal with the issue of its nuclear program in the reconciliation agreement with the South but promised to work on a separate North-South nuclear accord before the end of the year. This was facilitated on December 18, when after clearance from the United States, Roh announced publicly that the American nuclear weapons had been withdrawn.

On December 24 an important meeting of the Central Committee of the North Korean Workers Party heard Kim Il Sung praise the recent North-South nonaggression pact as "the first epochal event" since the start of inter-Korean diplomacy in 1972. The meeting, the first party plenum centered on North-South issues in nine years, ended with a public report that contained no criticism of South Korea or the United States.

The party meeting was significant for two other reasons, which may have been connected. Kim Jong Il, the son and designated successor to the Great Leader, was named supreme commander of DPRK armed forces. And in parallel moves that could not have been made without approval of Kim Jong Il and at least acquiescence by the armed forces commanders he now headed, the plenum apparently gave party clearance for international inspection of the country's nuclear program and for a bilateral nuclear accord to be worked out with the South. Selig Harrison of the Carnegie Endowment for International Peace was later told by a variety of North Korean and foreign observers that the plenum marked a conditional victory for pragmatists who argued for making a deal—compromising the nuclear issues in return for economic benefits and normalization of relations with the United States and Japan. Hard-line elements, according to Harrison, agreed to suspend the weapons program, but not to terminate it—being confident that U.S. and Japanese help would not be forthcoming.

The promised nuclear negotiations between the two Koreas convened at Panmunjom on December 26. As in the case of the nonaggression accords, the North's negotiators apparently had instructions to make a deal. On the second day of the talks, they appeared with a written proposal incorporating most of the sweeping South Korean language and dropping several earlier propositions that were unacceptable to the South. At one point the usually standoffish North Korean negotiators woke up their South Korean counterparts late at night for a series of one-on-one talks that made important progress. Some sensitive negotiations took place in whispered conversations in the corners of the meeting room, away from the formal conference table, with its microphones hooked up to offices in the two capitals.

A complicated issue for both Koreas was nuclear reprocessing, or obtaining plutonium from spent reactor fuel by chemical separation. Koreans were acutely conscious that nearby Japan operates reprocessing facilities for its civil nuclear program under arrangements with the United States that predate the time when Washington had focused on reprocessing as a proliferation risk. Some in the South were also eager not to foreclose the option of a future reprocessing plant on economic grounds and, some Americans suspected, as a potential source of weapons material. However, Roh agreed under heavy U.S. pressure to an unqualified commitment to forgo nuclear reprocessing, on grounds that it would better position the South to bargain against the North's then-suspected reprocessing capability. As for the North, the giant structure being built to house its reprocessing plant at Yongbyon was nearing completion—the most recent U.S. intelligence estimate was that it could be producing plutonium by mid-1992—but this did not seem to faze Pyongyang's negotiators when agreeing to ban reprocessing. When Representative Stephen Solarz met Kim Il Sung on December 18 in Pyongyang, the Great Leader declared, pounding the table at the end of a long and contentious meeting, "We have no nuclear reprocessing facilities!"

Under the bilateral deal as negotiated, the South agreed to cancel the 1992 U.S.–ROK Team Spirit military exercise in return for North Korean willingness to permit outside inspection of its nuclear facilities at Yongbyon. In retrospect, cancellation of Team Spirit was a ROK concession of crucial importance to the country's powerful military, which had consistently resisted compromises affecting the nuclear weapons program.

In the final agreement signed on December 31, both North and South pledged not to "test, manufacture, produce, receive, possess, store, deploy or use nuclear weapons" and not to "possess nuclear reprocessing and uranium enrichment facilities." Moreover, they agreed to reciprocal inspections of facilities of the other side, to be arranged and implemented by a Joint Nuclear Control Commission.

To achieve the agreement, which apparently had been ordered by Kim Il Sung, North Korean negotiators were uncharacteristically willing to compromise. While the South was exultant at the results, some of its officials felt in retrospect they had pushed the North too hard. Riding together in a car from Pyongyang to Kaesong nine months later, after signing protocols flowing from the December accords, DPRK Major General Kim Yong Chul complained to his counterpart, ROK Major General Park Yong Ok, that 90 percent of the language originated on the southern side and therefore "this is your agreement, *not* our agreement." At that moment, the South Korean officer began to doubt whether the concessions that had been made could be actually implemented.

At the time of the signing of the agreement on New Year's Eve, however, Kim Il Sung portrayed the North-South nuclear pact as a great victory. In a display of his enthusiasm, he dispatched a helicopter to bring his negotiators home from Panmunjom to Pyongyang in triumphant style. At the dawn of 1992 *The Economist,* the British weekly on international affairs, proclaimed that "the Korean peninsula looked a little safer this week."

## MEETING IN NEW YORK

Three weeks into 1992, the United States rolled out its biggest contribution to the positive trend—a bilateral American–North Korean meeting at the political level. Pyongyang had long sought direct discussions with senior levels in Washington, seeing the United States as the heart and head of the West, the superpower overlord of South Korea and Japan. Pyongyang also saw relations with the United States as an important victory in its zero-sum game with the South. Its leaders hoped that the beginning of a relationship with Washington could, to some extent, substitute for the collapse of its alliance with Moscow and the depreciation of its alliance with Beijing.

Starting in the fall of 1991, while exploring the range of incentives and disincentives that the United States could wield with the North, Washington officials had begun to discuss the possibility of a high-level meeting. The idea was highly contentious within the administration, but its advocates won approval to discuss it with the South Koreans, who approved it on the explicit condition that it would be only a one-time session that would not lead to further talks. Kim Chong Whi, Roh's national security adviser, as well as State Department experts, suggested that the meeting be with Kim Yong Sun, the relatively freewheeling Workers Party secretary for international affairs, who was close to Dear Leader Kim Jong Il, instead of the highly programmed and less voluble North Korean foreign minister.

In December, American officials informed the North Koreans, through the U.S.–DPRK political counsel channel in Beijing—which was limited to passing messages and little else—that a high-level meeting might be held if Pyongyang agreed to meet its nuclear inspection obligations. In the opinion of several U.S. officials, the promise that such a meeting represented had been an important factor in the North's decision to conclude the nuclear accord with the South and in its preparations to sign a nuclear safeguards agreement with the IAEA.

Shortly after ten A.M. on January 21, 1992, Kim Yong Sun and several aides arrived at the U.S. Mission to the United Nations in an ostentatious stretch limousine, to meet an American delegation headed by Arnold Kanter, the undersecretary of state for political affairs (and the third-ranking official in the State Department). Due to the intense antagonism to North Korea as an abhorrent society and a military threat and the unprecedented nature of the meeting, there had been fierce debates within the administration not only about whether to have the meeting but also about what Kanter could say. The bureaucratic compromise, according to Kanter, was "that the meeting would happen, but I would take a tough line."

Kanter's "talking points"—normally stripped-down notes of the main lines of presentation—were reviewed and approved in advance by an interagency committee and then by the South Korean and Japanese governments. They became virtually a script he had to read, though he did so in the most conciliatory and inoffensive way possible. While urging North Korea to permit IAEA inspections and to give up the nuclear weapons option, Kanter was forbidden to spell out what North Korea could expect in return. He was specifically not permitted even to mention the word *normalization* of American–North Korean relations. Although he referred vaguely to future meetings between the two countries as the principal incentive for Pyongyang, Kanter was required by the arrangement with Seoul to rule out follow-up meetings of this group, making clear that the session itself was not the start of a negotiating process.

The well-tailored Kim Yong Sun, who was wearing a more expensive suit than any of the Americans, impressed Kanter as shrewd and worldly, although he had never been in the United States before. While North Korea might be a hermit kingdom, Kanter concluded, his interlocuter was no hermit. Referring repeatedly to his intimacy with the Dear Leader, Kim Yong Sun said Kim Jong Il was now in charge of North Korea's foreign relations as well as the military. In the meeting and in a lengthy private talk with Kanter, Kim Yong Sun pushed hard for an agreement in principle to another meeting, or at least a joint statement at the conclusion of this one. When both were refused, he seemed disappointed but not angry. Later in the year, as tension mounted between Pyongyang and Washington, Kim sent a personal message to Kanter through the Beijing diplomatic channel appealing for another meeting to work things out—but this was rejected by the administration.

On January 30, eight days after the Kanter-Kim meeting, North Korea kept the promises it had made by signing the safeguards agreement with the IAEA in Vienna. It was ratified on April 9, in an unusual special meeting of the Supreme People's Assembly. The following day, the accord was presented to IAEA director general Hans Blix at the agency's headquarters in Vienna to bring it into force.

## THE COMING OF THE INSPECTORS

From its headquarters in the towers of the United Nations complex in Vienna, the International Atomic Energy Agency, created in 1957, runs the world's early-warning system against the spread of nuclear weapons. A semi-independent UN technical agency, it reports to the Security Council but is governed by a thirty-five-nation Board of Governors, in which the United States and other major powers have a large voice. Since the establishment of the Non-Proliferation Treaty in 1968, the most important task of the IAEA has been to send its multinational teams of inspectors to verify that nonnuclear weapon states are keeping their commitments not to manufacture or possess nuclear weapons.

Until 1991, the IAEA limited itself to checking civilian nuclear facilities and materials that NPT signatories reported in voluntary declarations to the agency. The aftermath of the U.S.–led Operation Desert Storm, however, disclosed that Iraq, which was an NPT signatory, had carried on an intensive and sophisticated nuclear weapons program at secret sites adjacent to those being inspected by the agency. The impact on the IAEA was profound.

In the face of withering criticism for ineffectiveness and timidity, the IAEA under Director General Hans Blix underwent an upheaval in personnel and a sea change in attitudes, from complacency to alertness about suspicious nuclear activities. Despite the misgivings of some third-world members of the IAEA board, Blix, a former Swedish foreign minister, established the right to accept intelligence information supplied by the United States and other member states in its investigations, and the right to demand access to suspicious facilities through mandatory "special inspections."

Starting in September 1991, in the wake of the Gulf War, the United States began supplying intelligence information to Blix and senior aides at his Vienna headquarters. In time, Washington also provided the services of its incomparably sophisticated national laboratories and supplied photos from U.S. spy satellites that were rarely shown to outsiders. Armed for the first time with extensive independent information about the nuclear programs that they were checking, the IAEA's leaders and its corps of international inspectors were determined not to be hoodwinked or embarrassed again. North Korea became the first test case of their new capabilities and attitudes.

◆　◆　◆

For six days in mid-May 1992, Blix led a team to North Korea to establish relations with the country's leaders and prepare for full-scale IAEA inspections. After preliminary discussions in Pyongyang, Blix and his party were taken to the nuclear facilities at Yongbyon. Despite the fact that North Korea had not joined the Non-Proliferation Treaty until 1985, the small Soviet-supplied research reactor there had been under regular IAEA inspection since 1977, at Soviet insistence. But the inspectors had formerly been allowed only in the area of the research reactor and had been carefully kept away from other parts of the growing complex. Not even visiting Russians were permitted to stray from the small research reactor they had supplied. As far as is known, Blix and his three technically expert companions were the first outsiders ever to see, from ground level, what the American surveillance cameras had been peering down on for nearly a decade.

Taking no chances that the IAEA chief would miss something of importance, U.S. officials provided intelligence briefings for Blix and his top aides in September 1991, March 1992, and on May 7, immediately before his departure. On the final occasion, Blix was given a "virtual reality" tour of Yongbyon using advanced computer modeling based on aerial photographs. Blix and his party were encouraged to memorize the shapes and relationships of the main facilities. The highlight of the intelligence tour was the reprocessing building. North Korea, after consistently denying that it had such a facility, listed the plant as a "radiochemical laboratory" in the declaration of its nuclear facilities provided a few days before Blix's visit.

When they were actually walking through this facility, Blix and his team had two surprises: first, that the six-story-high building, the length of two football fields, was even more imposing than they had expected from the CIA briefings; and second, that the building was only about 80 percent complete, and the equipment inside only about 40 percent ready for full-scale production. An IAEA official described the works inside the giant building as "extremely primitive" and far from ready to produce the quantities of plutonium needed for a stockpile of atomic weapons. This conclusion contradicted worst-case U.S. assessments, such as that by CIA director Robert Gates on March 27 that "we believe Pyongyang is close, perhaps very close, to having a nuclear weapon capability."

North Korea had reported to the IAEA in its initial declaration that in 1990 it had already produced about 90 grams of plutonium, roughly three ounces, on an experimental basis in the "radiochemical lab." In a third surprise, the seemingly obliging North Koreans shocked Blix by proudly presenting him with a vial of the plutonium in powdered form, which is deadly when inhaled. (Back in Vienna, the IAEA team underwent immediate medical exams that confirmed that they had not been contaminated.) This small amount was far short of the 8 to 16 pounds needed to produce a weapon. Nevertheless, if plutonium had been manufactured at all, it would be difficult to ascertain scientifically how much had been produced, raising the possibility that North Korea had squirreled some away.

While very small quantities of plutonium could be separated using test methods in a laboratory, IAEA officials found it illogical that North Korea would have erected a huge and expensive facility without first building a pilot plant to test its procedures. North Korea denied that such a pilot plant existed, but doubts persisted.

In late May, after Blix and his team returned to Vienna, the agency sent its first set of regular inspectors to Yongbyon. "The first inspection was just to get the picture," said Olli Heinonen, a sandy-haired IAEA veteran who eventually became chief inspector of the North Korean program. "The second inspection [in July] saw something that didn't fit the picture, the first signals that something was wrong." More discrepancies appeared beginning with the third inspection, which took place in September.

North Korea had reported that it had separated the three ounces of plutonium in an experimental procedure in 1990, when a small number of faulty fuel rods had been taken from its 5-megawatt indigenous reactor. To confirm what had been done, IAEA inspectors swabbed the inside of the steel tanks used to process the plutonium. The inspectors assumed that the North Koreans had previously scrubbed down the equipment, but the IAEA teams employed gamma ray detectors and other gear capable of finding minute particles clinging to grooved surfaces. The IAEA also convinced the North Koreans to cut into a waste storage pipe to obtain some of the highly radioactive waste that is a by-product of the plutonium production process.

Tests on some of this material were run at the IAEA's laboratory near its headquarters in Vienna. Far more sophisticated tests were conducted for the IAEA in supporting laboratories run out of the U.S. Air Force Technology Applications Center at Patrick Air Force Base, Florida. Much of the work of this laboratory, which had pioneered the analysis of Soviet nuclear tests, had been secret during the cold war.

Precise measurements of the rates of decay of the constituent elements of the plutonium samples indicated that three different episodes of plutonium separation could have taken place in 1989, 1990, and 1991—rather than the single operation in 1990 that North Korea had claimed. In another highly sophisticated set of tests, the isotopic signatures in the plutonium sample presented to Blix did not match those of the waste products that supposedly had been produced from the same operation. "It was like finding a left-hand glove of plutonium that is missing its right-hand glove, [and finding] a right-hand glove of nuclear waste that is missing its plutonium," Blix said in an interview for this book. From this mismatch in evidence, Blix and his experts reasoned that "there must be some more plutonium," but "whether it is grams or kilograms, we don't know."

Pyongyang's expectations about the nature and capabilities of the inspections probably had been shaped by the limited experiences of a North Korean who had worked as an IAEA inspector before the Gulf War and who in 1992 emerged as director of the safeguards liaison office of Pyongyang's Ministry of Atomic Energy. "It's hard to believe he had seen anything like this," said Heinonen, speaking of the greatly enhanced scientific prowess that provided detailed test results from tiny samples of radioactive material. Said Willi Theis, who initially was chief of the IAEA inspection team in North Korea: "North Korea grossly underestimated the agency's measurement capability. . . . They never expected us to be able to perform isotopic analyses. They could not understand this or explain the [test result] differences. The more they learned, the more they provided manufactured responses. We had to approach them harder and harder as they realized we were going to discover their wrongdoings."

## FROM ACCOMMODATION TO CRISIS

In the last half of 1992 and the early months of 1993, the euphoria that had resulted from opening North Korea's nuclear program to international inspection gave way to suspicion, antagonism, and, eventually, crisis. The rewards Pyongyang had expected from agreeing to nuclear inspections had not developed; instead, the presence of the inspectors provided the focal point for accusations of cheating and new international pressures. Contributing to the setback was a worsening political climate between the North and the South, brought about in part by preparations for ROK presidential elections in December 1992. The United States, which was distracted and largely immobilized by its own November presidential balloting, did nothing to forestall the approaching storm.

◆　◆　◆

Since the signing of the unprecedented series of accords between North and South the previous December, negotiations over their implementation had been going slowly. In the North-South Joint Nuclear Control Commission meetings which were charged with preparing the bilateral nuclear inspections called for under the accords, Pyongyang resisted Seoul's demands for short-notice "inspections with teeth" by South Koreans in addition to the ongoing IAEA inspections. This deadlock became more worrisome as the discrepancies accumulated, and conflict grew, between North Korea and the international inspectors, proving new ammunition for those who had believed all along that North Korea would never reveal crucial elements of its nuclear weapons activity.

With a record of foreign policy accomplishments behind him, President Roh Tae Woo was relatively relaxed, telling the *New York Times* in September that he believed North Korea's "determination to develop nuclear weapons has become weaker." Roh still hoped for a meeting with Kim Il Sung, although the previous spring he had been forced to reject an unexpected and secret invitation to travel to Pyongyang for the Great Leader's 80th birthday. To meet his counterpart on this occasion would make him seem to be a celebrant at Kim's party. Nevertheless, Roh secretly sent his intelligence chief to Pyongyang to wish Kim happy birthday and express continuing interest in a meeting.

Kim Young Sam, the former opposition leader who had joined the ruling party in 1990 and who became its presidential candidate in May 1992, was more apprehensive about the positive aspects of North-South relations. Kim and his political managers feared that continuation of the North-South euphoria of earlier months would benefit his old political rival, Kim Dae Jung, who was shaping up as once again his principal competitor, this time as opposition presidential candidate. As the political authority of Roh as a lame duck president began to ebb and that of his chosen successor grew in the late summer of 1992, South Korea slowed down its normalization process with the North, and its officials urged Americans to do the same.

In early October, as a part of a campaign of pressure and linkage, the U.S. and ROK defense ministers announced in Washington that they were resuming preparations for launching a new 1993 installment of the U.S.–ROK Team Spirit military exercise, "in the absence of meaningful improvement in South-North relations, especially on bilateral nuclear inspections." The 1992 exercise had been canceled in the period of mutual accommodation that led to the IAEA inspections of Yongbyon.

The South Korean military took the lead in demanding a renewal of Team Spirit, which was deemed important for readiness as well as a potent pressure point against the North. The U.S. Command, under General Robert RisCassi, was determined to go ahead with the exercise unless countermanded by higher-ups for political reasons. Surprisingly, interagency policy committees in Washington were neither informed nor consulted before the politically explosive decision was made in the defense ministers' annual meeting. To Korea experts in Washington and to Donald Gregg, U.S. ambassador to Seoul, it was an unpleasant bolt from the blue—he later called it "one of the biggest mistakes" of Korea policy on his watch.

For North Korea, the cancellation of the 1992 Team Spirit exercise had been the most tangible evidence of its improved relationship with the United States and the U.S. concession of greatest immediate benefit to the North Korean military establishment. While Americans tended to scoff at Pyongyang's fears that the annual field exercise was a threat to its national security, the landing of large numbers of additional American troops in South Korea by sea and air, the profusion of flights near the DMZ by American nuclear-capable warplanes, and the movement of heavily armed ROK and U.S. ground troops made a powerful impression on the North—as Team Spirit's planners had hoped from the start, nearly two decades earlier. Moreover, Team Spirit was personally important to Kim Il Sung, who had been complaining bitterly about it publicly and privately for many years. A U.S. official who visited Pyongyang in 1993 said the Great Leader's voice quivered and his hands shook with anger when he discussed Team Spirit in a conversation with Representative Gary Ackerman (D–N.Y.), calling it "a dress rehearsal for an invasion."

In a public statement, North Korea described the threat to resume the maneuvers in 1993 as "a criminal act" designed to "put the brakes on North-South relations and drive the North-South dialogue to a crisis." Within weeks, Pyongyang, citing the Team Spirit issue as the reason, abruptly canceled all North-South contacts in every forum except for those in the Joint Nuclear Control Commission. A short time thereafter, those talks also collapsed. For the first time, North Korea warned that it might refuse to continue the IAEA inspections, declaring that the decision to revive the Team Spirit exercise is "an act of provocation breaking the U.S. promise not to make nuclear threats.''

The day before the U.S.–ROK Team Spirit announcement, the Agency for National Security Planning (NSP), Seoul's renamed domestic and foreign intelligence agency, announced the arrest of sixty-two people in what it charged was the largest North Korean espionage ring in the history of the republic. More than three hundred others were implicated, the agency claimed, including a female member of the North Korean Workers Party hierarchy who had lived in the South under false identities several times in earlier decades. While there is no doubt that North Korea had long had spies in the South, the timing of the NSP's roundup and its revelations raised eyebrows within other elements of the South Korean government, especially because NSP officials—as well as the presidential campaign managers for ruling party candidate Kim Young Sam—were unhappy with the rapid improvement of relations with the North.

Before the spy ring announcement, Roh Tae Woo had authorized an ROK deputy prime minister to visit Pyongyang to pursue joint economic development with the North, and he ordered the Economic Planning Board (EPB) to prepare a team to travel to the North on a similar mission. In internal discussions, the intelligence agency opposed the EPB mission, according to Kim Hak Joon, who was chief Blue House spokesman at the time and an expert on unification policy. After the news of the spy ring arrests, which may have been ''greatly exaggerated or fabricated,'' according to the former official, Roh was forced to cancel the missions due to the political and public indignation. ''Everything stopped,'' the former spokesman recalled.

It was in this atmosphere that the IAEA, having received new U.S. satellite photographs indicating dissembling at Yongbyon, stepped up its efforts to force North Korea to reveal the full dimensions of its nuclear activity.

On the eve of a previous IAEA board meeting at which North Korea was to be discussed, Blix had obtained permission for his inspectors to ''visit'' two sites at Yongbyon that appeared to be nuclear-related but that had not been declared as such by North Korea. One of the sites was a building that had been constructed as a two-story structure but that had been partly covered by huge mounds of earth and landscaping to appear as a one-story building. American over-head photography had recorded the construction, in the original lower level, of thick-walled vaults made of reinforced concrete—suit-able for the storage of nuclear waste. When IAEA inspectors arrived, the lower floor was no longer visible, and the inspectors were told it did not exist. The top floor was filled with heavy weapons, including tanks and missiles on mobile carriages. North Korea subsequently refused to permit formal inspection of the facility on grounds it was a military site and therefore should be exempt from inspection. The IAEA does not accept such an exemption.

On November 12, in a telephone conversation from Vienna with Theis, his chief inspector on the ground at Yongbyon, Blix said the agency now possessed indisputable evidence that a trench had been dug and then covered up between the reprocessing plant and the "one-story building," whose basement was believed to be a nuclear waste storage facility. Blix said there was also clear evidence that the North Koreans had sought to camouflage a nearby outdoor nuclear waste facility. (While he did not say so over the telephone, U.S. satellites had photographed workers hastily covering up the sixteen-year-old waste site with dirt and planting dozens of shrubs and trees to hide it in between IAEA visits to the area.) Blix instructed his inspector to tell the North Koreans that they must declare these sites as nuclear facilities and permit their inspection.

Realizing that North Korean authorities had probably moni-tored the telephone conversation and that his demands would be diffi-cult for the North Koreans to swallow, Theis immediately summoned two senior nuclear officials of the Yongbyon facility and sought to work with them on amending their initial declaration to the IAEA to include the waste sites with as little admission of error as possible. At first the officials seemed amenable and even grateful. The next day, possibly after receiving instructions from Pyongyang, they reversed course, bitterly accusing Theis of being "an agent of the CIA" and performing inspections "on the basis of instructions from the U.S. State Department." With that, they refused to cooperate, widening and deepening the breach between North Korea and the IAEA.

The two sides sparred inconclusively over the next three months as the IAEA presented the North Koreans with new data on the chemical "inconsistencies" and referred vaguely to "information" on the true purposes of the two suspect sites that North Korea had refused to acknowledge as nuclear facilities. Pyongyang's officials made various explanations and denials, none of which were credible to the IAEA. In early January, the agency's experts identified two possible explanations for the chemical inconsistencies: some of the fissile material that had been separated to plutonium might have come from undeclared and undetected diversions from the very small Soviet-supplied research reactor at Yongbyon, or the additional fissile material might have been diverted from the 5-megawatt indigenous reactor.

If the latter was true, U.S. intelligence agencies calculated, it was at least theoretically possible that enough plutonium could have been obtained from a full load of irradiated fuel rods to produce one or two nuclear weapons (although very substantial additional efforts, of which North Korea was not believed to be capable, would be required to make the plutonium into bombs). This was the basis for worst-case U.S. intelligence estimates and public statements during the nuclear crisis.

Eventually the focus of contention became the two suspect sites that the IAEA, on the basis of U.S. satellite photographs, had identified as unacknowledged nuclear waste sites. In late December 1992, Blix requested "visits" to clarify the nature of the sites and make tests. In January, Pyongyang responded that "a visit by officials could not be turned into an inspection" and said that inspections of non–nuclear military facilities "might jeopardize the supreme interests" of the DPRK. This was a clear reference to the escape clause in the Non-Proliferation Treaty, which permits a nation to withdraw from the treaty to avoid jeopardizing its "supreme national interests." In a telex, Blix was also asked to "take into full consideration the political and military situation over the Korean peninsula."

In response, Blix, meeting a North Korean representative in Vienna, spoke explicitly for the first time of the possible requirement of a "special inspection"—in this context, an inspection of undeclared activities over the objections of the state involved. Except for the case of Iraq, the agency had never made such a demand inspection before. The UN Security Council, meanwhile, declared itself able to take punitive action if IAEA inspection requests were ignored, saying that nuclear proliferation constitutes a threat to international peace and security. Thus North Korea was set to become the first test of the more vigorous international consensus against nuclear proliferation that had arisen in the wake of the discoveries about Iraq's nuclear program.

In preparation for the IAEA board meeting in February, at which the agency's demands on North Korea would be considered, Blix asked the United States to approve the display of the satellite photographs at the heart of the agency's demand for inspection of the two suspect sites. The remarkable high-resolution pictures had been shown to Blix and his staff, but the CIA was much less willing to display them to a board that included officials of leftist third-world countries such as Libya, Syria, and Algeria and in the presence of North Korean representatives.

The CIA bureaucracy in Washington initially rejected showing the photos, but in response to urgent requests from the State Department, outgoing CIA director Robert Gates overruled his staff. Thirty years earlier, intelligence photos taken by a U-2 spy plane over Cuba had startled the world when they had been publicly displayed in the UN Security Council by the Kennedy administration during the Cuban missile crisis. In the meantime, orbiting satellites and high-resolution cameras had made further remarkable advances, placing every spot on earth within range of prying American eyes. Although the CIA was reluctant to advertise its prowess, Gates knew that sensitive intelligence photos had been displayed for the Security Council on the Chad issue in the early 1980s, on the Iran–Iraq War later in the 1980s, and on Iraq's invasion of Kuwait in 1991–92. "For me," Gates recalled, "the notion of sharing imagery with an international agency was not as new or as radical a step as it may have been to the bureaucracy."

Close to a dozen satellite photographs of North Korean installations and attempts at deception at Yongbyon were presented to a closed session of the IAEA board on February 22. The impact was electric. Although the senior North Korean representative at the meeting, Ho Jin Yun, denounced the photographs as fakery, the initially skeptical board was deeply and decisively impressed. At the end of its meeting, on February 25, the board demanded that North Korea permit the special inspection of the two disputed sites "without delay." As a concession to Chinese requests, it provided a one-month grace period for North Korean compliance, making clear that if Pyongyang did not act, it would take the issue to the Security Council for international sanctions or other actions.

By this time, the credibility and international standing of both the IAEA and North Korea were at risk, with the stakes very high for both sides. If the IAEA could not secure international backing for inspections when there was evidence of cheating, its newly asserted authority could be defied with impunity, and the post-Iraq drive against nuclear weapons proliferation would be set back decisively. For Pyongyang, the danger was that this would be only the first of increasingly intrusive inspections it regarded as masterminded by hostile U.S. intelligence.

Also at risk was the sensitive issue of respect, what Koreans call *ch'emyon* and Westerners call "face," a matter of tremendous, almost overwhelming, importance to the reclusive North Korean regime. "For us, saving face is as important as life itself," a senior North Korean told Representative Ackerman during his visit to Pyongyang, and experts on North Korea say that may not be much of an exaggeration. For although the "special inspections" were unlikely to clear up the inconsistencies in Pyongyang's program, they would almost certainly provide overwhelming evidence that North Korea had not told the IAEA the whole truth about its nuclear facilities and then had sought to cover up its misstatements. In the court of international opinion, North Korea would face demeaning condemnation. Such a prospect was intolerable for Pyongyang. As the tension increased, the country's minister of atomic energy, Choi Hak Gun, told IAEA inspectors, "Even if we had done it [cheated], we would never admit it."

As the conflict between the IAEA and North Korea was coming to a head in November 1992, Governor Bill Clinton was winning the American presidential election over incumbent George Bush. The outgoing administration was unwilling to contemplate long-range policies for dealing with North Korea and the issues posed by its nuclear noncompliance, and in the early months after its January 20 inauguration, the incoming administration was not organized well enough to do so either. Similarly in Seoul, Kim Young Sam, assisted by last-minute red-baiting against Kim Dae Jung, won the presidential election in mid-December and took office on February 25, far from well equipped to deal with immediate crisis.

The IAEA, however, did not wait for the new governments in Washington and Seoul to get settled before pressing its ultimatum. On February 26, the day after the IAEA Board of Governors formally endorsed the demand for mandatory "special inspection" of the two suspect sites, Blix sent a telex to the North Korean Foreign Ministry requesting that IAEA inspectors be permitted to travel to Yongbyon on March 16 to examine the two disputed places. Blix also notified the UN Security Council, which would be faced with enforcing the demand if North Korea refused to comply.

It was a tense time in North Korea. March 9 was the kickoff of the new Team Spirit exercise, this time downsized to a still-impressive 70,000 South Korean troops and 50,000 American troops, including the landing of 19,000 Americans from outside the country and the deployment of the aircraft carrier USS *Independence* offshore.

The day before the exercise, North Korea announced that Kim Jong Il, who had been supreme military commander for a little over a year, had ordered the entire nation and armed forces to "switch to a state of readiness for war" in view of the Team Spirit "nuclear war test aimed at a surprise, preemptive strike at the northern half of the country." Senior military officials, told that an attack might be imminent, were ordered to evacuate to underground fortifications. All military leaves were canceled, the heads of all soldiers were shaved, steel helmets were worn, and troops were issued rifle ammunition. In Pyongyang armored cars were drawn up in rows near security headquarters, and armed police checked military passes, while in the countryside the civilian population was mobilized to dig trenches near their homes as protection against air attack. In a message to the IAEA headquarters in Vienna, North Korea refused again to accept the special inspections, due to the Team Spirit exercise and the "state of semi-war" in the country. Blix rejected those excuses and repeated the inspection demand.

On March 12, North Korea announced it was withdrawing from the Nuclear Non-Proliferation Treaty, citing the treaty's escape clause

on defending supreme national interests. It gave two reasons: the
Team Spirit "nuclear war rehearsal," it charged, had violated the
spirit of the NPT and of the North-South denuclearization accord;
and the IAEA demand for special inspection of two suspect sites,
which it described as "an undisguised strong arm act designed to
disarm the DPRK and strangle our socialist system." Pyongyang recognized that under the treaty its withdrawal would not take effect
until after a three-month waiting period. If and when it became effective on June 12, North Korea's action would be the first withdrawal
by any nation from the treaty.

Although there had been abundant hints that North Korea
might withdraw from the NPT, many officials who had not been
monitoring the North Korean nuclear situation were unaware of
them. Most governments and publics were blindsided. The announcement of the withdrawal was treated as an incomprehensible act of
defiance and an ominous sign that North Korea was hell-bent on the
production of nuclear weapons. As the world reacted with shock and
dismay, North Korea's nuclear program suddenly leaped to the top of
the international agenda.

# 12

## WITHDRAWAL AND ENGAGEMENT

The first nuclear proliferation crisis of the post–cold war era came as an unwelcome surprise to the newly installed governments of Kim Young Sam in Seoul and Bill Clinton in Washington, which were both barely organized to deal with routine business, let alone a complex and dangerous confrontation with North Korea.

The South Korean government was in its fifteenth day in office on March 12, 1993, when the new foreign minister, Han Sung Joo, received word of North Korea's announcement that it intended to withdraw from the Non-Proliferation Treaty. A former professor of international relations with a Ph.D. from the University of California at Berkeley, Han was an expert on regional and global issues but a neophyte in governmental service. After trying in vain to reach the new South Korean president, who was attending a naval graduation ceremony outside Seoul, Han sat down to assess the potential consequences of North Korea's precipitating act.

The major concerns, as Han saw them, lined up in this order: first, the possibility that North Korea would actually produce nuclear weapons, thereby changing the strategic situation on the divided peninsula; second, the possibility that the United States and other nations would react so strongly that war would break out in Korea; third, the expectable demand inside South Korea to match the North Korean bomb program, touching off an arms race that could spur Japan as well as South Korea to become nuclear weapons powers and destroy the international nonproliferation regime that had retarded the spread of nuclear weapons for two decades. These possibilities would engage the two Koreas, the United States, and the international community over many months to come.

Two weeks after the announcement, Han traveled to Washington with the sketchy outlines of what he called a "stick and carrot" approach to persuading Pyongyang to change its mind during the ninety-day waiting period before its withdrawal would become effective. As Han saw it, the stick would be supplied by potential UN Security Council sanctions. Under chapter 7 of the UN Charter, which had been invoked after the Iraqi invasion of Kuwait, these sanctions could range from downgrading or severance of diplomatic relations to economic embargoes or military action. The carrots could include cancellation of the Team Spirit military exercise, security guarantees, trade, and other inducements to cooperate with the international community. "Pressure alone will not work," Han declared.

Han's approach was in line with the thinking of most officials in the State Department, whose business and tradition is to negotiate, but it was controversial among the more hawkish elements in Seoul and many sectors of the U.S. government. "The [U.S.] Joint Chiefs of Staff said, 'Under no circumstances should you engage [the North Koreans] in negotiations. You should not reward them. You should punish them,' " recalled a State Department official. But the official added, "As soon as you said, 'How do you mean, punish them?' of course the JCS would back away from any military options."

The absence of acceptable military options was also evident in Seoul. A few weeks after the North Korean announcement, when U.S. defense secretary Les Aspin made his first official visit to the ROK capital, Defense Minister Kwon Yong Hae warned that even a "surgical strike" against the Yongbyon reactor would lead to a major escalation of hostilities on the peninsula. The result, Kwon said, could be a general war that would wreak death and destruction on South Korea and immediately involve the military forces of the United States. Such an attack, even if completely successful, would probably not destroy any plutonium that might already be hidden away in North Korea.

Negotiations quickly emerged as the consensus solution in Washington, not because they appeared to be promising but because nobody could come up with another feasible plan to head off a crisis in Northeast Asia. However, talks with the North Koreans were highly controversial. With no strong signals coming from Clinton, the administration seemed unable to make a clear-cut decision to offer negotiations.

China, which was widely recognized as a crucial participant in the international maneuvering, was urging direct negotiations between the United States and North Korea, which were ardently desired by Pyongyang. South Korean Foreign Minister Han, in a meeting with Chinese Foreign Minister Qian Qichen in Bangkok on April 22, said Seoul would drop its long-standing opposition to Washington-Pyongyang talks if China, in return, would agree not to veto a UN Security Council resolution calling on the North to comply with international nuclear inspections rather than withdraw from the NPT. Qian did not immediately accept the deal, but in fact China did not veto the resolution.

With the precedent of the carefully limited 1992 New York meeting of Arnold Kanter and Kim Yong Sun before them, American officials were moving toward a decision to undertake direct negotiations with the North without the participation of the South, which was a reversal of often-declared U.S. policy. The Washington-Pyongyang talks were "the South Koreans' idea . . . they actually came to us and suggested it," according to Raymond Burkhardt, who was acting U.S. ambassador in Seoul at the time. Burkhardt added, however, that it was initially understood on both sides that the talks would be limited to nuclear issues, which were peculiarly the province of the United States as a nuclear power.

With Washington still unable to decide what approach to take, Pyongyang forced the issue. In early May, with about a month to go before the June 12 deadline, a diplomat at North Korea's UN Mission in New York telephoned C. Kenneth Quinones, the DPRK country officer in the State Department, to ask if the Americans wanted to meet and, if so, the sooner the better. Some of Quinones's colleagues were amazed that he had spoken on the telephone to North Koreans, but he pointed out that the North Koreans had placed the call. On further consideration, the State Department took North Korea's initiative as a hopeful sign of eagerness to avoid a confrontation over the nuclear issue. The administration decided to move ahead to talks.

The U.S. official chosen to negotiate with North Korea was Robert L. Gallucci, the breezy, Brooklyn-born assistant secretary of state for politico-military affairs. A man of abundant self-confidence and a good sense of humor, he was an expert on nuclear issues and a veteran of the postwar UN effort to dismantle Iraq's nuclear and chemical weapons programs. As Gallucci said later, he was "blissfully ignorant of profound regional contact," having previously spent only five days in South Korea and none in the North. Gallucci was picked largely because the negotiations were conceived as being narrowly focused on the proliferation question, and Washington did not wish to name a more politically oriented official whose outlook and responsibilities might alarm Seoul. Once he began the negotiations, however, Gallucci's perspective widened rapidly.

On the North Korean side, the negotiator was Kang Sok Ju, the deputy foreign minister whom I had met several times in New York and Pyongyang. Kang had attended the International Relations College in Pyongyang and had served in the international department of the Workers Party, the North Korean Mission in Paris, and as a deputy foreign minister for European affairs. A self-assured and evidently well-connected man (his older brother is head of the Workers Party History Research Institute), I had found him more direct and willing to engage than other senior North Korean diplomats, and less openly ideological. He had more experience in the west than most North Korean diplomats, and he told American negotiators at one point that one of his favorite books was *Gone with the Wind.* To their amazement, he quoted from it to prove the point.

After three lower-level exchanges to set it up, the first meeting between Gallucci and Kang took place at the U.S. Mission to the United Nations on Wednesday, June 2, only ten days before North Korea's withdrawal from the NPT was to become effective. Except for one or two career officials who had been present at the one-day

Kanter–Kim Yong Sun meeting the previous year, the American negotiators had never even met a North Korean before, and Kang and his team had never had a serious conversation with an American official. Each side was nervous and uncertain about what to expect from the other.

Speaking for the record as it would be read at home, Kang opened with a lengthy speech about the glories of Kim Il Sung and the *juche* system, which depressed the Americans but is obligatory for most North Korean presentations. The exchanges that followed did not get far, with North Koreans adamantly refusing to stay in the NPT and the Americans demanding that they do so. As the talks seemed to be getting nowhere, the U.S. team returned to Washington at the weekend and told the North Koreans essentially, if you want to meet again, call us and tell us what you have in mind.

On Monday morning, responding to a North Korean call, Quinones returned to New York and met three Pyongyang officials in a Forty-second Street coffee shop. There for the next three days, the American diplomat carried on a Socratic dialogue with the DPRK diplomats, drinking orange juice and coffee for hours at a time at a table by the front window of the coffee shop, where nobody paid any attention to them except (Quinones learned later) the FBI, which photographed the rendezvous. Quinones patiently explained to the uninformed visitors how the U.S. government and State Department were organized, what was or was not possible in the American system, and what types of security assurances might be provided to them in return for a decision to remain in the NPT.

After the coffee shop talks, Quinones and several other U.S. diplomats crafted prospective assurances against "the threat and use of force, including nuclear weapons" and against "interference in each other's internal affairs." To defend themselves against potential intra-administration criticism that they had given in to Pyongyang, they took the phrases directly from the UN Charter and previous official U.S. statements in other circumstances.

Meeting in lengthy sessions on June 10 and 11—the very eve of the June 12 date—Gallucci and Kang hammered out a six-paragraph joint statement. The key points were the American security assurances, an agreement to continue their official dialogue and, in return, a North Korean decision to "suspend" its withdrawal from the NPT for "as long as it considers necessary."

The joint statement removed the immediate threat of North Korean withdrawal from the Non-Proliferation Treaty and defused the sense of crisis, even though it did not resolve any of the inspection issues that had brought it on. The Americans who had participated in the negotiations were elated, especially because Pyongyang's negotiators proved to be open to argument and logic rather than the extraterrestrials some had expected. "I would make a point to Kang and he would make a point," said Gallucci, which would have been unremarkable in most negotiations but had by no means seemed assured in the case of North Koreans. After the opening lecture, Gallucci found Kang more open to reason than the Iraqis he had dealt with. Above all, Kang handled the nuclear questions in ways that suggested these were bargainable—that agreements could be made on many issues, if the two sides could agree on the price.

For the North Koreans, a joint statement with the United States was an achievement of immense importance. A year earlier, at the end of the Kanter–Kim Yong Sun talk, the Bush administration had refused to issue such a document. Even though vague in many respects, the joint statement this time was of great symbolic value to the Foreign Ministry and to others in Pyongyang who were arguing for making a serious effort to bargain with the Americans on the nuclear program. Even if it had only described the weather in New York, the statement would have been tangible evidence that the United States had recognized the legitimacy of North Korea and was willing to negotiate. By raising the stakes with its nuclear program, North Korea suddenly had become important to the United States. For the same reasons that Pyongyang was satisfied, the joint statement raised hackles in conservative circles in Seoul, where American relations with North Korea were anathema. This zero-sum pattern was to persist throughout the nuclear crisis.

In what had seemed only a minor piece of business at the end of the June 11 session, the American side suggested that follow-up communications take place through the North Korean UN Mission in New York. This move, which the DPRK officials immediately understood and accepted, gave the two countries a direct, authorized, and far more workable conduit for exchanges than the rigidly structured diplomatic talks in Beijing that had taken place periodically since 1988. If North Korea's objective had been to seize the attention of Washington and force it to negotiate seriously on a bilateral basis, its strategy had succeeded brilliantly.

## THE LIGHT-WATER REACTOR PLAN

On July 1, as Washington officials were preparing to continue the talks with Pyongyang on the outstanding nuclear issues, the new South Korean president, Kim Young Sam, voiced harsh criticisms of the negotiations in separate interviews with the British Broadcasting Company and *The New York Times.* In the *Times* interview, which drew the most attention in the U.S. capital, Kim charged that the North Koreans were manipulating the negotiations "to buy time to finish their project," and he expressed hope that the United States would "not continue to be led on by North Korea." American officials, who had undertaken the negotiations at the suggestion of the South and who had kept the South informed step by step, reacted with shock and anger.

This was only the first in a series of surprises from Kim Young Sam. Like much of the Korean public, whose feelings about the North are a complicated mixture of kinship, disdain, and fear, Kim's views on North Korea were replete with inconsistency.

Born on an island off the far south coast, Kim Young Sam had had little to do with North Korea issues during most of his career as an opposition political leader. Except for his strong prodemocracy stands, Kim was considered moderate to conservative on most political issues. As noted in Chapter 6, his mother had been murdered in 1960 by a North Korean agent who had invaded his parents' home. In 1992 his successful campaign for president featured anticommunist attacks on his longtime adversary Kim Dae Jung, whom he falsely accused of being endorsed by Pyongyang. On the other hand in his February 1993 inaugural address, Kim Young Sam offered to meet his North Korean counterpart "at any time and any place," and he declared that as members of the same Korean family, "no ally can be more valuable than national kinship." The latter remark, which implied a higher priority to reconciliation with the North than alliance with the United States, created something of a sensation on both sides of the DMZ.

What drove Kim Young Sam's northern policies above all were the tides of domestic public opinion. Unlike his military predecessors, Kim was a professional politician with a keen interest in the shifting views of the public. Known for relying more on his feel for the political aspects of issues than any overall strategy, he cited newspaper headlines or television broadcasts more often in internal discussions than official papers, which aides complained he did not read. According to a White House official, Kim constantly referred to polling data, public opinion, and political positioning in discussing his reactions to events, even in meetings and telephone calls with the U.S. president.

In mid-July, just prior to the second round of U.S.–North Korean negotiations, Kim was personally reassured about American policy by President Clinton, who came to Korea for a brief visit following the Group of Seven summit conference in Tokyo. Traveling to the DMZ for the traditional meeting with American troops, the U.S. president, clad in a fatigue jacket and "U.S. Forces Korea" cap, was taken to the very edge of the Bridge of No Return, which marks the border with North Korea—close to where the two American officers had been beaten to death in 1976 and much closer to the border than his predecessors had come during their visits to GIs. The North Korean soldiers manning a guard post on the other side of the bridge were in plain sight. Turning to a press pool accompanying him, Clinton held forth on the issue of the day: Due to U.S. security commitments, he said, "it is pointless for [North Koreans] to try to develop nuclear weapons because if they ever use them it would be the end of their country."

Clinton's remarks went over well in South Korea and at home, where he was considered suspect among many military-oriented people for evading the draft during the Vietnam War, but they were unwelcome in Pyongyang, where Foreign Ministry officials were preparing for the second round of talks with the Americans. When the negotiations convened on July 14 in Geneva, Kang protested that the United States had promised in June not to threaten the DPRK, yet Clinton had publicly threatened them with annihilation while standing in military garb on their very border. The Americans responded that when it came to bellicose language, Pyongyang had few peers. "The President of the United States went to South Korea. What did you expect him to say there?" Gallucci retorted. It soon became clear that Kang, while upset by Clinton's remarks, had no intention of breaking off the negotiations.

The second day of negotiations took place in the North Korean Mission in Geneva, the first time they had been on North Korea's home turf—all the meetings in New York and the first one in Geneva had been in American buildings. The DPRK Mission had been polished up for the occasion, complete with gleaming silver trays on which were arrayed delicate Swiss pastries. This was in startling contrast to the minimal hospitality of the rich Americans, who had had to scrape up their own private funds to provide even coffee and rolls served on paper plates. With appropriate fanfare in this elaborately prepared setting, North Korea put forward an initiative that would change the nature of the negotiations.

The DPRK had undertaken a peaceful nuclear program in good faith, Kang Sok Ju began, using natural uranium, which is mined in the country, and gas-graphite technology, which was widely available. While it had no intention of producing nuclear weapons, he insisted, other nations were concerned that the facilities had a big potential for weapons production. The DPRK, he announced, was willing to shift its entire nuclear development program to more up-to-date, less proliferation-prone light-water reactors (LWRs) to fill its energy needs, if these could be supplied by the international community.

Light-water reactors, originally so named to distinguish them from reactors using deuterium oxide, or heavy water, rely on ordinary water to moderate the nuclear reaction that produces energy. They are much more complex than the primitive gas-graphite reactors, which were in service or under construction in Yongbyon. Unlike the Yongbyon works, virtually all the key LWR components were beyond North Korea's technological capability and would have to be imported from abroad. LWRs would produce vastly more energy: If it were working well, Yongbyon's only operating reactor, rated at 5 megawatts (5 million watts), would produce only enough electricity to power perhaps five large American office buildings;

but two standard LWRs would produce 2,000 megawatts—nearly enough electricity to power the Washington metropolitan area.

The Americans at the conference table with technical expertise were unimpressed with what one called a "totally hare-brained" scheme, because of the expense and complexity involved. Energy experts realized that North Korea's electricity requirements could be met much more easily and cheaply with nonnuclear fuels. But other members of the U.S. team immediately saw Pyongyang's offer as a face-saving way to resolve the proliferation and inspection questions. It could modernize its nuclear power production without ever admitting it had been seeking to make atomic weapons. As soon as Kang announced his offer, Robert Carlin, the senior North Korea-watcher in the State Department's Bureau of Intelligence and Research, wrote on his note pad, "They want out of this issue."

Gallucci was skeptical at first that North Korea was serious about trading in its indigenous nuclear program, but he quickly saw the positive possibilities for international control of the North Korean program. He also saw the immense difficulties, especially the high costs involved. "The last time I looked, such reactors cost about $1 billion per copy," he told the North Koreans.

North Korea's quest for light-water reactors, although new to most of the Americans at the conference table, actually had a long history. The Soviet reactors that Pyongyang had requested in the mid-1980s were to have been of the light-water type. Although the Soviet–DPRK deal to supply them ultimately collapsed, the allure of more modern nuclear facilities remained undimmed in leadership circles in Pyongyang. When IAEA director general Hans Blix visited North Korea in May 1992, he was asked to help North Korea acquire light-water reactors and to guarantee a secure supply from abroad of the enriched uranium fuel they would require. Blix promised to try to help. Two months later, DPRK deputy premier Kim Dal Hyon, on a visit to Seoul, proposed that the two Koreas cooperate on an LWR plant, to be built in the North close to the DMZ, to provide power to both economies. Under this plan, South Korea would provide most of the capital and technology. The proposal, which was kept secret at the time, was shoved aside during the deterioration of North-South relations later in the year and went nowhere.

When the LWR proposal was resurrected in the Geneva negotiations with the United States, Gallucci was warned by senior State and Defense Department officials against making any commitment, especially a financial commitment, to the proposal. On July 19, at the end of six days of talks, Gallucci agreed in a formal statement that the United States would "support the introduction of LWRs and . . . explore with the DPRK ways in which LWRs could be obtained," but only as part of a "final resolution" of nuclear issues. Gallucci later said this gauzy statement was "seven times removed from any commitment" to provide LWRs.

The negotiations adjourned without progress on the contentious issue of permitting IAEA "special inspections" of the two suspected nuclear waste sites. The two sides agreed to continue meeting, but a U.S. statement specified that it would not begin the third round of negotiations until "serious discussions" were under way on nuclear issues in North-South channels and between North Korea and the IAEA.

## KIM YOUNG SAM BLOWS THE WHISTLE

The American–North Korean negotiations in June had had the limited objective of persuading Pyongyang not to withdraw from the Non-Proliferation Treaty, and Washington had offered limited benefits in return. Privately Gallucci characterized his initial negotiating posture as, "If they do everything we want, we send them a box of oranges." The North Korean offer in July, to give up its entire indigenous nuclear program in favor of the proliferation-resistant light-water reactors, had dramatically changed the bidding. Now the objective in view was much more ambitious—but it was also clear that Pyongyang would demand more extensive benefits in return. While American officials were intrigued and some elated, many in Seoul were unhappy with the shift from limited to virtually unlimited U.S.–DPRK talks.

As it turned out, progress toward meeting the American conditions for convening the third round of U.S.–DPRK talks, in which broader issues were to be discussed, was excruciatingly slow. Talks between North Korea and the Vienna-based IAEA quickly sank into exasperating arguments over the DPRK's obligations. As the IAEA saw it, North Korea was still required by treaty to comply with all nuclear inspection requirements that had been or would be imposed on it, like any other signatory, as long as it had not officially left the NPT. Pyongyang, however, insisted that in suspending its withdrawal from the treaty, it had entered a "special" and "unique" category in which it alone would determine what inspection requirements to accept. It was ready to accept very few.

To keep check on the North Korean program while the arguments continued, Washington invented an interim concept called "continuity of safeguards," which it insisted was essential. This required that agency inspectors be admitted to the Yongbyon site to replace films and batteries in monitoring equipment and to make other nonintrusive tests to check that no diversion of nuclear materials was taking place. While the IAEA was uncomfortable with this ad hoc concept—insisting that North Korea should comply in the fullest with its requirements—it went along. With film and batteries running down or even running out from time to time, the IAEA repeatedly threatened to declare that "continuity of safeguards" had been lost. It was clear that such a declaration would trigger an immediate demand for UN Security Council sanctions against North Korea.

IAEA inspectors were permitted to return to Yongbyon in August (as they had been in mid-May) but only to replace the film and batteries in the monitoring equipment. The IAEA protested vigorously that this was not enough and publicly criticized North Korea. Pyongyang reacted with bitter rhetoric. Under pressure, North Korea in September and October offered to accept another visit for film and battery replacement, but the IAEA rejected the conditions, declaring them to be insufficient. And so it went.

Action on the North-South front, the other prerequisite for convening the third round of U.S.–North Korean negotiations, was even less productive. In May, South Korea proposed meetings between the two sides to work on the nuclear issues, and North Korea counterproposed an exchange of "special envoys" to deal with unification issues and prepare a North-South summit. Despite a series of exchanges over the summer and fall, the two sides could not even agree to convene working-level meetings at Panmunjom to prepare for more important meetings. Working-level contacts were finally convened for three days in October but without results.

In early October 1993, with no progress being made on any front, Representative Gary Ackerman, the ebullient and earthy Democratic lawmaker from New York City, traveled to Pyongyang on a get-acquainted mission. Earlier in the year Ackerman had succeeded Stephen Solarz as chairman of the Asia-Pacific subcommittee of the House Foreign Affairs Committee, and thus he carried considerable weight in Congress. He bore a message from the administration, which he delivered in person to Kim Il Sung, that the United States wished to resolve its issues with the DPRK through dialogue and negotiations and wished to resume the bilateral engagement at the political level.

Accompanying Ackerman was C. Kenneth Quinones, the Korean-speaking State Department desk officer for North Korea who had helped get the talks started. After lengthy talks with Quinones on outstanding issues, Pyongyang's Foreign Ministry presented him with a paper proposing a series of trade-offs to settle the issues at stake with the United States. In the paper, written in English in longhand, the North Koreans said they were ready to remain in the NPT and submit to regular IAEA inspections and to discuss the contentious issue of the "special inspections" that the IAEA had demanded, in return for an end to U.S.–ROK Team Spirit military exercises, the lifting of American economic sanctions, and the convening of the long-delayed third round of U.S.–DPRK negotiations to tackle broader issues. The proposal for trade-offs, in retrospect, was a fundamental shift in the concept of the negotiations, which until that point had been based on making step-by-step progress toward accords rather than one simultaneous and comprehensive deal, later termed "a package solution." The Foreign Ministry officials said the handwritten proposals had been cleared with the top leadership of their country, meaning Kim Il Sung and Kim Jong Il.

When Quinones returned to Washington, he found a very skeptical group of U.S. policy makers, who insisted that details of potential accords be hammered out before proceeding further at the political level. In New York, Quinones and Gary Samore, Gallucci's top aide, engaged in a series of unannounced meetings with officials

of the North Korean UN Mission to try to work out a detailed accord. When this effort ran into trouble, a more senior State Department official, Deputy Assistant Secretary of State Thomas Hubbard,
began making frequent trips to New York to see the North Koreans.

With little progress being made, public as well as official frustration with the stalemate was soaring. On November 1, IAEA director
general Hans Blix reported to the UN General Assembly in pessimis-
tic terms on the agency's standoff with Pyongyang, though he
stopped just short of declaring the "continuity of safeguards" to be
lost. The General Assembly reacted with a resounding 140-to-1 vote
(with China abstaining and only Pyongyang dissenting) urging North
Korea "to cooperate immediately" with the IAEA, a demonstration
of how isolated Pyongyang had become.

At a press conference in Seoul, the exasperated South Korean
defense minister, Kwon Yong Hae, expressed concern about the
North Korean nuclear program and mentioned the possibility of using military action to stop it. In a meeting with visiting Secretary of
Defense Les Aspin, Kwon agreed to put off any decision about holding the Team Spirit exercise. Aspin said, "The ball is now in North
Korea's court. The world awaits."

On the way home from Seoul, Aspin gave a background briefing
to journalists aboard his plane that inadvertently gave rise to alarmist
reports that war was on the verge of breaking out. Reuters news
agency, which filed the most breathless dispatch, quoted a senior
U.S. defense official as saying, "We may be entering a kind of danger
zone," because North Korea had massed 70 percent of its military
force near South Korea (which in fact was nothing new) and might
launch a desperate conventional attack on the South sparked by
hunger and economic frustration in Pyongyang. In a precursor to
concerns which later were to be widely discussed, Aspin told the
reporters, "These guys are starving" and may feel that "you can
either starve or get killed in a war." The Aspin briefing gave rise to a
full-scale journalistic war scare—to the surprise and dismay of most
officials who had been following the situation.

On November 5 a passionate column by Charles Krauthammer
in *The Washington Post* demanded that Clinton "stop talking to the
North Koreans—it is time for an economic blockade—and start talk-

ing to the American people" about a military emergency in Asia. The administration was so jarred by Krauthammer's column that a State Department meeting was convened to discuss it. Two days later, President Clinton threw oil on the fire by warning on NBC's *Meet the Press* that "North Korea cannot be allowed to develop a nuclear bomb," implying that the United States would take military action to stop it. Weeks later, after various U.S. officials speculated that Pyongyang already had at least one bomb, the White House said Clinton had misspoken.

Suddenly North Korea was at the top of the news in the United States. An NBC/*Wall Street Journal* public opinion poll reported that North Korea's development of a nuclear weapon was considered the nation's most serious foreign policy problem by 31 percent of a nationwide sample—a larger proportion than any other single issue they picked.

On November 11, amid the war scare and in the absence of diplomatic movement, the chief DPRK negotiator, Kang Sok Ju, made public the proposed "package solution" in Pyongyang. Without revealing its earlier history, he set out the main elements of the handwritten paper that had been given to Quinones a month earlier and discussed inconclusively ever since.

On November 15, after fifteen midlevel meetings in New York and a host of letters back and forth to Pyongyang, the administration finally decided to put its own "package deal" on the table. The essence of the immediate bargain was North Korean resumption of regular IAEA inspections and a renewal of dialogue with the South, in return for cancellation of the 1994 Team Spirit military exercise and the convening of the long-delayed third round of U.S.–DPRK negotiations. Phase two, to be bargained in detail when American and North Korean negotiators finally began their third round, would deal with IAEA inspections of the two disputed Yongbyon waste sites, diplomatic recognition of North Korea, and trade and investment concessions from the United States, South Korea, and Japan.

The new administration proposal immediately leaked to *The Washington Post*'s R. Jeffrey Smith, who was following the maneuvering closely. The publicity was a bombshell in Seoul, which was always extremely sensitive to American concessions to North Korea, and especially to suggestions that South Korea was not the dominant force in policy toward Pyongyang. In addition, the proposal was anathema to President Kim Young Sam for another and highly personal reason: a "package deal" similar in name and concept had been publicly suggested in spring by his longtime rival in domestic politics, Kim Dae Jung. If *he* was for it, Kim Young Sam was automatically against it.

The South Korean president's views surfaced dramatically and unexpectedly on November 23, at the start of his first official visit to Washington. Ushered into the Oval Office for what had been planned as a brief meeting to put a pro forma stamp of approval on the proposal, Kim announced that it looked to him and his people as if the United States were accommodating North Korea without even giving Seoul a role in the decision process. His eyes flashing and his gestures emphatic, Kim insisted that he, not the Americans, have the final say on whether to cancel the Team Spirit exercise, and that he be the one to announce the decision when the time came. He also demanded that the long-discussed "exchange of envoys" between North and South actually take place before the third round of U.S.–North Korean negotiations begin.

Clinton was startled and his senior aides mystified by the nature and the vehemence of Kim's objections, since the various elements of the proposed offer had been discussed for months with officials of Kim's government. As the "brief" Oval Office meeting stretched on to eighty minutes, with senior American and Korean officials, including Kim's foreign minister, waiting with growing apprehension in another room, the Americans realized that Kim's objections had as much to do with appearance as with substance. A change in terminology to describe the proposal to North Korea as "thorough and broad" rather than as "comprehensive" or a "package" seemed to ease Kim's concern substantially. The White House also agreed to permit Kim to announce the final decision on postponement of Team Spirit if it came to that, and to make the exchange of North-South "special envoys" a prerequisite for the next round of U.S.–DPRK talks. The latter requirement proved to be an important stumbling block: North Korea bitterly resented being required to give in to the South's demand in order to deal with the Americans.

By the end of the Kim Young Sam visit, the Americans had begun to appreciate the complexity and difficulty of negotiating with North Korea on the nuclear issue. In fact, the parties were arrayed in a series of overlapping circles: between North Korea and the International Atomic Energy Agency, between North Korea and South Korea, and between North Korea and the United States. As in a combination lock, all three had to be in alignment simultaneously for the talks to succeed. Now a fourth circle of problems had been added: between Washington and Seoul. As the holiday season approached in 1993, negotiations with the DPRK seemed to portend more problems than progress.

## THE SEASON OF CRISIS BEGINS

In Pyongyang in early December 1993, the Workers Party Central Committee made a surprising admission. At a meeting marking the end of the country's current seven-year economic plan, the party announced publicly that the major targets of the plan had not been met, and it warned that the DPRK economy was in a "grave situation." Battered by the collapse of its allies and trading partners and by economic stagnation at home, "the socialist paradise" was suffering its fourth consecutive year of economic decline. Its GNP, once on a par with that of the South, was estimated at one-sixteenth the size of the booming ROK economy, and the gap was growing rapidly.

Instead of adopting a new seven-year plan with the usual emphasis on heavy industry, the party decreed a three-year period of transition, with top priority given to agriculture, light industry, and foreign trade. Behind the brave rhetoric about "socialist construction," the meaning of the shift was clear: the North's leaders had lowered their sights and were aiming at mere survival. They were failing to feed their people and to provide enough clothing and other consumer goods to avoid privation; hence the new emphasis on agriculture and light industry. In an attempt to ease the situation without making basic changes in its autarkic command economy, North Korea was looking to exports for salvation—but it had little to sell that the world wanted.

Kim Il Sung endorsed the economic shift in his annual New Year's address to the nation, typically the most important policy pronouncement of the year. Gone was the traditional goal, repeated incessantly by Kim since 1962, that North Koreans would soon be able to "eat rice and meat soup, wear silk clothes and live in a tile roofed house." Kim conceded that during the seven-year plan, "we came up against considerable difficulty and obstacles in the economic construction owing to the unexpected international events and the acute situation created in the country." Giving his personal blessing to the new priorities, Kim described the situation at home and abroad as "complicated and strained."

This abrupt departure from Kim Il Sung's eternal official optimism was like God announcing that things weren't what they should be in heaven. Adding to the impact of Kim's change in direction and tone was evidence that in his eighties he was emerging from semiretirement to reassert himself in day-to-day administration. American experts interpreted this as a sign of dissatisfaction with the work of his eldest son, Kim Jong Il, who had been openly designated as his chosen successor in 1980.

How much Kim Il Sung knew—or wanted to know—about the details of his country's problems in his latter years is a debatable point. According to a variety of North Korean and foreign sources, the younger Kim had increasingly assumed the management of governmental and party affairs. On the eve of his eightieth birthday in 1992, Kim Il Sung had told *The Washington Times* that he continued to carry out "some external work," but that "as far as the internal affairs of our country are concerned, everything is dealt with by [Kim Jong Il]."

Nonetheless, according to North Korean defector Kang Myong Do, a son-in-law of Prime Minister Kang Song San, the turning point in Kim Il Sung's reengagement in the economy had taken place by the time of the interview. In late 1991 or early 1992, the defector said, his father-in-law, who had been prime minister during two earlier periods and was the son of one of Kim Il Sung's guerrilla comrades, gave the Great Leader an unvarnished account of the desperate economic conditions in the strategic province along the Chinese and Russian borders where he was currently serving as provincial governor. Beginning in March 1992, startled by the contrast with rosier reports that he had been receiving through official channels, Kim Il Sung convened a series of extended Workers Party meetings on the economic situation. By the end of the year, the incumbent prime minister had been fired and Kang had been brought back for his third term in the job. In early 1993 Kim presided over an extended Politburo conference on the economic troubles, which led eventually to the new economic policies that he announced in December.

Toward the end of January, Kim Il Sung received an illustrious visitor. America's most famous evangelist, the Reverend Billy Graham, had often carried his crusades to communist and totalitarian countries, but he had a special interest in North Korea because his wife, Ruth, had spent part of her youth attending the American School in Pyongyang while her parents were missionaries in China. In 1992 the evangelist had paid a successful visit during which he preached in several small churches and brought a conciliatory message from President Bush. With tension growing again between Washington and Pyongyang, Graham had requested and received a message from Clinton in connection with his trip. This one, however, was only a few sentences long, with no salutations or good wishes and very blunt—it said, in essence, cooperate on the nuclear issue, and only then can relations improve.

The evangelist and his aides, especially Stephen Linton, a missionary's son who knows the culture and the language from years living in the South, sought to surround the Clinton pronouncement with grace notes and explanatory phrases that could make it more polite, less stark, and more acceptable to the eighty-one-year-old Korean leader. Nevertheless, when Graham conveyed the heart of the American president's message with its emphasis on North Korea's nuclear program, Kim became visibly angry, speaking loudly and shaking his fist. He harked back to the foreign policy pronouncements of his New Year's address, when he charged that the United States had raised "the nonexistent nuclear issue" and was itself to blame for bringing nuclear weapons into the Korean peninsula to threaten the DPRK. "Pressure and threat cannot work on us," Kim said in his address and repeated to Graham. The two countries needed to communicate with each other, Kim said, not confront each other—but if the United States used the language of threats, he declared, it would drive the situation to catastrophe.

As Graham was en route, a development in the United States had made North Korea's mood much less conciliatory. On January 26, the day before he arrived, *The New York Times* reported preparations for highly visible reinforcement of American forces in the Korean peninsula: deployment of Patriot missiles, the antimissile weapons used by American forces in the Gulf War. When Graham and his party landed in Pyongyang, antiaircraft missiles could be seen moving into place around the airport. Troops could be seen digging trenches in the capital, even in the subzero cold of the depth of winter. "The tension crackled," observed a Graham aide.

Deploying the Patriots had been under consideration since December, when they had been requested by the U.S. military commander in Korea, General Gary Luck, as a precautionary measure in case war broke out and North Korean Rodong missiles were fired against American military targets. Luck's December request had been temporarily shelved because of State Department objections that the deployments could upset the negotiations with North Korea over resuming the international inspections. But when Michael Gordon, the *Times* Pentagon correspondent, made a reporting trip to the South and returned with information about the potential Patriot deployment, "the White House went into a panic," Gordon recalled later. Fearful that the administration would be charged with withholding vital military equipment from American troops—as had been the case when a U.S. peacekeeping unit had been overwhelmed in Somalia the previous October—the White House immediately began briefing members of Congress on the Patriot request, and National Security Adviser Anthony Lake telephoned Gordon to tell him that Luck's request was in the process of being approved—giving rise to an exclusive story in the *Times.*

News stories and commentaries about the likely Patriot deployments were replete with references to their use by U.S. forces in Operation Desert Storm in the Persian Gulf. While North Korea was absorbing this decision, the South Korean Defense Ministry announced that the Team Spirit military exercise, which always brought a fierce reaction from Pyongyang and had been a factor in the breakdown of negotiations the previous year, would be held again in 1994 unless North Korea agreed to pending proposals for resumption of international nuclear inspections.

At this point, the tone of North Korean statements shifted from optimistic about the outcome of U.S.–DPRK talks to bitterly accusatory. American experts believed this reflected a shift in the preponderance of opinion among the North Korean leadership. "United States Must Be Held Totally Responsible for Catastrophic Consequences Arising From Its Perfidy" was the headline on the English-language version of a statement issued January 31 by the North Korean Foreign Ministry. The statement cited the decision on the Patriots and reports of the impending decision on Team Spirit as "new war maneuvers the United States has been pursuing behind the screen of the DPRK–USA talks." North Korea threatened to break off the talks, pull out of the NPT, and accelerate its nuclear program—threats that were repeated in a letter to Gallucci from DPRK chief negotiator Kang Sok Ju, one of a series of missives that had been going back and forth in private between Washington and Pyongyang.

The negotiations had been difficult enough without additional complications. Throughout the fall and winter, the main venue of U.S.–DPRK communications had been a dingy basement room at United Nations headquarters in New York, where Deputy Assistant Secretary of State Tom Hubbard had been meeting North Korean ambassador Ho Jong, with one or two aides on each side. Each time the Americans felt they had reached an agreement with the North Koreans on resumption of IAEA inspections and North-South negotiations, it collapsed, sometimes because the IAEA or South Korea refused to compromise its position, sometimes because Pyongyang pulled back from a seemingly agreed position.

After a new round of abortive negotiations, the IAEA established a February 21 deadline for continuing its inspections of the Yongbyon nuclear facilities. Unless an agreement could be reached by then, the international agency said, it would turn the stalemate over to the UN Security Council for action. In advance of the deadline, U.S. diplomats began informal discussions with the four other permanent members of the Security Council about economic and political sanctions to be levied against North Korea, and the Pentagon began preparations to order more than a thousand additional troops to South Korea for the Team Spirit exercise.

At this point in mid-February, the U.S. ambassador to South Korea, James Laney, came to Washington deeply concerned and angry that nobody seemed to be in charge of administration strategy as the situation veered toward conflict with North Korea. Laney, former president of Emory University and, in earlier days, an Army enlisted man and later a theology teacher in Korea, made the rounds of senior officials at the White House, the State Department, and the Pentagon, and reported that Seoul was calm but that the ROK government was worried—more about overheated rhetoric and brinksmanship in Washington than about a potential nuclear threat from North Korea. Laney expressed worry about the potential for "accidental war" on the peninsula as the United States unnecessarily "ratcheted up" the IAEA inspection issues and seemed to be pushing North Korea to violent action rather than relying primarily on deterrence as in the past. General Luck, he reported, agreed with his view. Above all, he insisted, the matter demanded far greater priority and coordination in Washington. Referring to U.S. military and civilian casualties in a new Korean war, Laney warned the White House, "You could have 50,000 body bags coming home."

The ambassador's pleas were sobering for Vice President Al Gore and others in Washington. Partly as a result, Gallucci eventually was named as overall coordinator of U.S. policy toward North Korea, with the rank of ambassador and a charter to coordinate or at least rationalize the disparate views of the White House, State Department, Defense Department, CIA, and various officials and offices within them. Nonetheless, disagreements continued within the executive branch and also in Congress and in the press.

On February 15, North Korea accepted minimum conditions for resumption of IAEA inspections but then, characteristically, refused to issue visas to the inspectors until a number of preconditions were met. Finally, in a renewed set of Hubbard–Ho Jong talks in New York—the twenty-second in a series that had begun the previous September—the two sides agreed on a broad set of measures to take effect simultaneously. On March 1, which American negotiators dubbed Super Tuesday, everything was to be settled at once: international inspectors were to return to Yongbyon for inspections to ensure "continuity of safeguards"; the United States and South Korea were to announce cancellation of the 1994 Team Spirit exercise; working-level North-South contacts were to be launched at Panmunjom in preparation for the exchange of "special envoys"; and the United States and North Korea were to announce that they would convene their long-awaited third round of high-level negotiations on March 21.

By this time, however, the U.S. government and public were thoroughly exasperated by North Korean foot-dragging and reversals. Under pressure from Congress and editorial columnists not to reward Pyongyang prematurely, American officials announced that the third round of negotiations would not start until the IAEA inspections and now-contentious exchange of North-South envoys had been successfully accomplished.

The caution was warranted. North-South working-level meetings began at Panmunjom but quickly deadlocked over a series of North Korean demands and a stiffening of South Korean positions. At Yongbyon, while IAEA inspectors were permitted to carry out their maintenance and inspection activities at six sites, they were barred from taking sophisticated measurements at key points in the seventh and most sensitive site, the plutonium reprocessing plant. While the North Koreans produced legalistic justifications for its refusal to permit the measurements, IAEA officials concluded that its real purpose was to apply pressure in connection with its dispute with the South over the exchange of envoys. Deputy Assistant Secretary of State Hubbard, who was heavily involved in the issue on the Washington end, said, "There were two different games here, linked together. The international need of the IAEA was linked to North-South dialogue where the two Koreas play games."

From that point on, it was all downhill. On March 15 the international agency ordered its inspectors home, announcing that since they had failed to complete their work, the agency could not verify that there had been no diversion of nuclear materials to bomb production. In a special meeting, the IAEA board finally voted to turn the matter over to the UN Security Council. "The general mood is that the IAEA has really been jerked around long enough," an administration official told *The Washington Post.*

The U.S. military immediately began consulting Seoul about rescheduling the Team Spirit military exercise. Washington canceled its plans for the third round of U.S.–DPRK negotiations and once again resumed preparations to seek UN sanctions.

On March 19, at a final North-South working-level meeting at Panmunjom to discuss the deadlocked exchange-of-envoys issue, North Korean negotiator Park Yong Su dramatically worsened the explosive atmosphere. After harsh words had flowed back and forth across the table, Park threatened his southern counterpart, Song Young Dae: "Seoul is not far from here. If a war breaks out, it will be a sea of fire. Mr. Song, it will probably be difficult for you to survive." Shortly after that, the northern team walked out of the meeting.

South Korean officials watched the exchange on closed circuit television, which was rigged up to allow a select group in each capital to observe the Panmunjom meetings, even meetings such as this one that were not open to the press. In an unprecedented move, the Blue House, with the approval of Kim Young Sam himself, ordered release of the videotape of the closed meeting to television stations, alarming the South Korean public.

After the breakdown of IAEA inspections and the "sea of fire" remark, Kim Young Sam summoned an emergency meeting of his national security cabinet to approve deployment of the U.S. Patriot missiles, which had been in limbo while the nuclear negotiations held promise of results. The South's action, in turn, inflamed leadership and military circles in Pyongyang. Suddenly the Korean situation was headed into a new downward spiral, with potentially calamitous consequences.

# 13

## SHOWDOWN OVER
## NUCLEAR WEAPONS

The crisis over North Korea's nuclear program that gripped the peninsula and engaged the major powers in the spring of 1994 had much in common with the confrontation a year earlier over North Korea's threat to withdraw from the Non-Proliferation Treaty. As before, the North-South dialogue had broken down, pressures from all sides were building up against Pyongyang, and the International Atomic Energy Agency touched off the crisis by publicly declaring North Korea to be in violation of its international obligations.

Since the early 1993 encounter, Pyongyang had been using its nuclear program as a bargaining chip to trade for recognition, security assurances, and economic benefits from the United States. A failing and isolated regime with few other cards to play, Pyongyang enhanced its bargaining power whenever its cooperation with the IAEA diminished and the threat increased that it might proceed to manufacture nuclear weapons. At the same time, such troublemaking actions, if they went too far, also increased the risk of being confronted and possibly overwhelmed by external forces. By this time, North Korea had become skilled at brinksmanship, increasing its leverage by playing close to the edge of the precipice; the problem was that it wasn't always clear just where the edge was.

In 1994 the crisis was intensified by serious military dimensions. As the United States and its allies pushed for UN Security Council sanctions against Pyongyang, North Korea repeatedly declared that "sanctions are a declaration of war." In response, the Pentagon accelerated a U.S. military buildup in and around Korea that had quietly begun several months earlier. Preparations were being made in Washington for a much more powerful buildup of men and materiel, with great potential for precipitating a military clash on the divided peninsula.

For Robert Gallucci, the spring of 1994 had an eerie and disturbing resemblance to historian Barbara Tuchman's account of "the guns of August," when, in the summer of 1914, World War I began in cross-purposes, misunderstanding, and inadvertence. As he and other policy makers moved inexorably toward a confrontation with North Korea, Gallucci was conscious that "this had an escalatory quality, that could deteriorate not only into a war but into a big war." Secretary of Defense William Perry, looking back on the events, concluded that the course he was on "had a real risk of war associated with it." Commanders in the field were even more convinced. Lieutenant General Howell Estes, the senior U.S. Air Force officer in Korea, recalled later that although neither he nor other commanders said so out loud, not even in private conversations with one another, "inside we all thought we were going to war."

## THE DEFUELING CRISIS

The issue that precipitated this showdown was the unloading of the irradiated fuel rods from the 5-megawatt reactor at Yongbyon, North Korea's only indigenous reactor so far in operation. Such rods, each a yard long and about two inches wide, could be chemically treated in the plant in the final stages of construction at Yongbyon to separate plutonium for atomic weapons from the rest of the highly radioactive material.

Based on satellite surveillance of smoke coming from the containment vessel of the reactor, the CIA estimated that it had been shut down for up to 110 days in 1989, during which period about half of its eight thousand fuel rods could have been replaced and thus been made available for fabrication into plutonium. North Korea said the reactor had been down only about 60 days and that only a few rods had been removed because they were damaged. Based on the higher figure, the CIA estimated at the end of 1993 that North Korea might have obtained enough plutonium for one or two bombs of about ten kilotons of explosive power each, similar to those exploded by the United States at Hiroshima in 1945. This CIA estimate was the basis for a December 1993 National Intelligence Estimate that there was a "better than even" chance that North Korea already had the makings of a bomb (though State Department and U.S. national laboratory analysts hotly dissented), and it was the basis for numerous public statements along similar lines by the secretary of defense, the CIA director, and other senior U.S. government officials. (Much later, after the crisis was over, the CIA "reassessed" its methods of observation and concluded that the lower figure cited by North Korea, 60 days, could well have been right. If this were the case, the theoretical weapons potential of North Korea's plutonium was considerably smaller than had been stated at the time.)

Others believed, even at the time of the crisis, that the U.S. intelligence estimate was, in the words of *The Bulletin of the Atomic Scientists,* a "worst-case scare-nario"—that it was highly unlikely that North Korea could have unloaded so many rods so quickly and successfully, or that the rods could have been so well made or fully irradiated, or that the reprocessing operation could have worked so effectively that Pyongyang had the plutonium for one or two bombs. Even in the worst case, skeptics pointed out, possession of the plutonium was several key steps away from having an explodable and deliverable nuclear weapon. There was so much disagreement within the administration, Clinton's national security adviser, Anthony Lake, told me, that the president often received diametrically opposite estimates on North Korea from the CIA and the State Department on the same day.

Unloading the reactor in 1994 was of great importance for two reasons, one having to do with the past and the other with the future. Regarding the past, IAEA experts believed that systematic sampling and careful segregation of rods from particular parts of the reactor's core under its supervision would disclose how long the fuel had been burned and at what intensity. In this way, they could compile a verifiable record of the operating history of the reactor, confirming how many fuel rods had been previously removed, and therefore identify the outer limit of the plutonium that might have been produced.

Such a disclosure would be a major step toward eliminating the ambiguity about the DPRK's past acquisition of nuclear weapons material. From Pyongyang's viewpoint, however, this was a no-win proposition: if it was established that Pyongyang had not diverted nuclear fuel clandestinely to manufacture plutonium in the past, its nuclear threat would diminish and with it the country's bargaining power; but if the supervised unloading established that Pyongyang had lied and produced more plutonium than it had admitted, it would lose face and the hunt would be on for the missing nuclear material.

The future of the eight thousand fuel rods that would now be unloaded from the reactor was of even greater importance. Secretary of Defense Perry estimated that this entire load of rods could be converted into enough plutonium for four or five nuclear weapons. While the United States was not prepared to go to war to clarify the past, it was determined to do so, if necessary, to prevent North Korea from converting these and future irradiated fuel rods into plutonium for nuclear weapons. Nearing completion at Yongbyon was a much larger 50-megawatt reactor that potentially could produce much more plutonium, and an even larger 200-megawatt reactor was under construction nearby. The North Koreans had promised to place the unloaded fuel from these facilities under the inspection of the IAEA, but like everything else, this was subject to agreement, and that seemed increasingly doubtful.

North Korean negotiator Kang Sok Ju had been warned repeatedly, during talks with Gallucci, that if the refueling of the 5-megawatt reactor took place without IAEA supervision, negotiations with the United States would be terminated, even though such action would be within North Korea's rights under the Non-Proliferation Treaty. However, a U.S. official familiar with the contents of the meetings said, "We didn't lay down with great force and clarity that this was a drop-dead issue." Moreover, this official said, most of the U.S.–North Korean discussion before the spring of 1994 had been about the *re*fueling of the reactor, not about *de*fueling, or unloading the current stock of irradiated fuel rods. "If North Korea understood, they chose to ignore it," he added.

On April 19, Pyongyang notified the IAEA of its intention to defuel the reactor "at an early date," and it invited agency inspectors to witness the unloading operations—but without specifying what procedures would be followed or what the inspectors would be able to see and do. There followed weeks of sparring over the procedures, with Pyongyang offering to permit inspectors to observe and take some measurements but not to segregate or sample the fuel rods in a way that would make it possible to determine their past history. The IAEA refused to send any inspectors unless its procedures for sampling fuel rods were fully accepted. Washington backed the IAEA, though some officials believed the agency was being too rigid.

Removal of the spent fuel rods began on May 8 without international observation or approval. To the shock of the IAEA, the operations proceeded much more rapidly than expected. North Korean technicians at Yongbyon produced a second homemade defueling machine that nobody had known they had. The two machines worked at top speed in three shifts around the clock.

At the end of May, in a last-ditch effort to preserve the reactor's verifiable operating history, the IAEA sent a high-level team headed by Dimitri Perricos, a twenty-two-year veteran of the agency and director of its East Asia division of safeguards operations. Perricos got nowhere. With about half of the fuel rods still to be removed, the North Koreans refused to slow down discharge operations or to accept the IAEA's method of segregating the rods to verify their history.

Instead, North Korea proposed a discharge method that the IAEA team judged would not guarantee preservation of the necessary data. Even worse, Perricos observed that the actual unloading of the rods by the DPRK reactor operators was "a big mess" that would make it impossible to learn much of anything of the past operations, and he concluded that this disarray was deliberate. On reflection, the struggle over the fuel rods reminded him of a poker game in which Pyongyang's ace was the outside world's uncertainty about how much plutonium it possessed. He believed that a political decision had been made, probably at the very top, that Pyongyang would not give up its high card. At the same time, however, North Korea permitted two IAEA inspectors to remain at Yongbyon to monitor the unloading of the fuel rods and the storage pond into which they were placed. This suggested that for the time being, at least, Pyongyang did not wish to alarm the world about its nuclear intentions.

At IAEA headquarters in Vienna, Director General Blix was indignant at North Korea's refusal to cooperate. Blix was uncomfortable with continuing to bend the agency's global rules and requirements to meet the self-proclaimed "unique status" of North Korea—partly in, partly out of the international nuclear inspection regime. So far as Blix was concerned, the DPRK was fully in the regime until its withdrawal was official and complete, and it should fully comply with IAEA requirements, even though some of the requirements had never been levied on any other state before. Blix feared that tolerating compromises with IAEA directives could damage the agency's shaky authority and credibility with other nations.

Washington officialdom was privately unhappy with the agency's legalistic mind-set. Gallucci, who had become increasingly imbued with the regional and political aspects of the dispute, described the workings of the IAEA in May as "medieval or perhaps Talmudic, depending on what religious metaphor you use." The administration did not know from one day to the next, he said, how Blix would react to North Korea's machinations. Gallucci could not pressure Blix, for fear it would be seen as American interference with nonproliferation objectives that everyone held dear. About the same time, a high-ranking Defense Department official whom I met on a social occasion described Blix as "a fanatic" who was single-mindedly protecting his agency with little thought for the overall consequences. Former ambassador to Korea Donald Gregg described the IAEA inspectors as "a bunch of eager proctologists, making painful inquiries without holding out any benefits to North Korea."

On June 2, when more than 60 percent of the fuel rods had been removed, Blix sent a strong letter to the UN Security Council that was an implicit call for international action. Blix reported that despite an earlier appeal from the Security Council president to heed the IAEA's proposal, "all important parts of the core" had been unloaded, and the agency's ability to ascertain with confidence whether reactor fuel had been secretly diverted "has been lost." The situation, he declared, is "irreversible." Blix's letter was the opening gun in the long-discussed drive for UN sanctions against the recalcitrant, often-maddening DPRK.

In Pyongyang, Kim Il Sung explained the situation as he saw it to his friend, Cambodian chief of state Norodom Sihanouk: "Please compare us to a man: They want us to take off our shirt, our coat and now our trousers, and after that we will be nude, absolutely naked. What they want us to be is a man without defense secrets, just a naked man. We cannot accept that. We would rather accept a war. If they decide to make war, we accept the war, the challenge we are prepared for." In case anyone failed to get the point, North Korea issued a formal statement on June 5 announcing that "sanctions mean war, and there is no mercy in war."

Undeterred, Washington proceeded with diplomatic consultations aimed at a sanctions vote in the Security Council and, in parallel, with plans for a stepped-up U.S. military presence in and around Korea, preparing for the possibility of war.

## THE MILITARY TRACK

Throughout the four decades since the armistice of 1953, the U.S. military considered the renewal of war in Korea to be one of its most dangerous potential challenges. Since the end of the Vietnam War in 1975, American military planners had consistently identified Korea as the most likely spot for hostilities involving the United States in Asia. Although U.S. troops had been reduced over the years to 37,000, the presence of these forces guaranteed that the United States would be instantly involved if the massive North Korean army should attack across the narrow demilitarized zone. With the demise of the Soviet Union and the end of the cold war, U.S. military forces were restructured as a "base force" whose main job was to be capable of fighting two regional wars at once—one of which was consistently identified as a renewal of war in Korea. Michael O'Hanlon, a Brookings Institution researcher, calculated that without the Korean contingency, the United States would be able to cut its military force structure by about one-fourth, saving $20–$30 billion per year. This is about as much as the federal government spends for all health research programs, or for natural resources and environmental cleanup. After the Gulf War, Joint Chiefs of Staff chairman General Colin Powell said breezily but with considerable truth, "I'm running out of villains. I'm down to Castro and Kim Il Sung."

In late 1993 and early 1994, as the international tension over North Korea's nuclear program heightened again, the U.S. Command in Korea began to prepare more seriously for new hostilities. For the first time in decades, the U.S. military war plan—Operations Plan 50-27—took on the flesh-and-blood colors of reality rather than remaining abstract papers in folders and computer programs. Although it kept the same designation number, the plan had been updated several times over the years, and its emphasis had shifted from defensive maneuvers to offensive action north of the DMZ, to take the fighting into North Korea after the start of hostilities. The early 1990s revision of the war plan under the supervision of General Robert RisCassi, who was chief of the U.S. Command at the time, authorized a massive U.S. and ROK counterattack to take Pyongyang and topple the North Korean regime, with an option to proceed farther north toward the Chinese border and essentially reunify the country. It also put heavier emphasis on military steps to be taken by the United States and South Korea in the "pre-hostility" phase leading up to a potential outbreak of war.

To the surprise of U.S. commanders, ROK defense minister Lee Pyong Tae publicly outlined the essence of the war plan in testimony to National Assembly on March 23, just four days after the North Korean "sea of fire" statement inflamed the South. "He did it as a threat to the North Koreans . . . as a deterrent measure," said a senior U.S. officer in Seoul, who was initially startled by the disclosure of the highly secret blueprint. For months, as its U.S. ally was becoming alarmed, the ROK military had been relatively complacent about the possibility of military conflict. Now the South Koreans had suddenly become "nervous as a cat," the senior officer said. "They thought we were going to war too."

As tension continued to rise over the unresolved nuclear inspections and defueling of the North Korean reactor, the U.S. Command and the Pentagon moved ahead with military preparations. The first shipment of Patriot antimissiles arrived in Pusan in mid-April and were deployed before the end of the month. A battalion of U.S. Apache attack helicopters were brought in to replace the older Cobras, with more on the way. Additional heavy tanks, Bradley fighting vehicles (the modern replacement for armored personnel carriers), advanced radar tracking systems to pinpoint North Korean artillery, aircraft spare parts, and new ammunition-loading equipment arrived. About a thousand more troops landed quietly with the additional weapons, bringing U.S. forces up to their full authorized strength of 37,000. More heavy combat gear was loaded aboard American ships, to be within easy reach of Korea if additional troops were needed.

I met with the then-CINC (commander in chief) of U.S. forces in Korea, General Gary Luck, for the first time on May 3 at Yongson, a sprawling former Japanese Army base in the heart of Seoul that had been headquarters of the command since the time of the Korean War. In the mid-1980s, Luck, 56, had commanded the Second Infantry Division in Korea and led the Eighteenth Airborne Corps into action against Iraq in Operation Desert Storm. Wearing fatigues with his four stars sewn on the collars and his sleeves rolled up showing his impressive muscles, the gray-haired, crew-cut general had the physique and disarming country-boy drawl that marked him as combat leader. Given his appearance and bearing, I was not surprised to learn that he often jogged with his troops and lifted weights, but I would not have guessed, and only learned much later, that Luck had earned a Ph.D. in business administration from George Washington University.

The situation in Korea, Luck told me, is "much more dangerous now than a year or two ago," because of a slow-paced but constant military buildup in the North and especially because of the nuclear maneuvering, which he called "the catalyst for a more tension-filled drama." Luck's intelligence officers had coined the phrase "incremental normalism" to describe the creeping buildup and improvement of Pyongyang's forces, so constant that it was now taken for granted. In 1994 roughly 65 percent of North Korean forces, including 8,400 artillery pieces and 2,400 multiple rocket launchers, were estimated to be stationed within sixty miles of the DMZ, compared with 45 percent a decade earlier. U.S. estimates were that in case of war, North Korea could pound Seoul with five thousand rounds of artillery within the first twelve hours, causing havoc, death, and destruction in the capital despite the fierce counterattack planned by U.S. and ROK forces.

At the same time, Luck was impressed with the fundamental weakness of the North Korean capacity to sustain a long war. Privation was taking a serious toll on its military, despite the fact that Pyongyang was estimated to be spending about 25 percent of its GNP on maintaining its huge force of 1.1 million troops. North Korean military pilots had long been able to fly only a few hours a year because of the desperate shortage of fuel. Food was scarce, even for the military. Luck was particularly struck with the condition of two Korean People's Army soldiers, 19 and 23 years old, who had been captured in the South earlier in the year when their small boat had drifted across the sea border. The North Koreans were barely five feet tall and weighed only about a hundred pounds each, which appeared to be typical of KPA regular troops. They were much smaller than average South Koreans of their age group. As they recuperated in the ROK military hospital before being sent back home at their own request, one of the North Koreans was overheard to say to the other that he could never marry a South Korean woman—"they're too big for us."

While fighting a war was never far from Luck's mind, he told me, "my job is deterrence," to make sure it does not happen. He acknowledged that his was a delicate balancing act, to improve the capabilities of U.S. and ROK forces in a very tense situation without the improvements themselves causing the explosion they were intended to deter. What he wanted to avoid, Luck said, was anything that could "spook" the North Koreans and cause them to react by striking out in a "cornered rat syndrome." For this reason, he said, it was not helpful for them to believe that the military balance on the peninsula was turning against them—as demonstrably it was. As I prepared to leave Luck's office, he paused and said gravely, "I just want you to know I'm comfortable in this job. I can do the job. If things go bad, I'm ready. I can handle it."

As North Korea began defueling its reactor and storm clouds darkened, Luck flew to Washington to join an extraordinary military meeting to prepare to fight in Korea. Secretary of Defense Perry and

Joint Chiefs of Staff chairman General John Shalikashvili summoned every active four-star general and admiral in the U.S. military, including several brought from commands across the world, to a Pentagon conference room on May 18. The subject was how the entire U.S. military would support Luck's war plan for Korea, with troops, materiel, and logistics. Among other things, the top military brass went over details of preparatory deployments of troops and transport from other commands, the shifting of U.S. aircraft carriers and land-based warplanes closer to the Korean coast, and plans for massive reinforcement—deployment of roughly half of all U.S. major combat forces—if hostilities actually got under way. Everyone was conscious that this was no paper exercise but "a real meeting of real war fighters to decide how they were going to fight a war," according to Navy Captain Thomas Flanigan, an officer on the Pentagon's Joint Staff who helped to set it up. Flanigan described it as "extremely sobering."

The following day Perry, Shalikashvili, and Luck took the results of the meeting to the ultimate commander-in-chief at the White House. There Clinton was officially informed of the gravity and consequences of the conflict shaping up in Asia. If war broke out in Korea, his military leaders told him, they estimated it would cost 52,000 U.S. military casualties, killed or wounded, and 490,000 South Korean military casualties in the first ninety days, plus an enormous number of North Korean and civilian lives, at a financial outlay exceeding $61 billion, very little of which could be recouped from U.S. allies. This horrendous tragedy would be by far the gravest crisis of Clinton's sixteen-month-old presidency, overwhelming nearly everything else he had planned or dreamed of doing at home or abroad.

As the enormity of the consequences sank in, Clinton summoned a meeting of his senior foreign policy advisers the next day, May 20, to discuss the Korean confrontation. To the surprise of most journalists and experts who had been following the crisis—but who did not know about the nature or conclusions of the military meetings—the administration suddenly veered back toward diplomatic efforts, offering to convene its long-postponed third round of high-level negotiations with Pyongyang despite the unloading of the nuclear reactor.

North Korea signaled its interest in the U.S. offer by resuming working-level meetings in New York with State Department officials on May 23 to plan for the third round. But before progress could be made, the IAEA declared on June 2 that its ability to verify the reactor's past history had been "lost" due to the faster-than-expected defueling. After receiving the IAEA assessment, the administration decided to seek UN Security Council sanctions against North Korea. "They have triggered this, not the United States or anyone else," Clinton told reporters. "I just don't think we can walk away from this."

Looking back on the crisis, Perry identified the defueling of the North Korean reactor as the turning point, when it appeared that dialogue and "preventive diplomacy" had failed and when U.S. strategy shifted to "coercive diplomacy" involving sanctions. In the view of American military planners, the unloaded fuel rods represented a tangible and physical threat that the DPRK could move ahead to manufacture nuclear weapons. If not stopped near the beginning, they believed, North Korea eventually could possess an entire arsenal of nuclear weapons, which it could use for threats and blackmail and even to sell to high bidders in the Middle East. That simply could not be permitted to happen. Thus, despite the serious risk of war, "we believed that it was even more dangerous to allow North Korea to proceed with a large-scale nuclear weapons program," according to the secretary of defense.

To prepare for the potential storm, the Pentagon moved full steam ahead on its plans for additional U.S. military deployments. Simultaneously, the State Department launched a new round of talks about the nature and timing of international sanctions in the capitals of major powers and at the United Nations.

## THE DEEPENING CONFLICT

The devastating possibilities of the deepening conflict were alarming to many of those most familiar with North Korea. Even administration officials conceded that sanctions were unlikely to force Pyongyang to reverse course: the isolated country was relatively invulnerable to outside pressures, since it had so little international commerce and few important international connections of any sort. Moreover, its fierce pride and often-repeated threats suggested that it might actually fight rather than capitulate.

A gaping omission in all that had been said and done was the absence of direct communication between the U.S. administration and the one person whose decisions were law in Pyongyang. Early in 1993, Les Aspin, Clinton's original secretary of defense, had proposed bringing the nuclear issue to a head by sending a delegation to make a bold and direct appeal to Kim Il Sung, but this was turned down as too risky. Under Perry, Aspin's successor, the Pentagon continued to urge direct contacts with Kim, but high-level dialogue by then had been identified by the State Department as a principal reward for good behavior, not to be permitted until North Korea earned it with agreements and performance.

However, in late May 1994, when the defueling crisis worsened and the Pentagon presented its alarming war plan, Clinton, at the urging of Perry and Ambassador Laney, asked Senators Sam Nunn and Richard Lugar to fly to Pyongyang to see Kim Il Sung. North Korea turned down the hastily prepared visit at the last minute, apparently because of a conflict with the Great Leader's schedule.

In early June, as Clinton opted for sanctions, former president Jimmy Carter reentered the Korea saga to play another historic role. Having been defeated for reelection in 1980, the successful broker of the Camp David accords in the Middle East carved out for himself a mission of promoting peaceful resolution of conflicts through his Atlanta-based Carter Center. At 69 years of age, the vigorous former president had already played a postpresidential intermediary role in the Middle East, Ethiopia, the Sudan, Somalia, and the former Yugoslavia.

Carter had received invitations from Kim Il Sung in 1991, 1992, and 1993 to visit Pyongyang, but each time he had been asked by the State Department not to go on grounds that his trip would complicate the Korean problem rather than help to resolve it. The ROK government, mindful of Carter's abortive efforts as president to withdraw U.S. troops, opposed Carter's return to Korean affairs.

As the sanctions drive got under way, Carter expressed his growing anxiety in a telephone call to Clinton. Briefed on June 5 by

Gallucci, who was sent to Plains for that purpose, Carter learned to his dismay that there was no American plan for direct contact with Kim Il Sung. He immediately dispatched a letter to Clinton telling him he had decided to go to Pyongyang in view of the dangers at hand. Clinton, on the advice of Vice President Gore, interposed no objection to the trip as long as Carter clearly stated that he was acting as a private citizen rather than as an official U.S. envoy. As Carter was launching his initiative and proceeding to Seoul en route to Pyongyang, a series of new developments added to the importance of his mission.

In the diplomatic field, the administration drew up a program of gradually enforced sanctions against North Korea for refusing to cooperate with the IAEA. As prepared for the Security Council, the sanctions resolution would have given North Korea a thirty-day grace period to change its policies, after which such relatively lightweight measures as a ban on arms sales and transfers of nuclear technology to Pyongyang would take effect. This would be followed, if necessary, by a second group of more painful sanctions, including a ban on remittances from abroad, such as those from pro–North Korean groups in Japan, and a cutoff of the vital oil supplies furnished by China and others. A potential third stage, if the others failed, was a blockade of shipping to and from North Korean ports.

Among the other major powers directly involved—Russia, Japan, and China—there was little enthusiasm for even the mildest set of sanctions.

Russia was in the process of attempting to rebuild relations with North Korea, which had nearly been destroyed in the abrupt 1990 Soviet turn toward South Korea. In March, in an effort to find a role for itself in the crisis, the Russian Foreign Ministry had proposed an international conference of the two Koreas, the four major outside powers, the UN, and the IAEA to resolve the nuclear issue. None of the other parties had accepted it, but Russia continued to advocate such a meeting prior to any UN sanctions.

For Japan, the crisis on the Korean peninsula was serious and close to home. Tokyo had been severely criticized in the West for failing to assist the American effort in the 1991 Gulf War, despite its dependence on gulf oil. To fail to do its part to back up sanctions and assist the U.S. military where its own security was potentially at stake would be far more damaging to its reputation and self-esteem and could have been devastating to the U.S.-Japanese alliance. Yet the difficulties were great.

The Japanese political system was in an especially volatile and vulnerable state. At the time of the crisis, the long-dominant Liberal Democratic Party had splintered and lost power, and the eight-party coalition government of Prime Minister Tsutomu Hata was in danger of collapsing. Its continuation in office depended on the acquiescence of the Japan Socialist Party, which had historically close relations with Pyongyang and was reluctant to take action against it.

If full-scale sanctions were to be voted by the UN Security Council, the Japanese government believed it would have no choice but to enforce a cutoff of the remittances from Koreans in Japan to North Korea, which were estimated at about $600 million annually. After extensive study, however, Japanese officials told their American counterparts it was unlikely they would be able to cut this off completely, since there were many ways beyond its control by which such money could flow, ranging from the transfer of suitcases full of currency to electronic transfers through Switzerland, Hong Kong, and other financial capitals. In a secret report, a government task force expressed concern that in case of such a crackdown, pro-Pyongyang residents of Japan would mount "severe protest activities" against Japanese government and UN offices in Japan and the U.S. Embassy, possibly involving violence and the destruction of property, verging on civil war.

An even more vexing problem was what Japan could or could not do to assist the U.S. military in a blockade or shooting war within the bounds of General Douglas MacArthur's post–World War II "no war" constitution, which sharply limits Japanese military actions outside its home islands. As its military buildup neared, U.S. Forces Japan drew up a planning list of 1,900 items of potentially needed assistance, ranging from cutting the grass at U.S. bases to supplying fuel, materiel, and weapons and using Japanese ships and planes for sweeping mines and gathering intelligence. The Japanese government, concerned that it might be unable to meet U.S. requests, set up a special headquarters to define what it would be able to do, and was preparing short-term legislation to permit military cooperation. Had this been put to the test, said a Japanese diplomat who was deeply involved, it would have been "a nightmare." As a result of this experience, Japan and the United States began an extensive review of Japanese guidelines for military crisis cooperation.

China, the main source of North Korea's energy and food imports, was by all estimates the most important Asian participant in the sanctions discussion. Since China had a veto in the UN Security Council, no sanctions resolution could be adopted without its acquiescence. While reluctant to use the veto, China consistently opposed sanctions against North Korea, saying that negotiations provided the only solution.

At the same time, the Chinese were privately irritated by North Korea's actions and apprehensive that its policies could lead to a disaster on China's borders. A key moment came on May 29, when Clinton, in a reversal of previous administration policy, announced he would grant U.S. most-favored-nation trade status to China without human rights conditions. This made it more attractive and politically acceptable for Chinese leaders to cooperate with the United States on the Korea issue.

In the view of White House national security adviser Anthony Lake, a principal purpose of the sanctions resolution was to press the Chinese to use muscle with the North Koreans in order to head it off. In a similar vein, ROK Foreign Minister Han told his Chinese counterpart, Qian Qichen, on June 9 in Beijing that there was only one way for China to avoid voting on sanctions in the UN Security Council—and that was to persuade North Korea in advance that it could not count on a Chinese veto, and therefore North Korea would have to defuse the situation on its own.

On June 10, according to accounts conveyed by the Chinese to a variety of American, South Korean, and Japanese diplomats, Chinese diplomats in Pyongyang and Beijing presented the North Koreans with a most unpleasant message: although China continued to oppose sanctions, the strength of international opinion was such that China might not be able to veto them. Therefore Beijing strongly urged Pyongyang to take action to accommodate international opinion on the nuclear issue in its own interest or face drastic consequences without Chinese protection. Many diplomats believe this warning had a substantial impact.

On the same day as the Chinese intervention, the IAEA board in Vienna sharply criticized North Korea and voted to suspend its technical assistance of about $500,000 yearly to Pyongyang's nuclear program. In practical effect, this was an international sanction. However, the Chinese ambassador in Vienna, rather than vote against it, merely abstained. In response to the vote, North Korea announced it would withdraw from the IAEA, expel the remaining international inspectors, and refuse to cooperate with "continuity of safeguards." If carried out, this would have ended the last vestige of international surveillance from the unloaded fuel rods and the extensive nuclear facilities in Yongbyon. This development set off new alarm bells in Washington, Seoul, Tokyo, and other world capitals, sharply increasing international concern about Pyongyang's nuclear intentions.

Even as these developments were taking place, North Korea was also beginning to sketch out areas of conciliation and compromise. On June 3, Pyongyang broadcast an unusual statement in the name of its chief negotiator. Kang Sok Ju announced that North Korea was prepared to dismantle its reprocessing plant ("radio-chemical laboratory") for manufacturing plutonium in connection with the replacement of its existing facilities by a light-water reactor project. This went one step beyond a written statement by Kim Il Sung to *The Washington Times* on his April 15 birthday, when he said the reprocessing plant "may not be needed" if the LWRs were supplied. In the swiftly moving tide toward collision, neither statement received much international attention.

The North Korean concession was further developed by Selig Harrison of the Carnegie Endowment for International Peace, who arrived in Pyongyang the day after Kang's statement. Harrison, *The Washington Post* correspondent for Northeast Asia in the early 1970s, had been one of the first American correspondents to interview Kim Il Sung. As a scholar since the mid-1970s, Harrison had kept a close eye on Korean developments, revisiting the North in 1987 and 1992 and making many visits to the South. Harrison was known in Washington policy circles for having an unusually positive view of Pyongyang's willingness to compromise in return for American relationships and concessions, which he believed its leaders badly wanted. Washington conservatives and many officials scoffed, but since Harrison had had a longer acquaintance with policy makers in Pyongyang than almost anyone else, it was difficult to dismiss him.

In his new trip, Harrison concentrated on finding a way to give operational significance to Pyongyang's willingness to abandon its reprocessing plant. In meetings with Kang and others, he argued that North Korea should freeze further development of the reprocessing plant and all the rest of its nuclear program when binding commitments were received for delivery and financing of the LWRs.

On June 9, when Harrison broached the freeze idea in a meeting with Kim Il Sung, the Great Leader seemed not to have heard of it from his aides. In a show of confidence in Kang that would be repeated with Carter, Kim turned to his chief negotiator for an explanation and discussed the possibilities with him for about five minutes in Korean. Then he turned to Harrison and said, "This is a good idea. We can definitely accept it if the United States really makes a firm commitment that we can trust."

Kim then repeated his denial that North Korea had nuclear weapons or any intention of producing them. "It gives me a headache when people demand to see something we don't have," said Kim. "It's like dogs barking at the moon. What would be the point of making one or two nuclear weapons when you have ten thousand plus delivery systems that we don't have. We would be a laughingstock. We want nuclear power for electricity, and we have shown this by our offer to convert to light-water reactors." Harrison left Pyongyang on June 11 believing that a freeze on the North Korean program in return for light-water-reactor commitments could produce the breakthrough that was desperately needed.

On June 13, however, when Carter arrived in Seoul en route to the North, Harrison's optimism was shared by very few in the South Korean capital. The ROK government, while counseling calm, had announced the largest civil defense exercise in many years to mobilize its citizens in case of war. Reacting to the growing atmosphere of crisis, the Seoul stock market dropped by 25 percent in two days and jittery South Koreans were jamming stores to stockpile rice, dried noodles, and candles. Carter found most members of the ROK government hostile to his mission. Before his arrival, ROK president Kim Young Sam had pronounced the mission to be "ill timed" and said it could help the North pursue "stalling tactics" on the nuclear issue.

The sense of inexorable drift toward military conflict that had been felt within the high ranks of the U.S. government since the defueling of the Yongbyon reactor in early May was now spreading to an increasingly aroused American public. In June, 46 percent of a nationwide sample of public opinion sponsored by NBC News and *The Wall Street Journal* said North Korea's nuclear development was the "most serious foreign policy issue facing the United States to-day," outdistancing the next most serious issue, instability in Russia, by more than three to one. At the same time, a nationwide poll for *Time* and CBS News reported that a majority (51 percent) favored military action to destroy North Korea's nuclear facilities if the DPRK continued to refuse international inspection, and a slimmer majority (48 percent yes, 42 percent no) said it was "worth risking war" to prevent North Korea from manufacturing nuclear weapons.

The predominant opinion of national columnists and commentators was that the United States should take a tough line with Pyongyang. Among the most prestigious voices were those of two former Bush administration officials, former national security adviser Brent Scowcroft and former undersecretary of state Arnold Kanter, the official who had met the North Koreans in New York in early 1992. In *The Washington Post* on June 15, the day Jimmy Carter crossed into North Korea, they advocated a U.S. military strike to destroy the reprocessing plant at Yongbyon unless the DPRK was prepared to permit "continuous, unfettered" international monitoring. "The stakes could hardly be higher. The time for temporizing is over," Scowcroft and Kanter wrote.

At the Pentagon, Secretary Perry had requested and received a detailed contingency plan for bombing the Yongbyon facilities and was told that the U.S. Air Force had the technical ability to take them out quickly and effectively, without spreading radiation far and wide. Perry's fear, as before, was that such an air strike "was highly likely to start a general war" on the peninsula. "We were looking for ways of avoiding a general war, not ways of starting a general war," he explained later.

Nevertheless, the Pentagon argued that if North Korea really meant that sanctions would be an act of war, it was incumbent on the United States to be ready. Consequently, in mid-June Perry and the Joint Chiefs of Staff drew up three options for increasing U.S. forces in and around Korea to heighten readiness further. General Luck estimated, on the basis of the experience in Vietnam and the Persian Gulf, that due to the colossal lethality of modern weapons in the urban environments of Korea, as many as 1 million people would be killed in the resumption of full-scale war on the peninsula, including 80,000 to 100,000 Americans, that the out-of-pocket costs to the United States would exceed $100 billion, and that the destruction of property and interruption of business activity would cost more than $1,000 billion (one trillion) dollars to the countries involved and their immediate neighbors. The extent of the death and destruction, in the American calculus, would depend to a great degree on the speed with which a counterattack could be mounted by the U.S. reinforcements called for in the war plan.

Option number one as drawn up at the Pentagon was the immediate dispatch to Korea of around 2,000 additional troops of the kind needed for rapid deployment of larger forces later—additional logistics, administrative, and supply elements—and additional counterbattery radars and reconnaissance systems, which had been most urgently requested by General Luck.

Option number two, which Perry and the Joint Chiefs of Staff favored, added squadrons of front-line tactical aircraft, including F-117 Stealth fighter-bombers and long-range bombers, to be based near Korea, available for immediate action; the deployment of several battalions of combat-ready U.S. ground troops, principally to augment artillery forces; and the stationing of a second U.S. aircraft-carrier battle group in the area, to reinforce the powerfully armed carrier group that had already been moved close to Korea. This would involve deployment of more than 10,000 U.S. troops, added to the 37,000 on duty in South Korea. Perry hoped that such a dramatic increase in American forces would combine more serious preparations for war with an element of additional deterrence, highly visible to the North Koreans.

Option number three called for the deployment of additional tens of thousands more army and Marine Corps ground troops and even more combat air power. Even this option did not provide enough U.S. forces to fight a general war on the peninsula—Operations Plan 5027 reportedly called for more than 400,000 reinforcements to do that.

The military concern was that if the flow of additional forces did not start quickly, Pyongyang might block it with an early preemptive strike. On the other hand, once the forces did begin to flow, North Korea might feel compelled to strike quickly to forestall an inexorable American buildup that would frustrate its chances for military success. Such an unstable military situation in an increasingly tense situation with an unpredictable foe was extremely worrisome; however, the U.S. military felt that it had little choice under the circumstances but to begin serious preparations for war.

Perry acknowledged in an interview for this book that it was difficult to calculate how Pyongyang might react. "We saw the deployment on the one hand as being provocative. That was the downside. On the other side, we saw it as demonstrating a seriousness of purpose. . . . We didn't know enough about the Korean mentality to know how to gauge the negative aspects versus the positive aspects of the signal we were sending. Therefore, I chose in my own thinking to set that signal aside, not knowing how to assess it, and recognizing we could have either of those two possibilities."

Some senior officers in the U.S. Command in Seoul were extremely concerned about the North Korean military reaction when they heard about the plans for these deployments. "I always got this feeling that the North Koreans studied the desert [Operation Desert Storm against Iraq] more than we did almost," said a general with access to all the available intelligence. "And they learned one thing: you don't let the United States build up its forces and then let them go to war against you. . . . So I always felt that the North Koreans were never going to let us do a large buildup. They would see their window of opportunity closing, and they would come." Adding to this officer's apprehension was a chilling fact not well known outside the U.S. Command: at Panmunjom in May, a North Korean colonel told a U.S. officer: "We are not going to let you do a buildup." He did not say, nor did anyone know, how much of a buildup of American forces might trigger a North Korean preemptive strike.

General Luck had played an integral role in earlier planning for augmentation of his forces under the existing war plan, but he received only a few hours' notice that the Pentagon would ask Clinton to authorize its execution on June 16. He was startled by the timing, concerned that the North Koreans would interpret the reinforcements as a signal of an American decision to destroy their regime, and intensely worried that no serious evacuation plan for 80,000 American dependents and other civilians in Korea had been put in place. Japan, which was the logical place for evacuees to go, had not agreed to receive them. Transportation for the evacuation had not been prepared. Most people had no idea an evacuation was imminent and no information about where to go or what to do. Moreover, an announcement of an evacuation of American civilians, and especially the loading of them onto planes and ships, was likely to panic South Koreans as well as many Americans.

Luck and Ambassador Laney met secretly at the ambassador's residence in Seoul the morning of June 16 (the evening of June 15 in Washington). Both felt there was no choice but to proceed with evacuation planning on an urgent basis. The ambassador did not wait for formal orders. He told his daughter and his three grandchildren, who were visiting at the time, that they should leave Korea by Sunday, three days thence.

## CARTER IN PYONGYANG

In the meantime Carter, accompanied by his wife Rosalynn and a small party of aides and security guards, had crossed the DMZ on June 15 on his way to see Kim Il Sung. Carter found walking across the dividing line at Panmunjom, then being handed over by U.S. and ROK military to North Korean military "a bizarre and disturbing experience, evidence of an incredible lack of communication and understanding." He was well aware of the risk to his reputation, believing that "the chances of success were probably minimal because so much momentum had built up on both sides of the sanctions issue."

In his initial meeting in Pyongyang, Carter found Foreign Minister Kim Yong Nam so uncompromising and negative that the former president awoke at three A.M. believing it likely that North Korea would go to war rather than yield to international sanctions. In desperation, he dispatched an aide, former ambassador Marion Creekmore, to the DMZ with a message to be sent through secure U.S. channels in South Korea, appealing to Clinton for authorization to agree to the start of the third round of U.S.–DPRK negotiations to head off a crisis. Carter instructed Creekmore not to send the message until receiving a go-ahead after his meeting with Kim Il Sung on the morning of June 16.

For Kim Il Sung, the meeting with the most prominent American ever to visit the DPRK was the culminating moment of his two-decades-long effort to make direct contact with American ruling circles, and a potential turning point in the escalating international crisis over his nuclear program. The Great Leader greeted his visitor with a booming welcome, a hearty handshake, and big smile, which was returned by Carter's characteristic toothy grin.

When the talks began, Carter explained that he had come as a private citizen rather than as a representative of the U.S. government, but that he had come with the knowledge and support of his government. The presence of Dick Christenson, the Korean-speaking deputy director of the State Department's Korea desk, was testimony to the semiofficial nature of the mission. Carter emphasized that the differences in the two governmental systems should not be an obstacle to friendship between the two nations, a point he repeated several times. If the current nuclear issues could be resolved, he said, then high-level negotiations on normalizing relations could move ahead.

Kim, responding on the high plane of generality and mutual recognition that is particularly important in Asia, said that the essential problem between the two nations was lack of trust and that therefore "creating trust is the main task." Kim expressed frustration that, although he had often announced that the DPRK couldn't make and didn't need nuclear weapons, he was not believed. The DPRK's requirement was for nuclear energy, he declared: if the United States helped to supply light-water reactors, North Korea would dismantle its gas-graphite reactors and return to the Non-Proliferation Treaty.

As part of a solution to the nuclear issue, Kim also requested U.S. guarantees against nuclear attacks on the DPRK. He expressed irritation that South Korea might interfere with whatever solution could be worked out, saying that whenever the prospect of making progress between Pyongyang and Washington came close, Seoul found a way to block it.

Carter, following talking points that he had cleared with Gallucci by telephone before traveling to Pyongyang, asked two things of Kim: that he temporarily freeze his nuclear program until the completion of the planned third round of U.S.–DPRK nuclear negotiations, and that the two remaining IAEA inspectors still at Yongbyon, who were scheduled to be expelled from the country on the next flight to Beijing, be permitted to remain. Even though the expulsions might seem a matter of course since North Korea had announced its withdrawal from the IAEA, they were certain to be taken as a sign that Pyongyang was going full speed ahead with a nuclear weapons program. Carter's request that Kim permit the inspectors to remain produced the most revealing and, as it turned out, the most important exchange of the meeting.

Apparently completely unfamiliar with the issue, Kim turned to Deputy Foreign Minister and chief DPRK negotiator Kang Sok Ju, who was among the few aides present, and asked what this request was about. Kang jumped to his feet and stood at attention, as all aides did when addressing the Great Leader. Then, as had been the case with Selig Harrison and the freeze proposal eight days earlier (about which Carter had not been informed), Kang patiently explained the issue. Kim seemed wary of giving something important away, but he asked his aide's opinion. Kang responded that keeping the inspectors on duty would be the right thing to do. Following this discussion, all in Korean, Kim turned to Carter and announced that North Korea would reverse the previous order and leave the inspectors in place.

This exchange, one of the few times when outsiders witnessed policy actually being made in North Korea, suggested that Kim Il Sung remained capable of making on-the-spot decisions of great importance without debate or fear of contradiction. It also suggested that he was willing to solicit and take the advice of aides in whom he had confidence—in this case, Kang. Kim's eldest son and anointed successor, Kim Jong Il, was nowhere in evidence in Carter's meetings, although Carter had asked to see him. The younger Kim rarely appeared in meetings with foreign visitors.

When Kim Il Sung agreed to the temporary freeze and to keep the international inspectors and monitoring equipment in place, a relieved Carter told him he would recommend that the U.S. government "support" North Korea's acquisition of light-water reactors (although he made it clear the United States could not finance or supply them directly) and that the long-awaited third round of U.S.–DPRK negotiations be quickly reconvened. Carter said he could speak with assurance that no American nuclear weapons were in South Korea or tactical nuclear weapons in the waters surrounding the peninsula. He and Kim agreed that the Korean peninsula should continue to be free of nuclear weapons from any source.

Believing that he had made an important breakthrough, Carter met later in the day with Kang to confirm the details. Kang warned against proceeding with the UN sanctions (which Carter had opposed from the beginning), telling him that "all the people in this country and our military are gearing up now to respond to those sanctions. If the sanctions pass, all the work you have done here will go down the drain." From the comments of Kang and his immediate superior, Foreign Minister Kim Yong Nam, Carter concluded that North Korea actually would have gone to war on a preemptive basis if sanctions had been imposed while the United States was engaging in a major military buildup in the area.

Cable News Network correspondent Mike Chinoy and a CNN film crew, who had been permitted to broadcast a rare series of reports from the North at the time of Kim Il Sung's eighty-second birthday two months earlier, had been allowed to return to cover the Carter visit. The only American journalists on hand, they were a channel for worldwide attention. Carter decided to give CNN an interview to announce the results of his meeting with Kim and to halt the rush toward armed conflict. But first it was necessary to inform the White House.

It was the morning of June 16 in Washington, a half-day behind Korea. President Clinton, Vice President Gore, Secretary of State Christopher, Secretary of Defense Perry, Joint Chiefs of Staff chairman Shalikashvili, CIA director James Woolsey, UN Ambassador Madeleine Albright, National Security Adviser Anthony Lake, and other senior foreign policy and defense officials were gathered in the Cabinet Room in the second hour of a climactic decision-making meeting about the Korean nuclear issue. At the outset, Clinton gave final approval to proceed with the drive for the sanctions against North Korea in the UN Security Council, where the American sanctions plan had been circulating in draft form for several days. That decided, General Shalikashvili began outlining the U.S. military buildup in and around Korea, which Perry and the Joint Chiefs had recommended in tandem with the sanctions decision. The President was informed that the dispatch of substantial additional forces, as contemplated in the meeting, would require a limited call-up to active duty of U.S. reservists. This would necessarily alert the country to the seriousness of the looming crisis.

The JCS chairman had explained the first option of modestly augmented forces and was well into his discussion of the Pentagon's preferred choice, the second option involving the dispatch of warplanes, another aircraft-carrier battle group, and more than 10,000 additional troops. Suddenly a White House aide entered the room with the news that Carter was on the telephone line from Pyongyang.

Gallucci, who was designated to take the call in an adjoining room, heard the enthusiastic former president say that Kim Il Sung had agreed to freeze the nuclear program and to allow the IAEA inspectors to remain. Carter said he believed the third round of U.S.–DPRK negotiations should be convened in the light of this breakthrough, and he was asking for White House permission to say so. Then he told Gallucci, who was startled but made no comment, that he planned to describe the progress he had made in a live interview shortly with CNN. Gallucci told Carter he would report his news to a meeting on these issues taking place as they spoke, and he promised a response later.

Gallucci's report was a bombshell in the Cabinet Room. Except for leaving the inspectors in place, the substance of Carter's accomplishments sounded to some like nothing new. But there was anger in the room about Carter's imminent CNN interview, which seemed likely to upstage and embarrass the administration just as it was reaching major new decisions on a problem it had been living with for more than a year. One participant viewed Carter's actions as "near traitorous." Another feared it was a stalling action by the North Koreans, just as the United States was about to "pull the trigger" on sanctions and the troop buildup. Whatever their private thoughts, Clinton and Gore decreed that it was essential to shape a substantive response, not indulge in mere Carter-bashing.

As Clinton left for another event, the others crowded in front of a television set where they stood or sat, some on the floor, as Carter spoke by satellite from halfway around the world in Pyongyang to CNN White House correspondent Wolf Blitzer, who was on the White House lawn a few steps away, and CNN diplomatic correspondent Ralph Begleiter, who was in a Washington office a few blocks away. Carter repeated Kim Il Sung's statements and declared them to be "a very important and very positive step toward the alleviation of this crisis." While saying that next steps would be up to the Clinton administration, Carter publicly proclaimed his preference: "What is needed now is a very simple decision just to let the already constituted delegations from North Korea and the United States have their third meeting, which has been postponed. That's all that's needed now, and that's all the North Koreans are addressing."

Suddenly a diplomatic-military crisis took on new political dimensions, as it was played out in public on live television in full view of Clinton's friends and foes at home as well as officials around the world. To the consternation of the White House team, the press saw administration officials as bystanders while a private citizen, former president Carter, appeared in control of U.S. policy.

After the officials filed back into the Cabinet Room, National Security Council aide Stanley Roth, a veteran of Asia policy making on Capitol Hill and at the Pentagon, suggested the course of action that was ultimately accepted: that the administration design its own detailed requirements for a freeze on the North Korean nuclear program and send them back to Pyongyang through Carter. In effect, the United States would say, "We agree and accept if you accept our version of the freeze." As was noted in the meeting, the tactic was similar to a celebrated U.S. ploy at the height of the 1962 U.S.–Soviet Cuban missile crisis, when the Kennedy administration had interpreted communications from Soviet premier Nikita Khrushchev in its own way to fashion an acceptable settlement.

Gallucci and two other aides left the room and drafted U.S. requirements for a North Korean freeze that was to be in effect while talks continued. In their version, North Korea would have to agree specifically not to place new fuel rods in the 5-megawatt reactor and not to reprocess the irradiated fuel rods that had been removed. By the time it ended, the marathon White House meeting had stretched on for more than five hours.

Lake then spoke to Carter in Pyongyang, where it was approaching dawn on June 17, and outlined the conditions, which went beyond what North Korea had offered and well beyond the legal restraints of the Non-Proliferation Treaty. Carter objected vociferously to upping the ante, noting that these new conditions had not been mentioned before his trip and that he had not presented them to Kim Il Sung or others in Pyongyang. It seemed far from certain, perhaps even unlikely, that the North Koreans would accept them. In fact, however, perhaps because of their own urgent desire to end the dangerous confrontation, the North Koreans quickly accepted. To make certain of agreement on the details, Gallucci subsequently sent the conditions in writing to Kang through the North Korean Mission in New York, and Carter sent a parallel letter to Kim Il Sung. Both received back formal acceptance.

To celebrate the easing of the crisis, Kim Il Sung invited Carter and his party to a celebration on the Taedong River aboard the presidential yacht. This cruise produced another informative decision-making episode, this one involving Kim Il Sung's wife, Kim Song Ae, who was rarely seen with her husband in public but who participated in the boat ride due to the presence of former first lady Rosalynn Carter. As the yacht sailed by North Korean villages and farmland, the former U.S. president proposed that joint U.S.–DPRK teams discover and return the remains of U.S. servicemen killed during the Korean War as a goodwill gesture to the American people and to forestall the kind of arguments that had long held up improved U.S. relations with postwar Vietnam. Kim was noncommittal, saying this could be discussed in future negotiations, but Carter persisted. At this point, the North Korean first lady spoke up, telling her husband she thought the joint recovery teams a good idea. "Okay, it's done, it's done," responded the Great Leader.

During the boat ride, the exhausted Carter mistakenly told Kim while CNN cameras were rolling that the American drive for economic and political sanctions at the UN Security Council had been halted due to their discussions the previous day. This action had not yet been taken. Carter's comment, which was played on American television, seemed to suggest once more that the White House had lost control of its Korea policies. This gaffe turned out to be the most controversial facet of Carter's trip in the U.S. press and dominated much of the immediate commentary.

The boat ride was also the occasion for the most important breakthrough of the mission from the South Korean standpoint. Sitting across a small table in the main cabin of the yacht, Carter brought up the unresolved state of North-South relations and the possibility of a North-South summit meeting, which ROK President Kim Young Sam had asked him to propose to his North Korean counterpart. Kim Il Sung recounted for Carter his version of the various attempts at agreement between the two halves of the divided country, and he expressed his frustration that little had been accomplished. In a remarkable statement coming from him, Kim said that the fault for the lack of progress lay on both sides, and that responsibility for the mistakes had to be shared. Kim said he had noted his southern counterpart's statements, in his inaugural address the previous year, about the primacy of national kinship and his offer of a summit meeting "at any time and in any place." He went on to say that he was ready to meet Kim Young Sam and that their meeting should be held without preconditions or extended preliminary talks. He invited Carter to pass along this message to the South Korean president.

How and why Kim Il Sung decided to proceed to a summit with the South Korean president in the last days of his life is a matter of great speculation, because he had only come that close to a meeting once before, when he had issued the invitation for Roh Tae Woo to attend his seventieth birthday observance in 1992. One theory holds that Kim sensed he did not have long to live and was seeking to arrange a smoother path for his son and successor. Another theory suggests he realized that it was necessary to improve relations with the South in order to improve fundamentally his relations with the United States. Still another theory is that the decision was a spur-of-the-moment response to Carter's proposal. There were persistent reports that some in the North Korean leadership, possibly including Kim Jong Il, were unenthusiastic or even opposed to a Kim Il Sung–Kim Young Sam meeting. Whatever lay behind Kim Il Sung's decision, it is clear that he never backed away from it but proceeded to plan energetically for the summit.

Shortly after Carter left North Korea through Panmunjom, he called on Kim Young Sam at the Blue House. The South Korean president was initially cool to Carter and his mission, believing that once again the fate of the peninsula had been under negotiation at a very high level without his participation. When Carter conveyed Kim Il Sung's summit offer, however, the South Korean president became visibly excited. Within the hour, Kim Young Sam announced his acceptance of an early and unconditional summit meeting, thereby turning Carter's mission into a personal initiative to achieve what his predecessors had tried and failed to do. In a sudden and entirely unexpected reversal of fortune, the immense tension and great danger in the Korean peninsula gave way to the greatest hope in years for a historic rapprochement between the leaders of the North and South.

Although delighted at the prospect of a summit meeting, the South Korean president privately rejected Carter's account of his counterpart's state of health, which Carter described as "vigorous" and "alert." The South Korean president's own father, whom he spoke to by telephone every morning, was just a year or two older than Kim Il Sung. From television pictures recorded by his intelligence agency, Kim Young Sam believed that his counterpart in the North wasn't all that well. "Carter is a smart man," Kim Young Sam told aides as the former U.S. president left his office, "but he doesn't know much about old people."

Carter called it "a miracle" that his meetings with Kim Il Sung had transformed a confrontation at the brink of war into new and promising sets of U.S.–DPRK and North-South negotiations. "I personally believe the crisis is over," he announced after briefing officials at the White House, and within a few days it was clear that this was so. The sanctions activity and plans for extensive reinforcement of U.S. troops were dropped. After obtaining written confirmation from Pyongyang of its acceptance of the U.S.-devised freeze on its nuclear program, Washington announced readiness to proceed to the third round of U.S.–DPRK negotiations, which were scheduled to begin on July 8 in Geneva.

Despite the positive results of his unorthodox initiative, Carter initially was the object of more criticism than praise. American politicians, public figures, and the press, emphasizing the contradictions between Carter's efforts and Clinton administration policies, were critical of his intervention. The former president was startled to be privately informed, as he came back across the DMZ, that the White House did not want him to return home through Washington or to even make a telephone report to Clinton. Later the administration relented, and Carter paid a visit to the White House en route to Atlanta, although Clinton remained at Camp David during the meeting with his Democratic predecessor and spoke to him only by telephone.

It will be years, perhaps many years, before it will be possible to know with certainty how close the Korean peninsula came to a devastating new outbreak of war in the spring of 1994. It is instructive that those in the U.S. and ROK governments who were closest to the decisions are among those who, in retrospect, rate the chances for hostilities to have been the highest. It is clear, however, that the United States responded to North Korea's nuclear challenge with a combination of force and diplomacy which, although often improvised and lacking coherence, was equal to the seriousness of the issue. While seeking a negotiated settlement, the United States demonstrated that it was prepared to sponsor UN sanctions and was ready to counter the North Korean threat of a violent response by adding powerfully to its military forces in the area. The American undertaking was backed by South Korea, whose diplomats urged a negotiated solution and whose military prepared for action even while its president and public wavered with the winds, and by China, whose deft and quiet diplomacy placed important limitations on Pyongyang's freedom of action. Japan, although uncertain how far it could go to back the application of international sanctions and American military operations in view of constitutional and political restrictions, was preparing to join the informal coalition.

Whether by blunder or design, North Korea discovered by early 1993 that its nuclear program, with its potential to destabilize Northeast Asia and affect the prospects for nuclear proliferation in other parts of the world, was its most valuable asset in transactions with the outside world, especially after the loss of its Soviet ally and the devaluing of its relations with China. Pyongyang played its card brilliantly, forcing one of the world's richest and most powerful nations to undertake direct negotiations and to make concessions to one of the world's least successful nations. The nuclear threat proved, up to a point, to be Pyongyang's great equalizer.

In the spring of 1994, however, the growing power of the forces arrayed against it strongly suggested that further escalation of tension would be dangerous and not necessarily to North Korea's advantage. By the time Carter arrived, Kim Il Sung was seeking a way to end the crisis without losing face or surrendering his bargaining card, and the former president provided the means. By cooperating with Carter, accepting a U.S.-designed nuclear freeze, and agreeing to a North-South summit meeting, the Great Leader defused the explosive confrontation while leaving the future open for further negotiations, which he planned to direct in the months to come.

# 14

## DEATH AND ACCORD

O n the morning of July 6, 1994, less than three weeks after he said
good-bye to Jimmy Carter, Kim Il Sung sat behind the desk in
his office and instructed senior officials on the economic goals for the
year ahead. From all outward signs, the 82-year-old Great Leader
was in good form, wearing a light blue Western-style suit and wagging his finger vigorously at two dozen officials arrayed in rows before him.

"Agriculture first. Light industry first. Foreign trade first," declared Kim, repeating the priorities he had announced in his New
Year's address after conceding that the economy was in trouble. In a
rich, husky rumble, which had been the voice of command in North
Korea for nearly half a century, he set forth specific targets for the
year: 850,000 tons of fertilizer, 12 million tons of cement, completion
of 100 ships, and special priorities for railways, and metal industries.
In remarks that would take on important meaning later, Kim gave
top priority to the urgent need for more electric power. Saying that
the much-discussed light-water nuclear reactors would take too long
to ease the shortage of energy, he laid down an immediate requirement for additional power plants burning heavy fuel oil.

The meeting with the economic aides was among the last activities of an aged head of state who had reengaged dramatically in the

affairs of his country, as if somehow he sensed that his time was short. In the month of June, Kim had taken part in seventeen events and activities, including on-the-spot inspections at two collective farms and meetings with a variety of visitors from overseas, compared to five appearances the previous month and even fewer in some earlier months.

Following the meeting with Carter, Kim's preoccupation was to prepare for the unprecedented summit meeting with his South Korean counterpart, Kim Young Sam, which had emerged from the talks with the former U.S. president and which was scheduled to begin in Pyongyang on July 25. After decades of haggling and disagreeing about such a meeting, the North and South this time had smoothly and quickly agreed on the overall plan and many of the details. Kim Il Sung personally intervened to facilitate agreement on some of the planning issues.

In Seoul, Kim Young Sam was spending days meeting with his ministers, staff, and experts on North Korea in preparation for the momentous conference. The two sides had agreed that the South Korean president would lead a hundred-member delegation to Pyongyang, accompanied by an eighty-member press corps equipped for live television broadcasts to the public back home. The actual meetings, which were to take place over two or three days, would be one-on-one discussions, with only two or three aides and a note-taker accompanying each president.

On the crucial subject of national reunification, Kim Young Sam was preparing to contest his counterpart's confederation plan calling for one country with two systems, which South Koreans found biased and unworkable, and to propose instead gradual steps to reconciliation such as the exchange of visits by separated families, exchange of correspondence, and mutual access to television and radio programs of the other side. The maximalist position of the North had often clashed in the past with the step-by-step position of the South, but the South Korean leader hoped that this time the recent danger of armed conflict on the peninsula, to which he attributed Kim Il Sung's willingness to meet, would make agreements possible.

Kim Young Sam believed it would take more than one meeting to iron out the historic trouble between the two Korean governments;

he therefore planned to propose that this be the first of a series of summits. To ease the way, he was preparing to surprise North Korea by offering to supply 500,000 tons of rice to help feed its people. This huge amount was more than double the 100,000 to 200,000 tons North Korea had been unofficially requesting through ROK businessmen.

Kim Il Sung was also making preparations. On the afternoon of July 6, after meeting his economic ministers in the morning, he traveled to his favorite place of respite from the summertime heat, the beautiful Myohyang Mountains (literally, Mountains of Delicate Fragrance) about a hundred miles north of Pyongyang. Kim maintained a sumptuous villa there with spectacular mountain views nestled amid a pine forest and ringed by guards and high fences. This is where he took special visitors whom he was seeking to impress, such as the Japanese parliamentarian Shin Kanemaru, and he had decided it was just the place to take the South Korean president.

On July 7, en route to the mountains, Kim made one of his on-the-spot inspections of a collective farm, where he may also have planned to take the South Korean president. The temperature was nearly 100 degrees Fahrenheit. In the mountains, he personally inspected a guest villa, which was being prepared for his South Korean visitor, checking bedrooms and bathrooms, even making certain that the refrigerators would be stocked with plenty of mineral water.

After these strenuous activities and his dinner, Kim complained of being tired. A short time later, he collapsed with a massive heart attack. Doctors were summoned, but heavy rains made helicopter flights impossible, and poor dirt roads delayed the arrival of a land convoy.* North Korean officials told Korean-American journalist Julie Moon, who obtained details of Kim's death, that doctors opened up his chest, hoping in vain to revive his heart, but it was too late. Kim Il Sung was pronounced dead at two A.M. on the morning of the eighth.

The death of the founding leader of the DPRK came at a time when the outside world was intruding increasingly on the unique

---

*Within a few months, the road to the Myohyang Mountains was paved in a top-priority operation, reportedly at the personal direction of Kim Jong Il.

dominion Kim had created in his unequaled reign of nearly half a century. In Kim's final months, he was seeking to adjust to the rapid decline of long-standing diplomatic, military, and economic arrangements and to explore new relationships with the United States, South Korea, and the world of his former enemies. Whether he was a leader of great vision or of great folly, he was without question the dominating figure on the stage that he trod. His sudden death, in retrospect, was among the most important events in the peninsula in the decades covered by this book. The absence of his controlling hand immensely complicated the problems of North Korea in the second half of the 1990s.

◆ ◆ ◆

As with other powerful authoritarian leaders, Kim's health had long been a state secret and a matter of intense interest to the outside world. From at least the early 1970s, a large lumpy external tumor had been visible on the back of his neck, but doctors determined it to be benign. German doctors informed Kim it could be removed surgically in two hours; however, since they also said it was not dangerous, he told them to leave it alone. South Korean and U.S. intelligence reports stating that Kim had heart trouble were confirmed by North Korea's official post-mortem medical bulletin, which said he had received treatment for arteriosclerosis, or hardening of the arteries. The official medical bulletin also said his fatal heart attack had been brought on by "heavy mental strains," a remark that has never been explained.

Personal impressions of Kim's health in his later years varied greatly, which may have reflected good days and bad days as well as the artifice of aides in presenting him in the best possible light. A CNN cameraman who photographed Kim during a birthday meeting with visitors two months before his death noticed tiny lights near the ceiling, which were turned on as Kim rose to speak, giving him an impressive rosy aura whose source was imperceptible to the casual onlooker.

A South Korean official who was among Kim's luncheon guests in February 1992, shortly before his eightieth birthday, found him hardly as fit as had been reported. The official said Kim dribbled food on his clothing, made a half-dozen incomprehensible statements, and left his eyeglasses on the table when he left the room at the end of the meal. Kim told the visitors on that occasion that due to doctors' orders, he could not smoke or drink very much. On the other hand, Korea expert William Taylor of the U.S. Center for Strategic and International Studies reported after luncheon with Kim just four months later, in June 1992, that "he walks and moves vigorously for age 80. His handshake is firm. When I left, he shook hands and pulled me toward him; his arm muscles are in good tone. His eyes are clear and his eye contact firm and compelling. Most important . . . his mind is quick and crystal clear."

Whatever Kim's private thoughts on his health and mortality, he was always upbeat. South Korean intelligence, which monitors satellite-based telephone transmissions from North Korea, overheard Kim in 1989 boasting to a daughter who was living in an Eastern European country, "I'm good for another ten years." Half a decade later, just weeks before he died, Kim told Jimmy Carter that he planned to remain active "for the next ten years."

✦　✦　✦

Kim Il Sung's death was kept secret for thirty-four hours, evidently to make sure arrangements were in place for the first succession in the country's history. On the morning of July 9, government ministries, offices, schools, and workplaces throughout North Korea were notified to watch television for an important announcement at noon. Many were expecting some good news, perhaps about the forthcoming summit meeting with the South. Instead they were greeted by an announcer dressed in black, who solemnly intoned a shocking announcement:

> To the Entire Party Members and People, our entire working class, cooperative farmers, officers and men of the People's Army, intellectuals, youth and students,
>
> The Central Committee of the Workers' Party, the Central Military Commission of the Party, the National Defense Commission, the Central People's Committee and the Administration Council of the Democratic People's Republic of Korea report to the entire people of the country with the

deepest grief that the great leader Comrade Kim Il Sung, General Secretary of the Central Committee of the Workers' Party of Korea and President of the Democratic People's Republic of Korea passed away from a sudden attack of illness at 02:00 on July 8, 1994. Our respected fatherly leader who has devoted his whole life to the popular masses' cause of independence and engaged himself in tireless activities for the prosperity of the motherland and happiness of the people, for the reunification of our country and independence of the world, till the last moments of his life, departed from us to our greatest sorrow.

There followed a lengthy obituary in praise of "a great revolutionary . . . genius in leadership . . . the greatest of great men . . . a great military strategist and ever-victorious iron-willed brilliant commander . . . the sun of the nation and lodestar of national reunification." Somber music followed, interspersed with readings from Kim's memoirs.

As the message sank in, officials in the Ministry of Foreign Affairs and many other places in the country broke down in front of the television sets and began weeping. Within a short time, residents of Pyongyang began converging on the giant statue of Kim on Mansu Hill near the city center, many of them crying hysterically. Before long, 15,000 to 20,000 people had gathered at the statue and in nearby streets, with lines of others stretching back as far as the eye could see. Ambulances were on duty, with aid workers assisting those who fainted or complained of feeling weak. Within a few hours, Pyongyang hospitals were overrun with heart attack victims. The areas around the many statues and other monuments to Kim elsewhere in the country were also overflowing with mourners.

In a strange coincidence, American and North Korean delegations headed by U.S. assistant secretary of state Robert Gallucci and DPRK deputy foreign minister Kang Sok Ju finally met to begin the long-awaited third round of nuclear negotiations on July 8, the day Kim died. Oblivious to the momentous but still secret event at home, the Pyongyang delegation reconfirmed the arrangements reached during the Carter mission to freeze its existing nuclear program in return for light-water reactors. From the American standpoint, surprisingly good progress was made. Following the meeting and private talks at a reception that night, Navy Captain Thomas Flanigan, the Joint Chiefs of Staff representative on the U.S. delegation, wrote an e-mail to his superior in the Pentagon, "They're here to deal. We need to understand that. Now it's an issue of what are we willing to negotiate."

At five A.M. local time on the morning of July 9, which was to be the second day of the talks, the news of Kim's death reached Geneva. Later in the morning, the shaken North Koreans, who had not been informed prior to the official announcement, prepared to return to Pyongyang, promising that the negotiations would continue as soon as possible.

In Washington, it was shortly after eleven P.M. local time when David E. Brown, the country director for Korea, got the news from the State Department Operations Center and began working on an official reaction. Senior officials were scattered around the world: President Clinton, Secretary of State Christopher, and their immediate staffs were in Naples at a Group of Seven summit meeting; Assistant Secretary for East Asian Affairs Winston Lord was en route home from a G-7 meeting between Clinton and Japanese prime minister Tomiichi Murayama; Ambassador Laney was in Ireland to receive an honorary degree; Gallucci and Deputy Assistant Secretary Thomas Hubbard were in Geneva; and other senior staff members were asleep in their beds in Washington.

In a globe-girdling telephone conference call that lasted most of the night, with various figures joining or leaving as their schedules and state of exhaustion dictated, it was decided to send condolences to "the North Korean people," in hopes of keeping the promising Geneva negotiations on track. Daniel Poneman, a National Security Council staff member, drafted the presidential statement that was promptly made public by the traveling White House:

> On behalf of the people of the United States, I extend sincere
> condolences to the people of North Korea on the death of
> President Kim Il Sung. We appreciate his leadership in
> resuming the talks between our governments. We hope they
> will continue as appropriate.

There was no consultation about the condolence statement with South Korea, a fact that prompted anger in some circles in Seoul. If there had been full consultation, according to a U.S. official involved in the decision, the statement might never have been issued.

Clinton's condolences were praised in Pyongyang but sharply condemned by Senate Republican leader Bob Dole, the president's eventual rival in the 1996 election. Dole called the statement "insensitive to the generation of Americans who suffered as a result of the Korean War" and heedless that "Kim Il Sung was a brutal dictator of a government that is neither a friend nor an ally of the United States—a government whose policies and actions have threatened and continue to threaten U.S. security and interests." Clinton responded that his statement was appropriate in view of the ongoing negotiations, and that "the veterans of the Korean War and their survivors, as much as any group of Americans, would very much want us to resolve this nuclear issue with North Korea and go forward."

In Seoul, Kim Young Sam placed the ROK armed forces on maximum alert at 12:39 P.M., within minutes after the news of the North Korean leader's death was broadcast. A National Security Council meeting was convened at the Blue House at two P.M., and an emergency cabinet meeting at five P.M. The only unusual military development in the North was that DPRK forces virtually stopped training and other visible activities, apparently to mourn the supreme leader and prepare for funeral activities.

As the days wore on, the reaction to Kim's death became the subject of political controversy in the South. When an opposition legislator, Lee Boo Young, suggested that the government express condolences in view of the grief being expressed by North Koreans, he touched off an impassioned debate in which conservatives went on the attack. After a week's delay, the government announced it would crack down on any domestic moves to pay tribute to Kim Il Sung and denounced the expression of condolences as "reckless" and "irresponsible behavior ignoring our history." The government also blocked a plan by leftist students to send a condolence mission to the North, and police warned that any expression of condolence would be met sternly as a violation of the National Security Law.

With old wounds reopened, emotions ran high. The Korean Broadcasting System was forced to terminate its broadcast of a fifty-five-minute Polish documentary about Kim Il Sung after twenty-five minutes due to a flood of complaints from viewers who felt it was too favorable. The same film had run on KBS two years earlier without incident. In a move that fanned the flames, the South Korean government, on the day after Kim's funeral, made public a hundred Soviet documents that had been given to Kim Young Sam during a visit to Moscow in early June, demonstrating that Kim Il Sung had been the moving figure behind the launching of the Korean War. Russian officials complained to Seoul about the inappropriate timing of the documents' release, which was decided without consultation with Moscow.

The actions and statements of Kim Young Sam's government, at a time of intense mourning in the North, generated bitter resentment in Pyongyang. North Korean authorities resumed virulent anti-South propaganda, which had been suspended by agreement in preparation for the summit, and they began refusing to accept official telephone messages from Seoul. Privately Kim Young Sam was unconcerned, since he was convinced that without its longtime leader, North Korea was on its last legs. The South Korean president's national security assistant, Chung Chong Uk, told his U.S. counterpart, Anthony Lake, in a telephone conversation that North Korea would collapse within six to twenty-four months. This conviction made Kim Young Sam more inclined to undercut than to accommodate the new leaders in Pyongyang.

## THE SUCCESSION OF KIM JONG IL

The plump, bespectacled, moon-faced man who stood apart and ahead of all others at the state funeral and the memorial service in Kim Il Sung Square was the most important mourner. Despite some expectations to the contrary, however, the eldest son and political heir of the Great Leader said nothing about his father, his loss, or his priorities for the country. Rather, he looked on enigmatically as others spoke in praise of the Great Leader, and of the ordained succession process that had been established more than a decade earlier.

In many respects, father and son were a study in contrasts. Kim Il Sung was a guerrilla fighter, the founder of the state, and a charismatic, outgoing, outspoken figure until the day he died. Kim Jong Il grew up in privilege from his teenage years, had never served a day in the military until he was named supreme commander of the People's Army in December 1991, wore his hair in an artsy pompadour, and was notably uncomfortable amid the roar of the crowd. Even when important pronouncements were made in his name, they were read by an announcer while he remained out of sight. As this is written, the only time the North Korean public has heard the voice of Kim Jong Il was in April 1992, when he uttered a single sentence during a ceremony marking the army's sixtieth anniversary: "Glory to the people's heroic military!"

A great deal about North Korea and its unique and inward-oriented system is mysterious; whatever pertains to Kim Jong Il is typically the most mysterious of all. His rise to power and selection as his father's successor were unacknowledged for many years, and his activities were masked under the vague euphemism "the party center." Since emerging from anonymity in 1980, he has rarely seen foreigners and is known to have traveled outside the country only twice: in 1983, when he toured Beijing and other Chinese cities for ten days; and in 1984, when he turned up briefly and unannounced in his father's entourage in Berlin. On the latter occasion, East German officials confirmed his presence only by studying photographs taken aboard Kim Il Sung's special train.

According to North Korean propagandists, Kim Jong Il was born in a log cabin on Mount Paekdu, the legendary birthplace of Tangun, the mythic father of the Korean people. More objective sources say the younger Kim was born on February 16, 1942, in a Russian military camp in the Far East, where his father's guerrilla band had taken refuge from the Japanese. After the Japanese surrender, at age three Kim Jong Il moved to Korea with his father but was evacuated to China at age eight during the Korean War. In his early years, a younger brother accidentally drowned, and his mother died while giving birth to a stillborn child, leaving Jong Il and a younger sister. Kim Il Sung remarried in the early 1960s and had two sons and two daughters by his second wife, Kim Song Ae.

North Korea has been aptly described by historian Bruce Cumings as "a corporate state and a family state." Kim Jong Il's sister, Kim Kyong Hui, is director of light industry in the Workers Party; her husband, Chang Song Taek, has become Kim Jong Il's right-hand man and one of the most powerful figures in the country. Kim Jong Il's half-brother, Kim Pyong Il, is ambassador to Finland after an earlier posting in Hungary. The husband of one of his half-sisters is a four-star general, and the other's husband is an ambassador. Family members and in-laws hold a very large number of the top leadership posts in the country.

Although passage of power from father to eldest son was traditional in Korean dynasties and Confucian families, it was heretical in a nominal "people's democracy." As recently as 1970, the official *Dictionary of Political Terminologies* published in Pyongyang defined hereditary succession as "a reactionary custom of exploitive societies." This entry was dropped in the early 1970s, when Kim Il Sung decided to make his son his closest aide and successor.

Kim Jong Il graduated from Kim Il Sung University in 1964 and went to work in the Central Committee of the Workers Party, with special responsibility for films, theater, and art, which became his lifelong passion. He is credited with the production of six major films and musicals in the early 1970s. Kim became a secretary of the Central Committee of the Workers Party in September 1973 and a member of its Politburo the following year. By then, songs were being sung about him among party cadres, who carried special notebooks to record his instructions.

Despite his prominence in the Workers Party, little was said about him publicly, which suggests that his father felt the need to fully prepare the domestic and external public for the first family succession of the communist world. North Korean media referred instead to a mysterious "party center" who was given credit for wise guidance and great deeds. The veil was lifted at the Sixth Workers Party Congress in October 1980, when the younger Kim was simultaneously awarded senior posts in the Politburo, the Military Commission, and the Party Secretariat and was openly proclaimed to be Kim Il Sung's designated successor. He was given the title of Dear Leader, close to that of the Great Leader. Both father and son were addressed and referred to in special honorific terms that were not used for any-one else.

Stories of Kim Jong Il's high living, hard drinking, and woman-izing are legion. Kim was married to his college sweetheart in 1966, but they divorced in 1971. He married his present wife, another Kim Il Sung University graduate who was a typist at Workers Party head-quarters, in 1973. He is widely reported to have had other liaisons, including a long-term affair in the early 1970s with a prominent ac-tress who was eventually sent off to live in a villa in Moscow.

For many years the most extensive glimpses of Kim Jong Il in action came from a prominent South Korean actress, Choi Eun Hee, and her former husband, film director Shin Sang Ok, who were kid-napped separately to North Korea from Hong Kong in 1978 on the younger Kim's orders. Without embarrassment, he baldly told the movie couple in a meeting that they surreptitiously tape-recorded that he had ordered their forcible abduction because "I absolutely needed you" to improve Pyongyang's unprofessional film industry. Speaking in matter-of-fact fashion about this bizarre kidnapping, Kim told them, "I just said, 'I need these two people, so bring them here,' so my comrades just carried out the operation."

Director Shin spent more than four years in North Korean pris-ons for trying to escape. After he was released and he and his wife were reunited, they made motion pictures for Kim Jong Il for almost three years. Kim Jong Il treated them as important artists and mem-bers of his social circle until their escape in Vienna in 1986. During this period they had extensive personal contact with him and his friends and entourage.

The country was struggling economically and was unable to pay its debts, but the filmmakers reported that Kim Jong Il spent money lavishly. He housed Choi and eventually Shin in luxurious surround-ings, including a house where he himself had previously lived. He gave each of them a new Mercedes 280 sedan with a license plate number beginning with 216, a reference to his February 16 birthday that is celebrated as a national holiday in North Korea, and that designates the automobile as that of a very important person. He built a new motion picture studio costing more than $40 million for their productions and put $2.3 million for their film company's use in a foreign bank account. An aide told Shin that the Dear Leader had use of the proceeds from a gold mine, which provided nearly unlimited funds for his gifts, motion picture hobby, and other activities.

In interviews shortly after their escape, Choi and Shin depicted Kim Jong Il as confident, bright, temperamental, quirky, and very much in charge of governmental as well as theatrical affairs. To his kidnapped "special guests," he could be privately self-deprecating, as when he said to actress Choi in their first dinner meeting, "What do you think of my physique? Small as a midget's turd, aren't I?" Or audacious, as when he summoned Choi at five A.M. to the final hours of an all-night party with his friends, a band, and lots of whiskey, of which he had imbibed too much.

While the kidnapping of Choi and Shin is the best documented of the many violent acts associated with the name of the younger Kim, it is not the only one. The terrorist bombing that killed South Korean cabinet members at Rangoon in 1983 was attributed to a clandestine agency reporting to him. Kim Hyon Hui, the female agent in the bombing of Korean Air Lines flight 858, in which 115 people were killed in 1987, was told that her orders came directly from Kim Jong Il in his own handwriting, although she did not see them. Various unconfirmed accounts suggest that the younger Kim had direct supervision of the North Korean nuclear weapons program.

At the same time, Kim Jong Il is believed to be more interested in modernizing than most others in the ruling circles. In a diplomatic dispatch to Berlin in 1982, the East German embassy remarked on the younger Kim's "modern" outlook and credited him with a loosening up of popular lifestyles, including the approval of more fashionable women's clothing, the reintroduction of dice, card, and board games, and the increased consumption of alcoholic beverages, especially beer.

In a tape recording brought out by the filmmakers, Kim Jong Il said in 1984, "After having experienced about thirty years of socialism, I feel we need to expand to the Western world to feed the people. The reality is that we are behind the West." At the same meeting, however, he said that North Korea could not open up, as even the Chinese were urging. "We have been stuck strategically" because opening up in his militarily embattled country, even for tourism, "would be naturally tantamount to disarmament." This could only be done after unification, he said.

In preparation for his succession, North Korean authorities went to extraordinary lengths to glorify Kim Jong Il: his portrait, along with that of his father, was placed in every home, office, and workplace. A fascinating example of the indoctrination was recounted to me by a Russian correspondent whose wife gave birth in the late 1980s at Pyongyang's maternity hospital during his assignment in the DPRK. The hospital is one of dozens around the country sponsored by Kim Jong Il in honor of his mother, who died in childbirth. After the correspondent's baby was born, the head nurse presented the newborn child to his father, declaring, "Congratulations from Comrade Kim Jong Il!" A few minutes later, several nurses paraded in military style into the birthing room with a large jar and a long-handled spoon. They ceremoniously placed a spoonful of honey into the mouth of the astonished new mother, chanting, "This is a gift from Comrade Kim Jong Il!" Sugar and honey were in such short supply among ordinary North Koreans that a spoonful of honey was a great delicacy. Despite such gestures, defectors and outside experts say that affection for Kim Jong Il in North Korea is much more limited than it was for his father.

The Dear Leader's health has been a matter of great speculation among foreign intelligence agencies. Over the years he has been variously reported to suffer from heart trouble, diabetes, epilepsy, and kidney disease. A Chinese military officer whose wife is a medical doctor told me he was treated by a Chinese medical team for head injuries sustained in a serious automobile accident in September 1993. A high-ranking official of South Korean intelligence, on the other hand, said he believes the younger Kim sustained injuries to his side and perhaps internal organs in 1993, in a fall sustained while horseback riding. None of the stories has been confirmed.

In July 1994, wearing a dark cadre suit with a black mourning armband, Kim Jong Il kept his own counsel at the ceremonies for his father. Pyongyang radio referred to him as "the Dear Leader, the sole successor to the Great Leader," and Korea experts speculated about how quickly he would assume his father's titles of general secretary of the Workers Party and president of the DPRK. Initial predictions were that he would claim the posts and titles of supreme leadership after a hundred days of mourning, then after one year of mourning; then after two years, and so on. His failure to take the two top posts stirred speculation that Kim Jong Il faced important opposition within the hierarchy.

## THE FRAMEWORK NEGOTIATIONS

The long-awaited third round of U.S.–DPRK nuclear negotiations, which had finally convened the day that Kim Il Sung died and was quickly interrupted, resumed in Geneva on August 5. American negotiators were relieved to discover that the death of Kim Il Sung had not altered the existing DPRK negotiating positions nor diminished the desire of its leadership to make a deal. From the outset of the Geneva talks, the North Koreans were impressively businesslike and determined to move ahead, in sharp contrast to their argumentative style on many previous occasions.

In a single week of talks ending with a postmidnight press conference on August 12, the two delegations were speedily able to agree on the rough outlines of a settlement of the central issues. Additional progress emerged from tougher bargaining when the negotiations resumed in September after a six-week recess.

As a result of the Carter mission, North Korea had already agreed to freeze its nuclear program while negotiations proceeded. In Geneva the two sides now pursued a permanent solution along the lines they had previously discussed: that Pyongyang would abandon all of its proliferation-prone gas-graphite nuclear facilities in return for modern light-water reactor nuclear power plants.

Beyond this basic provision, a comprehensive agreement had to take account of a number of lesser items of great concern to one side or the other. DPRK negotiator Kang, in private conversation with Gallucci, referred to several key items as "our chips": the eight thousand irradiated fuel rods that had been unloaded earlier in the year from the 5-megawatt nuclear reactor; the reprocessing facility that could extract from those fuel rods enough plutonium for four or five nuclear weapons; and the mandatory IAEA "special inspections" of the disputed nuclear waste sites, which might cast light on whether

North Korea already possessed hidden plutonium. The United States also had some important bargaining chips, especially the possible establishment of political and economic ties that could create a new environment for North Korea and substitute, in some degree, for the loss of the Soviet Union and the shifts in the policies of China.

Early on, the North Koreans asked to be compensated for the energy they would be giving up by shutting down their working reactor and stopping work on the two larger ones long before the promised light-water reactors were on the scene, a period estimated to take at least ten years. They made it clear that they needed something concrete to take home at the end of the negotiations. The Americans explored supplying various energy sources, including surplus Defense Department generators, coal-fired plants, and others. U.S. negotiators were delighted when the North Koreans asked for heavy oil, a little-used sludge-like commodity that is left over from the refining of petroleum. It had previously powered a large electricity plant near the northern border, supplied decades earlier by the East Germans and, unknown to the Americans, had been high on Kim Il Sung's wish list in connection with additional power plants.

How to structure the terms of what was emerging as a comprehensive deal consumed much of the bargaining. North Koreans feared they would be made to give up everything at the beginning and then the Americans would renege in the long run. Americans feared a sweeping agreement in principle that would not be fulfilled by the North Koreans. Gallucci observed that "there wasn't sufficient trust for one to take a very large step assuming the other would take the compensatory counter step. There had to be a series of smaller steps linked with constant checking on compliance." Thus, the core of the agreement was a detailed timetable of reciprocal actions, some of which were spelled out in confidential minutes that were not made public due to North Korean sensibilities.

The rapid progress toward a far-reaching accord in the first week, as well as continued progress when the negotiations resumed in September after a six-week recess, was surprising to many American officials. U.S. negotiators surmised that, especially after Kim Il Sung's death, the new leadership was under pressure to produce a deal that would enhance Kim Jong Il's stature. Moreover, Gallucci believed that the tangible threat of UN sanctions in the spring and American willingness to face down North Korea with a major infusion of additional ships, planes, and troops, as worrisome as it had been to all parties, was a crucial reason for his success. He called the events of June "a very good combination of political-military activity" that drove Pyongyang back to the bargaining table with a strong desire to reach a settlement.

One of the thorniest issues was the IAEA's demand, which Washington and the UN Security Council had endorsed, for "special inspections" of the two suspected nuclear waste sites at Yongbyon, which North Korea claimed were military facilities exempt from inspection. This dispute had been the immediate cause of Pyongyang's startling announcement eighteen months earlier that it was withdrawing from the Nuclear Non-Proliferation Treaty. In the meantime, private declarations of its chief negotiator, Kang Sok Ju, as well as public statements from Pyongyang, warned that North Korea would "never" submit to what it described as a violation of its national sovereignty. Gallucci, on the other hand, came with firm instructions that North Korean acceptance of the "special inspections" must be part of the final agreement. This was clearly a deal-breaker—until both sides began showing flexibility.

The State Department's senior North Korea watcher, Robert Carlin, who had spent more than twenty years listening for nuances in North Korean statements, noticed that beginning September 23, Kang had stopped saying "never" about the special inspections. Carlin thought the omission significant. The Pyongyang-watcher was even more certain that something was up when, on September 27, Pyongyang radio broadcast a puzzling press statement by "a spokesman for DPRK Ministry of the People's Armed Forces." In blustery language, the statement seemed to attack the ongoing Geneva talks being conducted by the Foreign Ministry, declaring that the army had never expected anything, did not recognize "talks accompanied by pressure," and could "never allow any attempt to open up military facilities through special inspections." CIA experts in Washington, whom I happened to meet that afternoon at a conference on Korea policy, interpreted the statement as presaging even fiercer North Korean opposition to special inspections and a deadlock in the negotiations. Carlin, however, was convinced that the opposite was true—that the strange military pronouncement had arisen from an outbreak of open bureaucratic warfare between the army and the Foreign Ministry in Pyongyang over making a key concession in Geneva.

Carlin was soon proven right. At the negotiating table on October 6, Kang proposed coolly that North Korea not be required to accept special inspections (he used a euphemism to avoid these words) until 70 to 80 percent of the components of the promised light-water reactors had been shipped. Suddenly "never" had been transformed into a discussion of the price. Carlin wrote an e-mail to his immediate superior at the State Department: "At 11:50 this morning we won the war. I can pinpoint the time because when Kang said what he said, I knew the game was over, and I looked at my watch." At that point it was left to Gallucci to nail down the terms and persuade Washington to permit special inspections to be postponed until the delivery of key nuclear components of the promised light-water reactors—probably five years or more away. The postponement became one of the agreement's most controversial features. Gallucci and the U.S. administration defended it as the best they could do.

South Korea had agreed to play the central role and pick up the lion's share of the costs of providing the light-water reactors, but Seoul was absent from the bargaining table at Geneva. Although its diplomats were briefed daily, its absence from direct participation in the U.S.–DPRK negotiations and resulting accords was a bitter pill for South Koreans, who saw themselves as relegated to a marginal role while their sponsor sat down with their peninsular foe. Conversely, a direct relationship with Washington was among the most important incentives for Pyongyang, which had been marginalized in the earlier South Korean breakthroughs with Moscow and Beijing.

The anxiety in Seoul emerged dramatically in mid-October, when President Kim Young Sam, in an interview with *The New York Times*, objected to the agreement nearing completion in Geneva on grounds that "North Korea faces the danger of imminent political and economic collapse" and that "any compromise [at this point] with North Korea will only help prolong its survival." He also declared that the United States, with far less experience than Seoul in negotiations with Pyongyang, was being deceived in Geneva. These comments contradicted the public positions of support for the negotiations that had been taken by Kim's government.

Kim's outburst was shocking to Gallucci and to officials in Washington, who feared their ally might torpedo the negotiations at the eleventh hour. Secretary of State Christopher, who was traveling in London, telephoned South Korean foreign minister Han Sung Joo at 2 A.M., London time, after receiving a phone call about Kim's interview from an unhappy President Clinton.

In the Blue House the following afternoon, Ambassador Laney bearded the South Korean president. "We wouldn't betray you at the DMZ; we wouldn't do it in Geneva," Laney declared. Speaking of the alliance's shared purposes about North Korea, he appealed to Kim to maintain unity when they were finally about to succeed in curbing Pyongyang's nuclear program. In response, Kim said flatly that he could not approve the Geneva accord because of promises he had made to the Korean people. He vehemently objected to postponing the "special inspections" to clear up North Korea's murky nuclear past, and to the absence of a North-South aspect of the proposed agreement. Laney countered that early "special inspections" could not be negotiated because Pyongyang would immediately lose all its nuclear leverage, and that Gallucci was actively seeking a commitment to North-South dialogue as part of the accord. Laney appealed to Kim as a statesman to rise above popular expectations.

President Kim was not convinced. In conversation with Foreign Minister Han the following morning, Kim initially resolved to denounce the U.S.–DPRK deal. Such a denunciation would have negated the Geneva negotiations, created a crisis between Seoul and Washington, and potentially led to a renewed confrontation with North Korea. In a series of telephone calls, Han persuaded his president that it was in the ROK's national interest to approve the agreement—but he was able to do so only after harsh words were exchanged. Han told his aide that the intense disagreement would probably cost him his job but that the issue was so important, it was worth the risk. Two months later, Kim dumped Foreign Minister Han and named a cautious career diplomat, Gong Ro Myung, in his place.

In view of this situation in Seoul, Gallucci in Geneva was instructed to insist that the U.S.–DPRK agreement include a clause committing North Korea to resume the dormant North-South dialogue. His opposite number, Kang, adamantly refused, on grounds that North-South relations were intra-Korean business and outside the legitimate concern of the United States. North Korean negotiators said flatly that they had instructions to break off the negotiations and return home if the U.S. side insisted on North-South issues as a precondition for the nuclear arrangements. Gallucci insisted that without a North-South commitment, there would be no agreement.

After threats from both sides to leave Geneva in failure, the North Koreans finally agreed to negotiate on the North-South issue. Several days of haggling over wording produced a paragraph declaring, "The DPRK will engage in North-South dialogue, as this Agreed Framework will help create an atmosphere that promotes such dialogue." The two sides had deadlocked on a timetable phrase, with the United States proposing the commitment to dialogue "at the earliest time." North Korea insisted on the "as" clause, which it later used as an excuse not to perform. Gallucci finally accepted these compromises, believing that no language could compel Pyongyang to negotiate with Seoul and that "the exact words were a matter of Talmudic significance to all those who lived on the Korean peninsula."

Although it was virtually a treaty in form and substance, with binding obligations on both sides, the accord was styled an Agreed Framework because the Clinton administration worried that it might not win approval if submitted to the Senate as a treaty. The North Koreans were gravely concerned that Congress would balk and that Washington would fail to uphold its end of the accord. The day before the signing, as agreed in Geneva, Clinton sent a letter to "His Excellency Kim Jong Il, Supreme Leader of the Democratic People's Republic of Korea" confirming that he would "use the full powers of his office . . . subject to the approval of the U.S. Congress" to arrange for light-water reactors and provide "interim energy alternatives" during the construction period. The North Koreans complained about the less-than-ironclad language, but the Americans explained that under the U.S. separation of powers, even a president cannot act independently of Congress.

The agreement was signed in ceremonies in Geneva on October 21 by Gallucci and Kang for the United States and the DPRK, respectively. According to its main provisions:

• The United States would organize an international consortium to provide light-water reactors, with a total generating capacity of 2,000 megawatts, by a target date of 2003. In return, North Korea would freeze all activity on its existing nuclear reactors and related facilities, and permit them to be continuously monitored by IAEA inspectors. The eight thousand fuel rods unloaded from the first reactor would be shipped out of the country.

• North Korea would come into full compliance with the IAEA—which meant accepting the "special inspections"— before the delivery of key nuclear components of the LWR project, estimated to be within five years. The DPRK's existing nuclear facilities would be completely dismantled by the time the LWR project was completed, estimated in ten years.

• The United States would arrange to supply 500,000 tons of heavy fuel oil annually to make up for energy forgone by North Korea before the LWRs came into operation.

• The two states would reduce existing barriers to trade and investment and open diplomatic liaison offices in each other's capitals as initial steps toward eventual full normalization of relations. The United States would provide formal assurances against the threat or use of nuclear weapons against North Korea.

• North Korea would implement the 1991 North-South joint declaration on the demilitarization of the Korean peninsula and reengage in North-South dialogue.

◆    ◆    ◆

North Korea greeted the accord as a triumph, which was neither surprising nor unjustified in view of the vastly unequal weight of the two countries. DPRK negotiator Kang Sok Ju called the agreement "a very important milestone document of historical significance" and was greeted with ceremonial honor at Pyongyang airport when he returned from Geneva. He and his team were honored at a banquet given in the name of (but not in the presence of) Kim Jong Il. The Workers Party newspaper, *Nodong Sinmun,* hailed the agreement as "the biggest diplomatic victory" and boasted, "We held the talks independently with the United States on an independent footing, not relying on someone else's sympathy or advice."

In Seoul, public opinion and the views of influential elite groups were extremely negative, even though the ROK government officially endorsed the agreement and pledged to cooperate to make it work. Arriving on one of my periodic visits a month after the signing of the accord, I was startled to run into so many objections expressed in such passionate terms, even by normally pro-American and pragmatic Koreans.

The objections ran the gamut from the failure to consult Seoul adequately to the belief that the U.S. negotiators could have obtained a better deal through tougher bargaining. Moreover, many South Koreans agreed with the sentiments expressed by President Kim Young Sam to *The New York Times* during the last days of the Geneva bargaining: any American deal would help shore up a Pyongyang regime on the verge of collapsing, thus postponing reunification.

However, the most important objection to the Agreed Framework was less specific but much more serious: South Koreans were in anguish that the United States, their great ally and closest friend, would establish any relationship with North Korea, about which nearly everyone had complex feelings and which many regarded as a bitter enemy. All the more infuriating was the fact that the U.S.–DPRK deal had been consummated without the direct involvement of the ROK. Suddenly Washington was dealing with "the evil twin," as one Seoulite put it to me, and doing so behind South Korea's back. The consequences of this shift in relationships with North and South, which were little understood in Washington, made the ROK government and its people immensely more difficult to deal with.

The agreement was greeted coolly by the American public, which had not been prepared for such a broad accord with a pariah nation. *The New York Times* headline was "Clinton Approves a Plan to Give Aid to North Korea." *The Washington Post* announced,

"North Korea Pact Contains U.S. Concessions; Agreement Would Allow Presence of Key Plutonium-Making Facilities for Years."

Seventeen days after the Agreed Framework was signed, its problems in Congress became more serious when Republicans in the 1994 elections unexpectedly won control of both houses for the first time in decades. Foreign policy had been only a minor issue in the political campaigns, but the new Republican Congress was much more conservative and more skeptical of any dealings with North Korea than the outgoing Democratic Congress had been.

## THE KIM JONG IL REGIME

On December 17, less than two months after the signing of the Agreed Framework, the new relationship between Washington and Pyongyang was tested in a way nobody had expected. That morning two U.S. Army warrant officers in an unarmed helicopter lost their way in snow-covered terrain and flew across the DMZ five miles into North Korean airspace before being shot down. Chief Warrant Officer David Hileman was killed, but the copilot, Chief Warrant Officer Bobby Hall, survived. He was immediately surrounded and captured by North Korean troops.

As these events were taking place, Representative Bill Richardson, a New Mexico Democrat, was on his way to Pyongyang via Beijing. When he arrived in the North Korean capital on the evening of the seventeenth, he tried strenuously but unsuccessfully to arrange the release of Airman Hall. He was told by Foreign Ministry officials that the case was in the hands of the less sympathetic Korean People's Army command. When Richardson left on December 22, he took with him the body of Airman Hileman but, despite pleas about the coming of Christmas, only a promise of best efforts to arrange the release of Hall "very soon."

On Christmas Day, Hall, still in captivity, wrote a "confession" accurately setting out the facts of his flight and asking forgiveness for his "grave infringement upon the sovereignty of the DPRK." The following day, the North Korean Foreign Ministry asked the State Department to send a senior official to Pyongyang, saying that the release of Hall probably could not be arranged through the military channels at the DMZ that were being used to deal with the issue.

Deputy Assistant Secretary of State Thomas Hubbard, who had participated in the framework negotiations and other exchanges, crossed the DMZ into North Korea on December 28. It was immediately clear that the Foreign Ministry was under orders to see what concessions could be gained in return for Hall's release. In two days of talks, Hubbard refused to grant the North Koreans any of the political concessions they sought, such as agreement to begin negotiating a U.S.–DPRK peace treaty, but he did agree to a statement of "sincere regret" for the "legally unjustified intrusion into DPRK air space."

An illuminating aspect of the negotiations were conspicuous differences between the Foreign Ministry, which was eager to protect and advance the framework accord with the United States, and the military, which was primarily concerned with the defense of borders. Foreign Ministry officials spoke openly of their frictions with military officers; at the DMZ, KPA officers spoke disparagingly to their American military counterparts of the "neckties," as they called the DPRK diplomats.

Such differences, in a less personal vein, had emerged during the course of the U.S.–DPRK negotiations in Geneva. To some extent conflicts with the harder-edged military were a useful bargaining ploy on the part of the diplomats, but Gallucci, Hubbard, and other American negotiators had become convinced that the differences were real. In Geneva the diplomats ultimately won most of the confrontations because they said their instructions had been personally signed by the new supreme leader, Kim Jong Il. At the climax of the Hall case, the military was also overruled, evidently by Kim Jong Il. While this appeared to show that Kim Jong Il retained ultimate authority even in policy disputes involving the powerful military, the openness with which differences were acknowledged suggested that the glue binding together disparate interest groups had become much thinner since the demise of the Great Leader.

On the evening of December 29, Hubbard received final approval from Washington for the public statement of U.S. regret that he proposed to make to accomplish Hall's release. At that point,

Deputy Foreign Minister Kang excused himself from an official dinner, taking a copy of the statement and saying he would submit it to "the supreme leader." At two A.M. another Foreign Ministry official called on Hubbard at the State Guest House to announce that the statement and the release of Hall had been "approved by Kim Jong Il." Hall was released the following morning at Panmunjom, where KPA officers made little effort to hide their displeasure. "I became convinced there was a supreme being there, and that probably it is Kim Jong Il," Hubbard told me later. However, neither he nor other foreign diplomats were able to meet the new North Korean leader in person.

Within minutes of Hall's return to South Korea, Clinton telephoned ROK president Kim Young Sam to reassure him that Hubbard's negotiations had not opened a new U.S. channel or line of policy toward North Korea. The telephone call was deemed necessary because South Korean news media and some officials were highly critical of the negotiations, worried that Hubbard was making new deals in the North and reading North Korean advantages into the brief statement Hubbard had made on Washington's authority. "Something strange is going on up there," Kim told Clinton, evidently referring to differences within North Korea's leadership. "We should not move too fast."

◆　◆　◆

In mid-January 1995, I was able to take a week-long look at North Korea in the Kim Jong Il era as part of a four-member academic delegation sponsored by George Washington University's Sigur Center for East Asian Studies. As in my 1991 visit, the small Russian-built airliner that brought us from Beijing was the only one to land in the entire country that day. By contrast, Seoul's busy Kimpo airport, one of dozens of commercial airports in the ROK, was recording more than 40,000 passengers a day arriving or departing from overseas on an incessant stream of jumbo jets.

Within an hour after landing, however, I was struck by notable changes from my previous trip three and a half years earlier. The first surprise was that our official Mercedes cars—and all other vehicles in sight—were stopped and their occupants examined at a military checkpoint. This had never happened on my previous trip. Moreover, army and internal security police, often armed with automatic weapons, were in much greater evidence in Pyongyang streets than they had been before, and a frequent European visitor said the military was more conspicuous in the countryside than previously. While there was no discernible challenge to the regime (nor would such a challenge have been tolerated), the notably greater military presence seemed intended to convey a message: but whether that message was increased vigilance against potential challenge or simply the increased importance of the military in the Kim Jong Il era, I did not know.

As our cars entered the city, we paused en route to our hotel for a new obligatory rite of passage: paying homage to Kim Il Sung at his giant bronze statue on Mansu Hill, overlooking the capital he built. Professor Young C. Kim, the Korean-American leader of our delegation, accepted bouquets of flowers from our hosts to place at the base of the statue, which was already bedecked with scores of other bouquets. Behind us in the subzero January chill were groups of schoolchildren, and then a group of children and adults, waiting their turn to pay tribute. While somber music came from loudspeakers and a sorrowful electronic voice invoked the memory of the Great Leader, television cameras recorded our respectful visit to the statue. The scene was broadcast the following evening on state television, the only TV outlet available and legally permitted to the people of North Korea.

Beginning with our stop at the statue and continuing throughout our stay, Kim Il Sung seemed as omnipresent in death as in life, dominating the television programs, publications, cultural programs, and even policy presentations of the regime he left behind. With rare exceptions, each official whom we met began his presentation with recognition of the grave historic misfortune suffered by the country and, they claimed, the entire world when the Great Leader died. While mention was made of his son and chosen successor, greater emphasis was placed on the fallen leader.

In all political systems, the death of the leader is a traumatic experience, especially in the case of totalitarian leaders such as Stalin, Mao, and Kim Il Sung, who reigned over their countries for decades. With the choice of his son to be his political heir, Kim had been seeking to avoid the years of confusion and the ultimate repudiation that followed the deaths of his Russian and Chinese contemporaries. The continuing and elaborate homage to Kim even after his death appeared to be calculated to minimize the perils of transition to his less-than-charismatic successor. To ensure that "Great Leader Comrade Kim Il Sung will be with us forever," as a ubiquitous slogan said, his body was being preserved, with the help of Russian experts who had prepared the bodies of Lenin and Mao for permanent display. Kim's former presidential office was being turned into a state mausoleum, which opened officially on the first anniversary of his death.

Whatever else his legacy might be, Kim Il Sung left his son an economy that was on the rocks. January 1995 marked the beginning of the sixth consecutive year of negative economic growth, as estimated by outside experts. Since 1990, the first year of decline, the North Korean GNP had contracted by about one-fourth, according to these estimates. Nonetheless, we saw little privation in our one-week visit that was limited to the capital city, whose specially chosen population obtains the best of whatever is available. Surprisingly, I noticed more cars, trucks, and buses on the streets, suggesting that the energy crisis had diminished since my previous visit in 1991.

The country's economic troubles were doubtless among the reasons that North Korea in early 1995 appeared eager to confirm and advance its new relationship with the United States. The importance of the U.S. relationship was explicit in the statements of officials whom we saw, including Foreign Minister Kim Yong Nam and the more freewheeling Kim Yong Sun, who after further ups and downs had become Workers Party secretary for North-South affairs. Our visit coincided with that of a team of experts from U.S. government agencies working with the nuclear authorities to arrange safe and continuously inspected storage of the fuel rods that had been unloaded from the now-dormant 5-megawatt reactor at Yongbyon. The visit also coincided with the arrival of two ships at the port of Sonbong carrying 50,000 tons of heavy fuel oil, the first of the U.S.-supplied energy to be delivered under the Agreed Framework in compensation for the shutdown of the North Korean nuclear program. Later I saw the brief cable from the Joint Chiefs of Staff in Washington to U.S. Commands in the Pacific notifying them that "the Secretary of Defense has directed the [merchant ships] *Da Quing* and *Lark Lake* to deliver 50,000 metric tons of heavy fuel oil to the DPRK." It was hard to believe that less than a year earlier, the United States and North Korea had been on the brink of war and that the Joint Chiefs had been contemplating very different orders about the DPRK to its Pacific commands.

On January 20, the day before we left Pyongyang, the State Department announced the easing of several economic sanctions against North Korea, as anticipated in the Agreed Framework. However, these were less than the administration had previously planned because of opposition to concessions on the part of the Republicans who were now in control of Congress. For the same reason, the first fuel oil shipments were paid for out of Pentagon contingency funds, which did not require new authorization from Capitol Hill. The Agreed Framework, while working as planned in North Korea, was on thin ice politically in the United States.

The central issue presented to us in nearly every meeting in Pyongyang was the desire to negotiate a U.S.–DPRK "peace insuring system" at the DMZ to replace the 1953 armistice agreement, which North Korea insisted was obsolete. The demand for a U.S.–DPRK peace treaty was more than twenty years old, but it had been given new impetus starting in April 1994, when North Korea reacted to the U.S. military buildup in technical violation of the armistice. Weeks later, the North withdrew its delegates from the Military Armistice Commission, forced the withdrawal of the Polish participants from the long-standing Neutral Nations Supervisory Commission at the DMZ, and launched a successful diplomatic drive to persuade China to withdraw from the Military Armistice Commission. A senior DPRK foreign ministry official, Kim Byong Hong, told us ominously that if the United States did not respond to the new "peace insuring" proposal, the DPRK would take "unilateral steps."

Due to the opposition to the armistice by then-President Syngman Rhee, South Korea was not a signatory to the armistice; therefore, North Korea insisted that the South not be included in talks about its future. From the American standpoint, it was out of the question to negotiate a bilateral peace treaty or other "peace insuring system" on the divided peninsula without the South Koreans, as our delegation told our hosts in no uncertain terms. Despite this imposing roadblock, the discussion of more permanent arrangements at the heavily fortified DMZ seemed to me a positive development.

The official attitude toward the South was the most troubling aspect of our talks in Pyongyang. Despite the North's reluctant commitment, in the Agreed Framework, to return to North-South dialogue, DPRK officials adamantly refused to deal with the ROK government, insisting it had irrevocably insulted North Korea by its conduct at the death of Kim Il Sung. The foreign minister and others insisted that the South must formally apologize, which was highly unlikely, before talks could restart.

How much of this was honest anger and how much a tactic to avoid North-South negotiations and bait the South while concentrating on Pyongyang's relationship with the United States was impossible to tell. It was clear enough, though, that the absence of movement toward accommodation or détente between North and South was a serious problem for the United States in moving between a former enemy and a close ally.

## THE STRUGGLE OVER THE REACTORS

The most important unresolved problem in implementing the Agreed Framework was the source and description of the light-water reactors to be furnished in exchange for North Korea's existing nuclear facilities. While the United States had negotiated the deal and sent a letter from Clinton to Kim Jong Il officially promising to provide the reactors, Washington did not propose to furnish or pay for them. South Korea had volunteered to provide them, and from the first, Washington called on Seoul to manufacture them in its sophisticated factories and underwrite most of their $4–$5 billion cost, with Japan putting up much of the rest. North Korea was reluctant to accept this high-tech export from its enemies in the South, but Gallucci and others insisted there was no alternative.

Three rounds of U.S.–DPRK expert talks on the topic in Beijing and Berlin ended in deadlock. Pyongyang was determined to avoid an open acknowledgment that South Korea might be the source of the reactors, insisting that it was up to the United States to provide them under an American label—but also saying that where they actually came from was Washington's business. Seoul, on the other hand, was determined that North Korea accept its central role in providing the light-water reactors, and that this role should be openly acknowledged by referring to the "South Korean type" reactors to be furnished.

A face-saving intermediary was the international consortium envisaged in the Agreed Framework. It was established by the United States, South Korea, and Japan in March 1995 as the Korean Peninsula Energy Development Organization (KEDO), with an American executive director, former diplomat Stephen Bosworth, giving overall direction to the project.

In the Agreed Framework the United States had pledged to make the "best efforts" to conclude a contract to supply the new reactors by April 21, 1995—six months after the signing of the accord. As that date approached with negotiations deadlocked on the origin and name of the new reactors, North Korea threatened to abandon the Agreed Framework, ending the freeze on its existing nuclear program by reloading its 5-megawatt reactor. The situation was made more complicated by Seoul's adamant demand that the North clearly acknowledge the origin of its new reactors, on grounds that this was necessary if the National Assembly was to furnish the billions of dollars required. At the Berlin talks in late March, when the United States proposed to offer the North face-saving language, South Korea refused to approve the talking points. Battered by criticism for ignoring the interests of the South, "we made a very conscious choice between pursuing what we thought was the most likely route to a solution and solidarity [with the South]. We opted for solidarity," according to a White House policy maker. Predictably, the talks ended in failure.

As tensions rose again, talk in Seoul and Washington turned again to a show of force to pressure North Korea. This time the adoption of sanctions by the UN Security Council seemed unlikely because the issue boiled down to North Korean pride versus South Korean pride. Moreover, Chinese cooperation was less likely because the United States and China were embroiled in a dispute over a U.S. visit by Taiwan's president.

To exert pressure on the North, ROK foreign minister Gong Ro Myung suggested bringing U.S. aircraft-carrier battle groups into both the seas around the Korean peninsula. Gong's idea was rejected, but officials in Washington began reconsidering the options for major augmentation of U.S. forces in Korea, such as had been on the table at the White House when Jimmy Carter met Kim Il Sung during the June 1994 crisis. According to a military officer who was involved, some senior administration officials, frustrated by the lack of agreement in April 1995 and angered by Pyongyang's threats, were saying, "Here we go again. There's only one way to play with North Korea, and that's very hard. Send in the troops." One option under active consideration at the Pentagon and in interagency discussions would have dispatched 75,000 additional U.S. troops—roughly double the 37,000 already stationed in Korea.

Once again, Ambassador Laney and the U.S. commander in Seoul, General Gary Luck, were more reluctant than some of their superiors in Washington to risk the beginning of rapid reinforcement, given that the reaction of the North Korean military was unforeseeable. On April 28 they sent an unsolicited joint message to Secretary of State Christopher and Secretary of Defense Perry strongly arguing that no emergency was at hand that justified a major augmentation of American forces. "Gen. Luck clearly viewed flowing lots of things as a precursor to war and that could lead to a conflict," said a Washington official familiar with his views. Luck's cabled objections arrived while Joint Chiefs of Staff chairman General John Shalikashvili and senior aides were meeting on the subject. It abruptly halted the drift toward large-scale reinforcement.

Unlike the crisis of the year before, this tension was unknown to the public, but it added salience to the diplomatic effort to resolve the LWR identity issue. The principal effort was negotiations held from May 19 to June 12 between U.S. deputy assistant secretary of state Thomas Hubbard and DPRK vice foreign minister Kim Gye Gwan in Kuala Lumpur, Malaysia. While nominally between the United States and North Korea, in reality much of the bargaining was on the sidelines between the United States and South Korea, which repeatedly rejected proposals that would permit North Korea to save face.

In the end, Washington persuaded Seoul to accept a sleight-of-hand solution. North Korea formally agreed, at Kuala Lumpur, that the project would consist of "two pressurized light-water reactors with two coolant loops and a generating capacity of approximately 1,000 megawatts each . . . the advanced version of U.S.-origin design and technology currently under production." This description perfectly described the South Korean standard reactors and no others in the world. Without explicitly mentioning South Korea, the agreement stipulated that KEDO, the U.S.-led consortium, would finance and supply the LWR reactors. However, as the accord was announced, the KEDO board, in a coordinated action that had been made known to the North in advance, announced simultaneously in Seoul that the state-run Korean Electric Power Corporation (KEPCO) would be the prime contractor for the project and that "Korean standard model reactors" would be provided.

"It is not a document of surrender but a product of diplomatic negotiations," said ROK foreign minister Gong, in defending the outcome of the Kuala Lumpur talks. The North Korean Foreign Ministry issued a statement claiming victory in the talks and declaring that "what KEDO does is the internal matter of the United States and we do not feel it necessary to interfere and do not care a bit." With the agreement in Kuala Lumpur, the nuclear crisis, while not over, seemed decisively on its way to resolution.

# 15

## NORTH KOREA IN CRISIS

With the waning of the nuclear struggle, North Korea only briefly left the list of pressing concerns of the major powers. Within months it was back, but this time with an abrupt shift in the angle of vision brought on by the regime's inability to feed its people and its unprecedented appeal for outside help. After dealing with the DPRK almost exclusively as a strong and nightmarish threat to peace, policy makers in Washington and other world capitals began to focus on a failing state whose very weakness was a menace, albeit of a different kind. The question being urgently discussed among the experts was, "Is this the beginning of the end for North Korea?" And if so, how would its neighbors and the world deal with a potential economic collapse, the flight of massive numbers of refugees across land and sea boundaries, and/or civil war that might spread across tense borders?

General John Shalikashvili, chairman of the Joint Chiefs of Staff, expressed the view of many when he said, "We are now in a period where most who watch the area would say it's either going to implode or explode—we're just not quite sure when that is going to happen." Secretary of Defense William Perry, who had been perhaps the most influential policy maker in the nuclear crisis, popularized the metaphor of North Korea as a disabled airliner rapidly losing altitude, as well as the metaphor of seeking a "soft landing," meaning a gradual unification or accommodation with the South, rather than a destructive crash.

The altered optic with which the great powers viewed the northern half of the Korean peninsula was evidence of how much the world had changed in the quarter-century since 1972, when the two Koreas had begun to interact peacefully with each other. South Korea had decisively won the economic race, with enormous consequences in the diplomatic and military fields. Although the North retained a formidable armed force, it was no longer a serious competitor to the South in any other field of endeavor, and the disparity of its resources was swiftly eroding its military competitiveness. Following the death of its Great Leader, it was forced to center its attention and energies on sheer survival and little else—and in so doing to ask the assistance of the outside world. Prideful North Korea sought to deal with this reversal of fortunes with a minimum of humiliation, but it was not easy.

The realization that North Korea was in deep trouble began with an act of nature. On the sticky midsummer day of July 26, 1995, the skies over the country darkened. Rains began to pound the earth, rains that were heavy, steady, and unrelenting and that soon turned into a deluge of biblical proportions. The DPRK Bureau of Hydro-Meteorological Service recorded 23 inches of rain in ten days; in some towns and villages, according to the United Nations, as much as 18 inches of rain fell in a single day, bringing floods that were considered the worst in a century.

As a self-proclaimed "socialist paradise," North Korea traditionally had said little or nothing about domestic disasters. This time, as the rains ended in mid-August, it broke its silence and described the tragedy in expansive terms, even exaggerating the admittedly severe impact of the flooding. In late August, for the first time in its history, the bastion of self-reliance openly appealed to the world for help, asking the United Nations for nearly $500 million in flood relief as well as fuel and medical assistance.

Because the United Nations agencies and other aid-givers had no confidence that aid they sent would reach the country's people, they demanded and obtained access to flood-stricken parts of the

North Korean countryside as a condition of providing assistance. This trailblazing access to some previously inaccessible areas was troubling to the secretive DPRK military and security forces, but they had no other choice than to accept it.

Trevor Page, chief of the newly opened UN World Food Program office in Pyongyang, visited the Korean hinterland late in 1995 and found malnutrition rampant and hungry people nearly everywhere. In the western province of Huanghei, Page observed "people scavenging in the fields looking for roots and wild plants to prepare soup for their families. People were anxious, restless. They are not getting enough to eat." Further south near the demilitarized zone, in one of the country's prime food-producing areas, Page found "not a cabbage to be seen" after authorities reduced the already-minimal food ration under the Public Distribution System to the bare subsistence level: a bowl or two of rice or corn per person per day. Even that was uncertain due to frequent supply failures.

Based on a visit to farming areas, cities, and DPRK government agencies in early December, a team of experts from the UN's Food and Agricultural Organization and its World Food Program reported that the floods "were extremely serious and caused extensive damage to agriculture and infrastructure." The experts also reported, however, that "the floods made an already and rapidly deteriorating food supply situation much worse, rather than caused the situation in the first place."

The DPRK had been historically able to till only about one-fifth of its mountainous territory and that usually for only one crop annually, since much of the northern land was frost free only six months of the year. In addition, overuse of chemical fertilizers in desperate pursuit of higher yields, failure to rotate crops, and short-sighted denuding of hillsides that accelerated erosion had all severely affected the country's capacity to grow sufficient food.

In the past, Pyongyang had coped with dwindling harvests by importing large amounts of grain under subsidized terms from its communist allies. Such imports were no longer possible when the Soviet Union collapsed and China, whose domestic consumption was rising in a swiftly growing economy, became a grain importer itself and began demanding hard cash for exports to Pyongyang. Despite its need to make up for massive shortfalls of more than 2 million tons of grain in both 1994 and 1995, North Korea lacked the foreign currency or access to credit to do more than very modest buying on international markets.

Long before the floods began, North Korea had been quietly asking selected countries for help in dealing with its food shortage. In the early 1990s, according to the then-director of the ROK intelligence agency, Suh Dong Kwon, the North requested 500,000 tons of rice from the South on condition that it be supplied secretly. The idea was dropped after Seoul responded that in its increasingly open society, it would be impossible to hide the rice shipments to the North. After a skimpy harvest in 1992, the regime began to propagandize to the public "Let's Eat Two Meals a Day," a program of austerity. Later, during the 1994 Geneva negotiations with the United States, DPRK officials had spoken with urgency of their severe food problems, but the U.S. team was so fixed on nuclear issues that the comments made little impression.

A more extensive effort began in January 1995, when Pyongyang appealed to Japan and South Korea for emergency food. Japan agreed to supply 500,000 tons. On June 21, after semiofficial North-South talks on the issue were held in Beijing, the ROK government announced it would donate 150,000 tons of rice to the North in unmarked bags "in a spirit of reconciliation and cooperation." President Kim Young Sam enthusiastically declared that the government would purchase the grain on international markets if domestic stocks were insufficient, telling the Blue House press corps that the rice would build trust with the North. In a grand gesture, Kim sent his popular prime minister, Lee Hong Koo, to the port to see off the first rice ships.

Within the next few days, two developments combined to turn enthusiasm into anger, laying the basis for an abrupt policy reversal. First, a DPRK local official, apparently without central authorization, required a South Korean rice ship to fly a North Korean flag as it entered port on June 27. Although the North promptly apologized, the ROK government demanded a more formal apology and suspended rice shipments until it was received. The incident infuriated the public in the South, as did a later incident in which a sailor on a

South Korean rice ship was arrested for taking photographs of a North Korean port.

The other key event was a series of dramatic losses by Kim Young Sam's ruling party in the June 27 nationwide elections for local offices—the first such elections since the military coup of 1961. It was widely perceived that Kim had been manipulating the rice aid for political gain before the vote and that his strategy had backfired. A political consultant told officials of the ruling party that anger at the aid package and at North Korean ingratitude cost the ruling party a million votes. Although the ROK government redeemed its pledge by eventually providing the undelivered portion of the 150,000 tons, the election results led to a sharp reversal in Kim Young Sam's posture.

As was evident in the nuclear negotiations, Kim had long been ambivalent about the North. A prominent South Korean told me, "I had the feeling from early in his administration, based on several private talks, that [the president] felt it was his destiny to bring about the collapse of North Korea on his watch, and be the man who made history by reunification of the country. He seemed to feel that if he pressed them hard, they'd give way." U.S. Ambassador James Laney who dealt with him frequently said Kim was a man divided in his own mind: "His more rational side says the collapse of North Korea would be a disaster, and he tells us all the things he's doing or is willing to do to cooperate with North Korea. On the other hand, his emotional side wants North Korea to collapse on his watch, so he can be the first to preside over a united Korea."

Kim's estimate of the situation in the North was repeatedly in flux. In July 1995, according to a State Department official, Kim told President Clinton, "I think [the North Koreans] are going down the tubes, and we should seek a gradual change" north of the thirty-eighth parallel. Four months later, after the flood, Kim told Vice President Gore in a bilateral meeting in Osaka, Japan, "There's no possibility of a soft landing. There's going to be a crash."

In early January 1996, Kim spoke out publicly against providing additional food aid for the North, declaring in his New Year policy speech that "it is a crime and a betrayal of the Korean people for North Korea to hope to receive aid from the international community while pouring all its natural resources into maintaining its military power." A senior aide to Kim, whom I saw shortly after the policy speech, made little effort to disguise the essentially domestic political nature of the president's turnabout, predicting that he would continue his hard line at least until after the National Assembly elections scheduled for April.

In the meantime, not only was Kim Young Sam's government unresponsive to UN and humanitarian appeals for food; it also sought to dissuade others from providing aid. In a Honolulu meeting with the United States and Japan in late January, Seoul officials argued that North Korea's plight was not so serious, and that in any case Pyongyang should be pressured to resume the formal North-South dialogue as a condition of obtaining more food. A week after the meetings ended, however, Washington announced a $2 million contribution to the UN's emergency appeal without conditions. It was intended as a signal of humanitarian concern about increasing hunger and malnutrition in the North.

Before the American contribution was announced, North Korean officials had been disheartened by the tepid response to the initial UN appeal for humanitarian aid. Washington's announcement, however, opened the way for additional contributions from governments and private groups. On March 29, after hesitation in Pyongyang due to conservatives who were disdainful of the appeals and who predicted they would produce little help, the DPRK ambassador in Geneva informed UN agencies of North Korea's "urgent need" for additional food and requested a second UN appeal on its behalf.

In this context, it was hard to understand that only a week later, North Korea announced it would no longer accept the duties and limitations of the Korean War armistice and sent 130 soldiers armed with AK-47 automatic rifles, light machine guns, and antitank recoilless rifles into the Joint Security Area at Panmunjom, in deliberate violation of the armistice. Under the agreement that had been generally observed for four decades, each side was limited to thirty enlisted men and five officers armed only with pistols. After two hours, the troops withdrew, but twice as many returned the next night in a further demonstration. After a third night of armistice violations, amid intense international nervousness and widespread condemnation, the demonstrations subsided.

Well before the DMZ incursions, intelligence analysts in Washington and Seoul had been closely watching the growing clout of the KPA in Pyongyang. Since succeeding his father in July 1994, most of Kim Jong Il's public appearances had been visits to military units, in his capacity as supreme commander of the armed forces. Moreover, since Kim Il Sung's death, high-ranking military officers had been elevated in the hierarchy of North Korean officialdom. A large-scale military parade was staged for the (fiftieth) anniversary of the founding of the Workers Party, an event that had previously been of a nonmilitary character; the newly appointed defense minister, Choe Kwang, made the keynote address. At the same time, however, Kim Jong Il seemed to have held the military in check on key policy issues involving the United States, overruling military objections in negotiating the Agreed Framework to halt the nuclear activities at Yongbyon and again in releasing American helicopter pilot Bobby Hall.

Equally curious were two unpublicized developments late in 1995. In the early fall, the Korean People's Army Sixth Corps, in the northeastern part of the country, was disbanded, its leadership purged, and its units submerged into others, under circumstances suggesting disarray in the ranks. Moreover, in early December the KPA suddenly halted its annual winter military maneuvers two months before their normal conclusion and embarked on new ideological education instead. This appeared to reflect a scarcity of resources even for top-priority military missions as well as problems of indoctrination and discipline.

During my trip to Pyongyang in early 1995, North Korean officials had spoken repeatedly of their long-standing dissatisfaction with the Korean War armistice and of their proposal to replace it with a U.S. DPRK "peace insuring system." Our delegation had been warned, as had others, that "unilateral steps" would be taken if there were no movement toward negotiations on the issue—and there had been no movement.

The greatest mystery in April 1995 was not what the KPA forces had done in the DMZ—clearly a demonstration that was intended to call attention to their demands—but how Pyongyang's leaders had calculated or tolerated the strange timing. Coming just as the DPRK government was appealing to the world anew for urgently needed food, the military actions made it more difficult to obtain. In another anomaly of timing, the incursions came less than a week before a new set of nationwide elections in South Korea, this time for seats in the National Assembly. The ruling party, which had been expected to do poorly because of the growing unpopularity of President Kim, did much better than expected, due in part to public alarm over the DMZ incursions which were heavily covered by South Korean media. Political experts in Seoul said that Kim's party probably won twenty to thirty seats as a result of the DMZ incidents—a crucial margin in assuring Kim legislative control. Twenty-eight percent of those questioned in a postelection poll said the incursions influenced their vote in favor of the ruling party.

The damaging lack of coordination of economic, political, and military objectives in the DMZ incursions was important evidence of Kim Jong Il's governing style. According to a South Korean intelligence official, the reclusive leader was "governing by memorandum," accepting separate reports, and making separate decisions in connection with the various functional groups constituting the North Korean party and governmental apparatus. Unlike his father, Kim Jong Il was reported to have little taste for official meetings at which a more coherent policy could have been thrashed out. With the death of Kim Il Sung, according to Adrian Buzo, an Australian academic and former diplomat, a transfer of power had taken place from an individual to a system. And the system was not working.

## POLITICAL EARTHQUAKE IN SEOUL

High school ties are cherished in South Korea, and high school alumni meetings are occasions for important celebrations. Such a meeting, in the Crystal Ballroom of the Lotte Hotel, one of Seoul's most glitzy skyscrapers, on October 16, 1995, was the occasion for a brief, unplanned encounter that touched off an earth-shaking political scandal, uncovering a system of payoffs that had undergirded South Korean politics for decades. Within a very short time, the burgeoning scandal brought about the arrest, conviction, and imprisonment of former presidents Roh Tae Woo and Chun Doo Hwan and the convictions of thirteen other former high-ranking military officers and of nine of the country's most important business leaders. The political earthquake made the ROK's democracy more responsive to public opinion and thereby less controllable by the central government, affecting and often complicating the government's dealings with the United States and with the North.

One of the celebrants at the school reunion, a businessman named Ha Chong Uk, was more glum than glad, being desperately worried about a problem involving money and politics. As toasts were being exchanged and a band was playing, Ha saw potential salvation in a fellow high school alumnus, Park Kye Dong, who had been elected to the National Assembly two years earlier. Ha asked Assemblyman Park to step out of the noisy ballroom into the hotel lobby, where he proceeded to explain his predicament.

His problem dated back to February 1993, as President Roh Tae Woo was leaving office. Ha, in a small family business with his father as brokers for shipping companies, received a strange request from the local branch of the Shinhan Bank, where his firm did business. The bank manager asked permission to deposit 11 billion won (about $14 million) of someone else's money in an account using the father's name. Because of favors owed to the bank, Ha agreed.

Ha did not think much about it until several other events occurred. In August 1993, in one of the most important of his domestic reforms, President Kim Young Sam decreed a "real name" bank deposit system, under which fictitious or borrowed names on bank accounts could no longer be used to hide or launder money for illegal political purposes or other shady dealings. The next step was a new tax system, to begin in January 1996, when taxes would be assessed on interest earned from all bank accounts.

At that point, businessman Ha had a serious problem. He had learned that the money in the account under his father's borrowed name actually belonged to former president Roh—yet his father would soon be liable for paying nearly $1 million in taxes on the accumulated interest. He couldn't pay it. Even if Roh provided the money to pay the taxes, Ha feared a tax audit could be launched to investigate how a small businessman had obtained such a big fund. Moreover, he learned that his father's account was one of three borrowed-name accounts at the same bank branch hiding money belonging to the former president. In desperation, Ha asked his fellow high school alumnus, the national assemblyman, to convince some big shots in government to fix the problem before the taxes came due.

Assemblyman Park, a member of the opposition Democratic Party, had long opposed the pervasive influence of illegal money in Korean politics. His indignation had been rekindled two months earlier when a government minister had told reporters that a former president had hidden 400 billion won ($500 million) in accounts at city banks, only to be fired for his indiscretion. Now, from the worried businessman Ha, Park obtained a statement of the status of the account, but instead of taking it to be "fixed," he rose on the floor of the National Assembly with the statement in his hand and delivered a bombshell accusation. Roh, he declared, had deposited the equivalent of $500 million in city banks around the time he left office, with 30 billion won ($37 million) deposited in the bank branch where Ha had his account. He then produced Ha's bank account documents as direct evidence of what had been going on.

The day the furor broke out, Roh Tae Woo's longtime chief bodyguard and his last intelligence agency director, Lee Hyun Woo, hurried to see the former president at his home in Seoul. Lee informed his boss that the money being discussed in the National Assembly indeed belonged to Roh—part of the funds that Lee had been managing since the two men had left government. Roh instructed Lee to report the facts to prosecutors but, before doing so, to destroy the account books containing the details of those who had contributed the money.

Eight days after the revelation in the National Assembly, via television from his home, Roh addressed the nation he had led for five years. The former president announced that while in office he had amassed a "governing fund" of 500 billion won ($625 million), an even more stupifying total than had been rumored, and that he had left office with 170 billion won ($212 million) of the money. (The amount was soon corrected to 185 billion won.)

Saying that raising and using such funds was "an old political practice," Roh declared the practice to be wrong and said, "I will wholeheartedly accept any kind of punishment you hand out to me." Roh said he hoped that nobody else, including the entrepreneurs who contributed the funds, would be hurt because of his misdeeds. Wiping tears from his eyes, he ended the broadcast by saying, "I have no other words to say as a man who has deeply hurt the pride of the nation. At this moment, I feel deeply ashamed of being a former president. I offer my apology again."

The gigantic size of the funds involved as well as Roh's retention of massive wealth after leaving office shocked the Korean public. His admissions were in startling contrast to his declarations of the late 1980s, when he pledged to create "a great era of ordinary people" after coming into office a hero for submitting to election by popular vote. Korean newspapers recalled that in his first presidential press conference, Roh had pledged to eliminate all forms of corruption and "to be recorded in history as a faithful and honest president." He declared his total assets then to be about 500 million won ($625,000), one-thousandth of the slush fund he admitted to raising in office. Several weeks after Roh's mea culpa statement, a public opinion poll in Seoul identified Roh as "the most loathsome politician" in the country by an overwhelming margin.

A secondary tremor from Roh's revelations was the announcement the same day by Kim Dae Jung, the opposition leader, that he had secretly accepted 2 billion won ($2.5 million) from Roh as a gift during the 1992 presidential campaign. This admission tarnished Kim's reformist image and also raised immediate questions about how much of Roh's money had gone to incumbent President Kim Young Sam, who had been the candidate of Roh's ruling party in the 1992 race. In making his startling admission, Kim Dae Jung charged that the incumbent president had received much more than he, "hundreds of billions of won," for his well-heeled and ultimately successful race. President Kim subsequently denied receiving any money personally, but he did not deny that his ruling party campaign might have received funds from Roh, in amounts that were not established or announced.

Roh was summoned for interrogation by prosecutors on November 15 and jailed on corruption charges the following day. Prosecutors soon extended their investigation to his predecessor Chun, who refused to cooperate and, like Roh, destroyed the account books of contributors to his off-the-books funds. According to prosecutors,

Chun collected 950 billion won ($1.8 billion) in slush funds—nearly twice as much as Roh—and left office with 212 billion won ($265 million). Chun later admitted in court that as president he gave 197 billion won to Roh for his 1987 election campaign. An aide testified he and the wives of both men were present when Chun personally handed over the majority of this illicit funding.

In an episode with almost as much popular impact as the overall size of the financial dealings, prosecutors discovered hundreds of stacks of 10,000-won notes belonging to Chun, totalling 6.1 billion won, stuffed into 25 apple boxes in the cement warehouse of the Ssangyong group, a Seoul conglomerate. Photographs of this mother lode of currency, prominently published and broadcast by the Korean press, disgusted the public.

Almost all the funds had come from leaders of Korea's vaunted *chaebol* conglomerates and other big business enterprises, whose executives had been called to meetings with Roh in an annex of the presidential residence on a regular basis and who had been expected to bring money. Business leaders insisted the payments were the equivalent of taxes, simply the cost of doing business in Korea, where presidents and their administrations were all-powerful arbiters of tax policy, loan funds, public contracts, and much more.

The chairman of the Kukje group, which had been one of South Korea's largest conglomerates in the early 1980s, recalled how Chun suggested he give $2.6 million to one of the then–First Lady's favorite charities. After the businessman declined, his bank credit was cut off at Blue House orders, and Chun's finance minister announced that Kukje was being dissolved because of insufficient financial backing— all of which quickly led to the firm's bankruptcy. Few tycoons were ready to risk such treatment.

In one of the rare specific revelations prior to the 1995 scandal, Hyundai group founder Chung Ju Yung said in early 1992 of his visits to Roh, "At first I gave him two to three billion won each time, but as I felt it was not enough, I gave him another five billion won and then, two years ago, the last time, I gave him ten billion won." Roh responded by saying he had received and spent Chung's funds to help "unfortunate neighbors." When Chung came to Washington in September 1992 as a maverick presidential candidate, he told me and other *Washington Post* editors and reporters that Roh was even more corrupt than Chun Doo Hwan had been. I found this hard to believe at the time and, to my regret, did not report this remark in my story on the meeting or press the industrialist for details.

As the furor following Roh's arrest continued, and with his own victorious presidential campaign suspect for taking some of Roh's money, President Kim Young Sam came under pressure to take stronger action. Earlier, Kim had taken the position that the December 12, 1979, military-backed takeover by Chun and Roh and the May 1980 killing of civilians in Kwangju did not warrant prosecution but should be left to "the judgment of history." After the scandal broke, Kim abruptly reversed his stand. With the backing of both the president and the opposition parties, a special law authorizing legal action against those responsible for the 1979 takeover and the 1980 Kwangju killings sailed through the National Assembly.

Even before passage of the law, Chun was arrested and jailed when he defiantly refused a prosecutors' summons to appear for questioning. Chun's lawyers argued that his arrest was unconstitutional because the ROK Constitution forbids retroactive statutes. Five of the nine members of the Constitutional Court agreed, but the legal action stood because the votes of six justices are required to overturn a statute.

From March until August 1996, the Korean public was presented with the regular spectacle of the two former presidents being taken before the court from their cells in loose-fitting prison uniforms and rubber shoes to respond to charges of bribery, insurrection, and treason. Former presidential aides in the economic field and the heads of the country's leading economic conglomerates also stood at the bar of justice in the bribery trial; fourteen retired military officers, eight of whom had left the service as four-star generals, were on trial with Roh and Chun in the insurrection case. Prisoner number 1042, former President Roh, adjusted quickly to prison life, continuing to express remorse and apologies but shedding little new light on the events under consideration. Prisoner number 3124, former President Chun, was defiant. Shortly after his arrest, he had protested by going on a hunger strike—an ironic counterpoint to a hunger strike against Chun by then-opposition leader Kim Young Sam in 1983—and persistently challenged the court's right to put him on trial for long-ago events.

On August 26, all but one of the defendants was found guilty by the three-judge court. Chun was sentenced to death, the announcement of which caused him to flinch momentarily before quickly regaining his composure. The court noted Chun's argument that while president he had contributed to the stabilizing of the economy and turned over power to his successor by peaceful means, but it said these acts could not offset his serious crimes. Roh was sentenced to twenty-two and a half years in prison, rather than life imprisonment as requested by the prosecutors. The court said it took into account Roh's "achievements in northern diplomacy and the nation's admission into the United Nations," as well as the fact that he had been popularly elected in 1987.

The other defendants in "the trial of the century," as the Korean press described it, were given lesser sentences. Many of the former generals were taken to jail cells from the courtroom to begin their sentences, but all the business leaders were released pending appeal or given suspended sentences on grounds that the nation continued to need their best efforts.

As they stood before the court to hear the announcement of their sentences, Chun and Roh, two old friends and military academy classmates who had become estranged after one succeeded the other in the presidency, linked their fingers in a public gesture of solidarity.

On December 16, 1996, the Seoul High Court commuted Chun's sentence to life imprisonment and reduced Roh's sentence to seventeen years. The court also reduced the sentences of all the other military and civilian defendants. It acquitted two of the *chaebol* leaders who had been convicted earlier and suspended the sentences of the other big businessmen. Under the ruling, none of the tycoons who contributed the funds were sent to jail.

A year later, in the Christmas season of 1997, President Kim Young Sam pardoned Chun and Roh, who returned quietly to private life.

## SUMMIT DIPLOMACY AND THE FOUR-PARTY PROPOSAL

As had been the case with Presidents Park Chung Hee, Chun Doo Hwan, and Roh Tae Woo, summit diplomacy with the American president was important to the domestic standing of President Kim

Young Sam, a fact that contributed to Washington's leverage in South Korea. In the summer of 1995 and the spring of 1996, the United States sought to use this leverage on North-South issues. Its efforts had mixed success.

President Kim was planning a visit to the U.S. capital in July 1995 to participate in the dedication of a monument on the Washington Mall to American veterans of the Korean War. Although President Clinton had visited Kim for two days in July 1993 and had hosted him in a three-day official visit in November 1993, including the Clintons' first big White House dinner for a foreign guest, Kim was eager to turn the mid-1995 trip into an important visit with even more protocol honors. The U.S. administration told Kim this could be done only if there was a substantive move toward accommodation or peace on the divided peninsula to justify a further allocation of Clinton's time and attention.

In response, the ROK Foreign Ministry devised and presented to Washington a "two plus two" formula, whereby the two Koreas would negotiate a permanent peace treaty to replace the Korean War armistice, with the United States and China acting as facilitators and eventual guarantors. The State Department welcomed the proposal as a step in the right direction if it were serious and well-prepared, and if Washington were kept informed of what Seoul's diplomats were doing.

The "two plus two" proposal, while still confidential, was enough to obtain the recognition Kim wanted. He was granted a four-day state visit with full honors, including an address to a joint session of Congress. In a conversation at the White House during the visit in late July, Kim looked Clinton in the eye and told him, "We are going to do this on August 15," the fiftieth anniversary of Korea's liberation from Japan and a day for important pronouncements in Seoul. Kim's aides leaked the proposal to the South Korean press, and the ROK president himself said in an interview with CNN that he planned to make "a refreshing and important initiative towards North Korea" on Liberation Day. Based on Kim's assurance, Secretary of State Warren Christopher took up the proposal with Chinese foreign minister Qian Qichen in a bilateral meeting in Brunei.

After returning to Seoul, however, Kim executed another of his sudden reversals in the face of the conservative political tide following North Korea's interference with ROK ships delivering rice to DPRK ports. Without consultation with or notification of the United States, Kim scuttled the initiative he had proposed to Clinton. American diplomats were not pleased.

In the spring of 1996, summit diplomacy reappeared when Clinton planned a state visit to Japan. At this point the U.S. administration was increasingly apprehensive about the reports of privation and instability in North Korea and none too happy with Kim's inconsistent and, lately, unresponsive policies. Although American presidents usually stopped in Korea when visiting Japan, Clinton was not inclined to do so this time. Considering Clinton's earlier visit to Seoul and Kim's two visits to Washington, "we thought we'd done enough" for Kim, said an administration official who was involved in the internal discussions. No stop in Korea was planned.

Kim, however, had different ideas. Clinton's schedule would bring him to Japan on April 16, just five days after the nationwide National Assembly elections in Korea that would have a crucial bearing on Kim's authority in his last two years in office. For it to be known in the campaign period that Clinton planned to visit Japan but bypass Korea could be a sign of little regard for Kim; indeed, there were reports in Seoul that the president's longtime rival, opposition leader Kim Dae Jung, was preparing to make the omission an issue. The ROK president was desperate to persuade Clinton to change his mind about a Korean stopover.

In a repeat of the previous year's discussions, Ambassador Laney, who was gravely concerned about the lack of movement in North-South diplomacy, told the Blue House that Clinton could only spare the time for such a visit if a serious peace initiative were to come out of it. Talks between Clinton's national security adviser, Anthony Lake, and his Korean counterpart, Yoo Chong Ha, produced agreement in principle for the two presidents to undertake and announce such an initiative. Lake and Yoo worked out the details by long distance in great secrecy, using the telephone instead of cables to bypass the established bureaucracy and other potential sources of leaks.

Kim got his meeting at 5:50 A.M. on April 16, 1996, when Air Force One touched down at Cheju Island, a colorful spot favored by honeymooners, off the southern end of the Korean peninsula. Five days earlier, Kim's party had won a commanding position in the National Assembly elections, due in part to the curiously timed North Korean military incursions in the DMZ. After taking an early morning walk through a garden of bright yellow flowers, Clinton and Kim settled down to discussions in the same hotel suite where presidents Roh Tae Woo and Mikhail Gorbachev had met in April 1991.

In a prearranged declaration that had already been presented informally to North Korea, China, Japan, and Russia, Clinton and Kim agreed to propose a four-power conference of the two Koreas, the United States, and China "to initiate a process aimed at achieving a permanent peace agreement" on the Korean peninsula. In a significant difference from the stillborn initiative of the previous year, this was a joint U.S.–ROK proposal rather than an ROK proposal backed by the United States.

Announcing the proposal in a press conference before Clinton flew on to Japan, both presidents expressed hope that North Korea would accept it. Clinton cautioned against expecting an immediate and positive response: "What is important is to put the offer out there and let it stand and be patient." Clinton and Kim were heartened when Pyongyang did not immediately reject the proposal but instead raised questions about the specific objectives of such a conference and about its procedures. Chinese president Jiang Zemin, in a letter to Kim a few days after the Cheju announcement, expressed Chinese support for the four-power talks. China ultimately would become an active and interested party in the talks, giving Beijing important diplomatic as well as strategic stakes in North-South stability.

As noted earlier, the idea of three-power talks involving Washington and the two Koreas had a history going back to the late 1970s and had been the subject of active diplomacy for a time in the early 1980s. The proposal for four-power peace talks, bringing in China as well, went back even further, to Secretary of State Henry Kissinger's speech to the UN General Assembly in September 1975. Secretary of State Cyrus Vance, as earlier noted, advanced the idea in 1977. The Reagan administration briefly resurrected the plan in the mid-1980s but put little effort into promoting it.

In 1996 North Korea, although continuing to seek bilateral peace talks with the United States, was in no position to take a rigid stand against the four-party proposal. The country had managed to get through the winter without actual starvation as a result of scrimping, the improvisation of its people, and a modest amount of international humanitarian assistance. However, the summer months before the next grain harvest posed a serious threat. In mid-May the UN World Food Program issued a special alert on North Korea, warning that "the food supply situation has deteriorated more seriously than had been anticipated." The UN agency reported that the DPRK government had reduced rations under its public distribution program to 300 grams (10.5 ounces) of grain per person per day, about 1,000 calories. The UN minimum standard for refugees was 1,900 calories per day. In South Korea, by contrast, food was so plentiful that the National Institute of Health and Social Affairs reported after an extensive survey that one in every four adults was on a diet to avoid putting on excess weight.

Diplomatic discussions with the United States, which had revolved around the nuclear issue and political relations in the previous three years, were increasingly dominated in the spring of 1996 by North Korea's urgent need for economic help. Calling on Deputy Assistant Secretary of State Thomas Hubbard, the State Department's senior point man on Korea following the assignment of Robert Gallucci to other duties, North Korea's external economic chief, Kim Jong U, offered a frank swap of ballistic missiles exports and food. Putting a blunter cast on a position taken in U.S.–DPRK talks about ballistic missiles in April, Kim said the North could either sell missiles to Middle Eastern countries to obtain money and food, as it had formerly done to American disapproval, or it could accept food from the United States to forgo those sales. Another high-ranking DPRK caller on Hubbard that spring, Ri Jong Hyok, pushed hard for additional food from the West, saying bluntly that "revolutions are made by hungry people."

Meeting in Jakarta, Indonesia, on July 24, Secretary of State Christopher and his South Korean and Japanese counterparts formally agreed to supply additional food aid and ease some American economic sanctions if North Korea would participate in a joint U.S.–ROK briefing on the four-power peace plan. The same day the skies over Northeast Asia darkened again, and the heavens opened up with new torrential downpours, three to five times the normal abundant rainfall of that time of year. While the resultant flooding was not as serious as that of the year before, this time it struck more of the country's principal food-producing areas. Once more the forces of nature, compounding the failure of the *juche* system, had dealt North Korea a painful blow.

## THE SUBMARINE INCURSION

A few minutes after midnight on the morning of September 18, 1996, a taxi driver speeding along a seaside road near Kangnung, on the east coast of South Korea, noticed a group of men crouched near the highway. Suspicious about what he had seen, cabbie Lee Jin Gyu, 31, returned to the area after dropping off his passenger and spotted a large object, which he thought at first to be a giant dolphin, in the water near the beach. On second look, it appeared to be a man-made object. Certain that it wasn't a fishing boat, he reported it to local police.

Within hours, ROK troops and police identified cab driver Lee's discovery as a thirty-seven-yard-long North Korean submarine of the Shark class that had run aground on the rocky coast and been abandoned by its passengers and crew. Before dawn came up that morning, the Defense Ministry was mobilizing 40,000 troops, helicopter gunships, and sniffer dogs in a massive search for the intruders from the North.

In midafternoon, on a mountain three miles from the landing site, an army squad came across a grisly scene: eleven bodies of North Korean infiltrators, all of whom had been executed with bullets to the back of the head, evidently with their own consent to avoid being captured. There was no sign of a struggle; one of the dead, a North Korean colonel, was armed with a pistol that was still in its holster.

About the same time, local police in a nearby area, acting on a tip from a villager, arrested Lee Kwang Su, a North Korean infiltrator from the sub, in a farmer's field. Lee, who was the only occupant of the submarine to be taken alive, said the personnel of the submarine belonged to the Reconnaissance Bureau of the North Korean People's Armed Forces, which is charged with the collection of tactical and strategic intelligence on U.S. and ROK forces. Their mission was to test ROK defenses and reconnoiter an ROK air base and radar facility near Kangnung.

In the ROK manhunt over the next two weeks, eleven subma- rine infiltrators were caught and killed in firefights. Two more held out for forty-eight days before being killed in early November, near the eastern end of the DMZ. This brought to twenty-five the number of North Koreans accounted for, one fewer than the lone captive believed had been on the submarine. At this point, the ROK Defense Ministry ended its intensive search and returned to normal opera- tions. The deaths of fourteen South Koreans—four civilians, eight military personnel, and two policemen—were attributed to the infil- trators, although some apparently had been killed by friendly fire.

South Korea, with dense vegetation close to the peninsula- spanning DMZ and fifteen hundred miles of irregular coastline dotted with offshore islands, is highly vulnerable to infiltration. North Korea has penetrated the South's defenses on many occasions. In the 1970s, as noted in Chapter 3, Kim Il Sung had boasted that his military reconnaissance teams kept American maneuvers in the South under surveillance, and the U.S. Command had concluded that "the North can infiltrate and exfiltrate its agents or special warfare units by land, sea or air to virtually any location within the ROK." By the mid- 1990s, only modest gains against these operations had been accom- plished. According to a Chinese military publication, North Korea equipped itself with at least forty-eight minisubmarines to transport undercover agents and disturb South Korean shipping lanes.

What made the September 1996 incursion different from those of the past was the fact that it was a spectacular failure, putting two dozen North Korean combatants into the countryside to fend for themselves and threaten ordinary citizens; its discovery, embarrass- ingly, by a cab driver rather than by coastal defenses; and the edgy political situation involving North Korea and the United States.

For the first time in such a conflict, Washington found itself positioned between the two Koreas, with important interests on both sides. On the one hand, it was seeking to protect its new relationship with North Korea, to keep the freeze of the DPRK nuclear program, and to advance peace negotiations on the peninsula, while on the other hand it was seeking to maintain solidarity with its longtime ally in the South and protect the security of ROK territory and U.S. troops. The ROK, which had received unqualified U.S. backing in military disputes in the past, was disappointed and angered by the altered American posture, all the more so because policy toward the North—once a taboo subject—had become a central political issue in Seoul.

After alternating for months between taking a hard line against the North, calculated to bring about its early collapse, and backing an accommodation to bring about a "soft landing," Kim Young Sam shifted powerfully to the hard side. He declared on September 20 that "this is an armed provocation, not a simple repeat of infiltration of agents of the past" and began almost daily condemnations of the North, eventually declaring that any further provocation against the South—which he said was likely—would bring a "real possibility of war." Announcing that his government was reconsidering its entire northern policy, Kim suspended inter-Korean economic cooperation and halted ROK activities in the Korean Peninsula Energy Development ment Organization (KEDO), which was charged with providing the light-water reactors under the 1994 Agreed Framework. In an interview with Kevin Sullivan of *The Washington Post* in early November, Kim said he would not proceed with the four-party peace proposal or provide aid to the DPRK until its leaders apologized for the submarine incursion.

North Korea initially issued a remarkably gauzy statement that "as far as a competent organ of the Ministry of the People's Armed Forces knows," the submarine encountered engine trouble and drifted south, leaving its crew "with no other choice but to get to the enemy side's land, which might cause an armed conflict." As the clash over the incursion deepened, however, the North's rhetoric hardened into threats of retaliation "a hundred or a thousand fold" against the killing of its personnel. When the activities of KEDO were halted by ROK objections, Pyongyang publicly threatened to abandon the Agreed Framework and resume its nuclear program at Yongbyon.

In diplomatic meetings, North Korea notified the United States that it was ready to express regret about the submarine incident and to accept a U.S.–ROK briefing on the proposed four-power peace talks, but it insisted on a package of economic benefits in return. A package deal including the briefing arrangement had been extensively discussed in U.S.–DPRK talks in May and June 1996 and virtually agreed to at the end of August, during an American visit by North Korean diplomat Lee Gun, deputy director of American affairs of the DPRK Foreign Ministry. Representative Bill Richardson, who had become a political-level emissary to North Korea, was heading to Pyongyang on his third trip, ready to conclude the arrangements, when news of the submarine incursion arrived. His trip was canceled.

Immediately after the incursion, South Koreans were angered by an off-the-cuff comment by Secretary of State Christopher that "all parties" should avoid further provocative steps, a statement that seemed to put the United States equidistant from both the antagonists. The State Department made corrective statements, but the damage had been done. A senior ROK official telephoned Daryl Plunk, a Korea expert at the conservative Heritage Foundation, to say that the highest levels of his government found the Clinton administration's response to the incursion "shameful" and its policies to be "appeasement" of the North.

As hard feelings festered and deepened, American civilian officials in Seoul became alarmed by the gap in thinking between themselves and their allies. In a symbol of the new mood, ROK officers were reluctant to permit a U.S. defense attaché to inspect the North Korean submarine and then, after relenting, subjected him to a body search when leaving the sub. The U.S. Embassy protested.

More ominously, the Korean-language *Joong-ang Daily News* reported in mid-October that ROK forces had selected twelve strategic targets in the North for air, naval, and ground retaliation in case of further provocations. The report shocked the U.S. Command, which had theoretical "operational control" of the ROK military in wartime but had heard nothing of these attack plans until publication of the newspaper report. Although ROK defense officials denied that the plans represented serious policy making, the Americans were unable to get what they considered satisfactory assurances that ROK forces would not launch retaliatory military action against the North without U.S. consultation and consent. The issue was quietly taken up by

Ambassador Laney and the new U.S. military commander, General John Tilelli; by ROK foreign minister Gong Ro Myung and Defense Minister Kim Dong Jin; by visiting CIA Director John Deutch with foreign minister Gong and others; and by Defense Secretary William Perry with Defense Minister Kim in a Washington conversation, all without clear resolution.

Adding to the American concern, in early November, was Kim Young Sam's abrupt ouster of Foreign Minister Gong, amid reports that he had expressed reservations about the president's hard line against the North. Gong's resignation was officially attributed to health reasons, but Korean and American officials close to him believed that the precipitating factor was a dossier of remarks reportedly provided to Kim by the NSP, the ROK intelligence agency. In these remarks, believed to have been gathered through telephone taps, Gong expressed personal differences with the president's policy in the aftermath of the submarine incursion. (Another former foreign minister told me he had been cautioned by aides when taking his job that he should assume his telephone conversations were tapped.) Gong was replaced as foreign minister by Yoo Chong Ha, Kim's Blue House assistant for national security, who was considered more independent of U.S. policies than any of his recent predecessors.

In mid-November, with these cross-currents flowing just beneath the surface of the nominally close alliance, *New York Times* correspondent Nicholas Kristof visited Seoul and summarized the consequences of the submarine incursion as "a surge of tension; fears of further military provocations or even war; stalling of the engagement process; a growing number of hungry North Korean peasants who can count on little international help; and a reminder that it is hard to find a place more dangerous and unpredictable than the Korean peninsula." ROK officials did not disagree with that analysis, but they were infuriated by Kristof's further observation that due to a newly created rift between the two allies, "some U.S. officials seem to feel that their biggest headache on the peninsula is the government in the South, not the North." As I learned from conversations in Washington and Seoul, Kristof was on the mark.

North-South relations and U.S.–ROK relations were still tense when President Clinton met President Kim Young Sam on the occasion of the summit of the Asia Pacific Economic Cooperation (APEC) forum in Manila on November 24. As a result of negotiations before the meeting, the two sides agreed on a three-paragraph statement that avoided the word, "apology," which Kim Young Sam had been demanding, but that called on the North "to take acceptable steps" to resolve the submarine incident, reduce tension, and avoid provocations in the future. Three days after the meeting, however, in the face of criticism that he had given in to Clinton, Kim reverted to his demand for a full-scale apology.

The most important exchange of the meeting took place in a private conversation between Clinton and Kim in a corner away from most of their aides. Clinton bluntly sought to obtain an ironclad commitment that South Korean forces would not initiate military action against the North without American consent. A senior ROK official who participated in the summit told me he believed Clinton had been reassured by Kim's remarks, but an American official said Kim's reaction had still left room for doubt.

Three months later, after Clinton began a new presidential term with a new foreign policy team, Kim moved preemptively to resolve the issue. During his first meeting with Madeleine Albright in late February, Kim began by volunteering that the new secretary of state could be assured that no South Korean military action would be undertaken without full coordination with the United States. Albright crossed it off her list of issues to discuss. General Tilelli said later he was completely satisfied there would be no unilateral military action on the part of ROK forces. Nevertheless, the top-level exchanges over the issue demonstrated how strained and mistrustful U.S. relations with South Korea had become.

In the wake of the Manila meeting of Clinton and Kim, the United States renewed its efforts to obtain a settlement of the submarine issue. Mark Minton, the State Department country director for Korea, met North Korea's director general of American affairs, Lee Hyong Chol on nine separate days in December to hammer out a multifaceted accord.

On December 29, North Korea issued a statement of "deep regret" for the submarine incursion and a pledge that "such an incident will not recur." Pyongyang also agreed to attend the long-offered joint U.S.-ROK briefing on the four-power peace talks. As part of a package accord, Washington agreed to resume the supply of heavy fuel oil, and Seoul removed its objections to continued work on the light-water nuclear reactors promised under the 1994 Agreed Framework accord. North Korea, in turn, permitted work to resume on preserving the fuel rods that had been unloaded from the Yongbyon reactor. In a last-minute accord arranged by the United States, South Korea agreed to return the remains of the North Korean personnel killed in the submarine incursion. When the transfer took place at Panmunjom, DPRK officials were shocked to find that they received only cremated ashes. U.S. officers believed the bodies were too riddled with bullets to be presentable.

Diplomatic delegations from the United States and the two Koreas met in New York in March 1997 for the "joint briefing," the first such talks about peace on the peninsula ever held among these three parties. Following this, higher-level diplomats from the three nations, plus a delegation from China, met in Geneva in December 1997 to officially begin the four-party peace talks that had been proposed the previous year. A second four-party meeting was held in Geneva in March 1998. The meetings quickly bogged down over procedural issues, but all sides agreed to continue the discussions in hopes of creating a permanent peace structure on the divided peninsula.

## NORTH KOREA'S STEEP DECLINE

By the winter of 1996, most observers who were following the situation in North Korea had watched the progressive sinking of the economy for many months and had become inured to the adverse trends. Portents of disaster and predictions of impending collapse had become commonplace, yet the North's ability to absorb external and internal reverses had been demonstrated time after time as it accepted the loss of its allies, the death of its founding leader, and the increasingly steep decline in its standard of living. Thus, it seemed possible to assume, in the face of all logic, that the country could continue indefinitely on its downward slope without experiencing a crisis.

Reports from travelers to North Korea, however, suggested this could hardly be the case. In fact, a principal debate among American government analysts was whether the DPRK economy was collapsing or had already collapsed. Deteriorating or flooded coal mines and reduced petroleum imports produced insufficient energy for industry, so many factories had closed or were operating at only a fraction of their previous output. Fuel was so scarce in some provincial cities that only oxcarts and bicycles could be seen on the streets. Many office buildings and dwellings, even in the much-favored capital, were unheated during large portions of a very cold winter. Electrical blackouts were commonplace. Even the state television station was off the air for long periods of time due to lack of power. Many trains, some of them coal-fired and others powered by electricity, were idle. An American intelligence official, who in the past had been sanguine about North Korea's prospects, compared its plight to that of a terminally ill patient, whose physical systems were weakening one after another, with each expiring organ reducing the performance of the others.

A drop in fertilizer production had diminished agricultural yields in the autumn 1996 harvest, adding to the serious shortages caused by flooding. In many cases crops that had been harvested could not be moved to where they were needed due to lack of transport, and more was lost to rain and rats. The meager public distribution of food in the countryside, which averaged three hundred grams per day earlier in the year, was cut back to half or less, barely enough to sustain life, or had stopped completely. To survive, North Koreans were consuming oak leaves, grasses, roots, tree bark, and other non-standard foods, many with little nutritive value, and buying or bartering food, clothing, and fuel at markets that had sprung up in many towns in violation of government policy. In some areas, dormant factories were being dismantled and turned into scrap metal, which was then bartered across the Chinese border for the cheapest food available.

Although the authorities had no choice but to accept these transgressions and local officials appear to have abetted or even sponsored them, the remarkable thing was that the authority and cohesion of the regime seemed undiminished, so far as the outside world could see. Song Young Dae, the former ROK vice-minister of national unification and longtime negotiator with the North, described the DPRK scene in late 1996 as "stability within instability," with Kim Jong Il at the top of a crisis-management system controlled by the military. Among the greatest unknown factors was how the trauma of the North Korean economy and society would affect the country's political and military systems.

In these dire circumstances Kim Jong Il paid a visit to Kim Il Sung University on December 7, on the occasion of the fiftieth anniversary of the founding of his alma mater, the nation's foremost institution of higher education. The transcript of his lengthy and rambling remarks, evidently delivered in confidence to several Workers Party secretaries who accompanied him, was brought out of North Korea by Hwang Jang Yop, who was not present but who was privy to such materials in his post as a party secretary. The text of the speech was eventually published in *Monthly Chosun* in Seoul. As of the spring of 1997, it was the only record of Kim Jong Il's candid utterances available outside North Korea, except for the tapes surreptitiously made by the kidnapped filmmakers over a decade earlier.

In his remarks Kim acknowledged to some extent the difficulties facing the country, saying that "the most urgent issue to be solved at present is the grain problem. . . . the food problem is creating a state of anarchy." Despite the onslaught of "heart-aching occurrences," Kim was highly critical of the street-corner food sellers and peddlers who had spontaneously emerged in response to urgent needs. "This creates egotism among the people, and the base of the party's class may come to collapse. Then, the party will lose popular support and dissolve. This has been well-illustrated by past incidents in Poland and Czechoslovakia."

Kim absolved himself of responsibility for the country's economic problems, maintaining that his father, who had spent much of his time in economic guidance, "repeatedly told me that if I got involved in economic work, I would not be able to handle party and army work properly." He implied that his job was too important to deal with mere economic issues: "If I handle even practical economic work, it will have irreparable consequences on the revolution and construction. . . . The people now unconditionally accept the directives of the Party Central Committee because of my authority, not because party organizations and functionaries carry out their work well. . . . No functionary assists me effectively. I am working alone."

The only institution to win unstinting praise from Kim Jong Il was the army, on which he had become increasingly reliant. Of forty-seven of his activities during 1996 made public in North Korea, thirty were visits to military units or other military-related activities. In contrast to the laggard youth he had observed at Kim Il Sung University, he declared, "all soldiers are politically and ideologically sound and their revolutionary military spirit is lofty." He was satisfied that the soldiers would "protect with their lives the nerve center of the revolution"—himself and other high-level leaders.

Kim's speech confirmed that, as suspected by American and South Korean intelligence, food shortages were affecting even the army. He proclaimed that the people must be told, "If you do not send rice to the army, even if the wretched Americans attack us, we cannot win. Then you will also become slaves, and your sons and daughters and grandsons and granddaughters will too."

In January 1997, despite the catastrophic state of the economy, Kim as commander-in-chief ordered a return to the full-scale conduct of the winter training exercises, which had been severely truncated the previous year. At great expense in fuel, ammunition, and other resources, a large proportion of North Korea's huge army moved along the roadways and trails to new positions, fired weapons, and practiced for combat operations. In March, Kim also ordered highly unusual "total mobilization" exercises in which cars in Pyongyang were covered with camouflage netting and thousands of people took refuge in underground shelters, as they would do in case of war. On April 25, the anniversary of the founding of the army, tens of thousands of troops paraded in mass formations in Pyongyang to mark the occasion.

At his headquarters in Seoul, General Tilelli watched the vigorous military activity in the North with deep concern. He was "intuitively" certain, he told me, that the DPRK military forces had been degraded by shortages and the general deterioration affecting the country. On the other hand, U.S. and South Korean forces had been continuously modernized and improved. While this had affected the military balance on the peninsula to the detriment of the North, he said, it was impossible to say by how much. The DPRK military continued to be highly capable, making up in mass what it lacked in modernization, the American commander said, and it "might be the only viable instrument of national power the regime has left."

What worried him and his staff was the possibility that the North Korean leadership could become so desperate that the combined power of the U.S. and South Korean forces might no longer deter a massive attack. Tilelli was certain that "the explosion," as such an attack was known among his military planners, would fail after a period of bloody and destructive fighting, which would wreak death and destruction in the South but would also destroy much that North Korea had built in its half-century of existence. Given the lack of what Pyongyang's leadership considers other options, said a member of Tilelli's staff, "I don't think a decision to attack would be irrational—though it might turn out to be wrong."

Beginning in 1997, the supply of food to alleviate the devastating situation at home became increasingly the central focus of North Korean diplomacy and of international concern, eclipsing other issues. This placed the United States and South Korea, and much of the world at large, in a terrible dilemma. North Korea was continuing to feed and supply a huge and menacing army even while many of its people were hungry or even starving. The regime's statist and short-sighted policies, as much or more than the floods, were to blame for its current crisis, but it refused to undertake major changes in economic policy. Few nations wished to aid such a regime. Yet a growing number of reports placed North Korea on the brink of a great humanitarian disaster, making it intolerable to do nothing to help. Moreover, for strategic reasons and considerations of international stability, most of North Korea's neighbors and the U.S. government as well, wished to stave off the sudden downfall of that regime, fearing it might bring devastating violence that could affect all of Northeast Asia.

The United States was willing to provide funds to purchase food on a humanitarian basis, and proceeded to do so in response to U.N. appeals. However, Washington rejected attempts by North Korean diplomats to link their attendance at peace talks and agreement to various tension-reducing steps to the supply of food assistance. Washington also ruled out supplying the massive amounts of aid that would be required to end the famine. The U.S. problem was essentially political: Congress would not support "aiding" North Korea, but would permit modest contributions to U.N. humanitarian efforts intended to feed its people.

South Korea was less hesitant about linking food to its diplomatic and political objectives. Early in 1997, ROK officials sought to use food as a bargaining chip, supplying or permitting private groups to supply only limited amounts in order to maximize diplomatic leverage over North Korea. As reports of starvation multiplied, however, public pain over the suffering of fellow Koreans brought a shift in government policy. Beginning in the spring, Seoul provided 50,000 tons of food through the Red Cross. In 1998, with a new administration in office, the ROK relaxed most restrictions on the non-governmental supply of food and other aid. In a spectacular consequence of the new policy, Hyundai group founder Chung Ju Yung, who was born in the North, brought 500 head of cattle through the DMZ in June and 501 in October 1998 for starving North Koreans. His private diplomacy led to unprecedented visits by South Korean tourists to the North, and promises of much bigger North-South economic deals to come.

After initial generosity Japan, whose warehouses were bursting with surplus grain, was held back by requests for restraint from Seoul and then by new revelations that several Japanese citizens, including a 13-year-old girl, had been kidnapped by North Korean agents in the 1970s and never returned. North Korea refused to accept responsibility for the kidnappings, and Japan refused to supply more food.

China, which announced modest contributions of grain to North Korea, was believed to be supplying much greater amounts at cut-rate prices and through private barter deals. Customs data suggested that at least 1.2 million tons of grain crossed the China-DPRK border in 1997. China also supplied more than 1 million tons of oil yearly. These flows of Chinese assistance were essential to the survival of the North Korean regime and maintenance of the status quo on the peninsula, which China strongly favored.

A variety of other nations and charitable organizations also contributed food or funds to purchase food. Yet the emergency continued, compounded by a serious drought in the summer of 1997, followed by tidal waves along the western coast that devastated additional growing areas. It was as if nature had conspired with the unyielding economic policies of their government to bedevil the lives of North Koreans.

The scale of the human tragedy was immense, yet impossible to measure with precision in the secretive country. A team of researchers from the Buddhist Sharing Movement interviewed 1,019 refugees from North Korea just across the Chinese border during eight months in 1997–8, and reported that a shocking 27 percent of the family members of the refugees had died since mid–1995. The movement's executive director estimated that 2.5 million people or more may die – "a famine that may be among the worst in human history." U.S. intelligence officials who had been accumulating and examining the evidence told me in September 1998 they had no precise data, but that "certainly hundreds of thousands" of North Koreans had died from starvation or starvation-related illnesses and that 1 million deaths up to that time seemed "not impossible." About the same time, a State Department official with direct responsibility for Korean relations said he believed that "easily more than 500,000 people" had died.

Jasper Becker, a Beijing-based journalist who wrote a book about the 1958–62 Chinese famine that killed at least 30 million people, found a chilling resemblance to that tragedy in the contemporary DPRK. "This is the world's least fashionable humanitarian crisis, but it is probably worse than anything the world has seen for nearly four decades," Becker wrote in 1998. Like the famine in China, Becker attributed the disaster in North Korea principally to government policy.

## THE PASSAGE OF HWANG JANG YOP

On the morning of February 12, 1997, a South Korean businessman in Beijing telephoned the South Korean Consulate in the Chinese capital with a momentous request: that a car and escort be sent to initiate the political asylum and defection of Hwang Jang Yop, one of North Korea's most prominent officials and the architect of its *juche* philosophy. ROK officials, who were expecting the call, declined to send one of their diplomatic vehicles to pick up the 74-year-old North Korean, fearing they would later be accused of kidnapping him. A few minutes later Hwang, accompanied only by his longtime aide and fellow defector,

Kim Duk Hong, arrived by taxi and walked into the consulate, asking for protection and safe transit to Seoul. Shortly after that he sat at the desk of the ROK consul-general and wrote a three-page declaration in his own hand:

> Starting with my family, all the people [in the North] will judge that I have gone mad when they learn that I have decided to go to the South, abandoning everything. I actually feel—on not a few occasions—that I have gone mad myself.
>
> But am I the only person who has gone mad? More than 50 years after the Korean people were divided, the two halves regard each other as an enemy and keep threatening to turn each other into a sea of flames while saying they want to realize national unification. How could we regard this as the behavior of sane people?
>
> In addition, at a time when workers and farmers are starving, how could we consider people sane who loudly say they have built an ideal society for them? . . .
>
> Only a few years remain for my life. I am a person that has failed in politics. I do not have the slightest idea of seeking personal fame and prosperity, working for one side. I do not want to live long either. I hope that my family consider me dead as of today. If possible, I only wish to help promote reconciliation between the South and the North until the last moment.

The passage of Hwang Jang Yop was the most sensational—and one of the most complex—defections from one side to the other in the half-century history of struggle between the two Koreas. Hwang was the first high-level insider ever to take refuge in the other side. His defection was a political blow to North Korea and a potential political bonanza for the South since he brought to the South a lifetime of experience in rarified circles in the North. However, what he had to say was complicated by his messianic belief that his mission was to prevent a devastating war on the peninsula, to liberate the North from feudalism, and to pave the way for the reunification of Korea.

Born in 1922, Hwang studied in Japan during World War II and majored in philosophy at Moscow University during the Korean War.

After returning home, he was professor of philosophy at Kim Il Sung University, where he had special responsibility for the education of Kim Jong Il. In 1965, the year after the Dear Leader graduated, Hwang was appointed president of the prestigious university. About the same time he began to assist Kim Il Sung in elaborating the *juche* philosophy, which Kim had mentioned a decade earlier but did not emphasize until the mid-1960s, after the deepening of the Sino-Soviet dispute between his two important sponsors.

Based on his close relationship with the Great Leader, Hwang became an important—and unusual—figure in Pyongyang. From 1972 until 1984 he was speaker of the Supreme People's Assembly, the country's compliant parliament, and after that secretary of the Workers Party for international affairs and chairman of the Foreign Affairs Committee of the parliament. His most important position, however, was that of principal authority on *juche,* which became the official credo of the DPRK in the 1972 constitution. In his dual capacity as a chief philosopher for the regime and an international affairs official, Hwang was freer than others to travel abroad, to have lengthy discussions and close relationships with foreign scholars, and to express opinions that were often less militant than those of others.

When Selig Harrison, the American scholar, was in Pyongyang in 1987, Hwang told him that a communist revolution in the South was "completely out of the question" and that "we must find a way for North and South to co-exist peacefully under different social and economic systems." The same year, Hwang met surreptitiously in Japan with Samuel Lee, a South Korean philosophy professor, who found him "a very reasonable thinker, and quite free from indoctrinated communist and North Korean ideology." Young C. Kim, of George Washington University in Washington, D.C., a political scientist who often visited Pyongyang, found Hwang far more interested in philosophy than in international affairs—and his philosophy abstract and difficult to fathom.

Following the death of Kim Il Sung in July 1994, Hwang helped to establish a trading company in Beijing under the aegis of the International Peace Foundation, to collect foreign currency in support of *juche* teachings and other activities in Pyongyang. The company was headed by Kim Duk Hong, who had been Hwang's senior aide at Kim Il Sung

University and later in the Workers Party. Hwang and Kim had many contacts with South Korean businessmen, clergy, and others in appealing for funds or other material support in exchange for access and appreciation in Pyongyang. These activities were authorized and encouraged, at least in general terms, by North Korean authorities.

In 1995 Hwang told an ROK contact in Beijing that despite the long-standing North Korean demand to the contrary, it was vital that U.S. military forces remain on the Korean peninsula. When I asked a senior American official about this information, he expressed shock that I had heard about it and urged me not to repeat it, saying that it "could cost [Hwang] his life" if it became widely known. (However, by that time North Korean diplomats and even generals had begun to tell Americans unofficially that U.S. troops should stay.)

In late 1995 and early 1996, in at least two more clandestine meetings in China with South Koreans, Hwang expressed grave concern about a dangerous shift of power in Pyongyang to the military. Hwang's views, made known to the U.S. Embassy in Seoul, were reported to Washington via secret intelligence channels. His heightened apprehensions roughly coincided with the notable rise of military influence in the North under Kim Jong Il, and the emergence in January 1996 of "Red Banner philosophy," emphasizing revolutionary and martial spirit, which quickly became more prominent than *juche*.

Hwang's first overt move of opposition, according to sources in Japan, had come in early February 1996, during an international seminar held in Moscow for delegates from thirty countries on "the *juche* idea." In this setting the high priest of *juche* expressed his determined opposition to war, calling it inhuman and comparing military combatants to animals, and he declared his support for Chinese-style market reforms, which were still anathema in Pyongyang.

On March 10 Hwang's world began to change when an article in *Nodong Sinmun* attacked "careerists and conspirators [who] outwardly pretend to uphold the leader and be faithful to the revolutionary cause while dreaming another dream inwardly and making conspiracies behind the scenes." It warned that "socialism will go to ruin if there are careerists and conspirators seated in the leadership." Although the article was one of a continuing series of such warnings and mentioned no names, Hwang was certain it was aimed at him. Surveillance of his activities was increased, and lectures were organized that criticized his views and weakened his authority, again without specific mention of his name. He noticed that government officials began avoiding him.

Meanwhile, Hwang's aide in Beijing had been meeting Lee Yon Kil, a 69-year-old South Korean businessman, born in the North, who had been leading a personal crusade to induce and assist defectors from the communist regime since serving as a commando under U.S. and ROK direction in the Korean war. This shadowy figure had befriended reporter Kim Yong Sam of *Monthly Chosun,* the magazine of the Seoul newspaper *Chosun Ilbo,* who had had repeated contacts with him for several years and later reported on his talks with Hwang and his aide. On March 14 Lee heard the first indirect hints from Kim Duk Hong that Hwang might defect because of his opposition to military dominance and the growing possibility of war. On July 3, while transiting Beijing on his way home from leading the official DPRK delegation to a congress of the Vietnamese Communist Party, Hwang himself met Lee. "War must be prevented at any cost," Hwang told him, and to do so South Korea should provide food to the people of the North, which is "50 years behind the South." Hwang emphasized the need for absolute secrecy, telling Lee that a North Korean agent was situated deep in the "power core" of the Seoul regime. While in Pyongyang Hwang had been privy to a report by such an agent on personal remarks in Seoul by Kim Kwang Il, who was chief of staff to the ROK president at the time.

In the late spring, in an attempt to stabilize his position at home, Hwang had taken the advice of high-ranking party figures to compose a self-criticism admitting to mistakes. Toward the end of July, however, a private speech by Kim Jong Il, published in the Workers Party theoretical journal *Kulloja,* returned to the attack against "social scientists" who erroneously interpreted *juche.* Hwang knew then that his self-criticism had been rejected, and that his ouster from the seat of power was inevitable. In Beijing Hwang's aide, Kim, spoke explicitly of defection for the first time on July 27 and reported that Hwang requested cyanide ampules in case suicide was his only option. He also asked for money to approach younger people in Pyongyang who he believed were less sympathetic to the regime. Hwang believes "North Korea is going opposite to the way he thinks. He is a man of peace and love," Kim told Lee, according to notes of their conversations later provided to the *Monthly Chosun* reporter.

Hwang now began to move decisively to the dissident camp. On August 21 he penned a lengthy treatise summing up his view that North Korea had become "neither a nationalist nor socialist state, but a full-fledged dictatorship" that "has nothing in common with the genuine *juche* idea." According to Hwang, "Anyone who conducts demonstrations or shows the slightest anti-government color, anyone who says or does anything humiliating the authority of the leader, is secretly shot to death. . . . From the intellectuals' standpoint, it can be said without hesitation that the entire country is a large prison."

As for Kim Jong Il, Hwang wrote that he "possesses vigorous energy, as well as unswerving will to protect his own interest. His political and artistic sense is very sharp, and his brain functions fast. Since he has only been worshipped by the people without being controlled by anyone, he has never experienced any hardships. As a result, he got to be impatient and has a violent character. He worshipped Germany's Hitler. . . . He never consults with anyone else. No one can make a direct telephone call to him, no matter how high his or her position is. He considers the party and military as his own and does not care about the national economy."

Regarding the possibility of war, Hwang wrote that "the North is developing nuclear, rocket and chemical weapons" and "believes it will win in a war." Therefore, he wrote, "the South should set up a social atmosphere of respecting the military; beef up military forces in all directions; and make impregnable readiness with proper preparations for war" in order to prevent armed conflict from breaking out. Reversing his previous stand, he wrote that to weaken the North, the South should discourage reforms in the DPRK. He advocated continuation of the economic blockade to isolate the North, with the exception of providing food and medicine for the North Korean people.

In mid-November Hwang hastily wrote three letters that were conveyed to Lee in Beijing. For the first time he identified February as a target date for defection and contemplated a postdefection future:

I have no desire for a political life in the South. If I had sought a political position, I would have gained more trust by using flattery in the North. I am old and have practically no aptitude for politics. I may be able to play an advisory role in this sector. I would like to spend the rest of my life simplifying the *juche* idea so that it is easier to understand for the people of the fatherland. I would also like to expend all my energy on avoiding the tragedy of fratricidal war to realize peaceful reunification.

All this time acting in his official capacity, Hwang continued to be the front man for the North Korean regime. In 1996, in his capacity as international affairs secretary of the Central Committee of the Workers Party, he received and exchanged views with thirty-six visiting delegations from Asia, Europe, the Middle East, and North and South America, and led North Korean delegations to Vietnam in June and to Thailand and India in September. Officiating at the October 15 celebration of the seventieth anniversary of the founding of the Down-With-Imperialism-Union, Hwang praised "Comrade Kim Jong Il [who] with unbounded love for the people subordinates everything in the interests and demands of the people. . . . Trust and love is his political philosophy and political mode."

A final letter smuggled from Pyongyang, written on the evening of January 2, provided advice to the South from a Hwang who was now intensely concentrating on his future life. Because of its content, this controversial letter raised doubts about its authenticity when published by *Chosun Ilbo* immediately after Hwang's defection. In the letter Hwang advised the South to strengthen its military, its ruling party, and the NSP intelligence agency. The ruling party had been campaigning for, and the opposition parties against, a strengthening of the NSP. Hwang also expressed opposition to the four-party talks, saying the North would seek to utilize them for its own purposes, and he warned again against encouraging reforms in Pyongyang. "For peaceful reunification, the gap between the North and South must be widened like the sky and the earth," he wrote.

On January 28 Hwang left Pyongyang to deliver the main address at a symposium in Japan sponsored by the Cho Chongryon, the pro-Pyongyang residents' association. He was closely guarded in visits to Tokyo, Kyoto, and Nagano, during which he extolled *juche* and paid tribute to Kim Il Sung and Kim Jong Il. He flew to Beijing on February

11 for an overnight stop before his scheduled train trip to Pyongyang the following afternoon. Instead, he left the North Korean Embassy on the morning of February 12, pleading that he needed to go shopping for gifts. A short time later he took refuge in the South Korean Consulate.

Hwang's defection posed a difficult issue for the Chinese government, which sought to maintain good relations with both Pyongyang and Seoul, until North Korea dropped its initial claim that Hwang had been kidnapped and announced that "a coward may leave" if he really wanted to defect. Still, in order to ease the embarrassment to Pyongyang, China did not permit Hwang to leave the ROK consulate in Beijing for five weeks, and then only for a third country rather than directly to South Korea. Under an arrangement worked out with Seoul, the Philippines provided a temporary refuge for Hwang before he was permitted to travel to Seoul on April 20. As he and Kim Duk Hong stepped out of a chartered Air Philippines jet at a military airport, the two defectors raised their arms in the air three times and shouted "Mansei!" a Korean expression of triumph and good wishes. The South Korean public, watching raptly on live television, suspended its mixed feelings about Hwang, at least for the moment, and warmly welcomed his arrival.

## THE TWO KOREAS IN TIME OF TROUBLE

By 1998, half a century after the creation of separate states following the division of the peninsula, the two Koreas were radically different, but both were facing serious difficulties.

South Korea, although far more advanced economically and politically and awash with riches when compared to the North, was beset by problems that would grow dramatically at the end of 1997. In November, the financial and economic crisis that had begun in Southeast Asia spread without warning to Korea. By December 31, South Korea's currency, the won, had lost 40 percent of its value against the U.S. dollar as investors fled the country, and the value of securities on the Seoul stock market had dropped by 42 percent. To avoid defaulting on the international debts of its banks and businesses, the country that in 1996 had joined the Organization of Economic

Cooperation and Development (OECD), known as the club of the world's richest nations, was forced to go hat in hand to the International Monetary Fund for $57 billion in loans—the largest international bailout on record, up to that point—in return for acceptance of stringent economic requirements. Bankruptcies and unemployment soared, with massive social and political consequences.

Amid this turmoil Kim Dae Jung, the longtime opposition leader, was elected president in the December 18 national election. "We're just entering a dark IMF tunnel," he told the public in a televised "town hall" meeting. "The real ordeal will begin from now on." As the Republic of Korea celebrated the fiftieth anniversary of its founding on August 15, 1998, its economy was still struggling to find the path to recovery. The economy bounced back dramatically in 1999, but began to slip back again in the second half of 2000, as it became clear that underlying problems in the banking and corporate structure were more serious and more damaging than had been anticipated.

Kim Dae Jung's policies toward the North were very different from those of his predecessor and rival, Kim Young Sam. From his first years in national politics in the early 1970s, Kim Dae Jung had outspokenly advocated a policy of easing North-South tension and engaging the North. For many years he was accused of pro-communism by military-dominated governments, but he persisted in his views. Now as president, he set out three principles in his inaugural address: "First, we will never tolerate armed provocation of any kind. Second, we do not have any intention to undermine or absorb North Korea. Third, we will actively push reconciliation and cooperation between the South and North beginning with those areas which can be most easily agreed upon." His administration established a program of engaging the North through positive gestures and lowered barriers to trade and other official and unofficial interactions. He reiterated this program, which had become known as his "Sunshine Policy," at the fiftieth anniversary observance. By then it had been sorely tested by the absence of progress in official relations with the DPRK and by public dismay over another failed North Korean submarine incursion, and the discovery of the body of a North Korean commando off the South Korean coast three weeks later. Kim Dae Jung persevered in his engagement policies, even though it appeared for many months that there was little sign of progress on a governmental level.

When I first saw Kim as president in March 1998, a month after his inauguration, he told me, "We're now waiting for the North Korean attitude. I think there is discussion among the North Korean leadership about how to change their policy toward South Korea." The following month, at Pyongyang's initiative, official bilateral talks were held in Beijing–but they broke up without results because the South insisted on reciprocity, in the form of guarantees of reunions of divided families, in return for 200,000 tons of fertilizer it was willing to provide. The North, however, insisted on obtaining the aid without conditions.

An important element in Kim Dae Jung's policy was the separation of politics from economics, which in practice meant permitting ROK businessmen to pursue deals with the North, even though there was little or no progress on intergovernment relations. This proved to be a key in preparing the way to broader contacts.

North Korea, meanwhile, continued to suffer devastating problems. As a result of failed policies, its economy continued to shrink in 1997 for the eighth consecutive year since the collapse of its alliance with the Soviet Union. An International Monetary Fund mission that visited Pyongyang in September 1997 issued a confidential report, on the basis of data largely provided by DPRK officials, that the economy had suffered "a severe contraction," with total national output in 1996 only half of what it had been five years earlier. Industrial output had fallen by two thirds, according to the report, and food production by 40 percent. Estimates of starvation varied widely, but U.S. Census Bureau estimates suggested that about 1 million North Koreans died as result of famine between 1994 and 1998.

Kim Jong Il, after the completion of a three-year mourning period for his father, was elected general secretary of the Workers Party in October 1997, placing him officially at the top of the political hierarchy he had headed since his father's death. All signs, however, suggested he was relying less on the party for control and governance than on the military from his posts as supreme military commander and chairman of the National Defense Commission.

# 16

## TURN TOWARD ENGAGEMENT

For most of the half century since the creation of its regime, North Korea's role on the world scene was that of menace to the peace. Its attack across the thirty-eighth parallel that started the Korean War, its massive and forward-deployed postwar military force, its practice of terrorism and its bristling vocabulary of threats made it a pariah state to be dealt with disapprovingly and as little as possible by most of the nations of the world. Beginning with the death of Kim Il Sung and the evidence of its poverty and deprivation in the middle 1990s, North Korea was seen less as a threat and more as an economic basket case and the object of humanitarian assistance. As Kim Jong Il gathered confidence and came into his own, especially after his June 2000 summit meeting with Kim Dae Jung, North Korea and its leader began to be accepted for the first time in terms befitting a normal state. What had been shrouded in mystery began to be explored; what had been cause for either anxiety or pity began to be engaged diplomatically and examined at high levels by many of the world's democratic governments.

North Korea's shift from self-reliance to engagement began amid very mixed portents. The launching of a long-range DPRK rocket late in 1998 accentuated fears in Japan and redoubled concern in the United States, while charges of nuclear duplicity in clandestine underground activity further marred the atmosphere. At the same time, below the level of most outside awareness, domestic developments in Pyongyang began to set the stage for dramatically different policies that would alter the central relationships on the Korean peninsula.

## INTO THE HEAVENS, UNDER THE EARTH

At seven minutes after noon on August 31, 1998, North Korea sent a three-stage rocket roaring into the heavens from a launching site on the shores of the Sea of Japan, which both North and South Koreans patriotically call "the East Sea." The first stage fell away from the rocket ninety-five seconds later and landed in the sea 156 miles away, short of Japan. The second stage flew over the northern tip of the main Japanese island of Honshu and landed in the Pacific 1,022 miles from the launch site. The third stage, a solid-fueled rocket that North Korea had not previously demonstrated or been known to possess, sought to place a small satellite in a global orbit broadcasting the revolutionary hymns, "Song of General Kim Il Sung" and "Song of General Kim Jong Il." So far as U.S. monitors could determine, the effort to launch a satellite failed. But the range of the rocket, especially its third stage, was a most unpleasant discovery for those concerned about North Korea's potential for launching ballistic missiles with highly lethal and destructive warheads.

The test launch of the rocket, called the Taep'o-dong by western analysts after the area where a mock-up of the projectile was first spotted, touched off an intense alarm, bordering on panic, in Japan. A manmade projectile from an unfriendly country flying over the Japanese islands was the most tangible physical threat to the country since the end of World War II, and a nightmare to many Japanese. The government of Prime Minister Keizo Obuchi sought to contain the furor with uncharacteristically quick responses. A Japanese official had been scheduled to sign an agreement in New York that very day to provide $1 billion toward the light-water reactors promised to North Korea under the 1994 Agreed Framework. After the test, Japan announced it would not sign (though it proceeded with the project under U.S. pressure several weeks later). Japan also announced that it was halting humanitarian food aid to North Korea and suspending its offer to continue talks on establishing diplomatic ties, which would be accompanied by large-scale reparations to Pyongyang. Most significantly, in the long run, the Taep'o-dong test emboldened the previously divided Japanese government to override its traditional pacifism and move into the arena of militarized space, deciding to produce its own satellite reconnaissance system for early warning and to move toward joining the controversial U.S. antiballistic missile project in the Asian region.

In the United States, the test came exactly two weeks after the *New York Times* reported that U.S. intelligence had detected what appeared to be a secret North Korean underground nuclear weapons complex in violation of the 1994 accord. Taken together, the possibility that North Korea was secretly continuing its quest for nuclear bombs, while rapidly improving its potential ability to deliver them via long-range missiles, sounded alarm bells in Congress, greatly enhancing the credibility of skeptics who had never accepted the idea of negotiating with North Korea to buy off its nuclear threat. In addition, the Taep'o-dong test, coming six weeks after a prestigious commission headed by former—and future—Secretary of Defense Donald Rumsfeld warned of a sooner-than-expected ballistic missile threat to the United States, was a gift to partisans of the controversial National Missile Defense plan (NMD). A Republican member of Congress gleefully told a White House official after the North Korean test, "That did it—we've got the NMD."

In all likelihood the timing of the test had little or nothing to do with these U.S. domestic developments, but was keyed to two significant DPRK milestones in early September: the fiftieth anniversary of the founding of the North Korean state and the formal elevation of Kim Jong Il to the top post in the North Korean government. Pyongyang had last tested a ballistic missile, the two-stage Nodong, in 1993. On a previous occasion in October 1996, North Korea was observed to be making physical preparations for a new test launch, but dismantled the preparations after U.S. protests that such a firing would seriously harm bilateral relations and the international environment. In August 1998, however, apparently for domestic reasons, it went ahead.

It would be difficult to exaggerate the damage to the existing U.S. policy inflicted by the twin blows of August 1998. Members of Congress who had reluctantly gone along with the U.S. commitments under the 1994 Agreed Framework were incensed by the developments and prepared to cut off the funds. "I think we ought to stop talking to [North Koreans], stop appeasing them," said the chairman of the House Appropriations Committee, Rep. Bob Livingston. "I see this as a pretty good excuse just to get out of this [1994 agreement]." A senior Clinton administration official with responsibilities in Asia told me, "the [secret] underground facility pulled the plug on the policy, and the missiles hurt even more." U.S. policy toward North Korea, he said, "is in deep shit." Should the United States abandon its commitments under the Agreed Framework, it was clear, North Korea would be free to resume its production of plutonium at Yongbyon, and it was saying it would do so. This activity had brought the two nations to the brink of a military crisis in 1994 and would almost certainly do so again.

Soon after the story broke regarding the secret underground facility, the United States demanded the opportunity to inspect it, in order to determine whether it was indeed a clandestine nuclear facility. After initial confusion about the site in question, North Korean diplomats were remarkably relaxed about this topic, expressing willingness to negotiate a site visit if the Americans would pay "a handsome lump-sum," later proposed to be $300 million, for the privilege. Negotiations that included this issue, in fact, were beginning in New York when the Taep'o-dong was launched, immensely complicating the U.S. political problem. North Koreans knew something the Americans were uncertain about: that the underground cavern in question, at a place called Kumchang-ni, was not a nuclear facility and was unsuitable for such a purpose. They also increasingly understood it was essential for American officials to obtain access, and therefore Pyongyang could drive a hard bargain.

The underground nuclear weapons issue was the creation of the Pentagon's Defense Intelligence Agency, a center of extreme skepticism, if not hostility, toward U.S. rapprochement with Pyongyang. American spy satellites had long been monitoring a variety of North

Korean military excavations, which were commonplace in a country under continual fear of air attack. In the case of the dig at Kumchang-ni, into a hard-rock mountain in a heavily militarized area northwest of Pyongyang near the Chinese border, excavation had begun a decade earlier, but had only attracted serious attention after U.S. intelligence suggested the area was linked to the Ministry of Atomic Power, and observation showed it was being heavily guarded. Calculating the size of the hole from the mounds of soil and rock being extracted and observing nearby dams and electrical facilities, the DIA proceeded to produce elaborate theories and assumptions, even creating small-scale models of nuclear reactors and plutonium-reprocessing facilities, which the agency believed could be under construction in the growing cavern beneath the surface of the earth.

Some other U.S. intelligence officials and competing intelligence agencies were dubious, but the DIA was insistent. The agency was permitted to begin briefings for U.S. allies and congressional committees in June 1998. With the acquiescence of the Central Intelligence Agency, an official intelligence "finding" was promulgated in mid-July that the Kumchang-ni cavern was "probably" a suspect nuclear facility, at which an active nuclear weapons program could be planned or under way. One month later, *New York Times* correspondent David Sanger was able to confirm rumors of the developments by interviewing former officials at a think-tank meeting outside Washington, D.C., and obtaining confirmation of the basic facts from the Clinton administration. Sanger's August 17 story put the issue on the record in highly visible fashion, making it the subject of political and public debate, just as North Korea was preparing its rocket launch.

It took five rounds and more than six months of negotiations between U.S. and DPRK diplomats, essentially over the extent of access and its price, to produce an agreement that a U.S. team could make multiple inspections at Kumchang-ni. The price was 600,000 tons of food, most of it to be supplied through the United Nations, plus a new potato-production program. Washington insisted officially that the inspections and the food were unrelated, but hardly anyone was fooled.

The inspection, by fourteen Americans, including several technical experts hired for the purpose, took place over three days in late May 1999. Inspectors found six miles of criss-crossing tunnels laid out in a grid pattern, plus one chamber near one of the entrances. Neither the tunnels nor the chamber was suitable to do what U.S. intelligence had suggested. North Korean officials who accompanied the team would not describe the purpose of the big dig except to say it was a "sensitive military facility." Following the on-site inspection, the State Department on June 25 announced that the Kumchang-ni excavation did not, after all, contain a nuclear reactor or reprocessing plant, either completed or under construction, and it had not been designed to do so. No one apologized or was penalized for the intelligence fiasco that had endangered U.S. policy in Korea for most of a year.

## TOWARD AN AID-BASED STATE

While the eyes of official Washington were riveted on North Korea's nuclear and missile programs, developments of fundamental importance were gathering momentum in Pyongyang. From the vantage point of hindsight, senior officials in both the United States and South Korea identified the final months of 1998 as the time when important shifts began to gather force in the regime north of the thirty-eighth parallel.

The Supreme People's Assembly, in theory the highest legislative authority in the country, met on September 5 for the first time since the death of Kim Il Sung four years earlier. As expected, it named his son and heir, Kim Jong Il, as the governmental leader of the country, although not as president—that post was reserved for the dead leader in perpetuity—but as head of the National Defense Commission, which was declared to be "the highest post of the state." The meeting enacted two other changes that proved to be of major significance. It amended the constitution to introduce some elements of a Chinese-style socialist market economy, and it brought into office a group of the younger, more pragmatic bureaucrats. The government's cabinet, which was given new powers, was henceforth to be composed of thirty-four officials, of whom twenty-three were new faces, replacing elderly figureheads. There was no doubt that these decisions, like nearly all others of central importance in North Korea, bore the personal imprimatur of Kim Jong Il.

The greatest questions, though, arose from Kim's decision to rule the country from a military post and the increasing prominence of military leaders in the Assembly, which suggested to outsiders a further militarization of the country's policies. Although Kim Jong Il, unlike his father, had no military background, since his father's death he had spent a great deal of time establishing and improving close relations with the armed forces, the only people in the country capable of challenging him. Large numbers of officers had been promoted at his direction. The overwhelming majority of his officially reported activities in his first five years of supreme power were visits to military units or had military-related connections. An American visitor to Pyongyang in 1997 noticed some of the extraordinary ways in which he was garnering military support. General officers, of whom there were now many, were being driven around the capital by uniformed drivers in new Mercedes and BMW limousines. Despite the famine in the countryside, a special floor of the Koryo Hotel, the capital's best, had been set aside for the lavish wining and dining of senior military officers. Outside the capital, Russia-style *dachas,* or recreational residences, were springing up for the use of military leaders. As it turned out, Kim Jong Il's new post and his policies appear to have cemented his grip on the military, setting the stage for greater diplomatic maneuvers.

For South Korea and most of the West, the first crack in the depiction of Kim Jong Il as a withdrawn, eccentric, and threatening ogre came in October 1998, a month after the Supreme Peoples Assembly meeting, when he met in Pyongyang with Chung Ju Yung, the eighty-two-year-old founder and honorary chairman of the South's giant Hyundai group. In his first meeting with an outsider since his formal elevation as head of government, Kim was described by his guest as polite, courteous, and deferential to an older man. Photographs of Kim welcoming South Korea's most illustrious industrialist, and of the two holding hands for the camera, were splashed on the front pages of Seoul's newspapers. Of more lasting significance were business deals that were sealed or seriously discussed during the Hyundai chairman's visit.

Chung Ju Yung, born in 1915, the son of a poor rice farmer in a village just north of the current DMZ, had long been determined to do what he could to improve the lives of the people of his original homeland. In January 1989 he had been the first prominent South Korean industrialist to be welcomed with honors in Pyongyang. In the early 1990s his attempts to return were blocked for political reasons by the government of President Kim Young Sam. By 1998, Kim Dae Jung's desire to engage the North and his policy of separating business from politics created an opening for a series of imaginative initiatives by Chung. In June he undertook high profile "cattle diplomacy" by transporting in big Hyundai trucks 500 head of cattle from his farm through the DMZ as a gift to North Korea, and by bringing in 501 more in October, plus 20 Hyundai automobiles, including several luxury models suitable for Kim Jong Il. In an unusual gesture, Hyundai also presented the North Korean leader with a solid gold replica of a crane, reminiscent of those that annually transit the DMZ, and a solid-gold replica of a cow. Each model was worth more than $3,000.

During the October trip North Korea granted Hyundai the right to bring tourists from South Korea to the famed Diamond Mountain (Mount Kumgang), just north of the DMZ, for payments totaling $942 million over six years. The tours in Hyundai-chartered ships began the following month, when the South Korean firm also began paying $25 million a month into a North Korean account at the Bank of China in Macao. The $150 million in unrestricted money in the first six months (to be reduced by agreement in later months) was hardly an impressive sum in the world of international finance, but it was a fortune to impoverished North Korea, whose largest single export, textiles, had been worth only $184 million in 1997. The deal proved to be instrumental in opening the door to more North-South economic engagement, but by June 2000, Hyundai had sustained losses of $206 million on the Diamond Mountain tours, which it could ill afford in a time of economic downturn. In early 2001 it was forced to appeal for an ROK government bailout.

The supply of so much cash to North Korea without restriction proved to be controversial in South Korea and among Washington policy-makers. Nevertheless, Kim Dae Jung's strategists believe the payments were crucial in demonstrating that the South would keep its economic promises toward the North consistently and reliably. "North Korea was suspicious whether the government would allow the Hyundai to pay cash," particularly in periods of tension between the two governments, a senior official told me. When it did so month after month, he said, "they began to trust us." Looking toward more important things to come, he added, the Hyundai deal was "a bite to catch a fish."

Shorn of trade and aid from its original Soviet Union and East European allies, uncertain of China's stopgap assistance, barred from most commercial loans due to the defaults on its debts in the 1970s, and excluded from international lending agencies due to its closed economic and political systems and the opposition of the United States and other key sponsors, cash-shy North Korea in recent decades has had its hand out for money on nearly every possible occasion. In 1994, it traded its nuclear activities at its production works at Yongbyon for the eventual supply of light-water reactors costing about $4 billion from a consortium of outside nations, plus heavy fuel oil from the United States, which has cost from $60 million to $100 million per year. As noted, it asked $300 million for U.S. inspection of the Kumchang-ni cavern. It initially asked $1 billion in cash yearly for three years for the United States to buy out its ballistic missile exports. Requests for payments from South Korea in food, fertilizer, and currency have been constant; much of the dialogue between the two Koreas in recent years has involved such transactions.

Owing to the reports of extreme famine in outlying areas, the international community began supplying large amounts of humanitarian assistance, principally food and medicine, to North Korea in the mid-1990s. The aid—through foreign government grants, the UN's World Food Program, private aid agencies, and the heavy fuel oil provided by the United States—is worth about $400 million annually, according to the Institute for International Economics' Marcus Noland, a careful independent record keeper of such data. This aid has come from forty-nine different countries, with the United States, South Korea, China, Japan, and the European Union being the largest contributors. In addition, North Korean income from missile sales, remittances from sympathetic Koreans living in Japan, and illicit activities such as counterfeiting and drug trafficking adds up to nearly as much, Noland has estimated. Altogether these sums are roughly equal to the aggregate value of all of North Korea's recorded exports of slightly less than $1 billion per year. Looking at these developments, Noland recently described the DPRK as "an increasingly aid-dependent economy."

The significance of this change has been great in political as well as economic terms, internally as well as externally. Although the regime continued to express fealty to Kim Il Sung's theory of *juche*, or self-reliance, North Korea by the end of the 1990s had become dependent on others for much of its sustenance. Unlike the assistance from communist countries during the cold war, most of this flow was not from ideological allies or sponsors, but from those who were not committed to survival of the regime. To keep money flowing and improve his standing abroad, Kim Jong Il was required to take greater account of the world outside than his father had done—or that anyone expected.

## PERRY TO THE RESCUE

At the moment of maximum peril to the administration's North Korea policy, it was widely agreed in the U.S. Congress, the executive branch, and such outside groups as the Council on Foreign Relations' Korea Task Force that the best chance for preservation was a high-level review and revision headed by a respected outsider. Nearly everyone's number-one choice to undertake this job was William J. Perry, the seventy-one-year-old former secretary of defense, who had led the nation's military establishment during the 1994 nuclear crisis. Perry was a figure of strength, maturity, and experience. More than almost anyone else, he had looked into the abyss of horrific bloodshed and destruction that had been threatened. Unknown to most outsiders, he had been seared by the experience. Having returned to the comfortable life of a Stanford University professor and board member of high-tech companies, he did not welcome the call from President Clinton asking him to become "North Korea policy coordinator" on an urgent basis. Perry saw it as "a difficult job, with a low probability of success . . . but I also remembered the 1994 crisis, which I thought then and still do was the most dangerous crisis we faced in this period. And I saw us moving toward another crisis as bad as that one."

Perry recruited Harvard University Professor Ashton Carter, who had been one of his assistants in the Pentagon, and assembled a small team of U.S. government officials headed by Ambassador Wendy Sherman, counselor of the State Department and a close confidant of Secretary of State Madeleine Albright. Perry concluded early that it was essential to present North Korea with an unshakably close alliance of the United States, South Korea, and Japan, rather than risk the possibility that Pyongyang would play one nation off against another as it had done with the Soviet Union and China during most of the cold war. To cement the alliance, Perry created a three-way Trilateral Coordination and Oversight Group of the United States, the ROK, and Japan to consider North Korean issues. Second, he concluded that U.S. policy could not be at odds with that of the South Korean president, who had made engagement with the North the major thrust of his newly installed administration.

The essence of Perry's plan was to offer North Korea's leaders a proposal with two alternative tracks. Track one was to end their long-range missile programs and reconfirm the stand-down of their nuclear weapons program, in return for full diplomatic relations with the United States, a peace treaty ending the Korean War, and improved relations with South Korea and Japan. Track two was to continue down the road of missile tests and nuclear uncertainty, in which case the United States and its allies would take actions to enhance their own security and containment of the North, increasing the likelihood of confrontations.

It was not simple for Perry to persuade the U.S. administration to accept both the positive and negative elements of his plan. The positive road would accord a greater degree of legitimacy and acceptance to the North Korean regime than had been the case before. Perry argued that even though North Korea was undergoing extreme economic hardships it was not likely to collapse and "therefore we must deal with the DPRK regime as it is, not as we might wish it to be." In successive cabinet-level meetings at the White House, Perry argued convincingly that the status quo was unsustainable, and spoke in graphic detail from his 1994 experience of the awesome dangers of the downward track. Madeleine Albright, normally a strong opponent of antidemocratic regimes, was persuaded by Perry's views and a private briefing by General John Tilelli, the U.S. military commander in South Korea, that the downward road was exceedingly dangerous and thus a serious effort to put North Korea on the upper path was essential. Albright, and she believes Clinton as well, were deeply affected by the views of Kim Dae Jung, in whom they had great trust and confidence.

It was clear to Perry from the beginning that he would have to travel to Pyongyang to learn which path the North would choose, if he could get an answer at all. He and his party flew into Pyongyang on May 25, 1999, aboard a U.S. Air Force special mission plane with "United States of America" emblazoned across its fuselage and the American flag on its tail. Before embarking, Perry and his team had spent an entire day at Stanford going over every word of a seventeen-page script, and over the Korean translation, to be used as the crucial presentation. After a lavish welcome banquet the night of his arrival, Perry made his presentation the following day, primarily to Kang Sok Ju, the First Deputy Foreign Minister who had negotiated the 1994 Agreed Framework and who was the closest diplomatic aide to Kim Jong Il, as he had been to Kim Il Sung. Perry was conscious that he was speaking through Kang to Kim Jong Il. Indeed, some members of the party believed he was speaking to Kim directly: an American official noticed that when he dropped a pencil on the conference table, he could hear an electronic echo, presumably from hidden microphones.

Reading from the script inside a file folder, Perry began with references to the difficult history of Korea and its great-power neighbors over the past 100 years, which included the Russo-Japanese War of 1904–5, in which Japan gained dominance over Korea. In those days, he said, "events [that] occurred and decisions made in capitals in Asia decisively and tragically influenced the course of the 20th century." Perry said he was there not to apologize for things the United States had done but to seek to work together to heal the wounds. He explained his own role in the nuclear crisis of 1994, how important his understanding of that crisis had been to him, and how perilously close the United States and the DPRK had come to a clash of arms.

The United States as a Pacific power would remain intimately bound up with Asia in the future as it had been earlier in the twentieth century, Perry told the North Koreans. Advancing a theme that was to recur in later ROK and U.S. conversations with Kim Jong Il, Perry said that a Korea surrounded by powerful states could benefit from a positive relationship with a power across the Pacific. The United States, he said, would be prepared to consider the legitimate defense concerns of the DPRK, but the DPRK in return must consider the defense concerns of others in the region. He observed that the status quo was not sustainable due to U.S. concerns about North Korean missile and nuclear programs.

Perry outlined in some detail the actions that North Korea must take to place itself on the positive track he recommended, leading step-by-step to full diplomatic, political, and economic relations with the United States. To obtain these benefits, North Korea must completely halt all missile exports, including related technology and equipment. Even more significantly, North Korea must cease development, production, testing and deployment of all missiles above the limit of the international Missile Technology Control Regime, which North Korea had not joined. This would eliminate the new Taep'o-dong as well as the Nodong that had been threatening Japan for most of a decade. This was a tall order for a country that was demanding $1 billion in cash yearly to cease its missile exports and had refused even to negotiate on its internal programs.

Should North Korea continue missile tests and other actions perceived to be hostile, in effect taking the second track, Perry said the United States, South Korea, and Japan were prepared to reverse positive steps that they had taken and to protect their security by military actions of their own. He did not specify what actions they would take and felt it was unnecessary for him to speak in detail, since North Koreans knew his history as defense secretary during the 1994 crisis.

Before leaving Pyongyang it was clear to Perry that deep divisions existed within the regime, or at least that North Korea wanted the United States to believe there were, about accepting his ideas. At U.S. requests for a meeting with a senior military figure, General Lee Yong Chol, a high-ranking member of Kim Jong Il's entourage, met the Perry team. "We don't normally meet with our enemies," he began bluntly, and proceeded to say he believed it was a bad idea even to discuss giving up North Korean missiles. Referring to the intensive U.S. bombing of Yugoslavia then taking place, he said this was because the Serbs were unable to fire back at the United States, and that North Korea was determined never to be in that position. Moreover, Lee referred to the Foreign Ministry officials as wimpish and said the military would pay little heed to what they thought.

Perry had made only pro-forma requests to see Kim Jong Il, the person who would ultimately decide what course North Korea would take, and no such meeting was arranged. On the final day of his visit, Perry summarized his proposals in a brief meeting with Kang. The United States had taken an important step in sending him to Pyongyang as the personal representative of President Clinton, and now it was up to North Korea to take the next step, he said. Kang was noncommittal. As the U.S. Air Force plane took off for Tokyo, Perry told his team that he believed his mission had failed. He doubted that the Foreign Ministry and the Workers Party could win a debate with the armed forces, although he conceded he did not know what the ultimate decision-maker, Kim Jong Il, might be thinking. The experienced Korean experts in his party read the tea leaves differently. They thought that Kang and some others were clearly intrigued with Perry's ideas and that they might well succeed in moving in a positive direction.

Before leaving Pyongyang, Perry suggested that if his proposals were too sweeping to digest all at once, North Korea might consider taking a smaller initial bite, such as placing a moratorium on further flight tests of its missiles. The United States could take its own small step by easing some U.S. economic sanctions. On June 23, less than a month after the Perry visit, North Korea's diplomats asked their U.S. counterparts in a meeting in Beijing for more details of what Perry had in mind, a clear sign that Pyongyang was interested. Serious discussions began in August in Geneva. A month later in Berlin, in mid-September 1999, North Korea agreed to a moratorium on further missile tests while talks continued. In return, President Clinton announced the lifting of sanctions that banned most U.S. exports to and imports from the DPRK. Pyongyang had initially accepted only a first bite-sized portion, but to a U.S. negotiator, "They had bitten; they had taken the hook." Albright declared publicly that the United States was heading down a new and more hopeful road in its relations with North Korea—but that Washington could reverse course if it became necessary. The missile test moratorium and the visit to the underground cavern took the edge off the anger in Congress that had erupted a year earlier. The future path of the U.S.-DPRK relationship, however, remained uncertain.

## TOWARD THE JUNE SUMMIT

For many summers North Korean fishermen had ventured south into a rich crab-harvesting area across an invisible line on the map that had been utilized as a sea border between the two Koreas since the 1950–53 war. Usually the crabbers had scuttled back north when confronted with southern ships, but in June 1999 they unaccountably did not do so, but stayed to fish under the protection of northern patrol craft. On June 10 a dozen North Korea crab-fishing boats, escorted by six North Korean patrol boats, were confronted by South Korean patrol boats, which began ramming the invading vessels to force them back across the dividing line. After a few minutes, the North Korean boats, several of which had been damaged, fled north.

On June 13, a renewal of the confrontation escalated into a mini-war. The southern side had strict orders not to fire first, but the first shot from a northern boat was answered by a hail of fire from more modern and better-armed southern vessels, initiating a fourteen-minute gun battle. A North Korean torpedo boat with an estimated twenty sailors on board was sunk before the rest of the flotilla fled.

The first serious naval clash between the two Koreas in the Yellow Sea since the Korean War put nerves on edge, prompted the dispatch of additional U.S. naval forces to the area, and created grave questions about relations between Seoul and Pyongyang. Yet, somehow, it did not escalate. After the shoot-out, the incursions, across a line the North had never officially recognized, did not continue. Despite fierce rhetoric, North Korea did not put its forces on alert, build up its forces near the battle zone, or counterattack with its nearby shore battery of 100-mm guns or its Silkworm antiship missiles.

Speculation was intense about why North Korea had sought to contest the sea border at that time. Some declared that the incident reflected an effort by hard-liners among the North Korean military to sabotage moves toward rapprochement with the South. Others suggested it was intended to improve Pyongyang's bargaining position in forthcoming talks with Seoul. Others saw the incident as a grave challenge to President Kim Dae Jung's engagement, or Sunshine, policy toward the North. In retrospect, high-ranking South Korean officials became convinced that the confrontation had been unintentional on the part of Pyongyang, and that it arose from a much more mundane cause: the fishing fleet's quota for crabs, which are sold by the North for scarce hard currency, had been raised to double that of the previous year, a new quota almost impossible to meet without tapping the southern waters.

The impact of the sea clash was substantial in all directions. Domestically, it appeared to validate the lesser-noticed "hard" side of Kim Dae Jung's Sunshine declaration, as expressed in his 1998 inaugural address: "We will never tolerate armed provocations of any kind." The military action improved his standing, at least temporarily, with those in South Korea who felt his policies toward the north were too accommodating. In an interview months later, Kim told me that the naval clash had been "a decisive success" that taught North Korea a great lesson, while improving the morale of South Korean armed forces. The embarrassed North, although it avoided any military response, reacted politically. Two weeks after the battle, long-delayed meetings of North and South Korean vice ministerial officials in Beijing broke down in arguments over the sea battle, and without a widely anticipated agreement on meetings of divided families in return for ROK economic assistance. Senior South Korean officials who subsequently dealt extensively with the North believe the clash in the Yellow Sea may have delayed Pyongyang's movement toward accommodation with the South by six months or more. If so, the delay proved to be a costly one in the developments on the divided peninsula.

In the summer and fall of 1999, North Korea was reaching out to a variety of key countries. In mid-May, Kim Jong Il summoned the Chinese ambassador, Wan Yongxiang, for the first meeting with a Chinese ambassador since his father's death. Kim applauded China's reform and open door policies and asked that China receive a mission to reestablish the high-level relations that had been dormant for five years; a few weeks later, he dispatched the mission headed by Kim Yong Nam, the former foreign minister who was nominally the head of state for protocol purposes. In November, Russian Foreign Minister Igor Ivanov was received in Pyongyang to make preparations for a new bilateral treaty on trade and cooperation, replacing the old Soviet military alliance. In early December the North welcomed a Japanese parliamentary group headed by former prime minister Tomiichi Murayama and including Hiromu Nonaka of the Liberal Democratic Party, which paved the way for resumption of Japan–North Korean normalization talks. Japan then announced the lifting of some economic sanctions.

Relations with the United States, however, appeared to be drifting if not stalled. In September 1999 North Korea proposed sending a high-level emissary to Washington to confirm officially the missile moratorium and move relations to the next level. Throughout the fall and winter, U.S. diplomats urged their Pyongyang counterparts to send the emissary soon, lest North Korean policy become embroiled in the U.S. presidential debate in 2000. From meeting to meeting North Korean diplomats were unable to set a date, suggesting to some of the Americans a policy debate in Pyongyang over what to do. Among other impediments, North Korean diplomats complained bitterly that the U.S. economic sanctions that President Clinton had publicly promised to lift were still in force. Neither they nor the public was told that the White House had made a private commitment in writing to Republican leaders of the Senate not to lift the sanctions until the high-level visit began to discuss elimination of long-range missiles–and nobody could say when that would be.*

I was in Seoul in early January 2000 and met privately with Kim Dae Jung to discuss North-South relations for the third time since he had become president two years earlier. The previous month, Kim had begun to receive signals from a variety of channels that Pyongyang wished to move again toward official cooperation and economic assistance, but he did not tip his hand. Asked about the lack of a clear-cut response to his overtures, Kim told me, "We told North Korea when they respond to our efforts for peace, we will respond." He expressed the belief that the activities of former secretary of defense Perry and the growing solidarity of the United States, South Korea, and Japan would have a positive influence on North Korea. Citing Pyongyang's efforts to reach out, he said, "they realized if they continue like this without cooperation with the outside, they cannot maintain their system." The day before our meeting, Italy had become the first Western European country to establish diplomatic relations with North Korea. Kim said the Italians had spoken to him ahead of time and "I told them to go ahead." His objective, he said, was "to liquidate the cold war structure on the Korean peninsula within three years"—the time remaining in his presidency. He did not predict what would happen next, but I sensed he was more confident than before.

In the early months of 2000, in fact, decisions were jelling in the North. On March 5, in the first observable sign to the outside that something different was happening, Kim Jong Il made a well-publicized visit to the Chinese embassy in Pyongyang. The nearly five-hour meeting was a farewell gesture to Ambassador Wan, who was soon to leave his post—but it had greater significance than that. Kim Jong Il normally did not receive ambassadors, and a visit by him to an embassy was astonishing in North Korean terms. It appears he used

*The sanctions were finally lifted in June 2000 after the North-South summit meeting and after DPRK diplomats furnished their American counterparts with a restatement of the missile test moratorium that was used to gain acquiescence of Senate leaders.

the evening to notify Chinese leaders what was coming, and to set the stage for an initially secret trip to see them in Beijing two months later.

Kim Dae Jung had decided early in the year that his top priority would be a summit meeting with Kim Jong Il, as difficult is that might be to arrange, because he believed the only way to negotiate success-fully with a dictatorial government was from the top down. On January 20 he publicly proposed a summit meeting to discuss issues of mutual cooperation, peaceful coexistence, and co-prosperity. In a pub-lic statement on February 6, he said he would not be bogged down by matters of location or format. His aim and flexibility were also made known in low-level channels that had been opened to the North. Perhaps more importantly, Kim began to speak publicly in startlingly positive terms about his potential opposite number at a North-South summit. A meeting of the top leaders is essential, the South Korean president said in February in an interview with the Tokyo Broadcasting System, and it is practical as well: "I believe [Kim Jong Il] is a man of good judgment, equipped with great knowledge." This surprising state-ment about a man who had been routinely and roundly condemned as the ultimate enemy brought a storm of protests from conservatives in the South, including those among the United Liberal Democrats, Kim Dae Jung's own coalition partner. No South Korean president had ever said such positive things about a North Korean leader.

On March 2, Kim left Seoul for state visits to Italy, France, and Germany. On March 9 at the Free University in Berlin, he called for a government-to-government dialogue with the North without delay and announced extensive new proposals for ROK assistance. These included a government role in expanding the North's "social infra-structure, including highways, harbors, railroads and electric and communications facilities." He proposed business-related treaties on investment guarantees and prevention of double taxation. To deal with the underlying causes of the North's famine he proposed "com-prehensive reforms in the delivery of quality fertilizers, agricultural equipment, irrigation systems and other elements of a structural nature," with the assistance of the South. U.S. officials, who were in the midst of negotiating with North Korean diplomats in New York, were taken aback by his ambitious offers, which they heard about only hours before the speech in Berlin. Secretary of State Albright protested the lack of advance notice to the ROK foreign minister, Lee Joung Binn, who apologetically said Kim had been working on the details of his speech right up until the time it was given.

Kim did not have long to wait for an answer from Pyongyang. On March 14, shortly after he returned from his trip, he received a message through the truce village of Panmunjom proposing a secret meeting in Shanghai to discuss the possibility of a summit. Kim called in Culture and Tourism Minister Park Jie Won and assigned him to be his negotiator. On March 17, Park flew to Shanghai after telling reporters and staff members that he was taking a leave of absence to be hospitalized for a checkup. The same day he began four rounds of talks with Song Ho Gyong, a veteran North Korean diplomat who was vice chairman of the DPRK's Asia-Pacific Peace Committee, an influential Workers Party unit in charge of policy toward the South. According to a high-ranking ROK official, the North sought to explore details of the economic assistance mentioned in the Berlin speech. There was also a question of where to meet and when to announce a meeting. No agreement was reached in the first two days of secret talks, nor in a second round the following week in Beijing. But when Park was summoned back to the Chinese capital by his negotiating partner on April 8, he and Song, "under instruction from the highest authority" of each side, signed an agreement on a North-South summit meeting to take place in Pyongyang on June 12–14. The agreement was announced on April 10, just three days before nationwide parliamentary elections in South Korea, generating skepticism and charges of "obvious politicking" from the political opposition. As it turned out, the announcement appeared to have little effect on the elections, in which the president's party failed in its bid to become the number-one party in the National Assembly.

## SUMMIT IN PYONGYANG

Following the announcement that the leaders of the two Koreas would meet, midlevel officials of the two governments met at Panmunjom in five sessions of preliminary talks from April 22 to May

18 to hammer out summit details: the agenda, participants, press attendees, travel arrangements, security. The central issue and the greatest unknown, however—the intentions and even the character of the North Korean leader—remained a mystery.

On the afternoon of May 27, Lim Dong Won, the South Korean president's closest adviser on North-South affairs, flew secretly from Beijing to Pyongyang in a North Korean airliner to find out. The diminutive former general, who had been born in the North but who became an army major general, a professor, and a military and diplomatic strategist in the South, was the most trusted and most powerful foreign-policy official in Kim Dae Jung's presidency. Lim had been deeply involved for many years in policy toward and negotiations with the North, but he had played little role in domestic politics until he joined Kim Dae Jung in 1995 as director general of Kim's Asia-Pacific Peace Foundation. Kim had been outspokenly determined for decades to pursue engagement with the North rather than confrontation; Lim, who agreed, brought expertise and enterprise in making it happen. After serving in two earlier senior posts, Lim in December 1999 became director general of the National Intelligence Service, the contemporary successor of the controversial Korean Central Intelligence agency (KCIA). In that post he had a hand on all intelligence concerning the North, and could direct and even participate in secret activities.

Before traveling to Pyongyang, Lim did not know what kind of man he would meet at the top of the North Korean hierarchy. He had collected ten books that had been written about Kim Jong Il, all from the negative side. Most of the intelligence that had been gathered and promulgated by the NIS was also harshly negative. Yet some other people and materials, including the accounts of Russian and Chinese officials who had met Kim Jong Il, were much more positive about his ability, his interests, and his inclinations.

In four hours of talks, Lim found a North Korean leader very different from most of the advance accounts. On returning to Seoul, he made a six-point report to Kim Dae Jung about his summit partner:

1. He is a strong dictator, stronger than his father, whom Lim had met on two occasions in the early 1990s.

2. He is the only person who is open-minded and pragmatic in the North Korean system.

3. He is a good listener. He took notes on the meeting with Lim, like a student with a professor.

4. When he is persuaded to another's point of view, he is decisive.

5. He is gentle and polite to older people around him, as he was to Hyundai founder Chung Ju Yung.

6. He has a sense of humor.

Lim sought to negotiate a joint statement to be issued at the end of the summit by the two leaders, but Kim Jong Il refused. He said he wished to work out such a statement in person with Kim Dae Jung during their meetings.

After a last-minute one-day postponement, the North-South summit began on the morning of June 13, when the special plane from Seoul bearing the ROK president; his wife, ministers, and aides; and an accompanying press corps, landed at Pyongyang airport. Meeting them on a red carpet laid on the tarmac was Kim Jong Il, clad in his characteristic quasi-military garb of khaki trousers and zippered khaki jacket, who greeted Kim Dae Jung with a warm two-handed handshake and words of welcome. As millions of South Koreans watched with high emotion via a television hookup, their president was accorded full honors, including a military band, an honor guard of North Korean soldiers with rifles and bayonets in salute position, and hundreds of women in traditional billowing gowns waving colorful flowers. The two leaders got in the back seat of Kim Jong Il's limousine for a forty-minute ride through the streets, which were lined with an estimated 600,000 cheering people waving pink and red paper flowers. En route to a state guest house, the two leaders occasionally held hands in a gesture of friendship as they chatted.

In three days of talks, accompanied by only a few aides during serious discussions, the leaders ranged widely over the issues between the two Koreas. They discussed the possibilities of South Korean assistance and of North Korean concessions on such issues as reunions of divided families, exchanges of cultural and sporting groups, and meetings of the military and civilian government officials that had long been desired by the South.

After much bargaining, the two Kims worked out, signed, and promulgated a joint declaration:

1. The South and the North have agreed to resolve the question of reunification on their own initiative and through the joint efforts of the Korean people, who are the masters of the country.

2. Acknowledging that there are common elements in the South's proposal for a confederation and the North's proposal for a federation of lower stage as the formulae for achieving reunification, the South and the North agreed to promote reunification in that direction.

3. The South and the North have agreed to promptly resolve humanitarian issues such as exchange visits by separated family members and relatives on the occasion of the August 15 National Liberation Day and the question of former long-term prisoners who had refused to renounce communism.

4. The South and the North have agreed to consolidate mutual trust by promoting balanced development of the national economy through economic cooperation and by stimulating cooperation and exchanges in civic, cultural, sports, public health, environmental and all other fields.

5. The South and the North have agreed to hold a dialogue between relevant authorities in the near future to implement the above agreement expeditiously.

   President Kim Dae Jung cordially invited National Defense Commission chairman Kim Jong Il to visit Seoul, and Chairman Kim Jong Il decided to visit Seoul at an appropriate time.

Some difficult moments and disagreements took place which, according to the South Korean president, nearly caused the talks to

break off. Among these were the complex and delicate issues of confederation versus federation; the question of whether Kim Jong Il
should sign the joint statement rather than Kim Yong Nam, the protocol head of state; and whether Kim Jong Il would commit himself
to a return summit in Seoul. In retrospect, the South Korean president said the success of the summit meeting "was due in large measure to [Kim Jong Il's] ability to be receptive to new ideas and a willingness to change his own views. . . . He didn't appear to be a cold-
minded theoretician, but a very sensitive personality who had a sharp
mind."

Some of the discussions went far beyond bilateral questions to
international issues. Kim Dae Jung handed his opposite a number of
written statements urging him to adhere strictly to the 1994 Agreed
Framework with the United States on nuclear issues, and to bring the
negotiations with Washington on curbing North Korean missiles to a
smooth and satisfactory conclusion. Without good North Korean
relations with the United States, the South Korean president said,
relations between North and South Korea could not continue to make
progress.

The presence of American troops on the peninsula will be needed even after unification to maintain regional balance and security,
Kim Dae Jung said. The North Korean leader replied that he agreed,
and said he had sent a message to this effect to Washington as early
as 1992 via Kim Yong Sun, who was sitting on his immediate right
and confirmed that he had given this message to Undersecretary of
State Arnold Kantor. However, the role of American troops on the
peninsula should be changed, the North Korean leader added. Rather
than defending the South against the North, he said, they should have
a peacekeeping purpose. This was a key point in a peace treaty he
wished to negotiate with United States, he said. When Kim Dae Jung
asked why North Korean radio broadcasts continued to attack the
presence of U.S. troops, Kim Jong Il responded this was for internal
propaganda purposes—and would continue.

"A new age has dawned for our nation," Kim Dae Jung declared
when he returned home on the afternoon of June 15. "We have
reached a turning point so that we can put an end to the history of ter-

ritorial division." Of his personal feelings, he told the South Korean people, "I found that Pyongyang, too, was our land, indeed. The Pyongyang people are the same as we, the same nation sharing the same blood. . . . We lived as a unified nation for 1300 years before we were divided 55 years ago against our will. It is impossible for us to continue to live separated physically and spiritually. I was able to reconfirm this fact first-hand during this visit. I have returned with the conviction that, sooner or later, we will become reconciled with each other, cooperate, and finally get reunified."

In the aftermath of the June summit, there was worldwide speculation about why Kim Jong Il suddenly emerged from the shadows and appeared to be opening his previously closed society. Was the change real or cosmetic? Had he changed strategy or only tactics? What were his main objectives?

Kim Dae Jung, in a dinner for Korea experts and friends in New York three months later, said he believed the most important reason for the opening was North Korea's desperate economic travail, which made assistance from the outside essential to its survival. "Without improved relations with South Korea, others won't help them," he said. Other reasons he cited were the failure of North Korea to sideline the ROK while responding to the United States; global pressure for détente from China, Russia, and other nations; and Pyongyang's growing trust that the South's policy was actually aimed at assisting the North rather than undermining it. Scholars also noted that a summit with the South had long been under consideration in Pyongyang and that Kim Il Sung had been preparing for a full-scale summit meeting with Kim Young Sam on the very day he died.

After the June summit, South Korea and the world were treated to a rapid, almost dizzying series of developments on the divided peninsula. Before the end of year, the two Koreas held four rounds of formal ministerial talks to authorize a wide range of cooperative activities, and aides agreed to four North-South pacts to encourage trade and investment. Kim Jong Il invited forty-six top executives of the South Korean media to Pyongyang and opened himself to a wide range of questions. Two sets of emotional meetings temporarily reuniting 100 families on each side were held, and more were scheduled, along with the first exchanges of mail between separated families. The DPRK defense minister came south to meet his opposite number, authorizing lower-level military working groups from the two opposing armies. The two sides agreed on plans to repair and reconnect the severed North-South railroad that ran through the peninsula until the outbreak of the Korean War, and to build a highway alongside the tracks to facilitate commerce and other exchanges through the heavily fortified DMZ. Harsh propaganda broadcasts against each other were toned down or stopped. In one of the most memorable moments of the 2000 Sydney Olympics, the athletes of North and South Korea marched together under a single peninsular flag, in sharp contrast to their bitter disputes over the 1988 Seoul Olympics. Hyundai and North Korea agreed to begin construction of a massive industrial park and export-processing zone at Kaesong, close to the northern edge of the DMZ, initially to involve hundreds of South Korean companies employing tens of thousands, eventually hundreds of thousands, of North Korean workers. The Hyundai-sponsored tourism to Diamond Mountain continued, although the losses on the tours and the company's overall economic difficulties cast a shadow over its continuing inter-Korean activities.

Many conservatives, who are powerful in the South, were uncomfortable with sudden warming and the rush of developments. After a period of muted criticism, the opposition Grand National Party began finding fault with Kim Dae Jung's policy, largely on the grounds of its lacking reciprocity for the South's concessions. Skeptics pointed out that despite symbolic acts, there had been no reduction in DPRK military forces or their potential threat to the South. As the ROK economy and stock market began to sink anew after the Pyongyang summit, disenchantment and impatience with the Northern policy mounted, although specific steps of DPRK cooperation continued to be applauded by the majority of the public. Even the awarding of the highly prized Nobel Peace Prize to President Kim in early December for his painstaking efforts at reconciliation with the North and his lifelong struggle for freedom and democracy provided only a temporary boost in Kim's popularity at home, while plaudits reverberated throughout the rest of the world.

In July, a month after the Pyongyang summit, North Korea joined its first regional security organization, the Asian Regional Forum sponsored by Southeast Asian nations. A month after that, it renewed its previous application for membership in its first international financial organization, the Asian Development Bank. Meanwhile, Kim Jong Il received Russian President Vladimir Putin, and prepared for his second journey in a year to meet Chinese leaders. In September his Foreign Ministry sent letters to the European Union and every European country proposing the opening of relations. Just prior to the summit, the DPRK established diplomatic relations with Italy and Australia. Between the summit and early 2001, North Korea established diplomatic relations with the Philippines, Great Britain, the Netherlands, Belgium, Canada, Spain, and Germany, and moved toward opening relations with several others. The whirlwind of diplomatic activity on the part of previously reclusive North Korea was startling.

## ENGAGING THE UNITED STATES

While the remarkable opening to the South was taking place, North Korea's engagement with the United States was marking time. From September 1999 to September 2000, U.S. and North Korean diplomats met in formal bilateral sessions five times in Berlin, Rome, and New York City, with only marginal progress on the issues before them. Additional meetings on such issues as missiles, terrorism, and the search for Americans missing in action from the Korean War also made little progress.

On September 27, 2000, North Korean Vice Foreign Minister Kim Gye Gwan sat down with Ambassador Charles Kartman, the chief U.S. negotiator with Pyongyang, in the twelfth-floor conference room of the U.S. Mission to the United Nations to begin a new round of comprehensive talks on issues between the two governments. Before bargaining could begin, however, Kim announced that Pyongyang at last was ready to send to Washington the special envoy it had long promised to advance the relationship. To the surprise of the Americans, he revealed that the visitor would be Vice Marshal Jo

Myong Rok, first vice chairman under Kim Jong Il of the ruling National Defense Commission and by most calculations the second most important person in the country. Moreover, Pyongyang proposed to send him right away. The dates for his visit were quickly fixed at October 9–12, less than two weeks away. The selection of such a high-level emissary—and especially a top-level military figure—suggested that Kim Jong Il was prepared to deal with Washington's central concerns, which were security issues.

After an overnight stopover in northern California, which was hosted by William Perry and included visits to Silicon Valley high-technology firms, Jo and his party, which included the highly trusted First Deputy Foreign Minister Kang Sok Ju, arrived in Washington on October 9. As a young man, Jo had been a minor aide to Kim Il Sung at the end of World War II and had cradled the toddler Kim Jong Il in his arms. A military pilot, he became commander of the DPRK Air Force around 1980. After the death of Kim Il Sung in 1994, he began a meteoric rise from 89th on the 273-man funeral committee to 11th among leaders of the party, the government, and the military in 1996, and second only to Kim Jong Il as first vice chairman of the ruling National Defense Commission in 1998. Although a military professional with a soldier's bearing who displayed little interest in politics, Jo was also chief of the General Political Department of the Korean People's Army, and was therefore in position as the senior political commissar of the armed forces to protect the interests of Kim Jong Il.

Jo appeared that morning in a conservative dark-blue suit at the State Department to meet Secretary Albright, but changed to his marshal's uniform, replete with row after row of campaign ribbons and decorations, for his meeting with President Clinton. In the Oval Office, he handed Clinton a letter from Kim Jong Il and then verbally stated his breathtaking objective: to invite Clinton to visit Pyongyang to iron out differences between the two governments in personal conversation with the North Korean leader. Tipped off by Albright, Clinton explained it would be impossible for him to undertake such a visit without thorough preparations and preliminary agreements. He proposed to send Albright first to accomplish these aims, with the hope he would be able to follow before he left office on January 20, only three months away.

While Jo toured the Air and Space Museum and other sights of Washington, Kang Sok Ju provided Wendy Sherman and several other officials with advance indications of the extraordinary compromises Kim Jong Il had in mind. Without firmly committing his leader, Kang suggested that North Korea was ready to contemplate steps down a positive path along the lines proposed by Perry in Pyongyang seventeen months earlier: an end to exports of ballistic missiles, technology, and equipment on negotiable terms of compensation, which might be food or other necessities rather than cash; termination of development, testing, production, and deployment of long-range ballistic missiles; potential stationing of U.S. military forces on the Korean peninsula on a long-term basis; and establishment of full diplomatic relations between the United States and the DPRK.

Under pressure of time to follow up, Secretary Albright flew into Pyongyang on October 23, only eleven days after Jo and Kang had left Washington. Hosting Albright the first night of her visit at a mass display of choreography and chorus by 100,000 people in a Pyongyang sports stadium—a repeat of a spectacle previously staged to celebrate the fifty-fifth anniversary of the founding of the Workers Party—Kim pointed to the depiction on a giant screen of the Taep'o-dong launch of August 1998, which had so unnerved Japan and worried the United States. He quipped to the U.S. visitor that this had been the first North Korean satellite launch—and that it would be the last.

Born in Czechoslovakia, the daughter of a diplomat, Madeleine Albright had spent much of her life studying communism and had been in nearly every other communist country. She found Pyongyang "not an unattractive place" given the heroic architecture, but was surprised by the lack of interest shown by the population in her entourage. Her greatest surprise was Kim Jong Il himself, with whom she had lengthy conversations. Despite his reputation as a strange and reclusive person she found him striving to be an affable, normal leader, even though it was clear that the adulation for him was extreme and that he was in complete control.

In their initial business session, Kim volunteered that he was prepared to give up further production and deployment of his long-range missiles. He also began to define what a ban on missile sales abroad might mean, including contracts not yet fulfilled, and made it clear that North Korea would accept such items as food, clothing, and energy instead of money to compensate for the sales it would lose.

In their next session, Albright presented to Kim, who was accompanied only by Kang and an interpreter, a list of missile-related questions the U.S. team had given to North Korean experts several hours earlier. After she commented that some of the questions were technical and might require study, Kim picked up the list and began immediately to provide answers one by one without advice or further study, in what Albright later called a "quite stunning" feat, which could only be performed by a leader with absolute authority. He agreed to ban future production and deployment of all ballistic missiles with a range exceeding 500 kilometers (310 miles), although he did not specify a payload weight limit or what would be done with missiles already produced. Such a range limit would preclude the Taep'o-dong I, which had been test-launched in 1998, as well as its reported intercontinental successor, Taep'o-dong II, which was believed to be capable of reaching the U.S. mainland, and which was among the principal motivations for the proposed U.S. national missile-defense plan. A 500-kilometer limit would also encompass the Nodong missiles, with a range of about 1,300 kilometers (807 miles), which had been a principal threat to Japan for several years. Under questioning by Albright, Kim accepted the need for verification of compliance with the missile agreements, but he also said that he could not accept "intrusive verification" because North Korea was neither an outlaw state nor a defendant on trial. Extensive progress had been made, but many details remained to be negotiated.

As partial compensation for the limits on his domestic missile programs, Kim proposed to Albright that other nations launch three or four North Korean scientific satellites per year into outer space, since the DPRK would no longer possess the rockets to do so itself. Such a possibility had been raised in general terms by U.S. negotiator Robert Einhorn in the bilateral missile talks a month after the August

1998 test, and also by Perry in his Pyongyang visit the following year. Kim Jong Il had first expressed interest in the idea during the visit of Russian President Vladimir Putin in July 2000, in a remark that Putin was quick to pass on to Clinton and other world leaders and that quickly became the subject of public speculation.

The most important compensation, it was clear, would be the visit to North Korea of the president of the United States, which in its view would end its pariah status and be tangible acceptance of its legitimacy and sovereignty for all the world to see. Even more than economic or other benefits, this had been the central objective of North Korea, especially since the collapse of the Soviet Union. The 1993 Joint Declaration with the United States, including its "assurances against the threat and use of force" and its "mutual respect for each other's sovereignty, and non-interference in each other's internal affairs" had been a key factor in persuading North Korea not to withdraw from the Non-Proliferation Treaty [see pp. 285–86]. The Agreed Framework of 1994, which specifically endorsed the earlier declaration, created the first nonhostile relationship between the two countries and was instrumental in ending the nuclear crisis [see pp. 356–58]. William Perry's statements of U.S. acceptance of North Korea had been among the most important aspects of his proposals. Most recently, a U.S.-DPRK joint communiqué issued on October 12 at the conclusion of Vice Marshal Jo's visit to Washington declared that "neither government would have hostile intent toward the other" and "reaffirmed that their relations should be based on the principles of respect for each other's sovereignty and non-interference in each other's internal affairs." All these were commitments that Pyongyang took seriously (perhaps more seriously than the Americans who drafted them) but still they were mere words. From Pyongyang's standpoint, the presence of a U.S. president on its soil would go far beyond words to create a new fact of great importance.

Until the events of October, virtually no progress had been made in six years of talks about curbing North Korea's missiles. Suddenly the prospect of nearly limitless agreement had opened up at the eleventh hour of the Clinton administration, with only two weeks to go before the election of a new President and less than three months before Clinton would leave office. Although many concessions and compromises had been outlined by Kim Jong Il, most details remained to be worked out. As Albright knew from watching decades of U.S.-Soviet arms control negotiations, the devil is in the details, especially in such matters as limitations on weapons and the verification thereof. Among details to be ironed out were terms of compensation by the United States and other nations, precisely which weapons would be covered, what would happen to missiles already produced or deployed, and the whole issue of verification.

It was clear that Clinton could neither sign nor endorse with his presence any vague or loosely worded agreement on such weighty matters; the signing of any agreement in North Korea, particularly in the final days of his presidency, would carry an additional political burden. Time was of the essence if a deal was to be struck. Albright and Kim agreed to send missile negotiators to Kuala Lumpur seven days later to discuss the details, with no expectation they would be able to settle the outstanding issues. The plan was for State Department Counselor Wendy Sherman, accompanied by an interagency team, to negotiate further in Pyongyang as the prelude to a presidential visit. In Seoul, Kim Dae Jung strongly endorsed the idea of a Clinton trip to Pyongyang, but many experts in Washington told Albright the time was too short and the gamble too great.

It was not to be. Instead of learning the identity of the new president a few hours after the polls closed on November 7, the disputed election dragged on for five weeks in the state of Florida, and the attitude of Governor George W. Bush toward such an accord with North Korea was unknown. In the meantime, serious violence had erupted between Israelis and Palestinians in the Middle East, creating the possibility of an emergency trip by Clinton to attempt to mediate. On the final weekend before the New Year of 2001, the State Department notified North Korea that Sherman would not be coming to try to close the deal, as it was now impossible for the outgoing U.S. president to travel to Pyongyang. Clinton telephoned Kim Dae Jung in Seoul to break the news, and the State Department notified all the other countries that had participated in the effort to capitalize on the dramatic opening in North Korea.

North Korean diplomats in New York expressed disappointment at the news, and said a great opportunity had been missed. Shortly before turning over her office to a new administration, Wendy Sherman received a New Year's card postmarked Pyongyang from Kang Sok Ju. It was the first such missive she had ever received from North Korea, and she took it as a positive sign.

On January 20, as Bill Clinton was turning over the U.S. presidency to George W. Bush, Kim Jong Il was ending a six-day visit to China, his second in less than a year, during which he visited the Shanghai stock market and a General Motors joint-venture plant making Buicks in China's largest city. The bustling Shanghai Kim experienced, with its towering skyscrapers and torrid industrial pace, was a far cry from the city he had seen during his only previous visit there in 1983, near the start of China's market-oriented reforms. Beijing's Foreign Ministry spokesman said the North Korean leader praised what had been accomplished by policies of economic reform and opening up. At the dawn of 2001 there was widespread hope that Kim Jong Il would steer his country in the same direction.

AFTERWORD

$A$ t the beginning of the twenty-first century, the struggle on the Korean peninsula remains unresolved, yet at this writing, the two Koreas appear once again to be on the verge of change. In the year 2000, South Korean President Kim Dae Jung's persistent and unwavering overtures to the North, combined with new policies of North Korea's leader, Kim Jong Il, produced the first peninsular summit meeting in the history of the two states, followed by substantial interaction in a variety of fields. In political terms, this change was the most significant since the Korean War half a century ago. If sustained, the surprising engagement has the capability of inaugurating a fundamentally new era in Korea and Northeast Asia.

It seems clear to me the two sides have reached a historical turning point in their relations, but it is not possible to forecast with any assurance the nature or even the direction of further change, whether toward greater cooperation or intensified hostility. I believe, however, that the future of their relationship is likely to be different from that of the past. To a greater degree than before, the two Koreas appear to have taken their fate into their own hands.

Nonetheless, the impact of the outside powers continues to be extensive. With the end of the cold war, the relationships among Russia, China, Japan, and the United States have been realigned, and their objectives on the Korean peninsula have shifted from furtherance of the status quo to more complex and flexible notions of national interest. The influence of Japan, although substantial, is less formidable today than in the pre–World War II era. Post-communist Russia has, probably only temporarily, lost much of its clout. China remains a vitally important factor in the calculus of both North and South, due to its proximity and its rising power. It kept North Korea on life support with food and fuel in its hour of peril, and is now providing a crucial connection in the DPRK's quest for economic renewal. China continues to exert a powerful influence on the future of the ROK.

The United States, however, continues to be the most important outside power in Korean affairs, maintaining a formidable troop presence on the peninsula, exerting a major influence on South Korean political and economic life, and continuing to be the most important negotiating target for North Korea. Yet while the United States has a large stake in the future of the peninsula, the uncertain nature of its policies toward the DPRK has diminished its effectiveness as the two Koreas move into a new relationship.

When I finished the first edition of this book in 1997, it seemed to me that the North Korean regime was unlikely to survive in its existing form without major changes, which I did not see as likely. Today, in the new century, Kim Jong Il has emerged from the shadows to show himself to be a more able and more flexible leader than he was in the first years after his father's death. He has done much more, more quickly and more smoothly, to take advantage of his opportunities than anyone had guessed. The prospects for survival of the DPRK appear to have improved, but they remain guarded due to its economic collapse, from which a return to health is problematic.

The experiences of former communist states in the post–cold war era suggest it is exceedingly difficult, although not impossible, to make the change from a centrally directed economy to some form of a market economy, even a guided market economy, which can thrive in the contemporary world. China has done it, although daunting problems remain, but other states have done less well. It is equally difficult, if not even more difficult, to convert a dictatorship to a stable political system resting on the foundation of the consent of the governed. Historically, North Korea is an extremely negative example, in both economic and political realms.

South Korea, despite many unresolved problems, continues to have a bright future at the dawn of the new century. Its industrious, well-educated people, who have been open to the rest of the world while North Korea has remained closed, have thrown off the authoritarian rule of military-led regimes and created a fractious but effective democracy. In spite of economic difficulties, the South continues to be a bustling factory producing a substantial portion of the world's ships, automobiles, electronics, and other goods, lifting most of its people to a living standard far above their previous bare-subsistence level. Among the many uncertainties of the peninsula's next stage is how the South will be affected by new decisions in the North. As of now, Seoul has opted decisively for cooperation rather than confrontation with Pyongyang in an effort to avoid a crisis of any sort.

While much has changed on the peninsula in the period covered by this account, one thing that will never change is its geography. Korea sits at the vital center of Northeast Asia, one of the world's most strategically important and dynamic regions. It is surrounded by three great powers, China, Japan, and Russia. No longer a passive factor in regional and world affairs, Koreans north and south will have an important impact on their neighbors and on the international scene in the years ahead. Whatever the future holds will likely develop with high drama, intense emotion, and powerful consequences. Hold on to your hats. Korea is a land of surprises.

# PRINCIPAL KOREAN FIGURES IN THE TEXT

## DEMOCRATIC PEOPLE'S REPUBLIC OF KOREA (NORTH KOREA)

Han Se Hae, Workers Party official and secret emissary to the ROK

Ho Dam, foreign minister and secret emissary to the ROK

Hwang Jang Yop, Workers Party secretary for international affairs and *juche* theoretician; defected to the ROK in 1997

Jo Myong Rok, vice marshal and first vice chairman of the National Defense Commission

Kang Sok Ju, deputy foreign minister and chief nuclear negotiator with the United States

Kim Gye Gwan, vice foreign minister and deputy negotiator with the United States

Kim Hyon Hui, DPRK agent; bomber of Korean Air Lines flight 858; incarcerated and pardoned in the ROK

Kim Il Sung, leader of the Workers Party; prime minister, later president of the DPRK

Kim Jong Il, eldest son of Kim Il Sung; leader of the DPRK following his father's death

Kim Yong Nam, deputy prime minister and foreign minister of the DPRK, later chairman of Supreme Peoples Assembly and nominal head of state

Kim Yong Sun, Workers Party secretary and head of the DPRK delegation in 1992 talks with the United States

Yun Ki Bok, Workers Party official; political adviser to the DPRK delegation to the Red Cross talks; secret emissary to the ROK

## REPUBLIC OF KOREA (SOUTH KOREA)

Choi Kyu Ha, prime minister of the ROK; briefly president after death of Park Chung Hee

Chun Doo Hwan, leader of the 1979 military takeover; president of the ROK

Chung Ju Yung, chairman of the Hyundai conglomerate; chairman of the campaign committee to win the Seoul Olympic games; presidential candidate in 1992

Gong Ro Myung, foreign minister of the ROK

Han Sung Joo, foreign minister of the ROK

Kim Chong Whi, national security assistant to President Roh Tae Woo

Kim Dae Jung, opposition political leader and presidential candidate in 1971, 1987, 1992, 1997; popularly elected president, 1997.

Kim Jae Kyu, director of KCIA; assassin of President Park Chung Hee

Kim Jong Pil, prime minister of the ROK; presidential candidate in 1987

Kim Woo Choong, chairman of the Daewoo conglomerate; unofficial envoy abroad and to the DPRK

Kim Young Sam, opposition political leader, later government party leader; popularly elected president in 1992

Lee Hu Rak, director of the KCIA

Lee Yon Kil, businessman and anti-communist activist who arranged the defection of Hwang Jang Yop from North Korea.

Lim Dong Won, senior adviser to President Kim Dae Jong on North-South affairs; secret emissary to DPRK in May 2000.

Park Chul Un, presidential staff and intelligence official; ROK secret emissary to the DPRK

Park Chung Hee, leader of the 1961 military coup; later president of the ROK

Roh Tae Woo, division commander in 1979 military takeover; popularly elected president in 1987

Sohn Jang Nae, KCIA minister in the ROK embassy, Washington; deputy director of the KCIA in Seoul

Yoo Chong Ha, national security assistant to President Kim Young Sam; later ROK foreign minister

## KOREANS IN JAPAN

Mun Se Kwang, attempted assassin of ROK president Park; killer of Yook Young Soo (Mrs. Park)

# ACKNOWLEDGMENTS

A great many people and institutions of many nationalities and points of view contributed to the research and writing of this book. I conducted more than 450 interviews in South and North Korea, the United States, China, Japan, Russia, Germany, and Austria in the course of the four years I was working on it. I was also aided immeasurably by documentary material from American, Russian, and East German archives, as well as journalistic and scholarly articles and books. All those who contributed, in large ways and small, have my thanks.

I am particularly grateful to Johns Hopkins University's Paul H. Nitze School of Advanced International Studies (SAIS), which accorded me a convenient and prestigious scholarly perch after my retirement from *The Washington Post* and which sponsored the book. I am also very grateful to the Rockefeller Brothers Fund, New York, and the Korea Foundation, Seoul, for grants that supported my extensive travel and research. I wish to thank SAIS students Narushige Michishita and Choo Yong Shik, who were my research assistants.

It was my good fortune that Carter Eckert, director of the Korean studies program at Harvard University, was on a fellowship in Washington during the final stages of my writing. He gave generously of his time and suggestions. A number of present and former officials of the United States and the ROK governments and personal friends also offered valuable comments on various parts of the manuscript.

I wish to thank The National Security Archive, Washington, for assisting my Freedom of Information Act (FOIA) requests and providing materials obtained by other researchers; the FOIA staff of the Department of State for processing my requests; the Gerald Ford Presidential Library, particularly archivist Karen Holzhausen, and the Jimmy Carter Presidential Library, particularly Assistant Director Martin Elzy and archivist James Yancey, for identifying and helping to declassify valuable documentation; the FOIA staff of the Eighth Army, Korea, for declassifying the intelligence portions of its command histories for 1972–87; Jim Mann of *The Los Angeles Times* for providing materials on U.S.-China diplomacy affecting Korea; and Tim Shorrock of the *Journal of Commerce* for sharing the extensive material he has obtained under FOIA.

*Joong-ang Ilbo*, one of South Korea's leading newspapers and the publisher of the Korean edition of this book, graciously provided many of the photographs.

I am very grateful to Mark B. M. Suh of the Free University of Berlin for obtaining important documents from the archives of the former East German Communist Party, the Socialist Unity Party (SED), including transcripts of meetings of East German leader Eric Honecker with Kim Il Sung and diplomatic dispatches from the East German embassy in Pyongyang.

In Seoul, former ambassador to the United States Kim Kyung Won accepted me as a guest scholar at the Institute of Social Sciences, which greatly facilitated my interviews there. I am grateful to him and his efficient secretary, Mrs. Park Soon Rye. I also appreciate the work of the Korean Overseas Information Service, Seoul, especially Suh Sang Myun, in arranging interviews with government officials.

My South Korean journalist friends, especially Kim Yong Hie and Kim Kun Jin of *Joong-ang Ilbo*, Cho Kap Che and Kim Dae Joong of *Chosun Ilbo*, Shim Jae Hoon of the *Far Eastern Economic Review*, and Lee Keum Hyun, special correspondent of *The Washington Post*, were especially helpful. Sam Jameson, the longtime Tokyo correspondent of *The Los Angeles Times*, now an independent journalist and scholar in Japan, provided information and suggestions.

My 1991 visit to North Korea was as a *Washington Post* diplomatic correspondent. My return visit in 1995 was under the sponsorship of George Washington University's Sigur Center for East Asian Studies, then headed by Young C. Kim, to whom I am grateful. I also wish to express appreciation to officials of the DPRK Mission to the United Nations for many courtesies, including providing me with copies of the works of President Kim Il Sung from 1965 to 1983.

In Beijing my 1993 research trip was sponsored by the Chinese Academy of Social Sciences, which also provided introductions and translating assistance, for which I am grateful.

My research and interviewing in Moscow was facilitated by the Moscow Bureau of *The Washington Post*, which generously treated me as a colleague even though I had retired. Anatoly Chernyayev and Pavel Palazchenko, who continue as aides to Mikhail Gorbachev, helped in obtaining materials from the Gorbachev archive.

David Kyd, the public information officer of the International Atomic Energy Agency, Vienna, provided information and arranged interviews for me there.

I wish to thank former president Jimmy Carter for his written responses to my questions about Korea policy in his administration, and especially for assistance in dealing with his 1994 mission to Pyongyang. Marion Creekmore and Dick Christenson, who accompanied him to North Korea, also helped me.

In Japan, Izumi Hajime of Shizuoka University was particularly helpful in providing insights and materials about the DPRK, on which he is a leading expert.

Among the many persons who agreed to interviews, I wish especially to thank


## IN THE UNITED STATES:

Former secretaries of state Cyrus Vance and George Shultz; former undersecretaries of state Michael Armacost, Robert Zoellick, Arnold Kanter, and Frank Wisner; former assistant secretaries of state for East Asian and Pacific affairs Marshall Green, Richard Holbrooke, Paul Wolfowitz, the late Gaston Sigur, Richard Solomon, and William Clark, as well as Winston Lord, who was assistant secretary during my research; former deputy assistant secretaries of state

Robert Oakley and Thomas Hubbard and the current holder of the post, Charles Kartman; former chief U.S. Korea coordinator and negotiator Robert Gallucci and his senior deputy, Gary Samore; former Korea country directors Robert Rich, Harry Dunlop, Spence Richardson, David E. Brown, and David G. Brown, and the current country director, Mark Minton.

At the Pentagon, former secretaries of defense James Schlesinger, Donald Rumsfeld, and Harold Brown, as well as William Perry, who held the post during my research; Morton Abramowitz; Admiral William Pendley; Captain Thomas Flanigan; and Mr. Wally Knowles.

At the White House, former national security advisers Zbigniew Brzezinski, Richard Allen, and Brent Scowcroft, as well as Anthony Lake, who held the post during my research; former National Security Council staff members William Hyland, Nick Platt, Jim Kelly, Doug Paal, Torkel Patterson, Kent Wiedemann, Stanley Roth, and Daniel Poneman.

In the intelligence community, former CIA director Robert Gates; the expert North Korea watchers in the State Department's Bureau of Intelligence and Research, Robert Carlin, Kenneth Quinones, and John Merrill, as well as nuclear expert Steve Fleischmann; former national intelligence officers Evelyn Colbert, John Despres, Nathanial Thayer, Carl Ford, and Ezra Vogel; Morgan Clippinger and other Korea experts of the Central Intelligence Agency; and former U.S. intelligence officials John Armstrong and the late Jim Hausman.

Former congressman Stephen Solarz.

From the U.S. embassy, Seoul, former U.S. ambassadors to the ROK William Gleysteen, Richard Walker, James Lilley, and Donald Gregg, as well as James Laney, who was U.S. ambassador during the period of my research; former deputy chiefs of mission Francis Underhill, Richard Ericson, Raymond Burkhardt, and Dick Christenson; former U.S. embassy political counselors Paul Cleveland and Daniel Russel; and former military attaché Jim Young.

In the U.S. Command, Korea, former commanders-in-chief Generals John Wickham, Robert Sennewald, Robert RisCassi, Gary

Luck, and current CINC General John Tilelli; Lieutenant General Howell Estes; retired Lieutenant Generals James Hollingsworth and John Cushman; special assistant to the USFK commander Stephen Bradner; USFK historian Major Thomas Ryan; former U.S. representative to the Military Armistice Commission (MAC) Jimmy Lee; former MAC secretary Colonel Forrest Chilton; public information officer Jim Coles and his predecessor Billy Fullerton.

Among Korea experts in the United States, Peter Hayes of the Nautilus Institute; nuclear weapons expert Bill Arkin; Bruce Cumings of Northwestern University; Joseph Ha of Lewis and Clark College; Dae-Sook Suh of the University of Hawaii; Charles Armstrong, then of Princeton University; Han S. Park of the University of Georgia; Edward Olsen of the Naval Postgraduate School; Manwoo Lee of Millersville University; and Sanghyun Yoon of George Washington University.

Also Larry Niksch and Rinn Sup Shinn of the Congressional Research Service; Tony Namkung of the Atlantic Council; Selig Harrison and Leonard Spector of the Carnegie Endowment for International Peace; Ralph Clough of SAIS; Daryl Plunk of the Heritage Foundation; Michael O'Hanlon of the Brookings Institution; Scott Snyder of the U.S. Institute of Peace; William Taylor of the Center for Strategic and International Studies; Chen You Wei; Norm Levin and Kongdan (Katy) Oh of the Rand Corporation; David Albright; Steve Linton and Robert Manning of the Progressive Policy Institute.

Also, *New York Times* correspondent Michael Gordon and managing editor Josette Shiner of *The Washington Times*.

## IN SOUTH KOREA:

President Kim Young Sam and former presidents Choi Kyu Ha and Roh Tae Woo; Blue House national security advisers Chung Jung Uk and Ban Ki Mun; former presidential press secretaries Kim Seong Jin and Kim Sung Ik; former Blue House economic advisers Oh Won Chol, Kim Ki Whan, and Kim Jong In; former spokesman Kim Hak Joon.

Former prime ministers Lho Shin Yang, Roh Jae Bong, and Lee Hong Koo; Deputy Prime Minister Kwon O-Kie and former DPMs Choi Yong Chol and Han Wan Sang.

Former ministers of foreign affairs Choi Kwang Su, Choi Ho Joong, Lee Sang Ok, Han Sung Joo, Gong Ro Myung; Foreign Minister Yoo Chong Ha; former deputy foreign minister Park Soo Kil; former minister of home affairs Chung Ho Young; former minister of culture and information Lee Kyu Hyun; former minister of science and technology Kim Jin Hyon; former chief of protocol Lee Byung Gi.

Former ROK ambassadors to the United States Kim Kyong Won, Hyun Hong Choo, and Han Seung Soo and the current ambassador, Park Kun Woo; ROK ambassador to the United Nations (and currently foreign minister) Yoo Chong Ha; ROK ambassadors to China Roh Jae Won and Whang Byong Tae; unofficial negotiator with China Lee Soon Sok; ROK ambassador to Russia Kim Suk Kyu.

Former minister of defense Choo Yong Bok; Lieutenant General Park Young Ok, assistant minister of defense; Retired General Kim Choi Chang; Han Yong Sup of the National Defense University.

Former directors of the Agency for National Security Planning Suh Dong Kwon and Kim Deok; Deputy NSP director Rhee Byong Ho and former deputy director Sohn Jang Nae; former NSP special assistant (now National Assembly member) Lee Dong Bok; former KCIA officials Kang In Duk and Chung Hong Jin.

Former North-South negotiator Lim Dong Won; former delegate to the North-South talks Chung Hee Kyung and former North-South spokesman Chung Choo Hyun; Kim Dal Sul, of the North-South dialogue office; Kil Jeong Woo and Ahn Inhay of the Research Institute on National Reunification; Yu Suk Ryul and Kim Choong Nam of the Institute of Foreign Affairs and National Security; former Vice Minister of Unification Song Yong Dae.

Chung Ju Yung, founder and honorary chairman of the Hyundai group, and Kim Woo Choong, founder and chairman of the Daewoo group.

Kim Dae Jung, opposition political leader; members of the National Assembly Chung Jey Moon, Hur Hwa Pyung, Kang Sin Ok,

Kim Yoon Hwan, Lee Boo Young, Park Kye Dong, and Park Se Jik.

North Korean defectors Koh Young Hwan, Kim Hyun Hui, Kang Myung Do, and Colonel Choi Ju Hwal.

Ahn Byung Joon of Yonsei University and Rhee Sang Woo of Sogang University.

Kim Jin, reporter of *Joong-ang Ilbo*, Kim Yong Sam of *Monthly Chosun*, and Songhee Stella Kim of *Time*.

I also wish to thank Russian diplomats in Seoul, Ambassador Georgi Kunaidze and Minister Georgi Toloraya; Siegfried Scheibe, former East German economic minister in the DPRK, now in the German Chamber of Commerce, Seoul; and David Steinberg, the representative in Seoul of the Asia Foundation.

## IN NORTH KOREA:

I met Deputy Prime Minister and Foreign Minister Kim Yong Nam; Workers Party secretary Kim Yong Sun; Vice Minister of External Economic Affairs Kim Jong U; and other officials during my January 1995 trip. I wish to acknowledge the assistance of the Institute of Disarmament and Peace, Pyongyang, which made the arrangements and was the host of this visit.

## IN CHINA:

Wu Dawei, deputy director of Asian Affairs, Li Bing of the Ministry of Foreign Affairs, and former Foreign Ministry official Li Xiang Wei.

Tao Bing Wei, a leading Chinese expert on Korea, now a senior fellow at the China Institute of International Studies; Pu Shan of the Chinese Academy of Social Sciences; Jin Zhen Ji of the Institute of Contemporary International Relations; Xu Man Zhang, former Chinese military attaché; and Colonel Shi Jin Kun of the Institute of International Strategic Studies.

At the Russian embassy, Beijing, Ambassador Igor Rogachev and Minister Sergei Goncharov.

Mike Chinoy, CNN correspondent, Beijing.

## IN RUSSIA:

Former president Mikhail Gorbachev; former national security adviser Anatoly Chernyayev; former foreign minister Alexander Bessmertnykh; former ambassador Anatoly Dobrynin; Sergei Tarasenko, former Foreign Ministry official; Vadim Tkachenko, former director of Korean affairs of the Central Committee of the CPSU; Igor Rakhmanin, former Asian affairs director of the Central Committee of the CPSU; Gorbachev aides Karen Brutents, Georgi Ostraumov, and Pavel Palazchenko.

Yevgeni Primakov, then chief of the Russian Foreign Intelligence Agency, now foreign minister; Deputy Foreign Minister Alexander Panov; Yevgeni Afanasyev, Valery Denisov, and Vladimir Rakhmanin of the Russian Foreign Ministry.

Mikhail Titerenko, director of the Institute of Far Eastern Studies, and Roald Seleviev of the Institute.

Vitaly Ignatenko, general director of ITAR-Tass news agency; Tass correspondent Vladimir Nadashkevich; journalists Yuri Sigov and Alexander Blatkovsky.

## IN JAPAN:

Kawashima Yutaka, director general of Asian Affairs, Ministry of Foreign Affairs; Okazaki Hisahiko, former Foreign Ministry official; Ambassador Endo Tetsuya, negotiator with North Korea; Takeuchi Yukio, deputy chief of mission, Washington.

Takemura Masayoshi, member of Japanese Diet.

Okonogi Masao of Keio University; Major General Tsukamoto Katsuichi of the Research Institute for Peace and Security.

## IN VIENNA:

Director General Hans Blix of the International Atomic Energy Agency; Dmitri Perricos, director of East Asian safeguards operations; Olli Heinonen, chief inspector for North Korea; Willy Theis, former chief inspector for North Korea.

John Ritch, U.S. ambassador to international organizations; Mike Lawrence and Marvin Peterson, U.S. mission officials.

## IN GERMANY:

Hans Maretzki, former ambassador of the GDR to North Korea; Gunter Unterbeck, former GDR diplomat; Ann-Katrin Becker, former correspondent of the GDR news agency in Beijing.

I also am grateful to several people whose insights were important but who asked that their names not be used, even in acknowledgment, and quite a few people who took the trouble to read and correct major chunks of the manuscript. You know who you are, and you have my thanks.

Finally, I would like to thank those whose work was essential to the writing and editing of this book: Tong Kim, for translations from Korean; Mary Drake, for transcription of interviews; Zhaojin Ji, the secretary of the SAIS Asia program; Joy Harris, my literary agent; Bill Patrick, formerly of Addison-Wesley, who saw the merit in the book, and his colleague Sharon Broll, a wonderful editor who found ways to make it better; and my wife, Laura, my own best editor and inspiration.

# NOTES AND SOURCES

According to an entry in the spiral-bound notebooks I kept as a journal, I first began thinking about a book on Korea in 1988, about the same time I began work on *The Turn*, my history of U.S.-Soviet relations at the end of the cold war. I realized even in that early note that this book would have to be a postretirement project, since it would take much time and travel that would be incompatible with full-time work for *The Washington Post*. While there were a few interviews earlier, work began seriously after my retirement in May 1993. Over the next four years, I conducted more than 450 interviews in a variety of countries, consulted books and archives, and obtained new information under the Freedom of Information Act. With a few confidential exceptions, the principal interviewees and sources of materials are mentioned in the Acknowledgments.

As in my earlier books, I am providing here information on the sources for *The Two Koreas*, except for those that were confidential or are well known to people in the field. In order to facilitate scholarly research, I deposited within the first half of 1998 copies of U.S. documents used in this book that were obtained under the Freedom of Information Act in the National Security Archive, an independent non-governmental research institute in Washington, where they will be available to any researcher.

The following abbreviations are used in the notes:

*Emb. cable:* Cable to the Department of State in Washington from the U.S. embassy in Seoul. Date and subject are given if available.

*DOS cable:* Cable from the Department of State in Washington to the U.S. embassy in Seoul. Date and subject are given if available.

*FBIS:* Foreign Broadcast Information Service, published by the U.S. government

*KH: The Korea Herald,* an English-language newspaper in Seoul

*KIS Works: Kim Il Sung Works* (Pyongyang: Foreign Languages Publishing House), in English.

*KT: The Korea Times,* an English-language newspaper in Seoul

*NYT: The New York Times*

*SED Archives:* Archives of the Socialist (Communist) Unity Party of the former East Germany, obtained in Berlin (in German)

*WP: The Washington Post*

*USFK Hist: U. S. Forces Korea /Eighth U.S. Army Annual Historical Reports,* the intelligence sections of which were declassified for me under the Freedom of Information Act. The year of the report quoted is given.

*US-PRC Chronology:* Richard H. Solomon, *US.-PRC Political Negotiations, 1967–1984: An Annotated Chronology* (Rand, 1985), secret (declassified 1994).

## CHAPTER 1: WHERE THE WILD BIRDS SING

DMZ setting, see Fran Kaliher of Two Harbors, Minn., research associate of International Crane Foundation; Yoon Moo Boo, "DMZ: Paradise for Migratory Birds," *Koreana* (Winter 1995); Jimmy Lee, interview, July 8, 1995.

*The Emergence of Two Koreas:* Historical details from Carter J. Eckert et al., *Korea Old and New: A History* (Ilchokak Publishers, Seoul, for the Korea Institute, Harvard University, 1990). Also, interviews with Eckert. For invasions and occupations, Donald S. Macdonald, *The Koreans*

(Westview, 1988), pp. 1–2. Stettinius's ignorance from Louis J. Halle, *The Cold War as History* (London: Chatto & Windus, 1967), p. 202n. The Whelan quote is from Richard Whelan, *Drawing the Line* (Little, Brown, 1990), p. 27. The Rusk quote is from Dean Rusk, *As I Saw It* (Penguin Books, 1990), p. 124. The Summers quote is from Summers telephone interview, Feb. 11, 1997. The Henderson quote is from Gregory Henderson's chapter in *Divided Nations in a Divided World* (David McKay, 1974), p. 43.

*War and Its Aftermath:* Kim Il Sung on not sleeping, Ciphered telegram from Shtykov to Vyshinsky, Jan. 19, 1950 in "Korea, 1949–50," *Cold War International History Project Bulletin* (Washington: Woodrow Wilson International Center for Scholars, Spring 1995), p. 8. For origins of Korean War, see especially Kathryn Weathersby's work for the Cold War International History Project. The casualty figures are from Whelan, *Drawing the Line*, p. 373. Kim Il Sung's secret emissary was Hwang Tae Sung; his mission was described by Chinese and Russian sources as well as by Lee Dong Bok, interview, July 15, 1993.

*The Origins of Negotiation:* For Kim Il Sung's presence in Beijing, see Henry Kissinger, *White House Years* (Little, Brown, 1979), p. 751. For Chinese military supply, see *USFK Hist. 1974*, secret (declassified 1994). Kim Seong Jin quote, Kim interview, Oct. 15, 1993. For Park remarks to correspondents, Son U Ryun, "Voice Testimony of Park Chung Hee," *Monthly Chosun* (Mar. 1993), in Korean.

For Park letter to Nixon, Theodore Eliot, "Reply to President Park Chung Hee's Letter on East Asian Problems," Department of State Memorandum, Nov. 4, 1971, secret (declassified 1978); "For Ambassador," Department of State Telegram (Dec. 13, 1971), secret (declassified, 1996); and "Seoul Receives Assurances from Nixon on China Talks," *NYT* Dec. 26, 1971. The Park quote on unprecedented peril is from Park Chung Hee, *Korea Reborn* (Prentice-Hall, 1979), p. 48.

For the secret plenum of the Workers Party, conversation of Hermann Axen (member of GDR Politburo) with DPRK ambassador Lee Chang Su (July 31, 1972), *SED Archives*. Henderson quote on KCIA is from Mark Clifford, *Troubled Tiger* (M.E. Sharpe, 1994), p. 85. Lee Hu Rak quotes are from Michael Keon, *Korean Phoenix* (Prentice-Hall International, 1977), pp. 129–130. This controversial book contains one of the few interviews with Lee on his Pyongyang mission. Lee was among a mere handful of Korean figures who declined to be interviewed for this book. On Lee Hu Rak's harrowing ride, see Kim Chung Shik, *Directors of KCIA,* vol. 1 (Dong-A Ilbo, 1992), in Korean.

*Kim Il Sung:* Separating fact from fiction about Kim's early life is a formidable task. I have relied primarily on the most authoritative biography in the West, Dae-Sook Suh's *Kim Il Sung: The North Korean Leader* (Columbia University Press, 1988). For Kim's Christian background, see Yong-ho Ch'oe, "Christian Background in the Early Life of Kim Il-Song," *Asian Survey* (Oct. 1986). For Kim's own account, see Kim Il Sung, *With the Century,* vol. 1 (Pyongyang: Foreign Languages Publishing House, 1992), pp. 105–107. Kim in Soviet uniform, Suh, *Kim Il Sung,* p. 60.

The Stalin quote on "young country, young leader" comes from U.S. expert John Merrill, who heard it from a Russian with extensive experience in Pyongyang. Medvedev on Kim as a "normal person" is from Vadim Medvedev, *Collapse* (Moscow: International Relations Publishing House, 1994), in Russian. For Kim's mansions and isolation from the people, see the memoir of Hans Maretzki (former East German ambassador to North Korea), *Kimism in North Korea* (Stuttgart: Anita Tykve Verlag, 1991), in German. The 1984 train procedure was told to me by a Soviet official who took part.

Special health arrangements for Kim in Germany, former East German diplomat, interview, June 10, 1994. The Rakhmanin quote is from Rakhmanin interview, Apr. 8, 1994. The Talleyrand quote is from Roald Seveliev (of the Institute of Far Eastern Studies, Moscow) interview, Apr. 8, 1994. On the early history of *juche,* see Michael Robinson, "National Identity and the Thought of Sin Ch'aeho: *Sadaejuui* and *Chuche* in History and Politics," *Journal of Korean Studies* (1984).

The Kim quote on "special emphasis" is from *KIS Works,* vol. 27, pp. 19–20. Han Park on *juche* is from his book *North Korea: Ideology, Politics, Economy* (Prentice-Hall, 1996), p. 10. On the 34,000 monuments, see Maretzki, *Kimism in North Korea.* The "cult of personality" quote is from Rakhmanin interview, Apr. 8, 1994. The Suh quote is from Suh, *Kim Il Sung,* pp. 314–315. South Korean visitor quotes, interview, Nov. 22, 1994.

Kim on the "situation at my fingertips," *KIS Works*, vol. 31, pp. 87–88. Kim to Solarz, transcript of Kim Il Sung–Solarz conversation, from the Jimmy Carter Library. On the ouster of high officials for new ideas, "Number One Taboo in Pyongyang: Challenging Kim's Authority," *Vantage Point* (Seoul, May 1995). Kim's words "said forever," former Communist diplomat, interview, June 10, 1994. On Kim's statue, Suh, *Kim Il Sung*, p. 316. Kim description from Harrison Salisbury, "North Korean Leader Bids U.S. Leave the South as Step to Peace," *NYT*, May 31, 1972.

*Conversations with the South*: For the Kim-Lee meeting, see the transcript published in *Monthly Joong-ang* (Mar. 1989), in Korean. Chong Hong Jin, who was present with Lee, told me in an interview (May 27, 1993) that it is essentially accurate. A North Korean version can be found in *KIS Works*, vol. 26, pp. 134ff. The story of twenty-one-year-old Poco Underhill is from his father in a telephone interview, Aug. 26, 1996. Ambassador Lee's presentation to the GDR, from conversation of Hermann Axen with Lee Chang Su (July 31, 1972), *SED Archives*. Kim Seong Jin's quotes on Park are from Kim interview, May 24, 1993.

## CHAPTER 2: THE END OF THE BEGINNING

On the Red Cross Exchange, the Chung quote is from Chung Hee Kyung interview, July 19, 1993. "Bringing all the tall buildings": This is one of the most oft-repeated anecdotes about the visit of the North Korean Red Cross delegation to Seoul and has been attributed to several different South Korean hosts. The Yun speech at the opening ceremony is from "Public 'Disappointed' in Propaganda," *KH* (Sept. 14, 1972), p. 14, and National Unification Board, ROK, *A White Paper on South-North Dialogue in Korea* (Seoul, 1982), p. 119. On the South Korean decision to televise the opening ceremony, Kim Seong Jin interview, Nov. 15, 1992; on intelligence management of South Korean protest, Chung Hee Kyung interview, July 19, 1993.

On the talks and meaningless agreement, National Unification Board, *White Paper on South-North Dialogue*, especially p. 119. On Park's views, Kim Seong Jin discussion, Nov. 15, 1992.

*Park Chung Hee*: For my interview with Park, see Don Oberdorfer, "Korea: Progress and Danger," *WP*, June 29, 1975. The story of Park's office safe is from a senior Korean diplomat who learned of it from a close aide to Park. On Park and the Yosu rebellion, James Hausman telephone interviews, Apr. 26, 1995 and Sept. 23, 1995. See also Allan R. Millett, "Captain James H. Hausman and the Formation of the Korean Army, 1945–50," unpublished paper from the Mershon Center, Ohio State University, p. 30. The embassy cable about Park is published in "Investigation of Korean-American Relations," *Appendices of the Report of the House Committee on International Relations,* Subcommittee on International Organizations, vol. 1 (Oct. 31, 1978), p. 64.

Military assessment of Park, *USFK Hist. 1975,* p. 47, confidential (declassified 1994). On Park's intelligence countermeasures, see No Chae Hyon, *Office of the Secretary of the Blue House,* vol. 2, (*Joong-ang Ilbo,* 1993), in Korean, p. 254. For the poll on Park's greatness, *Chosun Ilbo,* Mar. 5, 1995, in Korean. Park quote on "pilfered household," Frank Gibney, *Korea s Quiet Revolution* (Walker and Co., 1992), p. 50. On Park's plans and operations in the economic field, see the excellent book by Mark Clifford, *Troubled Tiger* (M.E. Sharpe, 1994), from which the quote from the first economic plan is taken. The same source is used for the ROK's Vietnam earnings (p. 57) and the Pohang steel mill (p. 67–75). Park as "orchestra conductor" quote, Michael Keon, *Korean Phoenix* (Prentice-Hall International, 1977), p. 79. The Kim quote on Park's economic choices is from Chung-yum Kim, *Policymaking on the Front Lines* (Washington, World Bank, 1994), p. 30.

On Park's honesty and modesty, Kim, *Policymaking on the Front Lines,* pp. 117–118, and an interview with Jim Kim, political writer for *Joong-ang Ilbo* and author of a book on Park, May 18, 1996. The Cho Soon quote is from his book *The Dynamics of Korean Economic Development* (Institute for International Economics, 1994), p. 180. The growth data are from Kihwan Kim and Danny M. Leipzinger, *Korea: A Case of Government-Led Development* (World Bank, 1993), p. 1. The income distribution data are from D. M. Leipziger, D. Dollar, A. F. Shorrocks, and S. Y. Song, *The Distribution of Income and Wealth in Korea* (World Bank, 1992), p. 7.

*Washington Blinks at Park s Coup:* On Habib and the *yushin* plan, *Emb. cable,* "ROKG Declaration of Martial Law and Plans for Fundamental Government Reform," Oct. 16, 1972, confidential (declassified 1996). On Habib's anger at lack of forewarning, Francis Underhill, telephone interview, July 29, 1996. Marshall Green quote, Green telephone interview, Aug. 13, 1996.

Habib's hands-off recommendation, *Emb. cable,* "Comment on Martial Law and Government Change in Korea," Oct. 16, 1972, secret (declassified 1996). Washington's reaction, *DOS cable,* Oct. 16, 1972, secret (declassified 1996). Habib's policy of disassociation, *Emb. cable,* "U.S. Response to Korean Constitutional Revision," Oct. 23, 1972, secret (declassified 1996). Washington's endorsement, *DOS cable,* "Ref Seoul 6119," Oct. 26, 1972, secret (declassified 1996). Nixon to Kim Jong Pil, Don Oberdorfer, "South Korean Abuses Tolerated," *WP,* May 19, 1976. The quote was supplied by Donald Ranard, then Korea country director, who obtained it from a White House participant.

*The Impact of Yushin:* On the harassment of Chang Chun Ha, see Don Oberdorfer, "Korea: The Silencing of Dissenters," *WP,* Dec. 31, 1972. Chang was the man referred to as "Mr. Lee." For his death, "Controversy over Dissident's Death Rekindled," *Newsreview,* Apr. 13, 1993. On the silencing of Korean press, see Don Oberdorfer, "The Korean Press," *WP,* Dec. 28, 1973.

On Donald Gregg's opposition to Lee Hu Rak, Gregg interview, Mar. 12, 1995. For country recognition data, see Samuel S. Kim, "North Korea and the United Nations," paper prepared for the 1996 Annual Conference of the International Council on Korean Studies, p. 31.

## CHAPTER 3: THE TROUBLE DEEPENS

This account of the assassination attempt on Park is based on my eyewitness recollection and several published accounts. The number of bullets fired and the issue of whose bullet killed the First Lady were extensively investigated by two of my colleagues who were also on the scene, Sam Jameson of *The Los Angeles Times* and Bruce Dunning of CBS News. They found many inconsistencies between the government's official account and their reporting but were unable to reach conclusive judgments. The Kim Seong Jin quote is from Kim interview, May 24, 1993. On the shoes and handbag (which I did not notice at the time), see Michael Keon, *Korean Phoenix* (Prentice-Hall, 1977), p. 199.

On students and Christians, see Koon Woo Nam, *South Korean Politics* (University Press of America, 1989), especially chap. 4. On the

Niedecker incident, Richard Ericson interview, Feb. 16, 1994, and Gregg interview, June 21, 1993. For Niedecker's account, memorandum from John E. Niedecker to General A. M. Haig Jr., July 29, 1974. Confidential (declassified 1997). It was also widely reported after the fact. For the intelligence assessment about student radicalism, *USFK Hist. 1974,* p. 37, confidential (declassified 1995).

*The Struggle with Japan:* Mun as a "jackal," interview with former Korean prosecutor, Oct. 23, 1992. On the plight of Koreans in Japan, see Don Oberdorfer, "An Assassin Comes 'Home' to Korea," *WP,* Sept. 3, 1974, my investigation of Mun Se Kwang's life and background in Osaka. The Chung Il Kwon quote is from Ericson interview, Feb. 16, 1994. Park's diary quotes from "Blue House Diary," *Minju Ilbo,* Nov. 24, 1989, in Korean, translation by Carter Eckert.

*The Underground War:* Material on the tunnels is based primarily on the tunnels sections of *USFK Hist. 1972–87,* which were declassified and released to me in 1995 under the Freedom of Information Act. See also Don Oberdorfer, "Korea's DMZ-Security Undermined?" *WP,* May 27, 1975. The "needle in haystack" quote is from *USFK Hist. 1979,* p. 44, secret (declassified 1995). For the psychics, see "US Spy Agencies Field Psychics to Pinpoint North Korean Tunnels under DMZ," *KT,* Dec. 2, 1995. Nathanial Thayer quote, Thayer interview, Aug. 1, 1995.

*Challenge from the North:* Retrospective U.S. military analysis, *USFK Hist. 1982,* p. 30, secret (declassified 1995). Chinese officer quote, Xu Xian Zhang interview, July 8, 1993. Gates on "black hole," interview, May 16, 1994. Gregg on intelligence failure, Gregg interview, Mar. 12, 1995. On JCS reduction of resources, see *USFK Hist. 1972,* p. 14, secret (declassified 1995).

Kim Il Sung on preparations for war, "Excerpts from Interview with North Korean Premier on Policy Toward the U.S.," *NYT,* May 31, 1972. 1974 U.S. intelligence estimate, *USFK Hist. 1974,* secret (declassified 1995). Hollingsworth section is based on a telephone interview with Hollingsworth, Aug. 26, 1995, as well as an interview with Gregg, June 21, 1993. See also John Saar, "The Army's Defiant Anachronism," *WP,* Feb. 15, 1976. NSC objections, Thomas J. Barnes, "Secretary Schlesinger's Discussions in Seoul," National Security Council Memorandum, Sept. 29, 1975, secret (declassified 1995).

For the U.S. Command's estimate of Soviet/Chinese intentions, *USFK Hist. 1974,* p. 21, secret (declassified 1995). For Kim Il Sung's speech, *FBIS, PRC International Affairs,* Apr. 21, 1975, p. A17. Kim had also used the formulation that there was nothing to lose but the DMZ on the eve of his Beijing journey, in a talk to the secretary of the Panama-Korea Association of Friendship and Culture. See *KIS Works,* vol. 30, p. 218. Chinese reaction, interview, former Chinese official, July 5, 1993. According to South Korean data, Chinese military assistance to North Korea diminished sharply following Kim's 1975 trip. On the Soviet reaction, Russian Foreign Ministry official, interview, Apr. 15, 1994. For Kim's roundabout flight avoiding Soviet air space, see Don Oberdorfer, "Korea: Progress and Danger," *WP,* June 29, 1975.

*Echoes of Saigon:* For Sneider on the review, *Emb. cable,* "Review of U.S. Policies toward Korea," Apr. 22, 1975, secret (declassified 1996). His more considered judgment, *Emb. cable,* "U.S. Policy towards Korea," June 24, 1975, secret (declassified 1996). On the NSC interpretation of Ford's promise and objections to Schlesinger's statements, see Thomas J. Barnes, "Secretary Schlesinger's Discussions in Seoul," National Security Council Memorandum, Nov. 29, 1975, secret (declassified 1995). For Schlesinger comments to Park, Memorandum of Conversation between President Park Chung Hee and Secretary of Defense James Schlesinger, Aug. 27, 1975, secret (declassified 1996).

For Park's actions in 1975, *USFK Hist. 1975,* p. 45, confidential (declassified 1995). For defense budget impact, *The Military Balance* (London: International Institute of Strategic Studies, 1975–76 through 1979–80). The South Korean military buildup data are from the Institute of International Strategic Studies' *Military Balance,* 1975–80.

*The South Korean Nuclear Weapons Program:* Oh Won Chol's comments, interview, June 24, 1996. See also his article, "Blood Battle between Park Chung Hee and Carter on Nuclear Development," *Shin Dong-A* (Nov. 1994), in Korean. See also Robert Gillette, "U.S. Squelched Apparent S. Korean A-Bomb Drive," *Los Angeles Times,* Nov. 4, 1978. For many years this well-researched article, based in part on congressional testimony, has been a key source on the South Korean nuclear program. On the South Korean reprocessing effort, the best source is Cho Kap Che,

"Nuclear Game on the Korean Peninsula," *Monthly Chosun* (June 1993), from which these details were taken. For the quote on "snapped into place," see Gillette, Los Angeles Times, Nov. 4, 1978 (as above). Cleveland quote from Cleveland interview, Mar. 8, 1994.

Embassy intelligence and Washington instructions, *DOS cable* "ROK Plans to Develop Nuclear Weapons and Missiles," Mar. 4, 1975, secret/nodis (declassified 1997).

The French ambassador's quote is from Steve Weissman and Herbert Krosney, *The Islamic Bomb* (Times Books, 1981), p. 252. Park's quote on nuclear capability is from Rowland Evans and Robert Novak, "Korea: Park's Inflexibility . . ." *WP,* June 12, 1975. The National Security Council Memorandum on persuading Seoul, Memorandum for Secretary Kissinger from Jan M. Lodal and Dave Elliott, July 24, 1975, secret (declassified 1995).

Schlesinger's meeting with Park, Schlesinger interview, July 6, 1995. For Sneider's "real consideration" statement, *Emb. cable,* December 16, 1975, nodis (declassified 1996). On the Rumsfeld threat against the ROK, Cho Kap Che, "Interview with Jae Nae Sohn," *Monthly Chosun* (Aug. 1995). For Sneider's postcrisis views, Memorandum of Conversation of Brent Scowcroft, Richard Sneider, William Gleysteen, Sept. 15, 1976, secret/sensitive (declassified 1995). On Carter-Giscard diplomacy, see Zbigniew Brzezinski, *Power and Principle* (Farrar Straus and Giroux, 1983), p. 134.

On Park's plan to unveil the A-bomb, Son U Ryun, "Voice Testimony of Park Chung Hee," *Monthly Chosun* (Mar. 1993), in Korean. For continuing development, "95 percent Development of Nuclear Weapons as of 1978," *Joong-ang Ilbo,* Oct. 2, 1993, in Korean; "Korea Close to N-bomb Development in Late 1970s," *KH,* Oct. 6, 1995.

*Murder in the Demilitarized Zone:* For this section, I relied heavily on materials obtained under mandatory declassification review from the Gerald Ford Presidential Library and from the Department of State under the Freedom of Information Act, as well as interviews with a number of former officials who were on the scene in Korea or Washington. Three books were also of great value: Richard G. Head, Frisco W. Short, and Robert C. McFarlane (the last a future White House national security adviser), *Crisis Resolution: Presidential Decision Making in the Mayaguez and Korean Confrontations* (Westview Press, 1978), which covers Washington policy making; Colonel Conrad DeLateur, *Murder at Panmunjom: The Role of the Theater Commander in Crisis Resolution,* research paper for the Senior Seminar, Foreign Service Institute, 1987, dealing primarily with General Stilwell's role; and Major Wayne A. Kirkbride, *DMZ: A Story of the Panmunjom Axe Murder* (Holly, 1984), which deals with the episode as seen by U.S. officers and men at the DMZ.

The CIA report, titled *DMZ Incident,* was dated Aug. 18, 1976; top secret (declassified 1996). The discussion at the WASAG meeting was taken from the minutes of the meeting obtained through the Ford Presidential Library, secret (declassified 1995). For the historical buildup cable, ComUSKorea to AIG Washington, Aug. 18, 1976, confidential (declassified 1996). For the warning effort by intelligence analysts, see Head, Short, and McFarlane, *Crisis Resolution,* p. 155. For Hyland's recommendation and discussion of punitive measures, see Memorandum for Brent Scowcroft from W. G. Hyland, Aug. 18, 1976, top secret/exclusively eyes only (declassified 1994).

On military views of punitive actions, see JCS Assessment and Addendum, top secret (declassified 1994). Scowcroft's "wimpish" quote is from Scowcroft interview, Mar. 29, 1995. For military "handwringing," William Hyland interview, May 15, 1995. Ford's summary quote is from Head, Short, and McFarlane, *Crisis Resolution,* p. 193.

For the Pyongyang radio programming and blackout, U.S. Liaison Office Beijing to SecState Washington, "Panmunjom Incident and Situation in Pyongyang," Aug. 21, 1976, confidential (declassified 1994). See also *South-North Dialogue in Korea* (Seoul: International Cultural Society, Nov. 1976), p. 64. On the military precautions in the DPRK, Colonel Choi Ju Hwal, a high-ranking DPRK defector, interview, June 24, 1996. For Ho Dam quote, AmEmbassy Colombo to SecState Washington, Aug. 20, 1976, unclassified.

Stilwell's reaction, cable from Stilwell to JCS, Aug. 19, 1976, secret (declassified 1995). Park's quotes are from Park Chung Hee, "Blue House Diary," *Minju Ilbo,* Nov. 24, 1989, in Korean. Stilwell quote on Park, cable from CINCUNC Korea (Stilwell) to JCS, Aug. 19, 1976, secret (declassified 1995). On the arms of the *tae kwan do* group, Lieutenant

General John Cushman telephone interview, May 4, 1995. Park quote on retaliation, *Emb. cable,* Aug. 20, 1976, secret (declassified 1994).

Stilwell's battle plan is set out in his cable to the JCS, Aug. 19, 1976, secret (declassified 1995). On North Korean notification, see DeLateur, *Murder at Panmunjom,* p. 20. Peter Hayes, *Pacific Powderkeg* (Lexington Books, 1991), p. 60, on "blew their minds."

Kim quote about North Korea not resisting, "Talk to a Professor of SOKA University in Japan," Nov. 13, 1976, in *KIS Works,* vol. 31, p. 401. Scowcroft quote on the impact on U.S. election, Scowcroft interview, Mar. 29, 1995. Lee's comments on North Koreans, Jimmy Lee interview, July 8, 1995.

## CHAPTER 4: THE CARTER CHILL

For Carter on the origin of his position, letter from Carter to me, Mar. 12, 1994. Brzezinski quote from "President Carter's Troop Withdrawal from Korea," Harvard University case study by Major Joseph Wood, 1990.

*Carter s Withdrawal: Origins and Implementation:* For Ford review, National Security Study Memorandum 226, "Review of U.S. Policy Toward the Korean Peninsula," May 27, 1975, secret/nodis (declassified 1994). A notation in the Ford Presidential Library file says that Scowcroft approved suspension of work on the study on May 29, with no reason given. For Powell quote and other details of my 1977 research on the origins of Carter's ideas, Don Oberdorfer, "Carter's Decision on Korea Traced to Early 1975," *WP,* June 12, 1977. For Carter's views on stationing troops and his recollection of poll data, Carter letter to me, Mar. 12, 1994. For priority given Korea, see Zbigniew Brzezinski, *Power and Principle* (Farrar Straus and Giroux, 1983), p. 51. Quotes from PRM–13 from "Presidential Review Memorandum/NSC 13," Feb. 26, 1977, secret (declassified 1991).

Abramowitz quote from interview, Apr. 22, 1995. For Sneider and Vessey meeting with Park, *Emb. cable,* "Meeting with President Park," Mar. 1, 1977, secret (declassified 1996). Carter's informal instructions are on a handwritten memo from "J.C." to "Zbig and Cy," Mar. 5, 1977, in the Carter Presidential Library, secret (declassified 1996).

Talking points from "Meeting with South Korean Foreign Minister Pak Tong-Chin," Memo from Brzezinski to Carter, Mar. 8, 1977, secret (declassified 1996). Foreign Minister Park's version is from his memoir, *One Will on a Long Road* (Seoul Dong-A Publishing Co., 1992), in Korean. Failure to approach Soviets and Chinese, "Approach to Soviets and Chinese on our troop withdrawals from Korea," Department of State Action Memorandum, June 10, 1977, confidential (declassified 1996).

Quote on "missing dimension," "Talks Between South Korea and North Korea with or without PRC Participation," Memorandum for the President (believed to be from Vance, about July 25, 1977), secret (declassified 1996). For Carter's response, see Zbigniew Brzezinski, "Talks between North Korea and South Korea," Memorandum for the Secretary of State, Aug. 5, 1977, secret (declassified 1996).

For Vance efforts in China, David Anderson for Peter Tarnoff, "Efforts to Promote a Dialogue Between South and North," Memorandum for Dr. Zbigniew Brzezinski, Sept. 2, 1977, top secret (declassified 1996). This was amplified by a telephone interview with William Gleysteen, who accompanied Vance to China, Nov. 19, 1996. Carter atomic weapons quote, *WP,* Mar. 21, 1976. For numbers of weapons at the time, William Arkin telephone interview, Mar. 4, 1995. For Harold Brown's view on nuclear weapons, Brown interview, July 12, 1995.

"Rebellion" against the president, Richard Holbrooke interview, Aug. 10, 1993. Harold Brown on limits of loyalty, interview, July 12, 1995. Cyrus Vance view, Vance interview, Feb. 4, 1994. Zbigniew Brzezinski on Carter's beliefs, Brzezinski interview, Mar. 1, 1994. Carter's withdrawal order, Presidential Directive/NSC-12, May 5, 1977, top secret/sensitive/eyes only (declassified 1991). The nuclear aspects of the decision remain classified.

For Park's comment to reporters, Sunwoo Ryun, "Voice Testimony of Park Chung Hee," *Monthly Chosun* (Mar. 1993), in Korean. For Park's position on withdrawal, former Korean official, interview, July 20, 1993. Brzezinski comments on "uphill battle" in Congress, Memorandum for the President from Zbigniew Brzezinski, "Congressional Reactions to our Korean Policy," July 21, 1977, confidential (declassified 1996).

Carter on cooperation with corruption probes, Memorandum from Robert Lipshutz and Zbigniew Brzezinski, "White House Role in

Congressional Investigation of Korean Misdoings," June 23, 1977, confidential (declassified 1997).

The Rich quote is from Robert G. Rich, Jr., *U.S. Ground Force Withdrawal from Korea: A Case Study in National Security Decision Making*, Executive Seminar, Foreign Service Institute, June 1982. Carter comment to Brzezinski, Brzezinski interview, Mar. 1, 1994; telephone conversation, Mar. 3, 1994. For Harold Brown on aide's dilemma, letter to me, July 23, 1996.

For senior aides meeting on withdrawal, Zbigniew Brzezinski Memorandum to the President, "Summary of April 11, 1978 Meeting on Korea and China," secret (declassified 1996). Carter irritation with Brown, Brown interview, July 12, 1995, and Brzezinski interviews.

*The View from Pyongyang:* North Korea on nepotism, cited in Jae Kyu Park, "North Korean Policy Toward the United States," *Asian Perspectives*, vol. 5 (Fall-Winter 1981), p. 144. The history of North Korean efforts to negotiate with Washington is recounted in Michael Armacost Memorandum for Zbigniew Brzezinski, "Contacts and Communications with North Korea," Feb. 28, 1977, secret (declassified 1996); Douglas J. Bennett Jr., Draft Letter to Rep. Lester Wolff, Apr. 28, 1978, secret (declassified 1996); and Don Oberdorfer, "North Korea Rebuffs Carter's Bid to Open 3-Country Negotiations," *WP*, July 15, 1979.

For Kim's quotes on Carter, *KIS Works*, "Talk to the Delegation of the International Liaison Committee" (June 15, 1978), vol. 33, p. 257; and "Talk with the Chief Editor of the Japanese Political Magazine *Sekai*," (Oct. 21, 1978), vol. 33, p. 493.

For Kim's discussion with Honecker, "Transcript of official talks between the party and state delegation of the GDR and North Korea in Pyongyang, 12/9–10/77," *SED Archive*. For CIA economic analysis, *Korea: The Economic Race Between the North and the South* (CIA: National Foreign Assessment Center, Jan. 1978), p. i. On South Korean military spending, *The Military Balance* (London: International Institute of Strategic Studies, 1976 and 1977). Chinese troops near DPRK border, "Conversation between Honecker and Kim, 5/31/84," *SED Archives*. U.S. Command on North Korean infiltration, *USFK Hist. 1977*, pp. 5455, secret/noforn (declassified 1995).

*End of the Carter Withdrawal:* The section on Armstrong's work is based on interviews with Armstrong July 7 and 20, 1974, Evelyn Colbert, Feb. 14, 1994, and Nathanial Thayer, Aug. 1, 1995, former CIA National Intelligence officers for East Asia; Alan MacDougall, former DIA senior analyst for Korea, Aug. 2, 1995; and an excellent case study, "President Carter's Troop Withdrawal from Korea," written for Harvard University in 1990 by Major Joseph Wood. For Vessey's intelligence request, *USFK Hist. 1978,* p. 57, secret (declassified 1995). New North Korean estimate, *USFK Hist. 1980,* p. 17, secret (declassified 1995). The Thayer quote is from Thayer interview, Aug. 1, 1995.

On Carter's suspicion of intelligence, letter to me, Mar. 12, 1994. Quote from new review, Presidential Review Memorandum/NSC–45, Nov. 22, 1979, secret (declassified 1991).

Carter's plan for meeting of Park and Kim, Nicholas Platt interview, Feb. 10, 1994; William Gleysteen interview, Sept. 29, 1993. Carter-Deng talks, Jimmy Carter, *Keeping Faith* (Bantam Books, 1982), pp. 205–206. See also *U.S.-PRC Chronology,* p. 75. Carter on three-way talks, Gleysteen interview.

For Carter-Park bilateral talks, interviews with Platt, Feb. 10, 1994, and Holbrooke, Aug. 10, 1993. Also White House Memorandum of Conversation, secret (declassified 1997). For argument in car, interviews with Gleysteen, Vance, Brown, Brzezinski, Holbrooke, Platt and Rich, and Vance, *Hard Choices* (Simon and Schuster 1993). For Carter proselytizing Park, "Private Meeting with President Park, Seoul, Korea," 7/1/79, notes by Carter, from Carter Library. Final strength figures from USFK, Nov. 25, 1996. On nuclear weapons, Arkin telephone interview, Mar. 24, 1995.

## CHAPTER 5: ASSASSINATION AND AFTERMATH

On the postassassination situation see Gleysteen's first dispatch, *Emb. cable,* "Initial Reflections on Post-Park Chung Hee Situation in Korea," Oct. 28, 1979, secret (declassified 1993). Gleysteen's postmidnight actions, interview, Oct. 12, 1993. On details of the White House meeting, see Chung Chin Suk, "Power Vacuum in Korea," *Hankook Ilbo* Dec. 13, 1996, in Korean. On the last days of Park and other late 1970s developments in Korea, I have relied on Koon Woo Nam's useful book,

*South Korean Politics: The Search for Political Consensus and Stability* (University Press of America, 1989).

Embassy on Pusan protests, *Emb. cable,* "Embassy Thoughts on Current Mood Following Declaration of Martial Law in Pusan," Oct. 20, 1979, confidential (declassified 1993). U.S. warnings about Kim Young Sam's expulsion, NCS Memorandum from Platt to Brzezinski, "Opposition Leader Ousted," October 4, 1979, confidential (declassified 1997). Brown-Gleysteen meeting with Park, *Emb. cable,* "Meeting with President Park Regarding Domestic Political Crisis," Oct. 18, 1979, confidential (declassified 1993).

"Pervasive worry" quote, *Emb. cable,* "Initial Reflections on Post–Park Chung Hee Situation in Korea," Oct. 28, 1979, secret (declassified 1993). Extraordinary security measures, William Chapman, "Park's Legacy: Prosperity and Fear," *WP,* Nov. 3, 1979. On the absence of grief, *Emb. cable,* "Surprisingly Few Mourn Park Chung Hee," Nov. 14, 1979, confidential (declassified 1993). Holbrooke's quote, Holbrooke interview, Aug. 10, 1993.

Kang Sin Ok quote, interview, Nov. 25, 1994. Gleysteen on noncomplicity, *Emb. cable,* "Charges of Complicity in President Park's Death," Nov. 19, 1979, secret (declassified 1993). Young's search, James V. Young, manuscript for *Monthly Chosun* (1994). Gleysteen on Kim Jae Kyu, Gleysteen interview, Sept. 9, 1993. Kim Il Sung's reaction, *KIS Works,* "Let Us Strengthen the People's Army," vol. 34, p. 419. On U.S. advice to Choi, Emb. cable, "Korea Focus: Meeting with Acting President November 29," Nov. 29, 1979, secret (declassified 1993).

*The Coming of Chun Doo Hwan:* For a report on the events of 12/12 as they emerged from the 1996 trial of Chun and Roh, see "Arrest of Two Ex-Presidents and May 18 Special Law," *Korea Annual 1996* (Yonhap News Agency, 1996), pp. 46–55. My account of 12/12 is based on interviews with Gleysteen and Wickham and on the written account by James V. Young, who was deputy U.S. military attaché at the time. Gleysteen's "bad news" cable is *Emb. cable,* "Younger ROK Officers Grab Power Positions," Dec. 13, 1979, secret (declassified 1993).

For Chun's family background, Sanghyun Yoon (Chun's son-in-law), *South Korea s Nordpolitik with Special Reference to Its Relationship with China,* Ph.D. diss. (George Washington University, 1994), p. 281. Chun's stoplight anecdote, Chun Doo Hwan interview, July 22, 1980. For Hana-hoe, see "Army Reforms Sweep Hana-hoe into History," *Newsreview,* Mar. 9, 1996. Gleysteen on Chun, Gleysteen interview, Oct. 12, 1993. Walker on Chun, Walker interview, Feb. 18, 1995. Gleysteen exchange with academic, *Emb. cable,* "Telegram from Professor Choi and Response," Dec. 19, 1979.

Gleysteen quote on not reversing coup, *Emb. cable,* "Discussions with the New Army Leadership Group," Jan. 26, 1979, secret (declassified 1993). On Gleysteen-Chun initial meeting, *Emb. cable,* "Korea Focus-Discussion with MG Chon Tu Hwan," Dec. 15, 1979, secret (declassified 1993). Carter letter and other details from *U.S. Government Statement on the Events in Kwangju, ROK, in May 1980,* June 19, 1989, supplemented by James V. Young's memoir written for *Monthly Chosun* in 1994. Gleysteen on U.S. dilemma, *Emb. cable,* "Korea—Ambassador's Policy Assessment," Jan. 29, 1980, secret (declassified 1993).

*The Kwangju Uprising:* Embassy reaction to KCIA appointment, Gleysteen interview, Feb. 10, 1997. Gleysteen on ROK contingency plans, *Emb. cable,* "Korea Focus: Building Tensions and Concern over Student Issue," May 8, 1980, secret (declassified 1993). State response, *DOS cable,* "Korea Focus-Tensions in the ROK," May 8, 1980, secret (declassified 1993). Chun's statement, meeting with Wickham, *U.S. Government Statement,* p. 10.

Intelligence officer's revelation, Park Hee Chung, "Chun Exaggerates North Korean Threat," *Hankuk Ilbo,* Dec. 13, 1995, in Korean. The flash cable, *Emb. cable,* "Crackdown in Seoul," May 17, 1980, secret (declassified 1993). Contradiction of Chun and Kim Dae Jung, *Emb. cable,* "Yet Another Assessment of ROK Stability and Political Development," Mar. 12, 1980, secret (declassified 1993).

Gleysteen on "incendiary arrest," *Emb. cable,* "May 17 Meeting with Blue House SYG Choi Kwang Soo," May 17, 1980, secret (declassified 1993). Warnberg and Huntley eyewitness account from Kwangju from Tim Warnberg, "The Kwangju Uprising: An Inside View," in *Korean Studies,* vol. 11 (1987). Gleysteen on "massive insurrection," *Emb. cable,* "The Kwangju Crisis," May 21, 1980, secret (declassified 1993). NSC meeting on Kwangju, "Summary of Conclusions," National Security Council Memorandum, secret (declassified 1994).

Regarding operational control and the U.S. role, see *U.S. Government Statement.* The troop movement cable, Defense Intelligence Agency, "ROKG Shifts SF Units," May 8, 1980, classified (declassified 1993). Tape recording of Wickham interview courtesy Sam Jameson. See also Sam Jameson, "U.S. Support Claimed for S. Korea's Chon," *Los Angeles Times,* Aug. 8, 1980. Choi's regrets, "Choi Terms Kwangju Incident 'Mistake,'" *KT,* Aug. 20, 1996.

On U.S. "cool and aloof" policy, Gleysteen interview, Oct. 12, 1993. For U.S. intelligence, Gregg and Aaron comments, Gregg to Brzezinski memo, July 1, 1979, secret (declassified 1997).

*The Fight to Save Kim Dae Jung:* Lilley on Kim Dae Jung, Lilley interview, June 8, 1993. Gregg on Chun's "terrific pressure," Gregg interview, Mar. 12, 1995. ROK contemporaneous notes of the discussions were published in Kwan Young Ki, "Behind the Scenes: Chun Doo Hwan-Reagan Relationship," *Monthly Chosun* (Aug. 1992). Chung Ho Young on Kim "card," Chung interview, Apr. 20, 1994. On Allen's discussions regarding Kim Dae Jung, Allen interviews, Dec. 27, 1993, and Jan. 14, 1994, plus interviews with Sohn Jang Nae on Apr. 21 and 29, 1994, and with Chung Ho Young, Apr. 20, 1994.

Gleysteen on Chun's visit to Washington, *Emb. cable,* "Agenda Suggestions for Reagan-Chun Meeting," Jan. 22, 1981, secret (declassified 1996). Haig views, Memorandum for the President from Alexander Haig, Jan. 29, 1981, secret (declassified 1993). The U.S. buildup data are from *USFK Hist.,* "Personnel Strength in Korea," Nov. 25, 1996. F-16 offer, *DOS cable,* "President Chun's Meeting with President Reagan February 2, 1981," Feb. 12, 1981, secret (declassified 1996). For Carter's refusal to approve F-16 sale, Memorandum for the President, "Harold Brown's November Asian Trip: Decision to Proceed with F-16 Sale to Korea," November 1, 1978, top secret (declassified 1997). Reagan's quote on dissenters, Zbigniew Brzezinski interview, Mar. 1, 1994. See also Jimmy Carter, *Keeping Faith* (Bantam Books, 1982), p. 578.

## CHAPTER 6: TERROR AND TALK

An authoritative account of the fate of KAL 007 is Murray Sayle, "Closing the File on Flight 007," *New Yorker,* Dec. 12, 1993. On Soviet decisions about trading, Georgi Toloraya interview, May 4, 1994. Details on the

Rangoon bombers and the bomb are taken from the official account of the Burmese government, as published in the *Guardian* newspaper, Rangoon; and from the Burmese government report to the UN General Assembly, reprinted in *KH*, Oct. 4, 1984. Koh on the African assassination plot, Koh Yong Hwan interview, Oct. 25, 1993.

On Chun's amended schedule in Rangoon, Lho Shin Yong interview, May 27, 1993; Richard L. Walker interview, Feb. 18, 1995. On North Korean plans after Chun's assassination, Kang Myung Do interview, Apr. 11, 1995. See also Don Oberdorfer, "N. Korea Reportedly Set Coordinated Offensives After Rangoon Blast," *WP*, Dec. 2, 1983.

Proposal to bomb North Korea in retaliation, Kang Kyong Shik (who had been minister of finance before Rangoon and was later Blue House chief of staff), conversation in Washington, Mar. 22, 1995. Chun on his talk to ROK commanders, Kim Sung Ik, *Voice Testimony of Chun Doo Hwan* (*Chosun Ilbo*, 1992), in Korean. Chun statements to Walker, Walker interview, Mar. 30, 1995; also Harry Dunlop (former U.S. political counselor, Seoul), interview, Jan. 12, 1994; Reagan's quotes, "Presidential Visit Meetings in Seoul," Memorandum from Assistant Secretary Paul Wolfowitz to Secretary Shultz, Nov. 19, 1993, secret/nodis (declassified 1995). The censure offer was in Shultz's bilateral talks with Korean foreign minister Lee Won Kyong.

*The Negotiating Track:* The Kissinger proposal was authorized by President Nixon in National Security Decision Memorandum 25 1, Mar. 29, 1974, top secret/sensitive (declassified 1996), which also involved substitution of a U.S.-ROK Command for the UN Command and negotiation of a nonaggression pact between the two Koreas. It evidently was discussed by Kissinger with the Chinese in Mar. 1974, Oct. 1974, and Oct. 1975. See *US-PRC Chronology*, pp. 40, 45, 54.

For the Deng-Weinberger talks, *US-PRC Chronology*, p. 110. For Deng's reaction to the Rangoon bombing, Ralph Clough, *Embattled Korea* (Westview, 1987), p. 269.

For the early history of the three-way talks proposal, see Kim Hak Joon, *Unification Policies of North and South Korea 1945–1991* (Seoul National University Press, 1992), especially pp. 380–385. On the continued promotion of three-way plan, William Gleysteen interview, Sept. 13, 1995. On U.S. backing for three-way talks, Don Oberdorfer, "North Korea

Says U.S. Proposals Merit Discussion," *WP,* Oct. 8, 1984. Wolfowitz on "boilerplate," Wolfowitz interview, July 19, 1994. Ho Dam's comments were in his report to the opening session of the SPA on Jan. 25, 1985. Kim Il Sung on "exposing" the United States, transcript of conversation between Kim Il Sung and Eric Honecker, May 30, 1984, *SED Archives.*

*Floods and Face-to-Face Talks:* Haberman dispatch, "North Korea Delivers Flood Aid Supplies to South," *NYT,* Sept. 30, 1984. On Liem's trip, Yang Chin Young, "Kim Il Sung Whom I Met," *Joong-ang Monthly* (Apr. 1989), in Korean; also Sohn Jang Nae interview, Apr. 29, 1994. On contention in Pyongyang, see "Kim Endorses Dialogue Amid Signs of Contention on Issue," *FBIS Trends* (CIA: Foreign Broadcast Information Service, Jan. 3, 1985), confidential (declassified 1995). For details of the Ho Dam–Chang Se Dong trips, see Park Bo Kyon, "Chang Se Dong–Ho Dam, Each Visited Pyongyang-Seoul," *Joong-ang Ilbo,* Jan. 7, 1994, and following days, in Korean. A transcript of the talks in the South was published as "Secret Talks Between Chun Doo Hwan and Ho Dam," *Monthly Chosun* (Nov. 1996), in Korean.

On Chun shutting down the nuclear weapons program, Kim Jin Hyun (former ROK minister of science and technology), interview, July 23, 1993. Sohn quote on talks, Sohn interview, Apr. 29, 1994. U.S. intelligence official on talks, interview, May 14, 1994. Kim Il Sung on "great losses" from Team Spirit, stenographic transcript of "Official Friendship Visit of North Korean Party and State Delegation to the GDR," May 30, 1984, *SED Archives.*

*Kim Il Sung and the Soviet Connection:* For Stalin's role in the armistice, Kathryn Weathersby, "Stalin and a Negotiated Settlement in Korea, 1950–53," paper prepared for conference on "New Evidence on the Cold War in Asia," Hong Kong, Jan. 1996. For Kim's situation in the Sino-Soviet split, see Dae-Sook Suh, *Kim Il Sung* (Columbia University Press, 1988), pp. 176–210. Tkachenko quote, Tkachenko interviews, Oct. 24, 1993, and Apr. 12, 1994.

For Central Committee quote on DPRK, Eugene Bazhanov, "Soviet Policy Toward North Korea," *Russia and Korea Toward the 21st Century* (Seoul: Sejong Institute, 1992), p. 65. Hu Yaobang to Reagan, *US-PRC Chronology,* p. 111. Rakhmanin on Kim in Moscow, Rakhmanin interview, Apr. 8, 1994. Gorbachev on Kim's "socialist monarchy," *Erinnerungen (Memories)* (Berlin: Siedler Verlag, 1995), the German-language version of his memoirs.

Kim's comments in Moscow 1984, "On the Visit of North Korea's Party and State Delegation led by Kim Il Sung to the USSR," May 29, 1984, *SED Archives,* in German and Russian. Kim's worry about China, from transcript of "Official Friendship Visit of North Korean Party and State Delegation to the GDR," Mar. 31, 1984, in German. Soviet official's quote, from "On the Visit of North Korea's Party and State Delegation."

The USSR-DPRK economic data are from an excellent analysis by Nicholas Eberstadt, Marc Rubin, and Albina Tretyakova, "The Collapse of Soviet and Russian Trade with the DPRK, 1989–1993," *Korean Journal of National Unification,* vol. 4 (1995). Details of Soviet military aid agreements in 1984 and 1986 from Joseph M. Ha, Ha interview, Feb. 21, 1995. Record of overflights, *USFK Hist. 1985,* p. 25, secret (declassified 1995). Satellite avoidance, *USFK Hist.,* with chapter headings on SATRAN, especially 1979 report, p. 51.

For the protests by North Korea in Moscow, see the outstanding scholarship of Eugene Bazhanov and his wife, Natalia Bazhanova (a Russian expert on Korean affairs who had access to Central Committee archives), especially her chapter, "North Korea and Seoul-Moscow Relations," in *Korea and Russia Toward the 21st Century* (Seoul: Sejong Institute, 1992). The Georgi Kim quote is from Eugene Bazhanov, "Soviet Policy Towards South Korea Under Gorbachev," *Korea and Russia Toward the 21st Century,* p. 65. On Kim Il Sung on flying, Vadim Tkachenko interview, Oct. 24, 1993. For Kim's quote and attitude in Gorbachev meetings, Vadim Medvedev, *Collapse* (Moscow: International Relations Publishers, 1994), in Russian. For the May 1986 Politburo document, Bazhanov, "Soviet Policy," p. 95. For Gorbachev's surprising declaration, Tkachenko interview, Oct. 24, 1993.

For the Gorbachev quote on the situation in 1986, Mikhail Gorbachev interview, Apr. 13, 1994. On North Korea as a privileged ally, Gorbachev, *Erinnerungen.* USSR weapons promises, Ha interview, Feb. 15, 1995. For aid levels, see Han Yong Sup, "China's Security Cooperation with North Korea: Retrospects and Prospects," paper prepared for conference on "Sino-Korean Relations and Their Policy Implications," American Enterprise Institute and George Washington University, Dec. 2–3, 1993, and additional details provided to me by Han. On Kim's view of Gorbachev as a revisionist, Koh Young Whan interview, Oct. 25, 1993.

## CHAPTER 7: THE BATTLE FOR DEMOCRACY IN SEOUL

For excellent descriptions of the 1987 events, see Manwoo Lee, *The Odyssey of Korean Democracy* (Praeger, 1990) and Sang Joon Kim, "Characteristic Features of Korean Democratization," *Asian Perspective* (Fall– Winter 1994).

*Chun s Succession Struggle:* Chun to Walker, Walker interview, Feb. 18, 1995. Lee Soon Ja views, from my journal, Feb. 1981, based on a conversation with the First Lady while sitting next to her at the luncheon for Chun at the National Press Club. Regarding the Ilhae Foundation, see Don Oberdorfer "Korean Conundrum," *WP,* May 25, 1986. On the forced contributions, see Donald Kirk, *Korean Dynasty* (M. E. Sharpe, 1994), p. 273. The Shultz quote is from his memoir, *Turmoil and Triumph* (Scribner's, 1993), pp. 977–998. Shultz's concerns were expressed to me in an interview, Mar. 16, 1995.

Chun pledge to Reagan, "Presidential Visit Meetings in Seoul," Memorandum from Assistant Secretary of State Paul Wolfowitz to Secretary Shultz, Nov. 19, 1983, secret/nodis (declassified 1995). Chun quote to Blue House reporters, *KH,* Jan. 9, 1988. For the Seoul National University poll, Se Hee Yoo, "The International Context of U.S.-Korean Relations: Special Focus on the 'Critical Views of the United States' in Korea since 1980," in *United States–Korea Relations* (Berkeley: Institute of East Asian Studies, 1986).

Shultz on Sigur speech, Gaston Sigur interview, Sept. 16, 1993. On dominance of Korea story in the American press, Don Oberdorfer, "U.S. Policy toward Korea in the 1987 Crisis Compared with Other Allies," in *Korea-U.S. Relations* (Berkeley: Institute of East Asian Studies, 1988). U.S. warning to Pyongyang, Michael Armacost telephone interview, Aug. 9, 1993. Pyongyang reaction, "Pyongyang Maintains Cautious Posture Toward Situation in South," *FBIS Analysis Note* (CIA: Foreign Broadcast Information Service, June 29, 1984).

Reagan's letter to Chun, dated June 17, 1989, in author's possession. Dunlop on "stonewalling," Dunlop interview, Jan. 12, 1994. Riot details are from John Burgess, "Seoul Says Crackdown 'Inevitable,'" *WP,* June 19, 1987. On June 19 meeting and Chun's previous statements to aides, Kim Sung Ik, *Voice Testimony of Chun Doo Hwan* (*Chosun Ilbo,* 1992), in Korean. Lilley's presentation to Chun, Lilley interviews, June 8, 1993, and Feb. 17, 1997. Chun on suspending the mobilization order, Kim Sung Ik, *Voice Testimony.* Chung Ho Yong on the military views, Chung interview, Apr. 20, 1994.

Roh Tae Woo's recollection, Roh interview, Oct. 21, 1993. Chun quote to Sigur, Sigur interview, Sept. 16, 1993. Roh's near-apology for Kwangju, Hyun Hong Choo interview, Oct. 17, 1995. Chun camp's version of June 29 origins: "The Truth of the 6/29 Declaration," *Monthly Chosun* (Jan. 1992), in Korean. Lee Soon Ja's declaration, "Wife says Chun Is Real Architect of the June 29, 1987 Declaration," *KT,* Dec. 19, 1996.

*The Election of 1987:* Chun's doubts about Roh, Kim Yoon Hwan interview, Oct. 18, 1993. Kim Young Sam's age has been a source of consistent confusion. He told Blue House reporters his birth date was misregistered at his birthplace and was actually December 4 (on the lunar calendar) 1927. "Kim's Birthday," *Korea Times,* Jan. 24, 1996.

Kim Young Sam's mother's death, Kim interview, Apr. 14, 1995. Cholla's disadvantages, Manwoo Lee, *The Odyssey of Korean Democracy* (Praeger, 1990), pp. 49–5 1. Lee quote on electoral territoriality from *Odyssey,* p. 47.

## CHAPTER 8: THE GREAT OLYMPIC COMING-OUT PARTY

*The Coming of the Olympics:* On Park Chung Hee's instructions, Park Seh Jik, *The Seoul Olympics* (London: Bellew Publishing Co., 1991), p. 5. On Korea's and Chung Ju Yung's efforts, Mark Clifford, *Troubled Tiger* (M. E. Sharpe, 1994), p. 289. For a full account of Chung's remarkable career, see Donald Kirk, *Korean Dynasty,* M. E. Sharpe, 1994. *Nodong Sinmun* quote, Park, *Seoul Olympics,* p. 8. Hwang Jang Yop on political significance, his letter to Hermann Axen (secretary of SED Central Committee), June 19, 1985, *SED Archives,* in German. Shevardnadze quote from "About the visits of Soviet Foreign Minister Eduard Shevardnadze to North Korea and the Mongolian People's Republic," Jan. 28, 1986, confidential, *SED Archives,* in Russian and German.

# 484 ◆ Notes to Pages 182–194

Maretzki quotes from his cable to Berlin, May 11, 1987, *SED Archives*.
North Korea "cornered" quote from Parks, *Seoul Olympics*, p. 20.

*The Bombing of KAL Flight 858:* My account is based on Kim Hyun Hui interview, Oct. 25, 1993; her memoir, *The Tears of My Soul* (William Morrow, 1993); a chapter in Eileen MacDonald's *Shoot the Women First* (Random House, 1993); and *Investigation Findings: Explosion of Korean Air Flight 858,* KOIS (Seoul: KOIS, Jan. 1988). Kim's "military order" quote, Kim interview, Oct. 25, 1993. The Shevardnadze quote is from Shultz, *Turmoil and Triumph,* p. 981.

*The Rise of Nordpolitik:* For Roh's interview, Don Oberdorfer and Fred Hiatt, "S. Korean President Urges End to Isolation of North," *WP,* July 2, 1988. On the early *Nordpolitik* policy-making, see Park Chul Un, "Northern Policy Makes Progress Toward Unification," *KH,* Mar. 13, 1991. Kim's July 1988 reaction, "Visit of an Official Military Delegation of the GDR to North Korea, Between July 19 and 13, 1988," *SED Archives.*

Kim Woo Choong in Hungary, from an unpublished manuscript furnished me by Daewoo in December 1994, "The Civilian Ambassador Kim Woo Choong"; Chong Bong Uk, "Ties with Budapest Result from Spadework," *KH,* Jan. 29, 1988; and interviews with several former Korean officials. Data on ROK-Hungarian economic deals from a confidential source. Bazhanova report from "North Korea and Seoul-Moscow Relations," in *Korea and Russia Toward the 21st Century* (Seoul: Sejong Institute, 1992), p. 334. On Soviet-ROK connections at the Olympics, see James F. Larson and Heung-Soo Park, *Global Television and the Politics of the Seoul Olympics* (Westview Press, 1993). For the booty the Russians took home, see the unpublished Daewoo manuscript, "The Civilian Ambassador Kim Woo Choong."

*Washington Launches a Modest Initiative:* State Department view, *DOS cable,* "ROK President Roh's Visit: US Policy re N. Korea," Oct. 25, 1988, secret (declassified 1995). Sigur quote, Sigur interview, Sept. 16, 1993. Clark quote, Clark interview, June 23, 1993. State cable on "staying in step," *DOS cable,* "ROK President Roh's Visit: U.S. Policy re N. Korea," Oct. 25, 1988, secret (declassified 1995).

State Department instructions, *DOS cable,* "Policy/Regulation Changes Regarding North Korea: Informing Seoul, Tokyo, Moscow and

Beijing," Oct. 28, 1988, confidential (declassified 1995). Burkhardt meetings, Burkhardt interview, Sept. 28, 1993. See also B. C. Koh, "North Korea's Policy Toward the United States," in *Foreign Relations of North Korea* (Seoul: Sejong Institute, 1994), a particularly helpful account of U.S.–North Korean diplomacy prior to 1994.

## CHAPTER 9: MOSCOW SWITCHES SIDES

My account of the Politburo meeting on Nov. 10, 1988, including quotes, is from notes by Gorbachev aide Anatoly Chernyayev. Minister's quote on the ROK as "most promising partner," Eugene Bazhanov, "Soviet Policy Towards South Korea Under Gorbachev," *Korea and Russia Toward the 21st Century* (Seoul: Sejong Institute, 1992), p. 94n.

*The Roots of Change:* Soviet news reports and journalists' quotes, from Yassen N. Zassoursky, "The XXIV Olympic Games in Seoul and Their Effect on the Soviet Media and the Soviet Public," in *Seoul Olympics and the Global Community* (Seoul Olympics Memorial Association, 1992). Pravda quote from Park Seh Jik, *The Seoul Olympics* (London: Bellew Publishing Co., 1991), p. 175. Muscovites survey, Park, *Seoul Olympics,* p. 175. The "Welcoming Soviets" quote is from Bazhanov, "Soviet Policy," p. 96.

The North-South economic comparisons are from Kwang Eui Gak's monumental study, *The Korean Economies* (Oxford: Clarendon Press, 1993). Soviet aid figures are found on p. 204. The subsidized trade figures are from an excellent account by Nicholas Eberstadt, Marc Rubin, and Albina Tretyakova, "The Collapse of Soviet and Russian Trade with the DPRK, 1989–1993," in *Korean Journal of National Unification,* vol. 4 (1995). The Soviet memorandum to the DPRK is quoted in Natalia Bazhanova, "North Korea and Seoul-Moscow Relations," *Korea and Russia Toward the 21st Century* (Seoul: Sejong Institute, 1992), p. 332. For the ROK proposed loans, Kyungsoo Lho, "Seoul-Moscow Relations," *Asian Survey* (Dec. 1989), p. 1153.

Shevardnadze's visit to Pyongyang, personal impressions of Pyongyang from Pavel Palazchenko, *My Years with Gorbachev and Shevardnadze,* (Pennsylvania State University Press, 1997), p. 111. For Shevardnadze's report, "The main results of Eduard Shevardnadze's visit to Japan, the Philippines and North Korea," memorandum of Feb. 2,

1989, *SED Archives*. Shevardnadze's "I am a communist" quote, Bazhanova, "North Korea and Seoul-Moscow Relations," p. 332–333.

*Gorbachev Meets Roh:* The Gorbachev memoirs quote is from the German version, *Erinnerungen* (Siedler Verlag, 1995). Gorbachev on the process of change, Gorbachev interview, Apr. 13, 1994. Roh on "smelling their intention," Roh interview, July 22, 1993. Lifting of Soviet restrictions, Bazhanov, "Soviet Policy Towards South Korea Under Gorbachev," p. 97. ROK industrialists in Moscow, Kim Hak Joon, "South Korea-Soviet Union Normalization Revisited," prepared for the Conference on Northeast Asia and Russia, Sigur Center for East Asian Studies, Mar. 17–18, 1994, p. 11. "Inventing new reasons" quote, Georgi Ostroumov interview, Apr. 12, 1994.

Chernyayev quote from Chernyayev interview, Apr. 12, 1994. Gorbachev–Li Peng exchange, Bazhanov, "Soviet Policy Towards South Korea Under Gorbachev," pp. 92–93. Impact of Moscow trip on Kim Young Sam's political fortunes, Yoon Sang Hyun, *South Korea s Nordpolitik with Special Reference to Its Relationship with China*, Ph.D. diss. (George Washington University, 1994), p. 255. Tkachenko quote from Tkachenko interview, Oct. 24, 1993. On the appeal to Germany, see Philip Zelikow and Condoleezza Rice, *Germany Unified and Europe Transformed* (Harvard University Press, 1995), p. 256ff.

Dobrynin quote and activities, Dobrynin interviews, June 22, 1993, and Feb. 23, 1994. Roh Tae Woo on Soviet desperation, Roh interview, July 26, 1993. Gregg on "stake through the heart," *Emb. cable*, "Roh Tae Woo on the Eve of Meetings with Soviet and U.S. Leaders," June 1, 1990, confidential (declassified 1995). Sensitivity about Soviet consulate, Kim Hak Joon, "South Korea-Soviet Union Normalization Reconsidered," p. 13. Gorbachev on "radical change," Bazhanov, "Soviet Policy Towards South Korea under Gorbachev," p. 103. Kim Jong In quote, Kim interview, Apr. 26, 1994.

Soviet meeting notes, "M. S. Gorbachev's Conversation with Roh Tae Woo in San Francisco," obtained by author from the Gorbachev archive, Moscow, in Russian. For Roh's requests to Gorbachev, "M. S. Gorbachev's Conversation." See also *Emb. cable*, "MOFA Readout on Roh-Gorbachev Meeting," June 12, 1990, secret (declassified 1995). Pyongyang's reaction, Bazhanova, "North Korea and Seoul-Moscow

Relations," p. 336. Dobrynin quote on photograph, Dobrynin interview, June 22, 1993. Roh on the road to Pyongyang, "Opening Remarks by President Roh," *Yonhap Annual* 1990, p. 410.

*The Shevardnadze Mission:* My account of Shevardnadze's Sept. 1990 trip to Pyongyang comes from interviews with three members of the Soviet delegation who were present. Shevardnadze on the "most difficult, unpleasant" mission, from former Soviet diplomat, interview, July 7, 1993. Bessmertnykh quote, Bessmertnykh interview, Apr. 14, 1994. Chernyayev quotes from Chernyayev interview, Apr. 12, 1994.

Choi's argument to Gorbachev, Choi interview, Apr. 25, 1995. Shevardnadze on "our friends," Sergei Tarasenko interview, Apr. 10, 1994. *Nodong Sinmun* on Soviet perfidy, "Commentary Denounces USSR Diplomatic Ties," *FBIS-EAS,* Oct. 5, 1990, p. 8. Economic data from Nicholas Eberstadt et al., "The Collapse of Soviet and Russian Trade with the DPRK, 1989–93," *Korean Journal of National Unification,* vol. 4 (1995); Young Namkoong, "An Assessment of North Korean Economic Capability," *Economic Problems of National Unification* (Seoul 1993); *North Korea: Insights into Economy and Living* (Seoul: Korean-German Chamber of Commerce and Industry, 1991), in German.

*"How Long Will the Red Flag Fly?":* On the Korea desk reaction, "North Korean Reaction to Roh-Gorbachev Meeting," Department of State Briefing Paper, June 1, 1990, confidential (declassified 1995). For the INR report, Douglas P. Hulholland, "Soviet Initiative in Asia," Information Memorandum, May 30, 1990, confidential (declassified 1995). On State's view, "Talking Points for the President's Use in His June 6 Meeting with President Roh," Memorandum for the White House from the Department of State, June 2, 1990, secret (declassified 1995).

The account of the Chinese meeting with Kim is from a former Chinese diplomat, interviews, Jan. 23 and Oct. 4, 1993. For Kanemaru's trip, my account is based on interviews with a senior parliamentarian and a Foreign Ministry official who accompanied Kanemaru; interviews and writings of Hajimi Izumi and Masao Okonogi, leading Japanese experts on Korea; and an excellent reconstruction by Ushio Shioda, "What Was Discussed by the 'Kanemaru North Korean Mission'?" in *Bungei Shunju* (Aug. 1994). On the shift in Japanese policy, see B. C.

Koh, "North Korea's Approaches to the United States and Japan,"
draft paper for a conference on "The Two Koreas in World Affairs,"
Nov. 1996. On "yellow skins" and "white skins," Japanese official,
interview, May 21, 1993. On Kanemaru's apology to the United States,
Michael H. Armacost, *Friends or Rivals?* (Columbia University Press,
1996), p. 147.

An account of the secret 1990 meetings can be found in "Secret Meeting
Between Suh Dong Won and Kim Il Sung and Kim Jong Il," *Monthly
Chosun* (Aug. 1994), in Korean. This account was verified for me by a
former high-ranking ROK official. For Kim's conciliatory speech, see
*FBIS–East Asia,* May 24, 1990. On the disarmament proposal, William
Taylor, "Shifting Korean Breezes," *Washington Times,* June 6, 1990.

*Soviet–South Korean Economic Negotiations:* On Medvedev's mission, see his
Collapse (Moscow: International Relations Publishing House, 1994),
in Russian. Roh on "exerting influence," from "M. S. Gorbachev with
the President of ROK (Roh Tae Woo)," Dec. 14, 1990, notes of conversation, from the Gorbachev archive, Moscow, in Russian. Roh's
"don't worry" quote is from Georgi Toloraya interview, Oct. 19, 1993.
On the Saudi loan, see James A. Baker, *The Politics of Diplomacy* (G. P.
Putnam's Sons, 1995), p. 294–295. For Roh's "out of the question"
quote, Kang Sung-chul, "'Foundation Laid for Ending Cold War':
Roh," *KH,* Dec. 18, 1990.

The Maslyukov exchange is from a confidential source. For military supply
data, Nicholas Eberstadt et al., "The Collapse of Soviet and Russian
Trade with the DPRK, 1989–1993," *Korean Journal of National
Unification,* vol. 1 (1995). Han Yong Sup of the National Defense
University, Seoul, has produced some different numbers that show the
most precipitous drop in Soviet military assistance to North Korea in
1990 and a further drop in 1991. Roh money to Gorbachev, discussion
with former Roh aide, June 1996. On Boldin's comment, see his book,
*Ten Years That Shook the World* (Basic Books, 1994), p. 283.

## CHAPTER 10: CHINA SHIFTS ITS GROUND

On Chinese casualties in the Korean War, see Richard Whelan, *Drawing the
Line* (Little Brown, 1990), p. 373. The quotes from Chou and Kim are
from Ilpyong J. Kim, "China in North Korean Foreign Policy," paper

for the East Asian Institute, Columbia University, May 31–June 1, 1996. The disparity between DPRK and ROK trade with China, Tai Ming Cheung, "More Advice Than Aid," *Far Eastern Economic Review,* June 6, 1991, p. 15.

*A Visit to North Korea:* My impressions of Pyongyang were recorded in my notebooks and in a *Washington Post Magazine* article, "Communism Lives," Sept. 22, 1991.

On the cutback on USSR-DPRK trade, see Nicholas Eberstadt, Marc Rubin, and Albina Tretyakova, "The Collapse of Soviet and Russian Trade with the DPRK, 1989–1993," *Korean Journal of National Unification,* vol. 4 (1995). On the cutback in DPRK energy consumption, see Chung Sik Lee, "Prospects for North Korea," in *Democracy and Communism* (Korean Association of International Studies, 1995). For the history of "own style" socialism, "North Korean Brand of Socialism," *Vantage Point* (Seoul: Naewoe Press, Feb. 1996), p. 42. The Pyongyang bombing quote is from Daewoo Lee, "Economic Consequences of the Korean War and the Vietnam War," *Korea Observer* (Autumn 1996), p. 413n.

My first interview with Kim Yong Nam was published on Oct. 8, 1984, in *WP* under the headline, "North Korea Says U.S. Proposals Merit Discussion." Koh quote on Kim Yong Nam, Koh interview, Oct. 25, 1993.

*China Changes Course:* Deng quote to Carter, *US-PRC Chronology,* p. 75. Sino-ROK trade figures, Kim Sung Yoon, "Prospects for Seoul's Entering Relations with Beijing and the Effects on Inter-Korean Relations," *East Asia Review,* vol. 4, no. 2 1992. Sino-DPRK trade, Nicholas Eberstadt (unattributed author), "China's Trade with the DPRK, 1990–1994: Pyongyang's Thrifty New Patron," North Korea Trade Project Memorandum, U.S. Bureau of the Census, May 1995. On the workings of China economic committee, former South Korean official, interview, Oct. 27, 1995.

On the North Korean protests about the hijacking negotiation, "Chinese Hijackers Sentenced," *Facts on File* (1983), p. 632. Torpedo boat crisis, Richard L. Walker interview, Mar. 30, 1995. Deng's refusal of massive military aid, former Chinese official, interview, Oct. 4, 1993. Roh's medical doctor emissary, Kim Hak Joon interview, Dec. 20, 1993. The "no filter" quote, former Roh Tae Woo aide, interview, Mar. 14, 1995.

On Roh's lobbying after Tienanmen, Kim Hak Joon, "The Establishment of South Korean–Chinese Diplomatic Relations," paper for American Enterprise Institute–George Washington University conference, Dec. 2–3, 1993. On unofficial Sunkyung contacts, Lee Sun Sok interview, Nov. 24, 1994. Trade offices, Roh Jae Won interview, Dec. 3, 1993.

On the new Chinese policy on DPRK trade, Ilpyong Kim, "North Korea's Relations with China," in *Foreign Relations of North Korea* (Seoul: Sejong Institute, 1994), p. 265. Lee Sang Ok–Qian Qichen meeting, Lee interview, Oct. 26, 1993. Roh-Qian meeting, from memorandum of conversation, "Dialogue with Foreign Minister Qian Qichen— 11/12/91," in Korean. Roh Tae Woo on Qian's "kowtow," Kim Hak Joon interview, Dec. 20, 1993.

China's 1992 normalization priority, former Chinese official, interview, Dec. 2, 1993. On the Apr. 13, 1992, meeting, interviews with Lee Sang Ok, Oct. 26, 1993; Roh Jae Won, Dec. 3, 1993. On Taiwan envoy's arguments, Lee Sang Ok interview. On the Taiwan threat to expand trade with the DPRK, Kim Hak Joon, "The Establishment of South Korean–Chinese Diplomatic Relations," p. 11. The source is Kim's diary, which he kept while he was an official of the Blue House. On China's face-saving statements to the DPRK, Japanese diplomat, interview, Nov. 8, 1993. Kim Yong Nam's quote on PRC-ROK normalization, Don Oberdorfer, "N. Korea Says U.S. Blocks Progress on Nuclear Inspection," *WP*, Sept. 29, 1992.

## CHAPTER 11: JOINING THE NUCLEAR ISSUE

Kim Chong Whi quote, from my personal journal, Nov. 15, 1991.

*The Origins of the Nuclear Program:* On Japanese and Soviet early activities, Joseph Bermudez interview, 1992. See also Bruce Cumings, "Spring Thaw for Korea's Cold War?" *Bulletin of the Atomic Scientists* (Apr. 1992), p. 17. MacArthur-Ridgeway requests, Cumings, "Spring Thaw," pp. 18–19. For Eisenhower's claims, see Michael J. Mazarr, *North Korea and the Bomb* (St. Martin's Press, 1995), pp. 15–16. Nixon also made this claim on several occasions, including one I covered in 1968. Dubna activities, Alexandre Y. Mansourov, "The Origins, Evolution, and Current Politics of the North Korean Nuclear Program," *Nonproliferation Review* (Spring–Summer 1995), p. 25–26.

On refusing the DPRK request for nuclear weapons, the quote is from a former Chinese Foreign Ministry official, interview, July 6, 1993. The Japanese expert is Major General (retired) Katsuichi Tsukamoto (executive director of the Research Institute for Peace and Security, Tokyo), interview, July 30, 1993. On Kim's 1974 request, Bermudez interview. Russian intelligence information from Mansourov, "Origins, Evolution," p. 26.

On the East German nuclear report, "Information for the Politburo," June 12, 1981, *SED Archives.* For key figures in the DPRK nuclear program, Tai Sung An, "The Rise and Decline of North Korea's Nuclear Weapons Program," *Korea and World Affairs* (Winter 1992), pp. 674–675. On Kim's requests to Chernenko, "On the visit of DPRK's Party and State Delegation led by Kim Il Sung to the USSR," memorandum dated May 29, 1984, *SED Archives,* confidential, in Russian and German.

For U.S. urging to the Soviets on the NPT, Paul Wolfowitz interview, July 14, 1994. On NPT and the power reactor deal, Mansourov, "Origins, Evolution," p. 37.

*Nuclear Diplomacy: The American Weapons:* Baker on the diplomatic strategy, in Baker's memoir, *The Politics of Diplomacy* (Putnam, 1995), p. 595. The ACDA concerns quote, Kathleen C. Bailey, memorandum to Solomon on Intelligence Briefings Concerning North Korea, June 23, 1989, secret (declassified 1994). My report and the DPRK reaction, Don Oberdorfer, "North Koreans Pursue Nuclear Arms," *WP,* July 29, 1989; "Preposterous Fabrication by Washington Post," Press Release of DPRK Permanent Observer Mission to the UN, Aug. 9, 1989. On Eisenhower's nuclear deployments, "U.S. Nuclear Warheads First Deployed to Korea in 1957," *Dong-A Ilbo* (Apr. 29, 1993).

William Arkin data, Arkin interview, Mar. 24, 1995, citing National Security Decision Memorandum 178 of July 18, 1972. My report on DMZ vicinity weapons, Don Oberdorfer, "U.S. Weighs Risk of Keeping A-Arms in Korea," *WP,* Sept. 20, 1974. Schlesinger quote is from AP, "Schlesinger Warns N. Korea U.S. May Use Nuclear Arms," *St. Louis Post-Dispatch,* June 22, 1975. On reduced deployments, Arkin interview. Gregg recommendation, Gregg interview, June 21, 1993. Crowe's views, Crowe and Alan D. Romberg, "Rethinking Security in the

Pacific," *Foreign Affairs* (Spring 1991), p. 34. Scowcroft's objections, Scowcroft interview, Mar. 29, 1995. Solomon's "hook a ride" quote, Solomon interview, Mar. 22, 1996.

*The December Accords:* Chinese advice to Kim Il Sung, Lim Dong Won interview, May 2, 1994. Roh's 1991 exchange with Kim Il Sung, Roh Tae Woo luncheon conversation, July 22, 1993. The seal quote from "Two Koreas Celebrate New Era of Rapprochement," *Korea Annual 1992* (Seoul: Yonhap News Agency), p. 88. For North Korean reaction to accords, Don Oberdorfer, "U.S. Welcomes Koreas' Nuclear Accord," *WP,* Jan. 1, 1992. Harrison on "conditional victory," Selig Harrison, "North Korea and Nuclear Weapons: Next Steps in American Policy," testimony to the Senate Foreign Relations Subcommittee on East Asian and Pacific Affairs, May 26, 1993.

Kim Il Sung's denial of reprocessing, Stephen Solarz, "Interview with DPRK President Kim Il Sung," Dec. 18, 1991, transcript in my possession. Kim Yong Chul quote from Park Yong Ok interview, Nov. 29, 1996. Kim's enthusiasm about accord, Han Yong Sup interview, Nov. 29, 1995. *Economist* quote from "The Koreas: Look, No Bomb," *Economist,* Jan. 4, 1992.

*Meeting in New York:* This section is based on my reporting at the time and a subsequent interview with Kanter, Feb. 25, 1994.

*The Coming of the Inspectors:* Gates quote, Don Oberdorfer, "N. Korea Is Far from A-bomb, Video Indicates," *WP,* June 4, 1992. Olli Heinonen quote on early inspections, Heinonen interview, June 21, 1994. An excellent description of the IAEA's sleuthing and the U.S. role, from which some of these details are taken, is R. Jeffrey Smith's "N. Korea and the Bomb: High-Tech Hide-and-Seek," *WP,* Apr. 27, 1993. Blix quote from Blix interview, June 22, 1994. Theis quote from Theis interview, June 21, 1994.

*From Accommodation to Crisis:* Gregg on Team Spirit "mistake," Gregg interview, Mar. 12, 1995. Kim anger -in Ackerman meeting, State Department official, interview, May 15, 1995. Kim Hak Joon on spy case, Kim interview, Jan. 5, 1994. Gates on imagery, Gates interview, May 16, 1994. Choi quote to IAEA, Heinonen interview, June 22, 1994. DPRK war alert, Lee Chung Kuk, *The Nuclear Weapons and Army of Kim Jong Il* (Tokyo: Kodansha, 1994), in Japanese. Also Colonel

Chjoi Ju Hwal (a high-ranking North Korean defector who experienced the alert), interview, June 24, 1996.

## CHAPTER 12: WITHDRAWAL AND ENGAGEMENT

Han Sung Joo on repercussions of withdrawal, Han interview, Apr. 12, 1995. Han's "stick and carrot" approach was outlined in a meeting with *Washington Post* editors and reporters, which was so close to all that he was saying privately that he was admonished to be less candid by some State Department officials. See Don Oberdorfer, "South Korean: U.S. Agrees to Plan to Pressure North," *WP,* Mar. 30, 1993. JCS on "punishing" North Korea, State Department official, interview, May 15, 1995. Burkhardt on ROK "suggestion," Burkhardt interview, Sept. 29, 1993.

Gallucci's initial impressions of Kang, Gallucci interviews, June 21, 1993, and Aug. 10, 1995.

*The Light-Water Reactor Plan:* On Kim Young Sam's objections to negotiations, David Sanger, "Seoul's Leader Says North Is Manipulating U.S. on Nuclear Issues," *NYT,* July 1, 1993. White House official on Kim's references to politics and polls, interview, May 3, 1995. Gallucci retort to Clinton threat, Gallucci interview, Sept. 1, 1993.

Contrast between U.S. and DPRK hospitality, Dan Russel interview, Nov. 7, 1996. Carlin quote on "they want out" from an excellent case study by Susan Rosegrant, for the Kennedy School, Harvard University, "Carrots, Sticks and Question Marks: Negotiating the North Korean Nuclear Crisis," p. 30. Gallucci's reaction to the LWR offer, Gallucci interview, Aug. 10, 1995. Request to Blix for LWRs, "IAEA Director General Completes Official Visit to the Democratic People's Republic of Korea," *IAEA Press Release,* May 15, 1992. See also R. Jeffrey Smith, "N. Korea May Consider Reducing Atom Program," *WP,* June 20, 1992.

DPRK plan for reactors in DMZ, Lim Dong Won interview, June 25, 1996. Warning to Gallucci, Gallucci interview, Aug. 10, 1995.

*Kim Young Sam Blows the Whistle:* Gallucci "seven times removed" and "box of oranges" quotes, Rosegrant, Harvard study, pp. 30 and 27. Aspin quote on "ball in their court," Michael J. Mazarr, *North Korea and the Bomb* (St. Martin's Press, 1995), p. 133. Smith report on package deal,

R. Jeffrey Smith, "U.S. Weighs N. Korean Incentives: New Approach Taken on Nuclear Inspection," *WP,* Nov. 17, 1993.

On Kim Young Sam in Oval Office, senior Clinton administration official, interview, Jan. 13, 1994.

*The Season of Crisis Begins:* North-South economic disparity, "N. Korea's Per-capita GNP at $904, eight times lower than South's $7,466," *KH,* June 11, 1994. The U.S. interpretation of Kim Il Sung's reemergence, State Department official, interview, Apr. 14, 1995. Kim Il Sung on Kim Jong Il activity, "Q&A: 'We don't need nuclear weapons,'" *Washington Times,* Apr. 15, 1992. Kang Myung Do on Kang Song San's role in reemergence, Kang Myung Do interview, Apr. 11, 1995.

The report on the Graham mission is based on interviews with Graham's aide Stephen Linton, Mar. 30, 1994, and (by telephone) Aug. 10, 1996, and several published reports including that in Mazarr, *North Korea and the Bomb,* pp. 123–125. On Michael Gordon and the Pershings, Gordon interview, Nov. 20, 1995. Laney quote on body bags, Laney interview, Nov. 22, 1994. IAEA on purpose of DPRK refusal to permit full inspections, David Kyd (IAEA spokesman) interview, Apr. 6, 1994. Hubbard quote, Hubbard interview, Mar. 31, 1994.

## CHAPTER 13: SHOWDOWN OVER NUCLEAR WEAPONS

Gallucci on *Guns of August,* Gallucci interview, Mar. 11, 1995. Perry quote on "risk of war," Perry address to World Affairs Council, Philadelphia, Nov. 3, 1994. Estes quote, Estes interview, Apr. 4, 1995. CIA reevaluation of reactor downtime, U.S. intelligence officials, interview, Nov. 1, 1996. "Scare-nario" quote, David Albright, "North Korea and the 'Worst-case' Scare'nario," *Bulletin of the Atomic Scientists* (Jan.–Feb. 1994). Lake on disparate intelligence findings, Lake interview, Apr. 5, 1994.

*The Defueling Crisis:* "Not a drop dead issue," senior U.S. official, interview, Nov. 14, 1994. Perricos on the DPRK "poker game," Perricos interview, June 16, 1995. Gallucci on the "medieval" IAEA, Gallucci interview, May 19, 1994. Gregg "proctologists" quote, Gregg interview, Mar. 12, 1995. Kim Il Sung "naked man" quote to Sihanouk, *Far East Economic Review,* June 23, 1994.

*The Military Track:* O'Hanlon estimates, O'Hanlon telephone interview, Feb. 20, 1997. On the war plan, "U.S.-Seoul 'Strategic Concept' on DPRK

Noted," *Joong-ang Ilbo,* Mar. 24, 1994, in *FBIS-EAS,* Mar. 24, 1994. See also the war plan description by Michael Gordon with David Sanger in "North Korea's Huge Military Spurs New Strategy in South," *NYT,* Feb. 6, 1994. ROK "nervous as a cat" quote, senior U.S. military officer, interview, Apr. 4, 1995. U.S. military preparations from various news reports and Perry's testimony before the Senate Foreign Relations Committee, Jan. 24, 1995. Luck comments, Luck interview, May 3, 1994. Flanigan on Pentagon preparatory meeting, Flanigan interview, Aug. 11, 1995. Flanigan "extremely sobering" quote from Rosegrant, Harvard study, p. 51.

Estimates given to Clinton, Captain Thomas Flanigan, letter to author, Sept. 20, 1995. Perry "even more dangerous" quote, Perry speech before the World Affairs Council, Philadelphia, Nov. 3, 1994.

*The Deepening Conflict:* On the Aspin appeal for direct negotiations with Kim Il Sung, Mazarr, *North Korea and the Bomb,* pp. 102–103. Estimates of remittances to the DPRK by Koreans in Japan are very uncertain, but $600 million was the figure used in governmental circles. A serious study by Nicholas Eberstadt of the American Enterprise Institute concluded from financial data that the transfers to North Korea from private groups in Japan has not exceeded $100 million yearly since 1990. On Japan's difficulty in cutting off remittances, former White House official, interview, Oct. 28, 1996. Secret Japanese report on effect of sanctions, Asao Iku, "North Korea Will Act This Way," *Bungei Shunju,* July 1994 in Japanese. Japanese preparations for assistance to United States, "Government Was Preparing Limited Legislation in 1994," *Asahi Shimbun,* Sept. 16, 1996, in Japanese. "Nightmare" quote from Japanese diplomat, interview, Nov. 6, 1996.

Selig Harrison's trip to Pyongyang, from interview with Harrison, July 14, 1994; a Carnegie Endowment press release with details of the Harrison trip published June 16, 1994, and Harrison's "The North Korean Nuclear Crisis: From Stalemate to Breakthrough," in *Arms Control Today* (Nov. 1994). Kim Young Sam's criticism of Carter mission, "Seoul Denounces Carter Trip as 'Ill-timed,'" DPA (German Press Agency), June 11, 1994. Poll data on opinion toward North Korea, *American Enterprise,* July 8, 1994, p. 83. Scowcroft and Kanter views, "Korea: Time for Action," *WP,* June 15, 1994.

The section on U.S. military preparations is based largely on an interview with William Perry, Apr. 25, 1995, as well as his testimony before the Senate Foreign Relations Committee, Jan. 24, 1995, and the Senate Armed Services Committee, Jan. 26, 1995, and on news reports and a variety of other sources. For Luck on casualties and the costs of war, testimony of Luck before Senate Armed Services Committee, Jan. 26, 1995. DPRK lessons from Gulf War, senior U.S. officer, interview, Apr. 4, 1995.

*Carter in Pyongyang:* Jimmy Carter, "Report of Our Trip to Korea, June 1994," unpublished manuscript from the Carter Center. The account of the Carter mission is also based on Marion Creekmore interview, Aug. 1, 1994, input from Carter to the author via his aides, and a variety of other published and unpublished sources. Carter's "chances are minimal" quote, Elizabeth Kurylo, "Revisiting a Mission to Korea," *Atlanta Journal-Constitution,* July 3, 1994.

My report of the crucial White House meeting is based on interviews with four of the participants. Carter clarified for me in October 1996 that it was he who brought up the topic of a potential summit in the conversation with Kim Il Sung.

## CHAPTER 14: DEATH AND ACCORD

A video of Kim's last year taken from official footage, containing good coverage of the final economic meeting, was broadcast on North Korean television and shown to me at my request during my January 1995 visit to Pyongyang. I also spoke about the meeting with Kim Jong U, one of the senior officials who were present. Other details, including Kim's intervention in summit planning, are from the North Korean official version of his final meetings in *KIS Works* (the Korean language edition), vol. 44, published June 21, 1996. For Kim's recent appearances, "Seoul Speculates Kim's Death May Be Result of Power Struggle," *KH,* July 10, 1994. Kim Young Sam discussed his plans for his summit meeting with Kim Il Sung with me in an interview in the Blue House, Apr. 14, 1995. Other than the official autopsy report, the details and circumstances of Kim Il Sung's death have never been made public by North Korea. My account relies on the reporting of Julie Moon, who was given special access to senior North Korean officials at the time of

Kim's funeral. A senior North Korean official confirmed the authenticity of her account in a conversation with me in Pyongyang in January 1995.

German doctors on the growth on Kim's neck, former East German diplomat, interview, Sept. 10, 1994. Kim's 1992 luncheon troubles, former ROK official, Oct. 1994. Taylor's assessment of Kim's health, "Report on Bill Taylor's Third Trip to North Korea, 23–29 June 1992," unpublished manuscript supplied by Taylor. Kim's "good for another ten years" quote, Cho Kap Che, "The Information War with North Korea," *Monthly Chosun* (Sept. 1990), in Korean. Kim to Carter on living another ten years, David Sanger, "Kim Il Sung Dead at 82," *NYT,* July 9, 1994.

Reactions to Kim's death, conversation with a senior North Korean official in Pyongyang in January 1995; see also "'Enormous Crowds' at Monument" from Kyodo News Agency and "'Mass Hysteria' in Pyongyang" from the Polish Press Agency, published in *FBIS-EAS,* July 11, 1994. Flanigan's e-mail on North Koreans "here to deal," Flanigan interview, Aug. 31, 1995. On KBS film incident, Sohn Tae Soo, "Some TV Programs on Kim Il Sung Draw Fire," *KH,* July 13, 1994.

On the inappropriateness of the documents release, Russian diplomat, interview, Mar. 27, 1995. On the DPRK reaction to the Seoul postdeath events, Steve Glain, "Turmoil Marks Relations Between Pyongyang, Seoul," *Asian Wall Street Journal,* Aug. 15, 1994. Chung quote to Lake on the DPRK collapse, U.S. official, interview, Dec. 11, 1996.

*The Succession of Kim Jong Il:* Kim Jong Il in Berlin on his father's train, former East German official, interview, June 10, 1994. On Kim Jong Il's birth date, Aiden Foster-Carter has written that Kim Jong Il was actually born a year earlier than acknowledged, in 1941, but his age was adjusted to make him exactly thirty years younger than his father. Aiden Foster-Carter, "Birth of a Legend," *Far Eastern Economic Review,* Feb. 21, 1991.

Cumings "corporate and family state" quote, Bruce Cumings, "The Corporate State in North Korea," in *State and Society in Contemporary Korea,* edited by Hagen Koo (Cornell University Press, 1993). DPRK dictionary on hereditary succession, Kong Dan Oh, *Leadership Change in North Korean Politics* (Rand, Oct. 88), p. 10.

About the filmmakers, some in South Korea and elsewhere have raised doubts about the credibility of Choi and Shin, but they returned with photographs and tape recordings of themselves with Kim Il Sung and Kim Jong Il that have been accepted by U.S. and ROK intelligence as authentic. I had three meetings with them, the first shortly after their escape through Vienna, and I believe they are credible. My report here is based in part on my three interviews with the couple for *The Washington Post* in the mid-1980s. The quotes are from Choi Eun Hee and Shin Sang Ok, "Kidnapped to the North Korean Paradise," unpublished manuscript (English translation of their Korean book), p. 246.

On Kim Jong Il's connection to the Rangoon bombing, Joseph Bermudez, *Terrorism: The North Korean Connection* (Crane Russak, 1990), p. 9. The East German report on Kim Jong Il's "modem" tendencies, "Information about current features in some of North Korea's cultural areas," Embassy of the GDR, June 9, 1982, *SED Archives*. The Kim Jong Il quotes are from the filmmakers' tape recording published by *Monthly Chosun* (Oct. 1995), in Korean.

*The Framework Negotiations:* This section is primarily based on interviews with Gallucci and several other members of the U.S. negotiating team. Carlin on Kang's failure to say "never," Carlin interview, Nov. 7, 1994. Carlin "game was over" quote, Carlin interview, Nov. 26, 1995. Gallucci on "Talmudic significance," Gallucci interview, Oct. 8, 1996.

*The Kim Jong Il Regime:* Hubbard discussions in Pyongyang, Hubbard interview, Jan. 6, 1995. DOD cable on heavy oil, Joint Staff, Washington D.C. cable, "Subject: Delivery of Heavy Residual Fuel Oil to the Democratic Peoples Republic of Korea," Jan. 14, 1995, unclassified.

*The Struggle over the Reactors* "We opted for solidarity," White House official, interview, Oct. 21, 1996. Luck's cable to Perry, Pentagon official, interview, Aug. 31, 1995.

## CHAPTER 15: NORTH KOREA IN CRISIS

Shalikashvili quote on "implode or explode," Mary Jordan, "Speculation Grows on Demise of N. Korea," *WP*, Apr. 6, 1996. For the North Korean rainfall figures, "Pyongyang Media Report on Flood to Get Aid," *Vantage Point* (Seoul, Sept. 1995). Also, "FAO/WFP Crop and Food Supply Assessment Mission to DPRK," FAO, Rome, Dec. 1995.

Trevor Page quotes, Pierre Antoine Donnet, "Widespread Signs of Famine in North Korea: U.N. Official," *KH*, Dec. 6, 1996. Floods "made situation worse," "FAO/WFP Crop and Food Supply Assessment Mission to DPRK."

The DPRK request to supply grain secretly, Suh Dong Kwan interview, Oct. 28, 1993. Quotes on Kim Young Sam as the man to bring down the DPRK, a prominent South Korean, interview, Nov. 25, 1996. Laney quote on Kim Young Sam, interview, June 27, 1996. For details of DMZ incursions, Oh Young Jin, "Heavily Armed NK Troops Enter JSA in Panmunjom," *KT*, Apr. 7, 1996.

Disbanding of Sixth KPA corps, curtailment of winter exercises, U.S. intelligence officials, interview, Nov. 1, 1996. On impact of DMZ incursions on election, Sun Phil Kwon, "Policy Issues in the 1996 General Election," *Korea Observer*, Spring 1997. Adrian Buzo quote from his article, "The DPRK and Late De-Stalinization," *Korean Journal of National Unification*, vol. 4 (1995).

*Political Earthquake in Seoul:* The account of the inception of the scandal is from an interview with Park Kye Dong, June 25, 1996. On Roh's postscandal unpopularity, "Roh Named as Most Hated Politician: Poll," *KH*, Nov. 19, 1995. Kukje episode, Sam Jameson, "Fall of Kukje Corporation Illustrates South Korea's Corruption," *KT* reprint of *Los Angeles Times*, Nov. 19, 1995.

Chung Ju Yung's revelation and Roh's response are reported in Park Byeong Seog, "Political Corruption in South Korea: Concentrating on the Dynamics of Party Politics," *Asian Perspective* (Spring–Summer 1995), p. 172.

*Summit Diplomacy and the Four-Party Proposal:* My account of the 1995 and 1996 diplomacy is based on interviews with four U.S. officials who were involved. For Kim Young Sam quote to Clinton about August 15, U.S. official, interview, Aug. 14, 1996. "We thought we'd done enough," U.S. official, interview, May 8, 1996.

Chinese response to four-way talks proposal, "Jiang Sends Letter to Kim to Support 4-Way Peace Talks," *KT*, May 22, 1996. On the Kissinger proposal of peace talks and others along this line, see Kim Hak Joon, *Unification Policies of South and North Korea, 1945–1991* (Seoul National University Press, 1992), pp. 371ff. The UN special alert, "WFP Warns

North Korea Food Situation Deteriorating Sharply," press release and report of World Food Program, United Nations, May 13, 1996. Contrast in South Korea, "One in Four Koreans Is on Diet: Survey," *KH,* Apr. 9, 1996.

*The Submarine Incursion:* For details on the submarine incident, see "Chronology of Events Surrounding Incursion on the Territory of the ROK by North Koreans," information office of the ROK Embassy, Washington, Oct. 4, 1996, and reporting in *KH* and *KT.* The 1976 quote on infiltration, *USFK Hist. 1976,* p. 53, secret (declassified 1995).

On DPRK submarines, "PRC Magazine on DPRK's Submarine Strength," *FBIS-EAS,* Feb. 21, 1995, p. 36. Kim Young Sam quotes on submarine incident, Shim Jae Hoon, "Submarine Shocker," *Far Eastern Economic Review,* Oct. 3, 1996; Chon Shi Yong, "Kim Sees 'Possibility of War.'" *KH,* Oct. 8, 1996. Kevin Sullivan's interview with Kim Young Sam, "S. Korea Demands Apology from North; Kim Suspends Nuclear Deal After Sub Incident," *WP,* Nov. 9, 1996. Initial DPRK announcement, "Statement by a Spokesman for North Korea's Armed Forces Ministry," Sept. 23, 1996, *Korea and World Affairs* (Fall 1996), p. 516.

Plunk quotes from senior ROK official, "No Way to Deal with North Korea," *WP,* Sept. 29, 1996; Plunk telephone interview, Feb. 6, 1997. Revelation about unilateral attack plans, "ROK Ready to Hit 12 DPRK Targets in Event of Attack," *FBIS-EAS,* Oct. 16, 1996. Kristof's article in the wake of the submarine incursion, "How a Stalled Submarine Sank North Korea's Hopes," *NYT,* Nov. 19, 1996.

U.S.-ROK discussions on unilateral military action, from confidential interviews in Seoul and Washington with officials involved. Tilelli on "complete" satisfaction, Tilelli interview, Apr. 22, 1997.

*North Korea s Steep Decline:* Song Young Dae on "stability within instability," his article, "Changes in North Korea and How to Respond," *Korea Focus,* Jan.–Feb. 1997. I also interviewed Song in Seoul, Apr. 22, 1997. The Kim Jong Il speech of Dec. 7, 1996, was published by *Monthly Chosun* in Mar. 1997. My English translation was from the BBC , Mar. 21, 1997. I learned that Hwang Jang Yop was the source of the speech from Kim Yong Sam, the *Monthly Chosun* reporter who obtained it, and whom I interviewed Apr. 16, 1997.

Tilelli quotes from Tilelli interview, Apr. 22, 1997. China customs data for food, fuel from U.S. Institute of Peace, Special Report on Korea, June 1998.

Kim Jong Il's military and nonmilitary activities in 1996 are listed in *Vantage Point* (Naewoe Press, Seoul), Dec. 1996 and Jan. 1997. The Tilelli quotes are from the Tilelli interview, Apr. 22, 1997.

*The Passage of Hwang Jang Yop:* This section is based largely on Hwang's letters and other documents provided to *Monthly Chosun* reporter Kim Yong Sam by intermediary Lee Yon Kil and published after Hwang's defection. It is also based on interviews with Kim Yong Sam on Apr. 16, 1997; with Hajime Izumi on Mar. 8, 1997; and with Songhee Stella Kim on Apr. 23, 1997, and on Kim Yong Sam's retrospective article in *Monthly Chosun* in June 1997.

The phone call to set up the defection, from interview with a senior ROK official, Apr. 21, 1997. Hwang's letter written in the South Korean Consulate was released by the ROK Foreign Ministry, Feb. 13, 1997.

On "Red Banner philosophy," see "Red Banner Philosophy as Kim Jong Il's Ruling Tool," *Vantage Point* (Naewoe Press, Seoul), Mar. 1997. Hwang's views as expressed in the Moscow meeting of Feb. 1996 are from the Izumi interview, Mar. 8, 1997.

*The Two Koreas in Time of Trouble:* South Korean economic data from Korea Economic Institute of America. North Korea in eighth year of economic decline, *Vantage Point,* July 1998, quoting the Bank of Korea (Seoul). IMF report on North Korea, Confidential, prepared by Asia and Pacific Department, IMF, Nov. 12, 1997. U.S. Census estimates from Nicholas Eberstadt.

## CHAPTER 16: TURN TOWARD ENGAGEMENT

*Into the Heavens, Under the Earth:* Satellite launch data from KCNA, September 4, 1998. Sanger's article, "North Korea Site an A-Bomb Plant, U.S. Agencies Say," *NYT,* Aug. 17, 1998. Livingston quotes from the *WP,* Sept. 1, 1998.

*Toward an Aid-Based State:* The new DPRK cabinet, from Yoo Young-ku, *Vantage Point* (Seoul), Mar. 1999. Marcus Noland's data from his paper, "North Korea's External Economic Relations," Institute for International Economics, 2001.

*Perry to the Rescue* and *Engaging the United States:* These sections are based in part on interviews with William J. Perry, Madeleine Albright, Wendy Sherman, Charles Kartman, Robert Einhorn, and other U.S. officials. Vice Marshal Jo's bio is from *Vantage Point* (Seoul), Mar. 1999, and ROK press reports.

*Summit in Pyongyang:* Translated text of Joint Declaration from ROK embassy, Washington, Mar. 23, 2001. Kim Dae Jung quote on one people, *Financial Times*, July 16, 2000.

INDEX